# THE COMPLETE PREFACES
## VOLUME 3: 1930–1950

# BERNARD SHAW

# THE COMPLETE PREFACES
## VOLUME 3: 1930–1950

EDITED BY DAN H. LAURENCE
AND DANIEL J. LEARY

ALLEN LANE
THE PENGUIN PRESS

ALLEN LANE
THE PENGUIN PRESS

Published by the Penguin Group
Penguin Books Ltd, 27 Wrights Lane, London W8 5TZ, England
Penguin Books USA Inc., 375 Hudson Street, New York, New York 10014, USA
Penguin Books Australia Ltd, Ringwood, Victoria, Australia
Penguin Books Canada Ltd, 10 Alcorn Avenue, Toronto, Ontario, Canada M4V 3B2
Penguin Books (NZ) Ltd, 182–190 Wairau Road, Auckland 10, New Zealand

Penguin Books Ltd, Registered Offices: Harmondsworth, Middlesex, England

First published 1997
1 3 5 7 9 10 8 6 4 2

Typeset by Rowland Phototypesetting Ltd,
Bury St Edmunds, Suffolk
Set in 11/13pt Postscript Bembo
Printed in England by Clays Ltd, St Ives plc

A CIP catalogue record for this book is available from the British Library

ISBN 0-713-99058-9

# Contents

═══

# Editors' Note

The *Complete Prefaces* contains, finally, 140 prefaces, introductions, forewords, and editor's notes, ranging in length from a single brief paragraph (*Against Corporal Punishment in Schools*, 1947) to the forty thousand words of the 'Preface on the Prospects of Christianity' (*Androcles and the Lion*, 1916).

Just after publication of the first volume a peeved letter writer to the London *Sunday Times* (22 August 1993) challenged our use, in the title, of the adjective 'complete' on the grounds that 'the editors . . . have chosen to reprint less than a third of Shaw's original 1893 preface to his first play, Widowers' Houses'. What we published was, in fact, the entire preface exactly as it appeared in 1893. What we did *not* publish was three appendices (clearly labelled as such) that had appeared in the 1893 edition and that were unexplainably included with the preface in the first collective edition of prefaces in 1934, and subsequently nowhere else. Shaw, admittedly, converted an afterword (to *The Adventures of the Black Girl in Her Search for God*, 1932) into a much revised preface for a Penguin edition in 1946; but there is no indication in the 1934 *Prefaces* that Shaw intended the appendices to be incorporated into the *Widowers' Houses* preface. And as that volume was assembled and edited by Shaw's wife, with the assistance of his Edinburgh printer William Maxwell from a list of works compiled by Shaw, the appendices may well have been included in error, without Shaw's knowledge.

Whatever the explanation, we declined to stretch our editorial mandate to the extent of treating appendices as prefatory matter. And though we took latitude in including significant private letters subsequently published (generally with Shaw's knowledge and consent) as prefaces, we ruled out inclusion of reprinted material like the 'Essay by Bernard Shaw' prefacing the Oxford University Press edition of Samuel Butler's *The Way of All Flesh* (1936), which is merely an abridged (otherwise unaltered) review of a 1919 biography, collected in Shaw's *Pen Portraits and Reviews* (1931).

In an appendix to Volume 3 we have gathered a few minor prefatory pieces that earlier eluded us, and two fragments, published posthumously as 'essays', that we believe to be draft portions of a preface (1922) intended for a volume of writings on religion Shaw was preparing for his Collected Edition but afterwards abandoned.

We apologize for an aberration that crept into our introduction in Volume 1 (eight lines from the foot of p. xxviii), where, as the context indicates, the title *Major Barbara*, not *Man and Superman*, was intended.

It has been our extreme good fortune to be assigned, at the Penguin Press (UK), to a dedicated, alert and painstaking trio of copy editors – Miranda McAllister, Sarah Coward and Monica Schmoller – and to have had our edition graced with the skilled indexing of David Bowron. We salute also the just retired Nancy Sadek, Special Collections Librarian of the McLaughlin Library, University of Guelph, and her indefatigable aides – Parvin Jahanpour, Ellen Morrison, Gloria Troyer and Darlene Wiltsie – for research assistance in the Laurence Collection of Shaw.

For enrichment of annotations we are most grateful to Jacques Barzun, John A. Bertolini, Nicholas Boyle, Georgeta Clinga (Director, Biblioteca Nationala a Romaniei), Fred D. Crawford, Joseph Dunlap, Samuel A. Freedman, Ruth S. Freitag (Senior Science Specialist, Library of Congress), Marion Harding (Department of Archives, National Army Museum, London), Guy Holborn (Librarian, Lincoln's Inn Library), Norman Kelvin, Mike Partington (Reference Librarian, Freiberger Library, Case Western Reserve University), Anne Summers (Curator, Department of Manuscripts, British Library), Susannah Thomas (Information Officer, University of Cambridge), Samuel A. Weiss and Stanley Weintraub.

Our thanks go as well to the staffs of the Music Division, New York Public Library for the Performing Arts; the Royal College of Surgeons, London; the Wellcome Institute for the History of Medicine, London; and the Elizabeth Coates Maddux Library, Trinity University, San Antonio, especially to Craig S. Likness, Assistant Director for Public Services and Collections. We wish also to acknowledge a debt to the contributors, past and present, to the *Encyclopaedia Britannica* for our several borrowings.

The hitherto unpublished preface 'Pugilism' appears by permission of the Trustees of the British Library; extracts from Shaw's letters of 16 and 21 October 1921 to Sidney Webb by kind permission of the Trustees of the Passfield Papers, British Library of Political and Economic Science, London School of Economics; and an extract from Charlotte Shaw's letter of 31 October 1917 to Apsley Cherry-Garrard by kind permission of the Trustees of the Will of Mrs Bernard Shaw.

D. H. L.

D. J. L.

## ABBREVIATIONS USED IN THIS EDITION

The following standard abbreviations are employed to identify sources of material:

| | |
|---|---|
| BBC | British Broadcasting Corporation |
| BL | British Library |
| *DNB* | *Dictionary of National Biography* |
| HRC | Harry Ransom Humanities Research Center, University of Texas at Austin |
| LC | Library of Congress |
| LSE | London School of Economics |
| NYPL | New York Public Library |
| *OED* | *Oxford English Dictionary* |
| ALS or TLS: | Autograph or Typewritten letter signed |

# THE COMPLETE PREFACES
## 1930–1950

# Immaturity

*Drafted in 1921; first published in the Collected Edition, 1930*

=====

The scene of one of Mr Arnold Bennett's novels [*The Roll-Call*, 1918] is laid in a certain *cul de sac* off the Brompton Road, nearly opposite the West Brompton District Post Office. He calls it Alexandra Grove; but its actual name is Victoria Grove. As he describes it, the houses now contrive a double rent to pay, as the gardens have been fitted up with studios, thus quietly modernizing London by the back-to-back housing so vehemently denounced as a relic of barbarism in Leeds. When I arrived there as an Irish emigrant of 20, this intensification of population had not occurred. The houses were semi-detached villas with plenty of air space round them (you could call it garden). On the other side of the back wall were orchards; for the huge Poor Law Infirmary which now occupies this space, with its tower on the Fulham Road, was not yet built. The land between West Brompton and Fulham and Putney, now closely packed with streets and suburban roads, had still plenty of orchard and market garden to give it a countrified air and to make it possible to live there, as I did for years [1876–80], without feeling that one must flee to the country or wither in the smoke. All the parallel Groves connected the Fulham Road with King's Road, Chelsea, where Cremorne Gardens, an unlaid ghost from the XVIII century, was desperately fighting off its final exorcism as a rendezvous of the half world. Hence these now blameless thoroughfares were then reputed Bohemian, whilst Victoria Grove, as a blind alley, remained as respectable as Clapham.

I came to London from Dublin in the spring of 1876, and found my mother and my one surviving sister (I had no brothers) established in No. 13 Victoria Grove, trying to turn their musical accomplishments to account: my mother by teaching, my sister by singing. My father, left in Dublin, spared us a pound a week from his slender resources; and by getting into debt and occasionally extracting ourselves by drawing on a maternal inheritance of £4000 over which my mother had a power of appointment, and which therefore could be realized bit by bit as her three children came of age, we managed to keep going somehow.

Impecuniosity was necessarily chronic in the household. And here let me distinguish between this sort of poverty and that which furnishes an element of romance in the early lives of many famous men. I am almost tempted to say that it is the only sort of poverty that counts, short of the privations that make success impossible. We all know the man whose mother brought him up with nineteen brothers and sisters on an income of eighteen shillings a week earned by her own labor. The road from the log cabin to the White House, from the bench in the factory to the Treasury Bench, from the hovel to the mansion in Park Lane, if not exactly a crowded road, always has a few well fed figures at the end of it to tell us all about it. I always assure these gentlemen that they do not know what poverty and failure is. Beginning with as much as they expected or were accustomed to, they have known nothing but promotion. At each step they have had the income of the society in which they moved, and been able to afford its clothes, its food, its habits, its rents and rates. What more has any prince? If you would know what real poverty is, ask the younger son of a younger son of a younger son. To understand his plight you must start at the top without the income of the top, and curse your stars that you were not lucky enough to start at the bottom.

Our institution of primogeniture may have been a feudal necessity. It kept the baronies together; and the barons and their retainers kept the king and the country supplied with an army, a magistracy, and a network of local governments. But it took no account of the younger sons. These unhappy ones were brought up in the baronial castle. Let us represent the income of the barony by the figure 1000. Both sons and daughters were brought up to know no other mode of life than life at this figure. When the eldest took all, what was there left for the girls' dowries and the boys' allowances? Only the scrapings and leavings of the mother's dowry, and such charity as the new baron might choose (if he could afford it) to bestow on his poor relations. A younger son's figure, especially if he had many brothers, might easily be 20 or less, even to zero. What was the poor wretch to do, knowing no other way of living but the way that cost 1000? Easy to tell him that he must cut his coat according to his cloth. Impossible to do it without being trained to that measure from childhood. Impossible anyhow without dropping every relative and friend in the world, and stepping down, a mistrusted, ridiculous, incongruous stranger, into the social circle of his mother's maid and his brother's butler. Impossible often even to go into the army, where an officer cannot live on his pay unless he is a promoted ranker in a line regiment, and not even then with any ease. There is nothing for it but to live beyond one's income, to spunge, to beg, to take credit at the shops without means, to borrow without the prospect of being able to repay, and to blackmail the baron by presenting him with a choice between paying up and having his brother haled before the criminal courts for swindling. The alternative (to marry the daughter of a rich *parvenu* [upstart], American or British) is not always available. Who would be an Honorable on such terms if he could help it?

But think of his son, and of his son's son: the undisguised commoner, for whom, because it costs too much, there is not even the public school and university education of the baron's cadet, and who cannot avail himself of the public elementary and secondary schools because such a step would disclass the man of family! Think of the attempt to go into business with some pitiful little capital! think of the struggle to make the loathed occupation yield a living! think of the son for whom there is nothing but a clerkship in the office of some goodnatured business acquaintance! and bear in mind that the descent implies that every generation is, like the original younger son, brought up to a mode of life more expensive than its income can compass; so that it is condemned to pull the devil by the tail from its adolescence to its grave! My able and flourishing friend A tells me that he knows what poverty is and what drink is: was he not brought up in The Borough[1] by a drunken mother? B [J. M. Barrie], rolling in wealth, tells me that when he was a boy he had meat only twice a year. C [H. G. Wells], wallowing in fame, calls me a snob, after gleefully narrating his experiences in the kitchen of his father's small shop, and how he was enabled to study country house society by a childish privilege of visiting the servants' hall. How easily I cap these zests to success by the simple statement that my father was second cousin to a baronet [Sir Robert Shaw, Second Baronet], and my mother the daughter of a country gentleman whose rule was, when in difficulties, mortgage. That was my sort of poverty. The Shaws were younger sons from the beginning, as I shall shew when I reveal my full pedigree. Even the baronetcy was founded on the fortunes of a fifth son who came to Dublin and made that city his oyster. Let who will preen himself on his Mother Hubbard's bare cupboard, and play for sympathy as an upstart: I was a downstart and the son of a downstart. But for the accident of a lucrative talent I should today be poorer than Spinoza; for he at least knew how to grind lenses, wheras I could not afford to learn any art. Luckily Nature taught me one.

This social *dégringolade* [tumble] never stops in these islands. It produces a class which deserves a history all to itself. Do not talk of the middle class: the expression is meaningless except when it is used by an economist to denote the man of business who stands in the middle between land and capital

1. Ancient name, still in common use, of the Borough of Southwark, in south central London.

on the one hand, and labor on the other, and organizes business for both. I sing my own class: the Shabby Genteel, the Poor Relations, the Gentlemen who are No Gentlemen. If you want to know exactly where I came in, you will get at such facts as that of my many uncles only one [William Bernard: 'Uncle Barney'], the eldest, contrived to snatch a university education. The rest shifted as best they could without it (rather better than he, mostly). One [Richard Frederick] distinguished himself as a civil servant. He had a gun, and went shooting. One [Henry] made a fortune in business, and attained to carriage horses; but he lost the fortune in a premature attempt to develop the mineral resources of Ireland without waiting for the new railways produced by the late war. Two [Edward Carr and Walter Stephen] emigrated to Tasmania, and, like Mr Micawber, made history there. One [Robert] was blind and dependent on his brothers: another [the aforementioned Walter Stephen] became blind later, but remained independent and capable. One aunt [Emily] married the rector [William George Carroll] of St Bride's (now demolished) in Dublin. The others married quite prosperously, except the eldest [Cecilia, the third daughter but the first to survive to adulthood], whose conception of the family dignity was so prodigious (the family snobbery being unmitigated in her case by the family sense of humor) that she would have refused an earl because he was not a duke and so died a very ancient virgin. Dead or alive, there were fourteen of them; and they all, except perhaps the eldest, must have had a very straitened time of it in their childhood after their father [Bernard Shaw, of Kilkenny] died, leaving my grandmother [Frances Carr Shaw] to bring up an unconscionable lot of children on very inadequate means. The baronet came to the rescue by giving her a quaint cottage, with Gothically pointed windows, to live in at Terenure (we called the place Roundtown). It stands in, or rather creeps picturesquely along, its little walled garden near the tram terminus to this day, though my grandfather's brass helmet and sword (he was in the Yeomanry or Militia as a gentleman amateur soldier) no longer hang in the hall. Professionally, he was some sort of combination of solicitor, notary public, and stockbroker that prevailed at that time. I suspect that his orphans did not always get enough to eat; for the younger ones, though invincibly healthy and long lived, were not athletic, and exhibited such a remarkable collection of squints (my father had a stupendous squint) that to this day a squint is so familiar to me that I notice it no more than a pair of spectacles or even a pair of boots.

On the whole, they held their cherished respectability in the world in spite of their lack of opportunity. They owed something perhaps, to the confidence given them by their sense of family. In Irish fashion they talked of themselves as the Shaws, as who should say the Valois, the Bourbons, the Hohenzollerns, the Hapsburgs, or the Romanoffs; and their world conceded the point to them. I had an enormous contempt for this family snobbery, as I called it, until I was completely reconciled to it by a certain Mr Alexander Mackintosh Shaw, a clansman who, instead of taking his pedigree for granted in the usual Shaw manner, hunted it up, and published 100 copies privately in 1877. Somebody sent me a copy; and my gratification was unbounded when I read the first sentence of the first chapter, which ran: "It is the general tradition, says the Rev. Lachlan Shaw [bless him!],★ that the Shaws are descended of McDuff, Earl of Fife." I hastily skipped to the chapter about the Irish Shaws to make sure that they were my people; and there they were, baronet and all, duly traced to the third son of that immortalized yet unborn Thane of Fife who, invulnerable to normally accouched swordsmen, laid on and slew Macbeth. It was as good as being descended from Shakespear, whom I had been unconsciously resolved to reincarnate from my cradle.

Years after this discovery I was staying on the shores of Loch Fyne [at Strachur, August 1903], and being cooked for and housekept by a lady named McFarlane, who treated me with a consideration which I at first supposed to be due to my eminence as an author. But she undeceived me one day by telling me that the McFarlanes and the Shaws were descended from the Thanes of Fife, and that I must not make myself too cheap. She added that the McFarlanes were the elder branch.

My uncles did not trouble about Macduff: it was enough for them that they were Shaws. They had an impression that the Government should give them employment, preferably sinecure, if nothing else could be found; and I suppose this was why my father, after essaying a clerkship or two (one of them in an ironworks), at last had his position recognized by a post in the Four Courts, perhaps because his sister [probably Frances Greene: 'Aunt Fanny'] had married the brother of a law baron. Anyhow the office he held was so undeniably superfluous that it actually got abolished before I was born; and my father naturally demanded a pension as compensation for the outrage. Having got it, he promptly sold it, and set up in business as a merchant dealing wholesale (the family dignity made retail business impossible) in flour and its cereal concomitants. He had an office and warehouse in Jervis Street in the city; and he had a mill in Dolphin's Barn on the country side of the canal, at the end of a rather pretty little village street called Rutland Avenue. The mill has now fallen to pieces; but some relics of it are still to be seen from the field with the millpond behind Rutland House at the end of the avenue, with its two stone eagles on the gateposts. My father used to take

★ Shaw's insertion.

me sometimes to this mill before breakfast (a long walk for a child); and I used to like playing about it. I do not think it had any other real use; for it never paid its way; and the bulk of my father's business was commissioned: he was a middleman. I should mention that as he knew nothing about the flour business, and as his partner, a Mr [George] Clibborn, having been apprenticed to the cloth trade, knew if possible less, the business, purchased readymade, must have proceeded by its own momentum, and produced its results, such as they were, automatically in spite of its proprietors. They did not work the industry: it worked them. It kept alive, but did not flourish. Early in its history the bankruptcy of one of its customers dealt it such a blow that my father's partner broke down in tears, though he was fortified by a marriage with a woman of property, and could afford to regard his business as only a second string to his bow. My father, albeit ruined, found the magnitude of the catastrophe so irresistibly amusing that he had to retreat hastily from the office to an empty corner of the warehouse, and laugh until he was exhausted. The business struggled on and even supported my father until he died, enabling him to help his family a little after they had solved a desperate financial situation by emigrating to London: or, to put it in another way, by deserting him. His last years were soothed and disembarrassed by this step. He never, as far as I know, made the slightest movement towards a reunion; and none of us ever dreamt of there being any unkindness in the arrangement. In our family we did not bother about conventionalities or sentimentalities.

Our ridiculous poverty was too common in our class, and not conspicuous enough in a poor country, to account wholly for our social detachment from my father's family, a large and (for Ireland) not unprosperous one. In early days the baronet, being a bachelor, was clannishly accessible: he entertained even his second cousins at Bushy Park, and was specially attentive to my mother. I was never at Bushy Park myself except once [February 1869], on the occasion of his funeral (the Shaw funerals were prodigies of black pomp); but if my father had been able to turn his social opportunities to account, I might have had a quite respectable and normal social training. My mother, socially very eligible, was made welcome in all directions. She sang very well; and the Shaws were naturally a musical family. All the women could "pick out tunes" on the piano, and support them with the chords of the tonic, subdominant, dominant, and tonic again. Even a Neapolitan sixth[2] was not

2. One of the chromatic chords: the first inversion (that is, the 'sixth' chord) of the major triad, built on the flattened supertonic (second degree of the scale). Usually associated with the eighteenth-century Neapolitan school of musicians: Scarlatti, Cimarosa, Paisiello, Pergolesi.

beyond them. My father played the trombone, and could vamp a bass on it to any tune that did not modulate too distractingly. My eldest uncle (Barney: I suppose I was called Bernard after him; but he himself was Uncle William) played the ophicleide, a giant keyed brass bugle, now superseded by the tuba. Berlioz has described it as a chromatic bullock; but my uncle could make it moo and bellow very melodiously. My aunt Emily played the violoncello. Aunt Shah (Charlotte) [Johnston], having beautiful hands, and refinements of person and character to match them, used the harp and tambourine to display them. Modern readers will laugh at the picture of an evening at Bushy Park, with the bachelor Sir Robert and his clan seated round an ottoman on which my uncle Barney stood, solemnly playing Annie Laurie on the ophicleide. The present distinguished inheritor of the title may well find it incredible. But in those days it was the fashion for guests to provide their own music and gentlemen to play wind instruments as a social accomplishment: indeed that age of brass is still remembered and regretted by the few makers of musical instruments whose traditions go back far enough.

And now you will ask why, with such unexceptional antecedents and social openings, was I not respectably brought up? Unfortunately or fortunately (it all depends on how you look at it) my father had a habit which eventually closed all doors to him, and consequently to my mother, who could not very well be invited without him. If you asked him to dinner or to a party, he was not always quite sober when he arrived; and he was invariably scandalously drunk when he left. Now a convivial drunkard may be exhilarating in convivial company. Even a quarrelsome or boastful drunkard may be found entertaining by people who are not particular. But a miserable drunkard—and my father, in theory a teetotaller, was racked with shame and remorse even in his cups—is unbearable. We were finally dropped socially. After my early childhood I cannot remember ever paying a visit at a relative's house. If my mother and father had dined out, or gone to a party, their children would have been much more astonished than if the house had caught fire.

How my mother rescued herself from this predicament by her musical talent I will tell elsewhere.[3] My father reduced his teetotalism from theory to practice when a mild fit, which felled him on our doorstep one Sunday afternoon, convinced him that he must stop drinking or perish. It had no worse effect; but his reform, though complete and permanent, came too late to save the social situation; and I, cut off from the social drill which puts one at one's ease in private society, grew up frightfully shy and utterly ignorant of social routine. My mother, who had been as carefully brought up as Queen

3. Preface to *London Music in 1888–89* (1937). See p. 320.

Victoria, was too humane to inflict what she had suffered on any child; besides, I think she imagined that correct behavior is inborn, and that much of what she had been taught was natural to her. Anyhow, she never taught it to us, leaving us wholly to the promptings of our blood's blueness, with results which may be imagined.

In England, if people are reasonably goodnatured and amiable, they are forgiven any sort of eccentricity of behavior if only they are unaffected and all of one piece. If when I came to London I had been merely shy provincially, with incorrect table manners and wrong clothes; if I had eaten peas with a knife and worn a red tie with an evening suit, kind people would have taken me in hand and drilled me in spite of the infernal and very silly Irish pride which will never admit the need of such tuition. But my difficulties were not of that easily remediable kind. I was sensible enough to inform myself so exactly as to what I should do with a finger bowl when it was placed before me on a dessert plate, that I could give a lead in such matters to other novices who were hopelessly floored by that staggering problem. Clever sympathetic women might divine at a glance that I was mortally shy; but people who could not see through my skin, and who were accustomed to respect, and even veneration, from the young, may well have found me insufferable, aggressive, and impudent. When a young man has achieved nothing and is doing nothing, and when he is obviously so poor that he ought to be doing something very energetically, it is rather trying to find him assuming an authority in conversation, and an equality in terms, which only conspicuous success and distinguished ability could make becoming. Yet this is what is done, quite unconsciously, by young persons who have in them the potentiality of such success and ability. Napoleon could hardly have felt much reverence for his average French generals before the French Revolution, when he was apparently only a by-no-means irreproachable subaltern from Corsica. No such general could possibly have liked him or his manners at that time, though after Austerlitz even first rate generals blushed with gratification at the most condescending word of praise from him. It must have been intolerable in Stratford-on-Avon in 1584 for a local magnate of mature age, knight of the shire and justice of the peace, to be contemplated *de haut en bas* [from high to low] by a dissolute young poacher, and even to amuse him by intellectual inadequacy. I am sure Shakespear was too civil by nature to make any such demonstration consciously; but it is inconceivable that the future author of Lear, who was to die a landowning magnate, and be described in the parish register as a Gent., could have treated Sir Thomas Lucy quite as an ordinary country gentleman of mature age expects to be treated by an ordinary poacher in his teens.

The truth is that all men are in a false position in society until they have realized their possibilities, and imposed them on their neighbors. They are tormented by a continual shortcoming in themselves; yet they irritate others by a continual overweening. This discord can be resolved by acknowledged success or failure only: everyone is ill at ease until he has found his natural place, whether it be above or below his birthplace. The overrated inheritor of a position for which he has no capacity, and the underrated nobody who is a born genius, are alike shy because they are alike out of place. Besides, this finding of one's place may be made very puzzling by the fact that there is no place in ordinary society for extraordinary individuals. For the worldly wiseman, with common ambitions, the matter is simple enough: money, title, precedence, a seat in parliament, a portfolio in the cabinet, will mean success both to him and his circle. But what about people like St Francis and St Clare? Of what use to them are the means to live the life of the country house and the west end mansion? They have literally no business in them, and must necessarily cut an unhappy and ridiculous figure there. They have to make a society of Franciscans and Poor Clares for themselves before they can work or live socially. It is true that those who are called saints are not saintly all the time and in everything. In eating and drinking, lodging and sleeping, chatting and playing: in short, in everything but working out their destiny as saints, what is good enough for a ploughman is good enough for a poet, a philosopher, a saint, or a higher mathematician. But Hodge's[4] work is not good enough for Newton, nor Falstaff's conversation holy enough for Shelley. Christ adapted himself so amiably to the fashionable life of his time in his leisure that he was reproached for being a gluttonous man and a winebibber, and for frequenting frivolous and worthless sets [Matthew 11: 19]. But he did not work where he feasted, nor flatter the Pharisees, nor ask the Romans to buy him with a sinecure. He knew when he was being entertained, well treated, lionized: not an unpleasant adventure for once in a way; and he did not quarrel with the people who were so nice to him. Besides, to sample society is part of a prophet's business: he must sample the governing class above all, because his inborn knowledge of human nature will not explain the anomalies produced in it by Capitalism and Sacerdotalism. But he can never feel at home in it. The born Communist, before he knows what he is, and understands why, is always awkward and unhappy in plutocratic society and in the poorer societies which ape it to the extent of their little means: in short, wherever spiritual values are assessed like Income Tax. In his nonage

4. A field-hand, servant to Gammer in the play *Gammer Gurton's Needle* (1575). Shaw employs the name generically for any peasant workman. See also p. 266.

he is imposed on by the prestige which the propertied classes have conferred on themselves and inculcated in the schools, and by the comfort and refinement and splendor of their equipment in contrast to the squalor of the proletariat. If he has been brought up to regard himself as one of the propertied classes, and has its whole equipment of false standards of worth, lacking nothing but the indispensable pecuniary equipment without which his education is utterly meaningless, his embarrassment and bewilderment are pitiable, and his isolation often complete; for he is left alone between the poor whom he regards as beneath him and the rich whose standards of expenditure are beyond his means. He is ashamed of his poverty, in continual dread of doing the wrong thing, resentfully insubordinate and seditious in a social order which he not only accepts but in which he actually claims a privileged part.

As I write, there is a craze for what is called psychoanalysis, or the cure of diseases by explaining to the patient what is the matter with him: an excellent plan if you happen to know what is the matter with him, especially when the explanation is that there is nothing the matter with him. Thus a bee, desperately trying to reach a flower bed through a window pane, concludes that he is the victim of evil spirits or that he is mad, his end being exhaustion, despair, and death. Yet, if he only knew, there is nothing wrong with him: all he has to do is go out as he came in, through open window or door. Your born Communist begins like the bee on the pane. He worries himself and everybody else until he dies of peevishness, or else is led by some propagandist pamphlet, or by his own intellectual impulses (if he has any), to investigate the economic structure of our society.

Immediately everything becomes clear to him. Property is theft:[5] respectability founded on poverty is blasphemy: marriage founded on property is prostitution: it is easier for a camel to go through the eye of a needle than for a rich man to enter the kingdom of heaven [Matthew 19: 24]. He now knows where he is, and where this society which has so intimidated him is. He is cured of his *mauvaise honte* [sense of shame], and may now be as much at his ease with the princes of this world as Cæsar was with the pirates whom he intended to crucify when, as presently happened, the fortune of war made their captive their conqueror.

If he be not a born Communist, but a predatory combative man, eager to do the other fellow down, and happy in a contrast between his prosperity and the indigence of others, happy also in a robust contempt for cowards and weaklings, the very same discovery of the nature of our Capitalism will nerve him to play the Capitalist game for all it and he are worth. But for the

5. Stated by Pierre-Joseph Proudhon in *Qu'est-ce que la propriété?* (1840).

most part men drift with the society into which they are born, and make the best of its accidents without changing its morals or understanding its principles.

As it happens, I was a born Communist and Iconoclast (or Quaker) without knowing it; and I never got on easy terms with plutocracy and snobbery until I took to the study of economics, beginning with Henry George and Karl Marx. In my twentieth year, at Victoria Grove, not being on Cæsarian easy terms with the pirates or their retainers, I felt much as Cæsar might have done if he had imagined the pirate ship to be the Mayflower, and was still more inclined to mistrust himself than to mistrust the crew, however little respect they might pay him. Not that my opinions were conventional. Read my preface to Back to Methuselah, and you will see me as the complete infidel of that day. I had read much poetry; but only one poet was sacred to me: Shelley. I had read his works piously from end to end, and was in my negations atheist and republican to the backbone. I say in my negations; for I had not reached any affirmative position. When, at a public meeting [10 March 1886] of the Shelley Society, I scandalized many of the members by saying that I had joined because, like Shelley, I was a Socialist, an atheist, and a vegetarian, I did not know that I could have expressed my position more accurately by simply saying that my conception of God was that insisted on in the first Article[6] of the Church of England, then as now vehemently repudiated by all pious persons, who will have it that God is a substantial gentleman of uncertain and occasionally savage temper, and a spirit only in the sense in which an archbishop is a spirit. I had never thought of reading the Articles of the Church of England; and if I had I should still have used the word atheist as a declaration that I was on the side of Bradlaugh and Foote and others who, as avowed Secularists and Atheists, were being persecuted and imprisoned for my opinions. From my childhood I had been accustomed to regard myself as a sceptic outside institutional religion, and therefore one to whom the conventional religious observances were fair game for scoffing. In this my manners were no better and no worse than those of my class generally. It never occurred to pious ladies and gentlemen to respect a sceptic; and it never occurred to a sceptic to respect a believer: reprobation and ostracism were considered natural and even obligatory on the one side, like derision,

6. The first of the 39 Articles of the Anglican *Book of Common Prayer* states: 'There is but one living and true God, everlasting, without body, parts, or passions; of infinite power, wisdom, and goodness; the Maker, and Preserver of all things both visible and invisible. And in unity of this Godhead there be three Persons, of one substance, power and eternity; the Father, the Son, and the Holy Ghost.'

even to blasphemy, on the other. In Ireland Protestants and Catholics despised, insulted, and ostracized oneanother as a matter of course. In England Church people persecuted Dissenters; and Dissenters hated the Church with a bitterness incredible to anyone who has never known what it is to be a little village Dissenter in a Church school. I am not sure that controversial manners are any better now; but they certainly were odious then: you thought it your right and your duty to sneer at the man who was a heretic to your faith if you could not positively injure him in some way. As my manners in this respect were no better than other people's, and my satirical powers much more formidable, I can only hope that my natural civility, which led me to draw back when I found I was hurting people's feelings, may have mitigated my offensiveness in those early days when I still regarded controversy as admitting of no quarter. I lacked both cruelty and will-to-victory.

It may be asked here how I came by my heterodox opinions, seeing that my father's alcoholic neurosis, though it accounts for my not going into society, does not account for my not going to church. My reply, if put in the conventional terms of that day, would be that I was badly brought up because my mother was so well brought up. Her character reacted so strongly against her strict and loveless training that churchgoing was completely dropped in our family before I was ten years old. In my childhood I exercised my literary genius by composing my own prayers. I cannot recall the words of the final form I adopted; but I remember that it was in three movements, like a sonata, and in the best Church of Ireland style. It ended with the Lord's Prayer; and I repeated it every night in bed. I had been warned by my nurse that warm prayers were no use, and that only by kneeling by my bedside in the cold could I hope for a hearing; but I criticized this admonition unfavorably on various grounds, the real one being my preference for warmth and comfort. I did not disparage my nurse's authority in these matters because she was a Roman Catholic: I even tolerated her practice of sprinkling me with holy water occasionally. But her asceticism did not fit the essentially artistic and luxurious character of my devotional exploits. Besides, the penalty did not apply to my prayer; for it was not a petition. I had too much sense to risk my faith by begging for things I knew very well I should not get; so I did not care whether my prayers were answered or not: they were a literary performance for the entertainment and propitiation of the Almighty; and though I should not have dreamt of daring to say that if He did not like them He might lump them (perhaps I was too confident of their quality to apprehend such a rebuff), I certainly behaved as if my comfort were an indispensable condition of the performance taking place at all.

The Lord's Prayer I used once or twice as a protective spell. Thunderstorms are much less common in Ireland than in England; and the first two I remember frightened me horribly. During the second I bethought me of the Lord's Prayer, and steadied myself by repeating it.

I continued these pious habits long after the conventional compulsion to attend church and Sunday School had ceased, and I no longer regarded such customs as having anything to do with an emancipated spirit like mine. But one evening, as I was wandering through the furze bushes on Torca Hill [Dalkey] in the dusk, I suddenly asked myself why I went on repeating my prayer every night when, as I put it, I did not believe in it. Being thus brought to book by my intellectual conscience I felt obliged in common honesty to refrain from superstitious practices; and that night, for the first time since I could speak, I did not say my prayers. I missed them so much that I asked myself another question. Why am I so uncomfortable about it? Can this be conscience? But next night the discomfort wore off so much that I hardly noticed it; and the night after I had forgotten all about my prayers as completely as if I had been born a heathen. It is worth adding that this sacrifice of the grace of God, as I had been taught it, to intellectual integrity synchronized with that dawning of moral passion in me which I have described in the first act of Man and Superman. Up to that time I had not experienced the slightest remorse in telling lies whenever they seemed likely to help me out of a difficulty: rather did I revel in the exercise of dramatic invention involved. Even when I was a good boy I was so only theatrically, because, as actors say, I saw myself in the character; and this occurred very seldom, my taste running so strongly on stage villains and stage demons (I painted the whitewashed wall in my bedroom in Dalkey with watercolor frescoes of Mephistopheles) that I must have actually bewitched myself; for, when Nature completed my countenance in 1880 or thereabouts (I had only the tenderest sprouting of hair on my face until I was 24), I found myself equipped with the upgrowing moustaches and eyebrows, and the sarcastic nostrils of the operatic fiend whose airs (by Gounod) I had sung as a child, and whose attitudes I had affected in my boyhood. Later on, as the generations moved past me, I saw the fantasies of actors and painters come to life as living men and women, and began to perceive that imaginative fiction is to life what the sketch is to the picture or the conception to the statue. The world is full of ugly little men who were taken to the theatre to see the Yellow Dwarf[7] or Rumpelstiltskin when they were children; and we shall soon have women in all directions with the features of Movie Vamps

7. A theatre burlesque (1842) by Gilbert à Beckett, which spawned a number of variants for the next quarter century.

because in childhood they were taken to the picture palaces and inspired with an ambition to be serpents of Old Nile.

My father disapproved of the detachment of his family from the conventional observances that were associated with the standing of the Shaw family. But he was in the grip of a humorous sense of anticlimax which I inherited from him and used with much effect when I became a writer of comedy. The more sacred an idea or a situation was by convention, the more irresistible was it to him as the jumping-off place for a plunge into laughter. Thus, when I scoffed at the Bible he would instantly and quite sincerely rebuke me, telling me, with what little sternness was in his nature, that I should not speak so; that no educated man would make such a display of ignorance; that the Bible was universally recognized as a literary and historical masterpiece; and as much more to the same effect as he could muster. But when he had reached the point of feeling really impressive, a convulsion of internal chuckling would wrinkle up his eyes; and (I knowing all the time quite well what was coming) would cap his eulogy by assuring me, with an air of perfect fairness, that even the worst enemy of religion could say no worse of the Bible than that it was the damndest parcel of lies ever written. He would then rub his eyes and chuckle for quite a long time. It became an unacknowledged game between us that I should provoke him to exhibitions of this kind.

With such a father my condition was clearly hopeless as far as the conventions of religion were concerned. In essential matters his influence was as good as his culture permitted. One of my very earliest recollections is reading The Pilgrim's Progress to him, and being corrected by him for saying grievious instead of grievous. I never saw him, as far as I can remember, reading anything but the newspaper; but he had read Sir Walter Scott and other popular classics; and he always encouraged me to do the same, and to frequent the National Gallery [of Ireland], and to go to the theatre and the opera when I could afford it. His anticlimaxes depended for their effect on our sense of the sacredness he was reacting against: there would have been no fun whatever in saying that the Adventures of Munchausen[8] (known to us as Baron Mun Chawzon) were a parcel of lies. If my mother's pastors and masters had had a little of his humor, she would not simply have dropped the subject of religion with her children in silent but implacable dislike of what had helped to make her childhood miserable, and resolved that it should not do the same to them. The vacuum she left by this policy had, I think, serious disadvantages for my two sisters (the younger of whom died just

8. A collection of exaggerative and fantastic tales by Rudolph Erich Raspe, *Baron Munchausen: the Narrative of his Marvellous Travels* (1785), published anonymously.

before I came to London); but in my case it only made a clear space for positive beliefs later on.

My mother, I may say here, had no comedic impulses, and never uttered an epigram in her life: all my comedy is a Shavian inheritance. She had plenty of imagination, and really lived in it and on it. Her brother, my uncle Walter, who stayed with us from time to time in the intervals of his trips across the Atlantic as a surgeon on the Inman Liners,[9] had an extraordinary command of picturesque language, partly derived by memory from the Bible and Prayer Book, and partly natural. The conversation of the navigating staffs and pursers of our ocean services was at that time (whatever it may be today) extremely Rabelaisian and profane. Falstaff himself could not have held his own with my uncle in obscene anecdotes, unprintable limericks, and fantastic profanity; and it mattered nothing to him whether his audience consisted of his mess-mates on board ship or his schoolboy nephew: he performed before each with equal gusto. To do him justice, he was always an artist in his obscenity and blasphemy, and therefore never sank to the level of incontinent black-guardism. His efforts were controled, deliberate, fastidiously chosen and worded. But they were all the more effective in destroying all my inculcated childish reverence for the verbiage of religion, for its legends and personifications and parables. In view of my subsequent work in the world it seems providential that I was driven to the essentials of religion by the reduction of every factitious or fictitious element in it to the most irreverent absurdity.

It would be the greatest mistake to conclude that this shocking state of affairs was bad for my soul. Insofar as the process of destroying reverence for the inessential trappings of religion was indecent, it was deplorable; and I wish my first steps to grace had been lighted by my uncle's wit and style without his obscenity. My father's comedy was entirely decent. But that the process was necessary to my salvation I have no doubt whatever. A popular book in my youth was Mark Twain's New Pilgrim's Progress [British title for *The Innocents Abroad*, 1869], which horrified the thoughtlessly pious by making fun of what they called sacred things. Yet Mark Twain was really a religious force in the world: his Yankee at the Court of King Arthur was his nearest approach to genuine blasphemy; and that came from want of culture, not from perversity of soul. His training as a Mississippi pilot must have been, as to religion, very like my training as the nephew of a Transatlantic surgeon.

Later on, I discovered that in the Ages of Faith the sport of making fun of the accessories and legends of religion was organized and practised by the

9. Transatlantic shipping company, founded in 1850, which used barque-rigged, canvas-spread, iron-screw-propeller steamers.

Church to such an extent that it was almost part of its ritual. The people were instructed in spiritual history and hagiology by stage plays full of comic passages which might have been written by my uncle. For instance, my uncle taught me an elaborate conversation supposed to have passed between Daniel in the lion's den and King Darius,[10] in which each strove to outdo the other in Rabelaisian repartee. The medieval playwright [probably the author of the Chester cycle of 25 mystery plays], more daring than my uncle, put on the stage comical conversations between Cain and his Creator, in which Cain's language was no more respectful than that of Fielding's Squire Western [in *Tom Jones*], and similarly indecent. In all Catholic countries there is a hagiology that is fit for publication and a hagiology that is not. In the Middle Ages they may have condemned a story as lewd or blasphemous; but it did not occur to them that God or His Church could be shaken by it. No man with any faith worth respecting in any religion worth holding ever dreams that it can be shaken by a joke, least of all by an obscene joke. It is Messieurs Formalist and Hypocrisy who feel that religion is crumbling when the forms are not observed. The truth is, humor is one of the great purifiers of religion, even when it is itself anything but pure.

The institution of the family, which is the centre of reverence for carefully brought-up children, was just the opposite for me. In a large family there are always a few skeletons in the cupboard; and in my father's clan there were many uncles and aunts and cousins, consequently many cupboards, consequently some skeletons. Our own particular skeleton was my father's drunkenness. It was combined with a harmlessness and humaneness which made him the least formidable of men; so that it was impossible for him to impress his children in the manner that makes awe and dread almost an instinct with some children. It is much to his credit that he was incapable of deliberately practising any such impressiveness, drunk or sober; but unfortunately the drunkenness was so humiliating that it would have been unendurable if we had not taken refuge in laughter. It had to be either a family tragedy or a family joke; and it was on the whole a healthy instinct that decided us to get what ribald fun was possible out of it, which, however, was very little indeed. If Noah had made a habit of drinking, his sons would soon have worn out the pious solicitude which they displayed on the occasion of his single lapse from sobriety. A boy who has seen "the governor" [his father], with an imperfectly wrapped-up goose under one arm and a ham in the same condition under the other (both purchased under heaven knows what delusion

10. Darius I ('the Great'), wise and liberal administrator, was King of Persia, 522–486 BC.

of festivity), butting at the garden wall in the belief that he was pushing open the gate, and transforming his tall hat to a concertina in the process, and who, instead of being overwhelmed with shame and anxiety at the spectacle, has been so disabled by merriment (uproariously shared by the maternal uncle) that he has hardly been able to rush to the rescue of the hat and pilot its wearer to safety, is clearly not a boy who will make tragedies of trifles instead of making trifles of tragedies. If you cannot get rid of the family skeleton, you may as well make it dance.

Then there was my Uncle William, a most amiable man, with great natural dignity. In early manhood he was not only an inveterate smoker, but so insistent a toper that a man who made a bet that he would produce Barney Shaw sober, and knocked him up at six in the morning with that object, lost his bet. But this might have happened to any common drunkard. What gave the peculiar Shaw finish and humor to the case was that my uncle suddenly and instantly gave up smoking and drinking at one blow, and devoted himself to his accomplishment of playing the ophicleide. In this harmless and gentle pursuit he continued, a blameless old bachelor, for many years, and then, to the amazement of Dublin, renounced the ophicleide and all its works, and married a lady [Caroline Purtland, of Bray] of distinguished social position and great piety. She declined, naturally, to have anything to do with us; and, as far as I know, treated the rest of the family in the same way. Anyhow, I never saw her, and only saw my uncle furtively by the roadside after his marriage, when he would make hopeless attempts to save me, in the pious sense of the word, not perhaps without some secret Shavian enjoyment of the irreverent pleasantries with which I scattered my path to perdition. He was reputed to sit with a Bible on his knees, and an opera glass to his eyes, watching the ladies' bathing place in Dalkey; and my sister [Lucy], who was a swimmer, confirmed this gossip as far as the opera glass was concerned.

But this was only the prelude to a very singular conclusion, or rather catastrophe. The fantastic imagery of the Bible so gained on my uncle that he took off his boots, explaining that he expected to be taken up to heaven at any moment like Elijah, and that he felt that his boots would impede his celestial flight. He then went a step further, and hung his room with all the white fabrics he could lay hands on, alleging that he was the Holy Ghost. At last he became silent, and remained so to the end. His wife, warned that his harmless fancies might change into dangerous ones, had him removed to an asylum in the north of Dublin. My father thought that a musical appeal might prevail with him, and went in search of the ophicleide. But it was nowhere to be found. He took a flute to the asylum instead; for every Shaw of that generation seemed able to play any wind instrument at sight. My uncle, still obstinately mute, contemplated the flute for a while, and then played Home Sweet Home on it. My father had to be content with this small success, as nothing more could be got out of his brother. A day or two later my uncle, impatient for heaven, resolved to expedite his arrival there. Every possible weapon had been carefully removed from his reach; but his custodians reckoned without the Shavian originality. They had left him somehow within reach of a carpet bag. He put his head into it, and in a strenuous effort to decapitate or strangle himself by closing it on his neck, perished of heart failure. I should be glad to believe that, like Elijah, he got the heavenly reward he sought; for he was a fine upstanding man and a gentle creature, nobody's enemy but his own, as the saying is.

Still, what sort of gravity could a boy maintain with a family history of this kind? However, I must not imply that all my uncles were like that. They were mostly respectable normal people. I can recall only two other exceptions to this rule. One of my uncles [Richard F.] married an elegant and brilliant lady [Georgina Waters], from whom he separated after scandalizing the family by beating her; but as Job himself would have beaten her when she lost her very unstable temper, nobody who knew her intimately ever blamed him. Though the neurosis which produced my father's joyless craving for alcohol had the same effect, with the same curious recalcitrance and final impermanence, in one or two other cases, and was perhaps connected with occasional family paroxysms of Evangelical piety, and some share of my father's comedic love of anticlimax, yet on the whole our collection of skeletons was not exceptionally large. But as, compared with similar English families, we had a power of derisive dramatization that made the bones of the Shavian skeletons rattle more loudly; and as I possessed this power in an abnormal degree, and frequently entertained my friends with stories of my uncles (so effectively, by the way, that nobody ever believed them), the family, far from being a school of reverence for me, was rather a mine from which I could dig highly amusing material without the trouble of inventing a single incident. What idle fancy of mine could have improved on the hard facts of the Life and Death of Uncle William?

Thus the immediate result of my family training in my Victoria Grove days was that I presented myself to the unprepared stranger as a most irreverent young man. My Mephistophelean moustache and eyebrows had not yet grown; and there was nothing in my aspect to break the shock of my diabolical opinions. Later on, when I had made a public reputation as an iconoclast, people who met me in private were surprised at my mildness and sociability. But I had no public reputation then: consequently expectation in my regard was normal. And I was not at all reticent of the diabolical opinions. I felt them to be advantageous, just as I felt that I was in a superior position as an Irishman, without a shadow of any justification for that patriotic arrogance. As it never occurred to me to conceal my opinions any more than my nationality, and as I had, besides, an unpleasant trick of contradicting everyone from whom I thought I could learn anything in order to draw him out and enable me to pick his brains, I think I must have impressed many amiable persons as an extremely disagreeable and undesirable young man.

And yet I was painfully shy, and was simply afraid to accept invitations, with the result that I very soon ceased to get any. I was told that if I wanted to get on, I must not flatly refuse invitations—actually dinner invitations—which were meant to help me, and the refusal of which was nothing short of a social outrage. But I knew very well that introductions could be of no use to one who had no profession and could do nothing except what any clerk could do. I knew I was useless, worthless, penniless, and that until I had qualified myself to do something, and proved it by doing it, all this business of calling on people who might perhaps do something for me, and dining out without money to pay for a cab, was silly. Fortunately for me, the realism that made me face my own position so ruthlessly also kept before me the fact that if I borrowed money I could not pay it back, and therefore might more candidly beg or steal it. I knew quite well that if I borrowed £5 from a friend and could not pay it back, I was selling a friend for £5, and that this was a foolish bargain. So I did not borrow, and therefore did not lose my friends; though some of them, who could have had no illusions about my financial capacity, hinted that they were quite willing, and indeed anxious, to call a gift a loan.

I feel bound to confess here, in reference to my neglect of the few invitations and offers of introductions that reached me, that behind the conviction that they could lead to nothing that I wanted lay the unspoken fear that they might lead to something I did not want: that is, commercial employment. I had had enough of that. No doubt it would have been a great relief to my mother if I could have earned something. No doubt I could have earned something if I had really meant to. No doubt if my father had died, and my mother been struck dumb and blind, I should have had to go back to the office desk (the doom of shabby gentility) and give up all hope of acquiring a profession; for even the literary profession, though it exacts no academic course and costly equipment, does exact all one's time and the best of one's brains. As it was, I dodged every opening instinctively. With an excellent testimonial and an unexceptionable character, I was an incorrigible Unemployable. I kept up pretences (to myself as much as to others) for some time. I answered advertisements, not too offensively. I actually took a berth in a telephone Company (then a sensational novelty) and had some difficulty in extricating myself from the Company which bought it up. I can remember an interview with a bank manager in Onslow Gardens (procured for me, to my dismay, by an officious friend with whom I *had* dined) with a view to employment in the bank.[11] I entertained him so brilliantly (if I may use an adverb with which in later years I was much plagued by friendly critics) that we parted on the best of terms, he declaring that, though I certainly ought to get something to do without the least difficulty, he did not feel that a bank clerkship was the right job for me.

I have said that I had an excellent testimonial as an employee in a business office. I had, as a matter of fact, spent four and a half years at a desk in Dublin before I emigrated. I have already given the economic reasons why boys of my class have to do without university education, just as they have to do without horses and guns. And yet I cannot deny that clergymen no better off than my father do manage somehow to start their sons in life with a university degree. They regard it as an absolute necessity, and therefore do not consider whether they can afford it or not. They must afford it. The need for it may be an illusion; but we are subject to such illusions: one man cannot live without a grand piano, another without a boat, another without a butler, another without a horse, and so on through a whole range of psychological imperatives. I have known women set up orphanages because they could not do without children to beat. Place their necessities in any rational order, and you will find that many of them cannot afford these things. They get out of the difficulty by simply rearranging your rational order as a psychological order, and putting their fancies at the top and their needs at the bottom. It is no use telling a woman that she needs good food and plenty of it much more vitally than she needs a seven guinea hat, a bottle of hair dye, a supply of face powder and rouge, a puff and a hares-foot. She will live on tea and rashers for months rather than forgo them. And men are just as unreasonable. To say that my father could not afford to give me a university education is like saying that he could not afford to drink, or that I could not afford to become an author. Both statements are true; but he drank and I became an author all the same. I must therefore explain, just as seriously as if my father had had fifty thousand a year, why I did not graduate at Trinity College, Dublin.

I cannot learn anything that does not interest me. My memory is not indiscriminate: it rejects and selects; and its selections are not academic. I

11. Shaw's interview in November 1878 was with a Mr Kretschmar of the Imperial Bank, South Kensington; the friend who introduced him was Captain R. H. Home.

have no competitive instinct; nor do I crave for prizes and distinctions: consequently I have no interest in competitive examinations: if I won, the disappointment of my competitors would distress me instead of gratifying me: if I lost, my self-esteem would suffer. Besides, I have far too great a sense of my own importance to feel that it could be influenced by a degree or a gold medal or what not. There is only one sort of school that could have qualified me for academic success; and that is the sort in which the teachers take care that the pupils shall be either memorizing their lessons continuously, with all the desperate strenuousness that terror can inspire, or else crying with severe physical pain. I was never in a school where the teachers cared enough about me, or about their ostensible profession, or had enough conviction and cruelty, to take any such trouble; so I learnt nothing at school, not even what I could and would have learned if any attempt had been made to interest me. I congratulate myself on this; for I am firmly persuaded that every unnatural activity of the brain is as mischievous as any unnatural activity of the body, and that pressing people to learn things they do not want to know is as unwholesome and disastrous as feeding them on sawdust. Civilization is always wrecked by giving the governing classes what is called secondary education, which produces invincible ignorance and intellectual and moral imbecility as a result of unnatural abuse of the apprehensive faculty. No child would ever learn to walk or dress itself if its hands and feet were kept in irons and allowed to move only when and as its guardians pulled and pushed them.

I somehow knew this when I began, as a boy entering on my teens, to think about such things. I remember saying, in some discussion that arose on the subject of my education, that T.C.D. men were all alike (by which I meant all wrong), and that I did not want to go through college. I was entirely untouched by university idealism. When it reached me later on, I recognized how ignorantly I had spoken in my boyhood; but when I went still further and learnt that this idealism is never realized in our schools and universities, and operates only as a mask and a decoy for our system of impressing and enslaving children and stultifying adults, I concluded that my ignorance had been inspired, and had served me very well. I have not since changed my mind.

However that may be, I decided, at thirteen or thereabouts, that for the moment I must go into business and earn some money and begin to be a grown-up man. There was at that time, on one of the quays in Dublin, a firm of cloth merchants, by name Scott, Spain, and Rooney. A friend of ours knew Scott, and asked him to give me a start in life with some employment. I called on this gentleman by appointment. I had the vaguest notion of what would happen: all I knew was that I was "going into an office." I thought I should have preferred to interview Spain, as the name was more romantic. Scott turned out to be a smart handsome man, with moustachios; and I suppose a boy more or less in his warehouse did not matter to him when there was a friend to be obliged: at all events, he said only a few perfunctory things and was settling my employment, when, as my stars would have it, Rooney appeared. Mr Rooney was much older, not at all smart, but long, lean, grave and respectable.

The last time I saw the late Sir George Alexander (the actor) he described to me his own boyhood, spent in a cloth warehouse in Cheapside, where they loaded him with bales, and praised him highly for his excellent conduct, even rewarding him after some years to the extent of sixteen shillings a week. Rooney saved me from the bales. He talked to me a little, and then said quite decisively that I was too young, and that the work was not suitable to me. He evidently considered that my introducer, my parents, and his young partner, had been inconsiderate; and I presently descended the stairs, reprieved and unemployed. As Mr Rooney was certainly fifty then at least, he must be a centenarian if, as I hope, he still lives. If he does, I offer him the assurance that I have not forgotten his sympathy.

A year later, or thereabouts, my uncle [Richard] Frederick, an important official in the Valuation Office, whom no land agent or family solicitor in Dublin could afford to disoblige, asked a leading and terribly respectable firm of land agents [C. Uniacke Townshend & Co.], carrying on business at 15 Molesworth Street, to find a berth for me. They did so; and I became their office boy (junior clerk I called myself) at eighteen shillings a month. It was a very good opening for anyone with a future as a land agent, which in Ireland at that time was a business of professional rank. It was utterly thrown away on me. However, as the office was overstaffed with gentlemen apprentices, who had paid large fees for the privilege of singing operatic selections with me when the principals were out, there was nothing to complain of socially, even for a Shaw; and the atmosphere was as uncommercial as that of an office can be. Thus I learnt business habits without being infected with the business spirit. By the time I had attained to thirty shillings a month, the most active and responsible official in the office, the cashier [Alexander Maclagan], vanished; and as we were private bankers to some extent, our clients drawing cheques on us, and so forth, someone had to take his place without an hour's delay. An elder substitute [William Townsend] grumbled at the strange job, and, though an able man in his way, could not make his cash balance. It became necessary, after a day or two of confusion, to try the office boy as a stopgap whilst the advertisements for a new cashier of appropriate age and responsibility were going forward. Immediately the machine worked again quite smoothly. I, who never knew how much money I had of my own (except when the figure was zero), proved a model of accuracy as to the money of others. I acquired my predecessor's very neat handwriting, my own being too sloped and straggly for the cash book. The efforts to fill my important place more worthily slackened. I bought a tailed coat, and was chaffed about it by the apprentices. My salary was raised to £48 a year, which was as much as I expected at sixteen and much less than the firm would have had to pay to a competent adult: in short, I made good in spite of myself, and found, to my dismay, that Business, instead of expelling me as the worthless impostor I was, was fastening upon me with no intention of letting me go.

Behold me therefore in my twentieth year, with a business training, in an occupation which I detested as cordially as any sane person lets himself detest anything he cannot escape from. In March 1876 I broke loose. I gave a month's notice. My employers naturally thought I was discontented with my salary (£84, I think, by that time), and explained to me quietly that they hoped to make my position more eligible. My only fear was that they should make it so eligible that all excuse for throwing it up would be taken from me. I thanked them and said I was resolved to go; and I had, of course, no reason in the world to give them for my resolution. They were a little hurt, and explained to my uncle that they had done their best, but that I seemed to have made up my mind. I had. After enjoying for a few days the luxury of not having to go to the office,[12] and being, if not my own master, at least not anyone else's slave, I packed a carpet bag; boarded the North Wall boat; and left the train next morning at Euston, where, on hearing a porter cry, in an accent quite strange to me (I had hardly ever heard an h dropped before) "Ensm' faw weel?" which I rightly interpreted as "Hansom or four wheel?" I was afraid to say hansom, because I had never been in one and was not sure that I should know how to get in. So I solemnly drove in a growler[13] through streets whose names Dickens had made familiar to me, London being at its spring best, which is its very best, to Victoria Grove, where the driver accepted four shillings as a reasonable fare for the journey.

I did not set foot in Ireland again until 1905, and not then on my own initiative. I went back to please my wife; and a curious reluctance to retrace my steps made me land in the south and enter Dublin through the backdoor

12. This is fantasy. Shaw worked out his month through Friday evening, 31 March, and set out for London the following morning.
13. Colloquial term for a horse-drawn four-wheeled cab introduced in the 1860s. It allegedly acquired its name from the hostile attitude of its drivers.

from Meath rather than return as I came, through the front door on the sea. In 1876 I had had enough of Dublin. James Joyce in his Ulysses [1922] has described, with a fidelity so ruthless that the book is hardly bearable, the life that Dublin offers to its young men, or, if you prefer to put it the other way, that its young men offer to Dublin. No doubt it is much like the life of young men everywhere in modern urban civilization. A certain flippant futile derision and belittlement that confuses the noble and serious with the base and ludicrous seems to me peculiar to Dublin; but I suppose that is because my only personal experience of that phase of youth was a Dublin experience; for when I left my native city I left that phase behind me, and associated no more with men of my age until, after about eight years of solitude in this respect, I was drawn into the Socialist revival of the early eighties, among Englishmen intensely serious and burning with indignation at very real and very fundamental evils that affected all the world; so that the reaction against them bound the finer spirits of all the nations together instead of making them cherish hatred of oneanother as a national virtue. Thus, when I left Dublin I left (a few private friendships apart) no society that did not disgust me. To this day my sentimental regard for Ireland does not include the capital. I am not enamored of failure, of poverty, of obscurity, and of the ostracism and contempt which these imply; and these were all that Dublin offered to the enormity of my unconscious ambition. The cities a man likes are the cities he has conquered. Napoleon did not turn from Paris to sentimentalize over Ajaccio, nor Catherine from St Petersburg to Stettin as the centre of her universe.[14]

On this question of ambition let me say a word. In the ordinary connotation of the word I am the least ambitious of men. I have said, and I confirm it here, that I am so poor a hand at pushing and struggling, and so little interested in their rewards, that I have risen by sheer gravitation, too industrious by acquired habit to stop working (I work as my father drank), and too lazy and timid by nature to lay hold of half the opportunities or a tenth of the money that a conventionally ambitious man would have grasped strenuously. I never thought of myself as destined to become what is called a great man: indeed I was diffident to the most distressing degree; and I was ridiculously credulous as to the claims of others to superior knowledge and authority. But one day in the office I had a shock. One of the apprentices, by name C. J. Smyth, older than I and more a man of the world, remarked that every young chap thought he was going to be a great man. On a really modest youth this commonplace would have had no effect. It gave me so perceptible a jar that

14. Ajaccio and Stettin were their birthplaces.

I suddenly became aware that I had never thought I was to be a great man simply because I had always taken it as a matter of course. The incident passed without leaving any preoccupation with it to hamper me; and I remained as diffident as ever because I was still as incompetent as ever. But I doubt whether I ever recovered my former complete innocence of subconscious intention to devote myself to the class of work that only a few men excel in, and to accept the responsibilities that attach to its dignity.

Now this bore directly on my abandonment of Dublin, for which many young Irishmen of today find it impossible to forgive me. My business in life could not be transacted in Dublin out of an experience confined to Ireland. I had to go to London just as my father had to go to the Corn Exchange. London was the literary centre for the English language, and for such artistic culture as the realm of the English language (in which I proposed to be king) could afford. There was no Gaelic League[15] in those days, nor any sense that Ireland had in herself the seed of culture. Every Irishman who felt that his business in life was on the higher planes of the cultural professions felt that he must have a metropolitan domicile and an international culture: that is, he felt that his first business was to get out of Ireland. I had the same feeling. For London as London, or England as England, I cared nothing. If my subject had been science or music I should have made for Berlin or Leipsic. If painting, I should have made for Paris: indeed many of the Irish writers who have made a name in literature escaped to Paris with the intention of becoming painters. For theology I should have gone to Rome, and for Protestant philosophy to Weimar. But as the English language was my weapon, there was nothing for it but London. In 1914 the Germans, resenting my description of their Imperial political situation as Potsdamnation [see vol. 2, p. 143], denounced me as a fatherlandless fellow. They were quite right. I was no more offended than if they had called me unparochial. They had never reproached me for making pilgrimages to Bayreuth when I could as easily have made them to the Hill of Tara. If you want to make me homesick, remind me of the Thuringian Fichtelgebirge,[16] of the broad fields and delicate airs of France, of the Gorges of the Tarn, of the Passes of the Tyrol, of the North African desert, of the Golden Horn,[17] of the Swedish lakes, or even of the Norwegian fiords where I have never been except in imagination, and

15. Founded in 1893 by Irish scholar Douglas Hyde.
16. A spruce-forested plateau in north-east Bavaria, one of its three highlands being the Thüringer Wald (Woods) in the north-west of the plateau.
17. Part of the harbour of Istanbul, formed by the arm of the Bosporus in European Turkey.

you may stir that craving in me as easily—probably more easily—as in any exiled native of these places. It was not until I went back to Ireland as a tourist that I perceived that the charm of my country was quite independent of the accident of my having been born in it, and that it could fascinate a Spaniard or an Englishman more powerfully than an Irishman, in whose feeling for it there must always be a strange anguish, because it is the country where he has been unhappy and where vulgarity is vulgar to him. And so I am a tolerably good European in the Nietzschean sense,[18] but a very bad Irishman in the Sinn Fein[19] or Chosen People sense.

For the first couple of years of my life in London I did nothing decisive. I acted as ghost for a musician who had accepted a berth as musical critic; and as such ghosts must not appear, and I was therefore cut off from the paper and could not correct proofs, my criticisms, mostly very ruthless ones, appeared with such misprints, such mutilations and venal interpolations by other hands, so inextricably mixed up with other criticisms most offensive to my artistic sense, that I have ever since hidden this activity of mine as a guilty secret, lest someone should dig out these old notices and imagine that I was responsible for everything in them and with them. Even now I can hardly bring myself to reveal that the name of the paper was The Hornet,[20] and that it had passed then into the hands of a certain Captain Donald Shaw, who was not related to me, and whom I never met. It died on his hands, and partly, perhaps, at mine.

Then my cousin, Mrs Cashel Hoey,[21] a woman of letters, daughter of the aunt who played the tambourine with her beautiful hands, gave me an introduction to Arnold White,[22] then secretary to the Edison Telephone Company. He found a berth for me in the Way Leave Department of that shortlived company; and I presently found myself studying the topography of the east end of London, and trying to persuade all sorts of people to allow

18. Nietzsche, in his *Untimely Meditations* (1873–6), was critical of German national-ism as an outgrowth of the Franco-Prussian War and its cultural associations, as in Wagner.
19. Sinn Féin (We Ourselves) was an Irish nationalist/separatist movement that flourished from 1900 to the creation of the Free State in 1922.
20. Satirical weekly, to which Shaw contributed his earliest music criticism, from 29 November 1876 to 26 September 1877, ghost-written.
21. Frances (Fanny) Johnston, a novelist who was the eldest child of Shaw's Aunt Charlotte.
22. Later a social and political commentator, editor and journalist (under the pseudo-nym 'Vanoc').

the Company to put insulators and poles and derricks and the like on their roofs to carry the telephone lines. I liked the exploration involved; but my shyness made the business of calling on strangers frightfully uncongenial; and my sensitiveness, which was extreme, in spite of the brazen fortitude which I simulated, made the impatient rebuffs I had to endure occasionally, especially from much worried women who mistook me for an advertisement canvasser, ridiculously painful to me. But I escaped these trials presently; for I soon had to take charge of the department, and organize the work of more thick-skinned adventurers instead of doing it myself. Further particulars will be found in the preface to my second novel, The Irrational Knot. The Edison Telephone Company was presently swallowed up by the Bell Telephone Company; and I seized the opportunity to recover my destitute freedom by refusing to apply for the employment promised by the amalgamation to the disbanded staff. This was the end of my career as a commercial employee. I soon dropped even the pretence of seeking any renewal of it. Except for a day or two in 1881, when I earned a few pounds by counting the votes at an election in Leyton, I was an Unemployable, an ablebodied pauper in fact if not in law, until the year 1885, when for the first time I earned enough money directly by my pen to pay my way. My income for that year amounted to £112; and from that time until the war of 1914–18 momentarily threatened us all with bankruptcy, I had no pecuniary anxieties except those produced by the possession of money, not by the lack of it. My penury phase was over.

The telephone episode occurred in 1879; and in that year I had done what every literary adventurer did in those days, and many do still. I had written a novel. My office training had left me with a habit of doing something regularly every day as a fundamental condition of industry as distinguished from idleness. I knew I was making no headway unless I was doing this, and that I should never produce a book in any other fashion. I bought supplies of white paper, demy size, by sixpennorths at a time; folded it in quarto; and condemned myself to fill five pages of it a day, rain or shine, dull or inspired. I had so much of the schoolboy and the clerk still in me that if my five pages ended in the middle of a sentence I did not finish it until next day. On the other hand, if I missed a day, I made up for it by doing a double task on the morrow. On this plan I produced five novels in five years. It was my professional apprenticeship, doggedly suffered with all the diffidence and dissatisfaction of a learner with a very critical master, myself to wit, whom there was no pleasing and no evading, and persevered in to save my self-respect in a condition of impecuniosity which, for two acute moments (I still recall them with a wry face), added broken boots and carefully hidden raggedness to cuffs whose edges were trimmed by the scissors, and a tall hat so limp with age that I had to wear it back-to-front to enable me to take it off without doubling up the brim.

I had no success as a novelist. I sent the five novels to all the publishers in London and some in America. None would venture on them. Fifty or sixty refusals without a single acceptance forced me into a fierce self-sufficiency. I became undiscourageable, acquiring a superhuman insensitiveness to praise or blame which has been useful to me at times since, though at other times it has retarded my business affairs by making me indifferent to the publication and performances of my works, and even impatient of them as an unwelcome interruption to the labor of writing their successors. Instead of seizing every opportunity of bringing them before the public, I have often, on plausible but really trivial pretexts, put off proposals which I should have embraced with all the normal author's keenness for publicity.

Thus, after five years of novel writing, I was a complete professional failure. The more I wrote and the better I wrote the less I pleased the publishers. This first novel of mine, though rejected, at least elicited some expressions of willingness to read any future attempts. Blackwood actually accepted and then revoked. Sir George Macmillan, then a junior, not only sent me a longish and evidently considered report by the firm's reader, John (afterwards Lord) Morley, but suggested to him that I might be of some use to him in his capacity as editor of the Pall Mall Gazette.[23]

All such responses ceased with my second novel; and I had no means of knowing, and was too young and inexperienced to guess, that what was the matter was not any lack of literary competence on my part, but the antagonism raised by my hostility to respectable Victorian thought and society. I was left without a ray of hope; yet I did not stop writing novels until, having planned my fifth effort on a colossal scale, I found at the end of what were to me only the first two sections of it, that I had no more to say and had better wait until I had educated myself much farther. And when, after an interval of critical journalism, I resumed the writing of fiction, I did so as a playwright and not as a novelist.

Four of the five novels of my nonage, as I call them, at last got into print as described in the preface already cited. But the first of them never got published at all. Opening the old parcel, as I do now (it is like opening a grave that has been closed for fortytwo years), I find a pile of cahiers of twenty pages each, and realize with some dismay that I am face-to-face

23. Morley was appointed editor of the *Pall Mall Gazette* in May 1880. In that same month he invited Shaw to submit a few specimens of critical writing, returning them as 'not quite suitable for this paper' (British Library, Add. Mss. 50508).

with a novel containing nearly 200,000 words. The title is Immaturity. The handwriting, which slopes slightly backwards, has all the regularity and legibility of my old cash book. Unfortunately, the mice have eaten so much of two of the cahiers that the ends of the lines are missing. This is awkward; for I have just told myself that I must make no attempt to correct the work of the apprentice with the hand of the master; that such as it is it must remain;[24] that I am too old now to touch it without producing new incongruities more disagreeable than any that are possible between the style of 1879 and the taste of 1921. Yet, if the mice have eaten much, I must play the sedulous ape, like Stevenson, and imitate my own youthful manner like any literary forger.

It may be asked why I should print the thing at all: why not let ill alone? I am quite disposed to do so; but somehow one must not do such things. If Beethoven had destroyed his septet for wind instruments when he had advanced to the ninth symphony and the Mass in D, many people who delight in the septet and cannot make head or tail of symphony or Mass would suffer a wanton deprivation; and though my early style now makes me laugh at its pedantry, yet I have a great respect for the priggish conscientiousness of my first efforts. They prove too that, like Goethe, I knew all along, and have added more to my power of handling, illustrating, and addressing my material than to the material itself.

Anyhow, I have little doubt that Immaturity will be at least readable by the easygoing bookbuyers who will devour anything in the shape of a novel, however ridiculously out of fashion it may be. I know that some readers will like it much better than my later works. There must be a certain quality of youth in it which I could not now recapture, and which may even have charm as well as weakness and absurdity. Having re-read the other four novels for publication and republication at one time or another, I can guarantee the propriety of my early style. It was the last thing in correctness. I have never aimed at style in my life: style is a sort of melody that comes into my sentences by itself. If a writer says what he has to say as accurately and effectively as he can, his style will take care of itself, if he has a style. But I did set up one condition in my early days. I resolved that I would write nothing that should not be intelligible to a foreigner with a dictionary, like the French of Voltaire; and I therefore avoided idiom. (Later on I came to seek idiom as being the most highly vitalized form of language). Consequently I do not expect to find the English of Immaturity idiomatic. Also, there will be nothing of the

24. Between the composition of the preface (1921) and publication of the novel (1930) Shaw silently amended the text extensively. See Nicholas Grene, 'The Maturing of *Immaturity*', *Irish University Review* (Dublin), XX (Autumn 1990), pp. 225–38.

voice of the public speaker in it: the voice that rings through so much of my later work. Not until Immaturity was finished, late in 1879, did I for the first time rise to my feet in a little debating club called the Zetetical Society,[25] to make, in a condition of heartbreaking nervousness, my first assault on an audience.

Perhaps I had better add a word as to the characters in the book. I do so with some reluctance, because it is misleading to mention even the smallest circumstance connecting a fictitious person with a living one. If Shakespear had happened to mention that he made the Prince of Denmark carry a set of tablets and make notes in them because he had seen Sir Walter Raleigh doing so, it would by this time be an invincible tradition in English literature that Raleigh was the original of Hamlet. We should have writers following up the clue, as they would call it, to the conclusion that Raleigh was the real author of the play. One day, as I was sitting in the reading room of the British Museum, beginning my fifth and last novel, An Unsocial Socialist, I saw a young lady with an attractive and arresting expression, bold, vivid, and very clever, working at one of the desks. On that glimpse of a face I instantly conceived the character and wrote the description of Agatha Wylie. I have never exchanged a word with that lady; never made her acquaintance; saw her again under the same circumstances but very few times; yet if I mention her name, which became well known in literature (she too was writing a novel then, probably, and perhaps had the hero suggested to her by my profile), she will be set down as Agatha Wylie to her dying day, with heaven knows how much more scandalous invention added to account for my supposed intimate knowledge of her character. Before and since, I have used living models as freely as a painter does, and in much the same way: that is, I have sometimes made a fairly faithful portrait founded on intimate personal intercourse, and sometimes, as in Agatha's case, developed what a passing glance suggested to my imagination. In the latter case it has happened sometimes that the incidents I have invented on the spur of such a glance have hit the facts so nearly that I have found myself accused of unpardonable violations of personal privacy. I hardly expect to be believed when I say that I once invented a servant for one of my models and found afterwards that he actually had just such a servant. Between the two extremes of actual portraiture and pure fancy work suggested by a glance or an anecdote, I have copied nature with many degrees of fidelity, combining studies from life in

25. Shaw's initial experience as a speaker occurred at the Zetetical (founded in 1878) when, on 8 February 1882, he read a paper 'On what is called The Sacredness Of Human Life, and its bearing on the question of Capital Punishment'.

the same book or play with those types and composites and traditional figures of the novel and the stage which are called pure fictions. Many of the characters in this first novel of mine owed something to persons I had met, including members of my family (not to mention myself); but none of them are portraits; and with one exception the models are unknown to the public.[26] That exception was Cecil Lawson,[27] whose early death lost us the only land-scape painter who ever reminded me of the spacious and fascinating experiments of Rubens in that branch of painting. When I lived at Victoria Grove the Lawsons: father, mother, Malcolm, and two sisters, lived in one of the handsome old houses in Cheyne Walk, Chelsea. Cecil and another brother, being married, boarded out. Malcolm was a musician; and the sisters sang. One, a soprano, dark, quick, plump and bright, sang joyously. The other, a contralto, sang with heartbreaking intensity of expression, which she deepened by dressing esthetically, as it was called then, meaning in the Rossettian taste. Miss Lawson produced this effect, not by the ugly extravagances which made the fashionable milliners' version of the esthetic mode ridiculous, but by very simple grey and brown gowns which somehow harmonized with her habitual expression of sadness and even suffering; so that when she sang "Oh, dont deceive me: oh, never leave me,"[28] she produced a picture as well as a tone poem. Cecil, who had just acquired a position by the few masterpieces which remain to us, was very much "in the movement" at the old Grosvenor Gallery (now the Aeolian Hall), then new, and passing through the sensational vogue achieved by its revelations of Burne Jones and Whistler.

Malcolm was conducting a Gluck Society, at which I had discovered Gluck through a recital of Alceste, in which Theo[dor] Marzials,[29] who had a charming baritone voice, sang the part of Hercules. My mother had met Marzials in the course of her musical activities: he introduced her to Malcolm Lawson: she lent him a hand in the chorus of the Gluck Society; and the

26. Shaw had apparently overlooked the dancer Erminia Pertoldi, the Alhambra Theatre's *prima ballerina* (called Bernardine di Sangallo in the 1879 text) of whom the young protagonist (a Shavian clone) was enamoured. When Shaw subsequently revised the text he substituted her real name.

27. English artist, who died in 1882, at the age of thirty-one. His brother Malcolm, a musician, was conductor of the Gluck Society and the St Cecilia Choir.

28. A line repeated in each of several verses of a traditional English tune, 'Early One Morning' (James F. Leisy, *The Folk Song Abecedary*, New York, 1966).

29. Young Belgian singer, a pupil of Malcolm Lawson; composer of popular songs and opera librettos. At twenty (1870) he became superintendent of the music division of the British Museum.

result was that I found myself invited to visit the Lawsons, who were at home in Cheyne Walk every Sunday evening. I suffered such agonies of shyness that I sometimes walked up and down the Embankment for twenty minutes or more before venturing to knock at the door: indeed I should have funked it altogether, and hurried home asking myself what was the use of torturing myself when it was so easy to run away, if I had not been instinctively aware that I must never let myself off in this manner if I meant ever to do anything in the world. Few men can have suffered more than I did in my youth from simple cowardice or been more horribly ashamed of it. I shirked and hid when the peril, real or imaginary, was of the sort that I had no vital interest in facing; but when such an interest was at stake, I went ahead and suffered accordingly. The worst of it was that when I appeared in the Lawsons' drawingroom I did not appeal to the goodnature of the company as a pardonably and even becomingly bashful novice. I had not then tuned the Shavian note to any sort of harmony; and I have no doubt the Lawsons found me discordant, crudely self-assertive, and insufferable. I hope they, and all the others on whom I jarred at this time, forgave me in later years, when it turned out that I really had something to assert after all. The house and its artistic atmosphere were most congenial to me; and I liked all the Lawsons; but I had not mastered the art of society at that time, and could not bear making an inartistic exhibition of myself; so I soon ceased to plague them, and, except for an occasional chance meeting with Malcolm, passed out of their lives after touching them very lightly in passing.

Cecil Lawson was the spoilt child of that household. He pontificated on art in a wayward grumbling incoherent musing fashion of his own. When, following my youthful and very irritating system of contradicting everyone from whom I thought I could learn anything, I suggested that Whistler was something short of the greatest artist of all time, he could not form a sentence to crush me with, but groaned inarticulately for a moment, like a clock about to strike, and then uttered the words Titian Turner Rembrandt Velasquez Whistler. He was goodlooking, not a big man, but trimly built, with just enough crisply curled hair to proclaim the artist without compromising the man. I had seen his work in the public exhibitions (never in private); and, thanks to my boyish prowlings in the Dublin National Gallery (as a boy I wanted to be a painter, never a writer), I knew its value. His untimely death, which occurred soon after my visits, must have broken up the Sunday evenings at Cheyne Walk very badly. I did not venture to intrude after it.

I used him in Immaturity as a model for the artist Cyril Scott, an invented name which has since been made famous by a British composer. I chose it because Cyril resembled Cecil metrically, and because I thought Lawson was a Scot (he was, I learn, born in Shropshire). But I must again warn the reader against taking the man in the book as an authentic portrait of the great painter, or inferring that his courtship and marriage or any of the circumstances I have invented for him, represent facts in Lawson's life. I knew nothing whatever about him except what I saw of him during my few visits to Cheyne Walk; and I have learnt nothing since. He set my imagination to work: that was all.

I have now told as much as seems to me necessary of the circumstances and relevant antecedents of my first book. It is the book of a raw youth, still quite out of touch with the country to which he had transported himself; and if I am to be entirely communicative on this subject, I must add that the mere rawness which so soon rubs off was complicated by a deeper strangeness which has made me all my life a sojourner on this planet rather than a native of it. Whether it be that I was born mad or a little too sane, my kingdom was not of this world: I was at home only in the realm of my imagination, and at my ease only with the mighty dead. Therefore I had to become an actor, and create for myself a fantastic personality fit and apt for dealing with men, and adaptable to the various parts I had to play as author, journalist, orator, politician, committee man, man of the world, and so forth. In this I succeeded later on only too well. In my boyhood [December 1868] I saw Charles Mathews act in a farce called Cool as a Cucumber.[30] The hero was a young man just returned from a tour of the world, upon which he had been sent to cure him of an apparently hopeless bashfulness; and the fun lay in the cure having overshot the mark and transformed him into a monster of outrageous impudence. I am not sure that something of the kind did not happen to me; for when my imposture was at last accomplished, and I daily pulled the threads of the puppet who represented me in the public press, the applause that greeted it was not unlike that which Mathews drew in Cool as a Cucumber. Certainly the growls of resentful disgust with which my advances were resisted closely resembled those of the unfortunate old gentleman in the farce whose pictures and furniture the young man so coolly rearranged to his own taste. At the time of which I am writing, however, I had not yet learnt to act, nor come to understand that my natural character was impossible on the great stage of London. When I had to come out of the realm of imagination into that of actuality I was still uncomfortable. I was outside society, outside politics, outside sport, outside the Church. If the term had

30. Mathews, an English actor-manager, was a popular light comedian. The role of Plumper in W. B. Jerrold's *Cool as a Cucumber* (1851), one of his most successful creations, remained in his repertory for quarter of a century.

been invented then I should have been called The Complete Outsider. But the epithet would have been appropriate only within the limits of British barbarism. The moment music, painting, literature, or science came into question the positions were reversed: it was I who was the Insider. I had the intellectual habit; and my natural combination of critical faculty with literary resource needed only a clear comprehension of life in the light of an intelligible theory: in short, a religion, to set it in triumphant operation. It was the lack of this last qualification that lamed me in those early days in Victoria Grove, and that set limits to this ungainly first novel of mine, which you will not lose very much by skipping.

AYOT ST LAWRENCE.
Summer, 1921.

# Poems of Mihail Eminescu

*A translation from the Romanian, rendered into the original metres by
E. Sylvia Pankhurst and I. O. Ştefanovici,*[1] *London, 1930. A holograph letter from
Shaw to Pankhurst, dated 12 September 1929, reproduced in facsimile,
is identified on the title as 'a Preface'*

═══

My dear Sylvia

After turning the whole house upside down in a despairing and finally maddened search for this typescript I collapsed into a chair utterly beaten, and immediately saw the thing lying at my elbow where it had been staring me in the face all the time. This gave the whole business such a supernatural air that under the influence of it and of exhaustion (I had begun the day with a hundred mile drive from Malvern, to find your imperious telegram awaiting me) I read Emperor & Proletarian and Ghosts and the rest over again.

If I were one of these young publishers with printing presses of their own, who dig up impossible old books and make collectors' editions of them I would just jump at this amazing book. Have you ever read Southey, or Burger's Lenore?[2] Have you ever seen the folios in the British Museum containing Delacroix' illustrations to Faust—great lithographs they are? Fifty years ago I used to try them on people to see whether they had any real original artistic sense and free imagination; but they hadnt; and since then I doubt whether the book and its companion Hamlet has ever been asked for: at least I have never heard them mentioned.[3]

Now if you could only find a Delacroix (young) and a publisher (also young), and a Press! No prosaic Macmillan-Murray-Constable issue would strike the right note. Music by Berlioz would also be desirable.

1. Sylvia Pankhurst, editor of the *Women's* (later *Workers'*) *Dreadnought*, is identified in vol. 2, p. 523. I. Olimpiu Ştefanovici-Svensk, Romanian author, scholar and translator of Wilde and H. G. Wells, studied for a doctorate in London 1924–7, then taught English in the Academia Comercialá, Cluj.
2. Gottfried Bürger, a German poet, was a force in the revival of folklore and development of ballad literature. *Lenore* (1773) is his best-known poetical work.
3. The artist Eugène Delacroix, who became interested in the new medium of lithography, produced a volume of seventeen engraved *Faust* subjects (1827) from Goethe, and sixteen *Hamlet* lithographs (1843).

The translation is astonishing and outrageous: it carried me away.

Sylvia: you are the queerest idiot-genius of this age—the most ungovernable, self-intoxicated, blindly and deafly wilful little rapscallion-condotierra [mercenary leader] that ever imposed itself on the infra-red end of the revolutionary spectrum as a leader; but that you had this specific literary talent for rhyming and riding over words at a gallop has hitherto been a secret.

Let me know what luck you have with the Moldavian,[4] who raised the XVIII–XIX *fin de siècle* from its grave.

faithfully
G. Bernard Shaw.

4. Mihail Eminescu, pseudonym of Mihail Eminovici, was a Romanian poet, whose pessimistic verse, collected in 1883, was permeated with folklore and legend.

# An Unsocial Socialist

*Preface for the Collected Edition, 1930*

======

This, the last of the Novels of My Nonage, is, according to my original design, only the first chapter of a vast work depicting capitalist society in dissolution, with its downfall as the final grand catastrophe. But when I had finished my chapter I found I had emptied my sack and left myself no more to say for the moment, and had better defer completion until my education was considerably more advanced. Thirtyseven[1] years having now been devoted to this process it is too late to resume the interrupted work; for events have outrun me. The contemplated fiction is now fact. My unsocial socialist has come to life as a Bolshevist; and my catastrophe has actually occurred in Communist Russia. The opinions of the fictitious Trefusis anticipated those of the real Lenin.

With the writing of this book my career as a novelist may be said to have ended before it had begun. As I have explained in the preface to Immaturity I employed myself in novel writing because nobody would employ me in any other sort of writing. It happened that just when I came to a standstill at the end of my first chapter as aforesaid my late friend William Archer pushed me into critical journalism by handing over to me certain jobs of his own for which he had little time and less inclination. I easily made good at criticism, which enabled me to make a living until, about ten years later, I discovered my main vocation in the profession of Shakespear and Molière, and thus returned to storytelling in its most highly specialized form.

I am not now likely to go back to novel writing. The novels of my nonage do not seem to me to call for a series of novels of my dotage. Their style seems quaintly oldfashioned nowadays; but fifty years hence my latest works will be indistinguishable from them in that respect. So, leaving them, with many apologies, to find what readers they can, I hasten on to the plays which succeeded them after that long interval during which I had left my novitiate behind and passed into middle age with its experiences and its freedom from the technical shyness of the beginner. In short, I had become, for better for worse, a different man.

AYOT ST LAWRENCE.                                                                    G. B. S.
18th February 1930.


1. Error for forty-seven years; the novel was written in 1883.

# To the Intelligent Hebrew Woman

*Written for the Hebrew translation, by Pessah Ginsburg, of* The Intelligent
Woman's Guide to Socialism and Capitalism, *Tel Aviv, 1931–3.
First published in its original English text in the* Manchester Guardian,
*15 July 1930*

When the Intelligent Woman is a Daughter of Jerusalem, let the Gentile
Author beware how he approaches her with an offer of guidance. I have no
illusions as to how I stand in the eyes of the chosen race. To them I am a
thing of yesterday, a barbarian, at best a creature into whose brutish hand
Jehovah has given a moment's power as a chastisement to the Jewess whose
pride will not permit her to walk humbly even with her God. How can I
expect her to walk humbly with me, accepting me as her leader in the paths
of wisdom?

Let me haste, then, to assure her that I am guilty of no such presumption.
I offer myself as a guide precisely as the poorest Bedouin in all humility might
offer himself to the Queen of Sheba to guide her through a strange corner
of the desert.

I am an Irishman; and to common Irishmen the Jew is a heathen who
barbarously killed his Savior and will go to hell for it. If you remind him
that the slain Savior was himself a Jew, he is shocked, for it has never occurred
to him to doubt that Jesus was a sound Irish Roman Catholic. I, being the
uncommon Irishman, do not entertain such illusions. For one thing, I do not
believe that Jesus was any more or less divine than Moses or myself; and as
that view is now widespread among the leaders of English culture, I now
often ask them wherein they differ from the Jews, seeing that the supernatural
character of Jesus is the only tenet on which the baptized and circumcized
fell out with oneanother. Jesus is now among the prophets; no modern
cultivated Jew reviles "Jeshu the Bastard" [see vol. 2, p. 176]; nor does any
cultivated Christian, even in Germany, speak or think of the Jews as "God
Murderers." It is true that there is the Law, and the observances that were
set up to prevent the Jews from going the way of St Paul. But these are not
fundamental; there are differences within Christendom in such matters just
as wide as between Christian and Jew.

But when we come upon the ground of Socialism the distinction becomes wholly absurd. From Karl Marx and Ferdinand Lassalle to Walter Rathenau[1] and the pioneers of Russian Communism, the Jew has been the inspirer, leader, and pleader of the European movement towards collectivism and Internationalism. I was converted to Socialism as a young man by Karl Marx, and Rathenau's mentality and outlook on life were far less foreign to mine than that of the anti-Semite statesmen who were then blundering into the war.

Zion must sink or swim with the whole of modern civilization, and the Jews can save themselves only by saving the Gentiles and sharing their salvation.

That is why I send my book unto the tents of Shem as earnestly as into the libraries of the Philistines.

1. German-Jewish industrialist, philosophical writer and democratic statesman, who became foreign minister in 1921. He was assassinated in June 1922 by fanatical nationalists.

# The Apple Cart

*First published in 1930*

The first performances of this play at home and abroad[1] provoked several confident anticipations that it would be published with an elaborate prefatory treatise on Democracy to explain why I, formerly a notorious democrat, have apparently veered round to the opposite quarter and become a devoted Royalist. In Dresden the performance was actually prohibited as a blasphemy against Democracy.[2]

What was all this pother about? I had written a comedy in which a King defeats an attempt by his popularly elected Prime Minister to deprive him of the right to influence public opinion through the press and the platform: in short, to reduce him to a cipher. The King's reply is that rather than be a cipher he will abandon his throne and take his obviously very rosy chance of becoming a popularly elected Prime Minister himself. To those who believe that our system of votes for everybody produces parliaments which represent the people it should seem that this solution of the difficulty is completely democratic, and that the Prime Minister must at once accept it joyfully as such. He knows better. The change would rally the anti-democratic royalist vote against him, and impose on him a rival in the person of the only public man whose ability he has to fear. The comedic paradox of the situation is that the King wins, not by exercising his royal authority, but by threatening to resign it and go to the democratic poll.

1. Warsaw: Teatr Polski, 14 June 1929; first Malvern Festival, 19 August 1929; London: Queen's Theatre, 17 September 1929 (258 performances); Berlin: Deutsches Theater, 19 October 1929 (197 performances in repertory in first season).
2. Dr [?Wilhelm] Bünger, Saxon Minister of Education, whose ministry controlled the State Theatre of Dresden, expressed misgivings about the ironic treatment of democracy in the play, as reported in *The Times*, 13 December 1929. Although the *Berliner Tageblatt* took the view that there was no legal basis for censoring the play and that Germany would incur much ridicule if the play were banned, Bünger's unassailable position, coupled with negative press reaction to the Berlin production in October, was sufficiently intimidating for the Dresden management to halt rehearsals and withdraw the production.

That so many critics who believe themselves to be ardent democrats should take the entirely personal triumph of the hereditary king over the elected minister to be a triumph of autocracy over democracy, and its dramatization an act of political apostasy on the part of the author, convinces me that our professed devotion to political principles is only a mask for our idolatry of eminent persons. The Apple Cart exposes the unreality of both democracy and royalty as our idealists conceive them. Our Liberal democrats believe in a figment called a constitutional monarch, a sort of Punch puppet who cannot move until his Prime Minister's fingers are in his sleeves. They believe in another figment called a responsible minister, who moves only when similarly actuated by the million fingers of the electorate. But the most superficial inspection of any two such figures shews that they are not puppets but living men, and that the supposed control of one by the other and of both by the electorate amounts to no more than a not very deterrent fear of uncertain and under ordinary circumstances quite remote consequences. The nearest thing to a puppet in our political system is a Cabinet minister at the head of a great public office. Unless he possesses a very exceptional share of dominating ability and relevant knowledge he is helpless in the hands of his officials. He must sign whatever documents they present to him, and repeat whatever words they put into his mouth when answering questions in parliament, with a docility which cannot be imposed on a king who works at his job; for the king works continuously whilst his ministers are in office for spells only, the spells being few and brief, and often occurring for the first time to men of advanced age with little or no training for and experience of supreme responsibility. George the Third and Queen Victoria were not, like Queen Elizabeth, the natural superiors of their ministers in political genius and general capacity; but they were for many purposes of State necessarily superior to them in experience, in cunning, in exact knowledge of the limits of their responsibility and consequently of the limits of their irresponsibility: in short, in the authority and practical power that these superiorities produce. Very clever men who have come into contact with monarchs have been so impressed that they have attributed to them extraordinary natural qualifications which they, as now visible to us in historical perspective, clearly did not possess. In conflicts between monarchs and popularly elected ministers the monarchs win every time when personal ability and good sense are at all equally divided.

In The Apple Cart this equality is assumed. It is masked by a strong contrast of character and methods which has led my less considerate critics to complain that I have packed the cards by making the King a wise man and the minister a fool. But that is not at all the relation between the two. Both play with equal skill; and the King wins, not by greater astuteness, but because he has the ace of trumps in his hand and knows when to play it. As the prettier player of the two he has the sympathy of the audience. Not being as pampered and powerful as an operatic *prima donna*, and depending as he does not on some commercially valuable talent but on his conformity to the popular ideal of dignity and perfect breeding, he has to be trained, and to train himself, to accept good manners as an indispensable condition of his intercourse with his subjects, and to leave to the less highly placed such indulgences as tempers, tantrums, bullyings, sneerings, swearings, kickings: in short, the commoner violences and intemperances of authority.

His ministers have much laxer standards. It is open to them, if it will save their time, to get their own way by making scenes, flying into calculated rages, and substituting vulgar abuse for argument. A clever minister, not having had a royal training, will, if he finds himself involved in a duel with his king, be careful not to choose the weapons at which the king can beat him. Rather will he in cold blood oppose to the king's perfect behavior an intentional misbehavior and apparently childish petulance which he can always drop at the right moment for a demeanor as urbane as that of the king himself, thus employing two sets of weapons to the king's one. This gives him the advantages of his own training as a successful ambitious man who has pushed his way from obscurity to celebrity: a process involving a considerable use of the shorter and more selfish methods of dominating the feebly recalcitrant, the unreasonable, the timid, and the stupid, as well as a sharp sense of the danger of these methods when dealing with persons of strong character in strong positions.

In this light the style of fighting adopted by the antagonists in the scrap between King Magnus and Mr Joseph Proteus is seen to be a plain deduction from their relative positions and antecedents, and not a manufactured contrast between democracy and royalty to the disadvantage of the former. Those who so mistook it are out of date. They still regard democracy as the under dog in the conflict. But to me it is the king who is doomed to be tragically in that position in the future into which the play is projected: in fact, he is visibly at least half in it already; and the theory of constitutional monarchy assumes that he is wholly in it, and has been so since the end of the XVII century.

Besides, the conflict is not really between royalty and democracy. It is between both and plutocracy, which, having destroyed the royal power by frank force under democratic pretexts, has bought and swallowed democracy. Money talks: money prints: money broadcasts: money reigns; and kings and labor leaders alike have to register its decrees, and even, by a staggering paradox, to finance its enterprizes and guarantee its profits. Democracy is no longer bought: it is bilked. Ministers who are Socialists to the backbone are as helpless in the grip of Breakages Limited as its acknowledged henchmen: from the moment when they attain to what is with unintentional irony called power (meaning the drudgery of carrying on for the plutocrats) they no longer dare even to talk of nationalizing any industry, however socially vital, that has a farthing of profit for plutocracy still left in it, or that can be made to yield a farthing for it by subsidies.

King Magnus's little tactical victory, which bulks so largely in the playhouse, leaves him in a worse plight than his defeated opponent, who can always plead that he is only the instrument of the people's will, wheras the unfortunate monarch, making a desperate bid for dictatorship on the perfectly true plea that democracy has destroyed all other responsibility (has not Mussolini said that there is a vacant throne in every country in Europe waiting for a capable man to fill it?), is compelled to assume full responsibility himself, and face all the reproaches that Mr Proteus can shirk. In his Cabinet there is only one friendly man who has courage, principle, and genuine good manners when he is courteously treated; and that man is an uncompromising republican, his rival for the dictatorship. The splendidly honest and devoted Die-hard lady is too scornfully tactless to help much; but with a little more experience in the art of handling effective men and women as distinguished from the art of handling mass meetings Mr Bill Boanerges might surprise those who, because he makes them laugh, see nothing in him but a caricature.

In short, those critics of mine who have taken The Apple Cart for a story of a struggle between a hero and a roomful of guys have been grossly taken in. It is never safe to take my plays at their suburban face value: it ends in your finding in them only what you bring to them, and so getting nothing for your money.

On the subject of Democracy generally I have nothing to say that can take the problem farther than I have already carried it in my Intelligent Woman's Guide to Socialism and Capitalism. We have to solve two inseparable main problems: the economic problem of how to produce and distribute our subsistence, and the political problem of how to select our rulers and prevent them from abusing their authority in their own interests or those of their class or religion. Our solution of the economic problem is the Capitalist system, which achieves miracles in production, but fails so ludicrously and disastrously to distribute its products rationally, or to produce in the order of social need, that it is always complaining of being paralyzed by its "overproduction" of things of which millions of us stand in desperate want. Our solution of the political problem is Votes for Everybody and Every Authority Elected by Vote, an expedient originally devized to prevent rulers from tyrannizing by the very effectual method of preventing them from doing anything, and thus leaving everything to irresponsible private enterprize. But as private enterprize will do nothing that is not profitable to its little self, and the very existence of civilization now depends on the swift and unhampered public execution of enterprizes that supersede private enterprize and are not merely profitable but vitally necessary to the whole community, this purely inhibitive check on tyranny has become a stranglehold on genuine democracy. Its painfully evolved machinery of parliament and Party System and Cabinet is so effective in obstruction that we take thirty years by constitutional methods to do thirty minutes work, and shall presently be forced to clear up thirty years arrears in thirty minutes by unconstitutional ones unless we pass a Reform Bill that will make a complete revolution in our political machinery and procedure. When we see parliaments like ours kicked into the gutter by dictators, both in kingdoms and republics, it is foolish to wait until the dictator dies or collapses, and then do nothing but pick the poor old things up and try to scrape the mud off them: the only sane course is to take the step by which the dictatorship could have been anticipated and averted, and construct a political system for rapid positive work instead of slow nugatory work, made to fit into the XX century instead of into the XVI.

Until we face this task and accomplish it we shall not be able to produce electorates capable of doing anything by their votes except pave the way to their own destruction. An election at present, considered as a means of selecting the best qualified rulers, is so absurd that if the last dozen parliaments had consisted of the candidates who were at the foot of the poll instead of those who were at the head of it there is no reason to suppose that we should have been a step more or less advanced than we are today. In neither case would the electorate have had any real choice of representatives. If it had, we might have had to struggle with parliaments of Titus Oateses and Lord George Gordons dominating a few generals and artists, with Cabinets made up of the sort of orator who is said to carry away his hearers by his eloquence because, having first ascertained by a few cautious feelers what they are ready to applaud, he gives it to them a dozen times over in an overwhelming crescendo, and is in effect carried away by them. As it is, the voters have no real choice of candidates: they have to take what they can get and make the best of it according to their lights, which is often the worst of it by the light of heaven. By chance rather than by judgment they find themselves represented in parliament by a fortunate proportion of reasonably honest and public spirited persons who happen to be also successful public speakers. The rest are in parliament because they can afford it and have a fancy for it or an interest in it.

Last October (1929) I was asked to address the enormous audience created by the new invention of Wireless Broadcast on a range of political and cultural topics introduced by a previous speaker under the general heading of Points of View. Among the topics was Democracy, presented, as usual, in a completely abstract guise as an infinitely beneficent principle in which we must trust though it slay us. I was determined that this time Votes for Everybody and Every Authority Elected by Vote should not escape by wearing its imposing mask. I delivered myself[3] as follows:

Your Majesties, your Royal Highnesses, your Excellencies, your Graces and Reverences, my Lords, Ladies and Gentlemen, fellow-citizens of all degrees: I am going to talk to you about Democracy objectively: that is, as it exists and as we must all reckon with it equally, no matter what our points of view may be. Suppose I were to talk to you not about Democracy, but about the sea, which is in some respects rather like Democracy! We all have our own views of the sea. Some of us hate it and are never well when we are at it or on it. Others love it, and are never so happy as when they are in it or on it or looking at it. Some of us regard it as Britain's natural realm and surest bulwark: others want a Channel Tunnel. But certain facts about the sea are quite independent of our feelings towards it. If I take it for granted that the sea exists, none of you will contradict me. If I say that the sea is sometimes furiously violent and always uncertain, and that those who are most familiar with it trust it least, you will not immediately shriek out that I do not believe in the sea; that I am an enemy of the sea; that I want to abolish the sea; that I am going to make bathing illegal; that I am out to ruin our carrying trade and lay waste all our seaside resorts and scrap the British Navy. If I tell you that you cannot breathe in the sea, you will not take that as a personal insult and ask me indignantly if I consider you inferior to a fish. Well, you must please be equally sensible when I tell you some hard facts about Democracy. When I tell you that it is sometimes furiously violent and always dangerous and treacherous, and that those who are familiar with it as practical statesmen trust it least, you must not at once denounce me as a paid agent of Benito Mussolini, or declare that I have become a Tory Die-hard in my old age, and accuse me of wanting to take away your votes and make an end of parliament, and the franchise, and free speech, and public meeting, and trial by jury. Still less must you rise in your places and give me three rousing cheers as a champion of medieval monarchy and feudalism. I am quite innocent of any such extravagances. All I mean is that whether we are Democrats or Tories, Catholics or Protestants, Communists or Fascists, we are all face to face with a certain force in the world called Democracy; and we must understand the nature of that force whether we want to fight it or to forward it. Our business is not to deny the perils of Democracy, but to provide against them as far as we can, and then consider whether the risks we cannot provide against are worth taking.

3. 'Points of View: III', BBC, 14 October 1929, relayed from Plymouth.

Democracy, as you know it, is seldom more than a long word beginning with a capital letter, which we accept reverently or disparage contemptuously without asking any questions. Now we should never accept anything reverently until we have asked it a great many very searching questions, the first two being What are you? and Where do you live? When I put these questions to Democracy the answer I get is "My name is Demos; and I live in the British Empire, the United States of America, and wherever the love of liberty burns in the heart of man. You, my friend Shaw, are a unit of Democracy: your name is also Demos: you are a citizen of a great democratic community: you are a potential constituent of the Parliament of Man, the Federation of the World." At this I usually burst into loud cheers, which do credit to my enthusiastic nature. Tonight, however, I shall do nothing of the sort: I shall say "Dont talk nonsense. My name is not Demos: it is Bernard Shaw. My address is not the British Empire, nor the United States of America, nor wherever the love of liberty burns in the heart of man: it is at such and such a number in such and such a street in London; and it will be time enough to discuss my seat in the Parliament of Man when that celebrated institution comes into existence. I dont believe your name is Demos: nobody's name is Demos; and all I can make of your address is that you have no address, and are just a tramp—if indeed you exist at all."

You will notice that I am too polite to call Demos a windbag or a hot air merchant; but I am going to ask you to begin our study of Democracy by considering it first as a big balloon, filled with gas or hot air, and sent up so that you shall be kept looking up at the sky whilst other people are picking your pockets. When the balloon comes down to earth every five years or so you are invited to get into the basket if you can throw out one of the people who are sitting tightly in it; but as you can afford neither the time nor the money, and there are forty millions of you and hardly room for six hundred in the basket, the balloon goes up again with much the same lot in it and leaves you where you were before. I think you will admit that the balloon as an image of Democracy corresponds to the parliamentary facts.

Now let us examine a more poetic conception of Democracy. Abraham Lincoln is represented as standing amid the carnage of the battlefield of Gettysburg, and declaring that all that slaughter of Americans by Americans occurred in order that Democracy, defined as government *of* the people *for* the people *by* the people, should not perish from the earth. Let us pick this famous peroration to pieces and see what there really is inside it. (By the way, Lincoln did not really declaim it on the field of Gettysburg;[4] and the American Civil

4. The speech was delivered in the National Cemetery at Gettysburg during its dedication on 19 November 1863. This cemetery was originally a part of the battlefield. Baron Charnwood, in his *Abraham Lincoln* (1916), which Shaw had read and praised, indicated that a number of State governors 'combined to institute a National

War was not fought in defence of any such principle, but, on the contrary, to enable one half of the United States to force the other half to be governed as they did not wish to be governed. But never mind that. I mentioned it only to remind you that it seems impossible for statesmen to make speeches about Democracy, or journalists to report them, without obscuring it in a cloud of humbug.)

Now for the three articles of the definition. Number One: Government *of* the people: that, evidently, is necessary: a human community can no more exist without a government than a human being can exist without a coordinated control of its breathing and blood circulation. Number Two: Government *for* the people, is most important. Dean [William Ralph] Inge[5] put it perfectly for us when he called Democracy a form of society which means equal consideration for all. He added that it is a Christian principle, and that, as a Christian, he believes in it.[6] So do I. That is why I insist on equality of income. Equal consideration for a person with a hundred a year and one with a hundred thousand is impossible. But Number Three: Government *by* the people, is quite a different matter. All the monarchs, all the tyrants, all the dictators, all the Die-hard Tories are agreed that we must be governed. Democrats like the Dean and myself are agreed that we must be governed with equal consideration for everybody. But we repudiate Number Three on the ground that the people cannot govern. The thing is a physical impossibility. Every citizen cannot be a ruler any more than every boy can be an engine driver or a pirate king. A nation of prime ministers or dictators is as absurd as an army of field marshals. Government by the people is not and never can be a reality: it is only a cry by which demagogues humbug us into voting for them. If you doubt this— if you ask me "Why should not the people make their own laws?" I need only ask you "Why should not the people write their own plays?" They cannot. It is much easier to write a good play than to make a good law. And there are not a hundred men in the world who can write a play good enough to stand daily wear and tear as long as a law must.

Now comes the question, If we cannot govern ourselves, what can we do

---

Cemetery upon the field of Gettysburg'; but present belief is that Lincoln's speech was delivered in the local Gettysburg cemetery, Evergreen Cemetery, on a rise outside and above the federal cemetery (Gary Wills, *Lincoln at Gettysburg*, 1992).

5. English prelate, Dean of St Paul's, London, 1911–34. Among his books are *Christian Mysticism* (1899), *Outspoken Essays* (first and second series, 1919, 1922), *England* (1926), and *Lay Thoughts of a Dean* (1926), all of which Shaw read.

6. In a lecture 'Democracy' delivered in Philadelphia in 1925, Inge commented: '[T]he right to equal consideration, to equality before the law, and the absence of social castes, is, I cannot help thinking, a good and Christian thing. Perhaps Democracy gives it . . . a better chance than any other form of government' (*More Lay Thoughts of a Dean*, 1931).

to save ourselves from being at the mercy of those who *can* govern, and who may quite possibly be thoroughpaced grafters and scoundrels? The primitive answer is that as we are always in a huge majority we can, if rulers oppress us intolerably, burn their houses and tear them to pieces. This is not satisfactory. Decent people never do it until they have quite lost their heads; and when they have lost their heads they are as likely as not to burn the wrong house and tear the wrong man to pieces. When we have what is called a popular movement very few people who take part in it know what it is all about. I once saw a real popular movement in London. People were running excitedly through the streets. Everyone who saw them doing it immediately joined in the rush. They ran simply because everyone else was doing it. It was most impressive to see thousands of people sweeping along at full speed like that. There could be no doubt that it was literally a popular movement. I ascertained afterwards that it was started by a runaway cow. That cow had an important share in my education as a political philosopher; and I can assure you that if you will study crowds, and lost and terrified animals, and things like that, instead of reading books and newspaper articles, you will learn a great deal about politics from them. Most general elections, for instance, are nothing but stampedes. Our last but one was a conspicuous example of this. The cow was a Russian one.[7]

I think we may take it that neither mob violence nor popular movements can be depended on as checks upon the abuse of power by governments. One might suppose that at least they would act as a last resort when an autocrat goes mad and commits outrageous excesses of tyranny and cruelty. But it is a curious fact that they never do. Take two famous cases: those of Nero and Tsar Paul the First of Russia. If Nero had been an ordinary professional fiddler he would probably have been no worse a man than any member of the wireless orchestra. If Paul had been a lieutenant in a line regiment we should never have heard of him. But when these two poor fellows were invested with absolute powers over their fellow-creatures they went mad, and did such appalling things that they had to be killed like mad dogs. Only, it was not the people that rose up and killed them. They were dispatched quite privately by a very select circle of their own bodyguards. For a genuinely democratic execution of unpopular statesmen we must turn to the brothers De Witt,[8] who were torn to pieces by a Dutch mob in the XVII century. They were neither tyrants nor

7. In the 1924 General Election campaign preceding Polling Day, 29 October, the press expressed great hostility towards Ramsay MacDonald's peace effort to enter into treaties with Russia, identifying the Labour Party with Bolshevism. The Red scare brought the Conservatives back to power with a vast majority.
8. Johan de Witt, seventeenth-century Dutch statesman, and his brother Cornelis were slain by a mob in The Hague during Orangist riots that followed a French invasion of the lowlands.

autocrats. On the contrary, one of them had been imprisoned and tortured for his resistance to the despotism of William of Orange; and the other had come to meet him as he came out of prison. The mob was on the side of the autocrat. We may take it that the shortest way for a tyrant to get rid of a troublesome champion of liberty is to raise a hue and cry against him as an unpatriotic person, and leave the mob to do the rest after supplying them with a well tipped ringleader. Nowadays this is called direct action by the revolutionary proletariat. Those who put their faith in it soon find that proletariats are never revolutionary, and that their direct action, when it is controled at all, is usually controled by police agents.

Democracy, then, cannot be government by the people: it can only be government by consent of the governed. Unfortunately, when democratic statesmen propose to govern us by our own consent, they find that we dont want to be governed at all, and that we regard rates and taxes and rents and death duties as intolerable burdens. What we want to know is how little government we can get along with without being murdered in our beds. That question cannot be answered until we have explained what we mean by getting along. Savages manage to get along. Unruly Arabs and Tartars get along. The only rule in the matter is that the civilized way of getting along is the way of corporate action, not individual action; and corporate action involves more government than individual action.

Thus government, which used to be a comparatively simple affair, today has to manage an enormous development of Socialism and Communism. Our industrial and social life is set in a huge communistic framework of public roadways, streets, bridges, water supplies, power supplies, lighting, tramways, schools, dockyards, and public aids and conveniences, employing a prodigious army of police, inspectors, teachers, and officials of all grades in hundreds of departments. We have found by bitter experience that it is impossible to trust factories, workshops, and mines to private management. Only by stern laws enforced by constant inspection have we stopped the monstrous waste of human life and welfare it cost when it was left uncontroled by the Government. During the war our attempt to leave the munitioning of the army to private enterprize led us to the verge of defeat and caused an appalling slaughter of our soldiers. When the Government took the work out of private hands and had it done in national factories it was at once successful. The private firms were still allowed to do what little they could; but they had to be taught to do it economically, and to keep their accounts properly, by Government officials. Our big capitalist enterprizes now run to the Government for help as a lamb runs to its mother. They cannot even make an extension of the Tube railway in London without Government aid. Unassisted private capitalism is breaking down or getting left behind in all directions. If all our Socialism and Communism and the drastic taxation of unearned incomes which finances it were to stop, our private enterprizes would drop like shot stags, and we should all be dead in a month. When Mr Baldwin tried to win the last election by declaring that Socialism had been a failure whenever and wherever it had been tried, Socialism went over him like a steam roller and handed his office to a Socialist Prime Minister.[9] Nothing could save us in the war but a great extension of Socialism; and now it is clear enough that only still greater extensions of it can repair the ravages of the war and keep pace with the growing requirements of civilization.

What we have to ask ourselves, then, is not whether we will have Socialism and Communism or not, but whether Democracy can keep pace with the developments of both that are being forced on us by the growth of national and international corporate action.

Now corporate action is impossible without a governing body. It may be the central Government: it may be a municipal corporation, a county council, a district council, or a parish council. It may be the board of directors of a joint stock company, or of a trust made by combining several joint stock companies. Such boards, elected by the votes of the shareholders, are little States within the State, and very powerful ones, too, some of them. If they have not laws and kings, they have by-laws and chairmen. And you and I, the consumers of their services, are more at the mercy of the boards that organize them than we are at the mercy of parliament. Several active politicians who began as Liberals and are now Socialists have said to me that they were converted by seeing that the nation had to choose, not between governmental control of industry and control by separate private individuals kept in order by their competition for our custom, but between governmental control and control by gigantic trusts wielding great power without responsibility, and having no object but to make as much money out of us as possible. Our Government is at this moment having much more trouble with the private corporations on whom we are dependent for our coals and cotton goods than with France or the United States of America. We are in the hands of our corporate bodies, public or private, for the satisfaction of our everyday needs. Their powers are life and death powers. I need not labor this point: we all know it.

But what we do not all realize is that we are equally dependent on corporate action for the satisfaction of our religious needs. Dean Inge tells us that our general elections have become public auctions at which the contending parties bid against oneanother for our votes by each promising us a larger share than the other of the plunder of the minority. Now that is perfectly true. The contending parties do not as yet venture to put it exactly in those words; but that is what it comes to. And the Dean's profession obliges him to urge his congregation, which is much wider than that of St Paul's (it extends across the Atlantic), always to vote for the party which pledges itself to go farthest in

9. Following Stanley Baldwin's defeat in June 1929 (Labour 287, Conservative 260, Liberal 59), MacDonald formed a minority Socialist government.

enabling those of us who have great possessions to sell them and give the price to the poor.[10] But we cannot do this as private persons. It must be done by the Government or not at all. Take my own case. I am not a young man with great possessions; but I am an old man paying enough in income tax and surtax to provide doles for some hundreds of unemployed and old age pensioners. I have not the smallest objection to this: on the contrary, I advocated it strongly for years before I had any income worth taxing. But I could not do it if the Government did not arrange it for me. If the Government ceased taxing my superfluous money and redistributing it among people who have no incomes at all, I could do nothing by myself. What could I do? Can you suggest anything? I could send my war bonds to the Chancellor of the Exchequer and invite him to cancel the part of the National Debt that they represent; and he would undoubtedly thank me in the most courteous official terms for my patriotism. But the poor would not get any of it. The other payers of surtax and income tax and death duties would save the interest they now have to pay on it: that is all. I should only have made the rich richer and myself poorer. I could burn all my share certificates and inform the secretaries of the companies that they might write off that much of their capital indebtedness. The result would be a bigger dividend for the rest of the shareholders, with the poor out in the cold as before. I might sell my war bonds and share certificates for cash, and throw the money into the street to be scrambled for; but it would be snatched up, not by the poorest, but by the best fed and most able-bodied of the scramblers. Besides, if we all tried to sell our bonds and shares—and this is what you have to consider; for Christ's advice was not addressed to me alone but to all who have great possessions—the result would be that their value would fall to nothing, as the Stock Exchange would immediately become a market in which there were all sellers and no buyers. Accordingly, any spare money that the Government leaves me is invested where I can get the highest interest and the best security, as thereby I can make sure that it goes where it is most wanted and gives immediate employment. This is the best I can do without Government interference: indeed any other way of dealing with my spare money would be foolish and demoralizing; but the result is that I become richer and richer, and the poor become relatively poorer and poorer. So you see I cannot even be a Christian except through Government action; and neither can the Dean.

Now let us get down to our problem. We cannot govern ourselves; yet if we entrust the immense powers and revenues which are necessary in an effective modern Government to an absolute monarch or dictator, he goes more or less mad unless he is a quite extraordinary and therefore very seldom obtainable person. Besides, modern government is not a one-man job: it is too big for

10. Shaw has freely expanded, re-interpreted, and re-written Inge's views as expressed in chapter five, 'Democracy', in *England* (1926).

that. If we resort to a committee or parliament of superior persons, they will set up an oligarchy and abuse their power for their own benefit. Our dilemma is that men in the lump cannot govern themselves; and yet, as William Morris put it, no man is good enough to be another man's master [see vol. 1, p. 237 fn]. We need to be governed, and yet to control our governors. But the best governors will not accept any control except that of their own consciences; and, as we who are governed are also apt to abuse any power of control we have, our ignorance, our passions, our private and immediate interests are constantly in conflict with the knowledge, the wisdom, and the public spirit and regard for the future of our best qualified governors.

Still, if we cannot control our governors, can we not at least choose them and change them if they do not suit?

Let me invent a primitive example of democratic choice. It is always best to take imaginary examples: they offend nobody. Imagine then that we are the inhabitants of a village. We have to elect somebody for the office of postman. There are several candidates; but one stands out conspicuously, because he has frequently treated us at the public-house, has subscribed a shilling to our little flower show, has a kind word for the children when he passes, and is a victim of oppression by the squire because his late father was one of our most successful poachers. We elect him triumphantly; and he is duly installed, uniformed, provided with a red bicycle, and given a batch of letters to deliver. As his motive in seeking the post has been pure ambition, he has not thought much beforehand about his duties; and it now occurs to him for the first time that he cannot read. So he hires a boy to come round with him and read the addresses. The boy conceals himself in the lane whilst the postman delivers the letters at the house, takes the Christmas boxes, and gets the whole credit of the transaction. In course of time he dies with a high reputation for efficiency in the discharge of his duties; and we elect another equally illiterate successor on similar grounds. But by this time the boy has grown up and become an institution. He presents himself to the new postman as an established and indispensable feature of the postal system, and finally becomes recognized and paid by the village as such.

Here you have the perfect image of a popularly elected Cabinet Minister and the Civil Service department over which he presides. It may work very well; for our postman, though illiterate, may be a very capable fellow; and the boy who reads the addresses for him may be quite incapable of doing anything more. But this does not always happen. Whether it happens or not, the system is not a democratic reality: it is a democratic illusion. The boy, when he has ability enough to take advantage of the situation, is the master of the man. The person elected to do the work is not really doing it: he is a popular humbug who is merely doing what a permanent official tells him to do. That is how it comes about that we are now governed by a Civil Service which has such enormous power that its regulations are taking the place of the laws of

England, though some of them are made for the convenience of the officials without the slightest regard to the convenience or even the rights of the public. And how are our Civil Servants selected? Mostly by an educational test which nobody but an expensively schooled youth can pass, thus making the most powerful and effective part of our government an irresponsible class government.

Now, what control have you or I over the Services? We have votes. I have used mine a few times to see what it is like. Well, it is like this. When the election approaches, two or three persons of whom I know nothing write to me soliciting my vote and enclosing a list of meetings, an election address, and a polling card. One of the addresses reads like an article in the Morning Post, and has a Union Jack on it. Another is like the Daily News or Manchester Guardian. Both might have been compiled from the editorial wastepaper baskets of a hundred years ago. A third address, more up-to-date and much better phrased, convinces me that the sender has had it written for him at the headquarters of the Labor Party. A fourth, the most hopelessly out of date of them all, contains scraps of the early English translations of the Communist Manifesto of 1848. I have no guarantee that any of these documents were written by the candidates. They convey nothing whatever to me as to their character or political capacity. The half-tone photographic portraits which adorn the front pages do not even tell me their ages, having been taken twenty years ago. If I go to one of the meetings I find a schoolroom packed with people who find an election meeting cheaper and funnier than a theatre. On the platform sit one or two poor men who have worked hard to keep party politics alive in the constituency. They ought to be the candidates; but they have no more chance of such eminence than they have of possessing a Rolls-Royce car. They move votes of confidence in the candidate, though as the candidate is a stranger to them and to everybody else present nobody can possibly feel any such confidence. They lead the applause for him; they prompt him when questions are asked; and when he is completely floored they jump up and cry "Let me answer that, Mr Chairman!" and then pretend that he has answered it. The old shibboleths are droned over; and nothing has any sense or reality in it except the vituperation of the opposition party, which is received with shouts of relief by the audience. Yet it is nothing but an exhibition of bad manners. If I vote for one of these candidates, and he or she is elected, I am supposed to be enjoying a democratic control of the government—to be exercising government *of* myself, *for* myself, *by* myself. Do you wonder that the Dean cannot believe such nonsense? If I believed it I should not be fit to vote at all. If this is Democracy, who can blame Signor Mussolini for describing it as a putrefying corpse? [*Gerarchia*, Milan, March 1923].

The candidates may ask me what more they can do for me but present themselves and answer any questions I may put to them. I quite admit that they can do nothing; but that does not mend matters. What I should like is a real test of their capacity. Shortly before the war a doctor in San Francisco discovered that if a drop of a candidate's blood can be obtained on a piece of blotting paper it is possible to discover within half an hour what is wrong with him physically.[11] What I am waiting for is the discovery of a process by which on delivery of a drop of his blood or a lock of his hair we can ascertain what is right with him mentally. We could then have a graded series of panels of capable persons for all employments, public or private, and not allow any person, however popular, to undertake the employment of governing us unless he or she were on the appropriate panel. At the lower end of the scale there would be a panel of persons qualified to take part in a parish meeting; at the higher end a panel of persons qualified to act as Secretaries of State for Foreign Affairs or Finance Ministers. At present not more than two per thousand of the population would be available for the highest panel. I should then be in no danger of electing a postman and finding that he could neither read nor write. My choice of candidates would be perhaps more restricted than at present; but I do not desire liberty to choose windbags and nincompoops to represent me in parliament; and my power to choose between one qualified candidate and another would give me as much control as is either possible or desirable. The voting and counting would be done by machinery: I should connect my telephone with the proper office; touch a button; and the machinery would do the rest.

Pending such a completion of the American doctor's discovery, how are we to go on? Well, as best we can, with the sort of government that our present system produces. Several reforms are possible without any new discovery. Our present parliament is obsolete: it can no more do the work of a modern State than Julius Cæsar's galley could do the work of an Atlantic liner. We need in these islands two or three additional federal legislatures, working on our municipal committee system instead of our parliamentary party system. We need a central authority to coordinate the federal work. Our obsolete little internal frontiers must be obliterated, and our units of local government enlarged to dimensions compatible with the recent prodigious advances in facility of communication and cooperation. Commonwealth affairs and supernational activities through the League of Nations or otherwise will have to be provided for, and Cabinet function to be transformed. All the pseudo-democratic obstructive functions of our political machinery must be ruthlessly scrapped, and the general

11. Dr Albert Abrams, referred to by Shaw in *Doctors' Delusions* (1931) as 'the electronic rayman', developed a theory of radioactivity of blood and the use of electrical currents for diagnosis of disease, inventing a rheostat for a process he called, in a book published in 1914, *Spondylotherapy*. An investigating committee of Britain's medical council indicated it was convinced of the soundness of Dr Abrams's diagnosis, but sceptical of the treatment by the instrument the London press dubbed 'the Abrams box'.

problem of government approached from a positive viewpoint at which mere anarchic national sovereignty as distinguished from self-government will have no meaning.

I must conclude by warning you that when everything has been done that can be done, civilization will still be dependent on the consciences of the governors and the governed. Our natural dispositions may be good; but we have been badly brought up, and are full of anti-social personal ambitions and prejudices and snobberies. Had we not better teach our children to be better citizens than ourselves? We are not doing that at present. The Russians *are*. That is my last word. Think over it.

So much for my broadcast on Democracy! And now a word about Breakages, Limited. Like all Socialists who know their business I have an exasperated sense of the mischief done by our system of private Capitalism in setting up huge vested interests in destruction, waste, and disease. The armament firms thrive on war; the glaziers gain by broken windows; the operating surgeons depend on cancer for their children's bread; the distillers and brewers build cathedrals to sanctify the profits of drunkenness; and the prosperity of Dives costs the privation of a hundred Lazaruses.

The title Breakages, Limited, was suggested to me by the fate of that remarkable genius, the late Alfred Warwick Gattie,[12] with whom I was personally acquainted. I knew him first as the author of a play. He was a disturbing man, afflicted—or, as it turned out, gifted—with chronic hyperæsthesia, feeling everything violently and expressing his feelings vehemently and on occasion volcanically. I concluded that he was not sufficiently coldblooded to do much as a playwright; so that when, having lost sight of him for some years, I was told that he had made an invention of firstrate importance, I was incredulous, and concluded that the invention was only a Utopian project. Our friend Henry Murray[13] was so provoked by my attitude that to appease him I consented to investigate the alleged great invention in person on Gattie's promising to behave like a reasonable being during the process, a promise which he redeemed with the greatest dignity, remaining silent whilst an engineer explained his miracles to me, and contenting himself with the reading of a brief statement shewing that the adoption of his plan would release from industry enough men to utterly overwhelm the Central Empires with whom we were then at war.

12. Inventor of a labour-saving cargo container-loader that was safe for breakables and explosives. His play was *The Honourable Member*, which Shaw reviewed in the *Saturday Review*, 18 July 1896.
13. Novelist, critic, and member of the publishing firm of Isbister & Co., with whom Shaw became acquainted in 1903.

I approached the investigation very sceptically. Our friend spoke of "the works." I could not believe that Gattie had any works, except in his fervid imagination. He mentioned "the company." That was more credible: anyone may form a company; but that it had any resources seemed to me doubtful. However, I suffered myself to be taken to Battersea; and there, sure enough, I found a workshop, duly labeled as the premises of The New Transport Company, Limited, and spacious enough to accommodate a double railway line with a platform. The affair was unquestionably real, so far. The platform was not provided with a station: its sole equipment was a table with a row of buttons on it for making electrical contacts. Each line of railway had on it a truck with a steel lid. The practical part of the proceedings began by placing an armchair on the lid of one of the trucks and seating me in it. A brimming glass of water was then set at my feet. I could not imagine what I was expected to do with the water or what was going to happen; and there was a suggestion of electrocution about the chair which made me nervous. Gattie then sat down majestically at the table on the platform with his hand hovering over the buttons. Intimating that the miracle would take place when my truck passed the other truck, he asked me to choose whether it should occur at the first passage or later, and to dictate the order in which it should be repeated. I was by that time incapable of choosing; so I said the sooner the better; and the two trucks started. When the other truck had passed mine I found myself magically sitting on it, chair and all, with the glass of water unspilled at my feet.

The rest of the story is a tragicomedy. When I said to Gattie apologetically (I felt deeply guilty of having underrated him) that I had never known that he was an engineer, and had taken him to be the usual amateur inventor with no professional training, he told me that this was exactly what he was: just like Sir Christopher Wren. He had been concerned in an electric lighting business, and had been revolted by the prodigious number of breakages of glass bulbs involved by the handling of the crates in which they were packed for transport by rail and road. What was needed was a method of transferring the crates from truck to truck, and from truck to road lorry, and from road lorry to warehouse lift without shock, friction, or handling. Gattie, being, I suppose, by natural genius an inventor though by mistaken vocation a playwright, solved the mechanical problem without apparent difficulty, and offered his nation the means of effecting an enormous saving of labor and smash. But instead of being received with open arms as a social benefactor he found himself up against Breakages, Limited. The glass blowers whose employment was threatened, the exploiters of the great industry of repairing our railway trucks (every time a goods train is stopped a series of 150 violent collisions is propagated from end to end of the train, as those who live within earshot know to their cost), and the railway porters who dump the crates from truck to platform and then hurl them into other trucks, shattering bulbs, battering cans, and too often rupturing themselves in the process, saw in Gattie an enemy of the human race, a wrecker of homes and a starver of innocent babes. He fought them undauntedly; but they were too strong for him; and in due time his patents expired and he died almost unrecognized, whilst Unknown Soldiers were being canonized throughout the world. So far, The Apple Cart is his only shrine; and as it does not even bear his name, I have written it here pending its tardy appearance in the roll of fame.

I must not leave my readers to assume that Gattie was an easy man to deal with, or that he handled the opposition in a conciliatory manner with due allowance for the inertia of a somewhat unimaginative officialdom which had not, like myself, sat on his trucks, and probably set him down as a Utopian (a species much dreaded in Government departments) and thus missed the real point, which was that he was an inventor. Like many men of genius he could not understand why things obvious to him should not be so at once to other people, and found it easier to believe that they were corrupt than that they could be so stupid. Once, after I had urged him to be more diplomatic, he brought me, with some pride, a letter to the Board of Trade which he considered a masterpiece of tact and good temper. It contained not a word descriptive of his invention; and it began somewhat in this fashion: "Sir: If you are an honest man you cannot deny that among the worst abuses of this corrupt age is the acceptance of city directorships by retired members of the Board of Trade." Clearly it was not easy for the Board of Trade to deal with an inventor who wished to interest them, not in his new machines, but in the desirability of its abolishing itself as infamous.

The last time I saw him he called on me to unfold a new scheme of much greater importance, as he declared, than his trucks. He was very interesting on that occasion. He began by giving me a vivid account of the pirates who used to infest the Thames below London Bridge before the docks were built. He described how the docks had come into existence not as wharves for loading and unloading but as strongholds in which ships and their cargoes could be secure from piracy. They are now, he declared, a waste of fabulously valuable ground; and their work should be done in quite another way. He then produced plans of a pier to be built in the middle of the river, communicating directly by rail and road with the shore and the great main lines. The ships would come alongside the pier; and by a simple system of hoists the contents of their holds would be lifted out and transferred (like myself in the armchair) to railway trucks or motor lorries without being touched by a human hand and therefore without risk of breakage. It was all so masterly, so simple in its complexity, so convincing as to its practicability, and so prodigiously valuable socially, that I, taking it very seriously, proceeded to discuss what could be done to interest the proper people in it.

To my amazement Gattie began to shew unmistakable signs of disappointment and indignation. "You do not seem to understand me," he said. "I have shewn you all this mechanical stuff merely by way of illustration. What I have come to consult you about is a great melodrama I am going to write, the scene of which will be the Pool of London in the XVII century among the pirates!"

What could I or anyone do with a man like that? He was naïvely surprised when I laughed; and he went away only half persuaded that his scheme for turning the docks into building land; expediting the Thames traffic; saving much dangerous and demoralizingly casual labor; and transfiguring the underpaid stevedore into a fullfed electrician, was stupendously more important than any ridiculous melodrama. He admitted that there was of course all that in it; but I could see that his heart was in the melodrama.

As it was evident that officialdom, writhing under his insults and shocked by his utter lack of veneration for bigwigs, besides being hampered as all our Government departments are by the vested interests of Breakages, Limited, would do nothing for him, I induced some less embarrassed public persons to take a ride in the trucks and be convinced that they really existed and worked. But here again the parallel between Gattie and his fellow-amateur Sir Christopher Wren came in. Wren was not content to redesign and rebuild St Paul's: he wanted to redesign London as well. He was quite right: what we have lost by not letting him do it is incalculable. Similarly, Gattie was not content to improve the luggage arrangements of our railways: he would not listen to you if your mind was not large enough to grasp the immediate necessity for a new central clearing house in Farringdon Market, connected with the existing railways by a system of new tubes. He was of course right; and we have already lost by sticking to our old ways more than the gigantic sum his scheme would have cost. But neither the money nor the enterprize was available just then, with the war on our hands. The Clearing House, like the Thames pier, remains on paper; and Gattie is in his grave. But I still hold that there must have been something great in a man who, having not only imagined them but invented their machinery, could, far from being crushed by their rejection, exclaim "Perish all my mechanical trash if only it provides material for one bad play!"

This little history will explain how it actually did provide material for Breakages, Limited, and for the bitter cry of the Powermistress General. Not until Breakages is itself broken will it cease to have a message for us.

Ayot St Lawrence.
March, 1930.

# The Philanderer

*First published in the Collected Edition, 1930*

===

There is a disease to which plays as well as men become liable with advancing years. In men it is called doting, in plays dating. The more topical the play the more it dates. The Philanderer [1893] suffers from this complaint. In the eighteen-nineties, when it was written, not only dramatic literature but life itself was staggering from the impact of Ibsen's plays, which reached us in 1889. The state of mind represented by the Ibsen Club in this play was familiar then to our Intelligentsia. That far more numerous body which may be called the Unintelligentsia was as unconscious of Ibsen as of any other political influence: quarter of a century elapsed before an impatient heaven rained German bombs down on them to wake them from their apathy. That accustomed them to much more startling departures from Victorian routine than those that shock the elderly colonel and the sentimental theatre critic in The Philanderer; but they do not associate their advance in liberal morals with the great Norwegian. Even the Intelligentsia have forgotten that the lesson that might have saved the lives of ten million persons hideously slaughtered was offered to them by Ibsen.

I make no attempt to bring the play up to date. I should as soon think of bringing Ben Jonson's Bartholomew Fair [1614] up to date by changing the fair into a Woolworth store. The human nature in it is still in the latest fashion: indeed I am far from sure that its ideas, instead of being 36 years behind the times, are not for a considerable section of the community 36 years ahead of them. My picture of the past may be for many people a picture of the future. At all events I shall leave the play as it is; for all the attempts within my experience to modernize ancient plays have only produced worse anachronisms than those they aimed at remedying.

1930.

# Ellen Terry and Bernard Shaw:
# A Correspondence

*Preface drafted and privately printed in rough proof, 1929.*
*First published, revised, 1931*

═══

In allowing everybody who cares about Ellen Terry to read this correspondence, I must warn them not to judge it according to the code of manners which regulate polite letter writing in cathedral country towns. As a correspondence between a churchwarden and a deaconess its implications would make its publication impossible. But the theatre, behind the scenes, has an emotional freemasonry of its own, certainly franker and arguably wholesomer than the stiffnesses of suburban society outside. The difference is less than it used to be; for actors, like the members of the other professions, have made their way into the general body of society and been accepted as ladies and gentlemen of the professional class rather than as players; and just as it was becoming difficult fifty years ago to imagine a medical baronet or a vicar or a prosperous solicitor or stockbroker accepting a position of social inferiority in a Bloomsbury mansion or a country house, which they had nevertheless had to do within living memory of that time, it is difficult now to imagine an actor being at any disadvantage in ordinary professional society in respect of his occupation, however he may happen to be disqualified in point of education and social habits. If there is nothing wrong with his table manners, his dress, and his accent, nobody will venture to snub or patronize an actor merely because he is an actor; and if he is not qualified in these respects he is at all events no worse off than any other professional man who has not taken the trouble to make himself presentable.

This social acceptance of the actor did not become quite unquestionable until Henry Irving insisted on its official recognition, even at the cost to his singular eminence of a much disrelished knighthood for himself, in 1895. The theatre into which Ellen Terry was born in 1848 [1847] enjoyed no such general consideration. Actors, like Jews, were a race apart; and like all segregated races they preserved manners and customs peculiar to themselves. My first youthful contacts with the stage were in connection with certain amateur enterprizes; and I well remember the puzzled mixture of amusement

and indignation with which a company of ladies and gentlemen of considerable social position who had engaged a professional London stage manager
(the modern Producer[1] had not then been invented) to direct their operations,
found themselves addressed by him, all the ladies as Darling and all the
gentlemen as Old Boy. No modern Producer says Old Boy; and Darling
survives only as an elderly joke to turn away the wrath of irritable stars at
critical moments; but to the stage manager of that day they were as conventional as the Sir and Madam of a well trained shop assistant.

But though that stage manager's Darling did not mean what it would have
meant if it had been addressed to the same ladies by a Dean, it is none the
less significant that the convention of the stage should have been one of
personal endearment whilst in other professions it was one of cold politeness.
That difference still exists, and will exist as long as acting remains an art.
When I was a boy, interested much more in music than in literature, I
managed to get admitted to the stage once or twice during an opera performance, and learned thereby that this is quite the worst way to enjoy it, and
that anyone behind the scenes who has no business there is as great a nuisance,
and is as little considered by those who have some business there, as Mr
Pickwick at the Chatham review [a regimental army manoeuvre, chapter 4].
But what is more to the present purpose is that, the opera being Donizetti's
Lucrezia Borgia, and Maffio Orsini and his comrades having overwhelmed
Lucrezia with their exposure of her infamies in the exciting *finale* to the first
act, the curtain had no sooner descended and Maffio ceased to be Maffio and
become [Zélie] Trebelli[-Bettini], and Lucrezia ceased to be Lucrezia and
become [Thérèse] Tietjens, than the two hurled themselves frantically into
oneanother's arms in a transport of some emotion that was certainly not any
of the emotions of ordinary life outside the theatre, but something peculiar
to their work that insisted on the most rapturous expression they could give
it. It cannot be explained by what people called the Italian temperament:
Trebelli was a Frenchwoman and Tietjens a German. It was something *sui
generis* that nobody who has not experienced it can credit, and that soon

1. Rehearsals until the late nineteenth century were conducted by the stage manager
of a company. By the turn of the century, resulting from the insistence of playwrights
(notably Gilbert, Pinero and Shaw) that they be permitted to control the staging of
their own works, a functionary known as the 'Producer' took charge of staging.
Eventually the American term 'Director' for the individual responsible for the conduct
of rehearsals came into universal use, with American employment of 'Producer' as
the one in charge of financial and production affairs paralleling British usage of the
term 'Manager'.

becomes second nature in those who have experienced it. The Initiates never resent its expression. When they say "he (or she) is one of us," they mean that the happy person is privileged to express any extremity of affection for an artist who achieves a fine piece of acting, and any extremity of disgust at one who wilfully acts basely. The measured public judgments of the critics cannot express this impulse or satisfy this need. The stage is not one fairyland but two: one for the public when the curtain rises, and another, which the public never discovers, for the theatre folk when the curtain falls. In that secret paradise genius excites a flush of adoration in the properly tuned recipient and is satisfied with nothing less. I adored Ellen Terry accordingly, and did not tell her so by halves. And it never occurred to her to say "Sir: how dare you insult a respectable female by such expressions?" *Honi soit qui mal y pense.*

Genius, I may add, is not commoner on the stage than elsewhere; but there, as elsewhere, it produces extravagance of language. The epithet beautiful is used by surgeons to describe operations which their patients describe as ghastly, by physicists to describe methods of measurement which leave sentimentalists cold, by lawyers to describe cases which ruin all the parties to them, and by lovers to describe the objects of their infatuation, however unattractive they may appear to the unaffected spectators. Within the magnetic field of the theatrical profession such hyperbole became conventional, and was finally used by the rank and file who had never felt the emotion until at last every actress was every stage manager's darling and every actor his old boy.

There is another peculiarity of the stage to be borne in mind. An actress is not a lady: at least when she is she is not an actress. Let me explain. A lady is—or in Ellen Terry's generation was—a person trained to the utmost attainable degree in the art and habit of concealing her feelings and maintaining an imperturbable composure under the most trying circumstances. An actress is a person trained even more severely in the art and habit of displaying her feelings so demonstratively that every occupant of the back row in a remote gallery can read them in her face and see them in her gestures. What to the lady is an emergency in which dissimulation is her first duty is to the actress an opportunity for explosive self-expression, however skilled her guidance of the explosion may be. Modern frankness has reduced this difference; but it remains, and is accentuated by the slovenliness of modern middle-class speech, which contrasts strongly with the distinct articulation of the actress who knows her business. Ellen Terry escaped the trials of our young actresses, who find themselves between silly producers who tell them that they must not articulate because it is not natural and not ladylike, and despairing authors who warn them that nobody in the theatre will know what they are saying unless they articulate very distinctly. When the author is experienced and wily, the lesson takes the form of a conversational remark that slovenly speech is middle class, and that great ladies owe much of their distinction to their scrupulous articulation, of which Queen Victoria, one of the most perfect speakers of her day, was a conspicuous example. To tell a young woman that if she speaks well she will be mistaken for an actress may spoil her for the stage; but there is a ready antidote in telling her that she may also be mistaken for a member of the royal family. Ellen Terry's articulation was perfect. Her slightly veiled voice reached the remotest listener in the theatre without apparent effort, though the nervous athleticism behind it was of championship quality.

Howbeit the fact remains that an actress, having to exaggerate to get her effects on the stage (on the film, by the way, the contrary is the case: an unnatural quietude and delicacy is the trade mark of the Movie Star), finally from mere habit exaggerates to get her effects off it; and the greater the actress the greater is her power of seizing on every emotional impulse and not only amplifying it as a microphone or a thermionic valve amplifies a sound, but uttering it with a muscular articulation which gives it an impressive driving power. The story of Mrs Siddons terrifying the shop assistant by the intensity with which she asked "Will it wash?" is quite probable.[2] And the playwright, supplying the verbal material for this skilled speech, develops the same quality in his writing. The reader of this budget of intimate letters must therefore not be surprised, and certainly not scandalized, by the reckless way in which the two correspondents express their delight in oneanother. I do not mean that they were insincere: all that the writers set down they felt at the moment. But their profession freed them from many of the inhibitions to which people outside that profession have to submit; and their language must be interpreted without the inferences which would be drawn from the same language on the part of a governess corresponding with a divinity student.

Possibly a little allowance should be made also for the very objectionable tradition of XVIII century gallantry into which I, as an Irishman, was born. "Remember" said the most attractive of my aunts to me by way of improving my young mind "that the least plain girl in a house is the family beauty." An English actress once expressed contemptuous impatience with women who want to be placed on a pedestal and worshipped. An Irish actress who

---

2. Thomas Campbell in *The Life of Mrs Siddons* (1834) reported that the actress, in response to a mercer praising the texture of his calico cloth, 'put the question to him, "*But will it wash?*" in a manner so electrifying as to make the poor shopman start back from his counter.'

was present exclaimed indignantly "I would not *look* at a man who did not place me on a pedestal." It was her right, by Irish tradition. Now I claim that no male writer born in the XIX century outside Norway and Sweden did more to knock Woman off her pedestal and plant her on the solid earth than I. But as, like all reactionaries, I was steeped in the tendency against which I was reacting, it was part of my conventional manners to concede a pedestal to every woman as such; and naturally in approaching a woman so goddesslike as Ellen Terry I did not pause to consider whether this attitude would have earned the approval of Ibsen or Strindberg. I do not justify it: it is really a relic of relations between men and women which are not only happily outmoded but insufferable. Still, there it was for what it was worth.

It must be borne in mind too, that we were both comedians, each acting as audience to the other, and each desiring to please and amuse the other without ulterior motives or what matchmaking mothers call intentions. A word, however, must be said about Ellen Terry's ethical position. She once said that what had supported her through all her trials was the consciousness that she had never done anything wrong; and this entirely sincere claim was quoted to me as an audacious hypocrisy. Ellen Terry was never called an advanced woman, the reason being that she was born, as Nietzsche put it, on the far side of good and evil as defined by the Victorian code. Such a play as Ibsen's Ghosts had no mission for her, because she had not had to break Mrs Alving's chains, never having worn them. She did not fight prejudices nor argue with them: like Mrs Stetson's heroine [see vol. 1, p. 307] she walked through them as if they were not there, as indeed for her they were not. This was partly individual character; but it must be remembered that in the old segregated theatre religion and morality were homemade: the actress did not live in ordinary society and go out to her work like a doctor or lawyer or clergyman or man of business: she belonged to a little world apart, with morals of its own; and though actors, being human beings, necessarily had the same morals as other people to the extent of, say, nine tenths, yet there was a difference in the other tenth. For instance, in the outside world ladies were not economically independent; and in the rare instances where a lady was paid for working she never dreamt of being paid as much as a gentleman, and felt herself heavily compromised socially by being paid at all. On the stage not only was the actress self-supporting, but if, as often happened, she attracted the public more than her male colleagues, she was paid more. Consequently the trade union view of marriage, from which the unmarried woman who is not a celibate must at all costs be boycotted as a blackleg, had no meaning in the theatre. Outside it women were held to a strict licitness in their sexual relations on penalty of ostracism, loss of employment, and every other injury that could express total reprobation by all decent people. In fact, a woman incurring this penalty used to be described as "ruined" until Ibsen set us laughing at the epithet by applying it to a man.[3] In the theatre illicit relations *as such* involved no penalty whatever. But please remark the italicized limitation. The notion that actors can behave wickedly without incurring the reprobation of their colleagues and being passed over and replaced by better conducted substitutes when any are available is a vulgar error. But the wickedness must be real wickedness, not mere disregard of the law. The result is that the standard of morals on the stage is in some important aspects higher than it is outside the theatre, where married couples regard the legal tie between them as justifying them in treating each other much worse than they dare treat an independent stranger. In the very important matter of sexual temperance a marriage licence is held to dispense with it as completely as is humanly possible. But it is impossible to keep in training for stage work on such terms. Behind the scenes self-preservation unites with lay opinion to make the life of the theatrical performer in many respects a model which might be followed in the most straitlaced suburb with considerable advantage to its matrimonial morals.

When a late well-known Roman Catholic critic[4] declared that no woman could be an actress and "a good woman," he was perhaps sufficiently answered by Robert Buchanan, who exclaimed "What! No good women on the stage! There are thousands of them—and only about six actresses." When Dumas *fils* publicly assured a young lady of good family who wanted to become an actress that it was quite out of the question for a person in her social position, and when Charles Dickens, himself an incorrigible actor, imposed the same prohibition on his daughter [Kate],[5] they were expressing a class prejudice, not a moral one; for the stage is socially quite promiscuous. As no extra money is attracted to the payboxes by the social standing of the performers, talent is everything and pedigree nothing. You must rub shoulders there with persons of every degree, accepting an order of precedence in which a person born in a caravan may be paid and estimated more highly than one born in a palace. It takes a revolution to produce such a state of things outside the

---

3. It is Nora's husband Torvald, in William Archer's translation of *A Doll's House* (1889), who laments that he is 'ruined'. In Rolf Fjelde's superlative new translation (Ibsen, *The Complete Major Prose Plays*, 1978) under the corrected title *A Doll House*, Torvald exclaims: 'Now you've wrecked all my happiness – ruined my whole future. Oh, it's awful to think of' (p. 187).
4. Clement Scott, dramatic critic of the *Daily Telegraph*.
5. See Gladys Storey, *Dickens and Daughter* (1939).

theatre: inside it is readymade and inevitable from the nature of the institution.

All this has to be grasped before the lay reader can understand how Ellen Terry could be a woman of very exceptional virtue without having the smallest respect for the law. She did not care enough about it to have even a prejudice against it. If the man of her choice was free, she married him. If the marriage was not a success, she left him. She had many enduring friendships, some transient fancies, and five domestic partnerships of which two were not legalized, though they would have been if the English marriage law had been decently reasonable. She was not in the least what is called a *grande amoureuse*. In the ordering of her life there was nothing of the infatuations and extravagances, the reckless expenditure, the fantastic equipment, the debts, the jewels, the caprices, the menagerie of strange pet animals and reptiles, and all the other affectations and fictions by which actresses' press agents advertize their mostly sober honest industrious economical and monogamous principals. Ellen Terry did not know what an actress's press agent was. And she was no fool: she lived and died within her means. She was certainly no skinflint: she would have run through her money too generously if she had not given it to businesslike friends to keep for her; but she died solvent, an honest woman with no vices.

Emotionally she was not quite so fortunate. She ran through her husbands, and ended as her own mistress and no man's housemate, though she retained the affection of her first husband [the painter G. F. Watts], who was much older than herself, and of her last [James Carew], who was much younger. One may say that her marriages were adventures and her friendships enduring. And all these friendships had the character of innocent love affairs: her friends were her lovers in every sense except the technical one; and she was incapable of returning their regard coolly: she felt either warmly or not at all. And yet she was critical, and never lost her head when it was necessary to keep it. Her soft side was her mothering side, her sensitive pity. She was drawn to men of brains because they interested her, and because she was very conscious of the holes left in her mind by the curious patchiness of theatrical culture and the ladylike ignorance of her day; yet she could not resist men who were so helplessly outside the world of intellect that their devotion to her was childlike and their distress at being repulsed by her more than she could bear unless they were personally repulsive to her. She seemed a mass of incalculable contradictions to people who had no analytic sense of character, and expected to find people either All Whites or All Blacks. But she was really as consistent off the stage as she was competent on it.

It must be noted also that she was not stagestruck. Her parents were actors. Like her famous contemporary Madge Robertson (Dame Madge Kendal) she

found it as impossible to keep off the stage as it is for many stagestruck
outsiders to get on it. You cannot say that Ellen Terry, like Garrick or Irving,
was a player by irresistible vocation. She was a player by force of circumstances.
I am not sure that she would have become a professional actress if she had
not been born with a property spoon in her mouth. Her natural taste was
for pictorial art, not for histrionics. Her first husband was a great painter. She
left the stage without hesitation for the best years of her youth to keep house
on £3 a week with Edward William Godwin, a distinguished architect with
a craze for stage pictures and pageantry, and was induced to return to it only
by an offer of £40 when she had two children to provide for. Although she
was soundly skilled in the technique of her profession she never needed to
perform any remarkable feat of impersonation: the spectators would have
resented it: they did not want Ellen Terry to be Olivia Primrose:[6] they wanted
Olivia Primrose to be Ellen Terry. Her combination of beauty with sensitive
intelligence was unique: a disguise would have been intolerable. Her instinct
was for beauty and for sincerity: she had only to play a part "straight," as
actors say, to transfigure it into something much better than its raw self. But
she could take this transfiguration home with her and fascinate her friends
with it. She was not the sort of actress who is a genius on the stage and a
nobody off it. She could do without the stage both as artist and woman. In
her letters she often speaks of wanting work and having to earn some money;
but there is no trace of the desperate need to be acting at any cost felt by
those who are so completely specialized for the stage that they hardly exist
except in fictitious characters.

This is almost a family characteristic. Her sister Kate, when she was in
the first rank of London actresses, retired after marriage apparently without
hesitation or regret. Miss Phyllis Neilson-Terry,[7] Ellen Terry's niece, does
not follow up her successes, though she seems to have every qualification for
a repetition of the career of her aunt. Ellen Terry's son, Edward Gordon
Craig, who succeeded with the greatest ease as an actor, cared so little for
acting or for the drama that he gave up acting whilst he was still a juvenile,
and engaged in a lifelong struggle to use the stage as a frame for the pictorial
architecture in which his father delighted.

6. Heroine of W. G. Wills's play *Olivia* (1878), adapted from Goldsmith's novel *The
Vicar of Wakefield*.
7. An actress admired by Shaw, who had appeared as Candida at Malvern a year
earlier, and would create the role of Queen Philippa in *The Six of Calais* in 1934
and appear as Epifania in the first London production of *The Millionairess*, at the 'Q'
Theatre in 1944.

I must now say a word about my own theatrical antecedents, as they explain the grudge against the old Lyceum Theatre, against Irving, and even against Ellen herself, which comes out so strongly in our correspondence, as it did publicly and in presentably measured terms through the series of my criticisms in the Saturday Review which ran alongside the correspondence during its main period.

From my birth in 1856 to my Hegira to London in 1876, I lived in Dublin, where the theatre had hardly altered, except for its illumination by coal gas, since the XVIII century. There were two theatres: the Queen's, which was then not respectable (I visited it, at most, twice, perhaps only once), and the old Theatre Royal, since unhappily burnt down, which maintained a stock company to support the stars who came to Dublin on their touring circuits, and to perform the Christmas pantomime and keep the house open in the occasional weeks left unfilled by the stars. As nobody nowadays has the least notion of what the old stock companies were like, and as my own plays are written largely for the feats of acting they aimed at, and as moreover both Ellen Terry and Irving were rooted like myself in that phase of the evolution of the theatre, I may as well say a word or two about them.

To begin with, the playgoers of their towns grew so desperately tired of them, and so hopelessly unable to imagine them to be any but their too familiar selves, that they performed in an atmosphere of hatred and derision which few of their members had talent or charm enough to conciliate. The modern practice of selecting for the performances actors and actresses suited to the parts they had to play was impossible: the stock company was a readymade cast that had to fit all plays, from Hamlet down to the latest burlesque; and as it never fitted any of them completely, and seldom fitted at all, the casts were more or less grotesque misfits. This system did not develop versatility: it destroyed it. Every member of the company except the utilities, as they called the worst actors who got parts that did not matter, had his or her specialty or "line." Thus there were leading juveniles with an age limit of fifty. There were walking gentlemen, first and second light comedians, first and second low comedians, first and second old men, heavies who played all the villains, and, as aforesaid, utilities. There were leading ladies and walking ladies, singing chambermaids (soubrettes), heavies to whom Lady Macbeth was all in the night's work, a pair of old women of whom one played the great ladies and the other the comic landladies, and, of course, female utilities. Each claimed as of right the part which came nearest to his or her specialty; and each played all his or her parts in exactly the same way. The low comedian was traditionally cast for Roderigo; and Roderigo consequently was presented, not as a foolish Venetian gentleman about town, but as a clown. The king in Hamlet and Ham Peggotty might have been twins except for the costume, because the heavy man had to play Ham, the juveniles being used up for Copperfield and Steerforth. On no other terms could stock actors play all the parts that had to be, not studied, but "swallowed"; for the stars and other traveling attractions came and went week after week, and had not only to be "supported," but eked out by farces to fill up what the playgoers of that time demanded as a sufficient program. At my first visit to the theatre I saw on the same evening Tom Taylor's three-act drama Plot and Passion followed by a complete Christmas pantomime, with a couple of farces as *hors d'œuvre*.[8] Tom Taylor's Joan of Arc had Massinger's New Way to Pay Old Debts as a curtain raiser. Under such circumstances serious character study was impossible; and the intensive elaboration of an impersonation which an actor can achieve when he can repeat his performance without having anything else to do in the theatre was out of the question. The actress learnt, not how to interpret plays, but how to appear sweet and gentle, or jealous and wicked, or funny, or matronly, or deaf and palsied, and how to make up her face and wear wigs. The actor learnt how to appear sprightly, or romantic, or murderous, or bucolic, or doddering, and to make funny faces. In addition he had one step dance, which he displayed annually in the pantomime, and one combat, which served for all stage duels.

These qualifications are not to be despised. In the modern cases in which they have been lost without being replaced by any discoverable technical qualifications at all they may well be sincerely regretted. The stock actor, with his conscientiously articulated elocution which reached the back row of the pit effectively (it is really more satisfactory to hear an actor say meechee-yah-eeld and know that he means my child than to hear him say msha and wonder what on earth the fellow thinks he is mumbling), his pompous entrance which invited and seized the attention of the audience, his momentous exit on the last word of his last speech (your modern novice as often as not finishes in the middle of the stage and stops the play until the audience has enjoyed the spectacle of his walking to the door), could plead that he knew the routine of his business and did not need a producer to teach him the A.B.C. of it. But only those who have seen him, as I have, in his native element, and lived to witness the effect of entrusting to his skilled hands a

8. The performance Shaw attended at the age of seven, at Dublin's Theatre Royal in January 1864, consisted solely of a pantomime *Harlequin Puss in Boots, or, The Fairies of the Gossamer Grove*, followed by the Tom Taylor play. Shaw was in error about the farces.

part in a play by Ibsen, can imagine how completely he could kill the dramatic illusion of a modern play.

The truth is, the style of work at which he aimed was wholly rhetorical and hyperbolical. Actors of gigantic or intense personalities could carry it off; but it made commonplace actors ridiculous, though commonplace actors could with ordinary diligence under good teachers acquire its technique only too easily. The teaching could give them style; but it could not give them taste or good sense or power, without which style is an affectation and an impertinence. The invariable effectiveness of the stock actor was a worse offence than the ineffectiveness of the generation which supplanted him, because it enabled and even obliged him to substitute himself for his part in and out of season. His blatant force, when he had any, was less impressive than the so-called "reserved force" of his comparatively impotent successor, who made a merit of either having no force to reserve or not knowing how to use it. When he was thrown on the world in the long interval between the break-up of the stock system in the latter half of the XIX century and the beginnings of the local repertory theatres in the XX, his plea that he knew his business, far from recommending him to the managers with whom he sought employment, only sealed his fate as a plague to be shunned at all hazards.

Conceive me then, a future playwright, with no conscious prevision of that destiny, gathering my practical knowledge of the stage from a company of such actors as I have just described playing round a star on tour. Of the English-speaking stars incomparably the greatest was Barry Sullivan, who was in his prime when I was in my teens, the last of the race of heroic figures which had dominated the stage since the palmy Siddons-Kemble days. Ellen Terry shrank from his acting as from a display of pugilism in which his trembling supporters had no part except to give him his cues and be played off the stage by him. His stage fights in Richard III and Macbeth appealed irresistibly to a boy spectator like myself: I remember one delightful evening when two inches of Macbeth's sword, a special fighting sword carried in that scene only, broke off and whizzed over the heads of the cowering pit (there were no stalls then) to bury itself deep in the front of the dress circle after giving those who sat near its trajectory more of a thrill than they had bargained for. Barry Sullivan was a tall powerful man with a cultivated resonant voice: his stage walk was the perfection of grace and dignity; and his lightning swiftness of action, as when in the last scene of Hamlet he shot up the stage and stabbed the king four times before you could wink, all provided a physical exhibition which attracted audiences quite independently of the play. To

John Coleman and T. C. King[9] and other provincial stars with whom he has been sometimes ignorantly classed by London stage historians he was as Hyperion to a very thirdrate satyr. He was as proud as Lucifer, and as imposing; but he was the only actor I ever heard come before the curtain at the end of a play to apologize for having acted badly. He had opened on Monday night in Hamlet (he was at his best in Hamlet and Richelieu) after a very rough passage from Holyhead. Certainly some of the usual charm was lacking; but only very sensitive Barry Sullivan connoisseurs could have noticed it. With an unanswerable dignity he informed the applauding Dublin playgoers that he had done justice neither to them nor to himself, and begged their indulgence. They were awestruck; and then their applause had a note of bewilderment; for most of them had thought it all very splendid.

Yet this great actor—for such of his kind and in his prime he was—had no notion of what we now require as artistic production. He went into a provincial theatre as into a rag and bottle shop; made them drag out the old scenes that the people of the town had seen hundreds of times in all sorts of plays; and, by summary methods that involved a good deal of swearing and bullying, drilled the stock company in a day's rehearsal into giving him his cues and playing up to his strokes of stage business that night. At first he brought with him nothing but his costumes and swords. Later on, he traveled with a fairly goodlooking young leading lady (possibly in consequence of an experience with a local Ophelia who reduced me to such paroxysms of laughter that I narrowly escaped ejection from the theatre) and an old actor, Cathcart,[10] who had supported Charles Kean, and who, as Richmond or Macduff, got the worst of all the stage fights[11] except the final fatal thrust under the arm, and who relieved the star of the worst drudgery of rehearsal when advancing age compelled him to husband his still mighty forces. In

9. Coleman was an actor-manager and dramatist, who leased London theatres for occasional seasons, but mostly toured the provinces. Thomas C. King, touring actor-manager (known as 'Handsome' King), popular in Dublin, was seen by Shaw at eleven, in Boucicault's *The Corsican Brothers* (March 1868).
10. The local Ophelia was Faucit Saville; the touring one, Louise Hibbert. James Faucit Cathcart was a member of Sullivan's troupe 1873–8. The backward view from 1929 (the year in which Shaw drafted the preface) to the childhood theatre experience of 1870 made Cathcart seem 'old'; in actuality he was only 42 when Shaw first saw him perform with Sullivan.
11. Robert M. Sillard in *Barry Sullivan and His Contemporaries* (1901) described these fights as 'veritable combats, such as only two accomplished swordsmen could go through with all the reality of a battlefield itself. The blades met with so stern a clash that sparks were often driven from the steel' (vol. II, pp. 177–8).

spite of this relief and of his haughty sobriety and irreproachable private life Barry Sullivan died paralyzed, exhausted by the impossible task of being superhuman for six nights in every week; for, clever as he was technically, he revelled in his work too keenly to keep within the limits of that passionless science of acting which enabled Salvini to make his audiences imagine him a volcano in eruption when he was in sober fact hardly moving, and Coquelin, without turning a hair, to get through a night's work that would have worn most of our actors to rags or driven them to stimulants to pull them through.

Had I passed my boyhood in London I should have seen nothing of the very important side of stage art represented by Barry Sullivan's acting. He had appeared there with Helen Faucit[12] as Hamlet at the Haymarket Theatre, and been hailed by The Times as the leading legitimate actor of the British stage. But when he found, as Irving found later, that this meant being skinned alive by the London landlords, he shook the dust of London off his feet, and, first in Australia and then in the English provinces and in Ireland and Scotland, set to work with a fixed determination that, however scanty the audience, whoever once saw him act would come again. He soon secured crowded houses every night, and died leaving £100,000 at about the age at which Irving had to abandon his London theatre penniless and fall back on America and the provinces. Had Barry Sullivan produced Shakespear's plays as handsomely as Irving did at the Lyceum they would not have drawn an extra farthing (for a theatre can be no more than full) and he would have had to spend much more money on them.

I certainly learnt nothing from Barry Sullivan's exploits of how far the grand style in acting can be carried by women. Most fortunately for me, however, a visit was paid to Dublin by Adelaide Ristori [in *Maria Stuart*], who completed my education in this respect, besides convincing me that an Italian stock company, when the novelty of its foreign conventions wears off, can become even more unbearably stale than an English one. The nearest English approach to a tragic actress was Ada Cavendish, whose performance as Wilkie Collins's New Magdalen [1873] made an extraordinary impression; but she only flashed across the sky and vanished, leaving no successor until Janet Achurch arrived fifteen years later and inaugurated the Ibsen movement. Both of them, like Edmund Kean, Robson, and many others, called to their aid powers that destroyed them. Ellen Terry did not visit Dublin, and was only a name to me when I came to London in 1876; but everything that the

12. Later Lady Martin, an intimate of Queen Victoria. She was celebrated for her Juliet, Portia and Desdemona, and one of her greatest successes was in Bulwer-Lytton's *The Lady of Lyons*, in which she appeared opposite William Macready.

perfection of technical accomplishment could do with youth, cleverness, wit, and irresistible charm in drawingroom drama was demonstrated by Madge Robertson, who came with Buckstone and the entire Haymarket company from London, and struck the first shattering blow at our poor old stock company.

The stock company was hard enough to bear when there was no alternative; but when the London successes began touring through the provinces and the Irish and Scottish capitals, and were performed there not as now by secondrate companies giving a mechanical imitation of the original London production, but by the London cast which had created the success, the stock companies fell dead at their impact. To say that they perished unwept, unhonored, and unsung would be to give only the faintest idea of their death and damnation. When we who had seen them scrambling anyhow through all sorts of plays in the way I have tried to describe first saw finished acting, careful production, thorough identification of the performers with parts for which they had been carefully selected as suitable, with new faces, new voices, new clothes, and new scenery, a return to the stock company was impossible.

And now I come to the link between all this theatrical history and the present volume. Among these London successes which brought London productions unchanged to Dublin was a play called The Two Roses [1870], by [James] Albery. One of the characters was a selfish old humbug named Digby Grant. It made the success of the piece by a certain egotistical intensity, sinister and yet dignified in its indignity, which was not in the play but in the actor: an actor with a tall thin figure, which if it could not be convicted of grotesqueness was certainly indescribably peculiar, and a voice which was dependent so much on the resonance of a cavernous nose that it was, compared to the powerful and musical chest voice of Barry Sullivan, a highly cultivated neigh. His name was Henry Irving. I instinctively felt that a new drama inhered in this man, though I had then no conscious notion that I was destined to write it; and I perceive now that I never forgave him for baffling the plans I made for him (always, be it remembered, unconsciously). His stage disguise was so perfect that I did not even know that he was still a young man: indeed the one effect he never could produce on the stage was a youthful effect: his Romeo was no younger than his Digby Grant. He was utterly unlike anyone else: he could give importance and a noble melancholy to any sort of drivel that was put into his mouth; and it was this melancholy, bound up with an impish humor, which forced the spectator to single him out as a leading figure with an inevitability that I never saw again in any other actor until it rose from Irving's grave in the person of a nameless cinema actor who afterwards became famous as Charlie Chaplin. Here, I felt, is something that leaves the old stage and its superstitions and staleness completely behind, and inaugurates a new epoch in the theatre.

The theatrical system to which the stock company belonged decomposed and broke up; and when I came to London it seemed to recede into a remote provincial past. I hastened to the famous little theatre [the Prince of Wales's] off Tottenham Court Road, where the Scala Theatre now stands,[13] to see the Cup and Saucer drama of Robertson handled by the Bancrofts. The play I hit on was Ours; and in it I saw Ellen Terry for the first time. She left on me an impression of waywardness: of not quite fitting into her part and not wanting to; and she gave no indication of her full power, for which the part afforded no scope. As her portraits had prepared me to find her interesting and singular (I have never been susceptible to mere prettiness) I was less struck than I should have been if she had been quite new to me. It was not until I saw her in New Men and Old Acres [produced at the Court Theatre, 2 December 1876], which was made a success by her performance as The Two Roses had been made a success by Irving's, that I was completely conquered and convinced that here was the woman for the new drama which was still in the womb of Time, waiting for Ibsen to impregnate it. If ever there were two artists apparently marked out by Nature to make a clean break with an outworn past and create a new stage world they were Ellen Terry and Henry Irving. Nobody can really understand my correspondence with Ellen Terry twenty years later without grasping this situation.

What actually happened was an anticlimax which in its public aspect was a glorious success for both of them. Irving fascinated London in a play [by Leopold Lewis] called The Bells [1871] under an oldfashioned management. His success was so great and so entirely personal that he was able to lift the theatre out of the grip of his manager and take its professional destiny into his own hands with all shackles cast off from his art, in the position as head of the English stage which he held almost unchallenged for thirty years. The earliest notable use he made of his freedom was to engage Ellen Terry as his leading lady. It was his first and last enlightened stroke of policy. For he immediately turned back to the old Barry Sullivan repertory of mutilated Shakespear and Bulwer Lytton, to which he actually added The Iron Chest of the obsolete [George] Colman. From the public point of view he never looked back: from my point of view he never looked forward. As far as the drama was concerned he was more oldfashioned than the oldest of his predecessors, and apparently more illiterate than the most ignorant of them. The taste and judgment which enabled him to achieve so much beauty and

13. The Scala Theatre was demolished in 1972.

dignity in scenery and costume and to rid his theatre of all the old vulgarities
when he had Ellen Terry to reveal such possibilities to him did not extend
to literature. He seemed the most pedantic of elocutionists, because his peculiar nasal method of securing resonance obliged him to pronounce our English
diphthongs as vowels; and though he delivered Shakespear's lines (what he
left of them) like one who had a sense of their music he would cut a purple
passage even out of his own parts quite callously. If any doubts remain as to
whether an actor who could look so profoundly and venerably scholarly did
not know the difference between Colman and Shakespear, much less between
Shakespear's poetry and Shakespear's verbiage, a glance at his acting version
of King Lear will dispel them. His henchmen Bram Stoker [business manager
of the Lyceum] and L. F. Austin [secretary and publicist] wrote his letters for
him; for he did not know how much more creditable to him were his own
simple and natural compositions than their displays of cleverness. He took
no interest in the drama as such: a play was to him a length of stuff necessary
to his appearance on the stage, but so entirely subordinate to that consummation that it could be cut to his measure like a roll of cloth. Of the theatre
at large he knew almost nothing; for he never left his own stage. I am
exaggerating when I say that he regarded an author as a person whose business
it was to provide plays at five shillings an act, and, in emergencies, to write
the fifth act whilst the fourth was being performed; and yet, in spite of his
intercourse with Tennyson, Traill, Wills, and Comyns Carr, I believe that
this caricature of his attitude gives a juster impression of it than any statement
of the sober facts. He composed his acting with extraordinary industry and
minuteness: his Matthias in The Bells and his Charles I [by W. G. Wills, in
1872] were wonderful mosaics of bits of acting thought out touch by touch.
His Macaire [*Robert Macaire*, by Charles Selby, in 1883] and Louis XI [by Dion
Boucicault, in 1878] will hardly be surpassed: they were limit achievements in
their *genre*. Even in his Shakespearean impostures (for such they were) there
were unforgettable moments. But he composed his parts not only without
the least consideration for the play as a whole, or even for the character as
portrayed by the author (he always worked out some fancy of his own), but
without any for the unfortunate actors whom he employed to support him.
A great deal of that absence of vulgarity which I have noted as characteristic
of his management was secured by the simple method of not allowing his
company to act. He worked hard to make them do what he wanted for his
own effects; but if they tried to make independent effects of their own, he
did not hesitate to spoil them by tricks of stage management. In this way
he threw on himself the enormous burden of attracting the public
singlehanded. He achieved the celebrated feat of performing Hamlet with

the part of Hamlet omitted and all the other parts as well, substituting for it and for them the fascinating figure of Henry Irving, which for many years did not pall on his audience, and never palled on himself. If those present could have remembered Barry Sullivan's Hamlet in the eighteen-sixties or foreseen Forbes-Robertson's Hamlet of the eighteen-nineties some of them might have said that Irving's Hamlet was neither skilled classic acting nor Shakespear's Hamlet, and that compared to Sullivan he was a limp duffer and compared to Robertson a freak; but most of them would have paid their money none the less to enjoy the performance as an avatar of Henry Irving.

When I use the word duffer I mean that when he began to play heroic parts he had neither the physique nor the technique needed for this sort of work, in which the actor must persuade the audience that he is sustaining bodily and vocal exertions which are, as a matter of fact, physically impossible. When Salvini electrified London with his Othello [1875], Irving had a golden opportunity of finding out how this can be done by a study of the Italian actor's very scientific methods; but he flatly refused to avail himself of it, whereat Salvini was some-what shocked. International courtesy apart, Irving was probably right in classing himself with the unteachables who have to find and go their own way rather than with the apprehensive geniuses who learn from everything and everybody.

I, being interested in the technique of acting, and having learned from Barry Sullivan, Ristori, and Salvini, what could be done in the grand school, was very conscious of Irving's technical shortcomings, and greatly relieved when, on his production of [Bulwer-Lytton's] The Lady of Lyons [in 1879], I found that he had at last learnt the limitations of the stage and of human faculty on it. Except for an occasional relapse into whinnying, he was main-taining his dignity and allowing the imagination of the audience to do its proper share of the work. Later on [2 April 1889] I saw him as Macbeth, his first assumption of which had provoked something like a storm of derision from the unconverted. I found it a performance of refined beauty. It was not any conceivable historical Macbeth; but then neither is Shakespear's. And I have not the faintest recollection of any other figure in the play, from which I infer that Ellen Terry cannot have played Lady Macbeth on that occasion, nor of any particular scene except the banquet scene, in which the violence of Macbeth's defiance of Banquo's ghost was rather ridiculously beyond the actor's resources; but still his performance was a fine piece of work within its limits. Mr Gordon Craig's idolatrous memoir of Irving [1930], though its judgments are invalidated by the misfortune that the author had no external standards except those set him by Irving himself, gives the most vivid extant pen-portrait of him both as actor and man.

To me, however, Irving's thirty years at the Lyceum, though a most imposing episode in the history of the English theatre, were an exasperating waste of the talent of the two artists who had seemed to me peculiarly fitted to lift the theatre out of its old ruts and head it towards unexplored regions of drama. With Lyceum Shakespear I had no patience. Shakespear, even in his integrity, could not satisfy the hungry minds whose spiritual and intellectual appetites had been whetted and even created by Ibsen; and Shakespear in his integrity was then unknown in the theatre, and remained so until William Poel and Harley Granville-Barker rediscovered and revived him. The shreds and patches which Irving and his predecessors tore out of his plays and tacked crudely together for performances which were interrupted four or five times by intolerable intervals, during which the women in the audience sat in silent boredom whilst the men wandered about the corridors and refreshment bars, were endurable only by people who, knowing no better, thought they were assisting at a very firstrate solemnization, and were helped by that illusion to persuade themselves that they were enjoying the best that a great institution and two great performers could do for them. I knew better. Irving, wasting his possibilities in costly Bardicide, was wasting Ellen Terry's as well. Her only rival as a Shakespearean actress was the great Ada Crehan (who by a printer's error became famous as Ada C. Rehan); and her genius too was being wasted by Augustin Daly, another master-mutilator of the unfortunate playwright whom he professed to adore. But as Daly did not himself act, his hackings and hewings were very largely addressed to the object of taking all the good lines out of the other parts and adding them to Ada Rehan's; and she spoke them so harmoniously that when listening to her it was impossible to care much about anything but the mere music of her voice and Shakespear's, wheras at the Lyceum Irving's peculiarities were the first consideration. To him professionally Ellen Terry was only the chief ornament of his theatre. Besides, his method was so slow that it was almost impossible to act with him. She had to stop too often and wait too long to sustain her part continuously when he was on the stage.

All this enraged me. I can keep my temper as well as most people; for my double training as a critic of highly sensitive living persons and a propagandist of seditious, not to say subversive, political views, kept me constantly on my guard against letting my temper get the better of me or my manners the worse of me: in short, against the least indulgence of personal malice. Besides, I am tolerant in matters of morals which provoke most people to censoriousness; for to me a great deal of current morality is unsound and mischievous. But when questions of art are concerned I am really malicious. Retrogressive art and wasted or unworthily used talent (the theatre is full of both) make me aware that I am capable of something as near to hatred as any emotion can be that has no taint of fear of it. This correspondence shews how, because Irving would not put his peculiar talent at the service of the new and intensely interesting development of the drama which had begun with Ibsen, and because he wasted not only his own talent but Ellen's, I destroyed her belief in him and gave shape and consciousness to her sense of having her possibilities sterilized by him. Then her position became unbearable; and she broke loose from the Ogre's castle, as I called it, only to find that she had waited too long for his sake, and that her withdrawal was rather a last service to him than a first to herself.

The castle did not long survive her departure. Irving, himself poorer and the landlords of the Lyceum Theatre richer than when he entered it, went to the provinces to exploit his great reputation and retrieve his fortunes as Barry Sullivan had built his up. When he died, he was buried as a prince of the theatre, in Westminster Abbey, with only one dissenting voice, which I, by good luck, succeeded in silencing.[14] His singleness of interest and purpose, his industry, his imagination, and his intensity had triumphed over his ignorance and self-sought isolation, and almost made qualities of them, forcing his audiences to attribute to him every talent, every dignity, and every accomplishment. Those who understood the art of the theatre and knew his limitations could challenge him on every point except one; and that one was his eminence. Even to call him eminent belittles his achievement: he was pre-eminent. He was not pre-eminent in or for this, that, or the other talent or faculty: his pre-eminence was abstract and positive: a quality in itself and in himself so powerful that it carried him to Westminster Abbey. Unlike Macready, Forbes-Robertson, and many of the best actors, he was stagestruck, and cared for nothing but acting: a craze and a limitation if you will, but one which saved him from being half ashamed of his profession, as Shakespear (the actor as distinct from the author) was, and thus enabled him finally to extort from the Government for his art the same official recognition which was accorded as a matter of course to painting and music.

Ellen Terry, not at all stagestruck, was extremely unlike Irving. She had had her professional technique hammered into her in her childhood by Mrs Charles Kean, who would sit in the gallery and see to it that every word of Ellen's reached her there. Thus she had skill at the back of her beauty and

---

14. A vindictive Lady Irving, upon learning in 1905 that she was left out of the will of her estranged husband, sought Shaw's assistance to prevent the Abbey interment by revelation of Irving's adulterous relationship with writer Eliza Aria. To forestall her, Shaw suggested she would forfeit by this act a civil list pension that would certainly be hers under quieter circumstances. Stifling her wrath and keeping her mouth shut, Florence Irving collected the pension.

charm. Success came to her without the asking. She never had to struggle, like Irving, against derision and dislike. The few and insignificant attempts that were made to caricature her were hopeless misfires, wheras caricature alone could give a truthful impression of Irving. The posthumous statue of him outside the National Portrait Gallery in London, though possibly quite accurate in its measurements, gives no notion of what he was like; and even the portrait by Millais is only Irving carefully drest up to be as unlike himself as possible, the ghostly impression of his Philip II by Whistler being more suggestive of him than either.[15] Artists were so eager to do Ellen Terry justice, and found it so difficult, that they had neither the time nor the desire to mock her. All this smoothing of her path had its disadvantages. She was not hardened and given the grim but invaluable quality of tenacity by having to struggle with an implacable resistance. Her value was so promptly and easily admitted that she did not realize it herself at all fully. I have already said that she trifled with her career by leaving the stage for years to devote herself to Godwin, an eminent architect in full practice outside the theatre. Irving would not have left the stage for a night to spend it with Helen of Troy. She squandered herself on all sorts of people and all sorts of interests until she lost the habit and power of mental concentration to such an extent that the slightest distraction made her forget her lines on the stage. She told me once that her memory was all right, but that if on the stage she saw the smallest thing (she instanced a matchbox) that had not been in exactly the same place the night before, it interested her so much that everything else at once went out of her head. Her sister Kate told me impatiently that Ellen could learn her parts well enough if she chose, but preferred to scatter her mind before the girls who crowded up to her to adore her. She was physically restless: when I reproached her for fidgeting she said "Do you know, I have no weight on the stage: unless I have heavy robes I cant keep on the ground." She literally did not think enough of herself: that was why her greatest self-squandering of all, her devotion of herself to the support of Irving at the Lyceum Theatre, did not until it was too late present itself to her otherwise than as a quite eligible professional opportunity.

And so, in the end, my early vision of the two as ideal instruments for a new drama did not come true.

15. The statue of Irving by Thomas Brock, R.A., was unveiled on 5 December 1910, at its present site at Charing Cross Road and Irving Street. The 1883 portrait by Sir John E. Millais is owned by the Garrick Club. The Whistler portrait of 1876, of Irving as Philip II of Spain in Tennyson's *Queen Mary*, is in the Metropolitan Museum of Art, New York.

When reading the letters which follow it must be borne in mind that long and intimate correspondence can occur only between people who never meet oneanother. Swift's journal to Stella would not have been written if they had met every day as Ellen Terry and Irving did, instead of living in separate islands. Ellen and I lived within twenty minutes of each other's doorstep, and yet lived in different worlds: she in a theatre that was a century behind the times, and I in a political society (the Fabian) a century ahead of them. We were both too busy to have any personal intercourse except with the people we were working with. Our correspondence began when I was a professional critic of music through a move she made to help a young musician [a soprano, F. Elvira Gambogi, 1892] in whom she was interested. Now critics, like dentists, are a good deal occupied in hurting sensitive people in sensitive places; and as they have to do it in an entertaining manner, which no doubt gives them an air of enjoying it, they produce an impression of Sadism. And so I, being a critic, and, I hope, an entertaining one, had been classed by Ellen Terry as an unamiable person. This was fortunate for me, because instead of having to live up to an exalted estimate of my merits I had only to be commonly civil and helpful to produce a surprised and pleased reaction in my favor. Finding her delightful as a correspondent, and having some gifts in that way myself, I improved the opportunity to such purpose that we presently became occupied with oneanother in a paper courtship, which is perhaps the pleasantest, as it is the most enduring, of all courtships. We both felt instinctively that a meeting might spoil it, and would certainly alter it and bring it into conflict with other personal relationships. And so I hardly ever saw her, except across the footlights, until the inevitable moment at last arrived when we had to meet daily at the rehearsals of the play I wrote for her: Captain Brassbound's Conversion. By that time Irving had passed out of her life, and indeed out of his own; and Ellen's heart was for the moment vacant. I could not help speculating as to the possibility of my filling the vacancy. But Providence had other views. At our first serious meeting [February 1906] in the rehearsal room at the Court Theatre, Ellen and I were talking together before business began when the door opened, and a young American actor, James Carew, who had been engaged to play the part of Captain Hamlin Kearney, came in. "Who is that?" said Ellen, looking at him with quick interest. "That's the American captain" I answered. Without an instant's hesitation she sailed across the room; put Mr Carew in her pocket (so to speak); and married him. The lucky captive naturally made no resistance; and some of the letters in this volume shew how far the marriage was successful, though I cannot believe that James had any choice of his own in the matter. I was awestruck; for I had not believed it possible for even the most wonderful of women to choose her man at a single glance and bear him off before he had time to realize who she was. Shooting a lion at sight is child's play in comparison, because it does not matter which lion it happens to be: if you do not kill it, it may kill you; so—bang! But it matters very much which man it is when marriage is in question; and so swift a decision by a huntress who, far from being promiscuous in her attachments, was highly fastidious, made me marvel and say to myself "There, but for the grace of God, goes Bernard Shaw."

After the play was disposed of our meetings were few, and all accidental. One of these chance meetings was on a summer day in the country near Elstree, where I came upon a crowd of people at work on a cinema film. Ellen Terry was there, acting the heroine.[16] She was astonishingly beautiful. She had passed through that middle phase, so trying to handsome women, of matronly amplitude, and was again tall and slender, with a new delicacy and intensity in her saddened expression. She was always a little shy in speaking to me; for talking, hampered by material circumstances, is awkward and unsatisfactory after the perfect freedom of writing between people who *can* write. She asked me why I did not give her some work in the theatre. "I do not expect leading parts" she said: "I am too old. I am quite willing to play a charwoman. I should like to play a charwoman." "What would become of the play?" I said. "Imagine a scene in which the part of a canal barge was played by a battleship! What would happen to my play, or to anyone else's, if whenever the charwoman appeared the audience forgot the hero and heroine, and could think of nothing but the wonderful things the charwoman was going to say and do?" It was unanswerable; and we both, I think, felt rather inclined to cry.

She became a legend in her old age; but of that I have nothing to say; for we did not meet, and, except for a few broken letters, did not write; and she never was old to me.

Let those who may complain that it was all on paper remember that only on paper has humanity yet achieved glory, beauty, truth, knowledge, virtue, and abiding love.

AYOT ST LAWRENCE.                                                    G. B. S.
26 June 1929.


16. Ellen Terry made five films between 1916 and 1922, including *Pillars of Society* (as Widow Bernick) and *The Bohemian Girl*. In her first, *Her Greatest Performance*, she played a retired stage star who disguises herself as a theatre dresser (played in the film by her daughter Edith Craig) to trap a murderer, thus clearing her son. Shaw visited her on the set.

# A Word First

*Preface to* Doctors' Delusions: Crude Criminology: Sham Education, *in the Collected Edition, 1931*

=====

Please do not class me as one who "doesnt believe in doctors." One of our most pressing social needs is a national staff of doctors whom we can believe in, and whose prosperity shall depend not on the nation's sickness but on its health. There should be no such thing as a poor doctor and no such thing as an ignorant one. The great majority of our doctors today are both poor and ignorant with the conceited ignorance of obsolete or spurious knowledge. Our surgeons obtain the highest official qualifications without having had a single hour of specific manual training: they have to pick up the art of carving us as paterfamilias picks up the art of carving a goose. The general education of our citizens (the patients) leaves them so credulous and gullible, that the doctor, to whom they attribute magical powers over life and death, is forced to treat them according to their folly lest he starve. Those to whom these menacing facts are known, and who are capable of understanding their gravity (including all our really able doctors), will not mistake my aim nor wish me anything but a sympathetic hearing. As for the simpletons (bless their anything-but-sacred simplicity!), if they dont like it, why, they must lump it.

Our mechanist-surgeons and chemist-physicians must, however, forgive me for differing fundamentally and flatly from the scientific basis (if it can be called scientific) of their crude practices. In my view surgeons and physicians should be primarily biologists. To tackle a damaged living organism with the outlook of a repairing plumber and joiner, or to treat an acid stomach by pouring an alkali into it, is to behave like a highly unintelligent artisan, and should entail instant and ignominious disqualification by the Privy Council. There are many unlearned amateur pathologists and hygienists, from Mary Baker Eddy to George Hackenschmidt,[1] who are safer guides than the Harley

---

1. Estonian wrestler, undefeated as professional freestyle wrestler (1900–08). After retirement he operated a physical culture school and published several books, including *Man and Cosmic Antagonism to Mind and Spirit* (1935). Shaw, introduced to him by the showman Charles Cochran, found him 'no fool'.

Street celebrities who laugh at them, their secret being simply that they have had the gumption to guess that it is the mind that makes the body and not the body the mind.

I also expect a doctor to be an evolutionist, and, as such, to regard all habits as acquired habits, a man being nothing but an amœba with acquirements. Any doctor found parroting the obsolete XIX century cackle about non-acquired heritable habits and non-heritable acquired habits should be removed to the nearest museum of quaint antiquities.

I hope this is clear. If not, please read the preface to my Back to Methuselah until it *is* clear.

1931.                                                                 G. B. S.

# Forty Years Later

*Preface to a reprint of* Fabian Essays in Socialism, *1931*

======

This set of essays is apparently inextinguishable. When it had very unexpectedly attained the age of twenty years, I, the original editor, had to provide
it with a fresh preface. Ten years passed; and it was still in steady demand.
Sidney Webb (now Lord Passfield) had to provide a preface for its thirtieth
anniversary. That, we supposed, must see it through; but no: its fortieth
birthday is now reached and passed; and I, somewhat surprised to find myself
alive, am called on to write my third preface to it.

I will not pretend that this longevity is a matter for jubilation. Everything
that is contained in the essays should by this time have become part of the
common education of every citizen. But our common education is centuries
out of date; and generations of Britons still crowd in on us with a laboriously
inculcated stock of ideas of which half belong to the courts of the Plantagenets
and the other half to the coffee houses under Queen Anne. This huge mass
of obsolescence rolls back like the stone of Sisyphus on every attempt to
advance thought and weed out ignorance. We the Fabian essayists, who made
such an attempt, and brought many of the Intelligentsia of our own generation
up to date in economic sociology, are facing a new generation with Queen
Anne and Henry VI still in possession, and the stage of Socialist thought
which we have ourselves outgrown still so far ahead of our youngest contemporaries that not only our essays but Henry George's ten-years-older Progress
and Poverty are still selling steadily.

Yet there is an air of amazing advance in our political circumstances. As I
write, a [former] Fabian Socialist [Ramsay MacDonald] is Prime Minister of
Britain. Two of our essayists are in the House of Lords: one of them [Sidney
Webb] a Cabinet minister and the other [Sydney Olivier] an ex-Cabinet
minister. Parliament swarms with Fabians and members of Socialist Societies
for which the Fabian Society is not extreme enough. Fabianism is now often
spoken of as an outmoded economic pedantry to which a few dotards cling
under the impression that they are still young pioneers. Socialist Cabinets,
Socialist Presidents, Socialist Dictators are all over Europe piecing together
the ruins of the empires. The largest country with a settled government in
Europe is now a Communist country in which persons with the Queen

Anne-Plantagenet mentality find it harder to live than Jesuits did in England under Elizabeth. Even in the British Isles, where the pupils of King Henry the Sixth's school [Eton College, 1440] are still in the ascendant, annual confiscation of the incomes of the capitalists on a scale rising to fifty per cent, and periodical raids on their capital on a similar scale by death duties, with immediate redistribution among the proletariat of much of it not only in kind but in hard cash, is taken as a matter of course.

Our airs of democratic advance are equally imposing. When the first Fabian essays were new the continent of Europe could shew only two republics (or three, if we count the toy republic of San Marino) as against four empires and eleven kingdoms. Today the four empires have disappeared and been replaced by republics. There are still twelve kingdoms left, including Iceland and Albania; but there are sixteen republics outnumbering them in population by 11 to 4. Over 300 millions of people have passed from monarchical to republican rule. Divine right is never mentioned: the sovereignty of the people is admitted everywhere, either by adult suffrage or by express declaration in the new constitutions. On paper at least Democracy is in the saddle and rides mankind.

If all this change were part of a developing Socialism it would be a matter for rejoicing. But being as it is an attempt to gain the benefits of Socialism under Capitalism and at its expense: a policy which has for its real slogan "What a thief stole steal thou from the thief," there is more threat of bankruptcy in it than promise of the millennium. When, as at present, the work of organizing civilization outgrows the scope and capacity of private adventurers and their personal interests, the first symptom of excessive strain is an abnormal increase of unemployment accompanied by reconstructions and amalgamations of commercial businesses, and appeals by them for State help: all of them desperate efforts to make private enterprize meet social needs which are more and more transcending its possibilities. When the number of unemployed runs into millions, and they consist to a considerable extent of demobilized soldiers who have learned in a war of unprecedented frightfulness to hold human life cheap, the unemployed become, in fact, an army living on the country.

In such straits, which have occurred before in the history of previous civilizations, Capitalism always tries to buy off those whom it cannot employ and no longer dares leave to starve. Unemployment thus becomes a recognized means of livelihood for the proletariat. As I write, there are young men in the prime of early manhood who have never worked, and proletarian children who have never seen their parents work. If two or three unemployed share the same house they can live "on the dole" quite comfortably according to their own standards of comfort by blackmailing Capitalism until it consents to share its social plunder with them. If the combinations of two or three become combinations of two or three hundreds or even thousands, as they will if the dole system attains a reputation for permanence, the Ritz Hostels of the unemployed will put to shame the humble dwellings of those for whom the Labor Exchanges can still find jobs. Members of seasonal trades now draw the dole through the off-season for which the on-season formerly provided. This state of things is clearly the "bread and circuses" of the ancient Roman proletariat over again; and the parallel will soon be more exact; for since our police have urged the opening of the cinemas on Sunday because they keep the streets empty and orderly, State-provided cinemas are quite likely to be instituted as a means of preventing riots of the unemployed. That must end as the Roman Empire ended, in bankruptcy.

It is not sufficiently realized, and is not made clear in these essays, that the Capitalist system is quite as Utopian, quite as artificial, quite as much a paper system founded on essays and treatises by clever idealist writers, as Socialism. Its elaborately worked out theory was that the solution of the great problem of how to keep our huge population alive in response to their necessary first prayer "Give us this day our daily bread" is to make the material sources of production private property, enforce all voluntary contracts made under this condition, keep the peace between citizen and citizen, and leave the rest to the operation of individual self-interest. This, it was claimed, would guarantee to every worker a subsistence wage whilst providing a rich leisured class with the means of upholding culture, and saturating them with money enough to enable them to save and invest capital without personal privation.

The theory worked wonderfully in the sphere of production and trade. It built up our factory system, our power machinery, our means of transport and communication, which have made the world a new world in which the iron Duke of Wellington would be as lost as Julius Cæsar. It has produced financial combinations which could buy up the England of Queen Anne as easily as Queen Anne could have bought up a shipyard. It keeps us amused and hopeful and credulous by miracle after miracle just as the Churches and creeds used to, except that the miracles are more authentic and can be performed by every cottager who can afford a pound for a wireless set, or a couple of pennies to drop into the slot in a telephone kiosk. And it has increased the possibilities of private income to a point at which kings are now relatively poor men.

Unfortunately these unprecedented achievements in production and finance have been accompanied by a failure in distribution so grotesquely inequitable and socially disastrous that its continuance is out of the question.

Desperate attempts are being made everywhere by redistributive taxation, State regulation of wages, and factory legislation, to remedy or at least palliate it, within the limits of the Capitalist system. But redistributive taxation within Capitalist limits means dole for idleness instead of wages for productive work; and regulation of wages and factories does not help the unemployed.

Distribution, it must be remembered, is not only distribution of material product, but of work and leisure. If modern methods of production enable a single machine tender to turn out more product in a day than an XVIII century worker in the same trade, without a machine, turned out in a year, there is a gain in leisure, realizable by a reduction in working hours, of 300 per cent or thereabouts. If this and all cognate gains in leisure were equally distributed the result would be a steady reduction in the hours of labor and a steady increase in the hours of individual liberty. But there is an alternative to this. It is just as possible to keep the workers working as long as before, or longer, and to increase the number or the luxury, or both, of the leisured rich. Now this is precisely what the Capitalist system does, and even aims at doing. And in its present stage, when it is adding an army of unemployed to the leisured rich, and thus burning the candle at both ends, the reform of distribution has become a matter of life and death to civilization.

No other remedy than the transformation of Capitalistic society into Socialistic society has so far been able to stand examination. The Fabian Society, founded to advocate that transformation, and to work out its political implications, is as much needed as ever.

The distinctive mark of the Fabian Society among the rival bodies of Socialists with which it came in conflict in its early days, was its resolute constitutionalism. When the greatest Socialist of that day, the poet and craftsman William Morris, told the workers that there was no hope for them save in revolution,[1] we said that if that were true there was no hope at all for them, and urged them to save themselves through parliament, the municipalities, and the franchise. Without, perhaps, quite converting Morris, we convinced him that things would probably go our way. It is not so certain today as it seemed in the eighties that Morris was not right. A European convulsion, of such extraordinary and sanguinary violence that all revolutions of which we have any record seem trifles in comparison, has changed the world more in four

---

1. In 'The Depression of Trade', addressed to the weavers of Oldham on 12 July 1885, Morris spoke of 'a propertyless, producing class, which as a class has no hope save revolution . . .' (*Unpublished Lectures of William Morris*, ed. Eugene D. Lemire, 1969). Shaw read all of the surviving manuscripts of Morris's lectures shortly after the latter's death in 1896.

years than Fabian constitutional action seems likely to do in four hundred. A staggering shock to constitutionalism has come from the settlement of the Irish question by crude force. Thirty years of constitutional agitation and parliamentary work had ended in the passing of a Home Rule Act. The Act was repudiated by its opponents, who armed themselves to resist it, and were seconded by a threat of mutiny from several army officers on service in Ireland. The Prime Minister assured the rebels that they would not be coerced; and their importation of arms was winked at by the authorities whilst similar operations by the Irish Nationalists were attacked by the forces of the Crown. Finally the Act was suspended: and the Irish question was settled by a savage campaign of incendiarism and murder of which the Irish, having the common people on their side, gave the English garrison the worse, thus producing a situation in which England had either to concede self-government to Ireland or engage in a sanguinary reconquest which public opinion would not support either in England or America. This very sensational object lesson, coming on top of the demonstration by the war that a British Government, when stimulated by a bayonet at its throat (a German one in this instance; but English steel is equally effective), could perform with precipitous celerity and the most satisfactory success all the feats of national organization it had declared impossible and Utopian when they were pressed on it by nothing sharper than the arguments of the Fabians and the votes of the Socialists in the country, greatly weakened the position of Constitutionalists and strengthened that of Militarist Terrorists in all parties and countries.

Besides, there was the Russian revolution of 1917. The attempt at Liberal constitutional parliamentarism which followed had almost instantly broken down and been swept away and replaced by a ruthless dictatorship of men of action who were also doctrinaire Marxians. These were very soon convinced by their opponents that the establishment of Socialism must be effected not by discussion and vote, but by those who actively desired it killing those who actively objected to it. Which they accordingly proceeded to do, and be done by, with terrific energy. And, far from alienating popular sympathy, they found the country rising to this sort of leadership with such enthusiasm that the Bolsheviks, beginning in an apparently hopeless condition of military inferiority as a mob with a casual equipment of pistols opposed by disciplined troops with full munitions provided largely by British money, succeeded in raising a Red Army which achieved the impossible by completely reversing the situation and driving the reactionary White armies out of the field in irretrievable defeat.

At the same time Signor Mussolini, banking on his belief that the people, out of all patience with the delays, obstructions, evasions, and hypocrisies of endlessly talking *fainéant* [sluggish] Parliaments, wanted not liberty (which he described boldly as a putrefying corpse) but hard work, hard discipline, and positive and rapid State activity: in short, real government, threw Constitutionalism to the winds, and became at once an acknowledged and irresistible dictator. Similar *coups d'état* followed in Spain, in Jugo-Slavia, in Poland, and in Hungary, all proving that the old Liberal parliamentary systems, which had grown up in opposition to monarchical autocracy, and had brought to perfection the art of paralyzing State enterprize under cover of preserving popular liberties, were falling into disillusioned contempt, and could be suspended or abolished without finding a single effective defender. The transfer of over three hundred million people from monarchical to republican rule resulted in a transfer of nearly two hundred and sixty millions from constitutional parliamentary rule to dictatorial despotism after a brief test by Trial and Error. Nobody wanted despotism as such; but the alternative would not work.

But dictatorships, like proclamations of martial law, are emergency measures; and they are subject to the standard objection to martial law that it is no law at all. When a nation's affairs drift into a hopeless mess some strongminded person seizes it by the scruff of the neck and bullies it into order when it has suffered so much from disorder that it is only too glad to be taken in hand and drilled, however autocratically. The effort usually exhausts the dictator; but even when it does not he finds that he cannot be everywhere and superintend the doing of everything like the chief of a small tribe: he must have a Constitution. It may be an electoral constitution or a dictatorial constitution with delegate dictators all over the place; but a constitution there must be; for autocratic one-man government of a modern State is physically impossible. What is more, it must be a positive constitution and not a negative one. That is, its object must be to enable the Government to control and even undertake every kind of business effectively and rapidly, and not, like our present British constitution, to obstruct, disable, and defeat every effort of the Government to go beyond police work, military defence, and diplomacy.

And here precisely is the rock which threatens to wreck the constitutionalism of the old Fabians. They have lived to see their political plans carried out with a success beyond all their reasonable hopes. The parliamentary Labor Party for which they bargained has been formed, and has already held office twice. The Treasury Bench has been filled with Socialists. Yet as far as Socialism is concerned it might as well have been filled by Conservative bankers and baronets. No industry has been nationalized; and the unemployed are bought off by doles in the disastrous old Roman fashion. The Party

System, under which "it is the business of the Opposition to oppose,"[2] still obstructs so effectively that bills to which nobody objects, and which could be disposed of in half an hour, take up as many months as really contentious measures. Fundamental changes are impossible: only the tinkerings necessary to prevent the State machine from jamming and stopping are introduced and pushed through by mere force of circumstances. Labor Governments, like other governments, end in disappointment and reaction with their millennial promises unfulfilled; whilst the revolutionary Left and the Fascist Right are supplied with daily evidence as to the futility of parliamentary action at home, and the swift effectiveness of hard knocks abroad.

Such being the very dangerous situation, the Fabian Society finds itself confronted with a task not contemplated in these essays. It must devize new instruments of government, designed, not to check governmental activity and neutralize the royal prerogative like our present instruments, but to organize and make effective the sovereignty of the community, and limit the usurped prerogative of private plutocratic interests. Until this is done all talk of reaching Socialism along constitutional paths is idle. The present paths simply do not lead there. They lead nowhere; and when people find themselves there they resort either to revolution or dictatorship.

Under such circumstances our old Plan of Campaign for Labor,[3] which has now been carried out only to land us in a no-thoroughfare, must be replaced by a new plan for the political reconstitution of British Society, eligible also as a model for the reconstitution of all modern societies. Sidney and Beatrice Webb came to the rescue in 1920 with their volume entitled A Constitution for the Socialist Commonwealth of Great Britain; but unfortunately they came too soon (the penalty of foresight); for the great industrial crash that followed the illusory boom after the war did not occur until a year later; and a whole decade passed before it began to dawn on the commercial and political world that anything worse was in question than the usual ephemeral moment of depression, to be followed by the usual revival of trade. Nor, in 1920, had the dictatorships come, nor any apprehensions of them, except in Russia, which did not count in England, as the Government and the Press insanely persisted in treating the Russian Revolution—a most beneficent event in spite of the incidental horrors which attend all too long delayed

2. Spoken by Edward Stanley, a Tory MP, in the House of Commons, in a caustic thrust at a former member, George Tierney, 'a great Whig authority', whom he quoted as saying 'The duty of an Opposition [is] . . . to oppose everything, and propose nothing' (Hansard, 4 June 1841, col. 1188).
3. Fabian Tract No. 49 (1894), drafted by Shaw.

revolutions—as a mere outburst of national crime which would presently be policed out of existence as the French Revolution, concerning which we made the same silly mistake, was supposed to have been policed on the field of Waterloo. At all events the Webb proposals made no perceptible impression on public opinion. The emergency was not grasped. The parliamentary leaders of the Labor Party, though baffled in their legislative plans, and worried by the murmurs of women impatient for practicality and back benchers rebelling against the waste of their time as mere chorus men (especially those who had served their apprenticeship to public work as municipal councillors), had no leisure for constitution making. At last the Fabian Society, pressed by Beatrice Webb, devoted one of its annual series of public lectures at Kingsway Hall to the subject in 1930, her own contribution being published by the Society as A Reform Bill for 1932. It is proposed to follow this by a second set of Fabian Essays on the constitutional machinery required for Socialism.[4]

To that volume readers must be referred for a detailed statement and explanation of the necessary changes. Two main features may be cursorily indicated here. First, the Party System must be scrapped ruthlessly. This ingenious device for disabling Parliament is very little understood. To most people, even to professional politicians, the words Party System mean nothing more than the inevitable division of any representative body into a conservative side and a progressive side, competing with oneanother for the direction of public affairs. As this tendency is an effect of human nature, and as one of our superstitions is that human nature cannot be changed (although changeability is one of the recognized qualities of human nature) proposals to drop the Party System are usually dismissed without examination as Utopian attempts to get rid of political parties. It must therefore be explained that the Party System, forced on William III at the end of the XVII century to secure the support of Parliament for his war against Louis XIV; vigorously repudiated by Queen Anne; but finally established during the XVIII century as our normal constitutional method of parliamentary Government, means simply the practice of selecting the members of the Government from one party only, that party being the one which commands a majority of votes in the House of Com-

---

4. The Fabian lecture series in October–November 1930 was titled 'The Unending Quest: An Inquiry into Developments in Democratic Government'. Beatrice Webb's lecture on 20 November was 'Can We Make British Parliamentary Government Equal to its Task?' Shaw followed on 27 November, to end the series of six lectures, with 'A Cure for Democracy'. The 'second set' of Fabian Essays did not come into being until after Shaw's death, in 1952.

mons, with its inevitable corollary that an adverse vote of the House on any Government measure obliges the Government to resign and "appeal to the country" by a general election.

The effect of this system is that measures brought before the House by the Government are never voted on their merits but solely on the question whether the Government shall remain in office or not, and whether all the members of the House shall be put to the expense and trouble of an immediate election at which their seats will be at stake. Cross-voting by members of independent character according to their conviction, information, or caprice, which made it impossible for William III to foresee from session to session whether the House of Commons would vote him supplies for his continental warfare, is eliminated: indeed such characters are eliminated from Parliament, as only candidates with a party label, pledged to vote for their party right or wrong, have more than the slenderest chance of being elected. Experience soon proved what Queen Anne's blunt common sense foresaw: that the System strengthens the hands of the Prime Minister and his Cabinet as much as it was at first intended to strengthen the hands of the King, though at the cost of spoiling the quality of the Government by restricting the King's choice of capable ministers; reducing their supporters to the rank of operatic choristers; and making all Governments factious and lopsided.

This system was never introduced in the municipalities. In them the corporation or council is elected for a fixed period during which there can be no appeal to the electorate. Business is conducted, not by a single Cabinet drawn from one party only, but by a string of committees on which all parties are represented, each dealing with its own special branch of public work. These committees, working independently, submit their measures to the general body of members, who vote on them quite freely, as nothing whatever is at stake except the measure itself, a rejection of it involving neither change of government nor general election. Obstruction, or opposition for the sake of opposition, which means an absolutely uncritical insincere opposition and thus destroys the whole value of opposition in Parliament, cannot occur: the conflict between the conservative and progressive temperaments is natural and honest: the Conservative is not, as in the House of Commons, repeatedly obliged to vote against advances of which he approves nor the Progressive for changes which he believes to be mistakes. The practical result is that the municipalities get through their work without excessive attendance at the Town Hall, whilst the House of Commons, sitting all day and sometimes all night, is hopelessly unable to keep abreast of its business, and finds that its overworked ministers have no control of the departments they are nominally responsible for, and often no real knowledge of the work done by them, the effective Government being really the bureaucracy or permanent Civil Service, which is unaffected by the Party System.

Hence the demand for the abolition of the Party System and a return to the older municipal system for all governing bodies.

The second main change needed is an adequate division of labor and specialization of function among our rulers. At present Cabinets of about twenty persons (complained of as being too numerous) assisted by a couple of dozen under secretaries, are expected to deal with a body of work which ranges from the widest and weightiest problems of world policy, finance, and constitutional legislation to the most trumpery details of the farmyard and the workshop. What is called devolution, or the delegation of the less comprehensive work to the urban and district local authorities, is baffled by the retention of our old local boundaries, which have been long since obliterated by the growth of villages into towns and the coalescence of towns into vast urban districts, accompanied by a development of intercommunication by motor traffic, air traffic, telephone, and wireless which reduces even the "regional" proposals of twenty years ago to absurdity. It is not now a question of regional councils but of additional central parliaments, with "home rule" for England and Scotland.

These constitutional reforms are, in relation to the ultimate aims of the Fabian Society, only means, not ends. That is why they have been excluded from this volume and made the subject of a new and more ephemeral series of Fabian Essays. Readers of the older series must be content for the moment with this hint that the ocean of Socialism cannot be poured into the pint pot of a XIX century parliament, and that a persistent attempt to do it must inevitably result, as it has already resulted for the majority of the European continental population, in personal dictatorships which, though they may save the situation for the moment, are as mortal as the men they have raised to power or shot out of it, and must, if civilization is to be preserved, be succeeded by effective modern constitutions and governments which really govern instead of helplessly taking their orders, as ours do, from unofficial, irresponsible, and practically secret dictatorships of private industrialists and financiers.

1930.                                        G. BERNARD SHAW.

# [*Troubetskoy*]

*Preface to the catalogue of an exhibition of sculpture by Prince Paul Troubetskoy at the P. & D. Colnaghi Galleries, London, 1931*

═══

Prince Paul Troubetzkoy[1] is one of the few geniuses of whom it is not only safe but necessary to speak in superlatives. He is the most astonishing sculptor of modern times.

When he models an animal, whether it is the tiniest domestic pet, or an overdriven carter's horse embodying all the sorrows of all the ill-used four-legged drudges that have ever perished without having known human pity, or the colossal brute dominated by the terrible Tsar, which stands irresistibly in the great square in Leningrad[2] amid the vacant sites of the conventional monuments which the Soviet wrath has swept away, the result is so perfect in its truth to nature and its power of conveying some lesson or appeal, that you are rushed to the conclusion that its sculptor, like [Antoine-Louis] Barye,[3] was born to model animals and nothing else.

Yet if your first confrontation is with his busts and statuettes of perfectly dressed leaders of society in Paris and London, you would say that his destiny was to extract the quintessence of elegance from the hang of a skirt and the carriage of the head and arms of an archduchess.

Or again, if you knew him only by the monuments which began with that grimly powerful Tsar mastering the horse which is not a gentleman's mount but a great earthy animal that symbolizes all the vast agricultural whole of oppressed Russia under the Imperial Crown, you would class him a supercharged portrayer of force *in excelsis*.

Yet when Troubetzkoy's neighbors on the Lago Maggiore [large lake in N. Italy, partially in Switzerland], where his famous Villa Cabianca stands, asked

1. Russian-born sculptor, who made busts of Shaw in 1908 and 1926, a statuette in 1926, and a life-size sculpture in 1927.
2. Troubetzkoy's equestrian statue of Alexander III was begun in 1899, completed in 1906, and erected in St Petersburg's Znamenskaya Square in 1909. It is now housed in the Russian Museum.
3. French sculptor, known for such animal figures as 'Jaguar devouring a hare' (Salon of 1850); 'Senegal elephant, running' (*c.* 1830–40); 'Lion crushing a serpent' (1833).

him to commemorate the great war for them, expecting something enormous and intense, he placed on a rock on the esplanade at Pallanza [resort town on west shore of Lago Maggiore] a simple figure of a young mother holding out her baby and asking "Is this what you are going to do with my son?"

For Troubetzkoy is a gigantic and terrifying humanitarian who can do anything with an animal except eat it.

Some of us remember the inaugural banquet in London of the International Society of Painters,[4] at which the late Lord Haldane, presiding, announced, when all the conventional speechmaking was over, that the illustrious sculptor Paul Troubetzkoy desired to address the company, and how a figure of Patagonian stature[5] arose amid polite applause, and began "Mr. President: is it not a monstrous thing that we, who are supposed to be artists and civilized men, and not savages, should be celebrating a great artistic occasion by gorging ourselves on the slaughtered corpses of our fellow creatures?"

As I am a vegetarian my withers were unwrung (it is as a faithful vegetarian that I am immortalized in bronze in this exhibition); but for the rest it was merciful that as the speech was in French they only pretended to understand it, and applauded they knew not what.

One sympathizes also with the unfortunate Russian committee of the Fine Arts who were instructed by the Tsar to see that the young Troubetzkoy produced a proper statue of him. They had him before them and admonished him that the statue must be accurate in detail and highly finished, like the statue of Charles XII in Stockholm and Louis XIV on the Pont des Arts.

"Did you say *finished*, gentlemen?" said the youthful sculptor. "Those statues have not even been begun." The puzzled councillors thereupon informed him that they would visit his statue every Monday morning to see how the work was progressing, and dictate any alterations that were necessary to bring it up to their imperial standard of excellence. He replied by a cordial invitation to them all to come when they pleased, adding that they would find delightful company in his two bears and eighteen wolfhounds, so much adored by all his friends. He saw nothing more of the councillors.

It is now many years—more's the pity—since an exhibition of Troubetzkoy's work has been seen in London. It should be welcome because we have

4. The 'inaugural' reference is curious, as the International Society of Sculptors, Painters and Gravers was founded in 1898 and held dinners annually for several years before the occasion to which Shaw refers. For many years its president was Auguste Rodin.
5. The aboriginal Indian stock of Patagonia (now absorbed by Chile and Argentina) was considered by many to be the tallest known race; hence a giant.

for so long seen ourselves reduced to our primitive elements by our modern sculptors, who take a duchess and reveal her as cave woman, that a sculptor of such incurable and inbred refinement that he can take even a postwar cave woman and make her into a duchess, is almost necessary to restore our respect.

However, his work is before you; and I must not trouble you further with my impertinences.

G. B. S.

# The Rationalization of Russia

*Following a visit to the USSR in July 1931 Shaw contemplated*
*a book to be called* The Rationalization of Russia. *He commenced to draft it in*
*January 1932, at sea en route to South Africa, but abandoned the work*
*after writing a preface and a single chapter. The surviving fragment, edited by*
*Harry M. Geduld, was published in 1964*

===

Most of what is current today in England and America about Communist Russia is written by persons who should never have been taught to write, and read by people who should never have been taught to read. For these accomplishments are as dangerous in the hands of the uneducated as a stick of dynamite in the hands of a baby. And today we are worse than uneducated: we are miseducated. Mr H. G. Wells understated the case when he complained that Gladstone, a typical product of public school and university education, was grossly ignorant.[1] If he had been, his natural mental power and character would have enabled him to learn easily all that he needed to know. But he began his political life with every corner of his mind so carefully stuffed with pernicious rubbish: tribal superstitions imposed on him as religion; glorifications of piracy, brigandage, slave-trading, and murder disguised as history; excuses for robbery, idleness, and mad pride labeled as political economy; and dishonest slacking and shirking of social duty idolized as liberty, that when he became Chancellor of the Exchequer he declared that England's prosperity was increasing by leaps and bounds when it was in fact a feebly palliated hell for nine tenths of the population, whilst the rest were wasting the plunder of the poor in digging their graves with their teeth, not having been taught even how to feed and clothe themselves healthily. A grossly ignorant person would have been a far safer leader of the nation; for he (or she) might have done the right thing by accident or sheer *naïveté*, wheras though Gladstone never said to himself "Evil, be thou my good" [Milton, *Paradise Lost*, IV: 109], yet having been carefully trained by his upbringing and schooling to mistake evil for good, his condition came to the same thing in an incurable form. That is why our Cabinets, consisting of men of unchallenged respectability, and often of the best intentions, are in effect

---

1. Wells's complaint, in *The Outline of History* (1920), was deleted from subsequent editions.

Cabinets of scoundrels, and why our bishops, who always have a saint or two among them as well as a blackguard or two, are at best in the position of chaplains to a pirate fleet. The corruption of a predatory society cannot be cured by reforms within that form of society: it is fundamental; and the remedy is the revolutionary one of a complete substitution of systematically enforced honesty for systematically encouraged predacity.

In our predacious society, politely called by my friend Mr [Richard Henry] Tawney an acquisitive society,[2] the Press invariably shares and voices the fundamental corruption. Its business is to hold a candle to the devil by flattering predacity and representing constitutional honesty as execrable villainy. This is the explanation of the Anti-Sovietism of the British and American newspapers, and consequently of the millions whose opinions are formed by them. I do not write this book with any intention of converting these good people. They will be converted exactly as they have been perverted. The day will come when their newspapers will say different things, as will their nurses and teachers; and their minds will be changed accordingly without any trouble to themselves. I am writing now as a revolutionist to revolutionists in the light of the accomplished revolution in Russia. I have often before written as a Socialist to Socialists; but Socialism means no more now than Christianity meant after its acceptance by Constantine: events have proved that we can have Governments of professed Socialists under Socialist Prime Ministers without the slightest constitutional change. Socialism is actually derided by the up-to-date young as a back number: a XIX century Fabian fad that is no longer in fashion. Social-Democracy, which in the days of Bismarck and Gladstone was the extreme Left in politics, is now the extreme Right of the bourgeois Left, and the recognized Opposition to Communism. We hear of Social-revolutionaries of the Right and of the Left, all classed as enemies by the Communists. The Ultra-Red Socialists of yesterday: Hyndman, [Karl] Kautsky, [Pavel] Miliukoff, [Alexandre] Kerensky,[3] figure in the newest Russian polemics as imperialist reactionaries and bourgeois democrats, the last epithet being the most contemptuous of all.

---

2. British economist and historian, who had a professorship at the London School of Economics, author of *The Acquisitive Society* (1920).
3. Hyndman was the leader of Britain's Social-Democratic Federation. Kautsky, German socialist leader and Marxist, private secretary to Engels, opposed Bolshevism and the Russian Revolution. Milyukov was founder (1905) of the Russian Constitutional Democratic Party (Kadets), who went into exile after the 1917 October Revolution. Kerensky, a Russian social-democrat, was a leader of the 1917 February Revolution, deposed by the Bolsheviks in the October Revolution, escaping to Paris.

Placid ladies and gentlemen who still classify the political world into Conservatives, Liberals, and ragtag and bobtail who have no business in it at all, are not conscious of this confusion. To them Socialism seems a perfectly solid and homogeneous sediment of wickedness and folly: consequently all Socialists are alike to them. But to the Socialists themselves—and common political thought has slipped much further into Socialism than it knows—the change of values, and the consequent new orientations of vituperation, are very puzzling; for all these people: Fabians, Social-Democrats, Right and Left Social Revolutionaries, Labor Party Left wings, and Communists, are Socialists, or at least think they are. They all believe in public control of industry for the common good, public ownership of the sources of production and the machinery of exchange, and public education of all children in the principles of Communism, including the inculcation of the belief that living by private ownership is simply a legalized method of theft. And when they say public they mean proletarian. In short, they are all fundamentally opposed to our Capitalist system, and contemptuous of its pretences to honesty, respectability, and piety.

How, then, has it happened that now that all their wildest hopes have been realized by the sudden transformation of the most backward of the European empires into a federation of Communist republics in which the advocacy of private property is high treason, they all, instead of finding themselves a happy family, come to loggerheads so fiercely that every section except one finds itself in the old Tsarist position of being in opposition to a Government which tolerates no opposition?

The answer is that it is possible to be a strongly convinced Socialist, and have cordial dislike of bourgeois society without any provision of the forms of government which Communism in practice will irresistibly create and impose. We cannot smash Capitalism without smashing its institutions; and its institutions include not only its predatory and oppressive organs but the defensive, humanitarian, palliative and popular brakes and checks and safeguards and franchises and "liberties" which it has consented to partly in fear of rebellion and partly in a natural recoil from its own worst villainy in pursuit of profits. And when Communism makes a clean sweep of the lot, Socialists who have spent their lives upholding [and] volunteering for these forlorn hopes and manning (and womanning) these bulwarks are horrified and often driven into flat reaction, never having reflected that when the Bastille has been stormed and demolished the regulations for the protection of its prisoners are no longer needed, and survive only as superstitions in the minds of the disbanded warders. For the thousandth time I have to note how hard superstitions die: how easy it is to induce people to adopt new ideas and how desperately difficult it is to induce them to scrap the old ones which the new have exploded. When I think of all the time and work I have wasted on parliamentary elections, for instance: the crowds that have come to hear me calling on them to vote for Tweedledum against Tweedledee and practising all the arts of the platform on them until they rose and sang "For he's a jolly good fellow" in a transport of delusion in which they seemed to themselves to be really doing something of intense political importance.

But this is not the case with revolutionary Communism. That is now a working reality, purged of all its old follies and adulterations; and the purpose of this book is to describe and explain this purgation by trial and error, as we shall no doubt go through it all ourselves as the penalty of our incapacity for learning from experience. Before getting to business let me make one statement of the general position.

About three-quarters of a century ago, a German Jew in exile in London, by name Karl Marx, published an epoch-making description and criticism of our capitalist system in which, after producing the necessary moral shock by shewing from our own official documents the atrocity of the system in its bearings on the huge proletarian majority of the nation, he proceeded to shew that the system had in its own nature and logic the seeds of its own disruption and dissolution. Though he lived most respectably with his wife and daughters at an unexceptionable address at Haverstock Hill, and was buried in Highgate Cemetery where his tomb is still visited by pious pilgrims, he was at once classed as an emissary of the devil, and took the place on the capitalist index occupied a century earlier by Voltaire, Rousseau, and Tom Paine, and in the Middle Ages by "the accurst Mahound."

Time passed; but the capitalist system shewed no signs of cracking up as Marx had prophesied: on the contrary it went from miracle to miracle in productive power, and the financiers who had thought in thousands in Marx's day now thought in millions, whilst the "surplus value" impetticosed by those who preyed on society instead of producing for it, piled up outrageously. And so Marx became a back number.

Then another prophet of evil arose: this time no German Jew exile and political suspect, but a professor of unimpeachable credentials, whose hobby was extinct civilizations. This academic ghoul [Sir Flinders Petrie]—if he will forgive me for calling him so—dug up no less than six civilizations of which we had never so much as heard, and coolly informed us in a convincing manner that they were just like our own, and when they had reached the stage at which the social symptoms tallied with those now being exhibited in the centre of the British Empire, had dissolved and left not a wrack behind [*Tempest*, IV: i] in the fashion adumbrated by Shakespear and specified by Karl Marx.

The thoughtful few now felt that this was becoming serious; but our statesmen, who never read anything but the newspapers and had no time to think, continued to assume that capitalist civilization, rooted in laboriously inculcated human vices (which they called human nature), is immortal and eternal, and went on as before, although they noticed that the old machine was requiring a great deal of patching and repairs of a kind dangerously inconsistent with its original design.

Still, they went on gaily enough until, having let their foreign policies relapse into the hands of the militarists, they suddenly found themselves up to the neck in a stupendous war, the upshot of which was that Germany, without being at the least disadvantage in point of fighting and military glory, found herself starved out and for the moment obliged to sue for mercy. The victors, not understanding that Germany is a vital organ of the international capitalism to which they all belong, and that her destruction must involve their own, proceeded at once to plunder her as recklessly and vindictively as if they were buccaneers and she a merchantman who had infuriated them by putting up a stiff fight and killing a good many of them. In spite of the clearest warnings from the few people who knew what they were talking about and were studying the figures whilst the others were wallowing in their gratified war passions, the victors demanded not only a ruinous ransom from Germany but more than she could possibly pay. And they got out of that difficulty by lending her the money to pay it. This silly game did not last very long. When Germany could borrow no more she could pay neither the instalments of the ransom nor the interest on the money she had borrowed to stave them off. This put the victorious allies into Queer Street;[4] for they had borrowed money for the war from England; and England had borrowed it from America; and they were depending on the German ransom to pay the interest on these huge debts. When Germany defaulted there was nothing for it but to face the facts and wipe the slates all round; but they had not the nerve to do this; and when they were at last convinced that the ransom neither would nor could be paid, announced with an air of magnanimity and a big word, moratorium, that they would wait a year for it. They did; and found themselves just where they were before. So they prolonged the moratorium, and will have to keep on prolonging it until the Day of Judgment; for any attempt to enforce payment of the ransom would drive Germany to flat repudiation, possibly by a revolutionary government.

---

4. Early nineteenth–century expression: any 'street' of difficulties, whose residents are in debt or ill or otherwise in trouble. Fledgeby, a villainous money-lender in Dickens's *Our Mutual Friend*, reports that 'Queer Street is full of lodgers just at present'.

Meanwhile, the Bank of England, presuming on the ransom, had lent money for long terms throughout Europe to such an extent that when the ransom dried up it was obliged to borrow for short terms to meet its immediate engagements. The moratorium [1931] created a financial panic throughout Europe; the bank's creditors were alarmed; there was a European run on it; and the Bank of England broke. But as the shutters did not go up, and business continued as usual at from thirteen to fifteen shillings to the pound, the crash was disguised by an auriferous phrase. It was called "going off the gold standard."

Unfortunately, in a desperate but quite unintelligent attempt to save the Bank at the last moment, this going off the gold standard had been held up *in terrorem* to the nation as the most horrible calamity that could befall a nation; and we were called on to submit patriotically to a general reduction in wages and increase in taxation, and, incidentally, to a Coalition Government, to save it. We submitted; and immediately the gold standard was not only repudiated but its repudiation was announced as a signal benefit to the community and a stimulus to the revival of trade. Brazen impudence and technical ignorance could go no further. But the British Public, short as its memory is and Cimmerian[5] as its darkness and bewilderment in matters of currency and finance as distinguished from individual business practice, could not help wondering how the national perdition of Tuesday could become the national salvation of Friday when nothing had happened between but a general election.

This gold business requires a word of explanation. Our statesmen spoke of going off the gold standard exactly as if the officers of a sinking ship in mid ocean had said "Dont be alarmed: all we have to do is to get off the ship." And no one was intelligent enough to say "Get off whither? Into the sea?" What is important on such occasions is not the standard you are going off from, but the one you are going on to. Your currency, when it ceases to represent one valuable commodity, must represent some other, or group of others; else nobody will accept it. If you withdraw your promise to pay in gold without at once promising to pay in something else you must go back to simple barter. There will be an interval during which your bills of exchange and the like will be discounted on the chance that you will be able to pay in meal or in malt; but presently you will have either to (a) make a new standard based on a group of commodities valued by an index number, (b) conduct your trade by barter, or (c) return to the gold standard.

---

5. A mythical people who inhabited a region described by Homer in the *Odyssey* as one of eternal mist and darkness.

The objection to the gold standard is that though gold is valuable everywhere, it is not producible everywhere, and can therefore be cornered, hoarded, and monopolized. A land may be flowing with milk and honey (or water power) and crammed with baser metals and minerals, and yet, if it must pay its debts in gold, be made bankrupt by States which either have gold mines or have cornered the available supply of gold and are sitting on it.

Now when the German ransom business began, Germany admittedly could not pay in gold, because she had none. When she was allowed, and indeed ordered, to pay in ships, the shipyards on the Tees, the Tyne, and the Clyde found their occupation gone, their workers unemployed, and their owners ruined. The ships had to be hastily countermanded. The mere suggestion that payments should be made in steel brought a threat of rebellion from the British steelsmelters. Coal was worse. South Wales was already on the dole because Germany was sending to France for nothing, as pure plunder, the supplies she had formerly bought from British collieries. Our Prime Minister [David Lloyd George] demanded payment in potash; but if there had been potash enough on earth to pay the ransom, England was not prepared to live on potash for thirty years. In the end, Germany, it appeared, must manage to buy gold and pay with it; and her creditors must pay England in gold, and England must pay America in gold. Gold flowed into America until she had more than she knew what to do with; so she simply hoarded it and thereby made it useless as currency; for the whole theory of gold money rests on the assumption that gold is a commodity in free general use and circulation. France, though some of the gold was pouring into her coffers, was the first of the victors to declare herself bankrupt. She also found a big word for it: Stabilization; but the fact was that she repudiated eighty per cent of her war debts by taking her tenpenny franc off the gold standard and replacing it thereon at two pence. Finally France managed to corner all the gold that was not being hoarded in America; and the Bank of England, not being able to procure gold enough to pay its debts, broke as aforesaid.

Now the bitter humor of the situation was that all this bankruptcy was produced, not by the losses of the Allies, but by their ill-gotten gains. For America, after draining Europe of its gold, crashed more sensationally than any of them, and had such budget deficits and millions of unemployed that her plight was more pitiable than Germany's.

At the bottom of all this welter of solvent insolvency, there were two main mistakes which may be called commercial complexes. First, it was assumed that what was going on was trade. Second, it was assumed that trade in itself was a desirable thing, and that without trade nothing could be done and nations must starve helplessly. Neither of these propositions will hold water. The payments made by Germany are not trade: they are tribute. And the payments of interest on investments are not trade: they also are a tribute paid by labor to land and capital for the right to exist. Trade means exchange of goods and services, imports paid for by exports and exports by imports, beneficial to both parties, a fair exchange being no robbery. Where there is payment without exchange, all on one side, the transaction, whatever its legal name may be, and for whatever reasons it may be tolerated, has all the economic effects of robbery, and the moral ones too. I keep bees and provide my breakfast table with honey by robbing them of all the honey they produce save what they must retain to keep them alive. But this is not trade; and when I receive dividends from my foreign investments, they do not give rise to trade with foreigners: I rob them as I rob the bees. The fact that years ago, I, or somebody from whom I have bought the power to exact this tribute, sent enough money abroad to support a body of workers whilst they were making a railway or digging a mine or building and equipping a factory or the like has no more to do with present trade than the fact that my beehives and artificial honeycombs cost me a few pounds say ten years ago creates trade between me and the bee.

Now all of us who have acquired more money than we need spend by applying the bee process to our own compatriots have been investing hundreds of millions of that spare money abroad as long as you or I can remember, and for many lifetimes before that too. If you take the enormous tribute resulting from this; pile on top of it the enormous ransom imposed on Germany; and persist in reckoning it as trade and applying the economics of trade to the solution of the problems it gives rise to, you will presently find yourself in an unholy mess, which is precisely where our statesmen and financiers and bankers are. And if, further, the tribute gets divided into reparations for damage done, of which France, having suffered most of the damage, takes the lion's share, and the rest goes to America as interest on the money borrowed from her for the war, and if again the pauperization of the workers and ruin of industries brought upon countries by receiving tributes instead of money honestly earned, forces them to bargain for payment in gold instead of miscellaneous commodities, then obviously America will automatically corner all the gold that is not cornered by France; and both of them have so much more than they can use that they will wallow in it helplessly like the giant Fafnir in the Niblung legend [Wagner's *Das Rheingold*], whilst the Bank of England breaks for lack of gold, and similar bankruptcies, with Stock Exchange closings, moratoriums, and the like, are occurring all over the commercial world.

The remedy seems ridiculously easy. Why does not the Bank of England buy gold from France and America with commodities? Simply because America refuses to have the commodities dumped on her to the ruin of her industries and the spread of an already crushing unemployment. Every attempt to buy gold with goods is met by a prohibitive tariff.

In the deadlock thus created we naturally say to America "Well, if you refuse to be paid in the only way we can pay you, had you not better cry off the debt?" And we say the same thing to France. And both America and France instantly shriek simultaneously "What! Forgo our just dues and let you cheat us!" They will have to all the same because the deadlock is only the practical expression of the eternal natural fact that nations[,] insofar as they are not wholly self-sufficing, must live by honest trade and not by military plunder and human bee-keeping in any of its forms. For the gods must be laughing very heartily at these terrestrial beggars on horseback vowing to deluge the world in blood again if they are not paid to the uttermost farthing, and then, when their perfectly solvent debtors rush to pay and overpay, scatter them with volleys of tariffs so meticulous that a woman cannot cross a frontier without the risk of being arrested for smuggling her hairpins.

The other delusion—that trade is a good thing in itself—turns all our city articles and commercial forecasts into fairy holes and foolishness. Trade is of course good business for the trader just as murder is good business for the executioner. But in itself it is simply a cost of distribution to be reduced, like other costs, as far as possible. When trade is at its maximum, the trader thinks it is at its optimum, though from the point of view of the consumer it is at its pessimum. The ideal is to have production and consumption within immediate reach of oneanother. Let me make this clear by an illustration which I have used again and again without being able to find a more effective one for bible-reading countries.

Ask any typical city editor to report on the condition of the Garden of Eden in its first year. His first care will be to ascertain the balance of trade by carefully computing and comparing the exports and imports. To his horror he will find that there are no exports, no imports, no balance of trade because there is no trade. He will report that the condition of the Garden is desperate, and that his stock remedy of a reduction in the Bank Rate is not available because there is no bank except the one on which the wild thyme grows ['blows': *A Midsummer Night's Dream*, II: ii]. The speedy death from starvation of Adam and Eve will be declared inevitable as long as Eve persists in plucking apples from the tree and Adam in immediately eating them.

Let us next suppose that Adam and Eve, through eating the fruit of the Tree of Knowledge (symbolizing a university education)[,] are impressed by the city editor[']s report, and, to save themselves from their prophesied doom, take to trade. Eve, instead of handing the apple to her hungry husband, sells it to a Persian fruit wholesaler, who sells it to a middleman, who sells it to another middleman, who sells it to an Afghan dealer, who sells it to a middleman, who sells it to another middleman, who sells it to a speculator, who sells it to an Indian, starting from whom it reaches successively Thibet, China, Manchuria, Japan, San Francisco, Vancouver, Montreal, London, Paris, Alexandria, Jerusalem, Baghdad, where it is sold to a firm specializing in expensive foreign fruits by whom it is sold in an almost uneatable and wholly innutritious condition to Adam at a price which must cover all its traveling expenses plus the commissions of the middlemen and the profits of the exporters in addition to a handsome profit for the Baghdad retailers.

The city editor, called on by Adam for a further report, would now declare that by an unprecedented extension of its foreign trade the Garden of Eden had been raised from an apparently hopeless state of moribund penury to a flourishing prosperity in which the shares of its fruit exporting companies might be regarded as his selection for the week of a particularly attractive investment. The simple facts would be a high death rate from eating rotten or icekilled fruit, and a grievous addition to the burden of labor needed to obtain even that deleterious refreshment.

This senseless cry of trade when there is no trade, and prosperity when things are getting dearer, has muddled us until we can no longer be dealt with as rational creatures; but that does not prevent some of us from being imposingly clever and ready with figures within the limits of our delusion. The unskilled public are dumb in the presence of experts whom they suppose to be starting from the general agreement that two and two make four, though they are really assuming that two minus four makes six.

These experts are far more dangerous than their XIX century predecessors, because the separation between industry and finance was not then nearly so complete as it has since become. When the industrialists had to finance their own concerns they knew that they had to deal with commodities, and that money was only a measure of their value. But today a financier knows nothing of commodities, having never been down a mine nor made a factory. He thinks in figures exclusively. And finally figures cease to represent even money to him: they represent credit; and he comes to believe that great industries are built of credit and not of bricks and mortar, machines and men, clothes, houses, and provisions. He believes that the war was fought on credit instead of on bully beef, trinitrotoluene [TNT: a high explosive], khaki clothing, steel and blood, and that the millions of dead were slain by bills of exchange and war loan scrip instead of by shells and bayonets. A quite able and earnest

American man of business sent me a book[6] containing a carefully thought out plan for paying for the war in I forget how many years painlessly. He did not know that wars have to be paid for on the nail, and that though those who find the money may do so in consideration of their being allowed to tax the future earnings of the nation until they too are repaid on the nail or have the debt extinguished politely by taxation or summarily by repudiation, the war is paid for and done and gone, and their money with it. Yet because their claim to be repaid an equivalent sum remains on record at the Bank of England, the bankers come to think that the money is there as well as the written figure; and grave statisticians count it[,] under the heading Capital, as an actual part of the nation's wealth: an asset instead of a liability.

The bankers who take care of our money for us only that they may make profits by lending it out, and are therefore creditors by profession, have lost all sense of men and things, and live in an imaginary world of credit. Now real credit is only the banker[']s opinion that if he gives (say) a woman a pint of milk, she will return the compliment presently by giving him a pint and a tablespoonful; and though what the woman or her baby consumes is not his opinion but actual milk from the cow, he comes to believe that as the woman has not only got the milk from him but the credit, the transaction, in terms of credit, represents two pints instead of one. Schemes for the financial regeneration of the country by "utilizing credit" (which means drinking non-existent milk) have been put before the country and been seriously discussed, and either advocated enthusiastically or rejected with portentous earnestness for every reason on earth except the simple and obvious one that they are blazing nonsense.

Now the appalling mess in which we have been bogged by this illusion of banking and stock exchange practice, and by the general contempt for scientific reasoning, is making many of us cry that Professor Flinders Petrie and Karl Marx were right, and that Capitalism is played out. That is not quite so. Karl Marx did not say that Capitalism would break up because the silly capitalists did not know their own silly business. Professor Flinders Petrie did not criticize Capitalism: he only told us what had hitherto invariably happened to it. Our modern realistic historians refuse to join the general scare caused by the mess: they say, in effect, that there is nothing new in Capitalism being in a mess, as the beastly thing has always been in a mess, more or less. Messes can be cleaned up; and the fact that we never do clean them up until they do us so much harm, and threaten to do so much more, that it is physically and morally impossible to keep on making them worse, does not excuse the

6. Arthur E. Stillwell, *The Great Plan: How to Pay for the War* (1918).

possibility of our cleaning up this one when we absolutely have to or perish. Without abandoning the Capitalist state we can for the moment wipe the slate of the war debt and the reparations and the unconditional annuities, and all the rest of it. We can discard the gold standard and substitute commodity standards grouped under index numbers. We can get rid of the fluctuation of foreign exchange by a managed international currency. We can abolish unnecessary trade by absolute prohibition of imports of the goods we had better produce for ourselves. We can make necessary trade free trade. We can steal a few tricks from Socialism by nationalizing banking, transport, mining, and power supply, and organizing and controling collective agriculture. We can reform and reconstruct our government machinery, and get sufficient effectual national control of industry to put an end to the present irresponsibility of purely venal private enterprize. I do not say that we shall have character enough or are teachable enough to do these things in the teeth of the bankers and billbrokers and shipowners and their retinues who live by foreign trade and domestic money lending, and in whose hands our Cabinets have all the helplessness of technical ignorance. I do not know whether Professor Flinders Petrie can produce any archæological evidence that the extinct civilizations ever prolonged their agony in this manner. The historians have exploded the old legend that the Roman Empire was assegaied summarily by barbarians tobogganing down the Alps on their shields like Buxton [College] schoolboys on tea trays: it seems to have been simple bankruptcy, financial and moral, and not a rejuvenating and easily absorbed immigration of outlandish folk that made an end of it. But I think our pessimists and catastrophists are hasty in thinking that the hour has arrived when the tremendous strain set up by competitive private capitalism has reached explosion point, and that the present deadlock is an impasse. The strains can still be relieved or shifted sufficiently to be bearable whilst the psychology of the masses is still capitalistic and nationalistic. Much as they have to bear they have borne worse before; and it is their hope and not their despair that capitalism has to dread, if indeed that dread does not itself turn to hope and the capitalists become enlightened enough to will their own destruction as such: a state of mind which I share with the best of my contemporaries.

I shall therefore not treat the present situation as a fulfilment of the forecast of Marx. The change from Capitalism to Communism has not come about as he predicted. It has been established in one State with Capitalism in full swing in all the other States. It has been established not in the most but in the least industrial State. It has been opposed by most of the doctrinaire Marxists. And the revolutionary situation which made it possible has been the accident of a foolish war produced by the assassination of an Archduke, not the culmination of a phase of social evolution. It was something that might happen anywhere, anyhow, instead of under the conditions laid down by Marx. The theory that a revolution cannot take place until there is a revolutionary situation, though it is one of the Marxist affectations, and is a convenient excuse for the large number of revolutionists who dread the revolution their principles oblige them to make, loses some of its apparent profundity in view of Marx's demonstration that under Capitalism there is always a revolutionary situation. All that can be said for it is that the inertia of an established State is so enormous that as long as the masses receive enough to keep them in the station of life to which they are accustomed, and the armed retainers of the State are paid punctually, a catastrophic revolution is impracticable unless it is deliberately desired and contrived by the Government itself as in the case of the Japanese change from Feudalism to Capitalism, or as a mere dynastic revolution desired by the governing class, like the revolution which substituted the House of Hanover for the House of Stuart on the British throne.[7] Even the French Revolution, in which the proletariat was only the catspaw of the bourgeoisie, might have been suppressed if the monarchy had been a capable one and the soldiers' wages paid up instead of being several years in arrear. Dictators' *coups d'état*, and palace revolutions, in which the controlers of the governmental forces and machinery are ousted violently by a new set, are not revolutions in the Marxian sense, and are very unstable if they produce no other change.

A revolution in a highly developed industrial State is extremely difficult because of the absolute dependence of the people on a complicated machinery which they do not understand and cannot work except under specialized direction and management. The old fable of the rebellion of the limbs against the belly has more point in modern times than it had in the mouth of Menenius.[8] A ferryman with a boat and a pair of oars can snap his fingers at organized society; and the village blacksmith can look the whole world in the face; but a sailor in a modern battleship or an assembler in an automobile factory is by himself much more helpless than a baby, who knows quite well where to clutch and how to suck for its subsistence. An Italian friend of mine who conducted a marine engineering establishment was informed by his men

7. This was the Glorious Revolution of 1688, in which James II was deposed in favour of William III and Mary. Anne (Mary's sister) succeeded William. As she had no issue, her throne (under the 1701 Act of Supplement) was given to George I, son of Sophie of Hanover (the heir of Anne, who had predeceased her).
8. Friend of Coriolanus, who, in Shakespeare's tragedy (I: i), relates a fable to a 'company of mutinous citizens'.

one day that they were syndicalists; that henceforth the factory belonged to them on the syndicalist principle of the factory to the factory hands, the mine to the miners, the railway to the railway workers and so forth; and that he had better clear out. He did so. A week later they came to him and told him to clear in again, as they could make nothing of the business.

Now this difficulty does not occur in a backward agricultural country cultivated by peasants. If they seize the land they can make something out of it. They may reduce big farms, ably managed and skilfully cultivated, to miserable strips which return a wretched living to incessant and brutalizing toil; but they do not find themselves in one day without artificial light, without driving power, without food, without water, and without the faintest notion how to set the supplies going again. The primitive peasant who has land has everything he is conscious of needing: the urban proletarian has nothing unless he has the cooperation of thousands of mates and a hierarchy of managers, mathematicians, chemical experts, designers, inventors, and technical specialists of all kinds, themselves cooperating with specialists in marketing, transport, and heaven knows what else.

The difference between the townsman and the countryman is more widely known than it used to be, because the great facility and speed of modern transport, which has filled the highway with motor vehicles which take us from door to door at a speed rivaled by long distance express trains only, and is filling the sky with still faster aeroplanes, has greatly multiplied the number of people who work in the city and sleep in rural bungalows which quickly become suburban. John Gilpin, living over his shop in Cheapside,[9] has to buy an acre in the country and put a house on it before he realizes that roads and paved streets, readymade boundaries marked by area railways and curbstones, water on tap and light in the open air at night are not natural phenomena. The same facility of transport which makes this possible for him also makes it so easy and economical to get implements of all sorts from the manufacturing towns that it is harder and harder to find anyone in the suburbs who can make anything or repair anything singlehanded. Even things which are still made by hands instead of by machines are made by so many hands that no individual possessing only two can pretend to make more than a fragment of anything. Thus the townsman can live only as a fragment in a jigsaw puzzle, wheras the husbandman can support himself independently and be his own master and slave to nature only, like a beaver.

9. A linen draper in a popular ballad by William Cowper, 'The Diverting History of John Gilpin' (1782), who has a series of comic misadventures in his attempts to ride a horse.

# Note on Puppets

*Prefatory note to Max von Boehn's* Dolls and Puppets, *tr. Josephine Nicoll, 1932.*
*In the original German edition* (Puppen und Puppenspiele, *1929) the text of a letter*
*from Shaw to the Italian puppeteer Vittorio Podreca was incorporated in the section*
*on marionettes. When Josephine Nicoll translated the book she sent her literal rendering*
*and von Boehn's German translation to Shaw, who, 'declaring that he could not now*
*"recapture the original wording" of the letter', generously provided a modified version.*
*Nicoll shifted the amended text from its previous position in the book to serve*
*as a prefatory note to the English-language edition*

═══

I always hold up the wooden actors as instructive object-lessons to our flesh-and-blood players. The wooden ones, though stiff and continually glaring at you with the same overcharged expression, yet move you as only the most experienced living actors can. What really affects us in the theatre is not the muscular activities of the performers, but the feelings they awaken in us by their aspect; for the imagination of the spectator plays a far greater part there than the exertions of the actors.

The puppet is the actor in his primitive form. Its symbolic costume, from which all realistic and historically correct impertinences are banished, its unchanging stare, petrified (or rather lignified) in a grimace expressive to the highest degree attainable by the carver's art, the mimicry by which it suggests human gesture in unearthly caricature—these give to its performance an intensity to which few actors can pretend, an intensity which imposes on our imagination like those images in immovable hieratic attitudes on the stained glass of Chartres Cathedral, in which the gaping tourists seem like little lifeless dolls moving jerkily in the draughts from the doors, reduced to sawdusty insignificance by the contrast with the gigantic vitality in the windows overhead.

G. B. S.

# A Glimpse of the Domesticity of Franklyn Barnabas

*Prefatory note to a deleted act of Part 2 of* Back to Methuselah. *First published in* Short Stories, Scraps and Shavings *in the Collected Edition, 1932*

=====

If you have read Back to Methuselah you will remember Franklyn Barnabas, the ex-clergyman who, with his gruff brother Conrad, the biologist, had come to the conclusion that the duration of human life must be extended to three hundred years, not in the least as all the stupid people thought because people would profit by a longer experience, but because it was not worth their while to make any serious attempt to better the world or their own condition when they had only thirty or forty years of full maturity to enjoy before they doddered away into decay and death. The brothers Barnabas were in fact the first discoverers of the staringly obvious truth that it is our expectation of life, and not our experience of it, that determines our conduct and character. Consequently the very vulgar proposition that you cannot change human nature, and therefore cannot make the revolutionary political and economic changes which are now known to be necessary to save our civilization from perishing like all previous recorded ones, is valid only on the assumption that you cannot change the duration of human life. If you can change that, then you can change political conduct through the whole range which lies between the plague-stricken city's policy of "Let us eat and drink; for tomorrow we die" and the long-sighted and profound policies of the earthly paradises of More, Morris, Wells, and all the other Utopians.

It was with this thesis of the Barnabases that I was concerned when I wrote Back to Methuselah; and though I got interested enough in Franklyn personally to go a little way into his domestic history, I had to discard my researches as both irrelevant and certain to sidetrack my main theme and confuse my biological drama with a domestic comedy.

Also I had amused myself by bringing Franklyn Barnabas into contact with a notable social philosopher [G. K. Chesterton] of our day for the mere fun of caricaturing him. But this proved a hopeless enterprize; for, like all really great humorists, he had himself exploited his own possibilities so thoroughly in that direction that I could produce nothing but a manifestly inferior copy of a gorgeous original. Still, even a bad caricature may have some value when the original has dissolved into its elements for remanufacture by the Life

Force. As we cannot now have a photograph of Shakespear, much less a portrait by a master, we cling to the inhuman caricature by [Martin] Droeshout as at least a corrective to the commonplace little bust of a commonplace little gent in the shrine in Stratford church;[1] and so I think it possible that my thumbnail sketch, inadequate and libelous as it is, may give a hint or two to some future great biographer as to what the original of Immenso Champernoon was like in the first half of his career, when, in defiance of the very order of nature, he began without a figure as a convivial immensity with vine leaves in his hair, deriding his own aspect, and in middle life slimmed into a Catholic saint, thereby justifying my reminder to those who took him too lightly of old, that Thomas Aquinas began as a comically fat man and ended as the Divine Doctor.

Until the other day I believed that my studies of the Barnabas home out Hampstead way, with my Champernoon caricature, had perished in the wastepaper basket which has swallowed many discarded pages of my works. But they have just turned up in the course of a hunt for matter wherewith to complete a collected edition of my works; and, being much at a loss for padding for this particular volume of scraps of fiction, I looked through them and thought they might prove not only readable, but perhaps useful to married ladies with interesting husbands who attract husband stealers. Such ladies, if they are at all bearable, have all the trumps in their hands, and need never be beaten if they understand the game and play it with the requisite audacity and contempt for the danger.

Here, then, are a few scraps of the scenes which took place in the suburban villa in which the brothers Barnabas made their famous attempt to persuade our political leaders in the first years after the war to discard their obsolete party programs and raise the slogan of Back to Methuselah.

1. Droeshout was a Flemish engraver resident in London, widely known for his portrait of Shakespeare in the 1623 first folio of the plays. The creator of the 'commonplace little bust' in Stratford Church is unknown.

# The Adventures of the Black Girl in
# Her Search for God

*First published as an afterword, 1932. Revised and converted into a preface for the 1947*
*Standard Edition,* The Black Girl in Search of God and Some Lesser Tales

=====

I was inspired to write this tale when I was held up in Knysna [South Africa] for five weeks in the African summer and English winter of 1932. My intention was to write a play in the ordinary course of my business as a playwright; but I found myself writing the story of the black girl instead. And now, the story being written, I proceed to speculate on what it means, though I cannot too often repeat that I am as liable as anyone else to err in my interpretation, and that pioneer writers, like other pioneers, often mistake their destination as Columbus did. That is how they sometimes run away in pious horror from the conclusions to which their revelations manifestly lead. I hold, as firmly as St Thomas Aquinas, that all truths, ancient or modern, are divinely inspired; but I know by observation and introspection that the instrument on which the inspiring force plays may be a very faulty one, and may even end, like Bunyan in The Holy War, by making the most ridiculous nonsense of his message.[1]

However, here is my own account of the matter for what it is worth.

It is often said, by the heedless, that we are a conservative species, impervious to new ideas. I have not found it so. I am often appalled at the avidity and credulity with which new ideas are snatched at and adopted without a scrap of sound evidence. People will believe anything that amuses them, gratifies them, or promises them some sort of profit. I console myself, as Stuart Mill did, with the notion that in time the silly ideas will lose their charm and drop out of fashion and out of existence; that the false promises,

1. Shaw apparently alludes to the explanation by Prince Emanuel (Christ) to Mansoul, at the end of *The Holy War* (1682), of his motivations for permitting evil: 'it is to keep thee wakening, to try thy love, to make thee watchful, and to cause thee yet to prize my noble captains, their soldiers and my mercy.' Christ as God is seen to be seeking gratitude from man for saving him from an evil that would not have existed if He had not permitted it to do so.

when broken, will pass through cynical derision into oblivion; and that after this sifting process the sound ideas, being indestructible (for even if suppressed or forgotten they are rediscovered again and again) will survive and be added to the body of ascertained knowledge we call Science.[2] In this way we acquire a well tested stock of ideas to furnish our minds, such furnishing being education proper as distinguished from the pseudo-education of the schools and universities.

Unfortunately there is a snag in this simple scheme. It forgets the prudent old precept, "Dont throw out your dirty water until you get in your clean" which is the very devil unless completed by "This also I say unto you, that when you get your fresh water you must throw out the dirty, and be particularly careful not to let the two get mixed."

Now this is just what we never do. We persist in pouring the clean water into the dirty; and our minds are always muddled in consequence. The educated human of today has a mind which can be compared only to a store in which the very latest and most precious acquisitions are flung on top of a noisome heap of rag-and-bottle refuse and worthless antiquities from the museum lumber room. The store is always bankrupt; and the men in possession include William the Conqueror and Henry the Seventh, Moses and Jesus, St Augustine and Sir Isaac Newton, Calvin and Wesley, Queen Victoria and H. G. Wells; whilst among the distraining creditors are Karl Marx, Einstein, and dozens of people more or less like Stuart Mill and myself. No mind can operate reasonably in such a mess. And as our current schooling and colleging and graduating consists in reproducing this mess in the minds of every fresh generation of children, we are provoking revolutionary emergencies in which persons muddled by university degrees will have to be politically disfranchised and disqualified as, in effect, certified lunatics, and the direction of affairs given over to the self-educated and the simpletons.

The most conspicuous example of this insane practice of continually taking in new ideas without ever clearing out the ideas they supersede, is the standing of the Bible in those countries in which the extraordinary artistic value of the English translation has given it a magical power over its readers. That

2. This concept of the evolution of inchoate thought into advanced and accepted ideas was, as Mill titled it in a series of articles for the *Examiner* (6 January–29 May 1831), 'The Spirit of the Age'. In chapter five of the *Autobiography* he wrote: 'I attempted . . . to embody . . . in the character of the present age, the anomalies and evils characteristic of the transition from a system of opinions which had worn out, to another only in process of being formed.' Alternating periods of criticism and negation are then examined.

power is now waning because, as XVI century English is a dying tongue, new translations are being forced on us by the plain fact that the old one is no longer intelligible to the masses. These new versions have—the good ones by their admirable homeliness and the ordinary ones by their newspapery everydayness—suddenly placed the Bible narratives in a light of familiar realism which obliges their readers to apply commonsense tests to them.

But the influence of these modern versions is not yet very wide. It seems to me that those who find the old version unintelligible and boresome do not resort to modern versions: they simply give up reading the Bible. The few who are caught and interested by the new versions, stumble on them by accidents which, being accidents, are necessarily rare. But they still hear Lessons read in church in the old version in a specially reverent tone; children at Sunday School are made to learn its verses by heart, and are rewarded by little cards inscribed with its texts; and bedrooms and nurseries are still decorated with its precepts, warnings, and consolations. The British and Foreign Bible Society has distributed more than three million copies annually for a century past; and though many of these copies may be mere churchgoers' luggage, never opened on weekdays, or gifts in discharge of the duties of godparents; yet they count. There is still on the statute book a law which no statesman dare repeal, which makes it [a] felony for a professed Christian to question the scientific truth and supernatural authority of any word of Holy Scripture, the penalties extending to ruinous outlawry;[3] and the same acceptance of the Bible as an infallible encyclopedia is one of the Articles of the Church of England [Article VI], though another Article, and that the very first, flatly denies the corporeal and voracious nature of God insisted on in the Pentateuch.

In all these instances the Bible means the translation authorized by King James the First of the best examples in ancient Jewish literature of natural and political history, of poetry, morality, theology, and rhapsody. The translation was extraordinarily well done because to the translators what they were translating was not merely a curious collection of ancient books written by different authors in different stages of culture, but the Word of God divinely

3. The Blasphemy Act, 'An Act for the more effectual suppressing of Blasphemy and Profaneness' (1697–8), 9 William III chapter 35, in *The Statutes of the Realm* (to 1714), 1820. According to Halsbury's *Laws of England*, second edition, vol. 9 (1933), para. 651, note (b), there never was a prosecution for an offence against the statute. It was repealed in 1967, the year before theatre censorship was abolished in Britain. Our thanks to Guy Holborn, Librarian of the Lincoln's Inn Library, for this information.

revealed through his chosen and expressly inspired scribes. In this conviction they carried out their work with boundless reverence and care and achieved a beautifully artistic result. It did not seem possible to them that they could better the original texts; for who could improve on God's own style? And as they could not conceive that divine revelation could conflict with what they believed to be the truths of their religion, they did not hesitate to translate a negative by a positive where such a conflict seemed to arise, as they could hardly trust their own fallible knowledge of ancient Hebrew when it contradicted the very foundations of their faith, nor could they doubt that God would, as they prayed, take care that his message should not suffer corruption in their hands. In this state of exaltation they made a translation so magnificent that to this day the common human Britisher or citizen of the United States of North America accepts and worships it as a single book by a single author, the book being the Book of Books and the author being God. Its charm, its promise of salvation, its pathos, and its majesty have been raised to transcendence by Handel, who can still make atheists cry and give materialists the thrill of the sublime with his Messiah. Even the ignorant, to whom religion is crude fetishism and magic, prize it as a paper talisman that will exorcise ghosts, prevent witnesses from lying, and, if carried devoutly in a soldier's pocket, stop bullets.

Now it is clear that this Bible worship, though at its best it may achieve sublimity by keeping its head in the skies, may also make itself both ridiculous and dangerous by having its feet off the ground. It is a matter of daily experience that a book taken as an infallible revelation, whether the author be Moses, Ezekiel, Paul, Swedenborg, Joseph Smith, Mary Baker Eddy, or Karl Marx, may bring such hope, consolation, interest and happiness into our individual lives that we may well cherish it as the key of Paradise. But if the paradise be a fool's paradise, as it must be when its materials are imaginary, then it must not be made the foundation of a State, and must be classed with anodynes, opiates, and anesthetics. It is not for nothing that the fanatically religious founders of the new Russia dismissed the religion of the Greek Church as "dope."[4] That is precisely what a religion becomes when it is divorced from reality. It is useful to ambitious rulers in corrupt political systems as a sedative to popular turbulence (that is why the tyrant always makes much of the priest); but in the long run civilization must get back to honest reality or perish.

At present one party is keeping the Bible in the clouds in the name of

4. The statement 'Religion is the opium of the people' appears in Marx's introduction to *A Contribution to the Critique of Hegel's Philosophy of Right* (1843–4).

religion, and another is trying to get rid of it altogether in the name of Science. Both names are so recklessly taken in vain that a Bishop of Birmingham once [October 1932] warned his flock that the scientific party is drawing nearer to Christ than the Church congregations.[5] I, who am a sort of unofficial Bishop of Everywhere, have repeatedly warned the scientists that the Quakers are fundamentally far more scientific than the official biologists.[6] In this confusion I venture to suggest that we neither leave the Bible in the clouds nor attempt the impossible task of suppressing it. Why not simply bring it down to the ground, and take it for what it really is?

To maintain good humor I am quite willing to concede to my Protestant friends that the Bible in the clouds was sometimes turned to good account in the struggles to maintain Protestant Freethought (such as it was) against the Churches and Empires. The soldier who had his Bible in one hand and his weapon in the other fought with the strength of ten under Cromwell, William of Orange, and Gustavus Adolphus. The very old-fashioned may still permit themselves a little romance about the Huguenots at La Rochelle, the psalm of the Ironsides at Dunbar,[7] the ships that broke the boom and relieved the siege of Londonderry,[8] and even about Dugald Dalgetty.[9] But the struggle between Guelph and Ghibelline is so completely over that in the 1914–18 war the ministers of the Guelph king did not even know what his name meant, and made him discard it in the face of the Ghibelline Kaiser and the Holy Roman Empire.[10] In the revival of that war the soldier, equipped with a few atomic bombs, fought with the strength of a million but the idolized Bible was still at the back of the popular newspapers, full of the spirit of the campaigns of Joshua, holding up our sword as the sword of the Lord and

5. Ernest William Barnes, controversial Anglican bishop of Birmingham 1924–53, took a provocative scientific approach to Christian dogma, as reflected in his 1927–9 Gifford lectures, published as *Scientific Theory and Religion* (1933).
6. Although Shaw discusses 'scientific religion' in the preface to *Back to Methuselah*, we can find in his writings or utterances no specific 'warning' to scientists relating to Quakers and 'official biologists'. See, however, the chapter 'Pacifism and the Quakers' in Warren Sylvester Smith's *The Bishop of Everywhere* (1982), pp. 65–72.
7. Perhaps Cromwell's greatest military triumph during the Civil War was against the Scots on 3 September 1650 at Dunbar. To Cromwell it was God's victory and at a halt in the battle he led his cavalry regiment – the Ironsides – in the singing of a psalm.
8. The siege, begun on 29 April 1689, was raised on 9–10 August after the blockade was broken by Capt. John Leake's ships on 7 August.
9. Soldier of fortune in Sir Walter Scott's *The Legend of Montrose* (1819).
10. See preface to *Heartbreak House*, in vol. 2, p. 330.

Gideon, and hounding us on to the slaughter of those modern Amalekites and Canaanites, the Germans, as idolators and children of the devil. Though the formula (King and Country) was different, the spirit was the same: it was the old imaginary conflict of Jehovah against Baal; only, as the Germans were also fighting for King and Country, and were quite as convinced as we that Jehovah, the Lord strong and mighty, the Lord mighty in battle, the Lord of Hosts (now called big battalions), was their God, and that ours was his enemy, they fought as hard and felt quite as virtuous. But the wounds to civilization were so serious that we do not as yet know whether they are not going to prove mortal, because they are being kept open by the Old Testament spirit and methods and superstitions.

The situation is past trifling. The ancient worshippers of Jehovah, armed with sword and spear, and demoralized by a clever boy with a sling, could not murder and destroy wholesale. But with machine gun and amphibious tank, aeroplane and gas bomb, operating on cities where millions of inhabitants are depending for light and heat, water and food, on centralized mechanical organs like great steel hearts and arteries, that can be smashed in half an hour by a boy in a bomber, we really must take care that the boy is better educated than Noah and Joshua. In plain words, as we cannot get rid of the Bible, it will get rid of us unless we learn to read it "in the proper spirit," which I take to be the spirit of intellectual integrity that obliges honest thinkers to read every line which pretends to divine authority with all their wits about them, and to judge it exactly as they judge the Koran, the Upanishads, the Arabian Nights, this morning's leading article in The Times, or last week's cartoon in Punch, knowing that all written words are equally open to inspiration from the eternal fount and equally subject to error from the mortal imperfection of their authors.

Then say, of what use is the Bible nowadays to anyone but the antiquary and the literary connoisseur? Why not boot it into the dustbin? Well, there is a *prima facie* case [a case established by the evidence adduced by the plaintiff] to be made out for that. Let us first do justice to it.

What about the tables of the law? the ten commandments? They did not suffice even for the wandering desert tribe upon whom they were imposed by Moses, who, like Mahomet later on, could get them respected only by pretending that they were supernaturally revealed to him. They had to be supplemented by the elaborate codes of Leviticus and Deuteronomy, which the most fanatically observant Jew could not now obey without outraging our modern morality and violating our criminal law. They are mere lumber nowadays; for their simpler validities are the necessary commonplaces of human society and need no Bible to reveal them or give them authority.

The second commandment, taken to heart by Islam, is broken and ignored throughout Christendom, though its warning against the enchantments of fine art is worthy [of] the deepest consideration, and, had its author known the magic of word-music as he knew that of the graven image, might stand as a warning against our idolatry of the Bible. The whole ten are unsuited and inadequate to modern needs, as they say not a word against those forms of robbery, legalized by the robbers, which have uprooted the moral foundation of our society and will condemn us to slow social decay if we are not wakened up, as Russia has been, by a crashing collapse.

In addition to these negative drawbacks there is the positive one that the religion inculcated in the earlier books is a crudely atrocious ritual of human sacrifice to propitiate a murderous tribal deity who was, for example, induced to spare the human race from destruction in a second deluge by the pleasure given him by the smell of roasting flesh when Noah "took of every clean beast and of every clean fowl, and offered burnt offerings on the altar" [Genesis 8: 20–22]. And though this ritual is in the later books fiercely repudiated, and its god denied in express terms, by the prophet Micah [Micah 6: 6–8], shewing how it was outgrown as the Jews progressed in culture, yet the tradition of a blood sacrifice whereby the vengeance of a terribly angry god can be bought off by a vicarious and hideously cruel blood sacrifice persists even through the New Testament, where it attaches itself to the torture and execution of Jesus by the Roman governor of Jerusalem, idolizing that horror in Noah's fashion as a means by which we can all cheat our consciences, evade our moral responsibilities, and turn our shame into self-congratulation by loading all our infamies on to the scourged shoulders of Christ. It would be hard to imagine a more demoralizing and unchristian doctrine: indeed it would not be at all unreasonable for the Intellectual Cooperation Committee of the League of Nations[11] to follow the example of the Roman Catholic Church by objecting to the promiscuous circulation of the Bible (except under conditions amounting to careful spiritual direction) until the supernatural claims made for its authority are finally and unequivocally dropped.

As to Bible science, it has over the XIX century materialistic fashion in biology the advantage of being a science of life and not an attempt to substitute physics and chemistry for it; but it is hopelessly pre-evolutionary; its descriptions of the origin of life and morals are obviously fairy tales; its astronomy is terracentric; its notions of the starry universe are childish; its history is

11. The Committee of Intellectual Co-operation (CIC) was created in 1921 by the League of Nations Assembly to promote appropriate international activity within the broad realm of art, science, literature and learning.

epical and legendary: in short, people whose education in these departments is derived from the Bible are so absurdly misinformed as to be unfit for public employment, parental responsibility, or the franchise. As an encyclopedia, therefore, the Bible must be classed with the first edition of the Encyclopedia Britannica as a record of what men once believed, and a measure of how far they have left their obsolete beliefs behind.

Granted all this, the fact remains that a great deal of the Bible is much more alive than this morning's paper and last night's parliamentary debate. Its chronicles are better reading than most of our fashionable histories, and less intentionally mendacious. In revolutionary invective and Utopian aspiration it cuts the ground from under the feet of Ruskin, Carlyle, and Karl Marx; and in epics of great leaders and great rascals it makes Homer seem superficial and Shakespear unbalanced. And its one great love poem is the only one that can satisfy a man who is really in love. Shelley's Epipsychidion [1821] is, in comparison, literary gas and gaiters.

In sum, it is an epitome, illustrated with the most stirring examples, of the history of a tribe of mentally vigorous, imaginative, aggressively acquisitive humans who developed into a nation through ruthless conquest, encouraged by the delusion that they were "the chosen people of God" and, as such, the natural inheritors of all the earth, with a reversion to a blissful eternity hereafter in the kingdom of heaven. And the epitome in no way suppresses the fact that this delusion led at last to their dispersion, denationalization, and bigoted persecution by better disciplined States which, though equally confident of a monopoly of divine favor earned by their own merits, paid the Jews the compliment of adopting their gods and prophets, as, on the whole, more useful to rulers than the available alternatives.

Now the difference between an illiterate savage and a person who has read such an epitome (with due skipping of its genealogical rubbish and the occasional nonsenses produced by attempts to translate from imperfectly understood tongues) is enormous. A community on which such a historical curriculum is imposed in family and school may be more dangerous to its neighbors, and in greater peril of collapse from intolerance and megalomania, than a community that reads either nothing or silly novels, football results, and city articles; but it is beyond all question a more highly educated one. It is therefore not in the least surprising nor unreasonable that when the only generally available alternative to Bible education is no liberal education at all, many who have no illusions about the Bible, and fully comprehend its drawbacks, vote for Bible education *faute de mieux* [for want of anything better]. This is why mere criticism of Bible education cuts so little ice. Ancient Hebrew history and literature, half fabulous as it is, is better than no history and no literature; and I neither regret nor resent my own Bible education, especially as my mind soon grew strong enough to take it at its real value. At worst the Bible gives a child a better start in life than the gutter.

This testimonial will please our Bible idolators; but it must not for a moment soothe them into believing that their fetichism can now be defended by the plea that it was better to be Noah or Abraham or Sir Isaac Newton than a London street arab. Street arabs are not very common in these days of compulsory attendance at the public elementary school. The alternative to the book of Genesis at present is not mere ignorant nescience, but H. G. Wells's Outline of History, and the host of imitations and supplements which its huge success has called into existence. Within the last two hundred years a body of history, literature, poetry, science, and art has been inspired and created by precisely the same mysterious impulse that inspired and created the Bible. In all these departments it leaves the Bible just nowhere. It is the Bible-educated human who is now the ignoramus. If you doubt it, try to pass an examination for any practical employment by giving Bible answers to the examiners' questions. You will be fortunate if you are merely plucked and not certified as a lunatic. Throughout the whole range of Science which the Bible was formerly supposed to cover with an infallible authority, it is now hopelessly superseded, with one exception. That exception is the science of theology, which is still so completely off the ground—so metaphysical, as the learned say, that our materialist scientists contemptuously deny it the right to call itself science at all.

But there is no surer symptom of a sordid and fundamentally stupid mind, however powerful it may be in many practical activities, than a contempt for metaphysics. A person may be supremely able as a mathematician, engineer, parliamentary tactician or racing bookmaker; but if that person has contemplated the universe all through life without ever asking "What the devil does it all mean?" he (or she) is one of those people for whom Calvin accounted by placing them in his category of the predestinately damned.

Hence the Bible, scientifically obsolete in all other respects, remains interesting as a record of how the idea of God, which is the first effort of civilized mankind to account for the existence and origin and purpose of as much of the universe as we are conscious of, develops from a childish idolatry of a thundering, earthquaking, famine striking, pestilence launching, blinding, deafening, killing, destructively omnipotent Bogey Man, maker of night and day and sun and moon, of the four seasons and their miracles of seed and harvest, to a braver idealization of a benevolent sage, a just judge, an affectionate father, evolving finally into the incorporeal word that never becomes flesh, at which point modern science and philosophy take up the problem with its *Vis Naturæ*, its *Élan Vital*, its Life Force, its Evolutionary Appetite, its still more abstract Categorical Imperative, and what not?

Now the study of this history of the development of a hypothesis from savage idolatry to a highly cultivated metaphysic is as interesting, instructive, and reassuring as any study can be to an open mind and an honest intellect. But we spoil it all by that lazy and sluttish practice of not throwing out the dirty water when we get in the clean. The Bible presents us with a succession of gods, each being a striking improvement on the previous one, marking an Ascent of Man to a nobler and deeper conception of Nature, every step involving a purification of the water of life and calling for a thorough emptying and cleansing of the vessel before its replenishment by a fresh and cleaner supply. But we baffle the blessing by just sloshing the water from the new fountain into the contents of the dirty old bucket, and repeat this folly until our minds are in such a filthy mess that we are objects of pity to the superficial but clearheaded atheists who are content without metaphysics and can see nothing in the whole business but its confusions and absurdities. Practical men of business refuse to be bothered with such crazy matters at all.

Take the situation in detail as it develops through the Bible. The God of Noah is not the God of Job. Contemplate first the angry deity who drowned every living thing on earth, except one family of each species, in a fit of raging disgust at their wickedness, and then allowed the head of the one human family to appease him by "the sweet savour" of a heap of burning flesh! Is he identical with the tolerant, argumentative, academic, urbane philosophic deity who entertained the devil familiarly and made a wager with him that he could not drive Job to despair of divine benevolence? People who cannot see the difference between these two Gods cannot pass the most elementary test of intelligence: they cannot distinguish between similars and dissimilars.

But though Job's god is a great advance on Noah's god, he is a very bad debater, unless indeed we give him credit for deliberately saving himself from defeat by the old expedient: "No case: abuse the plaintiff's attorney." Job having raised the problem of the existence of evil and its incompatibility with omnipotent benevolence, it is no valid reply to jeer at him for being unable to create a whale or to play with it as with a bird. And there is a very suspicious touch of Noah's God in the offer to overlook the complicity of Job's friends in his doubts in consideration of a sacrifice of seven bullocks and seven rams. God's attempt at an argument is only a repetition and elaboration of the sneers of Elihu, and is so abruptly tacked on to them that one concludes that it must be a pious forgery to conceal the fact that the original poem left the problem of evil unsolved and Job's criticism unanswered, as indeed it remained until Creative Evolution solved it.

When we come to Micah we find him throwing out the dirty water fearlessly. He will not have Noah's God, nor even Job's God with his seven bullocks and seven rams. He raises the conception of God to the highest point it has ever attained by his fiercely contemptuous denunciation of the blood sacrifices, and his inspired and inspiring demand "What doth the Lord require of thee but to do justly, and to love mercy, and to walk humbly with thy God?" [Micah 6: 8]. Before this victory of the human spirit over crude superstition Noah's God and Job's God go down like skittles: there is an end of them. And yet our children are taught, not to exult in this great triumph of spiritual insight over mere animal terror of the Bogey Man, but to believe that Micah's God and Job's God and Noah's God are one and the same, and that every good child must revere the spirit of justice and mercy and humility equally with the appetite for burnt flesh and human sacrifice, such indiscriminate and nonsensical reverence being inculcated as religion.

Later on comes Jesus, who dares a further flight. He suggests that godhead is something which incorporates itself in man: in himself, for instance [John 10: 30−31]. He is immediately stoned by his horrified hearers, who can see nothing in the suggestion but a monstrous attempt on his part to impersonate Jehovah. This misunderstanding, typical of dirty water theology, was made an article of religion eighteen hundred years later by Emanuel Swedenborg.[12] But the unadulterated suggestion of Jesus is an advance on the theology of Micah; for Man walking humbly before an external God is an ineffective creature compared to Man exploring as the instrument and embodiment of God with no other guide than the spark of divinity within him. It is certainly the greatest break in the Bible between the old and the new testament. Yet the dirty water still spoils it; for we find Paul holding up Christ to the Ephesians as "an offering and a sacrifice to God for a sweetsmelling savour" [Ephesians 5: 2], thereby dragging Christianity back and down to the level of Noah. None of the apostles rose above that level; and the result was that the great advances made by Micah and Jesus were cancelled; and historical Christianity was built up on the sacrificial altars of Jehovah, with Jesus as the sacrifice. What he and Micah would say if they could return and see their names and credit attached to the idolatries they abhorred can be imagined only by those who understand and sympathize with them.

Jesus could be reproached for having chosen his disciples very unwisely if

12. In *Heaven and Its Wonders, and Hell* (1758) Swedenborg wrote that 'the angels . . . are accustomed to say that the Lord alone is man and that they are men by derivation from Him; and that every one is a man so far as he receives Him' (Everyman's Library edition, 1909).

we could believe that he had any real choice. There are moments when one is tempted to say that there was not one Christian among them, and that Judas was the only one who shewed any gleams of common sense. Because Jesus had mental powers and insight quite beyond their comprehension they worshipped him as a superhuman and indeed supernatural phenomenon, and made his memory the nucleus of their crude belief in magic, their Noahism, their sentimentality, their masochist Puritanism, and their simple morality with its punitive sanctions, decent and honest and amiable enough, some of it, but never for a moment on the intellectual level of Jesus, and at worst pregnant with all the horrors of the later wars of religion, the Jew burnings under Torquemada, and the atrocious renewal of his persecution under Hitler in the present century.

Most unfortunately the death of Jesus helped to vulgarize his reputation and obscure his doctrine. The Romans, though they executed their own political criminals by throwing them from the Tarpeian rock, punished slave revolts by crucifixion. They crucified six thousand of the followers of the revolutionary gladiator, Spartacus, a century before Jesus was denounced to them by the Jewish high priest as an agitator of the same kidney. He was accordingly tortured and killed in this hideous manner, with the infinitely more hideous result that the cross and the other instruments of his torture were made the symbols of the faith legally established in his name three hundred years later. They are still accepted as such throughout Christendom. The crucifixion thus became to the Churches what the Chamber of Horrors is to a waxwork: the irresistible attraction for children and for the crudest adult worshippers. Christ's clean water of life is befouled by the dirtiest of dirty water from the idolatries of his savage forefathers; and our prelates and proconsuls take Caiaphas and Pontius Pilate for their models in the name of their despised and rejected victim.

The case was further complicated by the pitiable fact that Jesus himself, shaken by the despair which unsettled the reason of Swift and Ruskin and many others at the spectacle of human cruelty, injustice, misery, folly, and apparently hopeless political incapacity, and perhaps also by the worship of his disciples and of the multitude, had allowed Peter to persuade him that he was the Messiah, and that death could not prevail against him nor prevent his returning to judge the world and establish his reign on earth for ever and ever. As this romance came as easily within the mental range of his disciples as his social doctrine had been far over their heads, "Crosstianity" [see vol. 1, pp. 249, 265] became established on the authority of Jesus himself. Later on, in a curious record of the visions of a drug addict which was absurdly admitted to the canon under the title of Revelation, a thousand years was ordained as the period that was to elapse before Jesus was to return as he had promised. In 1000 A.D. the last possibility of the promised advent expired; but by that time people were so used to the delay that they readily substituted for the Second Advent a Second Postponement. Pseudo-Christianity was, and always will be, fact proof.

The whole business is in a muddle which has held out not only because the views of Jesus are above the heads of all but the best minds, but because his appearance was followed by the relapse in civilization which we call the Dark Ages, from which we are only just emerging sufficiently to begin to pick up Christ's most advanced thought and filter it from the dirty water into which the apostles and their successors poured it.

Six hundred years after Jesus, Mahomet made a colossal stride ahead from mere stock-and-stone idolatry to a very enlightened Unitarianism; but though he died a conqueror, and therefore escaped being made the chief attraction in an Arabian Chamber of Horrors, he found it impossible to control his Arabs without enticing and intimidating them by promises of a delightful life for the faithful and threats of an eternity of disgusting torment for the wicked after their bodily death, and also, after some honest protests, by accepting the supernatural character thrust on him by the childish superstition of his followers; so that he, too, now needs to be rediscovered in his true nature before Islam can come back to earth as a living faith.

And now I think the adventures of the black girl as revealed to me need no longer puzzle anyone. They could hardly have happened to a white girl steeped from her birth in the pseudo-Christianity of the Churches. I take it that the missionary lifted her straight out of her native tribal fetichism into an unbiased contemplation of the Bible with its series of gods marking stages in the development of the conception of God from the monster Bogey Man [to] the Everlasting Father, the Prince of Peace. She has still to consider the Church of England's sublimation of God to spirit without body, parts, nor passions, with its corollary that in spite of the fourth gospel God is not Love. Love is not enough (Edith Cavell made that discovery about Patriotism) and the Black Girl finds it wiser to take Voltaire's advice by cultivating her garden and bringing up her piccaninnies than to spend her life imagining that she can find a complete explanation of the universe by laying about her with her knobkerry.

Still, the knobkerry has to be used as far as the way is clear. Mere agnosticism is useless to the police. When the question of the existence of Noah's idol is raised on the point, vital to high civilization, whether our children shall continue to be brought up to worship it and compound for their sins by sacrificing to it, or, more cheaply, by sheltering themselves behind another's sacrifice to it, then whoever hesitates to bring down the knobkerry with might and main is ludicrously unfit to have any part in the government of a modern State. The importance of a message to that effect at the present world crisis is probably at the bottom of my curious and sudden inspiration to write this tale instead of cumbering theatrical literature with another stage comedy.

AYOT ST LAWRENCE.
1932–46.

# The Marketing of Literary Property

*Preface to a book by G. Herbert Thring, styled as*
*'A Letter to the Author', 1933*

My Dear Thring[1]

Now that you can look back on a long life devoted to the labor of protecting authors from the consequences of their own incorrigible unworldliness, do you regret it or glory in it? You had social and professional opportunities which put you within reach of a career much more brilliant and lucrative than that of secretary to a Society for organizing those unhappy fellowcreatures of yours whose traditional lot was described by one of the most eminent and successful of themselves as "toil, envy, want, the patron and the gaol" [Samuel Johnson's *The Vanity of Human Wishes*, 1749]. You got no thanks for it, and very few ha'pence for a man of your standing. I can only conclude that as you stuck to it incorruptibly and implacably you got some fun out of it. You certainly got plenty of satisfaction for your natural pugnacity in fighting the battles of authors who would not fight for themselves, though they were perfectly ready to quarrel with you when they had given themselves away so hopelessly that even you could do little or nothing to save them.

As for me, my ten years on the committee of management of the Society of Authors [1905–15] gave me, at intervals of a month or so, some insight into the troubles with which you were struggling daily. We consulted oneanother a good deal in the crises, usually quite abortive, caused by our efforts to improve our organization and establish standing treaties with the publishers and managers. Now that you have at last retired, and are confining yourself to giving our authors in print all the information they ought to possess and understand, and all the good advice they are likely to need, I feel that I owe you a public word or two, if only to express my melancholy conviction that they will not read the information, nor, having hopelessly unlegal minds, could understand it if they did, and that they will not take your advice, not because it would hurt them to take it (quite the contrary) but because they are afraid.

The public will never understand how an author's calling, when his department is that of fiction (as was the case with most of our members), unfits

1. Secretary of the Society of Authors, 1892–1930.

him for business and intercourse with business people. He works in an imaginary world in which he is absolute monarch, where everything suits him to perfection because it is created and arranged by his (or her) very self. It is peopled by villains as well as by heroes and heroines; but none of the villains can hurt him or talk back at him. Nor can the heroes be dishonorable nor the heroines unfaithful except at his own orders. He is more than a despot: he is a god.

Now it is one of the elementary facts of natural history that human beings who are given despotic powers go mad unless they have a very exceptional grip on reality and power of selfcriticism. And even in these rare cases their heads are not entirely unaffected. The proverbial beggar on horseback—and what more is the greatest of the great?—now has a motor car; but the change makes him all the more dangerous to the pedestrian. The difference between Nero, the fiddler driven mad by unnatural power, and Knut [Canute], who kept tight hold of the fact that, being but mortal, he could not rule the waves, was one of degree only; for nobody can persuade me that Knut was not occasionally a little more arbitrary than he would have been as an employee. Authors have a very feeble grip of reality, which is a grip that has to be developed by long and intense practice; and as to selfcriticism, many of them have not enough to correct their proofs, and have to be helped out by the printer's reader. Isolated as they are in a lonely study which their imagination can transfigure into a realm of romance in which they are far more despotic than any political ruler could possibly be, they become unreasonable and egocentred to an extent that only you, who have been all your life up against their petulance, can fully realize.

Not that they are cruel in their imaginary realm. On the contrary, they are magnanimous, generous, just, chivalrous, indignantly virtuous enough to qualify them for a heavenly throne. Why not? It costs them nothing and is even lucrative; for the nobler they are the better their readers like them. But introduce a vulgar substantial independent person into this paradise, preferably a publisher or manager, or a solicitor or agent, and the benevolent despot is either as terrified as a very small child confronted with a very big policeman, or, in the case of a best seller, as bumptious as a headmaster reluctantly compelled to deal with a juvenile delinquent. Both sorts are distractingly unmanageable when there is business to be done.

The intimidated ones are more common because their novitiate has been one of crushing poverty. And here we come to a ruinous defect in our social system. Have you ever wondered why I am a Communist? Well, it is largely because of my sense of the great importance of leisure in civilized society. Leisure is needed to produce art and religion, literature and science, without which we should be happier as birds or beasts than as humans. But it must be a leisure informed, trained, and disciplined by a share in the basic work of the world. If you bring up a class to live exempt from this share and wholly at leisure you will sterilize them as completely for cultural purposes as if you brought them up to work like slaves to the limit of human endurance without any effective leisure at all. Now this unnatural creation of two culturally sterilized classes is precisely what our social system of Manchester School Capitalism[2] inevitably and avowedly effects, with the result that the little religion and art, literature and science we can obtain, are frightfully corrupt, and confined to an unrepresentative and politically impotent minority of the population. The workers are too tired after their daily task of from eight to fourteen hours drudgery to educate themselves. The idlers, after learning in their enslaved and imprisoned childhood to loathe education, culture, literature, and everything suggestive of intellect, use their freedom from toil to cultivate the art of amusing themselves or letting other people amuse them (authors, for instance), the result being this time a positive one: namely, the creation of a great anti-culture of sport. In this the workers can participate to the extent of looking on at it from the cheap seats on half holidays, with very exceptional participation as "professionals," and, above all, by gambling. The final triumph and climax of our anti-culture is the mechanization of gambling by the invention of the Tote;[3] so that today every slum has its Tote Club; and the poorest laborer's wife can make a bid, with all the odds absurdly against her, for transfer to the leisured class as a millionairess.

Where, then, do such *belles lettres* as we have come from? Mostly from those upstarts of the literate working class and downstarts of the leisured class who are incorrigible daydreamers, without the muscle for manual labor, the acquisitive cunning for business, the long and expensive coaching for the civil service and professional examinations, or the income for leisure. They must either starve their way into the fine arts or into literature as best they can or else perish. Thus I, in my youth, when what I needed was work enough to prevent me from being a burden on others and leisure enough to qualify

2. A term first applied by Disraeli to a group of political individualists in Manchester, headed by Richard Cobden and John Bright, which organized as crusaders for universal peace through the throwing down of all commercial barriers in favour of free trade. The name later came to designate any policy of *laissez-faire*.
3. The Tote (totalizator) is a pari-mutuel machine in which gamblers deposit the amount they desire to wager on the horses they have chosen to bet on. It computes the odds and the pay-offs as the bets are placed, retaining a commission for the house.

myself as an author, found that I had either to work for so many hours a day that I had no leisure, or refuse to work and have no food except what I could induce or compel other people to give me for nothing. Had I not been unscrupulous enough to choose the latter alternative and lucky enough to inherit an expiring remnant of leisured property[4] I should have been lost to literature and unbearably unhappy. As it was I was for years so impoverished and isolated that if it had not been for the preceding spell of office work (of a nature for which I should have been shot in a Communist State) I should have come out as intimidated and unfit for any contact with the realities of civilization as most of my fellow-authors are. That, I think, was enough to make a Communist of any man with brains and knowledge enough to understand how easily a Communist State could organize and share out the necessary work of society so as to enable young persons to pay their way by a daily spell of ordinary bread-and-butter work, and yet have four or five untired hours of leisure for an apprenticeship to literature and the fine arts.

Anyhow, authors excreted by a class society in this fashion are the feckless creatures you had to protect. What about the parties against whom you had to protect them? the publishers? the managers? the speculators in copyrights? and sometimes the victims' own agents?

Byron said "Now Barabbas was a publisher."[5] In this book the worst examples you give of the extent to which some publishers are ready to take advantage of an author's poverty, timidity, and ignorance of his rights and their value, would make Barabbas blush. When Esau the author sells his copyright to Jacob the publisher for a mess of pottage—or rather when Jacob proposes the transaction and gets away with it—Esau comes to the Society of Authors (which meant for many years coming to you) to save him when he is past saving, and then reviles it because it tells him that the law is on the side of Jacob. It might seem that he is at least entitled to the satisfaction of being told that the publisher is a mean scoundrel, without honesty or compassion. But even this poor consolation is not available. In publishing, the author must take care of himself, because the nature of the business obliges the publisher to take all the advantages he can persuade the author to give

4. This refers to a small inheritance received in the late 1870s by Shaw's mother from a deceased relation. Shaw's own inheritance, in 1899 from his mother's brother, consisted of some rundown, heavily mortgaged property in Carlow (Ireland) that was actually a burden to him.

5. When the publisher John Murray sent Byron a Bible in acknowledgment of a favour, the poet returned it with the word 'robber' changed to 'publisher' in John 18: 40 (*Bartlett's*, sixteenth edition, 1992).

him; and if the publisher stops short of this, as many goodnatured publishers do, he is to that extent not running his business on business lines: literally, not playing the game.

For publishing is a game, and a game of hazard[6] at that. It is quite easy to shew—as the Society, let us confess it, was perhaps too fond of doing in its early days—that on a successful book the publisher, for his services as a wholesale distributor, and an advance of capital that is really made mostly by the long suffering printer and binder, is entitled to no more than an ordinary percentage of commercial profit plus the interest on the advance. But a publishing business cannot be kept going on successful books alone. The successful book must pay for many that leave the publisher no richer than he was before and for some that leave him poorer. If he could pick out the successful books in manuscript and confine his operations to them he would become as rich as a bookmaker who could infallibly spot winners, and retire with a handsome fortune in the prime of life. But there are no such publishers. It is true that there are some books which are assured of a lucrative circulation beforehand. Railway timetables, almanacks, and all indispensable books of reference with established reputations are in the forefront of this category; but they do not come the way of the speculative publisher. There are authors whose reputation is such that any work of theirs commands a minimum circulation sufficient to eliminate all risk of loss, the only uncertain factor being the magnitude of the profit. But these authors may be more than a match for any publisher in driving a bargain, and twice as rapacious. They may take advantage of the competition among publishers for the prestige conferred by famous clients to exact all the money they are worth and a bit more. Or they may refuse a speculative bargain and publish "on commission": a plan which leaves the author free to be as unbusinesslike as he pleases at his own expense. Thus the publisher can count only on speculative books for handsome profits. It may therefore be assumed that all publishers whose business is concerned with contemporary copyright literature are gambling on the inscrutable caprices of public taste.

It follows that there is no such thing as "a fair bargain" ascertainable when the untried author invites a publisher to speculate in his book, because the value of the book may be anything from zero to a silver mine. The best opinions the publisher can obtain from the ablest readers can establish nothing more than that the manuscript is presentable in print. They can eliminate the merely illiterate and ridiculous; but beyond that their judgments are worth

6. Game of chance, played with dice, brought back from the Holy Land in the twelfth century by King Richard's crusaders. Its direct descendant is craps.

no more than that of any racing tipster. In the eighteen eighties, when I tried to obtain a footing in literature by writing novels, I sent them to every publisher in London; and the publishers sent them to their corps of readers, which then included John Morley and George Meredith. I suppose I may now say that I was a winner; for these unlucky novels, having later on got themselves published uncommercially by pure accident, are alive to this day; yet their rejection was unanimous; and, what is more, I consider the advice to that effect given by Morley, Meredith and the rest, perfectly sound. I had to make my living by reviewing published books, many of which, though accepted by publishers on the best advice they could get, can hardly have repaid the cost of their manufacture. I take practically no interest in horse-racing; but the Derby has forced itself on my attention often enough to give me an impression that the favorites seldom win and the outsiders often do. The same thing happens in publishing; and I would urge authors, especially young authors, to treat publishers not as admiring benefactors who exist disinterestedly for the glory and profit of literature and its heroes, but as punters [bettors] whose business it is to inspect unpublished books and back their fancy, their stake being the cost of its manufacture and publication, whilst the author is a bookmaker betting against the said fancy, his stake being the work he has put into the writing of it. If the book prove a dud both of them lose their stakes. If it prove a best seller, each gains the share of the profits stipulated in the terms of the bet, and loses the rest.

It is in fixing these terms—offering the odds—that both publisher and author must have all their wits about them and understand their respective advantages and each other's advantages to a nicety. Each must take care of himself. The author who makes his bargain without the contents of this book in his head will get the worst of it unless, as sometimes happens, the publisher is a romantic novice or a routineer who does not understand his routine. If the author comes out with a few hundred pounds and the publisher comes out with several thousands, that is part of the game; and there is neither sense nor civility in denouncing him as a shark. If the publisher finds himself paying a handsome royalty year after year to an author or editor for a job which he could easily have got done for a modest lump sum, that also is part of the game; and it is only bad manners to call the author a Shylock. Both parties must know their business and be reasonable; and that, my dear Thring, is where your book comes in; for if they do not know all that it teaches them they will neither know their business nor be reasonable.

One of the author's disadvantages is that he has only one egg in his basket whilst the publisher has a score. The publisher's disadvantage is that nineteen out of the score may be bad eggs; and at best a good many of them will be indifferent. Also he must go on publishing, publishing, publishing merely to keep his business in being, whether he can find any books really worth publishing or not, wheras the author can cease working when it suits him for as long as he can afford to. Yet there is one overwhelming disadvantage at which the author who is a genuine artist must always stand in commercial transactions; and that is his indifference to money when he is not actually hungry nor under threat of eviction or the cutting off of his water and electric light, or the wearing-out of his clothes beyond the point at which they are useful or presentable. A publisher who staves off these emergencies for an author and flatters him sufficiently has very little to fear from him in the matter of hard bargaining. Literary agents live mainly by making soft bargains for authors, who are only too grateful to anyone who will relieve them of the abhorred necessity for bargaining at all. Now the publisher, as a man of business, is or ought to be totally insensible to every other consideration except that of making as much money as he possibly can. I know, of course, that many publishers fall short of this difficult ideal, and allow themselves, through love of literature, admiration of particular authors, and unbusinesslike compassion, to be seduced into giving the author better terms than he is in a position to extort. Some publishers have to protect themselves against this weakness by taking into partnership some born Harpagon [in Molière's *The Miser*, 1668] whose only joy and point of honor is to skin authors alive. I know also that there are authors—I am one of them myself—who like bargaining for its own sake, and are so interested in points of law and economics that for the mere fun of it they bargain keenly for money and concessions they do not really want. I have already intimated that there are unscrupulous and rapacious authors as well as unscrupulous and rapacious publishers. But, leaving these to balance oneanother, I would appeal to the typical authors who, either because they have private means and need not trouble about their professional incomes, or are so completely wrapt up in their art and so intimidated by the business world that they will stand out for nothing beyond enough to enable them to continue writing in a dry cottage, will sign any clause if they are assured that it is customary, and thereby very soon make it really customary. Fortunately these commercial imbeciles, incapable of taking thought for themselves, can often be stirred to take thought for other people. An author who accepts a low standard of income for himself, which he may think his own affair, is imposing that low standard on his fellow authors; and this is not his own affair: it is the affair of all his colleagues, and of literature with a large L. If the Society of Authors were powerful enough it would drive him out of his (or her) profession.

Authors have nothing to hope for from the courts beyond their bare legal rights; and we can both remember a time when even that was uncertain; for when the Society was founded [1884] it was still possible to find judges who refused to entertain the conception of literary property. They held that it is as ridiculous to pay an author to write as to pay a bird to sing; and they were fundamentally right as far as poetic literature is concerned. But as the judges who kept canaries discovered that birds cannot sing unless they are fed, an author can by this time appeal to the courts with a fair chance of finding a judge whose sense that a copyright is an exploitable property is nearly as strong as his sense of property in industrial patents and broad acres. But let not the author dream that it was for his sake that his old vague common law right to property in his work has been confirmed and defined by statute. The blunt truth is that as a man who has no property cannot be robbed, robbers have a strong interest in enabling him to acquire property. For the same reason publishers, theatre proprietors, picture dealers, and gramophone companies, who live by making money out of the productions of authors, composers, and artists, have the strongest interest in making these productions private property. A publisher who has all the works of Shakespear freely at his disposal will pay me for leave to print my plays, leaving Shakespear untouched, because I can give him a monopoly and thus enable him to charge a monopoly price whilst Shakespear can give him nothing; so that in publishing Shakespear he can get only an ordinary competitive profit on the cost of production unless he adds a copyright preface or commentary or set of illustrations; and for these he requires the protection of the Copyright Acts as much as the authors and artists do. Tolstoy, not understanding this, repudiated his copyrights and announced that anybody who pleased could publish his works, with the result that after a few experiments nobody would publish them until his wife took the matter in hand and practically reaffirmed his rights. I myself have had the experience of being asked for new articles in a country [USA] in which many early articles of mine had fallen into the public domain. I have pointed out that these works were at the disposal of the applicants without reference to me. But the applicants would not touch them because they were equally at the disposal of their competitors, and have offered me substantial sums for new copyright articles which, they explained, I need not even write, as they wanted only my name at the head or tail, and would undertake to get them written without troubling me.

Thus it is that the author owes all his rights to his exploiters, and by no means to his own futile appeals for justice, though these have always been made the pretext for the legislation which has established him as a person of property. You and I have good reason to know this from our experience of the passing of the Copyright Act of 1911: our Magna Charta (such as it is). For years the Society had clamored for the removal of the gross injustices and silly anomalies from which we suffered; but no Government could be persuaded to find the necessary time and attention for a new Copyright Act, though nobody questioned the need for it. At last, when hope deferred had become hope extinct, the resistance suddenly and mysteriously gave way, and we were told to hurry up with all the clauses we wanted in a new Act. We joyfully complied, and congratulated ourselves until the draft of the Government Bill reached us. It cleared up the mystery at once. It contained a clause, undreamt of by us, empowering the gramophone manufacturers to reproduce copyright music on their discs on payment of a modest statutory price whether the composer desired it or no.★

We protested vehemently. We were immediately told quite frankly by the Board of Trade that if we defeated this clause the Bill would be dropped. It was, in effect, the Gramophone Trust's Bill; and our grievances were only the pretext for it.

We had too much to gain by the Bill to run this risk; and we submitted. But the incident should be taken to heart by every author who imagines that authors, as such, have any political power or influence. They have none. Their handful of votes, which they very seldom exercise, are negligible: their business affairs interest nobody: in fact there is nothing the reading public hates more than to think of an author as having anything so sordid as business cares and bread-and-butter worries. And the reading public is only a fragment of the electorate.

But though our property has been blown to us by sidewinds it is all the more important that we should understand it and maintain it for all that it is worth. Writing is a poor profession, like all the professions, however the public may be dazzled by the celebrity and big incomes (mostly greatly overrated) of the handful of the supersuccessful at the top. But it has the advantage of property rights denied to other professions. A surgeon cannot patent an operation which he is the first to make practicable, nor levy royalties for the rest of his life and fifty years after on all surgeons performing it. A barrister cannot patent an original defence. Einstein has no copyright in relativity; nor can Dean Inge obtain a monopoly of what is original in his

---

★ In lobbying for this clause the manufacturers overlooked the fact that they were destroying the composer's power to grant a monopoly, which is the commercial essence of copyright. When they realize this they will probably lobby a repealing Act. [GBS]

neo-Platonic doctrine.[7] The Nelson touch and the tactics and strategy of Wellington are free to him that can get them. Of the great body of professional persons it is true that they must live from hand to mouth, their earnings stopping when their hands are put out of action by illness or accident. But the author is a person of property; and as long as his property is worth anything he can live by it if only he has the knowledge and nerve to stick to it and exact its full rent. With the aid of your book and the Society of Authors he and she should be able to do this without any greater strain on their character and faculties than other property holders have to face.

　　And so, my dear Thring, I wish you a wide circulation and am, as always,

Faithfully yours<br>BERNARD SHAW.

AYOT ST LAWRENCE.
22 November 1932.

---

7. In *The Platonic Tradition in English Religious Thought* (1926) Inge maintained that only a culture based on the transcendentals is securely founded.

# Where Stands Socialism To-day?

*Preface to a series of Fabian Society lectures in 1932, published under the above title in 1933, including Shaw's lecture 'In Praise of Guy Fawkes'*

═══

Unscientific Socialism is the cause of all our political messes. Politics are now as scientific as mathematics, and government is a highly technical art; but the more scientific and technical they become, the more infatuatedly do we leave them to the idle rich amateur, the superannuated commercial adventurer, and the rule-of-thumb banker, who know no more of politics and economics than a blackbeetle knows of electro-magnetism. They are expert in nothing but making private fortunes and doing the other fellow down. A century ago an Eatanswill elector [in *Pickwick Papers*] shouted "Success to the mayor; and may he never desert the nail and saucepan business as he got his money by!" Today England is so misruled by deserters from the nail and saucepan business that a demand is prevalent for a restoration of the rule of the robber baron and the cadi under the palm tree, whose military and judicial technique, picked up under turbulent public criticism and tested severely by its success, was more effective for constitutional purposes than nail and saucepan technique.

England leads the world in political science. She can boast—if only she knew what to boast about—that she produced the Fabian Society, which produced the London School of Economics. But as she keeps the Fabian Society and the Government in separate compartments without communicating doors she might just as well have no Fabian Society at all, and must get on as best she can with the international morality of Joshua and William the Conqueror and the modern business habits and practice of Cecil Rhodes, operating through an ingenious self-defeating parliamentary machine which tends more and more to make Guy Fawkes a popular hero. In his perception of the need for ending it by an explosion of the hot air which is its chief output Guy was before his time; but that time seems coming.

Meanwhile, as to where Socialism stands today, we told it to go to Russia and it has. We shall have to copy Russia presently in consequence, though Marxism was a genuine British Museum export.

G. Bernard Shaw.

# An Aside

*Preface to Lillah McCarthy's* Myself and My Friends, *1933. The original text was edited before publication by McCarthy and her husband Sir Frederick Keeble to delete all references to her former husband Harley Granville-Barker, at his request. No copy of the preface as first drafted is known to have survived*

———

I was very intimately concerned in the chapter of theatrical history[1] which is also a chapter of this autobiography of its leading actress. It did not seem an important chapter when we were making it; but now, twenty[-six] years after its close, it falls into perspective as a very notable one. I am often asked to write or speak of the development of the theatre, and to prophesy its future. I always reply that the theatre does not develop, and that it has, in the evolutionary sense, no future that will not repeat the past. From time to time dramatic art gets a germinal impulse. There follows in the theatre a spring which flourishes into a glorious summer. This becomes stale almost before its arrival is generally recognized; and the sequel is not a new golden age, but a barren winter that may last any time from fifteen years to a hundred and fifty. Then comes a new impulse; and the cycle begins again.

The impulse, like all creative impulses, is a mystery: that is, an unexplained phenomenon. Its outward and visible sign is a theatrical person of genius: a playwright or a player. The luckiest event is the coincidence of memorable playwriting with memorable acting. The present autobiography is the story of an actress who was caught by one of these germinal impulses; and, as it happened, I, as playwright, was its vehicle (or victim) when it stirred up the depths of our stagnant dramatic poetry and volatilized it into tragi-comedy in the last decade of the XIX century.

In 1889 the London stage had come into shattering collision with the Norwegian giant, Ibsen. I say shattering advisedly because nobody could follow up Ibsen. He knocked the fashionable drama of the day out of countenance without effectively replacing it, because his plays could never be forced on the London theatre for more than a fortnight at a time except when some player made a personal success in them. It was this that distinguished his case from that of Wagner, who not only delivered an equally smashing attack on

1. Vedrenne–Barker management of the Court and Savoy theatres, 1904–7.

the oldfashioned Italian opera houses but supplanted their repertories by his own operas and music dramas so completely that at last no one would pay a penny to hear Lucrezia Borgia or Semiramide whilst money poured in for Lohengrin, Die Meistersinger, Tristan, and even for The Ring. Wagner conquered and took possession: Ibsen passed like a tornado and left nothing behind but ruin. When I say that he made even Shakespear contemptible to inveterate Shakespeareans like myself his effect on the standing of lesser playwrights may be imagined. They began to write unhappy plays, and, worse still, embittered plays.[2] They lost their ease of handling and their sense of humor. They became a prey to doubts and compunctions which they could not define: above all, they lost their lightness of heart, without which nothing can succeed in the theatre except illiterate sob-stuff and police sensation. And the ground lost in this way was not occupied by Ibsen, who soon seemed as extinct as the least lucky of the playwrights he had destroyed.

And so the drama in London went staggering about crazily for fifteen years. Everybody wanted a new drama of Ibsenian novelty and importance, but pleasant and with plenty of laughs at the right side of the mouth. No such drama was forthcoming at the West End theatres. The playwrights were all shellshocked by the Norwegian broadside.

There was, however, one notable exception; and that was no less a person than myself. Ibsen had not shocked me in the least. Why was I immune? Because an earlier enchanter had taken me far outside the bounds of middle-class idealism within which Ibsen's bombshells were deadly. I am not by nature a good bourgeois any more than Shelley was; and I was a strong Shelleyan long before I ever heard of Ibsen from William Archer. And long after Shelley and yet still longer before Ibsen, came Karl Marx, whose indictment of bourgeois civilization, based wholly on English facts, utterly destroyed its high moral reputation and started throughout Europe a fire of passionate resolution to dethrone it and tear down its idols and laws and government, compared to which the commotion raised by Ibsen's Doll's House and Ghosts was a storm in a teacup. It is significant that though our press made a prodigious fuss about Ibsen as he sent the revolted daughters of the business and professional classes flying from the domestic hearth "to live their own lives" in all directions, the leaders of the proletarian movement which has overthrown Capitalism in Russia took no notice of Ibsen. They were not unaware of him; for at the first performance of A Doll's House in England [see also

2. Shaw's allusion is to social dramas like Pinero's *The Second Mrs Tanqueray* (1893) and *The Notorious Mrs Ebbsmith* (1895) and Henry Arthur Jones's *The Triumph of the Philistines* (1895) and *Michael and His Lost Angel* (1896).

vol. 1, p. 184], on a first floor in a Bloomsbury lodging house, Karl Marx's youngest daughter played Nora Helmer; and I impersonated Krogstad at her request with a very vague notion of what it was all about. But there is all the difference in the world between welcoming a dramatic poet as a useful auxiliary, which was the Marxist attitude towards Ibsen, and being wakened from a complacent satisfaction with Victorian respectability by a moral earth-quake which threatened to bring every suburban villa crashing to the ground in a hurricane of Feminism and Anti-Clericalism and anti-Idealism.

I had the advantage of that difference. I had read Karl Marx fourteen years before Lenin did; and the shock of Ibsen's advent did not exist for me, nor indeed for anyone who was not living in the Victorian fools' paradise. All the institutions and superstitions and rascalities that Ibsen attacked had lost their hold on me. Consequently, whilst the fashionable Victorian playwrights who had never heard of Marx were reeling all over the place from the Ibsen shock, my self-possession and gaiety and grip of the situation were completely undisturbed; and when in response to various external suggestions and pres-sures I began writing plays, they were just as amusing and undistracted as if Ibsen had never been born. But they were also so strange to the theatre of that day, kept alive by a little group of fashionable actors who brought their artistic skill and attractiveness to the rescue of every successive rehash of the adulteries and duels which were the worn-out stock-in-trade of the Parisian stage and its London imitation, that when little private clubs of connoisseurs like the Independent Theatre and the Stage Society ventured on single per-formances of them, the Strand (as theatre-land was then called) could not accept them as plays at all, and repudiated them as pamphlets in dialogue form by a person ignorant of the theatre and hopelessly destitute of dramatic faculty.

Behind the scenes, too, I had my difficulties. In a generation which knew nothing of any sort of acting but drawingroom acting, and which considered a speech of more than twenty words impossibly long, I went back to the classical style and wrote long rhetorical speeches like operatic solos, regarding my plays as musical performances precisely as Shakespear did. As a producer I went back to the forgotten heroic stage business and the exciting or impressive declamation I had learnt from oldtimers like Ristori, Salvini, and Barry Sulli-van. Yet so novel was my post-Marx post-Ibsen outlook on life that nobody suspected that my methods were as old as the stage itself. They would have seemed the merest routine to Kemble or Mrs Siddons; but to the Victorian leading ladies they seemed to be unleadingladylike barnstorming. When Kate Rorke played Candida [Court Theatre, 26 April 1904] I seized the opportu-nity to pay her a long deferred tribute to her beautiful performance of Helena in A Midsummer Night's Dream [Frank Benson's company, Globe Theatre, 19 December 1889], which she had treated as a piece of music from beginning to end. To my amazement she changed color, and reproached me for making heartless fun of her only failure. When I convinced her that I was in earnest she told me how her musical rendering of that most musical part had brought on her such a torrent of critical abuse and misunderstanding that she had never ventured to attempt anything of the sort again!

No wonder I often found actors and actresses nervously taking the utmost care to avoid acting, the climax being reached by an actor [A. G. Poulton] engaged for the broadly comic part of Burgess in Candida, who, after rehearsing the first act in subdued tones like a funeral mute, solemnly put up his hand as I vengefully approached him, and said: "Mr Shaw: I know what you are going to say. But you may depend on me. In the intellectual drama I never clown." And it was some time before I could persuade him that I was in earnest when I exhorted him to clown for all he was worth. I was continually struggling with the conscientious efforts of our players to underdo their parts lest they should be considered stagey. Much as if Titian had worked in black and grey lest he should be considered painty. It took a European war to cure them of wanting to be ladies and gentlemen first and actresses and actors after.

This difficulty was acute when I had to find a heroine for Man and Superman. Everybody said that she must be ultra-modern. I said that I wanted a young Mrs Siddons or Ristori and that an ultra-modern actress would be no use to me whatever in the part. I was in despair of finding what I wanted when one day there walked into my rooms in the Adelphi a gorgeously goodlooking young lady in a green dress and huge picture hat in which any ordinary woman would have looked ridiculous, and in which she looked splendid, with the figure and gait of a Diana. She said: "Ten years ago, when I was a little girl trying to play Lady Macbeth, you told me to go and spend ten years learning my business.[3] I have learnt it: now give me a part." I handed her the book of Man and Superman without a moment's hesitation, and said simply, "Here you are." And with that young lady I achieved

3. In a review of the Shakespeare Reading Society's staged production of *Macbeth* in aid of the Siddons Memorial Fund in 1895, Shaw pronounced Lillah McCarthy's performance 'bad', principally because she was too young for the role: 'I should', he added, 'like to see [her] play again: I venture on the responsibility of saying that her Lady Macbeth was a highly promising performance, and that some years of hard work would make her a valuable recruit to the London stage' (*Saturday Review*, 25 May 1895).

performances of my plays which will probably never be surpassed. For Lillah McCarthy was saturated with declamatory poetry and rhetoric from her cradle, and had learnt her business out of London by doing work in which you were either heroic or nothing. She was beautiful, plastic, statuesque, most handsomely made, and seemed to have come straight from the Italian or XVIII century stage without a trace of the stuffiness of the London cup-and-saucer theatres.

It is an actress's profession to be extraordinary; but Lillah was extraordinary even among actresses. The first natural qualification of an actress who is not a mere puppet, impotent without a producer, is imagination. Lillah had a great deal too much of it: she was of imagination all compact [*Midsummer Night's Dream*, V: i]. It was difficult to get her feet down to the ground, and almost impossible to keep them there. Her life was rich in wonderful experiences that had never happened, and in friendships with wonderful people (including myself) who never existed. All her geese were swans, flying about in an enchanted world. When, as inevitably occurred from time to time, real life and hard objectivity brought her down with a stunning collision, she could be tragically disappointed or murderously enraged; but she could not be disillusioned: the picture changed; but it remained a picture. On the stage she gave superb performances with a force and sureness of stroke and a regal authority that made her front rank position unassailable; but if by chance her imagination started a fresh hare before she went on the stage she would forget all about the play and her part in it, and, whilst mechanically uttering its words and moving through its business, revel in the feelings of some quite different character. The effect of seeing an actress going through the part of, say, Lady Macbeth, under the impression that she is giving a touching representation of Little Nell is curious: at the Court Theatre we described it by the occasional dismal announcement that Lillah was blithering. In this way she was sometimes disqualified by an excess of qualification, like Shelley, who could not write a big poem without smothering it under a whole universe of winds and clouds, mountains and fountains, glories and promontories (with the accent on the Tories) until its theme was lost like a roseleaf in a splendid sunset. The one fault that authors and producers had to find with her was that she would not "stay put." And her friends complained, not without reason, of the startling discrepancies between her daily visions and transfigurations and the much less lovely facts of the case. You could not say that she had the faults of her qualities. Her faults *were* her qualities.

However, her technique fell in with mine as if they had been made for oneanother, as indeed they had. She created the first generation of Shavian heroines with dazzling success.[4] Not merely playgoing London came to see her: indeed I doubt if playgoing London ever did to any great extent. Political London, artistic London, religious London, and even sporting London made the long series of performances in which she figured a centre of almost every vein of fashion except the hopeless old theatrical fashion. And she did this by playing my heroines exactly as she would have played Belvidera in [Thomas Otway's] Venice Preserved if anyone had thought of reviving that or any other of Mrs Siddons's great parts for her.

During the career of Mrs Siddons a play was regarded as an exhibition of the art of acting. Playwrights wrote declamatory parts for actors as composers did for singers or violinists, to display their technical virtuosity. This became an abuse: Wagner was quite justified in his complaint that singers thought only of how they sang, and never of what they were singing. Actors who had learnt how "to bring down the house" with a tirade were quite as pleased when the tirade was trash as when it was one of Shakespear's best. The cup-and-saucer drama, and the actor who, having no force to reserve, made a virtue of reserved force, were inevitable reactions against the resultant staginess, staginess being definable as much ado about nothing. The art of acting rhetorical and poetical drama, vulgarized and ridiculous, very soon became a lost art in the fashionable London theatres. Rhetoric and poetry vanished with it. But when I dragged rhetoric and poetry back its executive technique became again indispensable.

Lillah McCarthy describes in this book how she acquired and inherited from her father a love of verbal music in its loftiest ranges, and a physical necessity for declaiming it, with the inevitable accompanying craving for the beauty and dignity of noble architecture and statuary: a craving which could never be satisfied by dressmakers' and tailors' mannequins adorning "interiors" furnished by the best London establishments. Yet such actress-mannequins constituted the entire theatrical beauty stock in the cup–and–saucer drama. The continual efforts to give some sort of vital energy to these shop–window attractions by sex appeal, becoming less and less furtive until the interiors became bedrooms and the fashionable gowns had to be stripped off, mostly on no pretext whatever, in full view of the audience, seemed to Lillah poor

4. The roles she created included Ann Whitefield in *Man and Superman*; Jennifer Dubedat in *The Doctor's Dilemma*; Margaret Knox in *Fanny's First Play*; and Lavinia in *Androcles and the Lion*. In addition, during the Vedrenne–Barker seasons, she appeared in several performances of *Major Barbara*; succeeded Tita Brand as Gloria Clandon in *You Never Can Tell* and Ellen O'Malley as Nora in *John Bull's Other Island*; and played Raïna Petkoff in the 1907 revival of *Arms and the Man* at the Savoy Theatre.

stuff compared to a sonnet by Milton. When the new school arose she liked not only the matter of it (all the intelligent actresses did that) but its manner and method, in which she is today an adept, and in the part of it which consists in the delivery of English verse an unrivaled one. The horrible artificiality of that impudent sham the Victorian womanly woman, a sham manufactured by men for men, and duly provided by the same for the same with a bulbously overclothed "modesty" more lascivious than any frank sensuality, had become more and more irksome to the best of the actresses who had to lend their bodies and souls to it—and by the best of the actresses I mean those who had awakeningly truthful minds as well as engaging personalities. I had so little taste for the Victorian womanly woman that in my first play I made my heroine throttle the parlor maid. The scandal of that outrage shook the London theatre and its Press to their foundations: an easy feat; for their foundations were only an inch deep and very sandy at that; and I was soon shaking more serious impostures, including that of the whole rotten convention as to women's place and worth in human society which had made the Victorian sham possible. But for that I needed the vigorous artificiality of the executive art of the Elizabethan stage to expose and bring back to nature the vapid artificiality of the Victorian play.

Lillah McCarthy's secret was that she combined the executive art of the grand school with a natural impulse to murder the Victorian womanly woman; and this being just what I needed I blessed the day when I found her; and, if I become Dictator (which may happen to anybody nowadays), will most certainly engage and command her, for an enormous salary, to broadcast all the loveliest and splendidest pages of English literature everyday to them that have ears to hear her.

Ayot St Lawrence.                                                              G. B. S.
May, 1933.

# The Political Madhouse in America
# and Nearer Home

*Prefatory note, 'An Explanation', to the English edition of Shaw's lecture, delivered in New York on 11 April 1933, and published in America (without the note) as* The Future of Political Science in America, *1933*

By republishing in England a harangue addressed specifically to Americans in America I lay myself open to an accusation of wantonly holding up my sensitive American friends to British ridicule and contempt, not for their own good, which was my excuse in New York, but solely to gratify our British conceit of moral superiority and the vicious pleasure taken by the meanest of us in the defamation of persons not born in England (mostly in slums).

I am guiltless of any such incivility. It is to rebuke nationalist *Schadenfreude* [enjoyment of others' mishaps] that I have consented to supply a British counterpart to the edition of my address now circulating in the United States. It would be the silliest hypocrisy to keep up the pleasantry of implying, as I did at the Metropolitan Opera House in New York on the 11th of last April, that the follies and futilities I ascribed to our American cousins are peculiar to their Continent. To please my American audience I made fun of the Hundredpercent American; but the truth is that the Hpc American is a harmless and well-meaning child compared to the Hpc Englishman, Frenchman, German Nazi, or Japanese. The most complete and colossal example of the Hpc American I can recollect was the late William Jennings Bryan,[1] Bi-Metallist, Fundamentalist, and Hot Air Volcano. Shut him off from the rest of the world and measure him by an American scale and it is easy for me or any other critic to make him appear futile as a statesman, absurd as a thinker, and gaseous as an orator. But place him against the sinister figures of the leading British and Continental Hpcs of his generation and it becomes at once apparent that civilization would be much safer in the hands of a batch

---

1. American political leader, Democratic nominee for the presidency in 1896, 1900 and 1908. He was identified in the public mind as a champion of free coinage of silver.

of Bryans than in theirs. Bryan never said "My country, right or wrong,"[2]
though he may have sung "My country, 'tis of thee." He never declared that
the manifest divine destiny[3] of the entire human race is to be governed by
rich young Americans trained in the public schools and universities of the
United States. He never came back from a Geneva International Conference
and said that of course the United States came first with him, nor sat at a
Peace Conference declaring that absolute security for the country in which
he happened to be born comes before every other consideration, such absolute
security being attainable only by the extermination of everybody except his
compatriots, and incidentally of his God (if he believed in one). If he was
infatuated about silver he was at least faithful to it, and never won a general
election by rallying the nation to its defence immediately before announcing
that he was going to save the nation by repudiating it. He did not proclaim
the sacredness of ethnographical frontiers, and then, after sacrificing millions
of lives to re-establish them, use his victory to establish military frontiers
more pregnant with future wars than those he had sworn to redress.[4] In short,

2. Declared by Stephen Decatur, American naval officer, in a dinner toast at Norfolk,
Va., April 1816: 'Our country! In her intercourse with foreign nations may she
always be in the right, but our country, right or wrong!' The familiar phrase was
echoed by the politician Carl Schurz in the US Senate, 29 February 1872, when he
added 'if right, to be kept right; and if wrong, to be set right!'
3. The *Dictionary of American English* defines this as the doctrine of the inevitability
of Anglo-Saxon supremacy, the phrase being used by those who held that it was the
destiny of the United States or the Anglo-Saxon race to govern the entire western
hemisphere. It was widely used prior to the American Civil War to vocalize the
philosophy of territorial expansion in North America.
4. The 'sinister figures' alluded to in the foregoing passage can be identified despite
exaggeration and distortion. The 'manifest divine destiny' of youngsters trained in
private schools and universities calls to mind the never confirmed remark attributed
to the Duke of Wellington, 'The battle of Waterloo was won on the playing fields
of Eton.' Shaw, however, more likely was recalling a statement by Frederick Sleigh,
Lord Roberts, in the *Hibbert Journal*, October 1914, that Shaw earlier cited in *Common
Sense about the War* (November 1914), with its reference to 'young men, fresh from
the public schools of Britain, coming eagerly forward to carry on the high traditions of
Imperial Britain'. The man who returned from the Geneva International Conference
was Sir Austen Chamberlain, Foreign Secretary 1924–9, whose remarks were addressed
to the Birmingham Anglo-French Society, 26 April 1928. It was the supremely nationalistic Georges Clemenceau, premier of France and chairman of the Paris Peace Conference (1919), who stressed French national security as his principal concern, dwarfing
all other considerations. The leader accused of fiscal permutability (see also p. 105) was

Bryan might well pass for an angel of light in contrast with the nationalist patriots of the old world, with their hands against every man and every man's hand against them (except at Peace Conferences where all the said hands slipped surreptitiously into oneanother's pockets), their reproaches to honest Pacifists for being the friends of every country but their own, and their pride in the alternative of being the enemies of every country but their own. If I have said, as indeed I have, that the Hpc American is an idiot, he may well smile as he wrings my hand cordially for the hundredth time and replies with a smile "At least, dear friend, you do not call me a scoundrel as well."

The main points of my harangue obviously apply to England as urgently as to the United States. As I write, a folly called the World Economic Conference is collapsing in London[5] in an ignominy of failure and futility even greater than that of all the other Conferences by which our Parliament men try to stave off imminent disasters by another bout of talking round them. Obviously a World Economic Conference can succeed only on the assumption by its delegates that under all circumstances two and two make four, always have done so, and always will do so. The delegates in our Museum of Fossils, appropriately selected for their place of meeting, assumed, on the contrary, that the fate of their countries, and finally of the world, is continually being staked on the question whether two and two will make plus fifty million or minus five thousand, as on no other assumption is it worth a financier's while to add two and two together at all. The Conference was bound in the face of Nature to assume that the world must live from hand to mouth on the year's harvest, and can by no sleight of financial or other magic obtain a single grain of wheat from any future year's crop nor a slice from any future year's lamb. But the delegates all accepted as a familiar and unquestionable fact that the next twenty years' harvests are at the immediate

---

Ramsay MacDonald, whose government, weakened by a drain on gold reserves, resigned in July 1931. At the king's invitation he formed a National Government, immediately abandoning the Gold Standard it had been formed to defend. The General Election *followed*, in October. The man who sacrificed 'millions of lives' was Raymond Poincaré, president of the French Republic, who fought at the Peace Conference to eliminate Germany as a power by wresting from it the left bank of the Rhine, to be annexed to France or Belgium or to be given autonomy; and by annexation of the Saar by France and the ceding of Danzig to Poland, among other unsuccessful demands.
5. The World Economic Conference met in London in June 1933 to consider international monetary exchange and the problems of devaluation, deflation and social unrest. A global solution was made impossible by the Johnson Act, passed by the US Congress in January 1934, forbidding loans, either government or private, to any nation that had not paid its war debts.

disposal of everyone who can pay for them in paper money. The Conference depended on an unshakable conviction that all real trade is a barter of goods and necessary services, and that where there is no exchange there is robbery. Yet to the delegates trade was only a game at which the player who won the most paper money and lost the most goods was the winner. Nothing could differentiate the Conference from a conspiracy of brigands but a common aspiration to the utmost possible production and cheapening of the necessities and luxuries of a decent life. But the delegates with one voice declared that the only thing that can save the world is a general rise in prices and the destruction by natural calamity or deliberate sabotage of the existing supply of food for lack of which thirty millions of unemployed are perishing by inches. After that it is a mere anti-climax to mention that though sane finance depends on an unsleeping sense that credit is only an opinion, and that men can neither eat it, drink it, nor build houses with it, all the delegates believed that credit is a nourishing and succulent diet, and that as a man with food, drink, and bricks and mortar to the value of a thousand pounds has credit for that sum with his banker, he has in effect a thousand pounds in goods plus a thousand pounds credit, and is therefore "worth" two thousand pounds. "Credit schemes" on this basis are enjoying quite a vogue at present. Straitened nations ask, not for goods, but for credits.

I have not time to complete the analysis of the dust storm of delusions which constituted the mental equipment of the delegates. The Russian delegate[6] was the only one who proceeded on mentionable assumptions; and he confessed that his reason was giving way under the strain of having to argue with a World Conference of incurable lunatics. He was saved by his sense of humor; but his sense of humor could not save the world situation. The lunatics have gone home to their respective national asylums; but they are still in charge there; and if our affairs are not taken out of their hands we shall go to smash. For their greatest lunacy of all is that not one of them can see the smallest reason why any human being should be allowed to live unless in addition to supporting himself he can produce a privately appropriable profit for a share-holder or a rent for a landlord. Why, they argue, should anyone organize the work of propertyless men merely to produce their own food? Rather let them perish, or, if they shew signs of muttering "Thou shalt starve ere I starve,"[7] let the tax collector collect some crumbs for them from the owners'

6. Maxim M. Litvinov, Russian foreign commissar, who was chairman of the Russian delegation.
7. Spoken by Andrew Undershaft in the final act of *Major Barbara*: 'I moralized and starved until one day I swore that I would be a full-fed free man at all costs; that

tables. At such a point youths of spirit become car bandits and racketeers and kidnappers. What else do our crazy conferencemongers expect? It is easy to say "If you cannot produce a profit get off the earth: you have no right to live." Proletarians are so blind to this point of view that in the final issue they reply "Que messieurs les assassins commencent."[8]

I therefore conciliate my American friends by inviting my English ones to apply everything I say of the Americans in this book to themselves with the assurance that they deserve it no less, and that their day of judgment may be no further off, if so far.

AYOT ST LAWRENCE.                                                                       G. B. S.
16 July 1933.

nothing should stop me except a bullet, neither reason nor morals nor the lives of other men. I said "Thou shalt starve ere I starve"; and with that word I became free and great. . . . When it is the history of every Englishman we shall have an England worth living in.'

8. Written by the editor Alphonse Karr in the political and literary monthly, *Les Guêpes* (January 1840): 'Si l'on veut abolir la peine de mort, en ce cas que MM. les Assassins commencent' ('if, in such cases it is desired to abolish the death penalty, let the murderers begin').

# Too True to be Good

*First published in 1934*

═══

## MONEY AND HAPPINESS

Somehow my play, Too True to be Good, has in performance excited an animosity and an enthusiasm which will hardly be accounted for by the printed text. Some of the spectators felt that they had had a divine revelation, and overlooked the fact that the eloquent gentleman through whose extremely active mouth they had received it was the most hopeless sort of scoundrel: that is, one whose scoundrelism consists in the absence of conscience rather than in any positive vices, and is masked by good looks and agreeable manners. The less intellectual journalist critics sulked as they always do when their poverty but not their will consents to their witnessing a play of mine; but over and above the resultant querulousness to which I have long been accustomed I thought I detected an unusual intensity of resentment, as if I had hit them in some new and unbearably sore spot.[1]

Where, then, was the offence that so exceedingly disgruntled these unhappy persons? I think it must have been the main gist and moral of the play, which is not, as usual, that our social system is unjust to the poor, but that it is cruel to the rich. Our revolutionary writers have dwelt on the horrors of poverty. Our conventional and romantic writers have ignored those horrors, dwelling pleasantly on the elegances of an existence free from pecuniary care. The poor have been pitied for miseries which do not, unfortunately, make them unbearably miserable. But who has pitied the idle rich or really believed that they have a worse time of it than those who have to live on ten shillings a day or less, and earn it? My play is a story of three reckless young people who come into possession of, for the moment, unlimited riches, and set out to have a thoroughly good time with all the modern machinery of pleasure to aid them. The result is that they get nothing for their money but a multitude of worries and a maddening dissatisfaction.

1. Shaw almost certainly had in mind St John Ervine's vituperative notice in the *Observer*, on 9 October 1932, in which he opined that it would have been better if Shaw had 'died a dozen years ago than live to write this whining play . . . [in which he] recants all his beliefs'.

### THE VAMPIRE AND THE CALF

I doubt whether this state of things is ever intentionally produced. We see a man apparently slaving to place his children in the position of my three adventurers; but on closer investigation we generally find that he does not care twopence for his children, and is wholly wrapped up in the fascinating game of making money. Like other games it is enjoyable only by people with an irresistible and virtually exclusive fancy for it, and enough arithmetical ability and flair for market values to play it well; but with these qualifications the poorest men can make the most astounding fortunes. They accumulate nothing but powers of extracting money every six months from their less acquisitive neighbors; and their children accumulate nothing but obligations to spend it. As between these two processes of bleeding and being bled, bleeding is the better fun. The vampire has a better time than the calf hung up by the heels with its throat cut. The moneygetter spends less on his food, clothes, and amusements than his clerks do, and is happy. His wife and sons and daughters, spending fabulous sums on themselves, are no happier than their housemaids, if so happy; for the routine of fashion is virtually as compulsory as the routine of a housemaid, its dressing is as much dictated as her uniform, its snubbings are as humiliating, and its monotony is more tedious because more senseless and useless, not to mention that it must be pleasanter to be tipped than to tip. And, as I surmise, the housemaid's day off or evening off is really off: in those hard earned hours she ceases to be a housemaid and can be herself; but the lady of fashion never has a moment off: she has to be fashionable even in her little leisure, and dies without ever having had any self at all. Here and there you find rich ladies taking up occupations and interests which keep them so busy doing professional or public work that they might as well have five hundred a year as fifty thousand "for all the good it does them" as the poor say in their amazement when they see people who could afford to be fashionable and extravagant working hard and dressing rather plainly. But that requires a personal endowment of tastes and talents quite out of the common run.

I remember a soldier of the old never-do-well type drifting into a little Socialist Society which I happened to be addressing more than fifty years ago. As he had evidently blundered into the wrong shop and was half drunk, some of the comrades began to chaff him, and finally held me up to him as an example of the advantages of teetotalism. With the most complete conviction he denounced me as a hypocrite and a liar, affirming it to be a well-known and inexorable law of nature that no man with money in his pocket could pass a public house without going in for a drink.

## THE OLD SOLDIER AND THE PUBLIC HOUSE

I have never forgotten that soldier, because his delusion, in less crude forms, and his conception of happiness, seem to afflict everybody in England more or less. When I say less crude forms I do not mean truer forms; for the soldier, being half drunk, was probably happier than he would have been if quite sober, wheras the plutocrat who has spent a hundred pounds in a day in the search for pleasure is not happier than if he had spent only five shillings. For it must be admitted that a private soldier, outside that surprising centre of culture, the Red Army of Russia, has so little to be happy about when sober that his case is hardly a fair one. But it serves to illustrate the moral of my play, which is, that our capitalistic system, with its golden exceptions of idle richery and its leaden rule of anxious poverty, is as desperate a failure from the point of view of the rich as of the poor. We are all amazed and incredulous, like the soldier, when we hear of the multimillionaire passing the public house without going in and drinking himself silly; and we envy his sons and daughters who do go in and drink themselves silly. The vulgar pub may be in fact a Palace Hotel, and the pints of beer or glasses of whisky an elaborate dinner with many courses and wines culminating in cigars and liqueurs; but the illusion and the results are cognate.

I therefore plead for a science of happiness to cure us of the miserable delusion that we can achieve it by becoming richer than our neighbors. Modern colossal fortunes have demonstrated its vanity. When country parsons were "passing rich with forty pounds a year"[2] there was some excuse for believing that to be rich was to be happy, as the conception of riches did not venture beyond enough to pay for the necessities of a cultivated life. A hundred years ago Samuel Warren wrote a famous novel about a man who became enormously rich. The title of the novel was Ten Thousand a Year;[3] and this, to any resident Irish family in my boyhood, represented an opulence beyond which only Lords Lieutenant and their like could aspire. The scale has changed since then. I have just seen in the papers a picture of the funeral

2. 'A man severe he was, and stern / And passing rich with forty pounds a year': Oliver Goldsmith, *The Deserted Village* (1770).
3. The novel, one of the most popular sellers of the century, 'turns upon the validity of certain title-deeds, and a number of legal points are involved' (*DNB*). Its author was a former physician and barrister.

of a shipping magnate[4] whose income, if the capital value of the property left by him be correctly stated, must have been over four thousand pounds a day or a million and a half a year. If happiness is to be measured by riches he must have been fourteen thousand times as happy as the laborer lucky enough to be earning two pounds a week. Those who believe that riches are the reward of virtue are bound to conclude that he was also fourteen thousand times as sober, honest, and industrious, which would lead to the quaint conclusion that if he drank a bottle of wine a day the laborer must have drunk fourteen thousand.

## THE UNLOADING MILLIONAIRES

This is so obviously monstrous that it may now be dismissed as an illusion of the poor who know nothing of the lives of the rich. Poverty, when it involves continual privation and anxiety, is, like toothache, so painful that the victim can desire nothing happier than the cessation of the pain. But it takes no very extraordinary supply of money to enable a humble person to say "I want for nothing"; and when that modest point is reached the power of money to produce happiness vanishes, and the trouble which an excess of it brings begins to assert itself, and finally reaches a point at which the multimillionaires are seen frantically unloading on charitable, educational, scientific, religious, and even (though rarely) artistic and political "causes" of all kinds, mostly without stopping to examine whether the causes produce any effects, and if so what effects.[5] And far from suffering a loss of happiness every time they give away a thousand pounds, they find themselves rather in the enviable state of mind of the reveller in The Pilgrim's Progress [Part II] with his riddle "There was a man, though some did think him mad, the more he gave away the more he had."

4. Shipping magnate 'Captain' Robert Dollar, born in Scotland, emigrated to Canada in 1858 and to the United States in 1882, where he founded one of the greatest of shipbuilding families.
5. This is a toned-down reiteration of remarks made in *The Intelligent Woman's Guide to Socialism and Capitalism* (1928), in chapter 4, on 'a handful of hypertrophied capitalists gasping under the load of their growing millions, and giving it away in heaps in a desperate attempt, partly to get rid of it without being locked up as madmen for throwing it into the sea, and partly to undo, by founding Rockefeller institutes and Carnegie libraries, and hospitals and universities and schools and churches, the effects of the welter of ignorance and poverty produced by the system under which it has accumulated on their hands'.

## Delusions of Poverty

The notion that the rich must be happy is complemented by the delusion that the poor must be miserable. Our society is so constituted that most people remain all their lives in the condition in which they were born, and have to depend on their imagination for their notions of what it is like to be in the opposite condition. The upstarts and the downstarts, though we hear a great deal about them either as popular celebrities or criminals, are exceptional. The rich, it is said, do not know how the poor live; but nobody insists on the more mischievous fact that the poor do not know how the rich live. The rich are a minority; and they are not consumed with envy of the poor. But the poor are a huge majority and they are so demoralized by the notion that they would be happy if only they were rich, that they make themselves poorer, if hopefuller, by backing horses and buying sweepstake tickets on the chance of realizing their daydreams of unearned fortunes. Our penny newspapers now depend for their circulation, and consequently for their existence, on the sale of what are virtually lottery coupons. The real opposition to Socialism comes from the fear (well founded) that it would cut off the possibilities of becoming rich beyond those dreams of avarice which our capitalist system encourages. The odds against a poor person becoming a millionaire are of astronomical magnitude; but they are sufficient to establish and maintain the Totalizator as a national institution, and to produce unlimited daydreams of bequests from imaginary long lost uncles in Australia or a lucky ticket in the Calcutta or Irish Sweeps.[6]

## Trying it for an Hour

Besides, even quite poor people save up for holidays during which they can be idle and rich, if not for life, at least for an hour, an afternoon, or even a week. And for the poor these moments derive such a charm from the change from the monotony of daily toil and servitude, that the most intolerable hardships and discomforts and fatigues in excursion trains and overcrowded

6. A sweep is a pool in which the stakes contributed by the competitors are taken as a prize by a winner or multiple winners, after a percentage is deducted for charity or governmental tax. Most often it is related to horse races. In the Calcutta Sweep, however, it was held in conjunction with a gold competition, the gamblers being paid off through a prearranged scale of percentages.

lodgings seem delightful, and leave the reveller with a completely false notion
of what a lifetime of such revelry would be.

I maintain that nobody with a sane sense of values can feel that the sole
prize which our villainous capitalist system has to offer, the prize of admission
to the ranks of the idle rich, can possibly confer either happiness or health
or freedom on its winner. No one can convict me of crying sour grapes; for
during the last thirtyfive years I have been under no compulsion to work,
nor had any material privation or social ostracism to fear as a consequence
of not working. But, like all the intelligent rich people of my acquaintance,
I have worked as hard, ate and drunk no more, and dressed no better than
when I had to work or starve. When my pockets were empty I did not buy
any of the luxuries in the London shops because I had no money to buy
them with. When, later on, I had enough to buy anything that London could
tempt me with, the result was the same: I returned home day after day
without having made a single purchase. And I am no ascetic: no man alive
is freer than I from the fancy that selfmortification will propitiate a spiteful
deity or increase my balance in a salvation bank in a world beyond the grave.
I would and could live the life of the idle rich if I liked it; and my sole reason
for not living it is that I dont like it. I have every opportunity of observing
it both in its daily practice and its remoter results; and I know that a year of
it would make me more unhappy than anything else of an accepted kind that
I can imagine. For, just as the beanfeaster[7] can live like a lord for an afternoon,
and the Lancashire factory operative have a gorgeous week at Blackpool when
the wakes are on,[8] so I have had my afternoons as an idle rich man, and
know only too well what it is like. It makes me feel suicidal.

You may say that I am an exceptional man. So I am, in respect of being
able to write plays and books; but as everybody is exceptional in respect of
being able to do something that most other people cannot do, there is nothing
in that. Where I am really a little exceptional is in respect of my having
experienced both poverty and riches, servitude and selfgovernment, and also
having for some reason or other (possibly when I was assured in my infancy
that some nasty medicine was delicious) made up my mind early in life never
to let myself be persuaded that I am enjoying myself gloriously when I am,

7. A 'beanfeast' is British slang for an annual dinner or party hosted by an employer
for his workers.
8. Each Lancashire mill town shut down for a holiday 'Wakes' week (originally a
church festival), staggered through the season, and celebrated by workers at Blackpool's three piers, beaches, baths, Tower ballroom, Stanley Gardens, conservatories,
amusement park and golf courses.

as a matter of fact, being bored and pestered and plundered and worried and tired. You cannot humbug me on this point: I understand perfectly why Florence Nightingale fled from fashionable society in London to the horrors of the Crimean hospitals rather than behave like a lady, and why my neighbor Mr Apsley Cherry-Garrard, the sole survivor of what he calls with good reason "the worst journey in the world" through the Antarctic winter,[9] was no poor sailorman driven by his need for daily bread to make a hard living before the mast, but a country gentleman opulent enough to choose the best that London society could offer him if he chose. Better the wards of the most terrible of field hospitals than a drawingroom in Mayfair: better the South Pole at its blackest six months winter night and its most murderous extremities of cold than Sunday by the Serpentine in the height of the season.

## CONSOLATIONS OF THE LANDED GENTRY

To some extent this misery of riches is a new thing. Anyone who has the run of our country houses, with their great parks and gardens, their staffs of retainers, indoor and outdoor, and the local public work that is always available for the resident landed gentry, will at once challenge the unqualified assertion that the rich, in a lump, are miserable. Clearly they are nothing of the sort, any more than the poor in a lump. But then they are neither idle nor free. A lady with a big house to manage, and the rearing of a family to supervise, has a reasonably busy time of it even without counting her share in the routine of sport and entertainment and occasional travel which to people brought up to it is a necessary and important part of a well ordered life. The landed gentry have enough exercise and occupation and sense of social importance and utility to keep them on very good terms with themselves and their neighbors. If you suddenly asked them whether they really enjoyed their routine and whether they would not rather be Communists in Russia they would be more sincerely scandalized than if you had turned to them in church and asked them whether they really believed every clause in the Apostles' Creed. When one of their ugly ducklings becomes a revolutionist it is not because countryhouse life is idle, but because its activities are uncongenial and because

9. Cherry-Garrard was a member of Robert Scott's ill-fated second (*Terra Nova*) British Antarctic Expedition (1910–12). Invalided from military service in 1916 he retired to his country estate, which bordered on Ayot St Lawrence, where he wrote a book *The Worst Journey in the World* (1922) on the Antarctic experience. Shaw had recommended the title on hearing Cherry-Garrard utter the phrase in conversation.

the duckling has tastes or talents which it thwarts, or a faculty for social criticism which discovers that the great country house is not built on the eternal rock but on the sandy shore of an ocean of poverty which may at any moment pass from calm to tempest. On the whole, there is no reason why a territorial lady should not be as happy as her dairymaid, or her husband be as happy as his gamekeeper. The riches of the county families are attached to property; and the only miserable county people are those who will not work at their job.

## MISERIES OF THE VAGRANT ROOTLESS RICH

But the new thing is riches detached from real property: that is, detached from work, from responsibility, from tradition, and from every sort of pre-scribed routine, even from the routine of going to the village church every Sunday, paying and receiving calls, and having every month set apart for the killing of some particular bird or animal. It means being a tramp without the daily recurrent obligation to beg or steal your dinner and the price of your bed. Instead, you have the daily question "What shall I do? Where shall I go?" and the daily answer "Do what you please: go where you like: it doesnt matter what you do or where you go." In short, the perfect liberty of which slaves dream because they have no experience of its horrors. Of course the answer of outraged Nature is drowned for a time by the luxury merchants shouting "Come and shop, whether you need anything or not. Come to our palace hotels. Come round the world in our liners. Come and wallow in our swimming pools. Come and see our latest model automobile: we have changed the inventor's design for-better-for-worse solely to give you an excuse for buying a new one and selling your old one at scrap iron prices. Come and buy our latest fashions in dress: you cannot possibly be seen in last season's garments." And so on and so forth. But the old questions come home to the rich tourists in the palace hotels and luxury liners just as they do to the tramps on the highroad. They come up when you have the latest car and the latest wardrobe and all the rest of it. The only want that money can satisfy without satiating for more than a few hours is the need for food and drink and sleep. So from one serious meal a day and two very minor ones you go on to three serious meals a day and two minor ones. Then you work another minor one between breakfast and lunch "to sustain you"; and you soon find that you cannot tackle any meal without a cocktail, and that you cannot sleep. That obliges you to resort to the latest soporific drug, guaranteed in the advertisements to have none of the ruinous effects of its equally guaranteed forerunner. Then comes the doctor, with his tonics, which are simply additional cocktails, and his sure knowledge that if he tells you the truth about yourself and refuses to prescribe the tonics and the drugs, his children will starve. If you indulge in such a luxury as a clerical spiritual adviser it is his duty to tell you that what is the matter with you is that you are an idle useless glutton and drunkard and that you are going to hell; but alas! he, like the doctor, cannot afford this, as he may have to ask you for a subscription tomorrow to keep his church going. And that is "Liberty: thou choicest treasure."[10]

This sort of life has been made possible, and indeed inevitable, by what William Cobbett, who had a sturdy sense of vital values, denounced as the Funding System.[11] It was a product of war, which obliged belligerent governments to obtain enormous sums from all and sundry by giving them in exchange the right to live for nothing on the future income of the country until their money was returned: a system now so popular among people with any money to spare that they can be induced to part with it only on condition that the Government promises not to repay it before a certain more or less remote day. When joint stock companies were formed to run big industrial concerns with money raised on the still more tempting terms that the money is never to be repaid, the system became so extensive that the idle upstart rich became a definitely mischievous and miserable class quite different in character from the old feudal rich.

## THE REDEMPTION FROM PROPERTY

When I propose the abolition of our capitalistic system to redeem mankind from the double curse of poverty and riches, loud wailings arise. The most articulate sounds in the hubbub are to the effect that the wretched slaves of the curse will lose their liberty if they are forced to earn their living honorably. The retort that they have nothing to lose but their chains [Marx–Engels, *The Communist Manifesto*, 1848, sec. 4], with the addition that the gold chains are as bad as the iron ones, cannot silence them, because they think they are

10. Handel, *Judas Maccabeus* (1746), lyrics by Thomas Morell, Act 1.
11. Cobbett appears to have meant the consequences of carrying on government business on a basis of credit rather than on a cash–on–the–barrelhead system employing a metallic currency. Cobbett's resentment of government finance focused mainly on paper money and the national debt. In his writings from 1816 to 1835 he frequently forecast the imminent collapse of the Funding System. See, for example, *Cobbett's Weekly Political Register*, vol. 31, p. 595 (1816) and vol. 39, p. 409 (1821).

free, and have been brought up to believe that unless the country remains the private property of irresponsible owners maintaining a parliament to make any change impossible, with churches, schools and universities to inculcate the sacredness of private property and party government disguised as religion, education and democracy, civilization must perish. I am accused of every sort of reactionary extravagance by the people who think themselves advanced, and of every sort of destructive madness by people who thank God they are no wiser than their fathers.

Now I cannot profitably discuss politics, religion and economics with terrified ignoramuses who understand neither what they are defending nor what they are attacking. But it happens that Mr Gilbert Chesterton, who is not an ignoramus and not in the least terrified, and whose very interesting conversion to Roman Catholicism [in 1922] has obliged him to face the problem of social organization fundamentally, discarding the Protestant impostures on English history which inspired the vigorous Liberalism of his salad days, has lately taken me to task for the entirely imaginary offence of advocating government by a committee of celebrities. To clear up the matter I have replied to Mr Chesterton very fully and in Catholic terms. Those who have read my reply in the magazine in which it appeared need read no further, unless they wish, as I should advise, to read it twice. For the benefit of the rest, and to put it on permanent record, here it is.[12]

FUNDAMENTAL NATURAL CONDITIONS OF HUMAN SOCIETY

1. Government is necessary wherever two or three are gathered together—or two or three billions—for keeps.

2. Government is neither automatic nor abstract: it must be performed by human rulers and agents as best they can.

3. The business of the rulers is to check disastrously selfish or unexpected behavior on the part of individuals in social affairs.

4. This business can be done only by devizing and enforcing rules of social conduct codifying the greatest common measure of agreement as to the necessary sacrifice of individual liberty to the good of the community.

12. Chesterton and Shaw indulged in a debate in *Nash's–Pall Mall Magazine*, November 1933, Chesterton's contribution captioned 'Should We be Governed by Intellectuals? Ridiculous!', and Shaw's reply 'Why Not Give the Intellectuals a Chance?' The list of propositions reprinted by Shaw is extracted from his response to Chesterton. See also p. 174.

5. The paradox of government is that as the good of the community involves a maximum of individual liberty for all its members the rulers have at the same time to enslave everyone ruthlessly and to secure for everyone the utmost possible freedom.

6. In primitive communities people feed and lodge themselves without bothering the Government. In big civilizations this is impossible; so the first business of the Government is to provide for the production and distribution of wealth from day to day and the just sharing of the labor and leisure involved. Thus the individual citizen has to be compelled not only to behave himself properly, but to work productively.

7. The moral slavery of the compulsion to behave properly is a whole-time compulsion admitting of no liberty; but the personal slavery of the compulsion to work lasts only as many hours daily as suffice to discharge the economic duties of the citizen, the remaining hours (over and above those needed for feeding, sleeping, locomotion, etc.) being his leisure.

8. Leisure is the sphere of individual liberty: labor is the sphere of slavery.

9. People who think they can be honestly free all the time are idiots: people who seek whole-time freedom by putting their share of productive work on others are thieves.

10. The use of the word slavery to denote subjection to public government has grown up among the idiots and thieves, and is resorted to here only because it is expedient to explain things to fools according to their folly.

So much for the fundamental natural conditions of social organization. They are as completely beyond argument as the precession of the equinoxes; but they present different problems to different people. To the thief, for instance, the problem is how to evade his share in the labor of production, to increase his share in the distribution of the product, and to corrupt the Government so that it may protect and glorify his chicaneries instead of liquidating him. To Mr Chesterton the Distributist (or Extreme Left Communist) and Catholic (or Equalitarian Internationalist) it is how to select rulers who will govern righteously and impartially in accordance with the fundamental natural conditions.

The history of civilization is the history of the conflict between these rival views of the situation. The Pirate King, the Robber Baron, and the Manchester Man produced between them a government which they called the Empire, the State, the Realm, the Republic, or any other imposing name that did not give away its central purpose. The Chestertonians produced a government which they called The Church; and in due time the Last of the Chestertons joined this Catholic Church, like a very large ship entering a very small harbor, to the great peril of its many rickety old piers and wharves, and the swamping of all the small craft in its neighborhood. So let us see what the Catholic Church made of its governmental problem.

## THE CATHOLIC SOLUTION

To begin with, the Church, being catholic, was necessarily democratic to the extent that its aim was to save the souls of all persons without regard to their age, sex, nationality, class, or color. The nobleman who felt that God would not lightly damn a man of his quality received no countenance from the Church in that conviction. Within its fold all souls were equal before God.

But the Church did not draw the ridiculous conclusion that all men and women are equally qualified or equally desirous to legislate, to govern, to administer, to make decisions, to manage public affairs or even their own private affairs. It faced the fact that only about five per cent of the population are capable of exercising these powers, and are certain to be corrupted by them unless they have an irresistible religious vocation for public work and a faith in its beneficence which will induce them to take vows to abstain from any profit that is not shared by all the rest, and from all indulgences which might blunt their consciences or subject them to the family influences so bitterly deprecated by Jesus.

This natural "called" minority was never elected in the scandalous way we call democratic. Its members were in the first instance self-elected: that is, they voluntarily lived holy lives and devoted themselves to the public welfare in obedience to the impulse of the Holy Ghost within them. This impulse was their vocation. They were called from above, not chosen by the uncalled. To protect themselves and obtain the necessary power, they organized themselves, and called their organization The Church. After that, the genuineness and sufficiency of the vocation of the new recruits were judged by The Church. If the judgment was favorable, and the candidates took certain vows, they were admitted to the official priesthood and set to govern as priests in the parish and spiritual directors in the family, all of them being eligible, if they had the requisite ability, for promotion to the work of governing the Church itself as bishops or cardinals, or to the supreme rank of Pope or Vicar of Christ on earth. And all this without the smallest reference to the opinions of the uncalled and unordained.

## Need for a Common Faith

Now comes the question, why should persons of genuine vocation be asked to take vows before being placed in authority? Is not the vocation a sufficient guarantee of their wisdom?

No. Before priests can govern they must have a common faith as to the fundamental conditions of a stable human society. Otherwise the result might be an assembly of random men of genius unable to agree on a single legislative measure or point of policy. An ecumenical council consisting of Einstein and Colonel [Arthur] Lynch,[13] Aquinas and Francis Bacon, Dante and Galileo, Lenin and Lloyd George, could seldom come to a unanimous decision, if indeed to any decision except in the negative against a minority of one, on any point beyond the capacity of a coroner's jury. The Pope must not be an eccentric genius presiding over a conclave of variously disposed cardinals: he must have an absolutely closed mind on what Herbert Spencer called Social Statics;[14] and in this the cardinals must resemble and agree with him. What is more, they must to some extent represent the conscience of the common people; for it is evident that if they made laws and gave personal directions which would produce general horror or be taken as proofs of insanity their authority would collapse. Hence the need for vows committing all who take them to definite articles of faith on social statics, and to their logical consequences in law and custom. Such vows automatically exclude revolutionary geniuses, who, being uncommon, are not representative, more especially scientific geniuses, with whom it is a point of honor to have unconditionally open minds even on the most apparently sacred subjects.

## Russia Rediscovers the Church System

A tremendous importance is given to a clear understanding of the Catholic system at this moment by the staggering fact that the biggest State in the modern world, having made a clean sweep of its Church by denouncing its

13. Irish nationalist and former MP from West Clare, who commanded British troops in Ireland in 1918. He was author of *The Case against Einstein* (1932).
14. Spencer's first book, *Social Statics; or, the Conditions Essential to Human Happiness* (1851), was written, he stated, with the principal object to promulgate the individualist doctrine that 'every man has freedom to do all that he wills, provided he infringes not the equal freedom of any other man'.

religion as dope, depriving its priests and bishops of any greater authority than a quack can pick up at a fair, encouraging its most seriously minded children to form a League of the Godless, shooting its pious Tsar, turning its cathedrals into historical museums illustrating the infamies of ecclesiastical history and expressly entitling them anti-religious: in short, addressing itself solemnly and implacably to a root-and-branch extermination of everything that we associate with priesthood, has, under pressure of circumstances, unconsciously and spontaneously established as its system of government an as-close-as-possible reproduction of the hierarchy of the Catholic Church. The nomenclature is changed, of course: the Church is called the Communist Party; and the Holy Office and its familiars are known as the Komintern and the Gay Pay Oo.[15] There is the popular safeguard of having the symptoms of the priestly vocation verified in the first instance by the group of peasants or industrial workers with whom the postulant's daily life has been passed, thus giving a genuine democratic basis to the system; and the hierarchy elected on this basis is not only up to date for the moment, but amenable to the daily lessons of trial and error in its practical operations and in no way pledged against change and innovation as such. But essentially the system is that of the old Christian Catholic Church, even to its fundamental vow of Communism and the death penalty on Ananias and Sapphira for violating it.

If our newspapers knew what is really happening in the world, or could discriminate between the news value of a bicycle accident in Clapham and that of a capsize of civilization, their columns would be full of this literally epoch-making event. And the first question they would address to Russia would be "Why, seeing that the Christian system has been such a hopeless failure, do you go back to it, and invite us to go back to it?"

## WHY THE CHRISTIAN SYSTEM FAILED

The answer is that the Christian system failed, not because it was wrong in its psychology, its fundamental postulate of equality, or its anticipation of Lenin's principle that the rulers must be as poor as the ruled so that they can raise themselves only by raising their people, but because the old priests' ignorance of economics and political science blinded them to the mischief

---

15. Komintern (for Communist International), an ultraradical Communist organization (1919) founded in Moscow, uniting Communist groups throughout the world and advocating violent revolution. Gay Pay OO, also called GPU and Ogpu, was the secret police organization of the USSR, 1922–34.

latent in the selfishness of private property in the physical earth. Before The Church knew where it was (it has not quite located itself yet) it found itself so prodigiously rich that the Pope was a secular Italian prince with armies and frontiers, enjoying not only the rent of Church lands, but selling salvation on such a scale that when Torquemada began burning Jews instead of allowing them to ransom their bodies by payments to the Roman treasury, and leaving their souls to God, a firstrate quarrel between The Church and the Spanish Inquisition was the result.

But the riches of The Church were nothing compared to the riches of The Church's great rival, The Empire. And the poverty of the priest was opulence compared to the poverty of the proletarian. Whilst The Church was being so corrupted by its own property, and by the influence on it of the lay proprietors, that it lost all its moral prestige, the warriors and robbers of The Empire had been learning from experience that a pirate ship needs a hierarchy of officers and an iron discipline even more than police boats, and that the work of robbing the poor all the time involves a very elaborate system of government to ensure that the poor shall, like bees, continue to produce not only their own subsistence but the surplus that can be robbed from them without bringing on them the doom of the goose that lays the golden eggs. Naked coercion is so expensive that it became necessary to practise on the imaginations of the poor to the extent of making them believe that it is a pious duty to be robbed, and that their moment of life in this world is only a prelude to an eternity in which the poor will be blest and happy, and the rich horribly tortured.

Matters at last reached a point at which there was more law and order in The Empire than in The Church. Emperor Philip of Spain was enormously more respectable and pious, if less amiable, than Pope Alexander Borgia. The Empire gained moral prestige as The Church lost it until The Empire, virtuously indignant, took it on itself to reform The Church, all the more readily as the restoration of priestly poverty was a firstrate excuse for plundering it.

Now The Church could not with any decency allow itself to be reformed by a plutocracy of pirate kings, robber barons, commercial adventurers, moneylenders, and deserters from its own ranks. It reformed itself from within by its own saints and the Orders they founded, and thus "dished" the Reformation; whilst the Reformers set up national Churches and free Churches of their own under the general definition of Protestants, and thereby found themselves committed to a curious adulteration of their doctrine of Individualism, or the right of private judgment, with most of the ecclesiastical corruptions against which they had protested. And as neither Church nor Empire would share the government of mankind with the other nor allow the common people any say in the matter, the Catholics and Protestants set to work to exterminate oneanother with rack and stake, fire, sword, and gunpowder, aided by the poison gas of scurrilous calumny, until the very name of religion began to stink in the nostrils of all really charitable and faithful people.

## GOVERNMENT BY EVERYBODY

The moral drawn from all this was that as nobody could be trusted to govern the people the people must govern themselves, which was nonsense. Nevertheless it was assumed that by inscribing every man's name on a register of voters we could realize the ideal of every man his own Solon and his own Plato, as to which one could only ask why not every man his own Shakespear and his own Einstein? But this assumption suited the plutocrats very well, as they had only to master the easy art of stampeding elections by their newspapers to do anything they liked in the name of the people. Votes for everybody (called for short, Democracy) ended in government neither of the best nor of the worst, but in an official government which could do nothing but talk, and an actual government of landlords, employers, and financiers at war with an Opposition of trade unionists, strikers, pickets, and—occasionally—rioters. The resultant disorder, indiscipline, and breakdown of distribution, produced a reaction of pure disappointment and distress in which the people looked wildly round for a Savior, and were ready to give a hopeful trial to anyone bold enough to assume dictatorship and kick aside the impotent official government until he had completely muzzled and subjugated it.

## FAILURE ALL ROUND

That is the history of Catholicism and Protestantism, Church and Empire, Liberalism and Democracy, up to date. Clearly a ghastly failure, both positively as an attempt to solve the problem of government and negatively as an attempt to secure freedom of thought and facility of change to keep pace with thought.

Now this does not mean in the least that the original Catholic plan was wrong. On the contrary, all the disasters to which it has led have been demonstrations of the eternal need for it. The alternative to vocational government is a mixture of a haporth of very incompetent official government with an intolerable deal of very competent private tyranny. Providence, or Nature if you prefer that expression, has not ordained that all men shall have a vocation for being "servants of all the rest" as saints or rulers. Providence knows better than to provide armies consisting exclusively of commanders-in-chief or factories staffed exclusively with managing directors; and to that inexorable natural fact we shall always have to come back, just as the Russian revolutionists, who were reeking with Protestant Liberal superstitions at the beginning, have had to come back to it. But we have now thought out much more carefully than St Peter the basic articles of faith, without which the vocation of the priest is inevitably pushed out by the vocation of the robbers and the racketeers, self-elected as gentlemen and ladies. We know that private property distributes wealth, work, and leisure so unevenly that a wretchedly poor and miserably overworked majority are forced to maintain a minority inordinately rich and passionately convinced that labor is so disgraceful to them that they dare not be seen carrying a parcel down Bond Street. We know that the strains set up by such a division of interests also destroy peace, justice, religion, good breeding, honor, reasonable freedom, and everything that government exists to secure, and that all this iniquity arises automatically when we thoughtlessly allow a person to own a thousand acres of land in the middle of London much more completely than he owns the pair of boots in which he walks over it; for he may not kick me out of my house into the street with his boots; but he may do so with his writ of ejectment. And so we are driven to the conclusion that the modern priesthood must utterly renounce, abjure, abhor, abominate and annihilate private property as the very worst of all the devil's inventions for the demoralization and damnation of mankind. Civilized men and women must live by their ordered and equal share in the work needed to support the community, and must find their freedom in their ordered and equal share of the leisure produced by scientific economy in producing that support. It still takes some conviction to repudiate an institution so well spoken of as private property; but the facts must be faced: our clandestine methods of violating it by income tax and surtax, which mean only "What a thief stole steal thou from the thief," will no longer serve; for a modern government, as the Russians soon found out, must not take money, even from thieves, until it is ready to employ it productively. To throw it away in doles as our governing duffers do, is to burn the candle at both ends and precipitate the catastrophe they are trying to avert.

## OBSOLETE VOWS

As to the vows, some of the old ones must go. The Catholic Church and our Board of Education insist on celibacy, the one for priests and the other for schoolmistresses. That is a remnant of the cynical superstition of original sin. Married people have a right to married rulers; mothers have a right to have their children taught and handled by mothers; and priests and pastors who meddle with family affairs should know what they are talking about.

Another important modern discovery is that government is not a whole-time job for all its agents. A council of peasants derives its ancient wisdom from its normal day's work on the land, without which it would be a council of tramps and village idiots. It is not desirable that an ordinary parish priest should have no other occupation, nor an abnormal occupation, even that of a scholar. Nor is it desirable that his uniform should be too sacerdotal; for that is the method of idolatry, which substitutes for rational authority the superstitious awe produced by a contrived singularity. St Vincent de Paul knew thoroughly well what he was about when he constituted his Sisterhood of Charity on the rule that the sister should not be distinguishable from an ordinary respectable woman. Unfortunately, the costume prescribed under this rule has in the course of the centuries become as extraordinary as that of the Bluecoat boy;[16] and St Vincent's idea is consequently lost; but modern industrial experience confirms it; for the latest rediscovery of the Vincentian principle has been made by Mr Ford, who has testified that if you want a staff of helpful persons who will turn their hands to anything at need you must not give them either title, rank, or uniform, as the immediate result will be their partial disablement by the exclusion from their activities of many of the most necessary jobs as beneath their dignity.[17]

Another stipulation made by St Vincent, who already in the XVI century was far ahead of us, was that no sister may pledge herself for longer than a year at a time, however often she may renew her vows. Thus the sisters can never lose their freedom nor suffer from cold feet. If he were alive today St Vincent would probably propose a clean sweep of all our difficulties about marriage and divorce by forbidding people to marry for longer than a year, and make them renew their vows every twelve months. In Russia the members of

16. Christ's Hospital school for boys (known as the 'Bluecoat School'), whose alumni include Samuel Taylor Coleridge and Charles Lamb, was founded in the City of London in 1556. It moved to Horsham, Sussex, in 1902, where its boys still wear the traditional costume of long blue coat, breeches and yellow stockings. The school now accepts girls, equivalently clad.
17. Henry Ford indicated, in *My Life and Work* (1922), that 'the Ford factories . . . have no organization . . . no line of succession or of authority, very few titles'. In *Moving Forward* (1931) he stressed 'the single standard'. 'It is necessary', he wrote, 'to get away entirely from the thought that the relation between employer and employee has in it anything of meniality.' See also Ford's *My Philosophy of Industry* (1929).

the Communist Party cannot dedicate themselves eternally: they can drop out into the laity when they please, and if they do not please and nevertheless have become slack in their ministry, they are pushed out.

## SUPERNATURAL PRETENSIONS

Furthermore, modern priests must not make supernatural pretensions. They must not be impostors. A vocation for politics, though essentially a religious vocation, must be on the same footing as a vocation for music or mathematics or cooking or nursing or acting or architecture or farming or billiards or any other born aptitude. The authority which must attach to all public officials and councils must rest on their ability and efficiency. In the Royal Navy every mishap to a ship involves a court martial on the responsible officer: if the officer makes a mistake he forfeits his command unless he can convince the court that he is still worthy [of] it. In no other way can our hackneyed phrase "responsible government" acquire any real meaning. When a Catholic priest goes wrong (or too right) he is silenced: when a Russian Commissar goes wrong, he is expelled from the Party. Such responsibility necessarily makes official authority very authoritative and frightens off the unduly nervous. Stalin and Mussolini are the most responsible statesmen in Europe because they have no hold on their places except their efficiency; and their authority is consequently greater than that of any of the monarchs, presidents, and prime ministers who have to deal with them. Stalin is one of the higher functionaries with whom governing is necessarily a whole-time job. But he is no richer than his neighbors, and can "better himself" only by bettering them, not by buttering them like a British demagogue.

## ECLECTIC DEMOCRACY

I think my views on intellectual aristocracy and democracy and all the rest of it are now plain enough. As between the intentions of The Church and the intentions of The Empire (unrealized ideals both) I am on the side of The Church. As to the evil done by The Church with the best intentions and the good done by The Empire with the worst, I am an Eclectic: there is much to be learnt from each. I harp on Russia because the Moscow experiment is the only really new departure from Tweedledum and Tweedledee: Fascism is still wavering between Empire and Church, between private property and Communism. Years ago, I said that what democracy needed was a trustworthy anthropometric machine for the selection of qualified rulers. Since then I have elaborated this by demanding the formation of panels of tested persons eligible for the different grades in the governmental hierarchy.[18] Panel A would be for diplomacy and international finance, Panel B for national affairs, Panel C for municipal and county affairs, Panel D for the village councils and so forth. Under such a panel system the voters would lose their present liberty to return such candidates as the late Horatio Bottomley[19] to parliament by enormous majorities; but they would gain the advantage of at least knowing that their rulers know how to read and write, which they do not enjoy at present.

Nobody ventured to disagree with me when I urged the need for such panels; but when I was challenged to produce my anthropometric machine or my endocrine or phrenological tests, I was obliged to confess that they had not yet been invented, and that such existing attempts at them as competitive examinations are so irrelevant and misleading as to be worse than useless as tests of vocation. But the Soviet system, hammered out under the sternest pressure of circumstances, supplies an excellent provisional solution, which turns out to be the solution of the old Catholic Church purged of supernatural pretension, assumption of final perfection, and the poison of private property with its fatal consequences. Mr Stalin is not in the least like an Emperor, nor an Archbishop, nor a Prime Minister, nor a Chancellor; but he would be strikingly like a Pope, claiming for form's sake an apostolic succession from Marx, were it not for his frank method of Trial and Error, his entirely human footing, and his liability to removal at a moment's notice if his eminence should upset his mental balance. At the other end of the scale are the rank and file of the Communist Party, doing an ordinary day's work with the common folk, and giving only their leisure to the Party. For their election as representatives of the commons they must depend on the votes of their intimate and equal neighbors and workmates. They have no incentive to seek election except the vocational incentive; for success, in the first instance, means, not release from the day's ordinary work, but the sacrifice of all one's leisure to politics, and, if promotion to the whole-time-grades be achieved, a comparatively ascetic discipline and virtually no pecuniary gain.

If anyone can suggest a better practically tested plan, now is the time to

18. See 'Democracy' in 'The Revolutionist's Handbook', *Man and Superman* (1903), and, in the present volume, the preface to *The Apple Cart*, p. 56.
19. Unscrupulous political journalist, jingoist publisher and MP, whom Lloyd George labelled an independent Nationalist demagogue. His fraudulent financial activities led to imprisonment in 1922.

do it; for it is all up with the old Anarchist–Liberal parliamentary systems in the face of thirty millions of unemployed, and World Idiotic Conferences at which each nation implores all the others to absorb its unemployed by a revival of international trade. Mr Chesterton says truly that a government, if it is to govern, "cannot select one ruler to do something and another to undo it, one intellectual to restore the nation and another to ruin the nation." But that is precisely what our parliamentary party system does. Mr Chesterton has put it in a nutshell; and I hope he will appreciate the sound Catholicism with which I have cracked it.

AYOT ST LAWRENCE.
1933.

# On the Rocks

*First published in 1934*

===

## EXTERMINATION

In this play a reference is made by a Chief of Police to the political necessity for killing people: a necessity so distressing to the statesmen and so terrifying to the common citizen that nobody except myself (as far as I know) has ventured to examine it directly on its own merits, although every Government is obliged to practise it on a scale varying from the execution of a single murderer to the slaughter of millions of quite innocent persons. Whilst assenting to these proceedings, and even acclaiming and celebrating them, we dare not tell ourselves what we are doing or why we are doing it; and so we call it justice or capital punishment or our duty to king and country or any other convenient verbal whitewash for what we instinctively recoil from as from a dirty job. These childish evasions are revolting. We must strip off the whitewash and find out what is really beneath it. Extermination must be put on a scientific basis if it is ever to be carried out humanely and apologetically as well as thoroughly.

## KILLING AS A POLITICAL FUNCTION

That killing is a necessity is beyond question by any thoughtful person. Unless rabbits and deer and rats and foxes are killed, or "kept down" as we put it, mankind must perish; and that section of mankind which lives in the country and is directly and personally engaged in the struggle with Nature for a living has no sentimental doubts that they must be killed. As to tigers and poisonous snakes, their incompatibility with human civilization is unquestioned. This does not excuse the use of cruel steel traps, agonizing poisons, or packs of hounds as methods of extermination. Killing can be cruelly or kindly done; and the deliberate choice of cruel ways, and their organization as popular pleasures, is sinful; but the sin is in the cruelty and the enjoyment of it, not in the killing.

## THE SACREDNESS OF HUMAN LIFE

In law we draw a line between the killing of human animals and non-human ones, setting the latter apart as brutes. This was founded on a general belief that humans have immortal souls and brutes none. Nowadays more and more people are refusing to make this distinction. They may believe in The Life Everlasting and The Life to Come; but they make no distinction between Man and Brute, because some of them believe that brutes have souls, whilst others refuse to believe that the physical materializations and personifications of The Life Everlasting are themselves everlasting. In either case the mystic distinction between Man and Brute vanishes; and the murderer pleading that though a rabbit should be killed for being mischievous he himself should be spared because he has an immortal soul and a rabbit has none is as hopelessly out of date as a gentleman duellist pleading his clergy. When the necessity for killing a dangerous human being arises, as it still does daily, the only distinction we make between a man and a snared rabbit is that we very quaintly provide the man with a minister of religion to explain to him that we are not killing him at all, but only expediting his transfer to an eternity of bliss.

The political necessity for killing him is precisely like that for killing the cobra or the tiger: he is so ferocious or unscrupulous that if his neighbors do not kill him he will kill or ruin his neighbors; so that there is nothing for it but to disable him once for all by making an end of him, or else waste the lives of useful and harmless people in seeing that he does no mischief, and caging him cruelly like a lion in a show.

Here somebody is sure to interject that there is the alternative of teaching him better manners; but I am not here dealing with such cases: the real necessity arises only in dealing with untameable persons who are constitutionally unable to restrain their violent or acquisitive impulses, and have no compunction about sacrificing others to their own immediate convenience. To punish such persons is ridiculous: we might as reasonably punish a tile for flying off a roof in a storm and knocking a clergyman on the head. But to kill them is quite reasonable and very necessary.

## PRESENT EXTERMINATIONS

All this so far is mere elementary criminology, already dealt with very fully by me in my Essay on Prisons [see vol. 2, p. 437], which I recommend to those readers who may feel impelled to ramble away at this point into the prosings about Deterrence beloved by our Prison commissioners and judges. It disposes of the dogma of the unconditional sacredness of human life, or any other incarnation of life; but it covers only a corner of the field opened up by modern powers of extermination. In Germany it is suggested that the Nordic race should exterminate the Latin race. As both these lingual stocks are hopelessly interbred by this time, such a sacrifice to ethnological sciolism is not practicable; but its discussion familiarizes the idea and clears the way for practicable suggestions. The extermination of whole races and classes has been not only advocated but actually attempted. The extirpation of the Jew as such figured for a few mad moments in the program of the Nazi party in Germany.[1] The extermination of the peasant is in active progress in Russia, where the extermination of the class of ladies and gentlemen of so-called independent means has already been accomplished; and an attempt to exterminate the old Conservative professional class and the kulak or prosperous farmer class has been checked only by the discovery that they cannot as yet be done without. Outside Russia the extermination of Communists is widely advocated; and there is a movement in the British Empire and the United States for the extermination of Fascists. In India the impulse of Moslems and Hindus to exterminate oneanother is complicated by the impulse of the British Empire to exterminate both when they happen to be militant Nationalists.

## PREVIOUS ATTEMPTS MISS THE POINT

The novelty and significance of these instances consists in the equal status of the parties. The extermination of what the exterminators call inferior races is as old as history. "Stone dead hath no fellow" said Cromwell[2] when he

1. Shaw appears to distinguish here between 'extirpation' and 'execution'. Until Hitler came to power in 1933 there was no anti-Jewish policy publicly proclaimed by the National Socialists. Immediately after Hitler's appointment as Chancellor, however, a rooting out of Jews from German society commenced with a decree (on 1 April) proclaiming a national boycott of Jewish shops and another (on 7 April) dismissing most non-Aryans from government service and universities. During this period, according to William L. Shirer (*The Rise and Fall of the Third Reich*, 1960), a few thousand Jews were, however, robbed, beaten or murdered.
2. Macaulay, in a review of Howard Hallam's *Constitutional History of England* (1827), credited the statement to the Earl of Essex in reference to the just-executed Thomas Wentworth, Earl of Strafford, 1641. A correspondent, Hugh T. Dutton, informed Shaw on 25 July 1939 (Add. Mss. BL 50522) that it was John Pym, accuser of Strafford in Parliament, who had spoken the words. Shaw did not alter the text.

tried to exterminate the Irish. "The only good nigger is a dead nigger" say the Americans of the Ku-Klux temperament. "Hates any man the thing he would not kill?" said Shylock naïvely [*Merchant of Venice*, IV: i]. But we white men, as we absurdly call ourselves in spite of the testimony of our looking glasses, regard all differently colored folk as inferior species. Ladies and gentlemen class rebellious laborers with vermin. The Dominicans, the watchdogs of God, regarded the Albigenses as the enemies of God, just as Torquemada regarded the Jews as the murderers of God. All that is an old story: what we are confronted with now is a growing perception that if we desire a certain type of civilization and culture we must exterminate the sort of people who do not fit into it. There is a difference between the shooting at sight of aboriginal natives in the back blocks of Australia and the massacres of aristocrats in the terror which followed the foreign attacks on the French Revolution. The Australian gunman pots the aboriginal natives to satisfy his personal antipathy to a black man with uncut hair. But nobody in the French Republic had this feeling about Lavoisier,[3] nor can any German Nazi have felt that way about Einstein. Yet Lavoisier was guillotined; and Einstein has had to fly for his life from Germany. It was silly to say that the Republic had no use for chemists; and no Nazi has stultified his party to the extent of saying that the new National Socialist Fascist State in Germany has no use for mathematician-physicists. The proposition is that aristocrats (Lavoisier's class) and Jews (Einstein's race) are unfit to enjoy the privilege of living in a modern society founded on definite principles of social welfare as distinguished from the old promiscuous aggregations crudely policed by chiefs who had no notion of social criticism and no time to invent it.

## KING CHARLES'S HEAD

It was, by the way, the English Revolution which introduced the category of Malignant[4] or Man of Blood, and killed the King [Charles I] as an affirmation that even kings must not survive if they are malignant. This was much

3. Brilliant French chemist, founder of modern chemistry, whose principal work was *Traité élémentaire de chimie* (1789). His titular membership in the *Ferme Générale* having created suspicions in the Convention, he was tried, condemned and executed in a single day, by the revolutionary tribunal.
4. A Hebraic term, meaning one laden with bloodguiltiness. The *OED* classifies this as a special usage applied between 1641 and 1660 by supporters of the Parliament and the Commonwealth to their adversaries the Royalists or Cavaliers, who supported Charles I.

more advanced than the execution in the following century of Louis XVI as an ordinary traitor, or of the Tsar in our own time to prevent his being captured by the Tchekoslovakian contingent and used as a standard to rally the royalist reaction. Charles affirmed a divine personal right to govern as against the parliament and would keep no bargain with it. Parliament denied his right, and set up against it a divine right of election winners to govern. They fought it out; and the victorious election winners exterminated the king, very logically. Finding that their authority still needed a royal disguise they drove a hard bargain for a crown with his son [Charles II], and, after ejecting the next king [James II] who broke it, a still harder one with his Dutch grandson [William of Orange] before they allowed the title of king, with nine tenths of the meaning knocked out of it, to be used as a matter of convenience again in England. Nobody had a word to say against Charles's private character. It was solely for incompatibility of politics that he was eliminated, or "liquidated" as we say now. There was a real novelty in the transaction. The Church had for centuries before compelled the secular State to liquidate heretics; and the slaughter of rebels who tried to substitute one dynasty for another, or to seize the throne for themselves, was common routine. But Charles was neither a heretic nor a rebel. He was the assertor of a divine right to govern without winning elections; and because that right could not co-exist with the supremacy of a much richer and more powerful plutocracy off went his head.

Charles was only the first victim. After Culloden[5] the defeated Highland chiefs and their clansmen were butchered like sheep on the field. Had they been merely prisoners of war, this would have been murder. But as they were also Incompatibles with British civilization, it was only liquidation.

## Right to Exterminate conferred by Private Property

Having disposed of the divine right of kings the political liquidators turned their attention slowly to its derivatory the divine right of landlords, which had gradually disguised itself as private property in land. For when a tract of land becomes the private property of an individual who has to depend on it

5. The Battle of Culloden (near Inverness) on 16 April 1746 was the last battle of the Forty-five Rebellion, when Charles Edward the Young Pretender (Bonnie Prince Charlie) and the Jacobites were badly defeated by English forces under William, Duke of Cumberland, slaughtered by English cannonade and bayonets.

for his subsistence, the relation between him and the inhabitants of that tract becomes an economic one; and if they become economically superfluous or wasteful, he must exterminate them. This is continually happening wherever private property in land exists. If I possess land and find it profitable to grow wheat on it, I need many agricultural laborers to enable me to do it; and I tolerate their existence accordingly. If I presently find that it is more profitable to cover my land with sheep and sell their wool, I have to tolerate the existence of the sheep; but I no longer need tolerate the existence of the laborers; so I drive them off my land, which is my legal method of extermination, retaining only a few to act as shepherds. Later on I find that it is more profitable to cover my land with wild deer, and collect money from gentlemen and ladies who enjoy shooting them. I then exterminate my shepherds and keep only a few gamekeepers. But I may do much better by letting my land to industrialists for the erection of factories. They exterminate the sheep and the deer; but they need far more men than I needed even when I grew wheat. The driven-offs crowd into the factories and multiply like rabbits; and for the moment population grows instead of diminishing. But soon machines come along and make millions of proletarians economically superfluous. The factory owner accordingly sacks them, which is his legal method of extermination. During these developments the exterminated, or, as we call them, the evicted and sacked, try to avoid starvation partly by emigration, but mostly by offering themselves for all sorts of employment as soldiers, servants, prostitutes, police officers, scavengers, and operators of the immense machinery of amusement and protection for the idle rich classes created by the private property system. By organization in trade unions, municipal and parliamentary Labor Parties, and the like, and maintaining a sort of continual civil war consisting of strikes and riots, they extort from the proprietors enough to reduce the rate of extermination (shewn by the actuarial expectation of life of the unpropertied) for periods described as progressive, until the proprietors, by engaging in suicidal wars, are forced to intensify their economies, and the rate of extermination rises again.

## DISGUISES UNDER WHICH PRIVATE EXTERMINATION OPERATES

Note that during all this the Registrar General's returns do not give us the deaths of the exterminated as such, because the exterminated do not starve as lost travelers starve in the desert. Their starvation is more or less protracted; and when the final catastrophe arrives, it is disguised under an imposing array of doctors' names for moribundity. The victims die mostly in their first year, and subsequently at all ages short of the age at which properly nourished people die. Sometimes they are starved into attaining an age at which people with well filled pockets eat themselves to death. Either way and all ways the extermination is a real and permanent feature of private property civilization, though it is never mentioned as such, and ladies and gentlemen are carefully educated to be unconscious of its existence and to talk nonsense about its facts when they are too obvious or become too scandalous to be ignored, when they often advocate emigration or Birth Control or war as remedies. And against the facts there is a chronic humanitarian revolt expressing itself either underground or overground in revolutionary movements; making our political constitutions very unstable; and imposing an habitual disingenuousness on conservative statesmen.

## PRIVATE POWERS OF LIFE AND DEATH

Now the central fact of all these facts is that the private proprietors have irresponsible powers of life and death in the State. Such powers may be tolerated as long as the Government is in effect a committee of private proprietors; yet if such a committee be widened into or superseded by a Government acting in the interest of the whole people, that Government will not suffer any private class to hold the lives of the citizens at its mercy and thereby become their real masters. A popular Government, before it fully grasps the situation, usually begins by attempting to redistribute property in such a manner as to make everyone a petty proprietor, as in the French Revolution. But when the impossibility of doing this (except in the special case of agricultural land) becomes apparent, and the question is probed to the bottom by unpropertied political philosophers like Proudhon and Marx, private property is sooner or later excommunicated and abolished; and what was formerly called "real property" is replaced by ordinary personal property and common property administrated by the State.

All modern progressive and revolutionary movements are at bottom attacks on private property. A Chancellor of the Exchequer apologizing for an increase in the surtax, a Fascist dictator organizing a Corporate State, a Soviet Commissar ejecting a kulak and adding his acres to a collective farm, are all running the same race, though all of them except the Commissar may be extremely reluctant to win it. For in the long run the power to exterminate is too grave to be left in any hands but those of a thoroughly Communist Government responsible to the whole community. The landlord with his writ of ejectment and the employer with his sack, must finally go the way of the nobleman with his sword and his benefit of clergy, and of Hannibal Chollop[6] with his bowie knife and pistol.

Let us then assume that private property, already maimed by factory legislation, surtax, and a good deal of petty persecution in England, and in Russia tolerated only provisionally as a disgraceful necessity pending its complete extirpation, is finally discarded by civilized communities, and the duty of maintaining it at all costs replaced by the duty of giving effect to the dogma that every ablebodied and ableminded and ablesouled person has an absolute right to an equal share in the national dividend. Would the practice of extermination thereupon disappear? I suggest that, on the contrary, it might continue much more openly and intelligently and scientifically than at present, because the humanitarian revolt against it would probably become a humanitarian support of it; and there would be an end of the hypocrisy, the venal special pleading, and the concealment or ignoring of facts which are imposed on us at present because extermination for the benefit of a handful of private persons against the interests of the race is permitted and practised. The old doctrine of the sacredness of human life, which in our idiot asylums at Darenth [in north-west Kent] and elsewhere still terrifies us into wasting the lives of capable people in preserving the lives of monsters, was a crude expedient for beginning civilization. At present we discard it in dealing with murderers, heretics, traitors, and (in Scotland) vitriol throwers, who can be legally killed. A runaway convict can also be summarily shot by a warder to save the trouble of pursuing and recapturing him; and although the convict is not under capital sentence and the case is therefore clearly one of wilful murder, coroners' juries persist in treating it as a harmless and necessary incident in prison routine.

Unfortunately the whole question is bedeviled by our anti-Christian vice of punishment, expiation, sacrifice, and all the cognate tribal superstitions which are hammered into us in our childhood by barbarous scripturists, irascible or sadist parents, and a hideous criminal code. When the horrors of anarchy force us to set up laws that forbid us to fight and torture oneanother for sport, we still snatch at every excuse for declaring individuals outside the protection of law and torturing them to our hearts content.

6. 'Major' Chollop, in Dickens's *Martin Chuzzlewit*, a bully and bigot advocating lynch law and slavery, is described by his fellow Americans as 'a splendid sample of our native raw material'.

## CRUELTY'S EXCUSES

There have been summits of civilization at which heretics like Socrates, who was killed because he was wiser than his neighbors, have not been tortured, but ordered to kill themselves in the most painless manner known to their judges. But from that summit there was a speedy relapse into our present savagery. For Wallace, whom the Scots adored as a patriot and the English executed as a traitor, the most cruel and obscene method of killing that the human imagination could conceive at its vilest was specially invented to punish him for being a traitor (or "larn him to be a toad");[7] and this sentence has been passed, though not carried out, within the memory of persons now living. John of Leyden, for being a Communist, was tortured so frightfully before being hung up in a cage on the church tower to starve to death in sight of all the citizens and their little children, that the bishop who was officially obliged to witness it died of horror [see vol. 2, p. 158 fn 1]. Joan of Arc, for wearing men's clothes and being a Protestant and a witch, was burnt alive, after a proposal to torture her had been barely defeated. The people who saw her burnt were quite accustomed to such spectacles, and regarded them as holiday attractions. A woman's sex was made an excuse for burning her instead of more mercifully hanging her. Male criminals were broken on the wheel: that is, battered to death with iron bars, until well into the XIX century. This was a public spectacle; and the prolongation of the victim's suffering was so elaborately studied and arranged that Cartouche,[8] one of the kings of scoundrelism, was bribed to betray his accomplices by the promise that he should be killed by the sixth blow of the bar. The wheel and the stake have lately gone out of use; but the Sadist mania for flogging seems ineradicable; for after a partially successful attempt to discard it in Victorian times it has revived again with redoubled ferocity: quite recently a criminal was sentenced to a flogging and ten years penal servitude; and although the victim escaped his punishment and gave a sensational advertisement to its

7. Sir William Wallace, Scottish patriot who led insurgent Scots against the English, was hanged, drawn and quartered in 1305. To 'larn him to be a toad' was English dialect meaning to teach one through punishment the price for being a loathsome villain or enemy. Later, however, it was used merely to suggest a whipping for toadyism or minor crime.
8. Assumed name of Louis Bourguignon, French leader of a band of thieves, who was broken on the wheel (1721).

savagery by committing suicide,[9] nobody protested, though thirty years ago there would have been a strenuous outcry against it, raised by the old Humanitarian League, and voiced in Parliament by the Irish Nationalists. Alas! the first thing the Irish did when they at last enjoyed self-government was to get rid of these sentimental Nationalists and put flogging on their statute book in a series of Coercion Acts that would have horrified Dublin Castle. In a really civilized state flogging would cease because it would be impossible to induce any decent citizen to flog another. Among us a perfectly respectable official will do it for half a crown, and probably enjoy the job.

## LEADING CASE OF JESUS CHRIST

I dislike cruelty, even cruelty to other people, and should therefore like to see all cruel people exterminated. But I should recoil with horror from a proposal to punish them. Let me illustrate my attitude by a very famous, indeed far too famous, example of the popular conception of criminal law as a means of delivering up victims to the normal popular lust for cruelty which has been mortified by the restraint imposed on it by civilization. Take the case of the extermination of Jesus Christ. No doubt there was a strong case for it. Jesus was from the point of view of the High Priest a heretic and an impostor. From the point of view of the merchants he was a rioter and a Communist. From the Roman Imperialist point of view he was a traitor. From the commonsense point of view he was a dangerous madman. From the snobbish point of view, always a very influential one, he was a penniless vagrant. From the police point of view he was an obstructor of thoroughfares, a beggar, an associate of prostitutes, an apologist of sinners, and a disparager of judges; and his daily companions were tramps whom he had seduced into vagabondage from their regular trades. From the point of view of the pious he was a Sabbath breaker, a denier of the efficacy of circumcision and the advocate of a strange rite of baptism, a gluttonous man and a winebibber. He was abhorrent to the medical profession as an unqualified practitioner who healed people by quackery and charged nothing for the treatment. He was not anti-Christ: nobody had heard of such a power of darkness then; but he was startlingly anti-Moses. He was against the priests, against the judiciary,

9. James Spiers, an habitual criminal, committed suicide in Wandsworth Prison on 3 February 1930 after being sentenced to ten years' imprisonment plus fifteen strokes of the cat-o'-nine-tails for assault with intent to rob.

against the military, against the city (he declared that it was impossible for a rich man to enter the kingdom of heaven), against all the interests, classes, principalities and powers, inviting everybody to abandon all these and follow him. By every argument, legal, political, religious, customary, and polite, he was the most complete enemy of the society of his time ever brought to the bar. He was guilty on every count of the indictment, and on many more that his accusers had not the wit to frame. If he was innocent then the whole world was guilty. To acquit him was to throw over civilization and all its institutions. History has borne out the case against him; for no State has ever constituted itself on his principles or made it possible to live according to his commandments: those States who have taken his name have taken it as an alias to enable them to persecute his followers more plausibly.

It is not surprising that under these circumstances, and in the absence of any defence, the Jerusalem community and the Roman government decided to exterminate Jesus. They had just as much right to do so as to exterminate the two thieves who perished with him. But there was neither right nor reason in torturing him. He was entitled to the painless death of Socrates. We may charitably suppose that if the death could have been arranged privately between Pilate and Caiaphas Jesus would have been dispatched as quickly and suddenly as John the Baptist. But the mob wanted the horrible fun of seeing somebody crucified: an abominably cruel method of execution. Pilate only made matters worse by trying to appease them by having Jesus flogged. The soldiers, too, had to have their bit of sport, to crown him with thorns and, when they buffeted him, challenge him ironically to guess which of them had struck the blow.

## "CROSSTIANITY"[10]

All this was cruelty for its own sake, for the pleasure of it. And the fun did not stop there. Such was and is the attraction of these atrocities that the spectacle of them has been reproduced in pictures and waxworks and exhibited in churches ever since as an aid to piety. The chief instrument of torture is the subject of a special Adoration. Little models of it in gold and ivory are worn as personal ornaments; and big reproductions in wood and marble are set up in sacred places and on graves. Contrasting the case with that of Socrates, one is forced to the conclusion that if Jesus had been humanely exterminated his memory would have lost ninetynine per cent of its attraction

10. See vol. 1, p. 249.

for posterity. Those who were specially susceptible to his morbid attraction were not satisfied with symbolic crosses which hurt nobody. They soon got busy with "acts of faith" which consisted of great public shows at which Jews and Protestants or Catholics, and anyone else who could be caught out on a point of doctrine, were burnt alive. Cruelty is so infectious that the very compassion it rouses is infuriated to take revenge by still viler cruelties.

The tragedy of this—or, if you will, the comedy—is that it was his clearness of vision on this very point that set Jesus so high above his persecutors. He taught that two blacks do not make a white; that evil should not be countered by worse evil but by good; that revenge and punishment only duplicate wrong; that we should conceive God, not as an irascible and vindictive tyrant but as an affectionate father. No doubt many private amiabilities have been inspired by this teaching; but politically it has received no more quarter than Pilate gave it. To all Governments it has remained paradoxical and impracticable. A typical acknowledgment of it was the hanging of a crucifix above the seat of the judge who was sentencing evildoers to be broken on the wheel.

## CHRISTIANITY AND THE SIXTH COMMANDMENT

Now it is not enough to satirize this. We must examine why it occurred. It is not enough to protest that evildoers must not be paid in their own coin by treating them as cruelly as they have treated others. We still have to stop the mischief they do. What is to be done with them? It is easy to suggest that they should be reformed by gentleness and shamed by non-resistance. By all means, if they respond to that treatment. But if gentleness fails to reform them and non-resistance encourages them to further aggression, what then? A month spent in a Tolstoyan community[11] will convince anybody of the soundness of the nearest police inspector's belief that every normal human group contains not only a percentage of saints but also a percentage of irreclaimable scoundrels and good-for-noughts who will wreck any community unless they are expensively restrained or cheaply exterminated. Our Mosaic system of vindictive punishment, politely called "retributory" by Prison Commissioners, disposes of them temporarily; but it wastes the lives of honest citizens in guarding them; sets a horrible example of cruelty and malicious

11. Tolstoy's disciples, in his lifetime but not with his approval, organized colonies in which they attempted to live communally according to Tolstoy's religious and social precepts.

injury; costs a good deal of money that might be better spent; and, after all, sooner or later lets the scoundrel loose again to recommence his depredations. It would be much more sensible and less cruel to treat him as we treat mad dogs or adders, without malice or cruelty, and without reference to catalogues of particular crimes. The notion that persons should be safe from extermination as long as they do not commit wilful murder, or levy war against the Crown, or kidnap, or throw vitriol, is not only to limit social responsibility unnecessarily, and to privilege the large range of intolerable misconduct that lies outside them, but to divert attention from the essential justification for extermination, which is always incorrigible social incompatibility and nothing else.

### THE RUSSIAN EXPERIMENT

The only country which has yet awakened to this extension of social responsibility is Russia. When the Soviet Government undertook to change over from Capitalism to Communism it found itself without any instruments for the maintenance of order except a list of crimes and punishments administered through a ritual of criminal law. And in the list of crimes the very worst offences against Communist society had no place: on the contrary they were highly honored and rewarded. As our English doggerel runs, the courts could punish a man for stealing the goose from off the common, but not the man who stole the common from the goose [eighteenth-century epigram, authorship unknown]. The idler, that common enemy of mankind who robs everybody all the time, though he is so carefully protected from having his own pocket picked, incurred no penalty, and had actually passed the most severe laws against any interference with his idling. It was the business of the Soviet to make all business public business and all persons public servants; but the view of the ordinary Russian citizen was that a post in a public service was an exceptional stroke of good luck for the holder because it was a sinecure carrying with it the privilege of treating the public insolently and extorting bribes from it. For example, when the Russian railways were communized, some of the local stationmasters interpreted the change as meaning that they might now be as lazy and careless as they pleased, wheras in fact it was of life-or-death importance that they should redouble their activity and strain every nerve to make the service efficient. The unfortunate Commissar who was Minister of Transport found himself obliged to put a pistol in his pocket and with his own hand shoot stationmasters who had thrown his telegrams into the dustbin instead of attending to them, so that he might the more impressively ask the rest of the staff whether they yet grasped the fact that orders are meant to be executed.[12]

## INADEQUACY OF PENAL CODES

Now being Minister of Transport, or Minister of any other public service, is a whole time job: it cannot be permanently combined with that of amateur executioner, carrying with it the reputation in all the capitalist papers of the west of being a ferocious and coldblooded murderer. And no conceivable extension of the criminal code nor of the service disciplines, with their lists of specific offences and specific penalties, could have provided for instant exemplary exterminations of this kind, any more than for the growing urgency of how to dispose of people who would not or could not fit themselves into the new order of things by conforming to its new morality. It would have been easy to specify certain offences and certain penalties in the old fashion: as, for instance, if you hoard money you will be shot; if you speculate in the difference in purchasing power of the rouble in Moscow and Berlin you will be shot; if you buy at the Co-operative to sell at the private trader's shop you will be shot; if you take bribes you will be shot; if you falsify farm or factory balance sheets you will be shot; if you exploit labor you will be shot; and it will be useless to plead that you have been brought up to regard these as normal business activities, and that the whole of respectable society outside Russia agrees with you. But the most elaborate code of this sort would still have left unspecified a hundred ways in which wreckers of Communism could have sidetracked it without ever having to face the essential questions: are you pulling your weight in the social boat? are you giving more trouble than you are worth? have you earned the privilege of living in a civilized community? That is why the Russians were forced to set up an Inquisition or Star Chamber, called at first the Cheka and now the Gay Pay Oo (Ogpu), to go into these questions and "liquidate" persons who could not answer them satisfactorily. The security against the abuse of this power of life and death was that the Cheka had no interest in liquidating anybody

12. Feliks Dzerzhinski was head of the Russian secret police (the Cheka) until 1921, when he was appointed commissar of transport. Shaw relished this anecdote sufficiently to relate it at least three times in print: most detailedly in chapter 1 of the extant fragment (1932) of *The Rationalization of Russia* (published in 1964); in this preface to *On the Rocks*; and in the preface to *The Simpleton of the Unexpected Isles* (see p. 235).

who could be made publicly useful, all its interests being in the opposite direction.

## LIMITED LIABILITY IN MORALS

Such a novelty is extremely terrifying to us, who are still working on a system of limited liability in morals. Our "free" British citizens can ascertain exactly what they may do and what they may not do if they are to keep out of the hands of the police. Our financiers know that they must not forge share certificates nor overstate their assets in the balance sheets they send to their shareholders. But provided they observe a few conditions of this kind they are free to enter upon a series of quite legitimate but not the less nefarious operations. For example, making a corner in wheat or copper or any other cornerable commodity and forcing up prices so as to make enormous private fortunes for themselves, or making mischief between nations through the Press to stimulate the private trade in armaments. Such limited liability no longer exists in Russia, and is not likely to exist in the future in any highly civilized state. It may be quite impossible to convict a forestaller or regrator[13] under a criminal code of having taken a single illegal step, but quite easy to convince any reasonable body of judges that he is what the people call "a wrong one." In Russia such a conviction would lead to his disappearance and the receipt by his family of a letter to say that they need not wait up for him, as he would not return home any more.* In our country he would enjoy his gains in high honor and personal security, and thank his stars that he lived in a free country and not in Communist Russia.

But as the new tribunal has been forced on Russia by pressure of circumstances and not planned and thought out at leisure, the two institutions, the Ogpu and the ordinary police administering the criminal code, work side by side, with the odd result that the surest way to escape the Ogpu is to commit an ordinary crime and take refuge in the arms of the police and the magistrate, who cannot exterminate you because capital punishment has been abolished in Russia (liquidation by the Ogpu is not punishment: it is only "weeding

* Note, however, that a sentence of extermination should never be so certain as to make it worth the delinquent's while to avoid arrest by murdering his or her pursuers. [GBS]

13. A forestaller is one who manipulates commodities in large quantities to enhance the price. Regrator is a rarely used term for one who buys for resale: what we now call a retailer.

the garden"); and the sentence of imprisonment, though it may seem severe to us in view of the cruelty of our treatment of criminals, will be carried out with comparative leniency, and probably, if the culprit behaves well, be remitted after a while. As four years imprisonment is considered enough for any reasonable sort of murder, a cornerer who finds himself in imminent danger of detection and liquidation by the Ogpu would be well advised to lose his temper and murder his mother-in-law, thereby securing a lease of life for at least four years.

Sooner or later this situation will have to be thoroughly studied and thought out to its logical conclusion in all civilized countries. The lists of crimes and penalties will obsolesce like the doctors' lists of diseases and medicines; and it will become possible to be a judge without ceasing to be a Christian. And extermination, my present subject, will become a humane science instead of the miserable mixture of piracy, cruelty, vengeance, race conceit, and superstition it now is.

## NATURAL LIMIT TO EXTERMINATION

Fortunately the more frankly and realistically it is faced the more it detaches itself from the associations with crude slaughter which now make it terrible. When Charlemagne founded the Holy Roman Empire (as far as anyone can be said to have founded it) he postulated that all its subjects must be Catholic Christians, and made an amateurish attempt to secure this condition of social stability by killing everyone who fell into his power and refused to be baptized. But he cannot ever have got very far with it, because there is one sort of bird you must not kill on any pretext whatever: namely, the goose that lays the golden eggs. In Russia the Soviet Government began by a Charlemagnesque attempt to exterminate the bourgeoisie by classing them as intelligentsia, restricting their rations, and putting their children at the foot of the over-crowded educational list. They also proscribed the kulak, the able, hard-headed, hardfisted farmer who was richer than his neighbors and liked to see them poorer than himself. Him they rudely took by the shoulders and threw destitute into the lane.[14] There were plausible reasons for this beginning of

14. In 1928 Stalin abandoned Lenin's New Economic Policy for immediate state-controlled industrialization with the first of a series of five-year plans. When the kulaks, as landowners, resisted the collectivization of their farms, they were arrested *en masse*, most of them being slaughtered or exiled to Siberia. The result was famine for millions of Russian peasants.

selection in population; for the moral outlook of the bourgeoisie and the kulaks was dangerously anti-social. But the results were disastrous. The bourgeoisie contained the professional class and the organizing business class. Without professional men and business organizers nothing could be done in the industries; and the hope that picked members of the proletariat could take up professional and organizing work on the strength of their native talent in sufficient numbers was crushingly disappointed. When the kulak was thrown out of his farm, and his farming ability paralyzed, food ran short. Very soon the kulak had to be thrown back into his farm and told to carry on until his hour had come; and a pleasant convention was established whereby all educated persons, however obviously ladies or gentlemen, who were willing to assure the authorities that their fathers had "worked on the land with their hands" were accepted as genuine proletarians, and transferred from the infamous category of intelligentsia to the honorable one of "the intellectual proletariat." Even Lenin and his colleagues, all ultra-bourgeois (otherwise they would never have so absurdly overestimated the intellectual resources of the proletariat and been so contemptuous of the pretension of their own class to be indispensable), allowed their parents to be described as hornyhanded cultivators of the soil. The pretence has now become a standing joke; but you will still come up against it if you accuse any Russian of being a lady or gentleman.

## INCOMPATIBILITY OF PEASANTRY WITH MODERN CIVILIZATION

These, however, are merely expedients of transition. The Russian proletariat is now growing its own professional and organizing class; and the ex-bourgeois is dying out, after seeing his children receive a sound Communist education and being lectured by them on his old-fashioned prejudices. And the planners of the Soviet State have no time to bother about moribund questions; for they are confronted with the new and overwhelming necessity for exterminating the peasants, who still exist in formidable numbers. The notion that a civilized State can be made out of any sort of human material is one of our old Radical delusions. As to building Communism with such trash as the Capitalist system produces it is out of the question. For a Communist Utopia we need a population of Utopians; and Utopians do not grow wild on the bushes nor are they to be picked up in the slums: they have to be cultivated very carefully and expensively. Peasants will not do; yet without the peasants the Communists could never have captured the Russian Revolution. Nominally it was the Soviets of peasants and soldiers who backed Lenin and saved Communism when all Western Europe set on him like a pack of hounds on a fox. But as all the soldiers were peasants, and all the peasants hungry for property, the military element only added to the peasants' cry of Give us land, the soldiers' cry of Give us peace. Lenin said, in effect, Take the land; and if feudally minded persons obstruct you, exterminate them; but do not burn their houses, as you will need them to live in. And it was the resultant legions of petty landed proprietors that made Lenin's position impregnable, and provided Trotsky and Stalin with the Red soldiers who defeated the counter-revolutionists of 1918. For the counter-revolution, in which we, to our eternal shame, took part (England sets the example of revolution and then attacks all other countries which presume to follow it),[15] meant bringing the old landlords back; and the peasant fought against that as the mercenaries and conscripts of the Capitalist armies would not fight in favor of it.

## A Peasant Victory is a Victory for Private Property

So far so good for Lenin; but the war against the counter-revolutionists, when it ended in victory for the peasant proprietor, was really a victory for private property, and was therefore succeeded by a fiercer struggle between the fanatically Communist Government and the fiercely individualist peasant proprietor, who wanted the produce of his plot for himself, and had no notion of pooling it with anybody, least of all with the urban proletarians who seemed like another species to him. Left to themselves the moujiks [peasants] would have reproduced Capitalist civilization at its American worst in ten years. Thus the most urgent task before the victorious Communist Government was the extermination of the moujik; and yet the moujik, being still the goose that laid the golden eggs, could not be exterminated summarily without incidentally exterminating the whole Russian nation.

15. With Lenin, in November 1917, calling for an armistice for Russia and withdrawal of Russian troops from the war, resulting in the Brest-Litovsk treaty with the Germans, it was inevitable that the distressed Allies, fearful of Germany gaining an advantage, would intervene. The British blocked the port of Murmansk and, in May 1918, landed troops there to stem the flow of Russian war supplies to Germany. At Archangel they overthrew the local Soviet and set up a provisional government of the north. In August 1918 the British and French, with a Japanese division and two United States regiments, invaded Vladivostok, to protect railway lines and to give instruction and aid to Aleksander Kolchak's counter-revolutionary White Army.

The way out of this deadlock was obvious enough, though very expensive and tedious. You can exterminate any human class not only by summary violence but by bringing up its children to be different. In the case of the Russian peasantry the father lives in a lousy kennel, at no man's call but his own, and extracts a subsistence by primitive methods from a strip of land on which a tractor could hardly turn even if he could afford such a luxury, but which is his very own. His book is a book of Nature, from which all wisdom can be gathered by those who have been taught to read it by due practice on printed books; but he has not been so practised, and for cultural purposes has to be classed as ignorant, though he knows things that university professors do not know. He is brutalized by excessive muscular labor; he is dirty; his freedom from civilized control leaves him so unprotected from the tyranny of Nature that it becomes evident to his children that the highly regulated people in the nearest collectivist farm, where thousands of acres are cultivated by dozens of tractors, and nobody can put his foot on one of the acres or his hand on one of the tractors and say "This is my own to do what I like with," are better fed and housed, nicer, and much more leisured, and consequently free, than he ever is.

## PREVENTIVE EXTERMINATION: ITS DIFFICULTIES

In short, you exterminate the peasant by bringing up his children to be scientifically mechanized farmers and to live a collegiate life in cultivated society. It sounds simple; but the process requires better planning than is always forthcoming (with local famines and revolts as the penalty); for while the grass grows the steed starves; and when education means not only schools and teachers, but giant collective farms equipped with the most advanced agricultural machinery, which means also gigantic engineering works for the production of the machinery, you may easily find that you have spent too much on these forms of capitalization and are running short of immediately consumable goods, presenting the spectacle of the nation with the highest level of general culture running short of boots and tightening its belt for lack of sufficient food.

I must not suggest that this has occurred all over Russia; for I saw no underfed people there [on a visit in July 1931]; and the children were remarkably plump. And I cannot trust the reports; for I have no sooner read in The Times a letter from Mr Kerensky assuring me that in the Ukraine the starving people are eating oneanother, than M. Herriot, the eminent French statesman, goes to Russia and insists on visiting the Ukraine so that he may have ocular proof of the alleged cannibalism, but can find no trace of it.[16] Still, between satiety and starvation mitigated by cannibalism there are many degrees of shortage; and it is no secret that the struggle of the Russian Government to provide more collective farms and more giant factories to provide agricultural machinery for them has to be carried on against a constant clamor from the workers for new boots and clothes, and more varied food and more of it: in short, less sacrifice of the present to the future. As Stalin said quaintly "They will be demanding silver watches next."[17] The constant correction of the inevitable swerves towards one extreme or the other, analogous to the control of the Bank rate by the Bank of England (only enormously more laborious), strains all the wit and industry of the Russian rulers; and occasional sideslips must be inevitable during these years when the ablest and oldest Communists are still learners.

### Temperamental Difficulties

Even when the extinction of the bourgeoisie and the kulaks and the old aristocracy is complete, and the Russian population consists of citizens educated as Communists, there will still be questions to settle which are at bottom questions as to the sort of civilization that is desirable; and this involves a decision as to the sort of people that are desirable and undesirable. Some of us, believing that a more primitive life than ours would be happier and better, advocate "a return to nature." Others dream of a much more mechanized, specialized, and complicated life. Some of us value machinery because it makes a shorter working day possible for us: others value it because it enriches us by increasing the product per hour. Some of us would like to take things

16. Aleksander Kerensky, exiled leader of the February Revolution of 1917, stated in a letter 'The State of Russia' published in *The Times* on 24 June 1933, 'The last letter that I received from the Ukraine tells me that the people are now eating the carcasses of horses, cats, and even human flesh.' A report in *The Times* on 15 September 1933, of a talk two days earlier in Lyons, by Édouard Herriot, leader of the Radical Party and former premier of France, informed readers that 'in the Ukraine, which had been reported to be suffering from a grain scarcity, [Herriot] had seen nothing but prosperity, though he was taken at his request to the reported famine areas. The fact was . . . that the Russian question had been debated with passion on both sides, and many false judgments had been formed.'
17. Shaw may be recalling an offhand statement by Stalin during a two-and-a-half hour interview with Shaw and the other members of his travelling party in the Russian leader's Kremlin office on the evening of 29 July 1931.

easy and retire at 60: others would like to work their utmost and retire at 40. Some of us will say Let us be content with £200 a year: others No: let us live at the rate of £20,000 a year and strain every faculty to earn it. Some of us want a minimum of necessary work and a maximum of liberty to think and discover and experiment in the extension of science and art, philosophy and religion, sport and exploration: others, caring for none of these things, and desiring nothing more than to be saved the trouble of thinking and to be told what to do at every turn, would prefer thoughtless and comfortable tutelage and routine, not knowing what to do with themselves when at liberty. A life filled with scientific curiosity would be hell for the people who would not cross the street to find out whether the earth is flat or round; and a person with no ear for music would strenuously object to work for the support of municipal bands, whilst people of Shakespear's tastes would agitate for the extermination of the unmusical.

### IMPORTANCE OF LAZINESS FOR FALLOWING

Some of these differences could be settled on give-and-take lines. The division of society into classes with different tastes and capacities—different natures, as folks call it—would not shake social stability provided everyone had an equal share of the national dividend. It is not true that it takes all sorts to make a world; for there are some sorts that would destroy any world very soon if they were suffered to live and have their way; but it is true that in the generations of men continuous high cultivation is not expedient: there must be fallows, or at least light croppings, between the intense cultivations; for we cannot expect the very energetic and vital Napoleon to be the son of an equally energetic father or the father of an equally vital son. Nobody has yet calculated how many lazy ancestors it takes to produce an indefatigable prodigy; but it is certain that dynasties of geniuses do not occur, and that this is the decisive objection to hereditary rulers (though not, let me hasten to add, to hereditary figure heads). There is a large field for toleration here: the clever people must suffer fools gladly, and the easygoing ones find out how to keep the energetic ones busy. There may be as good biological reasons for the existence of the workshy as of the workmad. Even one and the same person may have spells of intense activity and slackness varying from weeks to years.

196     *The Complete Prefaces: Volume 3*

### STANDARD RELIGION INDISPENSABLE

Nevertheless there will be conflicts to the death in the creation of artificial humanity. There is nothing that can be changed more completely than human nature when the job is taken in hand early enough. Such artificial products as our agricultural laborers and urban mechanics, our country gentlemen and city plutocrats, though they are from the same human stock, are so different that they cannot live together without great discomfort, and are practically not intermarriageable. It is possible to get rid of their social incompatibility by giving them all the same education and income, and ranking them all in the same class. For example, Lord Lonsdale[18] is not in the least socially incompatible with Dean Inge, though a really critical naturalist would as soon class Shetland ponies with zebras as lump these two gentlemen under the same heading. But the question remains, what is this same education to be? The training of the scholar and the sportsman may split and diverge as they adolesce; but they must start from a common training and a common morality as children. And when the state has to prescribe a uniform moral curriculum the variety of our temperaments makes it impossible to please everybody. The Quaker and the Ritualist, the Fundamentalist and the Freethinker, the Vegetarian and the flesh eater, the missionary and the cannibal, the humanitarian and the sportsman-hunter, the military terrorist and the Christian, will not agree as to the faiths and habits to be inculcated upon the children of the community in order that they may be good citizens. Each temperament will demand the extermination of the other through the schools and nurseries, and the establishment of its temperamental faith and habits as standard in these factories of future citizens. All will agree to exterminate illiteracy by compulsory reading, writing, and arithmetic: indeed they have already done so. But all will not agree on a standard religion. Yet a standard religion is indispensable, however completely it may shed the old theologies. Every attempt to banish religion from the schools proves that in this respect Nature abhors a vacuum, and that the community must make up its mind, or have its mind made up for it by its official thinkers, as to what its children are to be taught to believe and how they should be trained to behave. Compromise is ruled out by the nature of the case. What compromise is possible between myself, for instance, who believe in the religion of Creative Evolution, the economics of Socialism, and a diet from which the

18. Hugh Lowther, fifth Earl of Lonsdale, was a noted sportsman, co-editor of the Lonsdale Library of Sports.

dead bodies of men, fish, fowls, and animals are rigidly excluded, and my Fundamentalist neighbors who believe that all Evolutionists go to hell; that children languish and die without beefsteaks; and that without private property civilization must perish? We cannot exterminate oneanother at present; but the time cannot be very far off when the education authorities will have to consider which set of beliefs is the better qualification for citizenship in Utopia.

## ECLECTIC RELIGIONS

They will probably pigeon-hole both, and proceed eclectically to compile several creeds suitable to the several capacities and ages of the children. For there is clearly no sense in offering the religion of a mature and scholarly philosopher to a child of five, nor attempting to bring the cosmogonies of Dante and Aquinas, Hegel and Marx, within the comprehension of a village dunce. Nurses rule their little charges by threatening them with bogies in whose existence no nurse believes, exactly as Mahomet ruled his Arabs by promises of a paradise and threats of a hell the details of which he must have known to be his own invention even if he did believe generally in a post mortem life of rewards and punishments for conduct in this world. Therefore I do not suggest that the education authorities in Utopia will seek for absolute truth in order to inculcate it though the heavens fall. Nor do I advise a return to Queen Elizabeth's plan of 39 Articles to please everybody by alternately affirming and denying all the disputed beliefs. The likeliest outcome is an elaborate creed of useful illusions, to be discarded bit by bit as the child is promoted from standard to standard or form to form, except such of them as adults may be allowed to comfort themselves with for the sake of the docility they produce.

There would be nothing new in this: it is what our authorities do at present, except that they do it unsystematically and unconsciously, being mostly more or less duped themselves by the illusions. Unfortunately they allow the illusions to fall behind the times and become incredible, at which point they become exceedingly dangerous; for when people are brought up on creeds which they cannot believe, they are left with no creeds at all, and are apt to buy pistols and take to banditry, bag snatching and racketeering when employment fails and they find themselves short of money. It is the importance of keeping our inculcated illusions up to date that throws our higher professional classes into wild alarm when the individual liberty of thought, speech, and conscience which they think they possess (this is one of their inculcated illusions) is threatened by the dictatorships which are springing up all over the world as our pseudo-democratic parliamentary institutions reduce themselves more and more disastrously to absurdity.

## IMPORTANCE OF FREE THOUGHT

Let me try to straighten this out for them. It was very generally believed as lately as in Victorian times that religious education consisted in imparting to children certain eternal, final, and absolute truths. I, for instance, being the son of an Irish Protestant gentleman, found myself, at the dawn of my infant conscience, absolutely convinced that all Roman Catholics go to hell when they die, a conviction which involved not only a belief in the existence of hell but a whole series of implications as to the nature and character of God. Now that I am older I cannot regard this as anything more than a provisional hypothesis which, on consideration, I must definitely reject. As the more pious of my uncles would have put it, I have lost my religious faith and am in peril of damnation as an Apostate. But I do not present my creed of Creative Evolution as anything more than another provisional hypothesis. It differs from the old Dublin brimstone creed solely in its greater credibility: that is, its more exact conformity to the facts alleged by our scientific workers, who have somehow won that faith in their infallibility formerly enjoyed by our priests. No future education authority, unless it is as badly educated as our present ones, will imagine that it has any final and eternal truths to inculcate: it can only select the most useful working hypotheses and inculcate them very much as it inculcates standard behavior throughout that vast field of civilized conduct in which it does not matter in the least how people act in particular situations provided they all act in the same way, as in the rule of the road. All the provisional hypotheses may be illusions; but if they conduce to beneficial conduct they must be inculcated and acted on by Governments until better ones arrive.

## TOLERATION MOSTLY ILLUSORY

But, cry the professors, are the hypotheses never to be questioned? Is disillusion to be punished as a crime? That will always depend a good deal on circumstances. One of the best religious brains in England has said that the war of 1914–18 was foolish and unnecessary;[19] and nobody now dreams of prosecuting him; but he would not have been allowed to go through the trenches from platoon to platoon saying so just before zero hour, with or without the addition "Sirs, ye are brethren: why do ye wrong one to another?" [Acts 7: 26] I have no illusion of being free to say and write what I please. I went round the world lately[20] preaching that if Russia were thrust back from Communism into competitive Capitalism, and China developed into a predatory Capitalist State, either independently or as part of a Japanese Asiatic hegemony, all the western States would have to quintuple their armies and lie awake at nights in continual dread of hostile aeroplanes, the obvious moral being that whether we choose Communism for ourselves or not, it is our clear interest, even from the point of view of our crudest and oldest militarist diplomacy, to do everything in our power to sustain Communism in Russia and extend it in China, where at present provinces containing at the least of many conflicting estimates eighteen millions of people, have adopted it. Now I was not physically prevented from saying this, nor from writing and printing it. But in a western world suffering badly from Marxphobia, and frantically making itself worse like a shrew in a bad temper, I could not get a single newspaper to take up my point or report my utterance. When I say anything silly, or am reported as saying anything reactionary, it runs like wildfire through the Press of the whole world. When I say anything that could break the carefully inculcated popular faith in Capitalism the silence is so profound as to be almost audible. I do not complain, because I do not share the professorial illusion that there is any more freedom for disillusionists in the British Empire and the United States of North America than in Italy, Germany, and Russia. I have seen too many newspapers suppressed and editors swept away, not only in Ireland and India but in London in my time, to be taken in by Tennyson's notion that we live in a land where a man can say the thing he will.[21] There is no such country. But this is no excuse for the extravagances of censorship indulged in by jejune governments of

---

19. Dean Inge, according to his successor, the Very Revd W. R. Matthews, attacked in a weekly article in the *Evening Standard* 'the optimism of those who thought that "the war to end war" had really succeeded in doing so'. In Inge's opinion the First World War '[was] unnecessary and could have been avoided by wiser statesmanship' (*DNB*).

20. The Shaws made a world tour aboard the liner *Empress of Britain* from mid-December 1932 to mid-April 1933.

21. Second stanza of an untitled poem (1833; printed 1842) '. . . the land, where girt with friends or foes / A man may speak the thing he will'.

revolutionists, and by Churches who imagine they possess the eternal truth about everything, to say nothing of hereditary autocrats who conceive that they are so by divine right. Our papers are silent about the suppression of liberty in Imperialist Japan, though in Japan it is a crime to have "dangerous thoughts." In my native Ireland, now nominally a Free State, one of my books is on the index;[22] and I have no doubt all the rest will follow as soon as the clerical censorship discovers their existence. In Austria my chronicle play St Joan had to be altered[23] to please Catholic authorities who know much less about Catholicism than I do. In America books which can be bought anywhere in Europe are forbidden.[24] The concentration of British and American attention on the intolerances of Fascism and Communism creates an illusion that they do not exist elsewhere; but they exist everywhere, and must be met, not with ridiculous hotheaded attacks on Germany, Italy, and Russia, but by a restatement of the case for Toleration in general.

## Leading Cases: Socrates and Jesus

It is a historical misfortune that the most world-famous victims of per-secution made no valid defence. Socrates and Jesus are the most talked of in Christian countries. Socrates at his trial was in full possession of his faculties, and was allowed to say everything he had to say in his defence; but instead of defending his right to criticize he infuriated his accusers by launching at them a damning contrast between their infamous corruption and mendacity and his own upright disinterestedness and blameless record as citizen and soldier. Jesus made no defence at all. He did not regard himself as a prisoner being tried for a vulgar offence and using all his wit to escape condemnation.

22. *The Adventures of the Black Girl in Her Search for God* (1932) was banned by the Irish censors as being 'in its general tendency indecent and obscene'. John Farleigh's woodcut illustrations apparently had much to do with this.
23. Shaw has confused two Austrian productions. Though the Austrian censors delayed issuance of a licence, the play opened at the Deutsches Volkstheater, Vienna, on 24 October 1924, with no substantive alteration or major deletion required. When, however, the censors attempted to delete all of scene 4 from the play for a scheduled revival at the same theatre in 1928, Shaw angrily demurred and the pro-duction was cancelled.
24. The work Shaw apparently alluded to was James Joyce's *Ulysses*, barred from the United States for a dozen years. The ban was lifted by court decision on 6 December 1933.

He believed that he was going through a sacrificial rite in which he should be slain, after which he should rise from the dead and come again in glory to establish his kingdom on earth for ever. It does not matter to our present purpose whether this was the delusion of a madman or a hard and holy fact: in either case the question of toleration was not at issue for him; therefore he did not raise it.

## The Case of Galileo

In the epoch which Jesus inaugurated, or at least in which his name was habitually taken in vain, we have Joan of Arc and John of Leyden, Giordano Bruno and Galileo, [Michael] Servetus[25] and John Hus and the heroes of Foxe's Book of Martyrs standing out in our imagination from thousands of forgotten martyrdoms. Galileo is a favored subject with our scientists; but they miss the point because they think that the question at issue at his trial was whether the earth went round the sun or was the stationary centre round which the sun circled. Now that was not the issue. Taken by itself it was a mere question of physical fact without any moral significance, and therefore no concern of the Church. As Galileo was not burnt and certainly not abhorred, it is quite credible that both his immediate judges and the Pope believed with at least half their minds that he was right about the earth and the sun. But what they had to consider was whether the Christian religion, on which to the best of their belief not only the civilization of the world but its salvation depended, and which had accepted the Hebrew scriptures and the Greek testament as inspired revelations, could stand the shock of the discovery that many of its tales, from the tactics of Joshua in the battle of Gibeon to the Ascension, must have been written by somebody who did not know what the physical universe was really like. I am quite familiar with the pre-Galileo universe of the Bible and St Augustine. As a child I thought of the earth as being an immense ground floor with a star studded ceiling which was the floor of heaven, and a basement which was hell. That Jesus should be taken up into the clouds as the shortest way to heaven seemed as natural to me as that, at the Opera, Mephistopheles should come up from hell through a trap in the floor. But if instead of telling me that Jesus was taken up into the clouds and that the disciples saw him no more, which still makes me feel quite holy, you tell me that he went up like a balloon into the stratosphere, I do not feel holy: I laugh obstreperously. The exalting vision has suddenly

25. Spanish theologian and learned physician, imprisoned and burned as a heretic.

become a ribald joke. That is what the Church feared; and that is what has actually happened. Is it any wonder that the Pope told Galileo that he really must keep his discoveries to himself, and that Galileo consented to deny them? Possibly it was the Pope who, to console him, whispered "E pur se muove."[26]

## FIGMENT OF THE SELFREGARDING ACTION

St Joan did not claim toleration: she was so far from believing in it that she wanted to lead a crusade of extermination against the Husites, though she was burnt for sharing their heresy. That is how all the martyrs have missed the point of their defence. They all claimed to possess absolute truth as against the error of their persecutors, and would have considered it their duty to persecute for its sake if they had had the power. Real toleration: the toleration of error and falsehood, never occurred to them as a principle possible for any sane government. And so they have left us no model defence. And there is no modern treatise known to me which quite supplies this need. Stuart Mill's Essay on Liberty satisfied the XIX century, and was my own first textbook on the subject; but its conclusion that selfregarding actions should not be interfered with by the authorities carries very little weight for Socialists who perceive that in a complex modern civilization there are no purely selfregarding actions in the controversial sphere. The color of a man's braces or a woman's garters may concern the wearers alone; but people have never been burnt for wearing black underclothes instead of white; and the notion that preaching a sermon or publishing a pamphlet can be classed as a selfregarding action is manifestly absurd. All great Art and Literature is propaganda. Most certainly the heresies of Galileo were not selfregarding actions: his feat of setting the earth rolling was as startling as Joshua's feat of making the sun stand still. The Church's mistake was not in interfering with his liberty, but in imagining that the secret of the earth's motion could be kept, and fearing that religion could not stand the shock of its disclosure, or a thousand such. It was idiotic to try to adapt Nature to the Church instead of continually adapting the Church to Nature by changing its teaching on physical matters with every advance made in our knowledge of Nature. In treating the legend of Joshua's victory as a religious truth instead of insisting

26. 'But still it moves': allegedly stated by Galileo following his enforced renunciation, before the Inquisition on 22 June 1633, of the truth he had discovered, that the earth moves round the sun.

that it did not make the smallest difference to religion whether Joshua was any more real than Jack the Giant Killer, and that Galileo might play skittles with the whole solar system without moving the Eternal Throne and the Papal Chair which was its visible tangible symbol on earth a single inch, it lost a great opportunity, as it has since lost many others, leaving itself open to the reproach of stupidity in not understanding Galileo's argument, of pride in not having humility enough to admit that it had been wrong in its astronomy, and of feebleness of faith and confusion of the temporal with the spiritual as aforesaid, laying itself open to much damaging Protestant and scientific disparagement, both mostly open to precisely the same reproaches.

## INCOMPLETENESS OF THE GREAT TRIALS

No doubt Galileo missed the real point at issue as completely as Socrates or Jesus. For this we need not blame him: he was a physicist and not a politician; and to him the only questions at issue were whether the earth moved or not, and whether a ten pound cannon ball would fall twice as fast as a five pound one or only just as fast and no faster. But Socrates was by vocation and habit a solver of problems of conduct, both personal and political; and Jesus, who had spent his life in propounding the most staggering paradoxes on the same subject, not by any means always in the abstract, but as personal directions to his followers, must, if he had any sense of moral responsibility, have been challenged by his own conscience again and again as to whether he had any right to set men on a path which was likely to lead the best of them to the cross and the worst of them to the moral destruction described by St Augustine. No man could expressly admit that his word would bring not peace but a sword without having satisfied himself that he was justified in doing so. He must have been told as frequently as I have been told that he was giving pain to many worthy people; and even with the fullest allowance for the strain of impishness with which the Life Force endows those of us who are destined by it to *épater le bourgeois*, he cannot have believed that the mere satisfaction of this Punchesque *Schadenfreude* [joy over another's misfortune] could justify him in hurting anyone's feelings. What, then, would have been his defence if, at his trial, he had been his old self, defending himself as an accused man threatened with a horrible penalty, instead of a god going through an inevitable ordeal as a prelude to the establishment of his kingdom on earth?

## A MODERN PASSION PLAY IMPOSSIBLE

The question is of such importance at the present crisis, when the kingdoms are breaking up, and upstart rulers are sowing their wild oats by such grotesque persecutions that Galileo's great successor Einstein is a plundered fugitive from officially threatened extermination, that I must endeavor to dramatize the trial of Jesus as it might have proceeded had it taken place before Peter uttered his momentous exclamation "Thou art the Christ" [Matthew 16: 16]. I have been asked repeatedly to dramatize the Gospel story, mostly by admirers of my dramatization of the trial of St Joan. But the trial of a dumb prisoner, at which the judge who puts the crucial question to him remains unanswered, cannot be dramatized unless the judge is to be the hero of the play. Now Pilate, though perhaps a trifle above the average of colonial governors, is not a heroic figure. Joan tackled her judges valiantly and wittily: her trial was a drama ready made, only needing to be brought within theatrical limits of time and space to be a thrilling play. But Jesus would not defend himself. It was not that he had not a word to say for himself, nor that he was denied the opportunity of saying it. He was not only allowed but challenged to defend himself. He was an experienced public speaker, able to hold multitudes with his oratory, happy and ready in debate and repartee, full of the illustrative hypothetical cases beloved of lawyers (called parables in the Gospels), and never at a loss when plied with questions. If ever there was a full dress debate for the forensic championship to be looked forward to with excited confidence by the disciples of the challenged expert it was this trial of Christ. Yet their champion put up no fight: he went like a lamb to the slaughter, dumb. Such a spectacle is disappointing on the stage, which is the one thing that a drama must not be; and when the disappointment is followed by scourging and crucifixion it is unbearable: not even the genius of our Poet Laureate [John Masefield, in *The Trial of Jesus*, 1926], with all the magic of Canterbury Cathedral for scenery, can redeem it except for people who enjoy horror and catastrophe for their own sake and have no intellectual expectations to be disappointed.

## DIFFERENCE BETWEEN READER AND SPECTATOR

It may be asked why the incident of the trial and execution must fail on the stage, seeing that the gospel narrative is so pathetic, and so many of us have read it without disappointment. The answer is very simple: we have read it in childhood; and children go on from horror to horror breathlessly, knowing nothing of the constitutional questions at issue. Some of them remain in this condition of intellectual innocence to the end of their lives, whilst the cleverer ones seldom reconsider the impressions they have received as little children. Most Christians, I suspect, are afraid to think about it critically at all, having been taught to consider criticism blasphemous when applied to Bible stories. Besides, there are a thousand things that will pass in a well told story that will not bear being brought to actuality on the stage. The evangelists can switch off our attention from Jesus to Peter hearing the cock crow (or the bugle blow) or to Pilate chaffering with the crowd about Barabbas; but on the stage the dumb figure cannot be got rid of: it is to him that we look for a speech that will take us up to heaven, and not to the weeping of Peter and the bawling of the mob, which become unbearable interruptions instead of skilful diversions.

For my part, when I read the story over again as an adult and as a professional critic to boot, I felt the disappointment so keenly that I have been ever since in the condition of the musician who, when he had gone to bed, heard somebody play an unresolved discord, and could not go to sleep until he had risen to play the resolution on his piano. What follows is my attempt to resolve Pilate's discord. I begin with the narrative of St John, the only one of the four which represents Jesus as saying anything more than any crazy person might in the same circumstances.

PILATE. Are you the king of the Jews?

JESUS. Do you really want to know? or have those people outside put it into your head to ask me?

PILATE. Am I a Jew, that I should trouble myself about you? Your own people and their priests have brought you to me for judgment. What have you done?

JESUS. My kingdom is not of this world: if it were, my followers would have fought the police and rescued me. But that sort of thing does not happen in my kingdom.

PILATE. Then you are a king?

JESUS. You say so. I came into this world and was born a common man for no other purpose than to reveal the truth. And everyone capable of receiving the truth recognizes it in my voice.

PILATE. What is truth?

JESUS. You are the first person I have met intelligent enough to ask me that question.

PILATE. Come on! no flattery. I am a Roman, and no doubt seem exceptionally intelligent to a Jew. You Jews are always talking about truth and righteousness and justice: you feed on words when you are tired of making money, or too poor to have anything else to feed on. They want me to nail you up on a cross; but as I do not yet see what particular harm you have done I prefer to nail you down to an argument. Fine words butter no parsnips in Rome. You say your vocation is to reveal the truth. I take your word for it; but I ask you what is truth?

JESUS. It is that which a man must tell even if he be stoned or crucified for telling it. I am not offering you the truth at a price for my own profit: I am offering it freely to you for your salvation at the peril of my own life. Would I do that if I were not driven by God to do it against all the protests of my shrinking flesh?

PILATE. You Jews are a simple folk. You have found only one god. We Romans have found many; and one of them is a God of Lies. Even you Jews have to admit a Father of Lies whom you call the devil, deceiving yourselves with words as usual. But he is a very potent god, is he not? And as he delights not only in lies but in all other mischief such as stonings and crucifixions of innocent men, how am I to judge whether it is he who is driving you to sacrifice yourself for a lie, or Minerva driving you to be sacrificed for the truth? I ask you again, what is truth?

JESUS. It is what you know by your experience to be true or feel in your soul must be true.

PILATE. You mean that truth is a correspondence between word and fact. It is true that I am sitting in this chair; but I am not the truth and the chair is not the truth: we are only the facts. My perception that I am sitting here may be only a dream; therefore my perception is not the truth.

JESUS. You say well. The truth is the truth and nothing else. That is your answer.

PILATE. Aye; but how far is it discoverable? We agree that it is true that I am sitting in this chair because our senses tell us so; and two men are not likely to be dreaming the same dream at the same moment. But when I rise from my chair this truth is no longer true. Truth is of the present, not of the future. Your hopes for the future are not the truth. Even in the present your opinions are not the truth. It is true that I sit in this chair. But is it true that it is better for your people that I should sit in this chair and impose on them the peace of Rome than that they should be left to slaughter oneanother in their own native savagery, as they are now clamoring to me to slaughter you?

JESUS. There is the peace of God that is beyond our understanding; and that peace shall prevail over the peace of Rome when God's hour strikes.

PILATE. Very pretty, my friend; but the hour of the gods is now and always; and all the world knows what the peace of your Jewish God means. Have I not read it in the campaigns of Joshua? We Romans have purchased the *pax Romana* with our blood; and we prefer it as a plain understandable thing which keeps men's knives off oneanother's throats to your peace which is beyond understanding because it slaughters man, woman and child in the name of your God. But that is only our opinion. It is not yours. Therefore it is not necessarily the truth. I must act on it, because a governor must act on something: he cannot loaf round the roads and talk beautifully as you do. If you were a responsible governor instead of a poetic vagrant, you would soon discover that my choice must lie, not between truth and falsehood, neither of which I can ever ascertain, but between reasonable and well informed opinion and sentimental and ill informed impulse.

JESUS. Nevertheless, opinion is a dead thing and impulse a live thing. You cannot impose on me with your reasonable and well informed opinion. If it is your will to crucify me, I can find you a dozen reasons for doing so; and your police can supply you with a hundred facts to support the reasons. If it is your will to spare me I can find you just as many reasons for that; and my disciples will supply you with more facts than you will have time or patience to listen to. That is why your lawyers can plead as well for one side as another, and can therefore plead without dishonor for the side that pays them, like the hackney charioteer who will drive you north as readily as south for the same fare.

PILATE. You are cleverer than I thought; and you are right. There is my will; and there is the will of Cæsar to which my will must give way; and there is above Cæsar the will of the gods. But these wills are in continual conflict with oneanother; therefore they are not truth; for truth is one, and cannot conflict with itself. There are conflicting opinions and conflicting wills; but there is no truth except the momentary truth that I am sitting in this chair. Yet you tell me that you are here to bear witness to the truth! You, a vagrant, a talker, who have never had to pass a sentence nor levy a tax nor issue an edict! What have you to say that I should not have the presumption scourged out of you by my executioners?

JESUS. Scourging is not a cure for presumption, nor is it justice, though you will perhaps call it so in your report to Cæsar: it is cruelty; and that cruelty is wicked and horrible because it is the weapon with which the sons of Satan slay the sons of God is [?as] part of the eternal truth you seek.

PILATE. Leave out cruelty: all government is cruel; for nothing is so cruel as impunity. A salutary severity—

JESUS. Oh please! You must excuse me, noble Governor; but I am so made by God that official phrases make me violently sick. Salutary severity is ipecacuanha to me. I have spoken to you as one man to another, in living words. Do not be so ungrateful as to answer me in dead ones.

PILATE. In the mouth of a Roman words mean something: in the mouth of a Jew they are a cheap substitute for strong drink. If we allowed you you would fill the whole world with your scriptures and psalms and talmuds; and the history of mankind would become a tale of fine words and villainous deeds.

JESUS. Yet the word came first, before it was made flesh. The word was the beginning. The word was with God before he made us. Nay, the word was God.

PILATE. And what may all that mean, pray?

JESUS. The difference between man and Roman is but a word; but it makes all the difference. The difference between Roman and Jew is only a word.

PILATE. It is a fact.

JESUS. A fact that was first a thought; for a thought is the substance of a word. I am no mere chance pile of flesh and bone: if I were only that, I should fall into corruption and dust before your eyes. I am the embodiment of a thought of God: I am the Word made flesh: that is what holds me together standing before you in the image of God.

PILATE. That is well argued; but what is sauce for the goose is sauce for the gander; and it seems to me that if you are the Word made flesh so also am I.

JESUS. Have I not said so again and again? Have they not stoned me in the streets for saying it? Have I not sent my apostles to proclaim this great news to the Gentiles and to the very ends of the world? The Word is God. And God is within you. It was when I said this that the Jews—my own people—began picking up stones. But why should you, the Gentile, reproach me for it?

PILATE. I have not reproached you for it. I pointed it out to you.

JESUS. Forgive me. I am so accustomed to be contradicted—

PILATE. Just so. There are many sorts of words; and they are all made flesh sooner or later. Go among my soldiers and you will hear many filthy words and witness many cruel and hateful deeds that began as thoughts. I do not allow those words to be spoken in my presence. I punish those deeds as crimes. Your truth, as you call it, can be nothing but the thoughts for which you have found words which will take effect in deeds if I set you loose to scatter your words broadcast among the people. Your own people who bring you to me tell me that your thoughts are abominable and your words blasphemous. How am I to refute them? How am I to distinguish between the blasphemies of my soldiers reported to me by my centurions and your blasphemies reported to me by your High Priest?

JESUS. Woe betide you and the world if you do not distinguish!

PILATE. So you think. I am not frightened. Why do you think so?

JESUS. I do not think: I know. I have it from God.

PILATE. I have the same sort of knowledge from several gods.

JESUS. Insofar as you know the truth you have it from my God, who is your heavenly father and mine. He has many names and his nature is manifold. Call him what you will: he is still Our Father. Does a father tell his children lies?

PILATE. Yes: many lies. You have an earthly father and an earthly mother. Did they tell you what you are preaching?

JESUS. Alas! no.

PILATE. Then you are defying your father and mother. You are defying your Church. You are breaking your God's commandments, and claiming a right to do so. You are pleading for the poor, and declaring that it is easier for a camel to pass through the eye of a needle than for a rich man to enter your God's paradise. Yet you have feasted at the tables of the rich, and encouraged harlots to spend on perfume for your feet money that might have been given to the poor, thereby so disgusting your treasurer that he has betrayed you to the High Priest for a handful of silver. Well, feast as much as you please: I do not blame you for refusing to play the fakir and make yourself a walking exhibition of silly austerities; but I must draw the line at your making a riot in the temple and throwing the gold of the moneychangers to be scrambled for by your partizans. I have a law to administer. The law forbids obscenity, sedition, and blasphemy. You are accused of sedition and blasphemy. You do not deny them: you only talk about the truth, which turns out to be nothing but what you like to believe. Your blasphemy is nothing to me: the whole Jewish religion is blasphemy from beginning to end from my Roman point of view; but it means a great deal to the High Priest; and I cannot keep order in Jewry except by dealing with Jewish fools according to Jewish folly. But sedition concerns me and my office very closely; and when you undertook to supersede the Roman Empire by a kingdom in which you and not Cæsar are to occupy the throne, you were guilty of the uttermost sedition. I am loth to have you crucified; for though you are only a Jew, and a half baked young one at that, yet I perceive that you are in your Jewish way a man of quality; and it makes me uneasy to throw a man of quality to the mob, even if his quality be only a Jewish quality. For I am a patrician and therefore myself a man of quality; and hawks should not pick out hawks' eyes. I am actually condescending to parley with you at this length in the merciful hope of finding an excuse for tolerating your blasphemy and sedition. In defence you offer me nothing but an empty phrase about the truth. I am sincere in wishing to spare you; for if I do not release you I shall have to release that blackguard Barabbas, who has gone further than you and killed somebody, wheras I understand that you have only raised a Jew from the dead. So for the last time set your wits to work, and find me a sound reason for letting a seditious blasphemer go free.

JESUS. I do not ask you to set me free; nor would I accept my life at the price of Barabbas's death even if I believed that you could countermand the ordeal to which I am predestined. Yet for the satisfaction of your longing for the truth I will tell you that the answer to your demand is your own argument that neither you nor the prisoner whom you judge can prove that he is in the right; therefore you must not judge me lest you be yourself judged. Without sedition and blasphemy the world would stand still and the Kingdom of God never be a stage nearer. The Roman Empire began with a wolf suckling two human infants. If these infants had not been wiser than their fostermother your empire would be a pack of wolves. It is by children who are wiser than their fathers, subjects who are wiser than their emperors, beggars and vagrants who are wiser than their priests, that men rise from being beasts of prey to believing in me and being saved.

PILATE. What do you mean by believing in you?

JESUS. Seeing the world as I do. What else could it mean?

PILATE. And you are the Christ, the Messiah, eh?

JESUS. Were I Satan, my argument would still hold.

PILATE. And I am to spare and encourage every heretic, every rebel, every lawbreaker, every rapscallion lest he should turn out to be wiser than all the generations who made the Roman law and built up the Roman Empire on it?

JESUS. By their fruits ye shall know them. Beware how you kill a thought that is new to you. For that thought may be the foundation of the kingdom of God on earth.

PILATE. It may also be the ruin of all kingdoms, all law, and all human society. It may be the thought of the beast of prey striving to return.

JESUS. The beast of prey is not striving to return: the kingdom of God is striving to come. The empire that looks back in terror shall give way to the kingdom that looks forward with hope. Terror drives men mad: hope and faith give them divine wisdom. The men whom you fill with fear will stick at no evil and perish in their sin: the men whom I fill with faith shall inherit the earth. I say to you Cast out fear. Speak no more vain things to me about the greatness of Rome. The greatness of Rome, as you call it, is nothing but fear: fear of the past and fear of the future, fear of the poor, fear of the rich, fear of the High Priests, fear of the Jews and Greeks who are learned, fear of the Gauls and Goths and Huns who are barbarians, fear of the Carthage you destroyed to save you from your fear of it and now fear worse than ever, fear of imperial Cæsar, the idol you have yourself created, and fear of me, the penniless vagrant, buffeted and mocked, fear of everything except the rule of God: faith in nothing but blood and iron and gold. You, standing for Rome, are the universal coward: I, standing for the kingdom of God, have braved everything, lost everything, and won an eternal crown.

PILATE. You have won a crown of thorns; and you shall wear it on the cross. You are a more dangerous fellow than I thought. For your blasphemy against the god of the high priests I care nothing: you may trample their religion into hell for all I care; but you have blasphemed against Cæsar and against the Empire; and you mean it, and have the power to turn men's hearts against it as you have half turned mine. Therefore I must make an end of you whilst there is still some law left in the world.

JESUS. Law is blind without counsel. The counsel men agree with is vain: it is only the echo of their own voices. A million echoes will not help you to rule righteously. But he who does not fear you and shews you the other side is a pearl of the greatest price. Slay me and you go blind to your damnation. The greatest of God's names is Counsellor; and when your Empire is dust and your name a byword among the nations the temples of the living God shall still ring with his praise as Wonderful! Counsellor! the Everlasting Father, the Prince of Peace.

## THE SACREDNESS OF CRITICISM

And so the last word remains with Christ and Handel; and this must stand as the best defence of Tolerance until a better man than I makes a better job of it.

Put shortly and undramatically the case is that a civilization cannot progress without criticism, and must therefore, to save itself from stagnation and putrefaction, declare impunity for criticism. This means impunity not only for propositions which, however novel, seem interesting, statesmanlike, and respectable, but for propositions that shock the uncritical as obscene, seditious, blasphemous, heretical, and revolutionary. That sound Catholic institution, the Devil's Advocate, must be privileged as possibly the Herald of the World to Come. The difficulty is to distinguish between the critic and the criminal or lunatic, between liberty of precept and liberty of example. It may be vitally necessary to allow a person to advocate Nudism; but it may not be expedient to allow that person to walk along Piccadilly stark naked. Karl Marx writing the death warrant of private property in the reading room of the British Museum was sacred; but if Karl Marx had sent the rent of his villa in Maitland Park to the Chancellor of the Exchequer, and shot the landlord's agents when they came to distrain on his furniture or execute a writ of ejectment, he could hardly have escaped hanging by pleading his right to criticize. Not until the criticism changes the law can the magistrate allow the critic to give effect to it. We are so dangerously uneducated in citizenship that most of us assume that we have an unlimited right to change our conduct the moment we have changed our minds. People who have a vague notion that Socialism is a state of society in which everyone gives away everything he possesses to everybody else occasionally reproach me because I, being a Socialist, do not immediately beggar myself in this fashion. People who imagined, more specifically, that a Socialist could not consistently keep a motor car, almost succeeded in making a public question of the possession of such a vehicle by a Prime Minister who at that time professed Socialism. But even if these idiots had really understood what they were talking about, they would have been wrong in supposing that a hostile critic of the existing social order either could or should behave as if he were living in his own particular Utopia. He may, at most, be a little eccentric at the cost of being indulged as slightly cracked.

On the other hand the Government, too, has not only a right but a duty of criticism. If it is to abandon once for all its savage superstition that whoever breaks the law is fair game for the torturers, and that the wrong wrought by the evildoer can be expiated and undone by a worse wrong done to him by judges and priests: if it is to substitute the doctrine of Jesus that punishment is only a senseless attempt to make a white out of two blacks, and to abolish the monstrous list of crimes and punishments by which these superstitions have been reduced to practice for routine officials, then there must be a stupendous extension of governmental criticism; for every crime will raise the essential critical question whether the criminal is fit to live at all, and if so whether he is fit to live under more or less tutelage and discipline like a soldier, or at normal liberty under an obligation to make good the damage he has cost.

For such functions as these we shall need critics educated otherwise than our judges of today; but the same may be said of all whose public functions transcend the application of a routine.

I have no doubt that the eradication of malice, vindictiveness, and Sadist libido on these terms from the personal contacts of citizens with their rulers, far from having a reassuring effect, is likely to be rather terrifying at first, as all people with any tenderness of conscience will feel the deepest misgivings as to whether they are really worth keeping alive in a highly civilized community; but that will wear off as standards of worth get established and known by practice. In the meantime the terror will act as a sort of social conscience which is dangerously lacking at present, and which none of our model educational establishments ever dreams of inculcating.

AYOT ST LAWRENCE.
22 October 1933.

# To Introduce the Prefaces

*Published as a preface to the first collective edition of Shaw's* Prefaces, *1934*

======

Ever since the issue of my plays in a single volume in 1931 the demand for a similar collection of my prefaces has been continuous. As these prefaces, forming a series of pamphlets and essays on current political and social problems, are quite journalistic in character, and cover a period of nearly thirty years, most of them should be by this time left completely behind the march of our supposedly progressive civilization. Alas! it is so stationary, not to say stuck-in-the-mud, that the prefaces are still rather ahead of the times than behind them; and I dare say many of their new readers will conclude that I am a daring young innovator of eighteen instead of what I am in fact: a sage of seventyeight who, having long ago given up his contemporaries as hopeless, looks to future generations, brought up quite differently, to make a better job of life than our present respectables and right honorables and reverends can.

My prefaces are not the only ones of which this can be said. The contrast between the wisdom of our literature and the folly of our rulers and voters is a melancholy proof that people get nothing out of books except what they bring to them, and that even when the books explode their prejudices and rebuke their villainies they will read their own dispositions into the books in spite of the authors, and hang up their instruments of torture and their bullet-riddled banners in the very temples of Mercy and Peace. All the preachers and writers who have been anything but mouthpieces and scribes for human vulgarity are still waiting for earnest attention, though their statues and epitaphs are all over the place, and their books in every library. The cross on which Jesus was horribly executed is adopted as an emblem more widely than the eagle, the lion, the swastika, or the fasces; but anyone attempting to take the sayings of Jesus seriously would get into trouble not only with his neighbors but with the law. Thomas More lived so long ago that he might have been the grandfather of Henry Fielding's grandfather; but the name [*Utopia*] More gave to his proposals for sane and neighborly living is used only to stigmatize all such proposals as impossible. Take up Henry Fielding's Tom Jones. It is divided into several sections; and every section has an admirable preface. For all the effect they have had on the British

Constitution or the Church of England they might just as well never have been written. Fielding might have been the great-grandfather of Charles Dickens, whose books, though classed as novels and duly hampered with absurd plots which nobody ever remembers, are really extraordinarily vivid parables. All the political futility which has forced men of the calibre of Mussolini, Kemal [Atatürk],[1] and Hitler to assume dictatorship might have been saved if people had only believed what Dickens told them in Little Dorrit. And Dickens might have been Mussolini's grandfather or my father.

And so it comes about that these prefaces of mine are no more out of date than the Gospels, or Utopia, or Tom Jones, or Little Dorrit, or even the plays of Aristophanes and Euripides and the Socratian dialogues of Plato.

You may well ask me why, with such examples before me, I took the trouble to write them. I can only reply that I do not know. There was no why about it: I had to: that was all.

I hope it is not necessary for me to remind critics unversed in literary tradition that the prefaces to my plays have nothing to do with the theatre. Most of them were written long after the plays to which they are attached had been repeatedly performed. The practice of weighting volumes of plays with political and philosophical disquisitions dates back to Dryden; and I have kept it up in a simple desire to give my customers good value for their money by eking out a pennorth of play with a pound of preface. It has ended, as you see, in this volume, which is all preface and no play.

AYOT ST LAWRENCE.
4 December 1933.

---

1. Soldier and statesman, who became president of Turkey in 1919.

*[The 1934 edition of the collected prefaces contained postscripts, drafted by*
*Shaw in 1933, to nine of the prefaces. Two of these, to* Man and Superman
*and* The Dark Lady of the Sonnets, *appear in Volumes 1 and 2*
*of the present edition, appended to their original prefaces.*
*The others, omitted by a regrettable oversight, are reproduced below.]*

## Widowers' Houses

*[Omitted from vol. 1, p. 13]*

POSTSCRIPT 1933. On the question of the slums this earliest play of
mine is still up to date more than forty years after its first performance. Not
only are the overcrowded tenements and cellar dwellings as bad as ever, but
highly respectable looking houses, covering whole residential districts formerly
inhabited by single families, are now partitioned to accommodate two families,
whilst gardens and backyards are filled up with quaintly called "villages" or
"studios," the result being back-to-back dwellings much worse than the
back-to-backs of Leeds so vehemently denounced there by housing reformers,
but left unnoticed in London because the change is invisible from the street.

The population question is still treated as if it were concerned solely with
the food supply and not with the supply of space. Plans for crowding up the
overpopulated quarters still more by covering in the railways and building
on the squares are still current although there are streets and streets of little
old two-storey houselets which could be replaced by commodious and sanitary
piles of flats. It seems as if nothing adequate can be done until the poor are
taught to burn their own dwellings instead of other people's when their
housing conditions become unbearable.

## Major Barbara

*[Omitted from vol. 1, p. 277]*

POSTSCRIPT 1933. In spite of the emphasis laid both in this preface and
in the play on the fact that poverty is an infectious pestilence to be prevented
at all costs, the lazy habit still prevails of tolerating it not only as an inevitable
misfortune to be charitably patronized and relieved, but as a useful punishment
for all sorts of misconduct and inefficiency that are not expressly punishable

by law. Until we have a general vital hatred of poverty, and a determination to "liquidate" the underfed either by feeding them or killing them, we shall not tackle the poverty question seriously. Long ago I proposed to eradicate the dangerous disease of hunger among children by placing good bread on public supply like drinking water.[2] No Government nor municipality has yet taken up that very sensible proposal.

## The Doctor's Dilemma

[*Omitted from vol. 1, p. 408*]

POSTSCRIPT 1933. The condition of the medical profession is now so scandalous that unregistered practitioners obtain higher fees and are more popular with educated patients than registered ones. I have dealt with this fully in my volume entitled Doctors' Delusions; but I may mention here that my demand for lay representation on the General Medical Council at last moved the Government to impose one of their best men, Sir Edward Hilton Young,[3] on that body. But as it immediately imposed on him several other whole-time jobs, culminating in the overwhelming business of Slum Clearance, it was evident that no serious importance was attached to his appointment. Until the General Medical Council is composed of hardworking representatives of the suffering public, with doctors who live by private practice rigidly excluded except as assessors, we shall still be decimated by the vested interest of the private side of the profession in disease.

2. Shaw discussed communization of bread ('there shall be public stores of bread, sufficient to satisfy everybody, to which all may come and take what they need without question or payment') in *The Impossibilities of Anarchism*, a paper read to the Fabian Society, 16 October 1891, published as Fabian Tract No. 45. It would, he added in *The Intelligent Woman's Guide to Socialism and Capitalism*, 'be an inestimable benefit to everybody if there were no such thing in the country as a hungry child' (chapter 6).
3. Liberal (later Conservative) MP, Minister of Health in MacDonald's National Government (1931), who became first lay member, for the Crown, on the General Medical Council (1926–31).

## Getting Married

[*Omitted from vol. 1, p. 470*]

POSTSCRIPT 1933. A fashion has set in among the theatre critics of declaring that Getting Married, and by implication its preface, are obsolete[4] because all the grievances and difficulties pointed out in them have been removed by recent legislation. This is a striking example of the delusion of progress which saves us from despair. The sole change made in our marriage laws since the Married Women's Property Act[5] created serious male grievances with one hand whilst abolishing some gross female ones with the other, is that by which a wife can now obtain a divorce just as a husband can for adultery alone,[6] instead of having to prove cruelty and desertion as well. In every other respect British marriage is what it was when the play was written: that is, so monstrously unreasonable that it is sustained only by the fact that in most marriages the couples, being ignorant of the law, do not realize the risks they are running, and seldom find them out later on because the unbearably hard cases are exceptional. Meanwhile in countries where marriages can be dissolved at the demand of either party without delay or serious expense, subject only to provision for the children, so that there is no longer any excuse for illicit and dissolute relations, public opinion on questions of sexual behavior is sterner than with us; and none of the disastrous consequences of unimpeded divorce predicted by our upholders of indissoluble marriage are complained of.

4. This probably alludes to reviews of the production at the Little Theatre on 25 November 1932.
5. Two Acts, of 1870 and 1882, abrogated all rights of a husband to his wife's property, giving a wife control over her own property, separate from her husband's. These laws were superseded by the Law Reform (Married Woman) Act of 1935.
6. Under the Matrimonial Causes Act, 1923, and the Judicature (Consolidation) Act, 1925, any single act of adultery by a husband could entitle his wife to a divorce.

## The Shewing-up of Blanco Posnet

[*Omitted from vol. 1, p. 530*]

POSTSCRIPT 1933. The censorship of plays remains unaltered, though of late years it has been much more liberally and intelligently exercised. None of my plays is now on the index.

But an unofficial censorship of films has been set up to safeguard their unprecedented licence in pornographic art. As an example of its operation I may cite the case of a lady [see vol. 1, p. 138] who, when doing charitable work among the outcasts on the Thames Embankment, was appalled by the extent to which men were lured to London by visions of unlimited employment there, and girls coming on the same errand found themselves helpless in the hands of White Slave traffickers because they did not know of the existence of the bodies which exist for the protection of unescorted young women travelers. She accordingly at great expense had a film made to warn the men, and not only to make known to young women the existence of the protective and rescue agencies but to make their addresses known by exhibition on the screen.

This film [*The Night Patrol*, 1930] was immediately banned as immoral by the unofficial trade censorship. The lady, bewildered by this attack on her personal character, appealed to me. I saw the film at a private exhibition, and satisfied myself that it was useful and quite irreproachable. In the same week I visited two leading picture houses in London. In one of them the dressing quarters of a company of ballet dancers were shewn; and the attraction of this scene, which did not further the story, and was introduced solely for its own sake, consisted in the row of dancers suddenly and simultaneously turning their backs to the audience, bending down, and changing their underclothing. The other film shewed a French seaport brothel in which two sailors began by watching an undressing woman through a skylight, and then entered the brothel and did everything that could be done without incurring a police prosecution.[7]

Without mentioning these films, and in the friendliest fashion, I begged the Censor to have a look at the lady's film, as I thought its prohibition must

7. The film with the 'ballet dancers' (a Shavian archaism for the then prevalent term 'chorus girls'), attended in the week following a private viewing on 23 January 1930 of *The Night Patrol* (subsequently retitled *City of Shadows*), was the American musical *The Gold Diggers of Broadway*. The second film has not been identified.

have been a mistake. My attempt at being conciliatory was thrown away: I was informed in the stiffest and loftiest manner that the prohibition was quite deliberate and fully justified. It was then stated in the Press without contradiction that the film was banned as an incitement to vice, at which breath-bereaving lie I had to drop the matter and assure the unfortunate benefactress that she had no remedy. The effect of the censorship was to leave pornography triumphant and to suppress the address of the Rescue Society. I cannot believe that this result was intended by the gentleman who took so high a tone with me; but, if not, the incident proves my contention that even the best intentioned and most highminded censors are often more disastrous than the Laodicean or corrupt ones.

As to my licensing proposal, I have never succeeded in making any of my critics understand it or any statesman notice it. Theatre critics assume that every member of a local authority is a Holy Willy fanatically biased against the theatre, and that I propose to set up a censorship of such persons, each reading all the plays and having a veto on its performances. Meanwhile, thanks to their hysterical ignorance, the drama remains at the mercy not only of the Lord Chamberlain, but of that most dangerous of Holy Willies, the common informer.

## Three Plays by Brieux

[*Omitted from vol. 1, p. 565*]

POSTSCRIPT 1933. The war of 1914–18 broke down the obscurantism as to venereal disease which led to the disablement of so many soldiers; and since then the work of Marie Stopes in England and of Margaret Sanger in America[8] has carried the propaganda of Birth Control into broader daylight and even established clinics to inculcate and teach its practice. Also the Church of England has for the first time flinched from condemning it. But as far as the law is concerned the situation is unchanged.

8. Stopes, a controversial British scientist and author, was founder and head of the Society for Constructive Birth Control and Racial Progress. Sanger, a nurse, was militant founder of the American Birth Control Movement and organizer of the first World Population Conference, at Geneva (1927).

# A Warning from the Author

*Preface to the second edition (1934) of the* Complete Plays *(first published in 1931).*
*The preface appeared also, in relation to a subscription edition for newspaper readers,*
*in the* Daily Herald, *3 October 1934*

━━━━

This is the first time I have ever attached any condition to the perusal of my books except the simple ceremony of walking into a bookshop and paying for them. I now find myself a party to a plan by which nobody, not even a millionaire, can obtain a copy of this edition of my plays unless he or she is a regular reader of one or other of certain newspapers or periodicals which credit their readers with brains beyond the ordinary and literary tastes not entirely vulgar. On this condition you can get the book for what it costs to manufacture, or less; and except on this condition you cannot get it at all.

This is an odd state of things; but what makes it odder is that I must warn you, before you attempt to enjoy my plays, to clear out of your consciousness most resolutely everything you have ever read about me in a newspaper. Otherwise you will not enjoy them: you will read them with a sophisticated mind, and a store of beliefs concerning me which have not the slightest foundation either in prosaic fact or in poetic truth. In some unaccountable way I seem to cast a spell on journalists which makes them recklessly indifferent not only to common veracity, but to human possibility. The person they represent me to be not only does not exist but could not possibly exist.

Now it may be that a pen portrait of an imaginary monster with my name attached to it may already have taken possession of your own mind through your inevitable daily contact with the newspaper press. If so, please class it with the unicorn and the dragon, the jabberwock and the bandersnatch, as a creature perhaps amusing but certainly entirely fabulous. If you are to get any good out of me you must accept me as a quite straightforward practitioner of the art I make my living by. Inasmuch as that living depends finally on you as reader or playgoer or both, I am your very faithful servant; and I should no more dream of pulling your leg or trifling with you or insulting you than any decent shopkeeper would dream of doing that to his best customers. If I make you laugh at yourself, remember that my business as a classic writer of comedies is "to chasten morals with ridicule"; and if I sometimes make you feel like a fool, remember that I have by the same action cured your folly, just as the dentist cures your toothache by pulling out your tooth. And I never do it without giving you plenty of laughing gas.

When you once get accustomed to my habit of mind, which I was born with and cannot help, you will not find me such bad company. But please do not think you can take in the work of my long lifetime at one reading. You must make it your practice to read all my works at least twice over every year for ten years or so. That is why this edition is so substantially bound for you.

G. B. S.

# Will No Man Understand?

*A play by Henry Norman, with an epistolary preface captioned 'A Letter to the Author about This Play and All Plays from Bernard Shaw', published in 1934*

═══

My dear Norman[1]

This play is full of difficulties. Not material difficulties, of course: as far as the mechanism of the stage is concerned nothing could be slicker: many authors of a hundred successful melodramas are illiterate bunglers beside you. But as you have never had to depend on the theatre for a livelihood you have never been forced to consider, on pain of starvation, what are the things that an accomplished man of letters can do very easily, and that the theatre cannot do at all. Or, to put it in another way, what are the things that will bear being read about, but will not bear being brought to life by a company of actors.

The extreme instance is the gospel narrative of the Passion, which is deeply moving when you read it, but when you put it on the stage (except as a village ritual at Oberammergau) becomes pathologically horrible and plays the most amazing tricks with all the characters, all the sympathy being with Pilate trying to bring an arrogant madman to reason. Masefield achieved a shocking demonstration of this.

At the other extreme you have drawingroom life as it actually exists. Baring[2] can write its dialogue and describe its airs and graces to perfection. So can you. But it will not stand the limelight and the magnification of the stage. In real life it is nothing but amateur acting; and that is exactly the effect it produces in the theatre. On that scale it is impossible to have any patience with it. No matter how lifelike the chatter and tittletattle may be or how delicate the comedy of its emptiness, you are forced to make the people either unnaturally witty, like Wilde, or give them something urgent and real to feel, so that they cease to be ladies and gentlemen and become heroes and heroines and criminals and buffoons just as in melodrama.

---

1. The Rt. Hon. Sir Henry Norman, coal magnate and former journalist, was a would-be playwright.
2. Maurice Baring, poet, unsuccessful playwright, and man of letters, was a former member of the British diplomatic corps, specializing in Russian and Balkan affairs.

You will see the bearing of this on your first Act, in which the maid with the obstacle would play the three society women off the stage. All these mock raptures about oneanother's dresses and good looks are true to life and good material for a miniaturist, but not for a scenepainter. It is not that the actors are not real ladies and gentlemen: it would be quite easy to pick a cast quite up to the mark in that respect; but the better they acted, the flimsier their material would appear.

But this is a trifle compared to the difficulty you raise when the play gets going. There are women who for some inscrutable cause are irresistible when they intend to please, and who cannot themselves resist the urge to exercise this power even when, as mostly happens, they are arrant coquettes: that is, they habitually excite passions which they have no intention of gratifying. It is useless to put these women, as such, on the stage. It has been tried over and over again since Shakespear produced Antony and Cleopatra, which is always a failure because the mysterious something cannot be acted. Even when, once in a thousand times, the actress has it by nature, she cannot act it. When she tries to do so she becomes that common stage figure a vamp, who is always unsympathetic. As something evil it goes down like mother's milk. As something angelic it just ceases to exist.

And yet the very first thing you do when you get to work in your play is to ask the actress to be a sympathetic vamp. You could not have made a more impossible demand.

But you have staked your play on a quite novel and interesting way of getting over the difficulty. Your vamp, though a complete coquette according to La Rochefoucauld's definition,[3] raises the question whether coquetry is not the true art of love, and copulation the mere piggery of it. This, and her difficulty in making any man understand it, is the whole point, substance and value of the play; and for its sake I should very much like to see the play acted. It ought to be acted. But the difficulty is tremendous; and it is the sense of this that makes theatrical people try to find hackneyed reasons for funking it, such as want of action and so forth.

One scene is so false that you must rewrite it. You do that very dangerous thing (you are always doing dangerous things), putting a poet on the stage and letting him recite one of his poems. Now you are a prose writer. Your poetry comes in prose rhythms. But you know what verse is; and you have

3. Of the three principal allusions to coquetry/coquettes in La Rochefoucauld's *Maximes*, none can be construed as a 'definition'. The most significant *maxime* states: 'Coquetry is the foundation of the temperament of women, but all do not put it into practice, because in some coquetry is restrained by fear or by reason.'

an ear and can construct a verse to order as easily as you can hum a fox-trot. But the result, perfectly correct, and dealing point by point with the job it has to do with the lady, is not in the least like a poem, which never serves any personal purpose of the poet, and has the authentic and magical music that comes to you only unconsciously in your prose. Once grasp this, and realize the shock that the listener gets when the authentic music of your prose stops and is suddenly changed into a manifest fake, and you will see what a chance the scene gives you. The woman would find out the imposture at once, and let him know that when he condescended to lay a trap for her he ceased to be a poet and became a mere metrician. She could make him understand that, if he couldnt understand her subtler point.

Your man of science who has made an immortal discovery which, as far as it is defined at all, suggests that he is the victim of a hopeless passion for Marie Stopes, ought to be a frantically comic character. Men of science are, as a matter of fact, quite the most ridiculous human products of our time; and to avoid as much as possible the monotony of every man in the play falling in love with the vamp you might with advantage take this savant a little less seriously.

I must stop. I think I have covered all the essential points as regards the play's difficulties.

Always yours
G. Bernard Shaw.

25 July 1933.

# Portraits and Figures of Sigismund de Strobl

*Published as a preface to a catalogue of an exhibition at the White Allom Galleries, London, 1935*

======

When Sigismund de Strobl[1] arrived on our shores at the age of fifty from Hungary I had never heard of him nor seen any of his work, though he was in the full maturity of his powers and one of the world's foremost sculptors. He informed me that a Hungarian patron of the arts,[2] equally unknown to me, had commissioned him to make an image of my venerable head for the information of Hungarian anthropologists and the admiration of mankind at large. I was not as flattered as I should have been; for I knew nothing of the great quality of the sculptor; and my friend H. G. Wells had complained vehemently that it is impossible to move about the world without coming up against some effigy of my too familiar beard and eyebrows. I had in fact been rather overdone in caricature and photograph, in clay, marble, and paint. After Rodin and Troubetskoy, Augustus John and the other Johns (Collier and Lavery), to say nothing of Davidson and the merciless Low,[3] what could any Hungarian add but my latest wrinkles, which I had no desire whatever to advertize?

De Strobl's reply was, in effect, his own personality, which made distinguished consideration something more than a stock phrase, and a portfolio of photographs of his works. There are invitations which it is impossible to refuse; and this was clearly one of them.

The sequel was startling. I had hardly taken shape in bronze and marble when I found that every celebrity in London, from Oswald Mosley to Arthur

1. Zsigmund Kisfaludi-Strobl, Hungarian sculptor, was appointed professor of sculpture at the Budapest Academy, 1923. Shaw sat to him in 1932.
2. Emanuel Ágoston, a textile manufacturer and one of Budapest's leading industrialists and socialites.
3. Shaw sat to Rodin at the sculptor's studio near Paris for two busts in 1907. For Troubetskoy see p. 97 in the present volume. Augustus John did two portraits in 1915, commissioned by Charlotte Shaw in Ireland. John Collier made two portraits in 1926–7. John Lavery of Ireland painted a portrait in 1935. The American sculptor Jo Davidson created a bust in 1930. David Low (later knighted), for whom Shaw sat in 1923, was a noted political cartoonist for the *Evening Standard*.

Henderson, from Ian Hamilton to Lord Parmoor, from Lady Astor[4] to royalty, were sitting to the new sculptor. The vogue of Rodin in London was not greater. And, what was surprising at the moment, none of the sitters had any reason to be ashamed of their busts. Anything of delicacy or nobility they possessed—and they all had some—was seized upon by the sculptor and expressed in a genuine poetry of form that made it possible for the first time for many years for a native of these islands to contemplate his own portrait without cursing the day he had consented to sit for it. For here was classic sculpture suddenly come to life again after dying and being buried in a state of dry decomposition.

To appreciate the effect of this resurrection one must take into account the circumstances in which it occurred. Long before the shock of the war, classicism in sculpture and painting were achieving nothing but senseless nudes with Greek outlines so dead that they could not produce even an aphrodisiac effect on the pruriently overclothed Victorians. When sunbathing set in after the war their stony nothingness left them fit only for the roadmender's hammer. But the moral shock of the war went deeper than the sunbath exposure. We had found out what destructive fools we all were; and a rage for rubbing in this discovery seized on our most sensitive artists. Had they lived a few centuries ago they would have confronted us with skulls and skeletons, and with the humors of Holbein's Dance of Death.[5] But now that they are all amateur psychoanalysts and evolutionary anthropologists, their delight is to reduce us to the primeval types from which, they imply, our evolution is only a hypocritical pretence. In doing so, however, they discovered that savages have a beauty of their own; that black women in Africa can outfascinate Rossetti's Rose of Sharon,[6] and brown women in Tahiti make painters

4. Mosley: sixth baronet, Independent (later Labour) MP, founder of the British Union of Fascists in 1932. Henderson: Labour MP and trade unionist, created a life peer in 1966. Hamilton: distinguished military leader and author. Parmoor: Charles A. Cripps, first Baron Parmoor, Conservative MP, who later became Lord President of the Privy Council in Labour's 1924 and 1929–31 governments. Astor: Viscountess, American-born politician, first woman to be seated in the House of Commons, in 1919. She retired in 1945.
5. Series of woodcuts (*c.* 1523–6, published 1538), one of the most celebrated works of Hans Holbein the Younger.
6. Shaw alludes to the same work in a letter of 2 September 1928 to Hall Caine (*Collected Letters 1926–1950*, 1988). There is, however, no painting of this title recorded in Virginia Surtees's *Catalogue raisonné* of Rossetti's work, and Rossettian specialists at the Tate Gallery and at the School of Art History (East Anglia) are unable to identify it.

unfaithful for ever to the models of the Parisian ateliers. An extraordinary muddle was the result. Our artists wanted to debunk their sitters morally by shewing them what savages they were underneath their civilized prettinesses, and yet at the same time wanted to force on them something of the beauty of savages. For instance, Jacob Epstein,[7] an American sculptor, would not have classicism on any terms: he rejected Greek outlines contemptuously as quite simply English lies, and broke up the brassy surfaces of his busts in his determination to make them flesh. Mestrovich[8] decivilized his sitters until they appeared as VIII century Balkanians; yet he sought for and found beauty in that type. It was a distinction to sit for these masters; but when the results were exhibited the sensation, to English ladies and gentlemen, was like that of being tarred and feathered and ridden on a rail. The sitter could not but admire the work; but he (or she) never admitted the resemblance.

Into this Walpurgisnacht Sigismond de Strobl did not crash like a thunderbolt, which was the usual manner of new arrivals. He walked sedately in and without any apology began making extremely handsome busts of contemporary civilized persons as such. He made no attempt to relate them visibly to the missing links in their remote ancestry. He did not impose on them the crude animal vitality which they had shed: he sought rather the beauty which was the outward and visible sign of their inward and spiritual grace. The critics called him a neo-classic; but even in his academic nudes there was not a single Greek line: his lines were the living lines of his own day, composed into noble forms exactly as Phidias and Praxiteles composed the quite different living lines of their day. Each bust was not only an authentic and instantly recognizable portrait of the sitter; but something quite beyond that: a work of art. The bust of myself which is before you in this exhibition is not only recognizable as what I look like: it is also what I ought to look like, and what I should like to look like. Perhaps I shall, someday, if I contemplate it with sufficient intensity. At all events, let posterity imagine me just so, in spite of the plastic protest of my friend Epstein, who will have it that I am a thinly disguised prehistoric monster.

MALVERN.
31 August 1935.

---

7. American-born British sculptor, who created a grotesque bust of Shaw in 1934.
8. Ivan Meštrović was a Yugoslavian sculptor much exhibited in London 1914–18.

# Preface on Days of Judgment
## (The Simpleton of the Unexpected Isles)

*First published in 1936*

═══

The increasing bewilderment of my journalist critics as to why I should write such plays as The Simpleton culminated in New York in February 1935, when I was described as a dignified old monkey throwing coconuts at the public in pure senile devilment.[1] This is an amusing and graphic description of the effect I produce on the newspapers; but as a scientific criticism it is open to the matter-of-fact objection that a play is not a coconut nor I a monkey. Yet there is an analogy. A coconut is impossible without a suitable climate; and a play is impossible without a suitable civilization. If author and journalist are both placid Panglossians, convinced that their civilization is the best of all possible civilizations, and their countrymen the greatest race on earth: in short, if they have had a university education, there is no trouble: the press notices are laudatory if the play is entertaining. Even if the two are pessimists who agree with Jeremiah that the heart of man is deceitful above all things and desperately wicked [Jeremiah 17: 9], and with Shakespear that political authority only transforms its wielders into angry apes [*Measure for Measure*, II: ii], there is still no misunderstanding; for that dismal view, or a familiar acquaintance with it, is quite common.

Such perfect understanding covers much more than nine hundred and ninety cases out of every thousand new plays. But it does not cover the cases in which the author and the journalist are not writing against the same background. The simplest are those in which the journalist is ignorant and uncultivated, and the author is assuming a high degree of knowledge and culture in his audience. This occurs oftener than it should; for some newspaper editors think that any reporter who has become stagestruck by seeing half a dozen crude melodramas is thereby qualified to deal with Sophocles and Euripides, Shakespear and Goethe, Ibsen and Strindberg, Tolstoy and Tchekov, to say nothing of myself. But the case with which I am concerned

1. This was by Percy Hammond in his review in the *New York Herald Tribune*, 19 February 1935.

here is one in which a reasonably well equipped critic shoots wide because he cannot see the target nor even conceive its existence. The two parties have not the same vision of the world. This sort of vision varies enormously from individual to individual. Between the superstatesman whose vision embraces the whole politically organized world, or the astronomer whose vision of the universe transcends the range of our utmost telescopes, and the peasant who fiercely resists a main drainage scheme for his village because others as well as he will benefit by it, there are many degrees. The Abyssinian Danakil[2] kills a stranger at sight and is continually seeking for an excuse to kill a friend to acquire trophies enough to attract a wife. [David] Livingstone[3] risked his life in Africa every day to save a black man's soul. Livingstone did not say to the sun colored tribesman "There is between me and thee a gulf that nothing can fill" [Luke 16: 26]: he proposed to fill it by instructing the tribesman on the assumption that the tribesman was as capable mentally as himself, but ignorant. That is my attitude when I write prefaces. My newspaper critics may seem incapable of anything better than the trash they write; but I believe they are capable enough and only lack instruction.

I wonder how many of them have given serious thought to the curious changes that take place in the operation of human credulity and incredulity. I have pointed out on a former occasion [preface to *Saint Joan*] that there is just as much evidence for a law of the Conservation of Credulity as of the Conservation of Energy. When we refuse to believe in the miracles of religion for no better reason fundamentally than that we are no longer in the humor for them we refill our minds with the miracles of science, most of which the authors of the Bible would have refused to believe. The humans who have lost their simple childish faith in a flat earth and in Joshua's feat of stopping the sun until he had finished his battle with the Amalekites [actually the Amorites, in Joshua 10: 12–13], find no difficulty in swallowing an expanding boomerang universe. They will refuse to have their children baptized or circumcized, and insist on their being vaccinated, in the teeth of overwhelming evidence that vaccination has killed thousands of children in a quite horrible way wheras no child has ever been a penny the worse for baptism since John the Baptist recommended it. Religion is the mother of scepticism: Science is the mother of credulity. There is nothing that people will not

2. Arabic name for the nomadic Afar people, a proud, independent and fearsome race who reside in north-east Ethiopia and Djibouti (Somaliland).
3. Scottish missionary and explorer, whose writings reflect principally his interest and participation in the lives of the native people and his efforts to interfere with Arab and Portuguese slave-trading.

believe nowadays if only it be presented to them as Science, and nothing they will not disbelieve if it be presented to them as religion. I myself began like that; and I am ending by receiving every scientific statement with dour suspicion whilst giving very respectful consideration to the inspirations and revelations of the prophets and poets. For the shift of credulity from religious divination to scientific invention is very often a relapse from comparatively harmless romance to mischievous and even murderous quackery.

Some credulities have their social uses. They have been invented and imposed on us to secure certain lines of behavior as either desirable for the general good or at least convenient to our rulers. I learned this early in life. My nurse induced me to abstain from certain troublesome activities by threatening that if I indulged in them the cock would come down the chimney. This event seemed to me so apocalyptic that I never dared to provoke it nor even to ask myself in what way I should be the worse for it. Without this device my nurse could not have ruled me when her back was turned. It was the first step towards making me rule myself.

Mahomet, one of the greatest of the prophets of God, found himself in the predicament of my nurse in respect of having to rule a body of Arab chieftains whose vision was not co-extensive with his own, and who therefore could not be trusted, when his back was turned, to behave as he himself would have behaved spontaneously. He did not tell them that if they did such and such things the cock would come down the chimney. They did not know what a chimney was. But he threatened them with the most disgusting penances in a future life if they did not live according to his word, and promised them very pleasant times if they did. And as they could not understand his inspiration otherwise than as a spoken communication by a personal messenger he allowed them to believe that the angel Gabriel acted as a celestial postman between him and Allah, the fountain of all inspiration. Except in this way he could not have made them believe in anything but sacred stones and the seven deadly sins.

The Christian churches and the Christian Kings were driven to the same device; and when I evolved beyond the cock and chimney stage I found myself possessed with a firm belief that all my Roman Catholic fellow children would inevitably burn in blazing brimstone to all eternity, and even that I myself, in spite of my Protestant advantages, might come to the same endless end if I were not careful. The whole civilized world seemed to be governed that way in those days. It is so to a considerable extent still. A friend of mine lately asked a leading Irish statesman why he did not resort to a rather soulless stroke of diplomacy. Because, replied the statesman, I happen to believe that there is such a place as hell.

Anywhere else than in Ireland the obsolescence of this explanation would have been startling. For somehow there has been a shift of credulity from hell to perishing suns and the like. I am not thinking of the humanitarian revolt against everlasting brimstone voiced by the late Mrs Bradlaugh Bonner,[4] nor of Tolstoy's insistence on the damnation on earth of the undetected, unpunished, materially prosperous criminal.[5] I am leaving out of the question also the thoughtful, sentimental, honorable, conscientious people who need no hell to intimidate them into considerate social behavior, and who have naturally outgrown the devil with his barbed tail and horns just as I outgrew the cock in the chimney.

But what of the people who are capable of no restraint except that of intimidation? Must they not be either restrained or, as the Russians gently put it, liquidated? No State can afford the expense of providing policemen enough to watch them all continually; consequently the restraint must, like the fear of hell, operate when nobody is looking. Well, a shift of credulity has destroyed the old belief in hell. How then is the social work previously done by that belief to be taken up and carried on? It is easy to shirk the problem by pointing out that the belief in hell did not prevent even the most superstitious people from committing the most damnable crimes. But though we know of these failures of infernal terrorism we have no record of its successes. We know that naïve attempts to bribe divine justice led to a trade in absolutions, pardons, and indulgences which proved by the hardness of the cash the sinners put down and the cost of the cathedrals they put up that there was a continual overdrawing of salvation accounts by firm believers in the brimstone; but we do not know, and never shall know, how many crimes were refrained from that would have been committed but for the dread of damnation. All we can do is to observe and grapple with the effect of the shift of credulity which has robbed hell of its terrors.

No community, however devout, has ever trusted wholly to damnation and excommunication as deterrents. They have been supplemented by crimi-

4. Hypatia Bradlaugh, reformist daughter of the famed secularist Charles Bradlaugh, married the printer Arthur Bonner.
5. We have found no direct statement in Tolstoy that confirms Shaw's interpretation. Tolstoy does observe, in *What is Religion?* (1902), that 'the [immoral] men of our world . . . become . . . proud of their perfections, which are necessary for a physical life, and of their refined, barren reasoning. They sink in their ignorance and depravity, fully convinced that they are standing upon such a height as has never before been reached by humanity and that every forward step of theirs on the road of ignorance and depravity raises them to a greater height of enlightenment and progress.'

nal codes of the most hideous barbarity (I have been contemporary with Europeans whose amusements included seeing criminals broken on the wheel). Therefore their effect on conduct must be looked for in that very extensive part of it which has not been touched by the criminal codes, or in which the codes actually encourage anti-social action and penalize its opposite, as when the citizen is forced by taxation or compulsory military service to become an accomplice in some act of vulgar pugnacity and greed disguised as patriotism.

Unless and until we get a new column in the census papers on the point we can only guess how far the shift of credulity has actually taken place in countries like our own in which children, far from being protected against the inculcation of the belief in brimstone, are exposed to it in every possible way, and are actually, when they have been confirmed, legally subject to ruinous penalties for questioning it. It happens, however, that in one of the largest States in the world, Russia, the children are protected from proselytizing (otherwise than by the State itself) not only by the negative method called Secular Education, but by positive instruction that there is no personal life after death for the individual, the teaching being that of Ecclesiastes in our own canon "Whatsoever thy hand findeth to do, do it with thy might; for there is no work, nor device, nor knowledge, nor wisdom, in the grave whither thou goest" [Ecclesiastes 9: 10]. We may take it that no civilized Russian born within the last twenty years has any apprehension of having to suffer after death for sins committed before it. At the same time the list of activities blacklisted by the Russian State as felonious has been startlingly extended; for the Russian Government has turned the country's economic morals downside up by breaking away from our Capitalist Utopia and adopting instead the views of the Bolshevist prophets whose invectives and warnings fill the last books of the Old Testament, and the Communist principles of Jesus, Peter, and Paul. Not that the Soviet Republic allows the smallest authority to Jesus or Peter, Jeremiah or Micah the Morasthite. They call their economic system, not Bolshevik Christianity, but Scientific Socialism. But as their conclusions are the same, they have placed every Russian under a legal obligation to earn his own living, and made it a capital crime on his part to compel anyone else to do it for him. Now outside Russia the height of honor and success is to be a gentleman or lady, which means that your living is earned for you by other people (mostly untouchables), and that, far from being under an obligation to work, you are so disgraced by the mere suggestion of it that you dare not be seen carrying a parcel along a fashionable thoroughfare. Nobody has ever seen a lady or gentleman carrying a jug of milk down Bond Street or the *rue de la Paix*. A white person doing such a thing in Capetown would be socially ruined. The physical activities called Sport, which are needed to keep the gentry in health, must be unpaid and unproductive: if payment is accepted for such activities the payee loses caste and is no longer called Mister. Labor is held to be a cross and a disgrace; and the lowest rank known is that of laborer. The object of everyone's ambition is an unearned income; and hundreds of millions of the country's income are lavished annually on ladies and gentlemen whilst laborers are underfed, ill clothed, and sleeping two or three in a bed and ten in a room.

Eighteen years ago this anti-labor creed of ours was the established religion of the whole civilized world. Then suddenly, in one seventh of that world, it was declared a damnable heresy, and had to be rooted out like any other damnable heresy. But as the heretics were carefully taught at the same time that there is no such thing as damnation, how were they to be dealt with? The well-to-do British Liberal, clamoring for freedom of conscience, objects to heretics being restrained in any way: his panacea for that sort of difficulty is Toleration. He thinks that Quakers and Ritualists should tolerate one-another; and this solution works quite well because it does not now matter a penny to the State or the individual whether a citizen belongs to one persuasion or the other. But it was not always so. George Fox, the heroic founder of the Quakers, could not hear a church bell without dashing into the church and upsetting the service by denouncing the whole business of ritual religion as idolatrous. The bell, he said, "struck on his heart." Consequently it was not possible for the Churches to tolerate George Fox, though both Cromwell and Charles II liked the man and admired him.

Now the heretic in Russia is like Fox. He is not content with a quiet abstract dissent from the State religion of Soviet Russia: he is an active, violent, venomous saboteur. He plans and carries out breakages of machinery, falsifies books and accounts to produce insolvencies, leaves the fields unsown or the harvests to rot unreaped, and slaughters farm stock in millions even at the cost of being half starved (sometimes wholly starved) by the resultant "famine" in his fanatical hatred of a system which makes it impossible for him to become a gentleman. Toleration is impossible: the heretic–saboteur will not tolerate the State religion; consequently the State could not tolerate him even if it wanted to.

This situation, though new to our generation of Liberal plutocrats, is not new historically. The change from paganism and Judaism to Christianity, from the worship of consecrated stones to an exalted monotheism under Mahomet, and from world catholicism to national individualism at the Reformation, all led to the persecution and virtual outlawry of the heretics who would not accept the change. The original official Roman Catholic

Church, which had perhaps the toughest job, was compelled to develop a new judicial organ, called the Inquisition or Holy Office, to deal with heresy; and though in all the countries in which the Reformation triumphed the Inquisition became so unpopular that its name was carefully avoided when similar organs were developed by the Protestant and later on by the Secularist governments, yet the Holy Office cropped up again under all sorts of disguises. Protestant England would never have tolerated the Star Chamber if it had called itself an Inquisition and given Laud the official title [inquisitor-general] borne by Torquemada. In the end all the specific Inquisitions petered out, not in the least through a growth of real tolerance, but because, as the world settled down into the new faiths, and the heretics stopped sabotaging and slaughtering, it was found that the ordinary courts could do all the necessary persecution, such as transporting laborers for reading the works of Thomas Paine, or imprisoning poor men for making sceptical jokes about the parthenogenesis of Jesus.

Thus the Inquisition came to be remembered in England only as an obsolete abomination which classed respectable Protestants with Jews, and burned both. Conceive, then, our horror when the Inquisition suddenly rose up again in Russia. It began as the Tcheka; then it became the Gay-pay-oo (Ogpu); now it has settled down as part of the ordinary police force. The worst of its work is over: the heretics are either liquidated, converted, or intimidated. But it was indispensable in its prime. The Bolsheviks, infected as they were with English Liberal and Agnostic notions, at first tried to do without it; but the result was that the unfortunate Commissars who had to make the Russian industries and transport services work, found themselves obliged to carry pistols and execute saboteurs and lazy drunkards with their own hands. Such a Commissar was Djerjinsky, now, like Lenin, entombed in the Red Square. He was not a homicidally disposed person; but when it fell to his lot to make the Russian trains run at all costs, he had to force himself to shoot a station master who found it easier to drop telegrams into the wastepaper basket than to attend to them. And it was this gentle Djerjinsky who, unable to endure the duties of an executioner (even had he had time for them), organized the Tcheka.

Now the Tcheka, being an Inquisition and not an ordinary police court dealing under written statutes and established precedents with defined offences, and sentencing the offenders to prescribed penalties, had to determine whether certain people were public spirited enough to live in a Communist society, and, if not, to blow their brains out as public nuisances. If you would not work and pull your weight in the Russian boat, then the Tcheka had to make you do it by convincing you that you would be shot if you persisted in your determination to be a gentleman. For the national emergencies were then desperate; and the compulsion to overcome them had to be fiercely in earnest.

I, an old Irishman, am too used to Coercion Acts, suspensions of the Habeas Corpus Act, and the like, to have any virtuous indignation left to spare for the blunders and excesses into which the original Tcheka, as a body of well-intentioned amateurs, no doubt fell before it had learnt the limits of its business by experience. My object in citing it is to draw attention to the legal novelty and importance of its criterion of human worth. I am careful to say legal novelty because of course the criterion must have been used in the world long before St Paul commanded that "if any would not work, neither should he eat" [II Thessalonians 3: 10]. But our courts have never taken that Communist view: they have always upheld unconditional property, private property, real property, do-what-you-like-with-your-own property, which, when it is insanely extended to the common earth of the country, means the power to make landless people earn the proprietors' livings for them. Such property places the social value of the proprietor beyond question. The propertyless man may be challenged as a rogue and a vagabond to justify himself by doing some honest work; but if he earns a gentleman's living for him he is at once vindicated and patted on the back. Under such conditions we have lost the power of conceiving ourselves as responsible to society for producing a full equivalent of what we consume, and indeed more. On the contrary, every inducement to shirk that primary duty is continually before us. We are taught to think of an Inquisition as a tribunal which has to decide whether we accept the divinity of Christ or are Jews, whether we believe in transubstantiation or merely in the Supper, whether we are prelatists or Presbyterians, whether we accept the authority of the Church or the conclusions of our private judgments as the interpreters of God's will, whether we believe in a triune godhead or a single one, whether we accept the 39 Articles or the Westminster Confession, and so on. Such were the tests of fitness to live accepted by the old Inquisitions. The public never dreams of an economic test except in the form of a Means Test[6] to baffle the attempts of the very poor to become sinecurists like ladies and gentlemen.

My own acquaintance with such a possibility began early in life and shocked

6. A stringent means test for collection of unemployment insurance was first imposed by the Government in 1922, with applicants further required to demonstrate to local employment committees that they were genuinely seeking work. This led to three million people being refused benefits between 1921 and 1930 (Martin Pugh, *State and Society: British Political and Social History, 1870–1992*, 1994).

me somewhat. My maternal grandfather [W. B. Gurly], a country gentleman who was an accomplished sportsman, was out shooting one day. His dog, growing old, made a mistake: its first. He instantly shot it. I learnt that he always shot his sporting dogs when they were past their work. Later on I heard of African tribes doing the same with their grandparents. When I took seriously to economic studies before electric traction had begun I found that tramway companies had found that the most profitable way of exploiting horses was to work them to death in four years. Planters in certain districts had found the like profitable term for slaves to be eight years. In fully civilized life there was no provision except a savagely penal Poor Law for workers[7] thrown out of our industrial establishments as "too old at forty."

As I happen to be one of those troublesome people who are not convinced that whatever is is right [Pope, *Essay on Man*, Epistle 1: 293] these things set me thinking. My thoughts would now be attributed to Bolshevik propaganda; and pains would be taken by our rulers to stop the propaganda under the impression that this would stop the thoughts; but there was no Bolshevik propaganda in those days; and I can assure the Foreign Office that the landed gentry in the person of my grandfather, the tramway companies, and the capitalist planters, made the question of whether individual dogs and men are worth their salt familiar to me a whole generation before the Tcheka ever existed.

It still seems to me a very pertinent question, as I have to pay away about half my earnings in tribute to the lady-and-gentleman business in order to get permission to live on this earth; and I consider it money very ill spent. For if the people who live on my earnings were changed by some Arabian Nights magician into dogs, and handed over to the sporting successors of my grandfather, they would be shot; and if they were changed into horses or slaves they would be worn out by overwork before their natural time. They are now worn out by underwork.

7. The Poor Law Act of 1834, which treated poverty as a crime, had as its principal purpose the stimulation of free trade in labour, by driving workers into the labour market through operations in workhouses that made labour, however poorly paid, a preferable alternative. As a concerned lawyer, Robert Pashley, observed in 1852: '[A] single English workhouse contains more that justly calls for condemnation in the principle on which it is established than is found in the very worst prisons or public lunatic asylums that I have ever seen. The workhouse as now organized is a reproach and disgrace peculiar to England: nothing corresponding to it is to be found throughout the whole Continent of Europe' (*Encyclopaedia Britannica*, fifteenth edition).

Nevertheless I do not plead a personal grievance, because though I still amuse myself with professional pursuits and make money by them, I also have acquired the position of a gentleman, and live very comfortably on other people's earnings to an extent which more than compensates me for the depredations of which I am myself the victim. Now my grandfather's dog had no such satisfaction. Neither had the tramway horses nor the slaves, nor have the discarded "too old at forty." In their case there was no proper account keeping. In the nature of things a human creature must incur a considerable debt for its nurture and education (if it gets any) before it becomes productive. And as it can produce under modern conditions much more than it need consume it ought to be possible for it to pay off its debt and provide for its old age in addition to supporting itself during its active period. Of course if you assume that it is no use to itself and is there solely to support ladies and gentlemen, you need not bother about this: you can just leave it to starve when it ceases to be useful to its superiors. But if, discarding this view, you assume that a human creature is created for its own use and should have matters arranged so that it shall live as long as it can, then you will have to go into people's accounts and make them all pay their way. We need no Bolshevik propaganda to lead us to this obvious conclusion; but it makes the special inquisitionary work of the Tcheka intelligible. For the Tcheka was simply carrying out the executive work of a constitution which had abolished the lady and gentleman exactly as the Inquisition carried out the executive work of a catholic constitution which had abolished Jupiter and Diana and Venus and Apollo.

Simple enough; and yet so hard to get into our genteel heads that in making a play about it I have had to detach it altogether from the great Russian change, or any of the actual political changes which threaten to raise it in the National-Socialist and Fascist countries, and to go back to the old vision of a day of reckoning by divine justice for all mankind.

Now the ordinary vision of this event is almost pure bugaboo: we see it as a colossal Old Bailey trial, with the good people helped up into heaven and the bad ones cast headlong into hell; but as to what code of law will govern the judgment and classify the judged as sheep or goats as the case may be, we have not troubled to ask. We are clear about Judas Iscariot going to hell and Florence Nightingale to heaven; but we are not so sure about Brutus and Cromwell. Our general knowledge of mankind, if we dare bring it into play, would tell us that an immense majority of the prisoners at the bar will be neither saints nor scoundrels, but borderland cases of extreme psychological complexity. It is easy to say that to divine justice nothing is impossible; but the more divine the justice the more difficult it is to conceive how it could deal with every case as one for heaven or hell. But we think we need not bother about it; for the whole affair is thought of as a grand finish to the human race and all its problems, leaving the survivors in a condition of changeless unprogressive bliss or torment for the rest of eternity.

To me this vision is childish; but I must take people's minds as I find them and build on them as best I can. It is no use my telling them that their vision of judgment is a silly superstition, and that there never will be anything of the kind. The only conclusion the pious will draw is that I, at all events, will go to hell. As to the indifferent and the sceptical, I may do them the mischief against which Jesus vainly warned our missionaries. I may root out of their minds the very desirable conception that they are all responsible to divine justice for the use they make of their lives, and put nothing in its place except a noxious conceit in their emancipation and an exultant impulse to abuse it. The substitution of irresponsibility for responsibility may present itself as an advance; but it is in fact a retreat which may leave its victim much less eligible as a member of a civilized community than the crudest Fundamentalist. A prudent banker would lend money on personal security to Bunyan rather than to Casanova. Certainly I should if I were a banker.

Who shall say, then, that an up-to-date Vision of Judgment is not an interesting subject for a play, especially as events in Russia and elsewhere are making it urgently desirable that believers in the Apocalypse should think out their belief a little? In a living society every day is a day of judgment; and its recognition as such is not the end of all things but the beginning of a real civilization. Hence the fable of The Simpleton of the Unexpected Isles. In it I still retain the ancient fancy that the race will be brought to judgment by a supernatural being, coming literally out of the blue; but his inquiry is not whether you believe in Tweedledum or Tweedledee but whether you are a social asset or a social nuisance. And the penalty is liquidation. He has appeared on the stage before in the person of Ibsen's button moulder. And as history always follows the stage, the button moulder came to life as Djerjinsky. My Angel comes a day after the fair; but time enough for our people, who know nothing of the button moulder and have been assured by our gentleman-ladylike newspapers that Djerjinsky was a Thug.

The button moulder is a fiction; and my Angel is a fiction. But the pressing need for bringing us to the bar for an investigation of our personal social values is not a fiction. And Djerjinsky is not a fiction. He found that as there are no button moulders and no angels and no heavenly tribunals available, we must set up earthly ones, not to ascertain whether Mr Everyman in the dock has committed this or that act or holds this or that belief, but whether he or she is a creator of social values or a parasitical consumer and destroyer of them.

Unfortunately the word tribunal immediately calls up visions not only of judgment but of punishment and cruelty. Now there need be no more question of either of these abominations than there was in the case of my grandfather's dog. My grandfather would have been horribly ashamed of himself if the dog's death had not been instantaneous and unanticipated. And the idea of punishment never entered either his mind or the dog's. (Djerjinsky, by the way, is believed to have devized a similar method of painless liquidation.) It may be expedient that one man should die for the people; but it does not follow in the least that he should be tortured or terrified. Public savagery may demand that the law shall torment a criminal who does something very provoking; for the Sermon on the Mount is still a dead letter in spite of all the compliments we pay it. But to blow a man's brains out because he cannot for the life of him see why he should not employ labor at a profit, or buy things solely to sell them again for more than he gave for them, or speculate in currency values: all of them activities which have for centuries enjoyed the highest respectability, is an innovation which should be carried out with the utmost possible delicacy if public opinion is to be quite reconciled to it. We have also to reckon with the instinctive shrinking from outright killing which makes so many people sign petitions for the reprieve of even the worst murderers, and take no further interest if a reprieve decrees that their lives shall be taken by the slow torture of imprisonment. Then we have a mass of people who think that murderers should be judicially killed, but that the lives of the most mischievous criminals should be held sacred provided they do not commit murder. To overcome these prejudices we need a greatly increased intolerance of socially injurious conduct and an uncompromising abandonment of punishment and its cruelties, together with a sufficient school inculcation of social responsibility to make every citizen conscious that if his life costs more than it is worth to the community the community may painlessly extinguish it.

The result of this, however, will finally be a demand for codification. The citizen will say "I really must know what I may do and what I may not do without having my head shot off." The reply "You must keep a credit balance always at the national bank" is sufficiently definite if the national accountancy is trustworthy and compulsory unemployment made impossible. In fact it is so definite that it finally takes the matter out of the hands of the Inquisition and makes an overdraft an ordinary offence to be dealt with by the police. But police measures are not enough. Any intelligent and experienced administrator of the criminal law will tell you that there are people who come up for punishment again and again for the same offence, and that punishing them is a cruel waste of time. There should be an Inquisition always available to consider whether these human nuisances should not be put out of their pain, or out of their joy as the case may be. The community must drive a much harder bargain for the privilege of citizenship than it now does; but it must also make the bargain not only practicable but in effect much easier than the present very imperfect bargain. This involves a new social creed. A new social creed involves a new heresy. A new heresy involves an Inquisition. The precedents established by the Inquisition furnish the material for a new legal code. Codification enables the work of the Inquisition to be done by an ordinary court of law. Thereupon the Inquisition, as such, disappears, precisely as the Tcheka has disappeared. Thus it has always been; and thus it ever shall be.

The moral of the dramatic fable of The Simpleton is now clear enough. With amateur Inquisitions under one name or another or no name at work in all directions, from Fascist *autos-da-fé* to American Vigilance Committees with lynching mobs as torturers and executioners, it is time for us to reconsider our Visions of Judgment, and see whether we cannot change them from old stories in which we no longer believe and new stories which are only too horribly true to serious and responsible public tribunals.

By the way, I had better guard myself against the assumption that because I have introduced into my fable a eugenic experiment in group marriage I am advocating the immediate adoption of that method of peopling the world for immediate practice by my readers. Group marriage is a form of marriage like any other; and it is just as well to remind our western and very insular Imperialists that marriage in the British Empire is startlingly different in the east from marriage in the British Isles; but I have introduced it only to bring into the story the four lovely phantasms who embody all the artistic, romantic, and military ideals of our cultured suburbs. On the Day of Judgment not merely do they cease to exist like the useless and predatory people: it becomes apparent that they never did exist. And, enchanting as they may be to our perfumers, who give us the concentrated odor of the flower without the roots or the clay or even the leaves, let us hope they never will.

ON THE INDIAN OCEAN.
April, 1935.

# The Six of Calais

*First published in 1936*

The most amusing thing about the first performance of this little play was the exposure it elicited of the quaint illiteracy of our modern London journalists. Their only notion of a king was a pleasant and highly respectable gentleman in a bowler hat and Victorian beard, shaking hands affably with a blushing football team. To them a queen was a dignified lady, also Victorian as to her coiffure, graciously receiving bouquets from excessively washed children in beautiful new clothes. Such were their mental pictures of Great Edward's grandson Edward III and his queen Philippa. They were hurt, shocked, scandalized at the spectacle of a medieval soldier-monarch publicly raging and cursing, crying and laughing, asserting his authority with thrasonic[al] ferocity and the next moment blubbering like a child in his wife's lap or snarling like a savage dog at a dauntless and defiant tradesman: in short, behaving himself like an unrestrained human being in a very trying situation instead of like a modern constitutional monarch on parade keeping up an elaborate fiction of living in a political vacuum and moving only when his ministers pull his strings. Edward Plantagenet the Third had to pull everybody else's strings and pull them pretty hard, his father having been miserably killed for taking his job too lightly. But the journalist critics knew nothing of this. A King Edward who did not behave like the son of King Edward the Seventh seemed unnatural and indecent to them, and they rent their garments accordingly.

They were perhaps puzzled by the fact that the play has no moral whatever. Every year or so I hurl at them a long play full of insidious propaganda, with a moral in every line. They never discover what I am driving at: it is always too plainly and domestically stated to be grasped by their subtle and far flung minds; but they feel that I am driving at something: probably something they had better not agree with if they value their livelihoods. A play of mine in which I am not driving at anything more than a playwright's direct business is as inconceivable by them as a medieval king.

Now a playwright's direct business is simply to provide the theatre with a play. When I write one with the additional attraction of providing the XX century with an up-to-date religion or the like, that luxury is thrown in gratuitously; and the play, simply as a play, is not necessarily either the better or the worse for it. What, then, is a play simply as a play?

Well, it is a lot of things. Life as we see it is so haphazard that it is only by picking out its key situations and arranging them in their significant order (which is never how they actually occur) that it can be made intelligible. The highbrowed dramatic poet wants to make it intelligible and sublime. The farce writer wants to make it funny. The melodrama merchant wants to make it as exciting as some people find the police news. The pornographer wants to make it salacious. All interpreters of life in action, noble or ignoble, find their instrument in the theatre; and all the academic definitions of a play are variations of this basic function.

Yet there is one function hardly ever alluded to now, though it was made much too much of from Shakespear's time to the middle of the XIX century. As I write my plays it is continually in my mind and very much to my taste. This function is to provide an exhibition of the art of acting. A good play with bad parts is not an impossibility; but it is a monstrosity. A bad play with good parts will hold the stage and be kept alive by the actors for centuries after the obsolescence of its mentality would have condemned it to death without them. A great deal of the British Drama, from Shakespear to Bulwer Lytton, is as dead as mutton, and quite unbearable except when heroically acted; yet Othello and Richelieu can still draw hard money into the pay boxes; and The School For Scandal revives again and again with unabated vigor. Rosalind can always pull As You Like It through in spite of the sententious futility of the melancholy Jaques; and Millamant, impossible as she is, still produces the usual compliments to the wit and style of Congreve, who thought that syphilis and cuckoldry and concupiscent old women are things to be laughed at.

The Six of Calais is an acting piece and nothing else. As it happened, it was so well acted that in the XVIII century all the talk would have been about Siddons as Philippa. But the company got no thanks except from the audience: the critics were prostrated with shock, damn their eyes!

I have had to improve considerably on the story as told by that absurd old snob Froissart, who believed that "to rob and pill was a good life" if the robber was at least a baron. He made a very poor job of it in my opinion.

On the High Seas.
28 May 1935.

# Preface on Bosses
## (The Millionairess)

*First published in 1936*

========

Though this play of The Millionairess does not pretend to be anything more than a comedy of humorous and curious contemporary characters such as Ben Jonson might write were he alive now, yet it raises a question that has troubled human life and moulded human society since the creation.

The law is equal before all of us; but we are not all equal before the law. Virtually there is one law for the rich and another for the poor, one law for the cunning and another for the simple, one law for the forceful and another for the feeble, one law for the ignorant and another for the learned, one law for the brave and another for the timid, and within family limits one law for the parent and no law at all for the child.

In the humblest cabin that contains a family you may find a *maîtresse femme*[1] who rules in the household by a sort of divine right. She may rule amiably by being able to think more quickly and see further than the others, or she may be a tyrant ruling violently by intensity of will and ruthless egotism. She may be a grandmother and she may be a girl. But the others find they are unable to resist her. Often of course the domestic tyrant is a man; but the phenomenon is not so remarkable in his case, as he is by convention the master and lawgiver of the hearthstone.

In every business street you will find a shopkeeper who is always in difficulties and ends his business adventures in the bankruptcy court. Hard by you will find another shopkeeper, with no greater advantages to start with, or possibly less, who makes larger and larger profits, and inspires more and more confidence in his banker, until he ends as the millionaire head of a giant multiple shop.

How does the captain of a pirate ship obtain his position and maintain his authority over a crew of scoundrels who are all, like himself, outside the law?

1. Most dictionaries translate this as 'female boss' or 'managing woman'. Spiers and Surenne's *French and English Pronouncing Dictionary* (1879) provides a Shavian translation: 'superior woman'.

How does an obscure village priest, the son of humble fisherfolk, come to wear the triple crown and sit in the papal chair? How do common soldiers become Kings, Shahs, and Dictators? Why does a hereditary peer find that he is a nonentity in a grand house organized and ruled by his butler?

Questions like these force themselves on us so continually and ruthlessly that many turn in despair from Socialism and political reform on the ground that to abolish all the institutional tyrannies would only deliver the country helplessly into the hands of the born bosses. A king, a prelate, a squire, a capitalist, a justice of the peace may be a good kind Christian soul, owing his position, as most of us do, to being the son of his father; but a born boss is one who rides roughshod over us by some mysterious power that separates him from our species and makes us fear him: that is, hate him.

What is to be done with that section of the possessors of specific talents whose talent is for moneymaking? History and daily experience teach us that if the world does not devize some plan of ruling them, they will rule the world. Now it is not desirable that they should rule the world; for the secret of moneymaking is to care for nothing else and to work at nothing else; and as the world's welfare depends on operations by which no individual can make money, whilst its ruin by war and drink and disease and drugs and debauchery is enormously profitable to moneymakers, the supremacy of the moneymaker is the destruction of the State. A society which depends on the incentive of private profit is doomed.

And what about ambitious people who possess commanding business ability or military genius or both? They are irresistible unless they are restrained by law; for ordinary individuals are helpless in their hands. Are they to be the masters of society or its servants?

What should the XIX century have done in its youth with Rothschild and Napoleon? What is the United States to do with its money kings and bosses? What are we to do with ours? How is the mediocre private citizen to hold his own with the able bullies and masterful women who establish family despotisms, school despotisms, office despotisms, religious despotisms in their little circles all over the country? Our boasted political liberties are a mockery to the subjects of such despotisms. They may work well when the despot is benevolent; but they are worse than any political tyranny in the selfish cases.

It is much more difficult to attack a personal despotism than an institutional one. Monarchs can be abolished: they have been abolished in all directions during the last century and a half, with the result, however, of sometimes replacing a personally amiable and harmless monarch, reigning under strict constitutional and traditional restraints, by energetic dictators and presidents who, having made hay of constitutions and traditions, are under no restraints at all. A hereditary monarch, on the throne because he is the son of his father, may be a normal person, amenable to reasonable advice from his councils, and exercising no authority except that conferred on him (or her) by the Constitution. Behead him, as we beheaded our Charles, or the French their Louis, and the born despot Cromwell or Napoleon (I purposely avoid glaring contemporary examples because I am not quite sure where they will be by the time this book is published) takes his place. The same mysterious personal force that makes the household tyrant, the school tyrant, the office tyrant, the brigand chief and the pirate captain, brings the born boss to the top by a gravitation that ordinary people cannot resist.

The successful usurpers of thrones are not the worst cases. The political usurper may be an infernal scoundrel, ruthless in murder, treachery, and torture; but once his ambition is achieved and he has to rule a nation, the magnitude and difficulty of his job, and the knowledge that if he makes a mess of it he will fall as suddenly as he has risen, will civilize him with a ruthlessness greater than his own. When Henry IV usurped the English crown he certainly did not intend to die of political overwork; but that is what happened to him. No political ruler could possibly be as wickedly selfish and cruel as the tyrant of a private house. Queen Elizabeth was a *maîtresse femme*; but she could have had her own way much more completely as landlady of the Mermaid Tavern than she had as sovereign of England. Because Nero and Paul I of Russia could not be made to understand this, they were killed like mad dogs by their own courtiers. But our petty fireside tyrants are not killed. Christina of Sweden would not have had to abdicate[2] if her realm had been a ten-roomed villa. Had Catherine II reigned over her husband only, she need not nor could not have had him murdered; but as Tsarina she was forced to liquidate poor Peter[3] very much against her own easy good nature, which prevented her from scolding her maids properly.

Modern Liberal democracy claims unlimited opportunities for tyranny: qualification for rule by heredity and class narrows it and puts it in harness and blinkers. Especially does such democracy favor money rule. It is in fact

2. Christina of Sweden was a private woman, bookishly intellectual and aesthetic. Confronted with the Thirty Years War with Germany, bitter class rivalries at home, and her nation in a precarious financial situation, she abdicated in 1654, after ten years of rule.
3. Peter III, a brutal and petty monarch, was removed from the throne in 1762 by a revolt of the regiments of the guard led by one of Catherine's favourites, Count Gregory Orlov. Officially the Tsar died several days later of 'apoplexy' and his wife became Tsarina.

not democracy at all, but unashamed plutocracy. And as the meanest creature can become rich if he devotes his life to it, and the people with wider and more generous interests become or remain poor with equal certainty, plutocracy is the very devil socially, because it creates a sort of Gresham law by which the baser human currency drives out the nobler coinage. This is quite different from the survival of the fittest in the contests of character and talent which are independent of money. If Moses is the only tribesman capable of making a code of laws, he inevitably becomes Lawgiver to all the tribes, and, equally inevitably, is forced to add to what he can understand of divine law a series of secular regulations designed to maintain his personal authority. If he finds that it is useless to expect the tribesmen to obey his laws as a matter of common sense, he must persuade them that his inspiration is the result of direct and miraculous communication with their deity. Moses and Mahomet and Joseph Smith the Mormon had to plead divine revelations to get them out of temporary and personal difficulties as well as out of eternal and impersonal ones. As long as an individual of their calibre remains the indispensable man (or woman) doing things that the common man can neither do without nor do for himself, he will be, up to a point, the master of the common man in spite of all the democratic fudge that may be advanced to the contrary.

Of course there are limits. He cannot go to the lengths at which the common man will believe him to be insane or impious: when measures of that complexion are necessary, as they very often are, he must either conceal them or mask them as follies of the sort the common man thinks splendid. If the ruler thinks it well to begin a world war he must persuade his people that it is a war to end war, and that the people he wants them to kill are diabolical scoundrels; and if he is forced to suspend hostilities for a while, and does so by a treaty which contains the seeds of half a dozen new wars and is impossible enough in its conditions to make its violation certain, he must create a general belief that it is a charter of eternal peace and a monument of retributive justice.

In this way the most honest ruler becomes a tyrant and a fabricator of legends and falsehoods, not out of any devilment in himself, but because those whom he rules do not understand his business, and, if they did, would not sacrifice their own immediate interests to the permanent interests of the nation or the world. In short, a ruler must not only make laws, and rule from day to day: he must, by school instruction and printed propaganda, create and maintain an artificial mentality which will endorse his proceedings and obey his authority. This mentality becomes what we call Conservatism; and the revolt against it when it is abused oppressively or becomes obsolete as social conditions change, is classed as sedition, and reviled as Radicalism, Anarchism, Bolshevism, or what you please.

When a mentality is created and a code imposed, the born ruler, the Moses or Lenin, is no longer indispensable: routine government by dunderheads becomes possible and in fact preferable as long as the routine is fairly appropriate to the current phase of social development. The assumption of the more advanced spirits that revolutionists are always right is as questionable as the conservative assumption that they are always wrong. The industrious dunderhead who always does what was done last time because he is incapable of conceiving anything better, makes the best routineer. This explains the enormous part played by dunderheads as such in the history of all nations, provoking repeated explanations of surprise at the littleness of the wisdom with which the world is governed.

But what of the ambitious usurper? the person who has a capacity for kingship but has no kingdom and must therefore acquire a readymade one which is getting along in its own way very well without him? It cannot be contended with any plausibility that William the Conqueror was indispensable in England: he wanted England and grabbed it. He did this by virtue of his personal qualities, entirely against the will of the people of England, who, as far as they were politically conscious at all, would have greatly preferred Harold. But William had all the qualities that make an individual irresistible: the physical strength and ferocity of a king of beasts, the political genius of a king of men, the strategic cunning and tactical gumption of a military genius; and nothing that France or England could say or do prevailed against him. What are we to do with such people?

When an established political routine breaks down and produces political chaos, a combination of personal ambition with military genius and political capacity in a single individual gives that individual his opportunity. Napoleon, if he had been born a century earlier, would have had no more chance of becoming emperor of the French than Marshal Saxe[4] had of supplanting Louis XV. In spite of the French Revolution, he was a very ordinary snob in his XVIII century social outlook. His assumption of the imperial diadem, his ridiculous attempt to establish the little Buonaparte family on all the thrones under his control, his remanufacture of a titular aristocracy to make a court for himself, his silly insistence on imperial etiquette when he was a dethroned and moribund prisoner in St Helena, shew that, for all his genius, he was and always had been behind the times. But he was for a time irresistible

4. Maurice, Comte de Saxe, French general, was created marshal-general of France in 1747 after his battle success in the War of Austrian Succession.

because, though he could fight battles on academic lines only, and was on that point a routineer soldier, he could play the war game on the established procedure so superbly that all the armies of Europe crumpled up before him. It was easy for anti-Bonapartist writers, from Taine to Mr H. G. Wells,[5] to disparage him as a mere cad; but Goethe, who could face facts, and on occasion rub them in, said simply "You shake your chains in vain."[6] Unfortunately for himself and Europe Napoleon was fundamentally a commonplace human fool. In spite of his early failure in the east he made a frightful draft on the manhood of France for his march to Moscow, only to hurry back leaving his legions dead in the snow, and thereafter go from disaster to disaster. [Jean-Baptiste] Bernadotte, the lawyer's son who enlisted as a common soldier and ended unconquered on the throne of Sweden [as Charles XIV] (his descendants still hold it), made a far better job of his affairs. When for the first time Napoleon came up against a really original commander at Waterloo, he still made all the textbook moves he had learnt at the military academy, and did not know when he was beaten until it was too late to do anything but run away. Instead of making for America at all hazards he threw himself on the magnanimity of the Prince Regent, who obviously could not have spared him even if he had wanted to. His attempt to wedge himself and his upstart family into the old dynasties by his divorce and his Austrian marriage ended in making him a notorious cuckold. But the vulgarer fool and the paltrier snob you prove Napoleon to have been, the more alarming becomes the fact that this shabby-genteel Corsican subaltern (and a very unsatisfactory subaltern at that) dominated Europe for years, and placed on his own head the crown of Charlemagne. Is there really nothing to be done with such men but submit to them until, having risen by their specialities, they ruin themselves by their vulgarities?

It was easy for Napoleon to make a better job of restoring order after the French Revolution than [Emmanuel-Joseph] Sieyès,[7] who tried to do it by

5. Hippolyte Taine, in *Origines de la France contemporaine* (1875–93), presents Napoleon as a ruthless cynic who considers 'horror of blood, respect for law' to be weaknesses. H. G. Wells, in *The Outline of History*, describes Napoleon as a 'dark little archaic personage, hard, compact, capable, unscrupulous, imitative, and neatly vulgar'.
6. Reported in a conversation of 21 April 1813 between Goethe and C. G. Körner, whose son had joined the famed Lützow corps of volunteers to fight the French in the name of a free Germany. For full text see *Goethes Gespräche*, eds. F. von Biedermann and W. Herwig (Zurich, 1929), vol. 2, pp. 794–5.
7. French churchman and revolutionist leader, who published a celebrated pamphlet on the Third Estate, *Qu'est-ce que le tiers-état?* (1789).

writing paper constitutions, or than a plucky bully like [Paul, Vicomte de] Barras,[8] who cared for nothing except feathering his own nest. Any tidy and publicspirited person could have done as much with the necessary prestige. Napoleon got that prestige by feeding the popular appetite for military glory. He could not create that natural appetite; but he could feed it by victories; and he could use all the devices of journalism and pageantry and patriotic braggadocio to make La Gloire glorious. And all this because, like William the Conqueror, he had the group of talents that make a successful general and democratic ruler. Had not the French Revolution so completely failed to produce a tolerable government to replace the monarchy it overthrew, and thereby reduced itself to desperation, Napoleon would have been only a famous general like Saxe or Wellington or Marlborough, who under similar circumstances could and indeed must have become kings if they had been ungovernable enough to desire it. Only the other day a man without any of the social advantages of these commanders made himself Shah of Iran.[9]

Julius Cæsar and Cromwell also mounted on the *débris* of collapsing political systems; and both of them refused crowns. But no crown could have added to the power their military capacity gave them. Cæsar bribed enormously; but there were richer men than he in Rome to play that game. Only, they could not have won the battle of Pharsalia.[10] Cromwell proved invincible in the field—such as it was.

It is not, however, these much hackneyed historical figures that trouble us now. Pharsalias and Dunbars[11] and Waterloos are things of the past: battles nowadays last several months and then peter out on barbed wire under the fire of machine guns. Suppose [Erich von] Ludendorff[12] had been a Napoleon, and Haig a Marlborough, Wellington, and Cromwell rolled into one, what more could they have done than either declare modern war impossible or

8. French revolutionist, appointed commander of the Army of the Interior and of the police by the Convention. It was he who summoned Napoleon in 1794 to maintain order in Paris. He was overthrown in Napoleon's coup (1799) and exiled.
9. Riza (also spelled Reza) Khan, an Iranian officer, staged a *coup d'état* in 1921, taking control of the military forces. In 1925 he was elected shah by the parliament, reigning as Reza Shah Pahlavi until 1941.
10. Caesar defeated Pompey at Pharsalia in Thessaly on 29 June 48 BC.
11. The Battle of Dunbar, 3 September 1650, was fought by the English under Oliver Cromwell and the Scots, who under their national leader David Leslie were routed, with an estimated loss of 3000 lives.
12. Ludendorff, as chief of staff to Field Marshal Paul von Hindenburg, insisted on unrestricted submarine warfare in 1917, thus prompting the United States to enter the war.

else keep throwing masses of infantry in the old fashion against slaughtering machinery like pigs in Chicago? Napoleon's booklearnt tactics and the columns that won so many battles for him would have no more chance nowadays than the ragged Irish pikemen on Vinegar Hill;[13] and Wellington's thin red line and his squares would have vanished in the fumes of T.N.T. on the Somme. "The Nelson touch"[14] landed a section of the British fleet at the bottom of the Dardanelles.[15] And yet this war, which, if it did not end civilized war (perhaps it did, by the way, though the War Office may not yet have realized it) at least made an end of the supremacy of the glory virtuoso who can play brilliant variations on the battle of Hastings, has been followed by such a group of upstart autocrats as the world had ceased to suppose possible. Mussolini, Hitler, Kemal and Riza Khan began in the ranks, and have no Marengos[16] to their credit; yet there they are at the top!

Here again the circumstances gave the men their opportunity. Neither Mussolini nor Hitler could have achieved their present personal supremacy when I was born in the middle of the XIX century, because the prevailing mentality of that deluded time was still hopefully parliamentary. Democracy was a dream, an ideal. Everything would be well when all men had votes. Everything would be better than well when all women had votes. There was a great fear of public opinion because it was a dumb phantom which every statesman could identify with his own conscience and dread as the Nemesis of unscrupulous ambition. That was the golden age of democracy: the phantom was a real and beneficent force. Many delusions are. In those days even our Conservative rulers agreed that we were a libertyloving people: that, for instance, Englishmen would never tolerate compulsory military service as the slaves of foreign despots did.

It was part of the democratic dream that Parliament was an instrument for carrying out the wishes of the voters, absurdly called its constituents. And as,

13. Vinegar Hill overlooks the town of Ennicorthy, taken by Cromwell in 1649; Irish rebels, encamped on the hill in 1798, stormed and burned the town in belated retaliation.
14. 'The Nelson touch' was an action or manner characteristic of Admiral Nelson (*OED*).
15. When a British naval bombardment of Turkey from the Dardanelles channel in February–March 1915 resulted in a loss of three British battleships and damage to three others, the operation was abandoned and, in May, First Sea Lord Admiral John Fisher resigned.
16. At Marengo (north-west Italy) the French under Napoleon seized victory from defeat on 14 June 1800, when, reinforced by the troops of General Louis-Charles Desaix de Veygoux, they overcame the Austrians.

in the XIX century, it was still believed that British individual liberty forbad Parliament to do anything that it could possibly leave to private enterprize, Parliament was able to keep up its reputation by simply maintaining an effective police force and enforcing private contracts. Even Factory Acts and laws against adulteration and sweating were jealously resisted as interferences with the liberty of free Britons. If there was anything wrong, the remedy was an extension of the franchise. Like Hamlet [III: ii], we lived on the chameleon's dish "air, promise crammed."

But you cannot create a mentality out of promises without having to face occasional demands for their materialization. The Treasury Bench was up for auction at every election, the bidding being in promises. The political parties, finding it much less troublesome to give the people votes than to carry out reforms, at last established adult suffrage.

The result was a colossal disappointment and disillusion. The phantom of Democracy, *alias* Public Opinion, which, acting as an artificial political conscience, had restrained Gladstone and Disraeli, vanished. The later parliamentary leaders soon learnt from experience that they might with perfect impunity tell the nation one thing on Tuesday and the opposite on Friday without anyone noticing the discrepancy. The donkey had overtaken the carrots at last; and instead of eating them he allowed them to be snatched away from him by any confidence trickster who told him to look up into the sky.

The diplomatists immediately indulged themselves with a prodigiously expensive war, after which the capitalist system, which had undertaken to find employment for everybody at subsistence wages, and which, though it had never fulfilled that undertaking, had at least found employment for enough of them to leave the rest too few to be dangerous, defaulted in respect of unprecedented millions of unemployed, who had to be bought off by doles administered with a meanness and cruelty which revived all the infamies of the Poor Law of a century ago (the days of Oliver Twist) and could not be administered in any kinder way without weakening the willingness of its recipients to prefer even the poorliest paid job to its humiliations.

The only way of escape was for the Government to organize the labor of the unemployed for the supply of their own needs. But Parliament not only could not do this, but could and did prevent its being done. In vain did the voters use their votes to place a Labor Government, with a Cabinet of Socialists, on the Treasury Bench [see p. 52]. Parliament took these men, who had been intransigent Socialists and revolutionists all their lives, and reduced them to a condition of political helplessness in which they were indistinguishable except by name from the most reactionary members of the

House of Lords or the military clubs. A Socialist Prime Minister, after trying for years to get the parliamentary car into gear for a move forward, and finding that though it would work easily and smoothly in neutral the only gear that would engage was the reverse gear (popularly called "the axe" because it could do nothing but cut down wages), first formed what he called a national government by a coalition of all parties, and then, having proved by this experiment that it did not make the smallest difference whether members of the Cabinet were the reddest of Bolsheviks or the bluest of Tories, made things easier by handing over his premiership to a colleague who, being a Conservative, and popular and amiable into the bargain, could steal a horse where a Socialist dare not look over a hedge. The voters rejected him at the next election; but he retained his membership of the Cabinet precisely as if he had been triumphantly returned.[17] Bismarck could have done no more.

These events, helped by the terrific moral shock of the war, and the subsequent exposure of the patriotic lying by which the workers of Europe had been provoked to slaughter oneanother, made an end of the XIX century democratic mentality. Parliament fell into contempt; ballot papers were less esteemed than toilet papers; the men from the trenches had no patience with the liberties that had not saved them from being driven like sheep to the shambles.

Of this change our parliamentarians and journalists had no suspicion. Creatures of habit, they went on as if nothing had occurred since Queen Victoria's death except a couple of extensions of the franchise and an epochmaking revolution in Russia which they poohpoohed as a transient outburst of hooliganism fomented by a few bloodthirsty scoundrels, exactly as the American revolution and the French revolution had been poohpoohed when they, too, were contemporary.

Here was clearly a big opportunity for a man psychologist enough to grasp the situation and bold enough to act on it. Such a man was Mussolini. He had become known as a journalist by championing the demobilized soldiers, who, after suffering all the horrors of the war, had returned to find that the men who had been kept at home in the factories comfortably earning good

---

17. MacDonald headed a National Coalition government from October 1931 until, in June 1935, he was obliged by failing health to trade positions with Stanley Baldwin, then Lord President of the Council, remaining in the Cabinet until his death two years later. Baldwin, in the October 1935 General Election, was not, as Shaw claimed, rejected by the voters; he retained his constituency (1931) and when the country at large returned a large Conservative majority in 1935 he formed a new Cabinet.

wages, had seized those factories according to the Syndicalist doctrine of "workers' control," and were wrecking them in their helpless ignorance of business. As one indignant master-Fascist[18] said to me "They were listening to speeches round red flags and leaving the cows unmilked."

The demobilized fell on the Syndicalists with sticks and stones. Some, more merciful, only dosed them with castor oil. They carried Mussolini to Rome with a rush. This gave him the chance of making an irreparable mistake and spending the next fifteen years in prison. It seemed just the occasion for a grand appeal for liberty, for democracy, for a parliament in which the people were supreme: in short, for XIX century resurrection pie. Mussolini did not make that mistake. With inspired precision he denounced Liberty as a putrefying corpse. He declared that what people needed was not liberty but discipline,[19] the sterner the better. He said that he would not tolerate Oppositions: he called for action and silence. The people, instead of being shocked like good Liberals, rose to him. He was able to organize a special constabulary who wore black shirts and applied the necessary coercion.

Such improvized bodies attracted young men of military tastes and old soldiers, inevitably including a percentage of ruffians and Sadists. This fringe of undesirables soon committed outrages and a couple of murders, whereupon all the Liberal newspapers in Europe shrieked with horror as if nothing else was happening in Italy. Mussolini refused to be turned aside from his work like a parliamentary man to discuss "incidents." All he said was "I take the responsibility for everything that has happened."[20] When the Italian Liberals joined in the shrieking he seized the shriekers and transported them to the Lipari Isles [north of Sicily]. Parliament, openly flouted, chastized, and humiliated, could do nothing. The people were delighted; for that was just how they wanted to see Parliament treated. The doctrinaires of liberty fled to France and England, preferring them to Lipari, and wrote eloquent letters to the papers demanding whether every vestige of freedom, freedom of speech,

18. Carlo Basile, author of *Discorsi Fascisti*, an acquaintance of the Shaws at Stresa, where they holidayed in 1926–7.
19. This was a frequently iterated theme in Mussolini's speeches. In October 1917 he proclaimed, '[W]e must abandon the great phrase "liberty". There is another which in this third winter of war should be on the lips of the cabinet when they address the Italian people, and it is "discipline"' (Margherita Sarfatti, *The Life of Mussolini*, 1925, p. 238).
20. In a speech on 3 January 1925 in the Chamber of Deputies in Rome after the murder of Giacomo Matteotti, a socialist deputy and one of Fascism's most outspoken critics.

freedom of the press, freedom of Parliament, was to be trampled under the heel of a ruthless dictator merely because the Italian trains were running punctually and travelers in Italy could depend on their luggage not being stolen without actually sitting on it. The English editors gave them plenty of space, and wrote sympathetic articles paraphrasing John Stuart Mill's Essay on Liberty. Mussolini, now Il Duce, never even looked round: he was busy sweeping up the elected municipalities, and replacing them with efficient commissioners of his own choice, who had to do their job or get out. The editors had finally to accord him a sort of Pragmatic Sanction by an admission that his plan worked better than the old plan; but they were still blind to the fact staring them in the face that Il Duce, knowing what the people wanted and giving it to them, was responding to the real democratic urge whilst the cold tealeaves of the XIX century were making them sick. It was evident that Mussolini was master of Italy as far as such mastership is possible; but what was not evident to Englishmen who had had their necks twisted the other way from their childhood was that even when he deliberately spat in the face of the League of Nations at Corfu,[21] and defiantly asked the Powers whether they had anything to say about it, he was delighting his own people by the spectacle of a great Italian bullying the world, and getting away with it triumphantly. Parliaments are supposed to have their fingers always on the people's pulse and to respond to its slightest throb. Mussolini proved that parliaments have not the slightest notion of how the people are feeling, and that he, being a good psychologist and a man of the people himself to boot, was a true organ of democracy.

I, being a bit of a psychologist myself, also understood the situation, and was immediately denounced by the refugees and their champions as an anti-democrat, a hero worshipper of tyrants, and all the rest of it.

Hitler's case was different; but he had one quality in common with Il Duce: he knew what the victorious Allies would fight for and what they would only bluster about. They had already been forced to recognize that their demands for plunder had gone far beyond Germany's utmost resources.

21. The Greek island of Corfu was occupied in 1923 by the Italians, allegedly in retaliation for the murder of an Italian general who was a member of an international boundary commission on Greek territory. Mussolini, infuriated by ensuing British protests and anti-Fascist press sentiments, threatened war with Britain, thundering that 'if the London press did not become more favorable to Fascist Italy he would find ways of making them regret it . . .' He added he would destroy the League of Nations if it attempted to intervene (Denis Mack Smith, *Mussolini: A Biography*, New York, 1982, p. 72).

But there remained the clauses of the Versailles treaty by which Germany was to be kept in a condition of permanent, decisive, and humiliating military inferiority to the other Powers, and especially to France. Hitler was political psychologist enough to know that the time had arrived when it would be quite impossible for the Allies to begin the war over again to enforce these clauses. He saw his opportunity and took it. He violated the clauses, and declared that he was going to go on violating them until a fully re-armed Germany was on equal terms with the victors. He did not soften his defiance by any word of argument or diplomacy. He knew that his attitude was safe and sure of success; and he took care to make it as defiant as that of Ajax challenging the lightning.[22] The Powers had either to renew the war or tear up the impossible clauses with a good grace. But they could not grasp the situation, and went on nagging pitifully about the wickedness of breaking a treaty. Hitler said that if they mentioned that subject again Germany would withdraw from the League of Nations and cut the Powers dead. He bullied and snubbed as the man who understands a situation can always bully and snub the nincompoops who are only whining about it. He at once became a popular idol, and had the regular executive forces so completely devoted to him that he was able to disband the brownshirted constabulary he had organized on the Mussolini model. He met the conventional democratic challenge by plebiscites of ninety per cent in his favor. The myopia of the Powers had put him in a position so far stronger than Mussolini's that he was able to kill seventyseven of his most dangerous opponents at a blow[23] and then justify himself completely before an assembly fully as representative as the British Parliament, the climax being his appointment as absolute dictator in Germany for life, a stretch of Cæsarism no XIX century Hohenzollern would have dreamt of demanding.

Hitler was able to go further than Mussolini because he had a defeated,

22. Aias (Ajax) the lesser, an arrogant warrior, raped Cassandra at Athene's statue, which he toppled. As punishment Zeus sent a great storm to the Greek fleet as it sailed home from the Trojan War, and Athene sank Aias's ship with a thunderbolt. As he swam ashore, bragging that he had defied the gods and survived, Zeus hurled a thunderbolt that drowned him.
23. Shaw's source for the 77 deaths has not been determined. Figures range widely, from Shirer's report (*The Rise and Fall of the Third Reich*) of 51 anti-Nazis listed as murdered during the 1932 *Reichstag* election campaign to the claim of Franklin Hittell, Visiting Professor of Religion at Baylor University, that even before the beer hall *Putsch* of 1923 Hitler's followers had murdered 344 opponents (*San Antonio Express-News*, 12 February 1994).

plundered, humiliated nation to rescue and restore, wheras Mussolini had only an irritated but victorious one. He carried out a persecution of the Jews which went to the scandalous length of outlawing, plundering, and exiling Albert Einstein, a much greater man than any politician, but great in such a manner that he was quite above the heads of the masses and therefore so utterly powerless economically and militarily that he depended for his very existence on the culture and conscience of the rulers of the earth. Hitler's throwing Einstein to the Antisemite wolves was an appalling breach of cultural faith. It raised the question which is the root question of this preface: to wit, what safeguard have the weaponless great against the great who have myrmidons at their call? It is the most frightful betrayal of civilization for the rulers who monopolize physical force to withhold their protection from the pioneers in thought. Granted that they are sometimes forced to do it because intellectual advances may present themselves as quackery, sedition, obscenity, or blasphemy, and always present themselves as heresies. Had Einstein been formally prosecuted and sentenced by the German National Socialist State, as Galileo was prosecuted by the Church, for shaking the whole framework of established physical science by denying the infallibility of Newton, introducing fantastic factors into mathematics, destroying human faith in absolute measurement, and playing an incomprehensible trick with the sacred velocity of light, quite a strong case could have been made out by the public prosecutor. But to set the police on him because he was a Jew could be justified only on the ground that the Jews are the natural enemies of the rest of the human race, and that as a state of perpetual war necessarily exists between them any Gentile has the same reason for killing any Jew at sight as the Roman soldier had for killing Archimedes.

Now no doubt Jews are most obnoxious creatures. Any competent historian or psychoanalyst can bring a mass of incontrovertible evidence to prove that it would have been better for the world if the Jews had never existed. But I, as an Irishman, can, with patriotic relish, demonstrate the same of the English. Also of the Irish. If Herr Hitler would only consult the French and British newspapers and magazines of the latter half of 1914, he would learn that the Germans are a race of savage idolaters, murderers, liars, and fiends whose assumption of the human form is thinner than that of the wolf in Little Red Riding Hood.

We all live in glass houses. Is it wise to throw stones at the Jews? Is it wise to throw stones at all?

Herr Hitler is not only an Antisemite, but a believer in the possibility and desirability of a pure bred German race. I should like to ask him why. All Germans are not Mozarts, nor even Mendelssohns and Meyerbeers, both of whom, by the way, though exceptionally desirable Germans, were Jews. Surely the average German can be improved. I am told that children bred from Irish colleens and Chinese laundrymen are far superior to inbred Irish or Chinese. Herr Hitler is not a typical German. I should not be at all surprised if it were discovered that his very mixed blood (all our bloods today are hopelessly mixed) got fortified somewhere in the past by that of King David. He cannot get over the fact that the lost tribes of Israel expose us all to the suspicion (sometimes, as in Abyssinia, to the boast[24]) that we are those lost tribes, or at least that we must have absorbed them.

One of my guesses in this matter is that Herr Hitler in his youth was fascinated by Houston Chamberlain's Foundations of the XIX Century, an interesting book which at the time of its appearance I recommended everybody to read [review in *Fabian News*, June 1911]. Its ethnology was not wholly imaginary. A smattering of Mendelism is all that one needs to know that the eternal fusion of races does not always blend them. The Jews will often throw up an apparently pure-bred Hittite or a pure-bred Philistine. The Germans throw up out-and-out blond beasts side by side with dark Saturnine types like the Führer himself. I am a blond, much less an antique Roman than a Dane. One of my sisters was a brunette: the other had hair of a flaming red seen only in the Scottish Highlands, to which my ancestry has been traced. All these types with which writers like Chamberlain play: the Teutons and Latins, the Apollonians and Dionysians, the Nordics and Southics, the Dominants and Recessives, have existed and keep cropping up as individuals, and exciting antipathies or affinities quite often enough to give substance to theories about them; but the notion that they can be segregated as races or species is bosh. We have nations with national characteristics (rapidly fading, by the way), national languages, and national customs. But they deteriorate without cross fertilization; and if Herr Hitler could put a stop to cross fertilization in Germany and produce a population of brainless Bismarcks Germany would be subjugated by crossfertilized aliens, possibly by cosmopolitan Jews. There is more difference between a Catholic Bavarian and a Lutheran Prussian, between a tall fair Saxon and a stocky Baltic Celt, than there is between a Frankfort Jew and a Frankfort Gentile. Even in Africa, where pink emigrants struggle with brown and black natives for possession of the land, and our Jamaican miscegenation shocks public sentiment, the sun sterilizes the pinks to such an extent that Cabinet ministers call for more emigration to maintain

24. The Abyssinians traced their lineage to the Hebrews maternally through Ethiop, son of Cush, who was in turn the son of Ham and grandson of Noah and, paternally, through Menelik I, son of Solomon and Sheba.

the pink population. They do not yet venture to suggest that the pinks had better darken their skins with a mixture of Bantu or Zulu blood; but that conclusion is obvious. In New Zealand, in Hawaii, there are pure-bred pinks and yellows; but there are hardly any pure-bred Maoris or South Sea Islanders left. In Africa the intelligent pink native is a Fusionist as between Dutch and British stock. The intelligent Jew is a Fusionist as between Jew and Gentile stock, even when he is also a bit of a Zionist. Only the stupidest or craziest ultra-Nationalists believe that people corraled within the same political frontier are all exactly alike, and that they improve by continuous inbreeding.

Now Herr Hitler is not a stupid German. I therefore urge upon him that his Antisemitism and national exclusiveness must be pathological: a craze, a complex, a bee in his bonnet, a hole in his armor, a hitch in his statesmanship, one of those lesions which sometimes prove fatal. As it has no logical connection with Fascism or National Socialism, and has no effect on them except to bring them into disrepute, I doubt whether it can survive its momentary usefulness as an excuse for plundering raids and *coups d'état* against inconvenient Liberals or Marxists. A persecution is always a man hunt; and man hunting is not only a very horrible sport but socially a dangerous one, as it revives a primitive instinct incompatible with civilization: indeed civilization rests fundamentally on the compact that it shall be dropped.

And here comes the risk we run when we allow a dominant individual to become a despot. There is a story told of a pious man who was sustained through a lifetime of crushing misfortune by his steady belief that if he fought the good fight to the end he would at last stand in the presence of his God. In due course he died, and presented himself at the gates of heaven for his reward. St Peter, who was for some reason much worried, hastily admitted him and bade him go and enjoy himself. But the good man said that he did not want to enjoy himself: he wanted to stand in the presence of God. St Peter tried to evade the claim, dwelling on the other delights of heaven, coaxing, bullying, arguing. All in vain: he could not shake the claimant and could not deny his right. He sent for St Paul, who was as worried and as evasive as his colleague; but he also failed to induce the newcomer to forgo his promised privilege. At last they took him by the arms and led him to a mighty cathedral, where, entering by the west door, he saw the Ancient of Days seated in silent majesty on a throne in the choir. He sprang forward to prostrate himself at the divine feet, but was held back firmly by the apostles. "Be quiet" said St Paul. "He has gone mad; and we dont know what to do." "Dont tell anybody" added St Peter. And there the story ends.

But that is not how the story ends on earth. Make any common fellow an autocrat and at once you have the Beggar on Horseback riding to the devil. Even when, as the son of his father, he has been trained from infancy to behave well in harness and blinkers, he may go as mad sadistically as a Roman emperor or a Russian Tsar. But that is only the extreme case. Uncommon people, promoted on their merits, are by no means wholly exempt from megalomania. Morris's simple and profound saying that "no man is good enough to be another man's master" holds good unless both master and man regard themselves as equally the fellow servants of God in States where God still reigns, or, in States where God is dead, as the subjects and agents of a political constitution applying humane principles which neither of them may violate. In that case autocrats are no longer autocrats. Failing any such religious or political creed all autocrats go more or less mad. That is a plain fact of political pathology.

Judged in this light our present predicament is lamentable. We no longer believe in the old "sanctions" (as they are called nowadays) of heaven and hell; and except in Russia there is not in force a single political constitution that enables and enjoins the citizen to earn his own living as a matter of elementary honesty, or that does not exalt vast personal riches and the organization of slaughter and conquest above all other conditions and activities. The financier and the soldier are the cocks of the walk; and democracy means that their parasites and worshippers carry all before them.

Thus when so many other tyrannies have been swept away by simple Liberalism, the tyranny of the talented individuals will remain. Again I ask what are we to do with them in self-defence? Mere liquidation would be disastrous, because at present only about five per cent of the population are capable of making decisions of any importance; and without many daily decisions civilization would go to pieces. The problem is how to make sure that the decisions shall be made in the general interest and not solely in the immediate personal interest of the decider. It was argued by our classical political economists that there is a divine harmony between these two interests of such a nature that if every decider does the best for himself the result will also be the best for everybody. In spite of a century of bitter experience of the adoption of these excuses for laziness in politics, shameless selfishness in industry, and glorification of idle uselessness in the face of the degrading misery of the masses, they are still taught in our universities, and, what is worse, broadcast by university professors by wireless, as authentic political economy instead of what they really are: that is, the special pleading put forward in defence of the speculators, exploiters, and parasitic property owners in whose grossly antisocial interests the country is misgoverned. Since Karl Marx and Friedrich Engels exposed the horrible condition of the working classes that underlies the pursepride and snobbery of the upper middle classes and the prestige of the landed gentry and peerage there has been no substantial excuse for believing in the alleged harmony of interests. Nothing more diabolical can be conceived than the destiny of a civilization in which the material sources of the people's subsistence are privately owned by a handful of persons taught from childhood that every penny they can extort from the propertyless is an addition to the prosperity of their country and an enrichment of the world at large.

But private property is not the subject of my demonstration in The Millionairess. Private property can be communized. Capitalists and landlords can be pressed into the service of the community, or, if they are idle or incorrigibly recalcitrant, handed over to the police. Under such circumstances the speculator would find his occupation gone. With him would disappear the routine exploiter. But the decider, the dominator, the organizer, the tactician, the mesmerizer would remain; and if they were still educated as ladies and gentlemen are educated today, and consequently had the same sort of consciences and ambitions, they would, if they had anything like our present proletariat to deal with, re-establish industrial anarchy and heritable private property in land with all their disastrous consequences and Gadarene destiny. And their rule, being that of able persons and not of nincompoops born with silver spoons in their mouths, would at first produce some striking improvements in the working of the public services, including the elimination of dud dignitaries and the general bracing up of plodders and slackers. But when dominators die, and are succeeded by persons who can only work a routine, a relapse is inevitable; and the destruction by the dominators of the organizations by which citizens defend themselves against oppression (trade unions, for example) may be found to leave society less organized than it was before the hand of the master had risen from the dust to which it has returned. For it is obvious that a business organized for control by an exceptionally omnipotent and omniscient head will go to pieces when that head is replaced by a commonplace numskull. We need not go back to Richard Cromwell or the Duke of Reichstadt to illustrate this.[25] It is occurring every day in commercial business.

Now the remedy lies, not in the extermination of all dominators and deciders, but on the contrary in their multiplication to what may be called their natural minority limit, which will destroy their present scarcity value.

25. Cromwell, English politician and son of Oliver Cromwell, was named by his father to succeed as Lord Protector. A Rump Parliament in 1659 dismissed him. François Bonaparte, called L'Aiglon (the Eaglet), was named as successor on the abdication of his father in 1814, but was not accepted by the Allies. He was created Duc de Reichstadt in 1818.

But we must also eliminate the mass of ignorance, weakness, and timidity which force them to treat fools according to their folly. Armies, fanatical sects and mobs, and the blackshirts complained of today by their black and blue victims, have consisted hitherto mostly of people who should not exist in civilized society. Titus Oates and Lord George Gordon owed their vogue to the London mob. There should not have been any London mob. The soldiers of Marlborough and Wellington were never-do-wells, mental defectives, and laborers with the minds and habits of serfs. Military geniuses could hunt with such products more easily than with a pack of hounds. Our public school and university education equips armies of this kind with appropriate staffs of officers. When both are extinct we shall be able to breathe more freely.

Let us therefore assume that the soldier and his officer as we know them, the Orange and Papist rioters of Belfast, the Moslem and Hindu irreconcilables of the east and the Ku-Klux-Klans and lynching mobs of the west, have passed away as the less dangerous prehistoric monsters have passed, and that all men and women are meeting on equal terms as far as circumstances and education are concerned. Let us suppose that no man can starve or flog his fellows into obeying him, or force upon them the alternative of risking their lives for him in battle or being shot at dawn. Let us take for granted armies intelligent enough to present their officers at any moment with the alternative of organizing a return home or being superseded out of hand. Let us narrow the case to the mysterious precedence into which certain people get pushed even when they lack ambition and are far too intelligent to believe that eminence and its responsibilities are luxuries. To be "greatest among you" is a distinction dearly bought at the price of being "servant to all the rest" [Matthew 23: 11]. Plato was quite right in taking reluctance to govern as a leading symptom of supreme fitness for it.[26] But if we insisted on this qualification in all cases, we should find ourselves as short of governors as the churches would be if they insisted on all their parish priests or rectors being saints. A great deal of the directing and organizing work of the world will still have to be done by energetic and capable careerists who are by no means void of vulgar ambition, and very little troubled by the responsibilities that attend on power. When I said that Napoleon was fundamentally a fool and a snob I did not mean for a moment to question his extraordinary capacity as a ruler of men. If we compare him with his valet-secretary [Louis-Antoine]

26. In the *Republic* we are told that 'No one of his own will chooses to hold rule and office and take other people's troubles in hand to straighten them out' (*Republic* I, p. 347, in *Collected Dialogues of Plato*, eds. Edith Hamilton and Huntington Cairns, 1961).

Bourrienne[27] we find that there were no external circumstances to prevent Bourrienne becoming the emperor and Napoleon the valet. They quarreled and parted with an exchange of epithets unprintable in polite English. Bourrienne was as much a Man of Destiny as Buonaparte. But it was his destiny to be ruled and Buonaparte's to rule; and so Buonaparte became Napoleon Bonaparte, First Consul and Emperor, as inevitably as Bourrienne remained a speculator, litterateur and diplomatist. I am not forgetting that Bourrienne saw Napoleon come and go, and had a much more comfortable and finally a more successful career than his quondam master; but the point is that Napoleon was master whilst their personal relations lasted. And please note that Napoleon did not and could not impose on Bourrienne and [Charles Maurice de] Talleyrand[-Périgord],[28] nor even on the more cultivated of his marshals (all planetary Napoleons) as he could and did on the soldiery and peasantry. They turned against him very promptly when his fortunes changed and he could no longer be of any use to them.

Now if a ruler can command men only as long as he is efficient and successful his rule is neither a tyranny nor a calamity: it is a very valuable asset. But suppose the nation is made up for the most part of people too ignorant to understand efficient government, and taught, as far as they are taught at all, to measure greatness by pageantry and the wholesale slaughter called military glory. It was this ignorance and idolatry that first exalted Napoleon and then smashed him. From Toulon to Austerlitz[29] Napoleon did what good he did by stealth, and had no occasion to "blush to find it fame,"[30] as nobody gave him the least credit for anything but killing. When the glory turned to shame on the road back from Moscow his good works availed him nothing, and the way was open to St Helena. Catherine of Russia, when she was faced with a revolt against the misery of her people, said, not "Let us relieve their misery by appropriate reforms," but "Let us give them a little war to amuse them."[31] Every tottering regime tries to rally its subjects to its

27. French diplomat, who, after serving as private secretary to Napoleon, became minister of state under Louis XVIII.
28. French statesman, who rose from church orders to become ambassador to Britain. He quarrelled and broke with Napoleon in 1809.
29. Napoleon, early in his career, commanded the artillery that successfully concluded the siege of Toulon (1793). At Austerlitz on 2 December 1805 he defeated the troops of Austria and Russia.
30. Alexander Pope, *Imitations of Horace*, Epilogue to the Satires, Dialogue 1 (1733–8).
31. Probably apocryphal. The remark was ascribed also to Vyacheslav Plehve, Russia's minister of the interior, in 1904.

support in the last resort by a war. It was not only the last card of Napoleon III before he lost the game:[32] it played a considerable part in the capitalist support of Hohenzollern sabre rattling which made the desperate onslaught of Germany in 1914 possible. Patriotism, roused to boiling point by an enemy at the gate, is not only the last refuge of a scoundrel in Dr Johnson's sense [*Dictionary*, 1755], it is far more dangerously the everyday resort of capitalism and feudalism as a red herring across the scent of Communism. Under such circumstances it is fortunate that war on the modern scale is so completely beyond the capacity of private capitalism that, as in 1915, it forces the belligerents into national factory production, public discipline, and rationed distribution: in short, into Socialism. Not only did national factories spring up like mushrooms, but the private factories had to be brought up to the mark by public control of prices and dictation of scientific business methods, involving such an exposure of the obsolescence and inefficiency of profitmongering methods that it took years of reckless lying from Press and platform to make the silly public believe the contrary. For war is like the seven magic bullets which the devil has ready to sell for a human soul [Weber, *Der Freischütz*, 1821]. Six of them may hit the glorymonger's mark very triumphantly; but the seventh plays some unexpected and unintended trick that upsets the gunman's apple cart. It seemed an astute stroke of German imperial tactics to send Lenin safely through Germany to Russia so that he might make trouble for the Tsar. But the bullet was a number seven: it killed the Tsar very efficiently; but it came back like a boomerang and laid the Hohenzollerns beside the Romanoffs.

Pageantry will lose its black magic when it becomes a local popular amusement; so that the countryside may come to know it from behind the scenes, when, though it will still please, it will no longer impose. For mere iconoclasm is a mistake: the Roundhead[33] folly (really a Thickhead one) of destroying the power of the pageant by forbidding all theatrical displays and dressings-up, and making everybody wear ugly clothes, ended in the flamboyant profligacy of the Restoration; and the attempt to enforce the second commandment by smashing the images soon smashed the second commandment. Give away the secret that the dressed-up performers are only amateurs, and the images works of art, and the dupes and worshippers will become undeluded connoisseurs.

32. When Charles-Louis Napoleon foolishly allowed Bismarck to involve France in the calamitous Franco-Prussian War (1870–71) he was deposed by the National Assembly.
33. Member or supporter of the Parliamentary (Puritan) Party during the English Civil War.

Unfortunately it is easier to produce a nation of artistic than of political connoisseurs. Our schools and universities do not concern themselves with fine art, which they despise as an unmanly pursuit. It is possible for a young gentleman to go through the whole educational mill of preparatory school, public school, and university with the highest academic honors without knowing the difference between a chanty and a symphony, a tavern sign and a portrait by Titian, a ballad by Macaulay and a stanza by Keats. But at least he is free to find out all this for himself if he has a fancy that way.

Not so in political science. Not so in religion. In these subjects he is proselytized from the beginning in the interests of established institutions so effectually that he remains all his life firmly convinced that his greatest contemporaries are rascally and venal agitators, villainous blasphemers, or at best seditious cads. He will listen to noodles' orations, read pompous leading articles, and worship the bloodthirsty tribal idols of Noah and Samuel with a gravity and sincerity that would make him infinitely pitiable if they did not also make him infinitely dangerous. He will feed his mind on empty phrases as Nebuchadnezzar fed his body on grass [Daniel 4: 33]; and any boss who has mastered these phrases can become his dictator, his despot, his evangelist, and in effect his god-emperor.

Clearly we shall be bossridden in one form or another as long as education means being put through this process, or the best imitation of it that our children's parents can afford. The remedy is another Reformation, now long and perilously overdue, in the direction and instruction of our children's minds politically and religiously. We should begin well to the left of Russia, which is still encumbered with XIX century superstitions. Communism is the fairy godmother who can transform Bosses into "servants to all the rest"; but only a creed of Creative Evolution can set the souls of the people free. Then the dominator will still find himself face to face with subordinates who can do nothing without him; but that will not give him the inside grip. A late rich shipowner,[34] engaged in a quarrel with his workmen in which he assumed that I was on their side, rashly asked me what his men could do without him. Naturally I asked him what he could do without them, hoping to open his eyes to the fact that apart from the property rights he had bought or borrowed he was as dependent on them as they on him. But I fear I

34. The shipowner was J. Bruce Ismay, of the White Star Line, whose stevedores, coalies and crews went on strike in Southampton, on 21 June 1911, to demand full recognition of their union. The strike was settled two days later. Shaw may, however, have met or corresponded with Ismay earlier, for there was much labour unrest in this period among the White Star's dockers in London and Liverpool.

impressed him most by adding, quite untruly, that no gentleman would have asked that question.

Save for my allusion to the persecution and exile of Einstein I have not said a word here about the miserable plight of the great men neglected, insulted, starved, and occasionally put to death, sometimes horribly, by the little ones. Their case is helpless because nothing can defend them against the might of overwhelming numbers unless and until they develop the Vril imagined by Bulwer Lytton[35] which will enable one person to destroy a multitude, and thereby make us more particular than we are at present about the sort of persons we produce. I am confining myself to the power wielded by the moneymakers and military geniuses in political life and by the dominant personalities in private life. Lytton's Vril was a fiction only in respect of its being available for everybody, and therefore an infallible preventive of any attempt at oppression. For that individuals here and there possess a power of domination which others are unable to resist is undeniable; and since this power is as yet nameless we may as well call it Vril as anything else. It is the final reality of inequality. It is easy to equalize the dominators with the commonplacers economically: you just give one of them half-a-crown and the other two-and-sixpence. Nelson was paid no more than any other naval captain or admiral; and the poverty of Mozart or Marx was worse than the voluntary holy poverty of the great heads of the religious orders. Dominators and dominated are already equalized before the law: shall not I, a playwright of Shakespearean eminence, be hanged if I commit a murder precisely as if I were the most illiterate call boy? Politically we all have at least the symbol of equality in our votes, useless as they are to us under political and economic institutions made to encourage William the Conqueror to slay Harold and exploit Hodge. But, I repeat, when all these perfectly feasible equalizations are made real, there still remains Epifania [Shaw's millionairess], shorn of her millions and unable to replace them, but still as dominant as Saint Joan, Saint Clare, and Saint Teresa. The most complete Communism and Democracy

35. In Edward Bulwer-Lytton's prophetic novel *The Coming Race* (1871), the narrator, in explaining vril to the reader, says: 'I should call it electricity, except that it comprehends in its manifold branches other forces of nature, to which, in our scientific nomenclature, differing names are assigned, such as magnetism, galvanism, etc. These people consider that in vril they have arrived at the unity in natural energetic agencies, which has been conjectured by many philosophers [of our world] . . .' Through vril conductors, we learn, these philosophers of the 'coming race' can 'exercise influence over minds, and bodies animal and vegetable, to an extent not surpassed in the romances of our mystics'.

can only give her her chance far more effectively than any feudal or capitalist society.

And this, I take it, is one of the highest claims of Communism and Democracy to our consideration, and the explanation of the apparently paradoxical fact that it is always the greatest spirits, from Jesus to Lenin, from St Thomas More to William Morris, who are communists and democrats, and always the commonplace people who weary us with their blitherings about the impossibility of equality when they are at a loss for any better excuse for keeping other people in the kitchen and themselves in the drawingroom. I say cheerfully to the dominators "By all means dominate: it is up to us to so order our institutions that you shall not oppress us, nor bequeath any of your precedence to your commonplace children." For when ambition and greed and mere brainless energy have been disabled, the way will be clear for inspiration and aspiration to save us from the fatheaded stagnation of the accursed Victorian snobbery which is bringing us to the verge of ruin.

MALVERN.
28 August 1935.

# Morris as I Knew Him

*First published as a preface to the second volume of May Morris's* William Morris:
Artist, Writer, Socialist, *London, 1936. Separately published as*
William Morris as I Knew Him, *New York, 1936*

======

Morris, when he had to define himself politically, called himself a Communist.[1] Very often, of course, in discussing Socialism he had to speak of himself as a Socialist; but he jibbed at it internally, and flatly rebelled against such faction labels as Social-Democrat and the like. He knew that the essential term, etymologically, historically, and artistically, was Communist; and it was the only word he was comfortable with.

It must not be inferred that he had any prevision of Soviet technique or any other developed method of Communist organization. Nobody had, or could have, in his time. He was on the side of Karl Marx *contra mundum* [against the world]; but he had none of the intellectual pretentiousness and pride of education that made Lassalle boast of being equipped with all the culture of his age,[2] and Marx elaborate a patent philosophic dialectic and an economic theory of bourgeois exploitation and surplus value. Far from being proud of his university education Morris declared that the only item in his past expenditure he thoroughly grudged was the twenty pounds his Oxford degree of Master of Arts had cost him. Going straight to the root of Communism he held that people who do not do their fair share of social work are

1. What Morris said, in a lecture 'Communism' (1893), was 'Communism is in fact the completion of Socialism: when that ceases to be militant & becomes triumphant, it will be Communism' and 'I do declare that any other state of society but communism is grievous & disgraceful to all belonging to it.'
2. Shaw's source was W. H. Dawson's *German Socialism and Ferdinand Lassalle* (1888), which he reviewed as 'The Messiah of Social Democracy' in the *Daily Chronicle*, 31 October 1888 (reprinted in *Bernard Shaw's Book Reviews*, vol. 2 (1884–1950), ed. Brian Tyson, 1996). Lassalle, said Dawson, 'would often assume a tone of lofty superiority when addressing even judges on the bench. "Ask friends and foes alike about me," he once exclaimed, "and if they are men who have themselves learned something, both will agree unanimously that I write every line armed with the entire culture of my century"' (p. 190).

"damned thieves,"[3] and that neither a stable society, a happy life, nor a healthy art can come from honoring such thieving as the mainspring of industrial activity. To him the notion that a British workman cannot arrive at this very simple fundamental conclusion except through the strait gate of the Marxian dialectic, or that the dialectic can be anything to such a one but a most superfluous botheration, was folly. He had read all the Socialist scriptures and economic textbooks: not only Marx's epoch-making exposure of capitalist civilization but John Stuart Mill's examination of Communism [*Principles of Political Economy*, 1848]; and he had seen at once that Mill's verdict was against the evidence, as Mill himself concluded later on. He had the authority of the eminent professor [John Elliott] Cairnes for the condemnation of *rentiers* as "drones in the hive", and disagreed with Cairnes only in seeing no sacredness whatever in contracts made under duress with drones.[4]

As a matter of fact Marx's theory of value and the explanation of surplus value he founded on it are academic blunders; and the dialectic, though it may have been a convenient instrument of thought a hundred years ago for a German university student soaked in Hegelianism, can now only make Communist thinking difficult and uncongenial. Morris put all that aside instinctively as the intellectual trifling it actually is, and went straight to the real issues on which he was quite simple and quite right. And I venture to prophesy that the Russians will presently do the same.

It was as an agitator in the Socialist movement of the eighteen eighties that I came into personal contact with Morris.[5] He was our one acknowledged

3. Morris expressed this sentiment in at least two of his lectures: 'The Depression of Trade' (1885) and 'What Socialists Want' (1888); see the *Unpublished Lectures of William Morris*, ed. Eugene D. Lemire (1969). The phrasing, however, is more apt to have been Shaw's, possibly recalled from his own lecture on the subject, 'Thieves', on 30 May 1886 at Morris's Kelmscott House, Hammersmith.
4. Cairnes, an Irish economist, Professor of Political Economy at University College, London, had been critical of the 'idle rich class' in his book *Some Leading Principles of Political Economy, Newly Expounded* (1874): '[W]hat they consume in luxury and idleness is not capital, and helps to sustain nothing but their own unprofitable lives. By all means they must have their rents and interest, as it is written in the bond; but let them take their proper place as drones in the hive, gorging at a feast to which they have contributed nothing' (p. 35).
5. Shaw first met Morris in 1884, the latter seeking Shaw out after reading the early chapters of *An Unsocial Socialist* serialized in *To-Day* from March 1884. Morris's first surviving letter to Shaw, 8 July 1884, invites him to Hammersmith for a Sunday visit, with a postscript 'I can always give you a bed' (Morris, *Collected Letters 1881–1884*, ed. Norman Kelvin, 1987, p. 292).

Great Man; but we knew very little about him. Of William Morris of the Red House,[6] head centre and organizer of a happy Brotherhood[7] of artists who all called him Topsy[8] and thought of him as a young man, we knew nothing. The small minority of us who had any contacts with the newest fashions in literature and art knew that he had become famous as the author of a long series of poems called The Earthly Paradise which few of us had read, though that magic line "the idle singer of an empty day" had caught our ears somehow. We knew that he kept a highly select shop in Oxford Street[9] where he sold furniture of a rum æsthetic sort, and decorated houses with extraordinary wallpapers. I myself had read enough of his work to know that his self-appointed work in poetry was the retelling of all the world's old stories in a tuneful dialect which went back past the pomposities of Dr Johnson and the rhetoric of Shakespear all the way to Chaucer, and which, though it rescued some good old English from disuse and oblivion, and was agreeable enough to my ear, seemed affected and ridiculous to the Philistines. And that was about all.

It was a curious situation for Morris (I have heard him discuss it). He had escaped middle age, passing quite suddenly from a circle of artistic revolution-ists, mostly university men gone Agnostic or Bohemian or both, who knew all about him and saw him as much younger and less important than he really was, into a proletarian movement in which, so far as he was known at all, he was venerated as an Elder. The atmosphere had changed from one of enthusiastic understanding and intimate good fellowship to an ignorant and uncertain reverence, poisoned at first by a class mistrust which he lived down by the irresistible evidence in himself that he was far above classification.

Once or twice, some tactless ghost from his past wandered into the Socialist world and spoke of him and even to him as Topsy. It was soon morally booted out in miserable bewilderment for being silly and impudent. Such

6. A small 'Palace of Art', set in an orchard some ten miles from London near Upton, dreamt up by Morris and designed by his architect friend Philip Webb, to which Morris brought his bride in 1859.
7. A cohesive group of artists (Burne-Jones, D. G. Rossetti and other Pre-Raphaelites) who founded a decorating firm that brought about a reform in Victorian taste in home decoration: furniture, fabric and wall decoration.
8. Morris acquired at Oxford (1853–6) the nickname 'Topsy' or 'Top', after the character in *Uncle Tom's Cabin*, because of his wild curly hair.
9. The shop of Morris, Marshall, and Faulkner, Decorators (1861) opened at 8 Red Lion Square. It removed to 26 Queen Square in 1865, and, in 1877, to 449 Oxford Street.

momentary incidents did not matter. What did matter was that many of the Socialists, especially the middle-class ones who presently organized themselves as Fabians, were arrant Philistines, regarding all poets and artists as undesirable cranks. However, there was no love lost on the other side. Morris heartily disliked the Fabians, not because they undervalued him, but as a species.

Anyhow we were a very mixed lot at that time; for the movement was at first one of pure reaction against the unrighteousness and cruelty of Capitalism, which had been tellingly exposed and traced to the institution of private property in land by the American Henry George, whose Progress and Poverty had just achieved a huge circulation. Marx's still more terrific exposure had not been translated into English (like Morris I had read all my Marx in French): and we were all out to *écraser l'infâme*[10] without in the least knowing how. We had not sorted ourselves out, and were for the moment far more Anarchists than Marxists. We were to break our chains, make a revolution, and live happily ever after.

I myself had always been a revolutionist in grain; but I had been occupied with the conflict between the Churches and Science, republicanism and monarchy, Irish Nationalism (which bored me) and Dublin Castle, and also good art and bad art, though here the art that concerned me most was modern music, especially in its dramatic applications by Mozart and Wagner. To train myself as a public speaker I frequented public meetings; and at one of these [5 September 1882] I discovered Henry George in person, a wonderful platform artist. His speech sent me to political economy, with which I had never concerned myself, as fundamental in any social criticism. I devoured Progress and Poverty and sought out the Socialist meetings [1883] of the Democratic Federation founded by Henry Mayers Hyndman, who had made the acquaintance of Karl Marx and been converted by him. At these meetings, on my advocating a rally round Henry George, I was told that I knew nothing because I had not read Karl Marx. I read Karl Marx and then found that none of the rest had. And so I took to the street corner as an evangelist of Socialism. In this way I became known to the leading Socialists of the moment before we had all quarreled and divided into rival societies; and so it came about that I found myself one evening at a social gathering of the Democratic Federation (later the Social-Democratic Federation or S.D.F.) with Hyndman

10. 'Down with the Infamy', written by Voltaire in a letter to Jean Le Rond d'Alembert, 27 January 1762. In a second letter to the same correspondent, on 28 November, he qualified the remark, saying he meant 'superstition' and not 'the Christian religion'.

and Morris present as colleagues in that body.[11] I have elsewhere described how I was the author of five novels which nobody would publish [see vol. 1, pp. 90ff and 172ff], and how I had dug them up to make padding for a Socialist magazine called To-Day, to which we all had to contribute as best we could. It really had not occurred to me that anyone would read this fifty times rejected stuff of mine: it was offered and accepted solely to bulk out the magazine to saleable size when the supply of articles ran short; but Morris, who read everything that came in his way, and held that nobody could pass a shop window with a picture in it without stopping [see p. 474], had read a chapter of An Unsocial Socialist, and been sufficiently entertained to wish to meet the author.

Here, then, was Morris in his blue suit and bluer shirt, his tossing mane which suggested that his objection to looking-glasses extended to brushes and combs, and his habit, when annoyed by some foolish speaker, of pulling single hairs violently from his moustache and growling "damned fool!" He maintained that his blue suit was aimed at when Andrew Lang wrote of the shock of meeting your favorite poet and finding that he looked like a ship's purser;[12] but Morris did not look like a purser; for pursers always smooth their hair, wheras the disarrangement of Morris's was so effectively leonine that I suspected him of spending at least a quarter of an hour every morning getting it just right.

I was soon in triple conversation with him and Hyndman, as our proletarian friends were a little out of it when we three got going. Hyndman could talk about anything with a fluency that left Morris nowhere. He was a most imposing man, and seemed to have been born in a frock coat and top hat. In old age he looked like God in Blake's illustrations to Job. In the prime of life, as he was then, he was more like the deity in Raphael's Vision of Ezekiel. He was a leading figure in any assembly, and took that view of himself with perfect self-confidence. Altogether an assuming man, quite naturally and unconsciously.

Morris was quite unassuming: he impressed by his obvious weight and quality. On this occasion he disclaimed all capacity for leadership, and said

11. The collaboration was brief: Morris joined H. M. Hyndman's Democratic Federation in 1883 and withdrew a year later, taking many of the Federation's members with him, to found the Socialist League. Shaw, who had been encouraged to join the Federation, chose instead to become a member of the newly founded Fabian Society.
12. Andrew Lang, a prolific journalist, published hundreds of 'middle leader' essays (of which Shaw was an avid reader) principally in the Daily News and the Morning Post, between 1875 and 1905. His remark has not been located.

he was ready to do anything he was told, presumably by Hyndman as chairman of the Federation, plus the leader who had called him as a disciple. I smiled grimly to myself at this modest offer of allegiance, measuring at sight how much heavier Morris's armament was; but Hyndman accepted it at once as his due. Had Morris been accompanied by Plato, Aristotle, Gregory the Great, Dante, Thomas Aquinas, Milton and Newton, Hyndman would have taken the chair as their natural leader without the slightest misgiving, and before the end of the month have quarreled with them all and left himself with no followers but the devoted handful who could not compete with him, and to whom he was a sort of god. But he was always excellent company as a perfect Victorian freethinking gentleman, like Meredith and [Charles] Dilke,[13] who had known everyone and was never at a loss for anecdotes about them. His talk was a most entertaining performance; and both Morris and I could listen to it without being bored for a moment. There was, however, an important difference between his talk and Morris's. What Morris said he meant, some-times very vehemently; and it was always worth saying. Of Hyndman's most brilliant conversational performances it was impossible to believe a single word. The people he described so entertainingly were not authentic human beings. The things he told as having happened to them could not possibly have happened to anybody.

In short, Hyndman was as unlike Morris as one mortal man can be unlike another. Only in one respect they were alike: they had been brought up in rich households where they had never been effectively controled nor forced by circumstances to control themselves. Consequently they both were petu-lant and subject to explosions of temper. The chances of their being able to work together were practically nil; and I was not at all surprised when the Hyndman-Morris combination exploded violently. What the immediate quarrel was about does not now matter: the two men were hopelessly incom-patible tactically and strategically; and neither of them could keep their tem-pers. Besides, Hyndman, like Marx, quarreled with everyone who challenged his leadership. Morris, after that first inevitable quarrel, was always a concili-atory force in the movement, and even went to extremes in making way for every goose who was crazy enough to fancy himself a swan.

In justice to Hyndman, who now goes out of the Morris saga, let it be remembered that though he could not work with anyone on terms which men of equal or greater ability would accept, he stuck to his Socialist guns

13. Radical MP, author of *Problems of Greater Britain* (1890), whose prominent career was devastated by a scandalous divorce action in which he was named as co-respondent.

nearly to the end, when the revolution for which he had been calling all his life took place in Russia. Now Hyndman, theoretically an Internationalist, was at heart a trueblue English patriot. When Lenin at Brest Litovsk backed out of the war[14]—England's war—Hyndman turned on him with a fury of invective which the Whitest of Tsarists could not have outdone. It was his only lapse from integrity as a Socialist. In private life he cannot have been an unamiable man; for he and his first wife, who lived long enough to be "old Matilda," were a model Darby and Joan. When she died and he was nearly eighty a young woman [Rosalind Travers] married him, and, when he too died, actually committed suttee after trying for a year to live without him. Those who can will like to think that she rejoined him in that heaven in which neither of them believed.

The importance of the Hyndman episode lies in Morris's action when the split took place. Morris had the majority of the committee on his side, and according to all constitutional precedent should have stood his ground and voted the Hyndman opposition down on issue after issue after endless debate on motion after motion and amendment after amendment. It was as clear to Morris as it has been later to Mussolini and Hitler that no business can be done in this way. He simply took his majority out of the Federation and formed a new body called the Socialist League, leaving the Federation to do what it could in its own way, and setting himself and his friends free to do the same instead of senselessly wasting all their time and energy in obstructing oneanother.

Morris certainly did not foresee that he had invented a new political technique having as its rule that the Opposition must step down and out instead of remaining to obstruct. That his followers on this point would nowadays include Fascists and autocrats as well as Communists would hardly have pleased him; but I believe he would have maintained, as a very practical man, that the parliamentary party system is, as Dickens had pointed out, the secret of How Not To Do It [*Little Dorrit*, chapter 10], and that when once it is decided that a thing has to be done the people who want to prevent its being done must leave the room.

The Socialist League did its share in that making of Socialists which was, as Morris held, the real business of the movement; but its attempt to extract from its proletarian members a Socialist Constitution was a grotesque failure. He bore with them for years, giving them every means of excogitating some plan that would hold water. Unfortunately they had no experience of the

14. Lenin signed a truce agreement with the Central Powers on 15 December 1917 and a peace treaty at Brest-Litovsk on 3 March 1918.

government of anything more complicated than a coster's barrow [a fruit-seller's cart]; and they were romantic anarchists to a man, strong on the negative side, but regarding the State as an enemy, very much as the child regards a policeman. Morris, like all original artists and thinkers, had a good deal of this feeling too, and though he would not countenance Anarchism on any terms, was genuinely anxious to discover how its appetite for freedom could be reconciled with the positive side of Communism. But he was an experienced business manager and knew what business management means and what personal qualities it needs. A very amateurish plan, called Anti-State Communism, was evolved;[15] and its authors, after spending a good deal of Morris's money, suddenly perceived that the logic of their plan involved the repudiation of Morris's directorship, which was keeping the whole affair together. So Morris, who had been holding the League up by the scruff of its neck, opened his hand, whereupon it dropped like a stone into the sea, leaving only a little wreckage to come to the surface occasionally and demand bail at the police court or a small loan.

After the Morris-Hyndman fission there were in the field four Socialist Societies, the Democratic Federation, which presently threw off that ambiguity and became the Social-Democratic Federation, with Hyndman as its Perpetual Grand; the Socialist League, which was really Morris and nothing else; an admirable group of Christian Socialist clergymen called the Guild of St Matthew captained by Stewart Headlam; and the Fabian Society, which I had picked out as the place for me, and which rapidly drew away from the others as the only one of them that could work as a purveyor of immediately constructive election programs. The explanation of this was very simple. The League and the Federation held their meetings in public halls and invited the working class to join them at a cost of a penny a week, the idea being that when the entire proletariat had been convinced by the speeches, and had joined in irresistible numbers, a revolution would be achieved by the Federation or the League, as the case might be. Each of them, I may add, denounced the other in terms of unmeasured vituperativeness. Both were incapable of real committee work because their councils were not homogeneous: a combination of one exceptionally brilliant gentleman politician and writer (Hyndman) or one man of genius of unique culture and mental power (Morris) with a handful of poor men coming from a different world seemed very

15. Joseph Lane, a joint founder and leader of the Labour Emancipation League, which merged with the Socialist League, read an Anti-State Communist Manifesto to a meeting in April 1887, calling for abolition of the state in every respect and foreseeing revolution for Britain.

democratic and equalitarian; but it made skilled criticism and genuine intellectual cooperation farcically impossible.

Now the Fabian Society was nominally open to all classes; but as it met in middle-class drawingrooms where a laborer would have been out of place and unbearably uncomfortable, the Society was a genuine society of equals, whose minds worked at the same speed, by the same methods, on the same common stock of acquired ideas. The ablest half dozen ran the Society as its executive committee, but always subject to a good deal of useful criticism from the rest in really competent discussions. We alone among the Socialist societies, much derided by them as a group of drawingroom snobs (which we were), enjoyed real equality, real cooperation, real freedom from any sort of arbitrary dictatorship by individuals. We enjoyed as much psychological and educational homogeneity as lay within human limits. When the societies came into collision, which they occasionally did, Morris was hopelessly handicapped by his disunited and academically unarmed following. They were decent fellows enough, some of them, and appealed to Morris far more deeply than the Fabians; but in public debate the Leaguers were like untaught novices opposed to skilled boxers: we could beat them at political skittles easily even when they were in the right and we in the wrong. As to Hyndman, he treated the Fabians with contempt and would not join battle.

It may be asked why Morris, as a practical man, did not join the Fabians. I joined them because I knew that I could work with them, and that I could not work with untrained colleagues. Why did not Morris do the same on the same grounds?

The answer is that he would have been more out of place in our drawingrooms than in any gang of manual laborers or craftsmen. The furniture would have driven him mad; and the discussions would have ended in his dashing out of the room in a rage, and damning us all for a parcel of half baked shortsighted suburban snobs, as ugly in our ideas as in our lives. He could be patient with the strivings of ignorance and poverty towards the light if the striver had the reality that comes from hard work on tough materials with dirty hands, and weekly struggles with exploitation and oppression; but the sophistications of middle-class minds hurt him physically. He had made his way through much opposition and ridicule; and he was a wise and great man *sub specie eternitatis* [in a universal sense]; but he was an ungovernable man in a drawingroom. What stimulated me to argument, or at least repartee, made him swear.

In due time, when he concluded that his Socialist League was doing nothing but wasting his money and never could do anything else, he did not fall back on the Social-Democratic Federation, which was just as hopeless, nor on the Fabian Society. The Guild of St Matthew was too clerical for him. He no longer told the working classes that their only hope was in revolution: he even said that no doubt Socialism would come in Sidney Webb's way: the Fabian way. But he did not pretend to take much interest in that process as a process, nor imagine that he could be of any use personally in working it out. There was, I feel sure, a prophetic misgiving at the back of his mind whether it would be so smooth a job as it looked on parliamentary assumptions, or indeed whether it was going to be a political job in the parliamentary sense at all. If so, the event has proved that he was quite right. He did not live to see the Irish Question, staved off by thirty years of verbiage in the House of Commons accompanied by an ugly seesaw of moonlighting and murder with police batoning and Coercion Acts, and nominally settled at last by a Home Rule Act, really settled when it came to the point by an orgy of château burning and blood and iron such as the Genghis Khan himself could hardly have worsened. Had Morris lived to be eightyfive, he would have seen a great Communist State founded in Russia (of all places!) by a revolution of peasants greedy for bits of land of their own, and deserter-soldiers bent on peace at any price, overthrowing a Liberal revolution and presently finding itself manipulated by a little group of Marxists into the last thing they desired or dreamt of: a Union of Communist republics.

Morris was right when he contracted his would-be world league into the little Hammersmith Socialist Society, and told it to go on with its job and make Socialists, *advienne que pourra* [come what may].

However, this was in the future when I made Morris's acquaintance at that *soirée*, and smiled to myself as aforesaid when he offered himself as a humble private to Generalissimo Hyndman. We must have got on fairly well together; for I presently found myself not only lecturing at the little meeting hall into which he had converted his Hammersmith coach house, but appearing with him at the neighboring street corners on Sunday mornings conducting what most of the passers-by took to be prayer meetings. He and I complemented oneanother admirably; for I had a positive taste for abstract economics, and used my knowledge so effectively against the capitalist enemy that Morris said in the course of one of his addresses "In economics Shaw is my master."[16] The shock this gave me, which I still remember vividly, shews how far I placed him above myself. I was positively scandalized.

The lectures in the little hall on Sunday nights were followed by a supper in the house, to which the lecturer was invited. In this way I penetrated to the Morris interior.

16. Spoken in reaction to Shaw's speech in a debate that followed Morris's lecture 'The Aims of Art', Bedford Debating Society, 11 March 1886.

Now though nobody gave me credit for it in those days (very few do even now) I had a keen sense of beauty, not at all blunted by the extent to which my poverty had obliged me to starve it as far as my private accommodations were concerned. But I also had a searching analytical faculty which was the secret of my subsequent success as a professional critic. The combination, I am afraid, is rare. Some people, going into Morris's house, and finding it remarkably unlike their own house, would say "What a queer place!" Others, with a more cultivated sense of beauty, would say "How very nice!" But neither of them would necessarily have seen what I saw at once, that there was an extraordinary discrimination at work in this magical house. Nothing in it was there because it was interesting or quaint or rare or hereditary, like grandmother's or uncle's portrait. Everything that was necessary was clean and handsome: everything else was beautiful and beautifully presented. There was an oriental carpet so lovely that it would have been a sin to walk on it; consequently it was not on the floor but on the wall and half way across the ceiling. There was no grand piano: such a horror would have been impossible. On the supper table there was no table cloth: a thing common enough now among people who see that a table should be itself an ornament and not a clothes horse, but then an innovation so staggering that it cost years of domestic conflict to introduce it.

I must not inflict an inventory; but throughout it all there had reigned an artistic taste of extraordinary integrity: not once had its owner been seduced by any other interest or association. I know a collector who has a specially prized book, totally uninteresting as a visual object, which he cherishes because it is bound in the skin of a celebrated murderer: an excellent reason for throwing it into the dustbin. You never had to fear that from Morris. Later on he collected early printed books and medieval manuscripts; but he never bought a book because it was early or a manuscript because it was medieval. There are plenty of ugly early printed books; and all medieval manuscripts are not beautiful. For the Codex Sinaiticus, recently sold to the British Museum for a hundred thousand pounds,[17] Morris would not have paid a hundred farthings; but when he came on a real beauty he snatched it up, tucked it tight under his arm, and was of course at the mercy of the dealer as to the price. Once, when he was remonstrated with for giving £800 for a manuscript which any experienced Jew could have bought for £300, and was looking thoroughly miserable and ashamed of himself for his weakness,

---

17. The purchase was announced in Parliament on 20 December 1933. The Government provided £50,000 of the purchase price; the balance was raised by public appeal.

I said, "If you want a thing you cannot bargain." He instantly recovered his selfrespect; and his gratitude to me was boundless.

I was useful to him in that way more than once. Morris was a very great literary artist: his stories and essays and letters no less than his poems are tissues of words as fine as the carpet on the ceiling; but he was quite often at a loss for a critical word in dealing with some uncongenial modern thing. On such occasions I would hand him the appropriate adjective, and he would grab at it with a gasp of relief. It was like giving a penny to a millionaire who had bought a newspaper and found his pockets empty.

An accident enabled me to gain his confidence on the artistic side. Up to then in any discussion of modern art he had pushed the subject away like a petulant veteran who had no tolerance for anything later than the pre-Raphaelite movement and had never had the patience to try to understand a picture by Whistler or Monet. But it happened that a sensation was made by a stupendously pretentious German writer named Max Nordau, who, having made himself famous by a book called The Conventional Lies of [Our] Civilization [1884], followed it up by a Jeremiad called *Entartung* [1892–3] (Degeneration [see vol. 1, p. 284]), in which he maintained that all modern art is pathological: Wagner's music, Rossetti's poems, Morris's wallpapers and the paintings of the Impressionists being symptoms of mental dissolution and corruption. The book was taken quite seriously by the Press in England and America; and its vogue was at its height when Mr Benjamin Tucker of Boston, U.S.A., intervened.

Mr Tucker was a philosophic anarchist, an "unterrified Jeffersonian Democrat," who ran a magazine called Liberty, which appeared to be in verse because the lines of print were not "justified" (made the same length by the printer) to save useless expense. Suddenly Mr Tucker wrote to me requesting me to ascertain the highest price ever paid for an article in the history of literature. That sum, whatever it might be, he offered me for a review devoted to the destruction of Nordau. He could not do the job himself, because he had not sufficient knowledge of art, and only felt instinctively that Nordau was all wrong; and it was his considered judgment that I was the only writer living who could cover the fine arts with enough knowledge of them to put my finger on all Nordau's weak spots.

The price offered was heroic and the reason given for it irresistibly flattering. I took the job on. As far as Nordau was concerned it was the easiest one since Macaulay slated Robert Montgomery.[18] It would not be fair to call

18. Author of religious poems severely criticized by T. B. Macaulay in the *Edinburgh Review* (1830).

Nordau an impudent impostor; for he was honestly too ignorant of art to know that he knew nothing about it; and his head was full of Lombroso's then fashionable "psychiatry" with its grotesque lists of stigmas, phobias, lalias,[19] criminal types and what not. It was child's play to slice him into a thousand pieces. But I seized the occasion to state the general case for the sanity of art (under which title, by the way, my essay is still on sale) and its necessity as both an instrument and an object of culture.

This greatly improved my relations with Morris. He had never talked freely to me about art because it was a fixed and very sound rule of his that it was no use arguing with a man who didnt know; and it was this that made him sometimes appear, as I have said, a petulant veteran wilfully and invincibly ignorant of the latest developments. But he had read the English translation of *Entartung* (he said he could read Martin Luther's Bible, but no later German) and witnessed its absurdly respectful reception with a disgust that was quite independent of Nordau's insulting and idiotic reference to himself; and when he saw the insult, not to himself, but to fine art generally, fearfully avenged by my hand, the petulant veteran disappeared; the real Morris took me on as one who knew; and I soon discovered that he knew as much about Whistler as he did about Van Eyck. You never knew how much Morris had up his sleeve until he thought you knew enough to understand him.

Meanwhile I had nearly ruined Benjamin Tucker, the onlie begetter of this episode. As I would not let him pay me for my contribution, which occupied a whole number of Liberty plus a considerable embolism, he printed an edition large enough to enable him to send a copy gratuitously to every editor in America and perhaps to several in Europe. It was the biggest thing I have ever heard of an editor doing; and it succeeded completely; for Nordau and his *Entartung* were never mentioned by the Press again, as far as I know. But it must have strained Benjamin's resources; for Liberty soon ceased and he retired to Monte Carlo, where I found him quite lately fresh as a daisy in spite of his advanced years.

And so, somehow, I found myself frequenting the Morris household instead of merely earning a supper there by lecturing occasionally on Sunday evenings in the ex-coach house. May Morris's description of the house is by no means

19. A terminal element, from the Greek 'chatter', used in forming words denoting disorders or unusual faculties of speech. Max Nordau, in *Degeneration*, dealt primarily with the disorder known as echolalia, a meaningless repetition of words or phrases. Shaw responded to this critically in the final section of his reply (issued, revised, as *The Sanity of Art*, 1908).

exaggerated or beglamored by youthful association. I had no association to bias me; yet I, the most irreverent of mankind, felt its magic instantly and deeply. Mrs Morris [née Jane Burden] made a startling impression on me. It was in the evening; and I had never been upstairs to her drawingroom before. I had time to take in all the lovely things that were in the room before she came in. Rossetti's pictures, of which I had seen a collection at the Burlington Fine Arts Club [1883], had driven her into my consciousness as an imaginary figure. When she came into the room in her strangely beautiful garments, looking at least eight feet high, the effect was as if she had walked out of an Egyptian tomb at Luxor. Not until she had disposed herself very comfortably on the long couch opposite the settle did I compose myself into an acceptance of her as a real woman, and note that the wonderful curtain of hair was touched with grey, and the Rossetti face ten years older than it was in his pictures.

I always felt apologetic with Mrs Morris. I knew that the sudden eruption into her temple of beauty, with its pre-Raphaelite priests, of the proletarian comrades who began to infest the premises as Morris's fellow-Socialists, must be horribly disagreeable to her (I knew how my mother felt about the more discordant of them); and as one of this ugly rag-tag-and-bobtail of Socialism I could not expect her to do more than bear my presence as best she might. Fortunately she did not take much notice of me. She was not a talker: in fact she was the silentest woman I have ever met. She did not take much notice of anybody, and none whatever of Morris, who talked all the time. When I presently found myself dining at Kelmscott House my position was positively painful; for the Morris meals were works of art almost as much as the furniture. To refuse Morris's wine or Mrs Morris's viands was like walking on the great carpet with muddy boots.

Now, as it happened, I practise the occidental form of Yoga: I am a vegetarian and teetotaller. Morris did not demur to the vegetarianism: he maintained that a hunk of bread and an onion was a meal for any man; but he insisted on a bottle of wine to wash it down. Mrs Morris did not care whether I drank wine or water; but abstinence from meat she regarded as a suicidal fad. Between host and hostess I was cornered; and Mrs Morris did not conceal her contempt for my folly. At last pudding time came; and as the pudding was a particularly nice one, my abstinence vanished and I shewed signs of a healthy appetite. Mrs Morris pressed a second helping on me, which I consumed to her entire satisfaction. Then she said "That will do you good: there is suet in it." And that is the only remark, as far as I can remember, that was ever addressed to me by this beautiful stately and silent woman, whom the Brotherhood and Rossetti had succeeded in consecrating. Happily she had a certain plain good sense which had preserved her sanity perfectly under treatment that would have spoiled most women.

There was, however, another member of the family who was also a member of all the families in the old circle of Morris & Co. She was by no means either silent or consecrated to beauty. This was Miss Mary de Morgan, sister to that William de Morgan who began as an artist-tile-maker, and at the end of his life suddenly became a pseudo-Dickens and filled his scanted pockets by writing prodigiously long novels[20] in the style of Nicholas Nickleby.

I had heard a good deal of Mary before I met her, and was persuaded by all I had heard that she must be the most odious female then alive, a woman who embroiled and wrecked every household she entered by mischiefmaking gossip and an unfailing instinct for laying down the law in the way most exquisitely calculated to infuriate her hosts. As she was not related to any of the families she frequented I could not understand why they not only tolerated her but seemed to consider her as necessary and inevitable, though they spoke of her as a devil incarnate. The truth of the matter was that Mary had in her a quality of helpfulness and efficiency that made her indispensable wherever there was illness or trouble; and with this she commanded a consideration and even affection that the dearest of women might have envied.

I was at Kelmscott Manor in Gloucestershire when we first collided [1884]. Her arrival was anticipated by us as a disaster which nothing could avert, and which would probably end in a clash with me and a first-class row with Morris. She bore my presence and the outrage of introduction to her with a stiffness that was barely within the limits of common civility. In revenge, I made up my mind to fascinate Mary. The opportunity came one afternoon when we were having tea in the garden, Morris drinking from an enormous vessel which he had purchased to enable him to keep a promise made to his doctor that he would never exceed a single cup.

And, sure enough, Mary began to lay down the law, on what subject I forget; but she contrived to say everything that could exasperate Morris, and to say it in the most unbearable way. He struggled visibly to control himself; and the apprehensions of the family could not be concealed. At last Mary had to stop for a moment to breathe; and I said, in my best manner, "Miss de Morgan: how *can* you sit there telling us such a monstrous string of lies?"

Morris's eyes glazed. He looked like a man who had heard the Last Trumpet, and was waiting for the end of the world. The rest sat paralyzed, hardly believing their ears. But a miracle happened. Mary smiled. She understood

20. His novels included *Joseph Vance* (1906), *Alice-for-Short* (1907), and *It Never Can Happen Again* (1909).

perfectly that she was being flirted with; and she liked it. She played the game with spirit; and that evening, when she was retiring for the night, she squeezed my hand.

This was the only occasion on which I can claim to have reduced Morris to a condition which can only be described as awestruck.

Years after, the word went round that Mary was in pecuniary straits. A purse was forthcoming instantly from everyone who had ever spoken ill of her: that is, from every one who had known her. She flung it back in our faces with an independence that recalled Queen Elizabeth telling her council that if they turned her out in her petticoat she could make her living with the best of them.[21] A great little woman Mary in her way.

Now it happened that among the many beautiful things in Morris's two beautiful houses[22] was a very beautiful daughter,[23] then in the flower of her youth. You can see her in Burne-Jones's picture coming down The Golden Stair, the central figure. I was a bachelor then, and likely to remain so; for I not only felt about marriage very much as Jack Tanner does in Man & Superman, but I was so poor that I could hardly have supported Morris's daughter on Morris's scale for a week on my income for a year; and nothing could have induced me to ask any woman to face the fate of my mother, who had been so "well brought up" that, knowing nothing of the value of money, she married an unsuccessful man whose means were quite inadequate to keep up her standard of expenditure. But these material considerations only made the Morris paradise more celestial and my part in it quite irresponsible. For if I could not immediately marry the beautiful daughter I could all the more lightheartedly indulge my sense of her beauty.

One Sunday evening after lecturing and supping, I was on the threshold

21. Elizabeth I, in a speech before Parliament on 5 November 1566, announced: 'I am your anointed Queen. I will never be by violence constrained to do anything. I thank God that I am endued with such qualities that if I were turned out of the realm in my petticoat, I were able to live in any place in Christendom' (J. E. Neale, *Elizabeth I and Her Parliaments, 1559–1581*, 1953).
22. Kelmscott Manor House in the upper Thames valley, near Lechlade, was rented in May 1871 by Morris in joint tenancy with D. G. Rossetti. His London abode was Kelmscott House at Upper Mall.
23. May Morris (who edited her father's *Complete Works*, 1910–15) was one of many women who fell under Shaw's spell in the 1880s. Shaw's romanticized rationalizations in this memoir veil the truth that, despite initial infatuation with Morris's daughter, he was in his early manhood a notorious trifler. After waiting in vain five years for a marriage proposal, May married her father's assistant and protégé Henry Halliday Sparling in 1890.

of the Hammersmith house when I turned to make my farewell, and at this moment she came from the diningroom into the hall. I looked at her, rejoicing in her lovely dress and lovely self; and she looked at me very carefully and quite deliberately made a gesture of assent with her eyes. I was immediately conscious that a Mystic Betrothal was registered in heaven, to be fulfilled when all the material obstacles should melt away, and my own position rescued from the squalors of my poverty and unsuccess; for subconsciously I had no doubt of my rank as a man of genius. Less reasonably I had no doubt that she, too, knew her own value, a knowledge that involved a knowledge of everyone else's. I did not think it necessary to say anything. To engage her in any way—to go to Morris and announce that I was taking advantage of the access granted to me as comrade-Communist to commit his beautiful daughter to a desperately insolvent marriage, did not occur to me as a socially possible proceeding. It did not occur to me even that fidelity to the Mystic Betrothal need interfere with the ordinary course of my relations with other women. I made no sign at all: I had no doubt that the thing was written on the skies for both of us.

So nothing happened except that the round of Socialist agitation went on and brought us together from time to time as before. Meanwhile Morris had finished his great incursion into the art of printing, which then took an extraordinary turn. To provide books for it he undertook an adventure which was nothing more nor less than the resuscitation of Don Quixote's burnt library. One of the literary tenets of the Brotherhood was that Cervantes was an abominable Philistine, and his book a collection of commonplace novelettes set in a framework that was an insult to beauty and chivalry, the crowning insult being the great conflagration made by Don Quixote's housekeeper and the curate of the romances that had made their owner so happy that they transfigured the world for him.

For three hundred years this unique library remained unreplaced and discredited by the derision of Cervantes. Then Morris, to fill the maw of the Kelmscott Press, began to pour out tale after tale of knights in armor, lovely ladies, slaughterous hand-to-hand combats, witches in enchanted castles changing humans into beasts, lovelorn heroes going mad in the mountains, haunted woods, quests after impossibilities, all under medieval conditions as far as their contacts with anything earthly were concerned: in short, all the troubadour romance of chivalry and love which Cervantes had condemned to the flames as pernicious trash. After John Ball, News from Nowhere, and the unique written lectures on the possibilities of the world's future, this was a startling relapse into literary pre-Raphaelitism; and the Socialist movement as such took no interest in it. I tried to check the voracity of the Kelmscott

Press by suggesting that as Morris had shewn the way in printing he should take up the manufacture of musical instruments, which were losing their old idiosyncrasies under commercial standardization. He went so far as to say that he would like to make a fiddle. But he needed a refuge from reality; and there was a limit to the number of times he could read the novels of Dumas *père*, his usual way of escape when his Socialist duties involved some specially grimy job in the police court or at the meetings of the League. I have used the Morris stories in that way myself, and found them perfectly effective. And so between the movement and the Press and the Merton factory with its continual demands for new designs as well as for management, he was kept far too busy to give any consideration to domestic and personal affairs that were not positively forced on him.

Suddenly, to my utter stupefaction, and I suspect to that of Morris also, the beautiful daughter married one of the comrades.

This was perfectly natural, and entirely my own fault for taking the Mystical Betrothal for granted; but I regarded it, and still regard it in spite of all reason, as the most monstrous breach of faith in the history of romance. The comrade was even less eligible than I; for he was no better off financially; and, though he could not be expected to know this, his possibilities of future eminence were more limited. But he was a convinced Socialist and regular speaker for the cause, and his character was blameless; so there was nothing to be done but accept the situation. Apparently my limitless imagination had deceived me in the matter of the Mystical Betrothal.

But it had not deceived me in the least. For it presently happened that the overwork and irregular habits of the combination of continual propaganda with professional artistic activities, which killed Morris ten years before his time, reduced me to a condition in which I needed rest and change very pressingly; and holidays of the usual sort were beyond my means. The young couple thereupon invited me to stay with them for a while. I accepted, and so found myself most blessedly resting and content in their house,[24] which had the Morris charm; for she had inherited her father's sense of beauty and also his literary faculty in a form curiously Miltonic as well as Morrisian. Everything went well for a time in that *ménage à trois*. She was glad to have me in the house; and he was glad to have me because I kept her in good humor and produced a cuisine that no mere husband could elicit. It was probably the happiest passage in our three lives.

But the violated Betrothal was avenging itself. It made me from the first

24. Shaw spent November–December 1892 and January 1893 in Hammersmith Terrace.

the centre of the household; and when I had quite recovered and there was no longer any excuse for staying unless I proposed to do so permanently and parasitically, her legal marriage had dissolved as all illusions do; and the mystic marriage asserted itself irresistibly. I had to consummate it or vanish.

I have in the scraps of autobiography I have written[25] described how my mother was enabled to bear a disappointing marriage by the addition to our household of a musician of genius who gave her a career as a singer, and plenty of occupation as his partner in all his general musical activities, and especially in a technique of singing which was an article of faith with her. I had therefore, to my own great advantage, been brought up in a *ménage à trois*, and knew that it might be a quite innocent and beneficial arrangement. But when it became evident that the Betrothal would not suffer this to be an innocent arrangement the case became complicated. To begin with, the legal husband was a friend whose conduct towards me had always been irreproachable. To be welcomed in his house and then steal his wife was revolting to my sense of honor and socially inexcusable; for though I was as extreme a freethinker on sexual and religious questions as any sane human being could be, I was not the dupe of the Bohemian Anarchism that is very common in socialist and literary circles. I knew that a scandal would damage both of us and damage The Cause as well. It seems easy in view of my later position to have sat down together as three friends and arranged a divorce; but at that time I could not afford to marry and I was by no means sure that he could afford to be divorced. Besides, I hated the idea of a prosaic and even mercenary marriage: that, somehow or other, was not on the plane of the Mystic Betrothal. The more I reasoned about the situation the worse it was doomed to appear. So I did not argue about it. I vanished.

Then the vengeance of the violated Betrothal consummated itself in a transport of tragedy and comedy. For the husband vanished too! The *ménage* which had prospered so pleasantly as a *ménage à trois* proved intolerable as a *ménage à deux*. This marriage which all the mystic powers had forbidden from the first went to pieces when the unlucky parties no longer had me between them. Of the particulars of the rupture I know nothing; but in the upshot he fled to the Continent and eventually submitted chivalrously to being divorced as the guilty party, though the alternative was technically arranged for him. If I recollect aright he married again, this time I hope more suitably,

25. The 'scraps' were provided for a preface to *London Music in 1888–89* (1937), written nine months earlier. The Morris preface, however, preceded it in publication by fourteen months.

and lived as happily as he might until his death, which came sooner than an actuary would have predicted.

The beautiful one abolished him root and branch, resuming her famous maiden name, and, for all I could prove, abolished me too. But I knew better.

Forty years or so later I was motoring one day through Gloster [Gloucestershire] when the spell of Kelmscott Manor came upon me. I turned off the high road from Lechlade to Oxford and soon found myself in the church with the tempting candlesticks that nobody ever stole, and at the grave of William and Jane Morris, which I had never seen before. I was soon on the garden flagway to the ancient door of the Manor House. It was opened by a young lady whose aspect terrified me. She was obviously strong enough to take me by the scruff of the neck and pitch me neck and crop out of the curtilage; and she looked as if for two pins she would do it as she demanded sternly who I was. I named myself apologetically. The Mystical Betrothal, strong as ever, operated at once, though the athletic lady (Miss [Mary Frances] Lobb[26]) could have known nothing about it. She threw the door wide open as if I belonged to the place and had been away for ten minutes or so; and presently the beautiful daughter and I, now harmless old folks, met again as if nothing had happened.

And now, how did all this affect my relations with William Morris, who is, after all, the subject of these reminiscences? Well, it really did not affect them at all. Morris was a complete fatalist in his attitude towards the conduct of his children, and of all human beings where sex was concerned. Once, when the eternal subject of the care of children under Communism cropped up, he said "The question of who are the best people to take charge of the children is a very difficult one; but it is quite certain that the parents are the very worst." He never discussed his family affairs with me; and I am not sure that he ever discussed them with his family. As to any sort of coercive interference on his part it was inconceivable. He knew that the world is full of precipices; but if people were determined to walk over them it was no use trying to hold them back: over they must go.

He seldom talked to me about his old associates of the Rossettian days. He had a certain respect for Rossetti; but he never spoke of his poetry or his painting. Apparently what awed him about Rossetti was that the poet–painter positively liked writing letters (Morris loathed it, and would never write one if he could possibly help it nor correct his slips and omissions by reading over

26. Former worker at the Kelmscott Press, who became May Morris's general factotum and lover.

what he had written) and was so clever in business and diplomacy that he sold his pictures for good prices long before he had any public reputation. Of Ruskin Morris said that he would write the most profound truths and forget them five minutes later, which is true of other writers than Ruskin. Of Swinburne, who, having ceased to be a drunken republican poet, had become a sober reactionary Jingo rhymester in Putney under the tutelage of Theodore Watts Dunton,[27] he said that he got everything from books and nothing from nature. "Read his poems about the sea" he said "and they will convince you that he never was near the sea in his life and had only read a lot about it; and yet the truth is that the fellow was never out of the sea: he was always swimming about." His favorite quotation from Swinburne was a little poem beginning "If Love were what the rose is" ['A Match' in *Poems and Ballads*, 1866] which sounds well but has absolutely no syntax. I gathered that Morris had always known that Swinburne's early revolutionary enthusiasms were epidemics caught from Victor Hugo, and that the Putney reactionary was the real man all the time. He demurred to the classification of Whitman as a poet on technical grounds: his stuff might have all sorts of merits, but it was not verse: anybody could write like that if they had anything to say. He delighted in Dickens, whom I fortunately had at my tongue's end, and was much too fond of Jorrocks, whom I knew only through Leech's pictures.[28] Shakespear was not in the Morris movement, which was strongly anti-rhetorical. He hated Wordsworth as far as any poet could hate the author of Intimations of Immortality; but this must be heavily discounted to allow for the overwhelming reaction against Fundamentalist Evangelicalism which made it impossible for the vanguard to be just to any poet who was under the smallest suspicion of piety. And all these sayings must be taken with the qualification that Morris was a practitioner in the arts and neither a professor of literature nor a vowed critic. Literary criticism was for him a side line open to any writer whose five senses were intact; but in art a man was what he was and did what he could; and what was the use of arguing about it?

There was one contemporary whom it was impossible to discuss with Morris. That was the painter Edward Burne-Jones. The most innocent joke

27. Watts-Dunton was for a number of years custodian of Algernon Swinburne, a helpless alcoholic, who from 1879 had required constant supervision to prevent a relapse.
28. John Jorrocks was a sporting character in Robert S. Surtees's *Jorrocks's Jaunts and Jollities* (1838), *Handley Cross* (1843), and *Hillingdon Hall* (1845). John Leech, who illustrated these works, was famed for sketches in *Punch*.

at his expense, to say nothing of any disparagement of his work, wounded Morris to a degree that roused him to fury. All offenders in this respect were excommunicated as damned fools; and there was an end of it. Fortunately most of them deserved it; for failure to appreciate Burne-Jones's very high rank among painters and designers was at that time a pretty sure sign of vulgar ignorance of art; but Morris was beyond reason on the subject: he seemed to have transferred to himself all the jealous sensitiveness on his friend's behalf which most artists feel on their own.

I did not see much of Morris after his health failed. The last meeting I can remember is one at Kelmscott House on a Sunday evening when I lectured there. Morris was in extreme trouble and low spirits; for many things had gone awry with him, and his mother had just died. He could not face the usual supper with a tableful of guests; and I tried to get away without adding to his trouble; but he insisted on my coming in alone to eat something. He found great difficulty in entertaining me; and I was at my wits' end to think of any way of cheering him. We had both given it up as a bad job and all but lapsed into silence when I had a fortunate inspiration. "Why dont you do a Pilgrim's Progress?" I said, meaning on the Kelmscott Press.[29] Instantly he shot up from the depths of misery to the liveliest interest. He was another man in a moment; and it ended in our having quite an eager time together. Nobody has ever described Morris as mercurial; but certainly no man could change more rapidly or through a larger scale.

It was, I think, some time before this that he made a final effort to make the Socialists stop quarreling. Now it was he himself who had set the first example of fission, and justified it as a necessary division of labor. But instead of each sect going its own way to Socialism they took to vituperating each other's leading personalities. In vain had the Guild of St Matthew, through the mouth of Stewart Headlam, said "Sirs: ye are brothers: wherefore do ye wrong one to another?" [Acts 7: 26]. At last Keir Hardie, simpleminded apostle of fraternity, forced the Societies, by a sentimental appeal to the rank and file, to form a committee to amalgamate them. The result was, first, to put a stop to every activity in the Societies except that of arguing fiercely about the resolutions sent in for approval by the amalgamating committee, and, second, Keir Hardie's discovery that the only way to secure unity was to expel the refractory sections one after another by the combined votes of all the rest. The last meeting of the amalgamators took place in the office of

29. Morris did not live to produce a Kelmscott *Pilgrim's Progress*. The Kelmscott Press published from 1891 to 1897.

the Fabian Society,[30] lent for the occasion. It terminated, amid roars of laughter, in the solemn expulsion of the Fabians from their own premises, leaving poor Hardie with a solidly unanimous few of his own personal followers in the room and all the others outside. Morris, who had taken no part in this comedy, again compelled the leaders to confer about it, but with a view, not to amalgamation, but to drawing up and jointly signing a manifesto of Socialist aims, which were becoming obscured and forgotten in the conflicts of the factions.

The conferences were held in Hammersmith at Kelmscott House. They consisted virtually of Hyndman representing the S. D. F., myself representing the Fabian Society, and Morris representing the Hammersmith Socialist Society. The proletariat was represented by a comrade whom we appointed secretary to our conference. He celebrated the compliment by turning up at the next meeting helplessly drunk, and thereby reducing himself to an attitude purely apologetic during the rest of the proceedings. Morris had drafted the manifesto.

The conferences began by we three, Hyndman, Shaw, and Morris, gathering up round the fire and having a good talk about everything on earth except the object of our meeting. Hyndman, as I have said, was a very good talker; and I am not afflicted with any sort of dumbness. We kept the ball rolling very pleasantly until after an hour or so the proletariat, who mostly slept through our performances, insisted mildly on our getting to business.

In drafting the manifesto Morris had taken care to give some expression to both the Fabian policy and the Social-Democratic Federation policy. Hyndman immediately proposed the omission of the Fabian program of

30. The formation of a Socialist Federation appears to have been suggested initially by Andreas Scheu of the Social-Democratic Federation. Morris's Hammersmith Socialist Society endorsed the concept on 10 February 1893, and invited Keir Hardie to speak on the aims of the Independent Labour Party. An 'Olive Branch' committee consisting of five delegates each from the SDF, the Hammersmith socialists, and the Fabian Society met on 23 February. Five days later a sub-committee consisting of three leaders of these organizations (Hyndman, Morris and Shaw) held its first meeting, at which time Shaw offered a 'sketch of a manifesto'. In March the 'Olive Branch' became the Joint Committee of Socialist Bodies. Morris eventually drafted, with help from Hyndman and Shaw, a manifesto published on 1 May as a *Manifesto of English Socialists*. It proved ineffective, and after a few more heated meetings, culminating on 20 July in what Shaw described in his diary as 'Lively scenes ... Hyndman and I squabbled all the time', the Fabian Society withdrew its delegates and the scheme collapsed.

municipal Socialism, and its explicit denunciation as "gas and water Socialism". I was equally determined not to endorse the policy of the S.D.F. Morris soon saw that we were irreconcilable. There was nothing for it but to omit both policies and substitute platitudes that any Church Congress could have signed. Morris's draft, horribly eviscerated and patched, was subsequently sold for a penny as the Joint Manifesto of the Socialists of Great Britain. It was the only document any of the three of us had ever signed and published that was honestly not worth a farthing. Hyndman soon characteristically persuaded himself that it was important and that he had drafted it; and bibliographers like [Harry] Buxton Forman[31] were presently asking me whether it should be included in their lists of Morris's works, finishing in considerable perplexity as to whether Hyndman or I was the greater liar. I submit that the internal evidence irresistibly bears me out.

Then came Morris's long illness and death. My old delicacy about Mrs Morris kept me away when he became bedridden, and even prevented me from attending his funeral, which I vainly regretted when I learnt that enough of the comrades had appeared to make one more or less a matter of indifference. A decent nation would have buried him in Westminster Abbey; but he himself would not have rested there as he does in the little grave at Kelmscott which has made the place the shrine of a saint.

Morris's writings about Socialism, which the most uppish of his friends regarded as a deplorable waste of the time and genius of a great artist, really called up all his mental reserves for the first time. His verse, though it cannot have been so effortless as it seemed, had not taken him to his limit. When people ask me whether it is difficult to write plays I always reply that it is either easy or impossible. It may be laborious: that is quite another matter; but unless the novice can do it from the first without any serious trouble or uncertainty he had better not do it at all: it is not his job. Morris knew this very well. There is no evidence of technical struggle with his medium; and the knowledge that he could go on writing lovely lines for ever as the idle singer of an empty day must have finally changed that exultant phrase to a self-criticism. To take my own case in those early days, I had never read The Earthly Paradise through; but I had read Atalanta's Race [first poem of *The Earthly Paradise*, 1868–70], which had to end very excitingly. I had then turned to The Life and Death of Jason [1867] and got through that very happily, because it described a journey by the Thames through the Thames

---

31. Editor, biographer of Shelley, and author of *The Books of William Morris Described, with Some Account of His Doings in Literature and in the Allied Crafts* (1897).

and Severn tunnel to its source.[32] Pharamond [*Love is Enough; or the Freeing of Pharamond*, 1873] was full of variety of verse, like a parterre of flowers; but the title repeated that irritating XIX century cliché "love is enough" (which is not its moral) and therefore suggested a very idle singer and a damnably empty day to anyone who had just read Marx and was raging for justice, not for love. And this must have been the reaction that carried Morris from Pharamond to John Ball.[33]

Iceland and the Sagas helped by changing the facile troubadour of love and beauty into the minstrel of strife and guile, of battle, murder, and death. Incidentally he achieved the summit of his professional destiny by writing the greatest epic since Homer, Sigurd the Volsung [1876]. He was quite aware of the greatness of this work, and used to recite passages from it, marking its swing by rocking from one foot to the other like an elephant. After one of these recitations he sat down beside me. I said "That is the stuff for me: there is nothing like it," whereupon he presented me with the copy he had read from. Epic was child's play to him: for pure pastime he translated that schoolboy's curse the Eneids of Virgil [1875] into long lolloping lines that in any other hands than his would have reduced the reader to idiocy, and later on The Odyssey [1887]: a nobler translation than the tale is worth. Samuel Butler's feminine prose variation [*The Authoress of the 'Odyssey'*, 1897] and [T.E.] Lawrence's (of Arabia) potboiler [1932] are nearer the mark; but nobody will look at either if Morris's versification is at hand.

Now all this was literature, romance, art for art sake, done with a natural facility that cost him nothing but the manual labor of writing it down. He was surprised when, in his college days, he was told that this gift constituted him a poet. I once told him that the reason I did not write verse was that instead of saying what I wanted to say in it I had to say something that would rhyme, and that to find the rhyme I had to go through the alphabet, so that

32. A fanciful linking of Morris's description of the Argo's passage upstream on a northern green river and through a 'cold, bat-haunted cavern low', in Book II of *The Life and Death of Jason* (1867), with the topography of the upper Thames in the Cotswold region and the tunnel built in 1873–86 to carry the railway beneath the Severn's estuary. It was Morris, Shaw claimed in 1949, who had informed him of the association. The recollection, in an undated letter (Harry Ransom Humanities Research Center: shorthand draft) to Lloyd Eric Grey, author of *William Morris: Prophet of England's New Order* (which Shaw was reviewing for the *Observer*), assumes a remarkable prescience on Morris's part.
33. *The Dream of John Ball* (1888) is a socialist romance in mixed prose and verse.

if my first line ended with my own name I had to follow it up with a caw or a daw, a flaw or a jaw, a paw or a saw, whether these things had anything to do with the subject or not. Morris looked at me exactly as if I had told him I was blind or deaf or impotent, or at best an utter fool. He could not understand anyone finding any difficulty in finding a rhyme or having to force it in any way, just as Elgar could not understand anyone inventing a tune without knowing at the same time what instrument should play it.

In short, Morris was a readymade poet and decorative draughtsman; but no man is a readymade street corner agitator if his subject is one which requires strenuous thought and makes him feel so deeply that he must preach it as a gospel in spite of all inaptitudes, timidities, and repugnances. Theretofore whenever Morris found the practice of an art troublesome and the result unconvincing he had very sensibly thrown it over as not being his job. For instance, he had tried his hand at figure painting in oils, the art of Burne-Jones, Madox Brown, and Millais, and given it up just as he had given up architecture, though it is fairly certain that if he had faced the necessary apprenticeship he could have qualified himself respectably in both these arts. But the world was none the worse for the renunciation; for there were plenty of born figure painters and trained architects to do all that he could have done.

Not so in the matter of Socialism. It is true that there was no lack of practised and even powerful speakers in the movement, spouting Marxism, Fabianism, and all the other brands; but not one of them could propagate his vision of the life to come on a happy earth, and his values that went so much deeper into eternity than the surplus value of Marx. This vision only he himself could propagate; and so he had to go to the street corner even though he was thoroughly miserable there, and to think out and write out for delivery in public halls lectures which were far too pregnant and profound to be extemporized as Hyndman and I and the rest extemporized. His intellectual conscience and his dislike of charlatanism, even legitimate charlatanism, prevented him from becoming a great platform artist like Bradlaugh, Henry George, Mrs Besant, Andreas Scheu, Jean Jaurès, Bebel,[34] or John Burns, who could hold an audience long after he had become so lightheaded with fatigue that his words had ceased to have any meaning. But their orations have gone

34. Scheu, an Austrian revolutionary active in Britain, was a close friend of Morris. August Bebel was leader of the German Social Democrats and editor of *Vorwärts*.

down the wind, whilst his painfully written lectures[35] survive as the best books in the Bible of Socialism.

I must add, however, that though Morris was rich in the enormous patience of the greatest artists, he went unprovided with the small change of that virtue which enables cooler men to suffer fools gladly. The provocations and interruptions of debate, which give experts such effective opportunities for retort that they are courted rather than resented, infuriated Morris, especially when they were trivial and offensive (he could bear with any serious and honest utterance like an angel); so that at last the comrades, when there was a debating job to be done, put it on me, knowing that I could play cat and mouse with any ordinary opponent whilst Morris, in the background, could only devastate his moustache and supply a growled *basso continuo* of "Damfool! Damfool!"

Another grievous task for him was to keep The Commonweal, the weekly paper of the League, going from number to number with topical paragraphs. Some of the stuff thus produced went to the rock bottom truth of the situation; but it did not come easily and happily: he would never have written Sigurd if it had cost him half the hard brain work Socialism extorted from him. But that was how the idle singer of an empty day became a prophet and a saint.

Bear in mind, you who read these casual memories, the difference in our ages. Morris was twentytwo before I was born; and I am now eighteen years older than he was when he died. I who was very much his junior now write as almost equally his senior. And with such wisdom as my years have left me I note that as he has drawn further and further away from the hurlyburly of our personal contacts into the impersonal perspective of history he towers greater and greater above the horizon beneath which his best advertized contemporaries have disappeared.

35. Several of the surviving manuscripts of the lectures (now in the British Library) were published in the *Collected Works* (1913) and others in the *Unpublished Lectures*, which contains a descriptive checklist of all of the known manuscripts of the lectures. See also Shaw's editor's note to 'Communism' in the appendix to the present volume (pp. 543–6).

# Memories of Early Years

*Preface to E. W. Walters's memoir of his brother,* Ensor Walters and the
London He Loves, 1937. *The prefatory text is preceded by an italicized note
by the author of the book: 'Bernard Shaw and Ensor Walters sat together for some years
on the St Pancras Vestry and, at a later date, on the new Borough Council.
Bernard Shaw here recalls the happenings of those remarkable years
and gives a vivid picture of Ensor Walters.'*

At the end of the XIX century the borough of St Pancras contained a quarter
of a million of the population of London. The culture of that quarter million
may be inferred from the fact that there was not a single bookshop in the
entire borough. It contained clusters of houses of ill-fame. It was cheerfully
corrupt politically: a cheque for £1000, placed in the right quarter, would
have secured the return of a baby in arms to Parliament or the County
Council for the southern division, where I resided. When cheques were not
forthcoming, as at the vestry elections, the little groups of politically-minded
local shopkeepers and men of business elected oneanother for no particular
reason except that they seemed likely to keep the rates down to the extreme
possible minimum. In fact they kept them below it, and were in debt to the
bank £17,000 deep when they were found out by the Local Government
Board auditor on the promotion of the Vestry to the rank of Borough Council
[1900] by Act of Parliament.

Into this stagnant bywater an energetic Methodist, Hugh Price Hughes,
and his wife, launched [1886] a devoted West London Mission which soon
found that it must make its way into local politics and stir them up in the
interest of the poor. I found earnest Methodist women calling on me as
election canvassers. I told them that they had not the least notion of how to
get votes, and explained to them how to vary their attack according to the
class and interests of the voter. At first they said they would rather see their
candidates dead than achieve their return by such ungodly duplicity; but as the
day of election came nearer and nearer they usually returned in a completely
demoralized condition to consult me as to how to get round some specially
obdurate elector. Anyhow, they soon proved that vestrydom could do nothing
where Methodism was really alive; when by some intrigue or other I became
a vestryman, I was not surprised to find myself sitting beside a young Methodist

minister named [Charles] Ensor Walters[1] at what was supposed to be the Progressive end of the long table on the Mayor's left. His figure, and a certain boyishly unconscious authority about him, reminded me of Pope Pius IX; and I at once set him down as likely to end as head of his Church, whatever that headship might be. All the more as he was quite natural and unassuming. The vestry, as far as it knew anything about me, classed me as a Socialist and therefore an atheist, sure to differ with the Methodist minister on every question. What actually happened was that he and I immediately formed a party two strong all to ourselves. And we troubled ourselves about no other party. There was a hopelessly outnumbered little section of the vestry which called itself the Progressive Party, and held party meetings under the presidency of an Irish doctor [Dr E. F. T. MacCarthy] who occasionally rose up at the council meetings and began his speech by the formula, "This is one of the most stinking scandals that has ever disgraced the annals of St Pancras." Nobody took offence at this: it was accepted as the rather amusing duty of a party leader. Naturally neither Ensor nor I had any use for that sort of thing. He was out to make a little corner for the Kingdom of God in St Pancras; and nothing could have suited me better.

As well as I remember, I did most of the talking. Ensor never wanted to hear himself talk; but when he let himself go the effect was startling. He would bear the follies of the old vestry gang in silence until they were going to do something unconsciously wicked or unintentionally cruel; and then he would explode, in righteous wrath, and, without wasting a word of argument on them, declare that he was not going to stand it and the thing was not to be done. And his word was like a fire: they cowered like naughty children caught at their tricks. Most men make fools of themselves when they lose their tempers. Ensor could lose his in a perfectly selfless way and be all the more effective for it.

In due time we two faded out of vestrydom, having more important work on our hands which took us out of oneanother's orbit; but I always held him in warm and special regard, and was delighted when he fulfilled my forecast and became Pope of the Methodists. His next promotion will be to the Communion of Saints; for he has reached the earthly top without, I will swear, having ever condescended to climb a single step, by sheer gravitation of a noble spirit.

17 February 1937.

---

1. Assistant to Revd Hughes at the West London Mission, elected to the Vestry in May 1898; Shaw had been elected on 18 May 1897, without contest.

# The Intelligent Woman's Guide to Socialism
# (Pelican edition)

*Shaw provided an 'Author's Note' and two chapters for this edition, No. 1
(in two volumes) of the Pelican series issued by the newly founded Penguin Books,
retitled* The Intelligent Woman's Guide to Socialism, Capitalism,
Sovietism and Fascism, *1937*

=====

As several newspapers have announced this Pelican edition of the Guide as rewritten, implying either that the original work was illwritten, or that the present issue is an abridged or cheapened version, I must assure its readers that they have in their hands the authentic original text in full, word for word, but with the addition of two new chapters dealing with events that have occurred since its first publication in 1928. The present edition is in fact a better bargain than the first edition was, though the price is so much more modest.[1]

The two new chapters deal respectively with Sovietism and Fascism. In the first I have been obliged to point out that had the Bolshevists studied our British post-Marxian Socialist literature after they had been converted to Socialism by Marx they might have avoided the ruinous business errors which so nearly wrecked the Russian revolution. I must also emphasize the weakness in economic theory which makes Socialists, in Russia as well as in the Capitalist States, still boggle at my demonstration that Socialism is economically a theory of distribution, and that from every practical point of view the only solution is equal distribution. The Russians, finding that equal distribution on the lowest proletarian level would make professional work impossible, and that piece work and gradation of labor and payment for different classes of work are indispensable stimulants to production at present, have hastily repudiated economic equality, protesting that Marx never postulated it. To this I must reply that I did. After preaching it for nearly quarter of a century I set it down in this book in 1928. The question is not worth pressing in Russia as yet, because the abolition of private property there, and the addition of exploitation of labor to the list of criminal offences, prevents the monstrous

1. Sixpence per volume.

misdistribution which Capitalism inevitably produces; but as this misdistribution is the main economic objection to Capitalism one must ask what ground the Russians will take if their all-powerful captains of industry, backed by the aristocracy of professional talents and the bureaucracy, should combine to reintroduce plutocracy? I can see nothing to prevent them if once they lose hold of the vital importance of equality for constitutional stabilization. Nor do I see any other test for practical as distinguished from arithmetical equality except the test of complete marriageability between all sections of the community.

Fascism breaks down, not on liberty and democracy, neither of which have any real existence under developed Capitalism, but on distribution; and if Fascism remedies that, it becomes Communism. Instead of sympathizing with the poor and abolishing the rich we must ruthlessly abolish the poor by raising their standard of life to that of the most favorably treated worker. Whoever has not clear ideas on this point has not clear ideas at all as to what Socialism means, no matter what party label the Intelligent Woman may adopt, or in what transport of indignation at the oppression of the proletariat she may declare herself Socialist or Communist or what not.

I find that in spite of my careful refusal to pretend that the change from Capitalism to Socialism is likely to be carried out reasonably without bloodshed, I am still cited, when I am cited at all, as a harmless and therefore negligible Fabian pacifist, still dreaming of revolution by Act of Parliament. Unhappily the history of our times, from our Curragh mutiny[2] to the present [civil] war in Spain, shews that the holders of property will make war on any Parliament that threatens their rights. Their money can always command proletarian troops who will fight for good wages without troubling themselves as to what cause they are defending or attacking. What I have pointed out is that the transition to Socialism is a positive constitutional and industrial operation that cannot be achieved by any negative process, much less a destructive one. If, as in Russia, the transition involves a sanguinary civil war, all the bloodshed will not advance Socialism: the most complete proletarian victory will leave all the constructive work, without which Socialism is only an empty word, still to be done. Only, it will be much more cruelly done after a civil war, when the vanquished will be mercilessly beggared or mercilessly

2. Britain was confronted with a threat of civil war in Ireland when, in March 1914, officers of The Curragh, a military training centre in Co. Kildare, revolted against orders issued by Lloyd George's government for the carrying out of an anticipated Home Rule policy in Ireland, and submitted their resignations. In consequence, Sir John French resigned as Chief of the Imperial General Staff.

massacred, as the case may be. The proper way to effect the transition is to throw our present constitution to the winds and, taking a hint from the successful Russian experiments in multiformity, institute several governing bodies. We have one parliament of gentlemen-amateurs and ex-tradesmen to deal with industry, with agriculture, with transport, with education and religion, with distribution in wages, incomes and taxation, with production and new capital, with foreign policy, with national policy: in short with every form and department of national activity in the little time it can spare from its own little party intrigues. The result, of course, is that Great Britain is 99.5% not nationally governed at all. Our wretched little offices and boards and ministries huddled together in Whitehall should multiply and expand into separate governments; and their ministers should be real directors instead of party politicians in whom any knowledge of the work of their departments or any ability to control their officials is a rare and unwelcome accident. The coordination of such structures, financially and socially, would employ political talent of an order very different from that employed in our present Cabinets, which exclude no depth of common stupidity or social ignorance if it can flourish an old school tie.

As I write these lines it is announced that the Government is about to make a plunge into Socialism by buying the coal mines from their owners.[3] The millions it will cost will not matter, because the taxation to meet it will fall finally on rent; so that the coalowners will be paid out of their own pockets and those of their fellow proprietors. But what is to be done with the mines when they have become national property? There is no organ of government at present capable of managing them; and as they must be carried on without a day's respite they will be handed back to private companies for exploitation unless an adequate organ is created. The transaction will demonstrate how nationalizations are possible without civil war; but it will also demonstrate the uselessness of such operations until we have national machinery enough to do national work instead of a handful of gentlemen mouthing phrases about Liberty and the like.

At all events what this book has to deal with is Socialism and its requirements. It is not concerned with the extent to which we may consider it necessary to murder oneanother in bringing it about.

3. Britain nationalized its mines under the Coal Act of 1938, acquiring all the unworked coal then privately owned for the sum of £66,450,000.

# Great Expectations

*First published as a preface to the Dickens novel in the Limited Editions Club issue, New York, 1937. Revised for an edition in the Novel Library, London, 1947*

=====

Great Expectations is the last of the three full-length stories written by Dickens in the form of an autobiography. Of the three, Bleak House, as the autobiography of Miss Esther Summerson, is naturally the least personal, as Esther is not only a woman but a maddening prig, though we are forced to admit that such paragons exist and are perhaps worthy of the reverent admiration with which Dickens regarded them. Ruling her out, we have David Copperfield and Great Expectations. David was, for a time at least, Dickens's favorite child, perhaps because he had used him to express the bitterness of that episode in his own experience which had wounded his boyish self-respect most deeply.[1] For Dickens, in spite of his exuberance, was a deeply reserved man: the exuberance was imagination and acting (his imagination was ceaseless, and his outward life a feat of acting from beginning to end); and we shall never know whether in that immensely broadened outlook and knowledge of the world which began with Hard Times and Little Dorrit, and left all his earlier works behind, he may not have come to see that making his living by sticking labels on blacking bottles and rubbing shoulders with boys who were not gentlemen, was as little shameful as being the genteel apprentice in the office of Mr Spenlow[2] [DC], or the shorthand writer [young Dickens] recording the unending twaddle of the House of Commons and electioneering bunk on the hustings of all the Eatanswills [PP] in the country.

That there was a tragic change in his valuations can be shewn by contrasting Micawber [DC] with William Dorrit [LD], in which light Micawber suddenly becomes a mere marionette pantaloon with a funny bag of tricks which he repeats until we can bear no more of him, and Dorrit a portrait of the

---

1. At the age of twelve Dickens was sent out to earn his own living as a hand in a blacking warehouse at Old Hungerford Stairs, on a salary of six shillings a week.
2. Characters, places and agencies in the novels are identified in the text with bracketed initials. BH: *Bleak House*; DC: *David Copperfield*; D&S: *Dombey and Son*; GE: *Great Expectations*; LD: *Little Dorrit*; MC: *Martin Chuzzlewit*; OCS: *The Old Curiosity Shop*; OMF: *Our Mutual Friend*; PP: *Pickwick Papers*.

deadliest and deepest truth to nature. Now contrast David with Pip [GE]; and believe, if you can, that there was no revision of his estimate of the favorite child David as a work of art and even as a vehicle of experience. The adult David fades into what stage managers call a walking gentleman. The reappearance of Mr Dickens in the character of a blacksmith's boy may be regarded as an apology to Mealy Potatoes [DC].

Dickens did in fact know that Great Expectations was his most compactly perfect book. In all the other books, there are episodes of wild extravagance, extraordinarily funny if they catch you at the right age, but recklessly grotesque as nature studies. Even in Little Dorrit, Dickens's masterpiece among many masterpieces, it is impossible to believe that the perfectly authentic Mr Pancks really stopped the equally authentic Mr Casby in a crowded street in London and cut his hair; and though Mr F's aunt is a first-rate clinical study of senile deficiency in a shrewd old woman, her collisions with Arthur Clennam are too funny to be taken seriously. We cannot say of Casby, Pancks, and the aunt, as we can say of Sam Weller [PP], that such people never existed; for most of us have met their counterparts in real life; but we can say that Dickens's sense of fun ran away with him over them. If we have absolutely no fun in us we may even state gravely that there has been a lapse from the artistic integrity of the tragic picture of English society which is the subject of the book.

In Great Expectations we have Wopsle and Trabb's boy; but they have their part and purpose in the story and do not overstep the immodesty of nature. It is hardly decent to compare Mr F's aunt with Miss Havisham; but as contrasted studies of madwomen they make you shudder at the thought of what Dickens might have made of Miss Havisham if he had seen her as a comic personage. For life is no laughing matter in Great Expectations; the book is all of one piece and consistently truthful as none of the other books are, not even the compact Tale of Two Cities, which is pure sentimental melodrama from beginning to end, and shockingly wanting in any philosophy of history in its view of the French Revolution.

Dickens never regarded himself as a revolutionist, though he certainly was one. His implacable contempt for the House of Commons, founded on his experience as parliamentary reporter, never wavered from the account of the Eatanswill election and of Nicholas Nickleby's interview with Pugstyles to the Veneering election in Our Mutual Friend, his last book (Edwin Drood is only a gesture by a man three-quarters dead). And this was not mere satire, of which there had been plenty. Dickens was the first writer to perceive and state definitely that the House of Commons, working on the Party system, is an extraordinarily efficient device for dissipating all our reforming energy and ability in Party debate and when anything urgently needs to be done, finding out "how not to do it." It took very little time to get an ineffective Factory Act. It took fifty years to make it effective, though the labor conditions in the factories and mines were horrible. After Dickens's death, it took thirty years to pass an Irish Home Rule Bill, which was promptly repudiated by the military plutocracy, leaving the question to be settled by a competition in slaughter and house burning, just as it would have been between two tribes of savages. Liberty under the British parliamentary system means slavery for nine tenths of the people, and slave exploitation or parasitic idolatry and snobbery for the rest. Parliament men—one cannot call them statesmen—and even historians keep declaring that the British parliamentary system is one of the greatest blessings British political genius has given to the world; and the world has taken it at its self-valuation and set up imitations of it all over Europe and America, always with the same result: political students outside Parliament exposing the most frightful social evils and prescribing their remedies, and Parliament ignoring them as long as possible and then engulfing their disciples and changing them from reformers into partisans with time for nothing but keeping their party in power or opposing the Government, rightly or wrongly ("it is the duty of the Opposition to oppose" [see p. 93]), as the case might be. In the middle of the XIX century Dickens saw this and said it. He had to be ignored, as he would not stand for Parliament and be paralyzed.

Europe has had to learn from hard experience what it would not learn from Dickens. The Fascist and Communist revolutions which swept the great parliamentary sham into the dustbin after it had produced a colossal Anarchist war, made no mention of Dickens; but on the parliamentary point he was as much their prophet as Marx was the economic prophet of the Soviets. Yet a recent reactionist against Dickens worship declares that he "never went ahead of his public."[3]

Marx and Dickens were contemporaries living in the same city and pursuing the same profession of literature; yet they seem to us like creatures of a different species living in different worlds. Dickens, if he had ever become conscious of Karl Marx, would have been classed with him as a revolutionist. The difference between a revolutionist and what Marx called a bourgeois is that the bourgeois regards the existing social order as the permanent and natural order of human society, needing reforms now and then and here and there, but essentially good and sane and right and respectable and proper and everlasting. To the revolutionist it is transitory, mistaken, objectionable, and pathological: a social disease to be cured, not to be endured. We have only to compare Thackeray and Trollope with Dickens to perceive this

3. Hugh Kingsmill, *The Sentimental Journey: A Life of Dickens* (1934).

contrast. Thackeray reviled the dominant classes with a savagery which would have been unchivalrous in Dickens: he denied to his governing class characters even the common good qualities and accomplishments of ladies and gentlemen, making them mean, illiterate, dishonest, ignorant, sycophantic to an inhuman degree, whilst Dickens, even when making his aristocrats ridiculous and futile, at least made gentlemen of them. Trollope, who regarded Thackeray as his master and exemplar, had none of his venom, and has left us a far better balanced and more truthful picture of Victorian well-off society, never consciously whitewashing it, though allowing it its full complement of black sheep of both sexes. But Trollope's politics were those of the country house and the hunting field just as were Thackeray's. Accordingly, Thackeray and Trollope were received and approved by fashionable society with complete confidence. Dickens, though able to fascinate all classes, was never so received or approved except by quite goodnatured or stupid ladies and gentlemen who were incapable of criticizing anyone who could make them laugh and cry. He was told that he could not describe a gentleman and that Little Dorrit is twaddle. And the reason was that in his books the west-end heaven appears as a fool's paradise that must pass away instead of being an indispensable preparatory school for the New Jerusalem of Revelation. A leading encyclopedia tells us that Dickens had "no knowledge of country gentlemen."[4] It would have been nearer the mark to say that Dickens knew all that really mattered about Sir Leicester Dedlock [BH] and that Trollope knew nothing that really mattered about him. Trollope and Thackeray could see Chesney Wold [BH]; but Dickens could see through it. And this was no joke to Dickens. He was deeply concerned about it, and understood how revolutions begin with burning the châteaux.

The difference between Marx and Dickens was that Marx knew that he was a revolutionist whilst Dickens had not the faintest suspicion of that part of his calling. Compare the young Dickens looking for a job in a lawyer's office and teaching himself shorthand to escape from his office stool to the reporters' gallery, with the young Trotsky, the young Lenin, quite deliberately facing disreputable poverty and adopting revolution as their profession with every alternative of bourgeois security and respectability much more fully open to them than to Dickens.

4. This appears to be a misrecollection. What G. K. Chesterton wrote in his Dickens article published in the *Encyclopaedia Britannica* (fourteenth edition) was: 'The poverty and anarchy of Dickens's early life had stuffed his memory with strange things and people never to be discovered in Tennysonian country houses or even Thackerayan drawing-rooms.'

And this brings us to Dickens's position as a member of the educated and cultured classes who had neither education nor culture. This was fortunate for him and for the world in one way, as he escaped the school and university routine which complicates cultural Philistinism with the mentality of a Red Indian brave. Better no schooling at all than the schooling of Rudyard Kipling and Winston Churchill. But there are homes in which a mentally acquisitive boy can make contact with the fine arts. I myself learnt nothing at school, but gained in my home an extensive and highly educational knowledge of music. I had access to illustrated books on painting which sent me to the National Gallery [of Ireland]; so that I was able to support myself as a critic of music and painting as Dickens supported himself by shorthand. I devoured books on science and on the religious controversies of the day. It is in this way, and not in our public schools and universities that such culture as there is in England is kept alive.

Now the Dickenses seem to have been complete barbarians. Dickens mentions the delight with which he discovered in an attic a heap of XVIII century novels. But Smollett was a grosser barbarian than Dickens himself; and Don Quixote and The Arabian Nights, though they gave the cue to his eager imagination, left him quite in the dark as to the philosophy and art of his day. To him a philosopher, an intellectual, was a figure of fun. Count Smorltork [PP] is the creation by a street Arab: Dickens did not even know that the Count's method of studying Chinese metaphysics by studying metaphysics and China and "combining the information" was not only sensible and correct, but the only possible method. To Dickens as to most Victorian Englishmen metaphysics were ridiculous, useless, unpractical, and the mark of a fool. He was musical enough to have a repertory of popular ballads which he sang all over the house to keep his voice in order; and he made Tom Pinch [MC] play the organ in church as an amiable accomplishment; but I cannot remember hearing that he ever went to a classical concert, or even knew of the existence of such entertainments. The articles on the National Gallery [London], in All the Year Round, though extremely funny in their descriptions of "The Apotheosis" of "William the Silent" (the title alone would make a cat laugh), and on some profane points sensible enough, are those of a complete Philistine. One cannot say that he disliked all painters in the face of his friendship with [Daniel] Maclise and Clarkson Stanfield;[5]

---

5. Daniel Maclise provided the frontispieces and titles for three of Dickens's Christmas Books: *The Chimes* (1844), *The Cricket on the Hearth* (1845), and *The Battle of Life* (1846). Clarkson Stanfield supplied some of the drawings for woodcuts in the Christmas Books. *Little Dorrit* was dedicated to him.

but it was not a cultural friendship: Stanfield was a scene painter who appealed to that English love of landscape which is so often confused with a love of art; and Maclise was a pictorial anecdotist who presented scenes from Shakespear's plays exactly as they were presented on the stage. When Dickens introduced in his stories a character whom he intensely disliked he chose an artistic profession for him. Henry Gowan in Little Dorrit is a painter. Pecksniff [MC] is an architect. Harold Skimpole [BH] is a musician. There is real hatred in his treatment of them.

Now far be it from me to imply that they are false to nature. Artists are often detestable human beings; and the famous Anti-Scrape, officially The Society for the Protection of Ancient Buildings, was founded by William Morris and his friends to protect ancient buildings from architects. What is more, the ultra-artistic sets, the Pre-Raphaelites and the aesthetes grouped round Rossetti and Morris and Ruskin, were all Dickens worshippers who made a sort of cult of Trabb's boy and would have regarded me as a traitor if they had read what I am now writing. They knew better than anyone else that Leigh Hunt deserved all he got as Harold Skimpole, that Gowan's shallow sort of painting was a nuisance, and that architecture was just the right profession for a parasite on Salisbury Cathedral like Pecksniff. But all their Dickensian enthusiasm, and all the truth to life of Dickens's portraiture cannot extenuate the fact that the cultural side of art was as little known to Dickens as it is possible for a thing so public to remain to a man so apprehensive. You may read the stories of Dickens from beginning to end without ever learning that he lived through a period of fierce revivals and revolutionary movements in art, in philosophy, in sociology, in religion: in short, in culture. Dean Inge's remark that "the number of great subjects in which Dickens took no interest whatever is amazing"[6] hits the nail exactly on the head. As to finding such a person as Karl Marx among his characters, one would as soon look for a nautilus in a nursery.

Yet Little Dorrit is a more seditious book than Das Kapital. All over Europe men and women are in prison for pamphlets and speeches which are to Little Dorrit as red pepper to dynamite. Fortunately for social evolution Governments never know where to strike. Barnacle and Stiltstalking [both in LD] were far too conceited to recognize their own portraits. Parliament,

6. The statement, which does not appear in any of Dean Inge's books, may have originated in one of the many dozen columns contributed to the *Evening Standard* between 1921 and 1946 that were not subsequently collected – or from personal conversation with Shaw on one of the several occasions when they dined at each other's homes.

wearying its leaders out in a few years in the ceaseless drudgery of finding out how not to do it, and smothering it in talk, could not conceive that its heart-breaking industry could have any relation to the ridiculous fiction of the Coodle-Doodle [BH] discussions in Sir Leicester Dedlock's drawing-room. As to the Circumlocution Office [LD], well, perhaps the staffs, owing their posts to patronage and regarding them as sinecures, were a bit too insolent to the public, and would be none the worse for a little chaff from a funny fellow like Dickens; but their inefficiency as a public service was actually a good thing, as it provided a standing object lesson in the superiority of private enterprize. Mr Sparkler [LD] was not offended: he stuck to his job and never read anything. Little Dorrit and Das Kapital were all the same to him: they never entered his world; and to him that world was the whole world.

The mass of Dickens readers, finding all these people too funny to be credible, continued to idolize Coodle and Doodle as great statesmen, and made no distinction between John Stuart Mill at the India Office and Mr Sparkler. In fact the picture was not only too funny to be credible: it was too truthful to be credible. But the fun was no fun to Dickens: the truth was too bitter. When you laugh at Jack Bunsby [D&S] or at The Orfling [Clickett, in DC] when the handle of her corkscrew came off and smote her on the chin, you have no doubt that Dickens is laughing with you like a street boy, despite Bunsby's tragic end. But whilst you laugh at Sparkler or young Barnacle, Dickens is in deadly earnest: he means that both of them must go into the dustbin if England is to survive.

And yet Dickens never saw himself as a revolutionist. It never occurred to him to found a Red International, as Marx did, not even to join one out of the dozens of political reform societies that were about him. He was an English gentleman of the professional class, who would not allow his daughter to go on the stage because it was not respectable. He knew so little about revolutionists that when [Giuseppe] Mazzini called on him and sent in his card,[7] Dickens, much puzzled, concluded that the unknown foreign gentleman wanted money, and very kindly sent him down a sovereign to get rid of him. He discovered for himself all the grievances he exposed, and had no sense of belonging to a movement, nor any desire to combine with others who shared his subversive views. To educate his children religiously and historically he wrote A Child's History of England [3 vols., 1852–4] which had not even the excuse of being childish, and a paraphrase of the gospel

7. Famed Italian patriot who made England his home and London his base of operations from 1837. He and Dickens became friends.

biography which is only a belittling of it for little children.[8] He had much better have left the history to Little Arthur and Mrs Markham and Goldsmith,[9] and taken into account the extraordinary educational value of the Authorized Version as a work of literary art. He probably thought as seldom of himself as a literary artist as of himself as a revolutionist; and he had his share in the revolt against the supernatural pretensions of the Bible which was to end in the vogue of Agnosticism and the pontificate of Darwin. It blinded that generation to the artistic importance of the fact that at a moment when all the literary energy in England was in full eruption, when Shakespear was just dead and Milton just born, a picked body of scholars undertook the task of translating into English what they believed to be the words of God himself. Under the strain of that conviction they surpassed all their normal powers, transfiguring the original texts into literary masterpieces of a splendor that no merely mortal writers can ever again hope to achieve. But the XIX century either did not dare think of the Bible in that way, it being fetish, or else it was in such furious reaction against the fetishism that it would not allow the so-called Holy Scriptures even an artistic merit. At all events Dickens thought his Little Nell [OCS] style better for his children than the English of King James's inspired scribes. He took them (for a time at least) to churches of the Unitarian persuasion, where they could be both sceptical and respectable; but it is hard to say what Dickens believed or did not believe metaphysically or metapolitically, though he left us in no doubt as to his opinion of the Lords, the Commons, and the ante-Crimean Civil Service.

On the positive side he had nothing to say. Marxism and Darwinism came too late for him. He might have been a Comtist—perhaps ought to have been a Comtist, but was not. He was an independent Dickensian, a sort of unphilosophic Radical, with a complete disbelief in government by the people and an equally complete hostility to government in any other interest than theirs. He exposed many abuses and called passionately on the rulers of the people to remedy them; but he never called on the people themselves. He would as soon have thought of calling on them to write their own novels.

Meanwhile he overloaded himself and his unfortunate wife with such a host of children that he was forced to work himself to death prematurely to

8. *The Life of Our Lord*, written for Dickens's children in 1849; first published in 1934.

9. 'Little Arthur' was the pseudonym of Maria, Lady Callcott, author of the eight-volume *Little Arthur's History of England* (1835). 'Mrs Markham' was the pen name of Elizabeth Penrose, author of popular school histories of England and France. Oliver Goldsmith wrote a *History of England* (1771).

provide for them and for the well-to-do life he led. The reading public cannot bear to think of its pet authors as struggling with the economic pressures that often conflict so cruelly with the urge of genius. This pressure was harder on Dickens than on many poorer men. He had a solid bourgeois conscience which made it impossible for him to let wife and children starve whilst he followed the path of destiny. Marx let his wife go crazy with prolonged poverty whilst he wrote a book which changed the mind of the world. But then Marx had been comfortably brought up and thoroughly educated in the German manner. Dickens knew far too much of the horrors of impecuniosity to put his wife through what his mother had gone through, or have his children pasting labels on blacking bottles. He had to please his public or lapse into that sort of poverty. Under such circumstances the domestic conscience inevitably pushes the artistic conscience into the second place. We shall never know how much of Dickens's cheery optimism belied his real outlook on life. He went his own way far enough to make it clear that when he was not infectiously laughing he was a melancholy fellow. Arthur Clennam is one of the Dismal Jemmies[10] of literature. For any gaiety of heart we have to turn to the impossible Dick Swiveller [OCS], who by the way, was designed as a revoltingly coarse fortune hunter, and still appears in that character in the single scene which precedes his sudden appeal to Dickens's sense of fun, and consequent transformation into a highly entertaining and entirely fantastic clown. This was a genuine conversion and not a concession to public taste; but the case of Walter Gay in Dombey and Son, whose high spirits were planned as a prelude to his degeneration and ruin, is a flagrant case of a manufactured happy ending to save a painful one. Martin Chuzzlewit begins as a study in selfishness and ends nowhere. Mr Boffin [OMF], corrupted by riches, gets discharged without a stain on his character by explaining that he was only pretending for benevolent purposes, but leaves us with a feeling that some of his pretences were highly suspicious. Jarndyce [BH], a violently good man, keeps on doing generous things, yet ends by practising a heartlessly cruel and indelicate deception on Esther Summerson for the sake of giving her a pleasant melodramatic surprise. I will not go so far as to say that Dickens's novels are full of melancholy intentions which he dares not carry through to their unhappy conclusions; but he gave us no vitally happy heroes and heroines after Pickwick (begun, like Don Quixote, as a contemptible butt). Their happy endings are manufactured to make the books pleasant. Nobody who has endured the novels of our XX century emancipated women, enormously

10. Jem Hutley in *Pickwick Papers*, an itinerant actor who specializes in 'heavy business', is known as 'Dismal Jemmy' (a jemmy being a sheep's head).

cleverer and better informed than the novels of Dickens, and ruthlessly calculated to leave their readers hopelessly discouraged and miserable, will feel anything but gratitude to Dickens for his humanity in speeding his parting guests with happy faces by turning from the world of destiny to the world of accidental good luck; but as our minds grow stronger some of his consolations become unnecessary and even irritating. And it happens that it is with just such a consolation that Great Expectations ends.

It did not always end so. Dickens wrote two endings, and made a mess of both.[11] In the first ending, which Bulwer Lytton persuaded him to discard, Pip takes little Pip for a walk in Piccadilly and is stopped by Estella, who is passing in her carriage. She is comfortably married to a Shropshire doctor and just says how d'y'do to Pip and kisses the little boy before they both pass on out of oneanother's lives. This, though it is marred by Pip's pious hope that her husband may have thrashed into her some understanding of how much she has made him suffer, is true to nature. But it is much too matter-of-fact to be the right ending to a tragedy. Piccadilly was impossible in such a context; and the passing carriage was unconsciously borrowed from A Day's Ride: A Life's Romance, the novel by Lever which was so unpopular that Great Expectations had to be written to replace it in All The Year Round.[12] But in Lever's story it is the man who stops the carriage, only to be cut dead by the lady. Dickens must have felt that there was something wrong with this ending; and Bulwer's objection confirmed his doubt. Accordingly, he wrote a new ending, in which he got rid of Piccadilly and substituted a perfectly congruous and beautifully touching scene and hour and atmosphere for the meeting. He abolished the Shropshire doctor and left out the little boy. So far the new ending was in every way better than the first one.

Unfortunately, what Bulwer wanted was what is called a happy ending, presenting Pip and Estella as reunited lovers who were going to marry and live happily ever after; and Dickens, though he could not bring himself to be quite so explicit in sentimental falsehood, did, at the end of the very last line, allow himself to say that there was "no shadow of parting" between

11. Shaw's recollection of having as a boy read an 'unhappy' ending to the novel led to an extensive correspondence: see the brochure *The Mystery of the Unhappy Ending*, Limited Editions Club, 1937. For a comprehensive account of the two endings, including Shaw's involvement, see Edgar Rosenberg, 'Last Words on *Great Expectations*', *Dickens Studies Annual*, IX (1981).
12. *A Day's Ride* actually was published uninterruptedly from 18 August 1860 to its conclusion on 23 March 1861, running concurrently with *Great Expectations*, which commenced serialization on 1 December 1860.

them. If Pip had said "Since that parting I have been able to think of her without the old unhappiness; but I have never tried to see her again, and I know I never shall" he would have been left with at least the prospect of a bearable life. But the notion that he could ever have been happy with Estella: indeed that anyone could ever have been happy with Estella, is positively unpleasant. I can remember when the Cowden Clarks[13] ventured to hint a doubt whether Benedick and Beatrice had a very delightful union to look forward to; but that did not greatly matter, as Benedick and Beatrice have none of the reality of Pip and Estella. Shakespear could afford to trifle with *Much Ado About Nothing*, which is avowedly a potboiler; but *Great Expectations* is a different matter. Dickens put nearly all his thought into it. It is too serious a book to be a trivially happy one. Its beginning is unhappy; its middle is unhappy; and the conventional happy ending is an outrage on it.

Estella is a curious addition to the gallery of unamiable women painted by Dickens. In my youth it was commonly said that Dickens could not draw women. The people who said this were thinking of Agnes Wickfield [DC] and Esther Summerson, of Little Dorrit and Florence Dombey, and thinking of them as ridiculous idealizations of their sex. Gissing put a stop to that by asking [in *Charles Dickens: A Critical Study*, 1898] whether shrews like Mrs Raddle [PP], Mrs MacStinger [D&S], Mrs Gargery [GE], fools like Mrs Nickleby and Flora Finching [LD], warped spinsters like Rosa Dartle [DC] and Miss Wade [LD], were not masterpieces of woman drawing. And they are all unamiable. But for Betsey Trotwood [DC], who is a very lovable fairy godmother and yet a genuine nature study, and an old dear like Mrs Boffin [OMF], one would be tempted to ask whether Dickens had ever in his life met an amiable female. The transformation of Dora [DC] into Flora is diabolical, but frightfully true to nature. Of course Dickens with his imagination could invent amiable women by the dozen; but somehow he could not or would not bring them to life as he brought the others. We doubt whether he ever knew a little Dorrit; but Fanny Dorrit is from the life unmistakably. So is Estella. She is a much more elaborate study than Fanny, and, I should guess, a recent one.

Dickens, when he let himself go in *Great Expectations*, was separated from his wife and free to make more intimate acquaintances with women than a domesticated man can. I know nothing of his adventures in this phase of his career, though I daresay a good deal of it will be dug out by the little sect of anti-Dickensites whose fanaticism has been provoked by the Dickens

13. Charles and Mary Cowden-Clarke were joint authors of *The Shakespeare Key* (1879).

Fellowships.[14] It is not necessary to suggest a love affair; for Dickens could get from a passing glance a hint which he could expand into a full-grown character. The point concerns us here only because it is the point on which the ending of Great Expectations turns: namely, that Estella is a born tormentor. She deliberately torments Pip all through for the fun of it; and in the little we hear of her intercourse with others there is no suggestion of a moment of kindness: in fact her tormenting of Pip is almost affectionate in contrast to the cold disdain of her attitude towards the people who were not worth tormenting. It is not surprising that the unfortunate Bentley Drummle, whom she marries in the stupidity of sheer perversity, is obliged to defend himself from her clever malice with his fists: a consolation to us for Pip's broken heart, but not altogether a credible one; for the real Estellas can usually intimidate the real Bentley Drummles. At all events the final sugary suggestion of Estella redeemed by Bentley's thrashings and waste of her money, and living happily with Pip for ever after, provoked even Dickens's eldest son to rebel against it,[15] most justly.

Apart from this the story is the most perfect of Dickens's works. In it he does not muddle himself with the ridiculous plots that appear like vestiges of the stone age in many of his books, from Oliver Twist to the end. The story is built round a single and simple catastrophe: the revelation to Pip of the source of his great expectations. There is, it is true, a trace of the old plot superstition in Estella turning out to be Magwitch's daughter; but it provides a touchingly happy ending for that heroic Warmint. Who could have the heart to grudge it to him?

As our social conscience expands and makes the intense class snobbery of the XIX century seem less natural to us, the tragedy of Great Expectations will lose some of its appeal. I have already wondered whether Dickens himself ever came to see that his agonizing sensitiveness about the blacking bottles and his resentment of his mother's opposition to his escape from them was not too snobbish to deserve all the sympathy he claimed for it. Compare the case of H. G. Wells, our nearest to a XX century Dickens. Wells hated being

14. The Dickens Fellowship was founded in London in 1902.
15. Dickens's son, in an introduction to the novel, agreed there was 'undoubted truth' in the objection that the conclusion 'is faulty and inartistic'. The revised ending, he commented, may have been acceptable 'to those readers who are never satisfied without "a happy ending," but it is certain that the only really natural as well as artistic conclusion to the story was that which was originally intended . . . which kept Pip and Estella apart' (*Works of Charles Dickens*, with introductions by Charles Dickens the Younger, 21 vols., 1892–1926, vol. 16, 1895).

a draper's assistant as much as Dickens hated being a warehouse boy; but he was not in the least ashamed of it, and did not blame his mother for regarding it as the summit of her ambition for him. Fate having imposed on that engaging cricketer Mr Wells's father an incongruous means of livelihood in the shape of a small shop, shopkeeping did not present itself to the young Wells as beneath him, wheras to the genteel Dickens being a warehouse boy was an unbearable comedown. Still, I cannot help speculating on whether if Dickens had not killed himself prematurely to pile up money for that excessive family of his, he might not have reached a stage at which he could have got as much fun out of the blacking bottles as Mr Wells got out of his abhorred draper's counter.

Dickens never reached that stage; and there is no prevision of it in Great Expectations; for in it he never raises the question why Pip should refuse Magwitch's endowment and shrink from him with such inhuman loathing. Magwitch no doubt was a Warmint from the point of view of the genteel Dickens family and even from his own; but Victor Hugo would have made him a magnificent hero, another Valjean. Inspired by an altogether noble fixed idea, he had lifted himself out of his rut of crime and honestly made a fortune for the child who had fed him when he was starving. If Pip had no objection to be a parasite instead of an honest blacksmith, at least he had a better claim to be a parasite on Magwitch's earnings than, as he imagined, on Miss Havisham's property. It is curious that this should not have occurred to Dickens; for nothing could exceed the bitterness of his exposure of the futility of Pip's parasitism. If all that came of sponging on Miss Havisham (as he thought) was the privilege of being one of the Finches of the Grove,[16] he need not have felt his dependence on Magwitch to be incompatible with his entirely baseless self-respect. But Pip—and I am afraid Pip must be to this extent identified with Dickens—could not see Magwitch as an animal of the same species as himself or Miss Havisham. His feeling is true to the nature of snobbery; but his creator says no word in criticism of that ephemeral limitation.

The basic truth of the situation is that Pip, like his creator, has no culture and no religion. Joe Gargery, when Pip tells a monstrous string of lies about Miss Havisham, advises him to say a repentant word about it in his prayers; but Pip never prays; and church means nothing to him but Mr Wopsle's orotundity. In this he resembles David Copperfield, who has gentility but neither culture nor religion. Pip's world is therefore a very melancholy place, and his conduct, good or bad, always helpless. This is why Dickens worked

16. A club of rich young men that Pip and Herbert Pocket join.

against so black a background after he was roused from his ignorant middle-class cheery optimism by Carlyle. When he lost his belief in bourgeois society and with it his lightness of heart he had neither an economic Utopia nor a credible religion to hitch on to. His world becomes a world of great expectations cruelly disappointed. The Wells world is a world of greater and greater expectations continually being fulfilled. This is a huge improvement. Dickens never had time to form a philosophy or define a faith; and his later and greater books are saddened by the evil that is done under the sun; but at least he preserved his intellectual innocence sufficiently to escape the dismal pseudo-scientific fatalism that was descending on the world in his latter days, founded on the preposterous error as to causation in which the future is determined by the present, which has been determined by the past. The true causation, of course, is always the incessant irresistible activity of the evolutionary appetite.

# Collaborator's Note
## (Cymbeline Refinished)

*First published as a leaflet distributed with the programme for a production of Shakespeare's* Cymbeline *with a revised fifth act by Shaw, London, 1937. Revised and expanded as a foreword to* Cymbeline Refinished, *1947*

The practice of improving Shakespear's plays, more especially in the matter of supplying them with what are called happy endings, is an old established one which has always been accepted without protest by British audiences. When Mr Harley Granville-Barker, following up some desperate experiments by the late William Poel, introduced the startling innovation of performing the plays in the West End of London exactly as Shakespear wrote them [see vol. 2, p. 432], there was indeed some demur; but it was expressed outside the theatre and led to no rioting. And it set on foot a new theory of Shakespearean representation. Up to that time it had been assumed as a matter of course that everyone behind the scenes in a theatre must know much better than Shakespear how plays should be written, exactly as it is believed in the Hollywood studios today that everyone in a film studio knows better than any professional playwright how a play should be filmed. But the pleasure given by Mr Granville-Barker's productions shook that conviction in the theatre; and the superstition that Shakespear's plays as written by him are impossible on the stage, which had produced a happy ending to King Lear, Cibber's Richard III, a love scene in the tomb of the Capulets between Romeo and Juliet before the poison takes effect,[1] and had culminated in the crude literary butcheries successfully imposed on the public and the critics as Shakespear's plays by Henry Irving and Augustin Daly at the end of the last century, is for the moment heavily discredited. It may be asked then why I, who always fought fiercely against that superstition in the days when I was a journalist-critic, should perpetrate a spurious fifth act to Cymbeline, and

---

1. Nahum Tate's version of *King Lear* (1681) omits the Fool and has Cordelia survive and marry Edgar; Colley Cibber's adaptation of *Richard III* (1700) removed major speeches and added others he considered more dramatic; David Garrick's version of *Romeo and Juliet* (1748) provides the tragic pair with a plaintive parting conversation.

do it too, not wholly as a literary *jeu d'esprit* [witticism], but in response to an actual emergency in the theatre when [on 3 December 1936] it was proposed to revive Cymbeline at no less sacred a place than the Shakespear Memorial Theatre at Stratford-upon-Avon.

Cymbeline, though one of the finest of Shakespear's later plays now on the stage, goes to pieces in the last act. In fact I mooted the point myself by thoughtlessly saying that the revival would be all right if I wrote a last act for it. To my surprise this blasphemy was received with acclamation; and as the applause, like the proposal, was not wholly jocular, the fancy began to haunt me, and persisted until I exorcised it by writing the pages which ensue.[2]

I had a second surprise when I began by reading the authentic last act carefully through. I had not done so for many years, and had the common impression about it that it was a cobbled-up affair by several hands, including a vision in prison accompanied by scraps of quite ridiculous doggerel.

For this estimate I found absolutely no justification nor excuse. I must have got it from the last revival of the play at the old Lyceum theatre [22 September 1896], when Irving, as Iachimo, a statue of romantic melancholy, stood dumb on the stage for hours (as it seemed) whilst the others toiled through a series of *dénouements* of crushing tedium, in which the characters lost all their vitality and individuality, and had nothing to do but identify themselves by moles on their necks, or explain why they were not dead. The vision and the verses were cut out as a matter of course; and I ignorantly thanked Heaven for it.

When I read the act as aforesaid I found that my notion that it is a cobbled-up *pasticcio* [patchwork] by other hands was an unpardonable stupidity. The act is genuine Shakespear to the last full stop, and late phase Shakespear in point of verbal workmanship.

The doggerel is not doggerel: it is a versified masque, in Shakespear's careless woodnotes wild, complete with Jupiter as *deus ex machina*, eagle and all, introduced, like the Ceres scene in The Tempest, to please King Jamie, or else because an irresistible fashion had set in, just as at all the great continental opera houses a ballet used to be *de rigueur*. Gounod had to introduce one into his Faust, and Wagner into his Tannhäuser, before they could be staged at the Grand Opera in Paris. So, I take it, had Shakespear to stick a masque into Cymbeline. Performed as such, with suitable music and enough pictorial splendor, it is not only entertaining on the stage, but, with the very

2. Shaw's revised fifth act was performed, not at Stratford, but by Ronald Adam's company at the Embassy Theatre, London, on 16 November 1937.

Shakespearean feature of a comic jailor which precedes it, just the thing to save the last act.

Without it the act is a tedious string of unsurprising *dénouements* sugared with insincere sentimentality after a ludicrous stage battle. With one exception the characters have vanished and left nothing but dolls being moved about like the glass balls in the game of solitaire until they are all got rid of but one. The exception is the hero, or rather the husband of the heroine, Leonatus Posthumus. The late Charles Charrington, who with his wife Janet Achurch broke the ice for Ibsen in England, used to cite Posthumus as Shakespear's anticipation of his Norwegian rival. Certainly, after being theatrically conventional to the extent of ordering his wife to be murdered, he begins to criticize, quite on the lines of Mrs Alving in Ghosts, the slavery to an inhuman ideal of marital fidelity which led him to this villainous extremity. One may say that he is the only character left really alive in the last act; and as I cannot change him for the better I have left most of his part untouched. I make no apology for my attempt to bring the others back to dramatic activity and individuality.

I should like to have retained Cornelius as the exponent of Shakespear's sensible and scientific detestation of vivisection. But as he has nothing to say except that the Queen is dead, and nobody can possibly care a rap whether she is alive or dead, I have left him with her in the box of puppets that are done with.

I have ruthlessly cut out the surprises that no longer surprise anybody. I really could not keep my countenance over the identification of Guiderius by the mole on his neck. That device was killed by Maddison Morton, once a famous farce writer, now forgotten by everyone save Mr Gordon Craig and myself.[3] In Morton's masterpiece, Box and Cox [1847], Box asks Cox whether he has a strawberry mark on his left arm. "No" says Cox. "Then you are my long lost brother" says Box as they fall into oneanother's arms and end the farce happily. One could wish that Guiderius had anticipated Cox.

Plot has always been the curse of serious drama, and indeed of serious literature of any kind. It is so out-of-place there that Shakespear never could invent one. Unfortunately, instead of taking Nature's hint and discarding plots, he borrowed them all over the place and got into trouble through having to unravel them in the last act, especially in The Two Gentlemen of Verona and Cymbeline. The more childish spectators may find some delight

3. Gordon Craig acted the role of Abel Quick in Morton's one-act farce *A Regular Fix* at Irving's Lyceum Theatre on 2 June 1891.

in the revelation that Polydore and Cadwal are Imogen's long lost brothers and Cymbeline's long lost sons; that Iachimo is now an occupant of the penitent form and very unlike his old self; and that Imogen is so dutiful that she accepts her husband's attempt to have her murdered with affectionate docility. I cannot share these infantile joys. Having become interested in Iachimo, in Imogen, and even in the two long lost princes, I wanted to know how their characters would react to the *éclaircissement* [enlightenment] which follows the battle. The only way to satisfy this curiosity was to rewrite the act as Shakespear might have written it if he had been post-Ibsen and post-Shaw instead of post-Marlowe.

In doing so I had to follow the Shakespearean verse pattern to match the 89 lines of Shakespear's text which I retained. This came very easily to me. It happened when I was a child that one of the books I delighted in was an illustrated Shakespear, with a picture and two or three lines of text underneath it on every third or fourth page. Ever since, Shakespearean blank verse has been to me as natural a form of literary expression as the Augustan English to which I was brought up in Dublin, or the latest London fashion in dialogue. It is so easy that if it were possible to kill it it would have been burlesqued to death by Tom Thumb, Chrononhotonthologos, and Bombastes Furioso.[4] But Shakespear will survive any possible extremity of caricature.

I shall not deprecate the most violent discussion as to the propriety of meddling with masterpieces. All I can say is that the temptation to do it, and sometimes the circumstances which demand it, are irresistible. The results are very various. When a mediocre artist tries to improve on a great artist's work the effect is ridiculous or merely contemptible. When the alteration damages the original, as when a bad painter repaints a Velasquez or a Rembrandt, he commits a crime. When the changed work is sold or exhibited as the original, the fraud is indictable. But when it comes to complete forgery, as in the case of [William H.] Ireland's Vortigern, which was much admired and at last actually performed as a play by Shakespear,[5] the affair passes beyond the sphere of crime and becomes an instructive joke.

But what of the many successful and avowed variations? What about the additions made by Mozart to the score of Handel's Messiah? Elgar, who adored Handel, and had an unbounded contempt for all the lesser meddlers,

4. All are burlesque tragedies, by, respectively, Henry Fielding (1730; expanded as *The Tragedy of Tragedies*, 1731); Harry Carey (1734); and W. B. Rhodes (1810).
5. Forger of many legal documents and personal papers supposedly by or relating to Shakespeare, as well as of a play *Vortigern and Rowena*, staged as Shakespeare's at Drury Lane in 1796.

loved Mozart's variations, and dismissed all purist criticism of them by maintaining that Handel must have extemporized equivalents to them on the organ at his concerts. When Spontini found on his visit to Dresden that Wagner had added trombone parts to his choruses, he appropriated them very gratefully.[6] Volumes of variations on the tunes of other composers were published as such by Mozart and Beethoven, to say nothing of Bach and Handel, who played Old Harry with any air that amused them. Would anyone now remember Diabelli's vulgar waltz but for Beethoven's amazing variations, one of which is also a variation on an air from Don Giovanni?

And now consider the practice of Shakespear himself. Tolstoy declared that the original Lear is superior to Shakespear's rehandling, which he abhorred as immoral.[7] Nobody has ever agreed with him. Will it be contended that Shakespear had no right to refashion Hamlet? If he had spoiled both plays, that would be a reason for reviving them without Shakespear's transfigurations, but not for challenging Shakespear's right to remake them.

Accordingly, I feel no qualm of conscience and have no apology to make for indulging in a variation on the last act of Cymbeline. I stand in the same time relation to Shakespear as Mozart to Handel, or Wagner to Beethoven. Like Mozart, I have not confined myself to the journeyman's job of writing "additional accompaniments": I have luxuriated in variations. Like Wagner dealing with Gluck's overture to Iphigenia in Aulis[8] I have made a new ending for its own sake. Beethoven's Ninth Symphony towers among the classic masterpieces; but if Wagner had been old enough in his Dresden days not only to rescore the first and greatest movement as he did, but to supply the whole work with a more singable ending I should not have discouraged him; for I must agree with Verdi that the present ending, from the change to six-four onward, though intensely Beethovenish, is in performance usually a screaming voice-destroying orgy.

6. When Gasparo Spontini took personal direction of his opera *La Vestale* at the Dresden Court Theatre late in 1844, Wagner asked him why he had failed to use trombones in the first-act Triumphal March. Spontini urged Wagner to introduce them into the march in time for the next rehearsal, and, pleased with the result, later wrote from Paris 'begging me to forward him a copy of this instrumental addition' (Wagner, 'Mementoes of Spontini', *Prose Works*, tr. W. A. Ellis, vol. III: *The Theatre*, 1894).
7. *Tolstoy on Shakespeare*, tr. V. Tchertkoff (1906), which contains extracts from undated correspondence by Shaw to the translator.
8. In 1846–7 Wagner edited Gluck's *Iphigénie en Aulide* (1774), making both textual and musical alterations.

I may be asked why all my instances are musical instead of literary. Is it a plot to take the literary critics out of their depth? Well, it may have that good effect; but I am not aiming at it. It is, I suppose, because music has succeeded to the heroic rank taken by literature in the XVI century. I cannot pretend to care much about what Nat Lee did in his attempts to impart Restoration gentility to Shakespear,[9] or about Thomas Corneille's bowdler-ization [1677] of Molière's Festin de Pierre, or any of the other literary precedents, though I am a little ashamed of being found in the company of their perpetrators. But I do care a good deal about what Mozart did to Handel, and Wagner to Gluck; and it seems to me that to discuss the artistic morality of my alternative ending without reference to them would be waste of time. Anyhow, what I have done I have done; and at that I must leave it.

I shall not press my version on managers producing Cymbeline if they have the courage and good sense to present the original word-for-word as Shakespear left it, and the means to do justice to the masque. But if they are halfhearted about it, and inclined to compromise by leaving out the masque and the comic jailor and mutilating the rest, as their manner is, I unhesitatingly recommend my version. The audience will not know the difference; and the few critics who have read Cymbeline will be too grateful for my shortening of the last act to complain.

AYOT ST LAWRENCE.                                                    G. B. S.
January, 1937–December, 1945.

9. Although Lee, the most popular playwright of his time, revealed strong influences of Shakespeare in his heroic verse tragedies, there is no evidence that he ever edited, produced or performed Shakespeare. Shaw may be suggesting merely that Lee wrote in a classic tradition, mannered and rhetorical, combining heroic drama with Jacobean tragedy, in the elegant style of the French tragedians.

# London Music in 1888–89

*First published in 1937*

When my maiden novel, called Immaturity, was printed fifty years after it was written, I prefaced it with some account of the unhappy-go-lucky way in which I was brought up, ending with the nine years of shabby genteel destitution during which my attempts to gain a footing in literature were a complete and apparently hopeless failure.

I was rescued from this condition by William Archer, who transferred some of his book reviewing work to me, and pushed me into a post as picture critic which had been pushed on him, and for which he considered himself unqualified, as in fact he was. So, as reviewer for the old Pall Mall Gazette and picture critic for Edmund Yates's then fashionable weekly, the World, I carried on until I found an opening which I can explain only by describing the musical side of my childhood, to which I made only a passing allusion in my Immaturity preface, but which was of cardinal importance in my education.

In 1888, I being then 32 and already a noted critic and political agitator, the Star newspaper was founded under the editorship of the late T. P. O'Connor (nicknamed Tay Pay by Yates), who had for his very much more competent assistant the late H. W. Massingham. Tay Pay survived until 1936; but his mind never advanced beyond the year 1865, though his Fenian sympathies and his hearty detestation of the English nation disguised that defect from him. Massingham induced him to invite me to join the political staff of his paper; but as I had already, fourteen years before Lenin, read Karl Marx, and was preaching Socialism at every street corner or other available forum in London and the provinces, the effect of my articles on Tay Pay may be imagined. He refused to print them, and told me that, man alive, it would be five hundred years before such stuff would become practical political journalism. He was too goodnatured to sack me; and I did not want to throw away my job; so I got him out of his difficulty by asking him to let me have two columns a week for a *feuilleton* on music. He was glad to get rid of my politics on these terms; but he stipulated that—musical criticism being known to him only as unreadable and unintelligible jargon—I should, for God's sake, not write about Bach in B Minor. I was quite alive to that danger: in fact I had made my proposal because I believed I could make musical criticism readable even by the deaf. Besides, my terms were moderate: two guineas a week.

I was strong on the need for signed criticism written in the first person instead of the journalistic "we"; but as I then had no name worth signing, and G.B.S. meant nothing to the public, I had to invent a fantastic personality with something like a foreign title. I thought of Count di Luna (a character in Verdi's Trovatore), but finally changed it for Corno di Bassetto, as it sounded like a foreign title, and nobody knew what a corno di bassetto was.

As a matter of fact the corno di bassetto is not a foreigner with a title but a musical instrument called in English the basset horn. It is a wretched instrument, now completely snuffed out for general use by the bass clarinet. It would be forgotten and unplayed if it were not that Mozart has scored for it in his Requiem, evidently because its peculiar watery melancholy, and the total absence of any richness or passion in its tone, is just the thing for a funeral. Mendelssohn wrote some chamber music for it, presumably to oblige somebody who played it; and it is kept alive by these works and by our Mr [Roughton H.] Whall.[1] If I had ever heard a note of it in 1888 I should not have selected it for a character which I intended to be sparkling. The devil himself could not make a basset horn sparkle.

For two years I sparkled every week in the Star under this ridiculous name, and in a manner so absolutely unlike the conventional musical criticism of the time that all the journalists believed that the affair was a huge joke, the point of which was that I knew nothing whatever about music. How it had come about that I was one of the few critics of that time who really knew their business I can explain only by picking up the thread of autobiography which I dropped in my scrappy prefix to Immaturity. For the sake of those who have not read the Immaturity preface, or have forgotten it, I shall have to repeat here some of my father's history, but only so far as is necessary to explain the situation of my mother.

Technically speaking I should say she was the worst mother conceivable, always, however, within the limits of the fact that she was incapable of unkindness to any child, animal, or flower, or indeed to any person or thing whatsoever. But if such a thing as a maternity welfare centre had been established or even imagined in Ireland in her time, and she had been induced to visit it, every precept of it would have been laughably strange to her.

1. Musician, organist for thirty years at Holy Trinity, Stroud, and music instructor at Wycliffe College in Gloucestershire. He was frequently co-opted by symphonic orchestras when a 'bass clarionet' part had to be supplied.

Though she had been severely educated up to the highest standard for Irish "carriage ladies" of her time, she was much more like a Trobriand islander as described by Mr [Bronislaw] Malinowski[2] than like a modern Cambridge lady graduate in respect of accepting all the habits, good or bad, of the Irish society in which she was brought up as part of an uncontrolable order of nature. She went her own way with so complete a disregard and even unconsciousness of convention and scandal and prejudice that it was impossible to doubt her good faith and innocence; but it never occurred to her that other people, especially children, needed guidance or training, or that it mattered in the least what they ate and drank or what they did as long as they were not actively mischievous. She accepted me as a natural and customary phenomenon, and took it for granted that I should go on occurring in that way. In short, living to her was not an art: it was something that happened. But there were unkind parts of it that could be avoided; and among these were the constraints and tyrannies, the scoldings and browbeatings and punishments she had suffered in her childhood as the method of her education. In her righteous reaction against it she reached a negative attitude in which, having no substitute to propose, she carried domestic anarchy as far as in the nature of things it can be carried.

She had been tyrannously taught French enough to recite one or two of Lafontaine's fables; to play the piano the wrong way; to harmonize by rule from [Johann] Logier's Thoroughbass [1818]; to sit up straight and speak and dress and behave like a lady, and an Irish lady at that. She knew nothing of the value of money nor of housekeeping nor of hygiene nor of anything that could be left to servants or governesses or parents or solicitors or apothecaries or any other member of the retinue, indoor and outdoor, of a country house. She had great expectations from a humpbacked little aunt [Ellen Whitcroft], a fairylike creature with a will of iron, who had brought up her motherless niece with a firm determination to make her a paragon of good breeding, to achieve a distinguished marriage for her, and to leave her all her money as a dowry.

Manufacturing destinies for other people is a dangerous game. Its results are usually as unexpected as those of a first-rate European war. When my mother came to marriageable age her long widowed father married again. The brother of his late wife [Lucinda Whitcroft], to whom he was considerably in debt, disapproved so strongly that on learning the date of the approaching

2. British anthropologist, author of *The Sexual Life of Savages in N. W. Melanesia* (1929), which dealt with sexual relations among the natives of the Trobriand Islands, a coral archipelago lying to the north-east of New Guinea.

ceremony from my mother he had the bridegroom arrested on his way to church. My grandfather naturally resented this manœuvre, and in his wrath could not be persuaded that his daughter was not my grand-uncle's accomplice in it. Visits to relatives in Dublin provided a temporary refuge for her; and the affair would have blown over but for the intervention of my father.

My father was a very ineligible suitor for a paragon with great expectations. His family pretensions were enormous; but they were founded on many generations of younger sons, and were purely psychological. He had managed to acquire a gentlemanly post in the law courts. This post had been abolished and its holder pensioned. By selling the pension he was enabled to start in business as a wholesaler in the corn trade (retail trade was beneath his family dignity) of which he knew nothing. He accentuated this deficiency by becoming the partner of a Mr [George] Clibborn, who had served an apprenticeship to the cloth trade. Their combined ignorances kept the business going, mainly by its own inertia, until they and it died. Many years after this event I paid a visit of curiosity to [No. 67] Jervis St, Dublin; and there, on one of the pillars of a small portico, I found the ancient inscription "Clibborn & Shaw" still decipherable, as it were on the tombs of the Pharaohs. I cannot believe that this business yielded my father at any time more than three or four hundred a year; and it got less as time went on, as that particular kind of business was dying a slow death throughout the latter half of the XIX century.

My father was in principle an ardent teetotaller. Nobody ever felt the disgrace and misery and endless mischief of drunkenness as he did: he impressed it so deeply on me in my earliest years that I have been a teetotaller ever since. Unfortunately his conviction in this matter was founded on personal experience. He was the victim of a drink neurosis which cropped up in his family from time to time: a miserable affliction, quite unconvivial, and accompanied by torments of remorse and shame.

My father was past forty,[3] and no doubt had sanguine illusions as to the future of his newly acquired business when he fell in love with my mother and was emboldened by her expectations and his business hopes to propose to her just at the moment when marriage seemed her only way of escape from an angry father and a stepmother. Immediately all her relatives, who had tolerated this middleaged gentleman as a perfectly safe acquaintance with an agreeable vein of humor, denounced him as a notorious drunkard. My mother, suspicious of this sudden change of front, put the question directly to my father. His eloquence and sincerity convinced her that he was, as he claimed to be, and as he was in principle, a bigoted teetotaller. She married

3. George Carr Shaw, born in 1814, was married in 1852.

him; and her disappointed and infuriated aunt disinherited her, not foreseeing that the consequences of the marriage would include so remarkable a phenomenon as myself.

When my mother was disillusioned, and found out what living on a few hundreds a year with three children meant, even in a country where a general servant could be obtained for eight pounds a year, her condition must have been about as unhappy and her prospects as apparently hopeless as her aunt could have desired even in her most vindictive moments.

But there was one trump in her hand. She was fond of music, and had a mezzo-soprano voice of remarkable purity of tone. In the next street to ours, Harrington Street, where the houses were bigger and more fashionable than in our little by-street, there was a teacher of singing, lamed by an accident in childhood which had left one of his legs shorter than the other, but a man of mesmeric vitality and force. He was a bachelor living with his brother, whom he supported and adored, and a terrible old woman who was his servant of all work. His name was George John Vandeleur Lee, known in Dublin as Mr G. J. Lee. Singing lessons were cheap in Dublin; and my mother went to Lee to learn how to sing properly. He trained her voice to such purpose that she became indispensable to him as an amateur *prima donna*. For he was a most magnetic conductor and an indefatigable organizer of concerts, and later on of operas, with such amateur talent, vocal and orchestral, as he could discover and train in Dublin, which, as far as public professional music was concerned, was, outside the churches, practically a vacuum.

Lee soon found his way into our house, first by giving my mother lessons there, and then by using our drawingroom for rehearsals. I can only guess that the inadequacies of old Ellen in the Harrington Street house, and perhaps the incompatibilities of the brother, outweighed the comparative smallness of our house in Synge Street. My mother soon became not only *prima donna* and chorus leader but general musical factotum in the whirlpool of Lee's activity. Her grounding in Logier's Thoroughbass enabled her to take boundless liberties with composers. When authentic band parts were missing she thought nothing of making up an orchestral accompaniment of her own from the pianoforte score. Lee, as far as I know, had never seen a full orchestral score in his life: he conducted from a first violin part or from the vocal score, and had not, I think, any decided notion of orchestration as an idiosyncratic and characteristic part of a composer's work. He had no scholarship according to modern ideas; but he could do what Wagner said is the whole duty of a conductor: he could give the right time to the band; and he could pull it out of its amateur difficulties in emergencies by sheer mesmerism. Though he could not, or at any rate within my hearing never did sing a note, his taste in singing was classically perfect. In his search for the secret of *bel canto* he had gone to all the teachers within his reach. They told him that there was a voice in the head, a voice in the throat, and a voice in the chest. He dissected birds, and, with the connivance of medical friends, human subjects, in his search for these three organs. He then told the teachers authoritatively that the three voices were fabulous, and that the voice was produced by a single instrument called the larynx. They replied that musical art had nothing to do with anatomy, and that for a musician to practise dissection was unheard-of and disgusting. But as, tested by results, their efforts to teach their pupils to screech like locomotive whistles not only outraged his ear but wrecked the voices and often the health of their victims, their practice was as unacceptable to him as their theory.

Thus Lee became the enemy of every teacher of singing in Dublin; and they reciprocated heartily. In this negative attitude he was left until, at the opera, he heard an Italian baritone named Badeali,[4] who at the age of 80, when he first discovered these islands, had a perfectly preserved voice, and, to Lee's taste, a perfectly produced one. Lee, thanks to his dissections, listened with a clear knowledge of what a larynx is really like. The other vocal organs and their action were obvious and conscious. Guided by this knowledge, and by his fine ear, his fastidious taste, and his instinct, he found out what Badeali was doing when he was singing. The other teachers were interested in Badeali only because one of his accomplishments was to drink a glass of wine and sing a sustained note at the same time. Finally Lee equipped himself with a teaching method which became a religion for him: the only religion, I may add, he ever professed. And my mother, as his pupil, learnt and embraced this musical faith, and rejected all other creeds as uninteresting superstitions. And it did not fail her; for she lived to be Badeali's age and kept her voice without a scrape on it until the end.

I have to dwell on The Method, as we called it in the family, because my mother's association with Lee, and the *ménage à trois* in which it resulted, would be unpleasantly misunderstood without this clue to it. For after the death of Lee's brother, which affected him to the verge of suicide, we left our respective houses and went to live in the same house, number one Hatch Street, which was half in Lower Leeson Street. The arrangement was economical; for we could not afford to live in a fashionable house, and Lee

---

4. Cesare Badiali, highly reputed Italian basso, first sang in London in 1859. Shaw was misled by Lee, who claimed to have heard Badiali sing 'when he was nearly eighty' (Shaw, 'Beethoven's Ninth', *Shaw's Music*, 1981, vol. 2, p. 131, reprinted from the *World*, 23 July 1890). Badiali died in 1865, at the age of 55.

could not afford to give lessons in an unfashionable one, though, being a bachelor, he needed only a music room and a bedroom. We also shared a cottage in Dalkey, high up on Torca Hill, with all Dublin Bay from Dalkey Island to Howth visible from the garden, and all Killiney Bay with the Wicklow mountains in the background from the hall door. Lee bought this cottage and presented it to my mother, though she never had any legal claim to it and did not benefit by its sale later on. It was not conveniently situated for rehearsals or lessons; but there were musical neighbors who allowed me to some extent to run in and out of their houses when there was music going on.

The *ménage à trois*, alternating between Hatch St and Dalkey, worked in its ramshackle way quite smoothly until I was fifteen or thereabouts, when Lee went to London and our family broke up into fragments that never got pieced together again.

In telling the story so far, I have had to reconstruct the part of it which occurred before I came into it and began, as my nurse put it, to take notice. I can remember the ante-Lee period in Synge St when my father, as sole chief of the household, read family prayers and formally admitted that we had done those things which we ought not to have done and left undone those things which we ought to have done,[5] which was certainly true as far as I was personally concerned. He added that there was no health in us; and this also was true enough about myself; for Dr Newland, our apothecary, was in almost continual attendance to administer cathartics; and when I had a sore throat I used to hold out for sixpence before submitting to a mustard plaster round my neck. We children (I had two sisters older than myself and no brothers) were abandoned entirely to the servants, who, with the exception of Nurse Williams, who was a good and honest woman, were utterly unfit to be trusted with the charge of three cats, much less three children. I had my meals in the kitchen, mostly of stewed beef, which I loathed, badly cooked potatoes, sound or diseased as the case might be, and much too much tea out of brown delft teapots left to "draw" on the hob until it was pure tannin. Sugar I stole. I was never hungry, because my father, often insufficiently fed in his childhood, had such a horror of child hunger that he insisted on unlimited bread and butter being always within our reach. When I was troublesome a servant thumped me on the head until one day, greatly daring, I rebelled, and, on finding her collapse abjectly, became thenceforth uncontrolable. I hated the servants and liked my mother because, on the one or two rare and delightful occasions when she buttered my bread for me, she

5. Anglican *Book of Common Prayer;* see act one of *Major Barbara.*

buttered it thickly instead of merely wiping a knife on it. Her almost complete neglect of me had the advantage that I could idolize her to the utmost pitch of my imagination and had no sordid or disillusioning contacts with her. It was a privilege to be taken for a walk or a visit with her, or on an excursion.

My ordinary exercise whilst I was still too young to be allowed out by myself was to be taken out by a servant, who was supposed to air me on the banks of the canal or round the fashionable squares where the atmosphere was esteemed salubrious and the surroundings gentlemanly. Actually she took me into the slums to visit her private friends, who dwelt in squalid tenements. When she met a generous male acquaintance who insisted on treating her she took me into the public house bars, where I was regaled with lemonade and gingerbeer; but I did not enjoy these treats, because my father's eloquence on the evil of drink had given me an impression that a public house was a wicked place into which I should not have been taken. Thus were laid the foundations of my lifelong hatred of poverty, and the devotion of all my public life to the task of exterminating the poor and rendering their resurrection for ever impossible.

Note, by the way, that I should have been much more decently brought up if my parents had been too poor to afford servants.

As to early education I can remember our daily governess, Miss [Caroline] Hill, a needy lady who seemed to me much older than she can really have been. She puzzled me with her attempts to teach me to read; for I can remember no time at which a page of print was not intelligible to me, and can only suppose that I was born literate. She tried to give me and my two sisters a taste for poetry by reciting "Stop; for thy tread is on an empire's dust" [Byron, *Childe Harold's Pilgrimage*, Canto III] at us, and only succeeded, poor lady, in awakening our sense of derisive humor. She punished me by little strokes with her fingers that would not have discomposed a fly, and even persuaded me that I ought to cry and feel disgraced on such occasions. She gave us judgment books and taught us to feel jubilant when after her departure we could rush to the kitchen crying "No marks today" and to hang back ashamed when this claim could not be substantiated. She taught me to add, subtract, and multiply, but could not teach me division, because she kept saying two into four, three into six, and so forth without ever explaining what the word "into" meant in this connection. This was explained to me on my first day at school; and I solemnly declare that it was the only thing I ever learnt at school. However, I must not complain; for my immurement in that damnable boy prison [Wesleyan Connexional School] effected its real purpose of preventing my being a nuisance to my mother at home for at least half the day.

The only other teaching I had was from my clerical Uncle William George (surnamed Carroll) who, being married to one of my many paternal aunts (my father had no end of brothers and sisters), had two boys of his own to educate, and took me on with them for awhile in the early mornings to such purpose that when his lessons were ended by my being sent to school, I knew more Latin grammar than any other boy in the First Latin Junior, to which I was relegated. After a few years in that establishment I had forgotten most of it, and, as aforesaid, learnt nothing; for there was only the thinnest pretence of teaching anything but Latin and Greek, if asking a boy once a day in an overcrowded class the Latin for a man or a horse or what not, can be called teaching him Latin. I was far too busy educating myself out of school by reading every book I could lay hands on, and clambering all over Killiney hill looking at the endless pictures nature painted for me, meanwhile keeping my mind busy by telling myself all sorts of stories, to puzzle about my vocabulary lesson, as the punishments were as futile as the teaching. At the end of my schooling I knew nothing of what the school professed to teach; but I was a highly educated boy all the same. I could sing and whistle from end to end leading works by Handel, Haydn, Mozart, Beethoven, Rossini, Bellini, Donizetti and Verdi. I was saturated with English literature, from Shakespear and Bunyan to Byron and Dickens. And I was so susceptible to natural beauty that, having had some glimpse of the Dalkey scenery on an excursion, I still remember the moment when my mother told me that we were going to live there as the happiest of my life.

And all this I owed to the meteoric impact of Lee, with his music, his method, his impetuous enterprize and his magnetism, upon the little Shaw household where a thoroughly disgusted and disillusioned woman was suffering from a hopelessly disappointing husband and three uninteresting children grown too old to be petted like the animals and birds she was so fond of, to say nothing of the humiliating inadequacy of my father's income. We never felt any affection for Lee; for he was too excessively unlike us, too completely a phenomenon, to rouse any primitive human feeling in us. When my mother introduced him to me, he played with me for the first and last time; but as his notion of play was to decorate my face with moustaches and whiskers in burnt cork in spite of the most furious resistance I could put up, our encounter was not a success; and the defensive attitude in which it left me lasted, though without the least bitterness, until the decay of his energies and the growth of mine put us on more than equal terms. He never read anything except [John] Tyndall on Sound [1867], which he kept in his bedroom for years. He complained that an edition of Shakespear which I lent him was incomplete because it did not contain The School for Scandal, which for some reason he wanted to read; and when I talked of Carlyle he understood me to mean the Viceroy of that name[6] who had graciously attended his concerts in the [Dublin] Antient Concert Rooms. Although he supplanted my father as the dominant factor in the household, and appropriated all the activity and interest of my mother, he was so completely absorbed in his musical affairs that there was no friction and hardly any intimate personal contacts between the two men: certainly no unpleasantness. At first his ideas astonished us. He said that people should sleep with their windows open. The daring of this appealed to me; and I have done so ever since. He ate brown bread instead of white: a startling eccentricity. He had no faith in doctors, and when my mother had a serious illness took her case in hand unhesitatingly and at the end of a week or so gave my trembling father leave to call in a leading Dublin doctor, who simply said "My work is done" and took his hat. As to the apothecary and his squills [herbal expectorants], he could not exist in Lee's atmosphere; and I was never attended by a doctor again until I caught the smallpox in the epidemic of 1881. He took no interest in pictures or in any art but his own; and even in music his interest was limited to vocal music: I did not know that such things as string quartets or symphonies existed until I began, at sixteen, to investigate music for myself. Beethoven's sonatas and the classical operatic overtures were all I knew of what Wagner called absolute music. I should be tempted to say that none of us knew of the existence of Bach were it not that my mother sang My Heart Ever Faithful ['*Mein gläubiges Herze. Frohlocke, sing, Scherze*', in Cantata 68 (1725)], the banjo-like *obbligato* of which amused me very irreverently.

Lee was like all artists whose knowledge is solely a working knowledge: there were holes in his culture which I had to fill up for myself. Fortunately his richer pupils sometimes presented him with expensive illustrated books. He never opened them; but I did. He was so destitute of any literary bent that when he published a book entitled The Voice, it was written for him by a scamp of a derelict doctor whom he entertained for that purpose, just as in later years his prospectuses and press articles were written by me.[7] He

6. George W. F. Howard, seventh Earl of Carlyle, was Lord-Lieutenant of Ireland 1855–8, 1859–64.
7. *The Voice: Its Artistic Production, Development, and Preservation* (1869) was ghosted, probably by Malachi J. Kilgarriff, Demonstrator at the Ledwich School of Anatomy. In 1883 Shaw provided a publicity release for Lee's contemplated production of *Patience*, which appeared in the *Court Journal* on 30 June. In 1886 Shaw drew up a prospectus for him on 'How to Cure Clergyman's Sore Throat', an ailment that plagued singers who misused their voice.

never visited the Dublin National Gallery, one of the finest collections of its size in Europe, with the usual full set of casts from what was called the antique, meaning ancient Greek sculpture. It was by prowling in this gallery that I learnt to recognize the work of the old masters at sight. I learnt French history from the novels of Dumas *père*, and English history from Shakespear and Walter Scott. Good boys were meanwhile learning lessons out of school-books and receiving marks at examinations: a process which left them pious barbarians whilst I was acquiring an equipment which enabled me not only to pose as Corno di Bassetto when the chance arrived, but to add the criticism of pictures to the various strings I had to my bow as a *feuilletonist*.

Meanwhile nobody ever dreamt of teaching me anything. At fifteen, when the family broke up, I could neither play nor read a note of music. Whether you choose to put it that I was condemned to be a critic or saved from being an executant, the fact remains that when the house became musicless, I was forced to teach myself how to play written music on the piano from a book with a diagram of the keyboard in it or else be starved of music.

Not that I wanted to be a professional musician. My ambition was to be a great painter like Michael Angelo (one of my heroes); but my attempts to obtain instruction in his art at the School of Design presided over by the South Kensington Department of Science and Art only prevented me from learning anything except how to earn five shilling grants for the masters (payment by results) by filling up ridiculous examination papers in practical geometry and what they called freehand drawing.

With competent instruction I daresay I could have become a painter and draughtsman of sorts; but the School of Design convinced me that I was a hopeless failure in that direction on no better ground than that I found I could not draw like Michael Angelo or paint like Titian at the first attempt without knowing how. But teaching, of art and everything else, was and still is so little understood by our professional instructors (mostly themselves failures) that only the readymade geniuses make good; and even they are as often as not the worse for their academic contacts.

As an alternative to being a Michael Angelo I had dreams of being a Badeali. (Note, by the way, that of literature I had no dreams at all, any more than a duck has of swimming.) What that led to was not fully explained until [F.] Matthias Alexander, in search, like Lee, of a sound vocal method, invented his technique of selfcontrol.[8]

8. Alexander, a young Australian actor, began his work as a method of restoring psycho-physical equilibrium to the maladjusted individual. Eventually this developed into a new science of living, by which one changes oneself, not mentally or physically,

I had sung like a bird all through my childhood; but when my voice broke I at once fell into the error unmasked by Alexander of trying to gain my end before I had studied the means. In my attempts to reproduce the frenzies of the Count di Luna, the sardonic accents of Gounod's Mephistopheles, the noble charm of Don Giovanni, and the supernatural menace of the Commendatore, not to mention all the women's parts and the tenor parts as well (for all parts, high or low, male or female, had to be sung or shrieked or whistled or growled somehow) I thought of nothing but the dramatic characters; and in attacking them I set my jaws and my glottis as if I had to crack walnuts with them. I might have ruined my voice if I had not imitated good singers instead of bad ones; but even so the results were wretched. When I rejoined my mother in London and she found that I had taught myself to play accompaniments and to amuse myself with operas and oratorios as other youths read novels and smoke cigarets, she warned me that my voice would be spoiled if I went on like that. Thereupon I insisted on being shewn the proper way to sing. The instructive result was that when, following my mother's directions, I left my jaw completely loose, and my tongue flat instead of convulsively rolling it up; when I operated my diaphragm so as to breathe instead of "blowing"; when I tried to round up my pharynx and soft palate and found it like trying to wag my ears, I found that for the first time in my life I could not produce an audible note. It seemed that I had no voice. But I believed in Lee's plan and knew that my own was wrong. I insisted on being taught how to use my voice as if I had one; and in the end the unused and involuntary pharyngeal muscles became active and voluntary, and I developed an uninteresting baritone voice of no exceptional range which I have ever since used for my private satisfaction and exercise without damaging either it or myself in the process.

Here I must digress for a moment to point a moral. Years after I learnt how to sing without spoiling my voice and wrecking my general health, a musician-reciter (Matthias Alexander aforesaid) found himself disabled by the complaint known as clergyman's sore throat. Having the true scientific spirit and industry, he set himself to discover what it was that he was really doing to disable himself in this fashion by his efforts to produce the opposite result. In the end he found this out, and a great deal more as well. He established

---

but psycho-physically, finding a better way to use one's 'instrument', whether body or voice. The technique has had worldwide theatrical adoption as a principal working tool for performers. Shaw undertook a course of forty sessions with Alexander, October–December 1936. See Alexander, *Constructive Conscious Control of the Individual* (1924) and *The Use of the Self* (1931), and Louise Morgan, *Inside Yourself* (1954).

not only the beginnings of a far reaching science of the apparently involuntary movements we call reflexes, but a technique of correction and selfcontrol which forms a substantial addition to our very slender resources in personal education.

Meanwhile a Russian doctor named [Ivan] Pavlov devoted himself to the investigation of the same subject by practising the horrible voodoo into which professional medical research had lapsed in the XIX century. For quarter of a century he tormented and mutilated dogs most abominably, and finally wrote a ponderous treatise on reflexes [*Twenty Years of Objective Study of the Higher Nervous Activity (Behaviour) of Animals*, Leningrad, 1922] in which he claimed to have established on a scientific basis the fact that a dog's mouth will water at the sound of a dinner bell when it is trained to associate that sound with a meal, and that dogs, if tormented, thwarted, baffled, and incommoded continuously, will suffer nervous breakdown and be miserably ruined for the rest of their lives. He was also able to describe what happens to a dog when half its brains are cut out.

What his book and its shamefully respectful reception by professional biologists does demonstrate is that the opening of the scientific professions to persons qualified for them neither by general capacity nor philosophic moral training plunges professional Science, as it has so often plunged professional Religion and Jurisprudence, into an abyss of stupidity and cruelty from which nothing but the outraged humanity of the laity can rescue it.

In the department of biology especially, the professors, mostly brought up as Fundamentalists, are informed that the book of Genesis is not a scientific document, and that the tribal idol whom Noah conciliated by the smell of roast meat is not God and never had any objective existence. They absurdly infer that the pursuit of scientific knowledge: that is, of all knowledge, is exempt from moral obligations, and consequently that they are privileged as scientists to commit the most revolting cruelties when they are engaged in research.

Their next step in this crazy logic is that no research is scientific unless it involves such cruelties. With all the infinite possibilities of legitimate and kindly research open to anyone with enough industry and ingenuity to discover innocent methods of exploration, they set up a boycott of brains and a ritual of sacrifice of dogs and guinea pigs which impresses the superstitious public as all such rituals do. Thereby they learn many things that no decent person ought to know; for it must not be forgotten that human advancement consists not only of adding to the store of human knowledge and experience but eliminating much that is burdensome and brutish. Our forefathers had the knowledge and experience gained by seeing heretics burnt at the stake and harlots whipped through the streets at the cart's tail. Mankind is better without such knowledge and experience.

If Pavlov had been a poacher he would have been imprisoned for his cruelty and despised for his moral imbecility. But as Director of the Physiological Department of the Institute of Experimental Medicine at St Petersburg, and Professor of the Medical Academy, he was virtually forced to mutilate and torment dogs instead of discovering the methods by which humane unofficial investigators were meanwhile finding out all that he was looking for.

The reaction against this voodoo is gathering momentum; but still our rich philanthropic industrialists lavish millions on the endowment of research without taking the most obvious precautions against malversation of their gifts for the benefit of dog stealers, guinea pig breeders, laboratory builders and plumbers, and a routine of cruel folly and scoundrelism that perverts and wastes all the scientific enthusiasm that might otherwise have by this time reduced our death and disease rates to their natural minimum. I am sorry to have to describe so many highly respected gentlemen quite deliberately as fools and scoundrels; but the only definition of scoundrelism known to me is anarchism in morals; and I cannot admit that the hackneyed pleas of the dynamiter and the assassin in politics become valid in the laboratory and the hospital, or that the man who thinks they do is made any less a fool by calling him a professor of physiology.

And all this because in 1860 the men who thought they wanted to substitute scientific knowledge for superstition really wanted only to abolish God and marry their deceased wives' sisters![9]

I should add that there is no reason to suppose that Pavlov was by nature a bad man. He bore a strong external resemblance to myself, and was well-meaning, intelligent, and devoted to science. It was his academic environment that corrupted, stultified, and sterilized him. If only he had been taught to sing by my mother no dog need ever have collapsed in terror at his approach; and he might have shared the laurels of Alexander.

And now I must return to my story. Lee's end was more tragic than Pavlov's. I do not know at what moment he began to deteriorate. He was a sober and moderate liver in all respects; and he was never ill until he treated himself to a tour in Italy and caught malaria there. He fought through it without a doctor on cold water, and returned apparently well; but whenever he worked too hard it came back and prostrated him for a day or two. Finally

9. Marriage to a deceased wife's sister was a prohibited affinity as laid down in the *Book of Common Prayer* and in Britain's Marriage Act of 1836. A statutory exception was made in the revised Marriage Act of 1949.

his ambition undid him. Dublin in those days seemed a hopeless place for an artist; for no success counted except a London success. The summit of a provincial conductor's destiny was to preside at a local musical festival modelled on the Three Choirs[10] or Handel Festivals. Lee declared that he would organize and conduct a Dublin Festival with his own chorus and with all the famous leading singers from the Italian opera in London. This he did in connection with an Exhibition [of Arts, Industries and Manufactures, 1872] in Dublin. My mother, of course, led the chorus. At a rehearsal the contralto, Madame [Emilie] de Meric Lablache, took exception to something and refused to sing. Lee shrugged his shoulders and asked my mother to carry on, which she did to such purpose that Madame Lablache took care not to give her another such chance.

At the Festivals Lee reached the Dublin limit of eminence. Nothing remained but London. He was assured that London meant a very modest beginning all over again, and perhaps something of an established position after fifteen years or so. Lee said that he would take a house in Park Lane, then the most exclusive and expensive thoroughfare in the west end, sacred to peers and millionaires, and—stupendous on the scale of Irish finance— make his pupils pay him a guinea a lesson. And this he actually did with a success that held out quite brilliantly for several seasons and then destroyed him. For wheras he had succeeded in Dublin by the sheer superiority of his method and talent and character, training his pupils honestly for a couple of years to sing beautifully and classically, he found that the London ladies who took him up so gushingly would have none of his beauty and classicism, and would listen to nothing less than a promise to make them sing "like [Adelina] Patti" in twelve lessons. It was that or starve.

He submitted perforce; but he was no longer the same man, the man to whom all circumstances seemed to give way, and who made his own musical world and reigned in it. He had even to change his name and his aspect. G. J. Lee, with the black whiskers and the clean shaven resolute lip and chin, became Vandeleur Lee, whiskerless, but with a waxed and pointed moustache and an obsequious attitude. It suddenly became evident that he was an elderly man, and, to those who had known him in Dublin, a humbug. Performances of [Filippo] Marchetti's Ruy Blas [1869] with my sister as the Queen of Spain, and later on of [Arthur] Sullivan's Patience [1881] and scraps of Faust and Il Trovatore were achieved; but musical society in London at last got tired of the damaged Svengali who could manufacture Pattis for twelve guineas; and

10. Annual musical event of six days' duration, based in turn in the cathedrals of Gloucester, Worcester and Hereford, from 1715.

the guineas ceased to come in. Still, as there were no night clubs in those days, it was possible to let a house in Park Lane for the night to groups of merrymakers; and Lee was holding out there without pupils when he asked me to draft a circular for him announcing that he could cure clergyman's sore throat. He was still at Park Lane when he dropped dead in the act of undressing himself, dying as he had lived, without a doctor. The postmortem and inquest revealed the fact that his brain was diseased and had been so for a long time. I was glad to learn that his decay was pathological as well as ecological, and that the old efficient and honest Lee had been real after all.[11] But I took to heart the lesson in the value of London fashionable successes. To this day I look to the provincial and the amateur for honesty and genuine fecundity in art.

Meanwhile, what had happened to the *ménage à trois*? and how did I turn up in Park Lane playing accompaniments and getting glimpses of that artstruck side of fashionable society which takes refuge in music from the routine of politics and sport which occupies the main Philistine body?

Well, when Lee got his foot in at a country house in Shropshire whither he had been invited to conduct some private performances, he sold the Dalkey cottage and concluded his tenancy of Hatch Street. This left us in a house which we could afford less than ever; for my father's moribund business was by now considerably deader than it had been at the date of my birth. My younger sister was dying of consumption caught from reckless contacts at a time when neither consumption nor pneumonia were regarded as catching. All that could be done was to recommend a change of climate. My elder sister had a beautiful voice. In the last of Lee's Dublin adventures in amateur opera [1873] she had appeared as Amina in [Vincenzo] Bellini's La Sonnambula [1831], on which occasion the tenor lost his place and his head, and Lucy obligingly sang most of his part as well as her own. Unfortunately her musical endowment was so complete that it cost her no effort to sing or play anything she had once heard, or to read any music at sight. She simply could not associate the idea of real work with music; and as in any case she had never received any sort of training, her very facility prevented her from becoming a serious artist, though, as she could sing difficult music without

11. Neither the death certificate nor the newspaper report (*Westminster Times*) of the post-mortem says anything about 'brain disease', the certificate reading 'Natural angina pectoris. Found dead on floor.' Shaw may have confused this with Lee's alleged father, who was reported to have died of 'softening of the brain'; or perhaps he was designedly seeking in this manner to exculpate Lee for questionable behaviour during his last years in London.

breaking her voice, she got through a considerable share of public singing in her time.

Now neither my mother nor any of us knew how much more is needed for an opera singer than a voice and natural musicianship. It seemed to us that as, after a rehearsal or two, she could walk on to the stage, wave her arms about in the absurd manner then in vogue in opera, and sing not only her own part but everybody else's as well, she was quite qualified to take the place of Christine Nilsson[12] or Adelina Patti if only she could get a proper introduction. And clearly Lee, now in the first flush of his success in Park Lane, would easily be able to secure this for her.

There was another resource. My now elderly mother believed that she could renounce her amateur status and make a living in London by teaching singing. Had she not the infallible Method to impart? So she realized a little of the scrap of settled property of which her long deceased aunt had not been able to deprive her; sold the Hatch Street furniture; settled my father and myself in comfortable lodgings at 61 Harcourt St; and took my sisters to the Isle of Wight, where the younger one died. She then took a semi-detached villa in a *cul-de-sac* off the Fulham Road, and waited there for Lucy's plans and her own to materialize.

The result was almost a worse disillusion than her marriage. That had been cured by Lee's music: besides, my father had at last realized his dream of being a practising teetotaller, and was now as inoffensive an old gentleman as any elderly wife could desire. It was characteristic of the Shavian drink neurosis to vanish suddenly in this way. But that Lee should be unfaithful! unfaithful to The Method! that he, the one genuine teacher among so many quacks, should now stoop to outquack them all and become a moustachioed charlatan with all the virtue gone out of him: this was the end of all things; and she never forgave it. She was not unkind: she tolerated Lee the charlatan as she had tolerated Shaw the dipsomaniac because, as I guess, her early motherless privation of affection and her many disappointments in other people had thrown her back on her own considerable internal resources and developed her self-sufficiency and power of solitude to an extent which kept her up under circumstances that would have crushed or embittered any woman who was the least bit of a clinger. She dropped Lee very gently: at first he came and went at Victoria Grove, Fulham Road; and she went and came at 13 Park Lane, helping with the music there at his At Homes, and even singing the part of Donna Anna for him (elderly *prima donnas* were then tolerated as matters of course) at an amateur performance of Don Giovanni.

12. Outstanding, sweet-voiced Swedish soprano at Covent Garden, 1867–87.

But my sister, who had quarreled with him as a child when he tried to give her piano lessons, and had never liked him, could not bear him at all in his new phase, and, when she found that he could not really advance her prospects of becoming a *prima donna*, broke with him completely and made it difficult for him to continue his visits. When he died we had not seen him for some years; and my mother did not display the slightest emotion at the news. He had been dead for her ever since he had ceased to be an honest teacher of singing and a mesmeric conductor.

Her plans for herself came almost to nothing for several years. She found that Englishwomen do not wish to be made to sing beautifully and classically: they want to sing erotically; and this my mother thought not only horrible but unladylike. Her love songs were those of Virginia Gabriel and Arthur Sullivan, all about bereaved lovers and ending with a hope for reunion in the next world. She could sing with perfect purity of tone and touching expression

> Oh, Ruby, my darling, the small white hand
> Which gathered the harebell was never my own.[13]

But if you had been able to anticipate the grand march of human progress and poetic feeling by fifty years, and asked her to sing

> You made me love you.
> I didnt want to do it.
> I didnt want to do it,[14]

she would have asked a policeman to remove you to a third-class carriage.

Besides, though my mother was not consciously a snob, the divinity which hedged an Irish lady of her period was not acceptable to the British suburban parents, all snobs, who were within her reach. They liked to be treated with deference; and it never occurred to my mother that such people could entertain a pretension so monstrous in her case. Her practice with private pupils was negligible until she was asked to become musical instructress at the North London College. Her success was immediate; for not only did her classes leave the other schools nowhere musically, but the divinity aforesaid exactly suited her new *rôle* as schoolmistress. Other schools soon sought her services; and she remained in request until she insisted on retiring on the ground that her age made her public appearances ridiculous. By that time all the old

13. 'Ruby', a ballad (*c.* 1865), was composed by Virginia Gabriel to lyrics by J. J. Lonsdale.
14. Music by Joseph McCarthy, lyrics by James V. Monaco; performed by Al Jolson in the Broadway musical *The Honeymoon Express* (1913).

money troubles were over and forgotten, as my financial position enabled me to make her perfectly comfortable in that respect.

And now, what about myself, the incipient Corno di Bassetto?

Well, when my mother sold the Hatch Street furniture, it never occurred to her to sell our piano, though I could not play it, nor could my father. We did not realize, nor did she, that she was never coming back, and that, except for a few days when my father, taking a little holiday for the first time in his life within my experience, came to see us in London, she would never meet him again. Family revolutions would seldom be faced if they did not present themselves at first as temporary makeshifts. Accordingly, having lived since my childhood in a house full of music, I suddenly found myself in a house where there was no music, and could be none unless I made it myself. I have recorded elsewhere[15] how, having purchased one of Weale's Handbooks [piano tutors] which contained a diagram of the keyboard and an explanation of musical notation, I began my self-tuition, not with [Karl] Czerny's five-finger exercises, but with the overture to Don Giovanni, thinking rightly that I had better start with something I knew well enough to hear whether my fingers were on the right notes or not. There were plenty of vocal scores of operas and oratorios in our lodging; and although I never acquired any technical skill as a pianist, and cannot to this day play a scale with any certainty of not foozling it, I acquired what I wanted: the power to take a vocal score and learn its contents as if I had heard it rehearsed by my mother and her colleagues. I could manage arrangements of orchestral music much better than piano music proper. At last I could play the old rum-tum accompaniments of those days well enough (knowing how they *should* be played) to be more agreeable to singers than many really competent pianists. I bought more scores, among them one of Lohengrin, through which I made the revolutionary discovery of Wagner. I bought arrangements of Beethoven's symphonies, and discovered the musical regions that lie outside opera and oratorio. Later on, I was forced to learn to play the classical symphonies and overtures in strict time by hammering the bass in piano duets with my sister in London. I played Bach's Inventions and his Art of Fugue. I studied academic textbooks, and actually worked out exercises in harmony and counterpoint under supervision by an organist friend named [J. Maude] Crament,[16] avoiding consecutive fifths and octaves, and having not the faintest notion of what the result

15. 'The Religion of the Pianoforte', *Fortnightly Review*, February 1894; reprinted in *Shaw's Music*, III.
16. Shaw in 1878 studied under Crament, a church composer and organist of the Brompton parish church.

would sound like. I read pseudo–scientific treatises about the roots of chords which candidates for the degree of Mus.Doc. at the universities had to swallow, and learnt that Stainer's commonsense views would get you plucked at Oxford, and Ouseley's pedantries at Cambridge.[17] I read Mozart's Succinct Thoroughbass [basso continuo] (a scrap of paper with some helpful tips on it which he scrawled for his pupil Sussmaier[18]); and this, many years later, Edward Elgar told me was the only document in existence of the smallest use to a student composer. It was, I grieve to say, of no use to me; but then I was not a young composer. It ended in my knowing much more about music than any of the great composers, an easy achievement for any critic, however barren. For awhile I must have become a little pedantic; for I remember being shocked, on looking up Lee's old vocal score of Don Giovanni, to find that he had cut out all the repetitions which Mozart had perpetrated as a matter of sonata form. I now see that Lee was a century before his time in this reform, and hope some day to hear a performance of Mozart's Idomeneo in which nothing is sung twice over.

When I look back on all the banging, whistling, roaring, and growling inflicted on nervous neighbors during this process of education, I am consumed with useless remorse. But what else could I have done? Today there is the wireless, which enables me to hear from all over Europe more good music in a week than I could then hear in ten years, if at all. When, after my five years office slavery, I joined my mother in London and lived with her for twenty years until my marriage, I used to drive her nearly crazy by my favorite selections from Wagner's Ring, which to her was "all *recitative*," and horribly discordant at that. She never complained at the time, but confessed it after we separated, and said that she had sometimes gone away to cry. If I had committed a murder I do not think it would trouble my conscience very much; but this I cannot bear to think of. If I had to live my life over again I should devote it to the establishment of some arrangement of headphones and microphones or the like whereby the noises made by musical maniacs should be audible to themselves only. In Germany it is against the law to play the piano with the window open. But of what use is that to

17. Sir John Stainer, author of *A Theory of Harmony* (1876), and Sir Frederick Ouseley, who wrote theoretical works on counterpoint and harmony, were British composers. Shaw apparently had got it into his head that Ouseley taught at Cambridge, for he'd made the same error before. Both men were professors of music at Oxford.
18. Mozart's supposititious *Kurzgefasste Generalbass-Schule* (Vienna, 1818) was translated by Sabilla Novello as *A Succinct Thorough-bass School* (London, 1854). Franz Süssmayer, Austrian conductor and opera and theatre composer, was the 'pupil'.

the people in the house? It should be made a felony to play a musical instrument in any other than a completely soundproof room. The same should apply to loud speakers on pain of confiscation.

Readers with a taste for autobiography must now take my Immaturity preface and dovetail it into this sketch to complete the picture. My business here is to account for my proposal to Tay Pay and my creation of Bassetto. From my earliest recorded sign of an interest in music when as a small child I encored my mother's singing of the page's song from the first act of Les Huguenots (note that I shared Herbert Spencer's liking for Meyerbeer) music has been an indispensable part of my life. Harley Granville-Barker was not far out when, at a rehearsal of one of my plays, he cried out "Ladies and gentlemen: will you please remember that this is Italian opera."

I reprint Bassetto's stuff shamefacedly after long hesitation with a reluctance which has been overcome only by my wife, who has found some amusement in reading it through, a drudgery which I could not bring myself to undertake. I know it was great fun when it was fresh, and that many people have a curious antiquarian taste (I have it myself) for old chronicles of dead musicians and actors. I must warn them, however, not to expect to find here the work of the finished critic who wrote my volumes entitled Music in London, 1890–94, and Our Theatres in the Nineties.[19] I knew all that was necessary about music; but in criticism I was only a beginner. It is easy enough from the first to distinguish between what is pleasant or unpleasant, accurate or inaccurate in a performance; but when great artists have to be dealt with, only keenly analytical observation and comparison of them with artists who, however agreeable, are not great, can enable a critic to distinguish between what everybody can do and what only a very few can do, and to get his valuations right accordingly. All artsmen know what it is to be enthusiastically praised for something so easy that they are half ashamed of it, and to receive not a word of encouragement for their finest strokes.

I cannot deny that Bassetto was occasionally vulgar; but that does not matter if he makes you laugh. Vulgarity is a necessary part of a complete author's equipment; and the clown is sometimes the best part of the circus. The Star, then a hapenny newspaper, was not catering for a fastidious audience: it was addressed to the bicycle clubs and the polytechnics, not to the Royal Society of Literature or the Musical Association. I purposely vulgarized musical criticism, which was then refined and academic to the point of being unreadable and often nonsensical. Editors, being mostly ignorant of music,

19. Collected music criticism from the *World* and dramatic criticism (1895–8) from the *Saturday Review*, both published in the Collected Edition in 1931.

would submit to anything from their musical critics, not pretending to understand it. If I occasionally carried to the verge of ribaldry my reaction against
the pretentious twaddle and sometimes spiteful cliquishness they tolerated in
their ignorance, think of me as heading one of the pioneer columns of what
was then called the New Journalism; and you will wonder at my politeness.

You may be puzzled, too, to find that the very music I was brought up
on: the pre-Wagner school of formal melody in separate numbers which
seemed laid out to catch the *encores* that were then fashionable, was treated
by me with contemptuous levity as something to be swept into the dustbin
as soon as possible. The explanation is that these works were standing in the
way of Wagner, who was then the furiously abused coming man in London.
Only his early works were known or tolerated. Half a dozen bars of Tristan
or The Mastersingers made professional musicians put their fingers in their
ears. The Ride of the Valkyries was played at the Promenade Concerts, and
always encored, but only as an insanely rampagious curiosity. The Daily
Telegraph steadily preached Wagner down as a discordant notoriety-hunting
charlatan in six silk dressing-gowns, who could not write a bar of melody, and
made an abominable noise with the orchestra. In pantomime harlequinades the
clown produced a trombone, played a bit of the pilgrims' march from
Tannhäuser *fortissimo* as well as he could, and said "The music of the future!"
The wars of religion were not more bloodthirsty than the discussions of the
Wagnerites and the Anti-Wagnerites. I was, of course, a violent Wagnerite;
and I had the advantage of knowing the music to which Wagner grew up,
wheras many of the most fanatical Wagnerites (Ashton Ellis, who translated
the Master's prose works, was a conspicuous example) knew no other music
than Wagner's, and believed that the music of Donizetti and Meyerbeer had
no dramatic quality whatever. "A few *arpeggios*" was the description Ellis gave
me of his notion of Les Huguenots.

Nowadays the reaction is all the other way. Our young lions have no use
for Wagner the Liberator. His harmonies, which once seemed monstrous
cacophonies, are the commonplaces of the variety theatres. Audacious young
critics disparage his grandeurs as tawdry. When the wireless strikes up the
Tannhäuser overture I hasten to switch it off, though I can always listen with
pleasure to Rossini's overture to William Tell, hackneyed to death in
Bassetto's time. The funeral march from Die Götterdämmerung hardly keeps
my attention, though Handel's march from Saul is greater than ever. Though
I used to scarify the fools who said that Wagner's music was formless, I should
not now think the worse of Wagner if, like Bach and Mozart, he had combined the most poignant dramatic expression with the most elaborate decorative design. It was necessary for him to smash the superstition that this was

obligatory; to free dramatic melody from the tyranny of arabesques; and to give the orchestra symphonic work instead of *rosalias* [cheap, stale musical sequences] and rum-tum; but now that this and all the other musical superstitions are in the dustbin, and the post-Wagnerian harmonic and contrapuntal anarchy is so complete that it is easier technically to compose another Parsifal than another Bach's Mass in B Minor or Don Giovanni I am no longer a combatant anarchist in music, not to mention that I have learnt that a successful revolution's first task is to shoot all revolutionists. This means that I am no longer Corno di Bassetto. He was pre- and pro-Wagner; unfamiliar with Brahms; and unaware that a young musician named Elgar was chuckling over his irreverent *boutades* [caprices or conceits]. As to Cyril Scott, [Arnold] Bax, [John] Ireland, [Eugene] Goossens, [Arthur] Bliss, [William] Walton, [Arnold] Schönberg, [Paul] Hindemith, or even Richard Strauss and [Jean] Sibelius, their idioms would have been quite outside Bassetto's conception of music, though today they seem natural enough. Therefore I very greatly doubt whether poor old Bassetto is worth reading now. Still, you are not compelled to read him. Having read the preface you can shut the book and give it to your worst enemy as a birthday present.

MID-ATLANTIC.
Sunday, 2 June 1935.

# New Architecture

*Published as a foreword to a souvenir book of an exhibition* New Architecture:
An Exhibition of the Elements of Modern Architecture, *sponsored by MARS
(Modern Architectural Research Group), New Burlington Galleries, London, 1938*

═══

If you would see how extravagantly architecture has been valued, go to
Baalbek.[1] It was there that the Romans set to work to impose their god
Jupiter Ammon on the world as the god of gods. They did it quite successfully
(as such efforts go) by building a stupendous temple, the remains of which
still impress even American engineers as the handiwork of a superhuman
force. For how these colossal monoliths could have been hoisted to the tops
of those gigantic columns, or even how they were transported from the
quarries in which some of them lie hewn out and still awaiting that transport,
is beyond all speculation. Experts tell you calmly that they were lifted by
inclined planes. I prefer the explanation that angels carried them up Jacob's
ladder as being much more plausible.

There are few of these columns left with their incredible entablatures; but
in the great acreage of the temple as the Romans left it there were scores of
them. People came from all parts of what was known of the world at the
time; and when they saw that humanly impossible temple they knew that
Jupiter was indeed verigod. As long as the temple stood there was no resisting
him. That was why, when the Arabs came, bearing the standard of Allah
(save in Whom is no majesty and no might) they saw at a glance that the
great temple must come down, and not one stone of it be left on another,
before Jupiter could be dethroned.

Amazing as the building of the temple was, its demolition and desecration
must have been at least equally laborious and dangerous. Even Arab fanaticism
could not go quite through with it. Or it may be that the destroyers deliberately calculated that a visible wreck and ruin of Jupiter's famous temple would
shew how Allah had dealt with him better than an annihilation that could
shew nothing. Anyhow there is the wreck for all the world to see. It is easier
to get to than the Shetland Isles [northern Scotland]; and I advise you not to

1. Site in east Lebanon of ruins of ancient Heliopolis, which Shaw visited in March
1931.

miss it when you visit the Holy Land, as everyone with money enough ought to nowadays.

Yet as pure architecture Baalbek is not, and never was, worth twopence. Its builders relied on magnitude and apparent impossibility for the effect of their work. The esthetic part of it was conventionally Roman. To anyone who has seen Ely Cathedral, or Chartres, or St Sophia, or even the Parthenon, it is null and dull. But it illustrates, as no other existing ruin within my reach does, the fact that you cannot destroy a religion until you have destroyed or assimilated what it has built.

Architecture of this kind may be called impressive architecture. It persists from Baalbek to the country seats of our landed gentry, to the terraces, gardens, and squares of Bayswater and Bloomsbury, South Kensington, and Regent's Park, and to the newest fanes of Christian Science. I lived for thirty years in Adelphi Terrace, which was built to reproduce in London the splendors of the palace of Diocletian in Split (*ci-devant* Spalato) [Croatia], and for nearly twenty years in Fitzroy Square, where you may still see what the impressive architects call *façades*. As to the Terrace, it has just been razed to the ground and even deeper. I speak with the authority of personal experience when I say that in neither of these residences was there a bathroom, and in both the sanitary arrangements had had no place in the original plans. In impressive architecture it is the outside that matters most; and the servants do not matter at all.

The MARS group represents a violent reaction against impressive architecture. It has no religion to impose; and however it may operate incidentally as an advertisement of wealth and respectability, this is not its object. It considers the health and convenience not only of the inmates but of their neighbors and of the whole town, as far as it is allowed to have its own way, though of course it is often baffled on this point just as Christopher Wren was. To the classical Baalbekian list of building materials, stone and bricks and mortar, it adds concrete with a steel skeleton, glass, and steel without any concrete. I must not say that in using these materials for utilitarian ends it is indifferent to the aspect of the result. Indeed, artistic instinct is at the very root of the matter even if the more fanatical Martians do produce buildings that are staggeringly unlike Adelphi Terrace and Fitzroy Square.

No matter: we shall have to get used to them, even if the only way to escape from their unusualness is to get inside them. At all events they do not keep out the light, and when one considers that the curse of London is the three months of all but Arctic darkness which descends on it every winter, this alone is an overwhelming recommendation.

Martian architecture is part of a new artistic movement. Its unprejudiced search for new beauties of form is in its favor; for the seekers after what Dickens's blacksmith [Joe Gargery in *Great Expectations*] happily called the Architectooralooral always find themselves back again at Lancaster Gate[2] or the Tate Gallery.[3] And we have had enough of that. At least I have.

I think I have now put the MARS case intelligibly before you, though I need hardly say that no individual member of the group is in any way responsible for my view of it.

2. Lancaster Gate is a London street just north of Bayswater Road, with a Victorian gate at its east end, designed in 1857 by Sancton Wood.
3. The Tate Gallery, on Millbank, Westminster, designed by Sidney R. J. Smith, opened in 1897 as the National Gallery of British Art.

# The Dark Lady of the Sonnets
## (BBC broadcast)

*Written and read by Shaw as prologue to a wireless broadcast of the play, 22 April 1938. First published in the* Listener, *London, 27 April 1938*

=====

This play which you are going to hear is all about Shakespear and Queen Elizabeth; but it is really only an appeal for the Shakespear Memorial National Theatre which we have been trying to make the English nation establish for thirty years past. Dame Edith Lyttelton [see vol. 2, p. 105] invented the play in 1910; I wrote the dialogue; and we had a grand performance at the Haymarket Theatre with Mr Granville-Barker in the part of Shakespear. But I am not going to talk to you about the National Theatre. Shakespear does this so eloquently in the play, and Queen Elizabeth is so up-to-date with her reply to him, that if I anticipate them I shall spoil their speeches for you. So let me tell you how far the play is historical. It takes place in the old royal palace of Whitehall, where Shakespear often acted for the amusement of King James. We have Ben Jonson's word for it. He says it was "on banks of Thames" that Shakespear "did oft delight Eliza and our James" ['To the Memory of . . . Shakespeare'].

Now I have my doubts about Eliza. She was a bit of a scholar; but she was a great out-of-doors woman; and when she was not taken up with her queen business she liked riding, hunting, staying in country houses, dancing, flirting, and ordering the most magnificent dresses ever worn by mortal woman. There is no evidence that she took any interest in the theatre. A stage player was to her at best a nobleman's servant of much less importance to her than his cook, and at worst a rogue and a vagabond. Still, a playwright whose works got printed had to be able to put his stage directions into good Latin; for in Eliza's time playwrights were not so illiterate as they are today. Chapman and Ben Jonson would have died rather than write "he exits" "she exits" "they exit" instead of the good Latin *exit* and *exeunt*. Even Shakespear, who, according to Ben Jonson had "little Latin and less Greek," knew better than that; and so Queen Elizabeth, if she had ever heard of Shakespeare, would have allowed him a disreputable sort of middle-class professional rank. But my own belief is that she never did hear of him, and that the name Will

Shakespear meant absolutely nothing to her. When Dame Edith planned this play, we both thought it was high time to introduce them to oneanother.

And now, as there is nothing about either Will or Eliza in the title of the play, you may be wondering who on earth the dark lady was. Well, nobody knows; but there *was* a dark lady all the same. Shakespear, in addition to his plays, wrote a batch of 154 sonnets, most of them addressed to a certain young man known as Mr W. H., who was one of those very attractive people whom we call world's sweethearts. They are mostly film stars nowadays. They are adored equally by men and women because their attraction is one of beauty and charm, and has nothing to do with sex. Shakespear's sonnets to this young gentleman are far more affectionate and admiring than any that he would have addressed to a woman. And the proof of this is that the sonnets to Mr W. H. are interrupted by some that were addressed to a woman with whom Shakespear had fallen in love. He was furious about it; for Shakespear did not like being captured in this way; especially by a lady for whose character he had no respect, and whose personal appearance was by no means satisfactory; for it happened that she was a blackhaired beauty; and as Queen Elizabeth had red hair, black hair was very unfashionable. And so the lady is known to us only as Shakespear's dark lady. He was fascinated by her; but he revenged himself by writing savage sonnets, one of which [129] is the most terrible denunciation of that sort of love in existence; and another [130] points out all the lady's defects so mercilessly that she can hardly have been consoled by the concluding lines "And yet, by Heaven, I think my love as rare as any she belied by false compare." It may gratify a woman to be told "I love you." But to be told *"and yet* I love you" after a whole string of insults, is quite another pair of shoes. No wonder the dark lady preferred Mr W. H. and thereby provoked a first class quarrel between him and Shakespear.

In the play I have assumed that the dark lady was a maid of honor at Elizabeth's court. A friend of mine, the late Thomas Tyler [see vol. 2, pp. 93–5], discovered that one of Elizabeth's maids of honor named Mary Fitton got into scrapes at court by her gallantries. Well, I had to get the dark lady into Whitehall Palace somehow; so let us pretend that she was Mary Fitton.

Whitehall Palace was burnt long before I arrived in London 62 years ago; but it still exists in my imagination; and the place where it stood is now right under my bedroom window. It ought to bear Shakespear's name; but they call it Horseguards Avenue because all the tourists and the country folk and the provincial football fans congregate at the end of it to stare at the two mounted guardsmen in their sentry boxes and cuirasses. Not one of them ever turns round to look at the spot where the sweet swan of Avon upon banks of Thames did oft delight Eliza and our James. I wanted the National

Theatre to be there; and when the Government announced their intention of pulling down the old houses which are now all Government offices, with the old-fashioned grates which make more smoke every morning when the charladies arrive than the whole city of Edinburgh, I claimed a place for Shakespear's National Theatre there. But the Government had never heard of Shakespear; and my dream of seeing the National Theatre from my window was shattered by an assurance that when the site was filled up with new offices I should not be able to see anything at all. So we have had to buy a magnificent site in Kensington,[1] which Shakespear knew only as a far-off village.

And now I ask you to imagine the old palace still standing. You may find it hard to imagine it by daylight; but if you imagine it at 11 o'clock at night with everybody gone to bed except the warders on duty it will be as easy as any other dream. As I see it the place is a terrace overlooking the river, with the Queen's apartments on one side, and a gateway on the other. Have you got it? Right; then up goes the curtain.

1. For a history of the National Theatre Shakespeare Memorial see vol. 2, p. 118 fn 27.

# My Apprenticeship

*Foreword to Beatrice Webb's* My Apprenticeship, *1938, a slightly revised appreciation first published as 'Beatrice Webb, Octogenarian', in the* Spectator, *London, 21 January 1938*

=====

We must admit that Beatrice Webb is a very notable woman. In the main mass of her work she is inseparable from the firm of Sidney and Beatrice Webb, whom a Labor Government tried vainly to disguise as Baron and Lady Passfield. The collaboration is so perfect that her part in it is inextricable. I who have been behind the scenes of it, cannot lay my hand on a single sentence and say this is Sidney or that is Beatrice.

Nevertheless there is in literature a separate Beatrice; and later on there will be more. She is one of those terrible women who keep diaries.[1] Sidney, the least autobiographical of human creatures, is no more capable of keeping a diary than I or you. I have never been able to find out where or when or how this diary contrived to get written, though I have spent months in Mrs Webb's household and seen her working every day to the limit of human endurance at the great joint masterpieces all the time. But it exists; and the world will some day learn what a very clever woman, quite free from any sort of sentimental veneration, thought of the celebrities, nonentities, obscurities and real live wires who made up the public life of her time.

Besides, she was at work long before she collided with Sidney Webb. She had written a history of Co-operation [*The Co-operative Movement in Great Britain*, 1891] and thereby not only made the co-operators class-conscious, but established the importance and success of Consumers' Co-operation as distinguished from the futile attempts at co-operative production which had had no chance against Capitalism. That was the sort of thing she liked doing, though all the joys of the West End and the country houses were open to her. She was a born industrial investigator, and was satisfied by nothing short

1. Portions of Beatrice Webb's diaries were published by her in *My Apprenticeship* (1926) and, after her death, in *Our Partnership* (1948), *Beatrice Webb's Diaries 1912–24* (1952), and *Beatrice Webb's Diaries 1924–32* (1953), edited by Margaret Cole. The complete diaries 1873–1943 were published in 1982–5, edited by Norman and Jeanne MacKenzie.

of personal contacts with the personalities operating the proletarian side of industry. Hunting, shooting, dancing and adventures in the marriage market, in which she was a desirable catch, were to her a waste of time when there were so many intensely important things to be investigated at the East End and in the manufacturing towns. When her relative, Charles Booth, financed his great enquiry into poverty [*Life and Labour of the People in London*, 1891– 1903] to prove that it did not exist and that Karl Marx's world-shaking description of it was a fable, she joined him, and instead of consulting wage-lists and official figures, disguised herself and worked in sweaters' dens until her hopeless inferiority as a needlewoman and her obviously extreme eligibility as an educated managing woman to be the bride of young Ikey or Moses, the sons of the house, made further experiment in that direction impossible. But enough was enough. Marx won hands down.

It was this determination to sample movements and their leaders instead of reading about them that brought her into contact with the Fabian Society, which was making stir enough at the time to call for investigation. They were, as usual, a mixed lot, but with unerring judgment she fixed on Sidney Webb as a unique lump of solid ability without any complications. She had no difficulty in appropriating him with a completeness which was part of the fundamental simplicity of his nature; for she was an attractive lady; and when Sidney fell in love he did not do it by halves. Her family was amazed and scandalized, as she had seemed of all the young women in London the most certain to choose and marry a Cabinet Minister, if not a Prime Minister. And in those days Cabinet Ministers were not six a penny. Her choice needs no justification now. Cabinets have flamed and crackled and died down like thorns under a pot; but Sidney Webb remains, piling up an authority and an eminence that have never been shaken. Asquith the contemptuous lived to canonize him.[2]

In fact, the sole drawback to her choice was myself, a useful member of the Webbs' Fabian retinue, but highly obnoxious to Beatrice for the technical reason that I could not be classified. All her interest was in social organization. Her job was the discovery of the common rules by which men bind themselves to co-operate for social ends. She had no use for exceptional people: degrees of ability and efficiency she could deal with; but the complications introduced by artists, Irishmen and the eccentric and anarchic individuals who infest revolutionary movements and have to be shot when the revolution succeeds,

2. In a letter of 4 March 1926 to Hilda Harrisson, Asquith wrote that Beatrice Webb 'at the age of thirty married Sidney Webb, a highly-knowledgeable *Saint*' (*Letters from Lord Oxford to a Friend*, 1934, II, p. 159).

were, in her business of social definition and classification, simply nuisances. She would probably have got rid of me as most women get rid of their husbands' undesirable bachelor friends, but for one qualification which I possessed. I knew Webb's value. And so I was not only tolerated but heroically made much of until the joyous day when she discovered a classification for me. I was a Sprite;[3] and in that category I became happily domesticated at holiday times with the newly wed pair until my own marriage six years later.

We were all three heavily afflicted with what Tolstoy's children called *Weltverbesserungswahn* [world-improvement mania], and went on solving all the social problems, and being completely ignored by the Press whilst noodles' orations in the official key were solemnly reported every day at length, provided the orator was a parliamentary careerist. As Beatrice had made the co-operators class conscious singlehanded, the two Webbs proceeded by the same contactile method to do the same for the Trade Unionists by their History of Trade Unionism [1894], and followed this up by extending the field to the whole Labor movement in their Industrial Democracy [1897]. In the famous Minority Report on the Poor Law,[4] Beatrice was extraordinarily active, whilst the monumental seven volumes on [English] Local Government kept steadily growing [to 11 vols., 1903–29] through miracles of investigation until the pair, having become the most skilled and best-informed investigators on earth as far as we know, were ready for the great Soviet experiment, and in their advanced age were able to give the first competent account [*Soviet Communism: A New Civilisation?* 1935] of the new social structures that are evolving in Russia, whilst the Press either screamed curses at the Red Spectre or represented the new Russia as an earthly paradise.

Meanwhile, not only does the diary go on ruthlessly: the diarist from time to time detaches herself from the firm to burst into autobiography in My Apprenticeship, with the design of teaching us all how to set about social investigation if our destiny, like hers, lies in this direction. Most of us care little for that, having neither any bent towards her profession nor much urgent *Weltverbesserungswahn*; yet the treatise on method holds us as a unique volume of confessions, to say nothing of its record of contacts with all sorts and conditions of men, from the most comfortably corrupt and reactionary

3. Shaw informed Ellen Terry (8 September 1897) that Beatrice had said 'You cannot fall in love with a *sprite*; and Shaw is a sprite. . . not a real person' (Shaw, *Collected Letters 1874–1897*, p. 801).
4. The Report of the Royal Commission on the Poor Law, published in February 1909, was written by the Webbs in collaboration with the Royal Prebendary Russell Wakefield, Francis Chandler and George Lansbury.

functionaries to the most devoted revolutionists of the gutter, or from Herbert Spencer, whom her genial unmetaphysical father entertained much as he might have kept a pet elephant, to all the parliamentary figures who passed as great, from Joseph Chamberlain to—well, to the present moment. And these are no mere staring and gabbling reminiscences, but judgments and generalizations which give depth to the narrative and value to the time spent in conning it.

It is amazing that such a woman should survive in apparently undiminished vigor after eighty years among fools and savages who will rise to nothing but ecstasies of wholesale murder: still, if only because she has proved that such a feat is possible to an able Englishwoman, her statement of how she has done it must be placed within the reach of all her countrywomen, and incidentally of their male followers with political pretensions, mostly quite unfounded.

Its worth is guaranteed by her ancient and faithful colleague.

G. B. S.

# Oscar Wilde

*Preface to a new edition of Frank Harris's* Oscar Wilde, *1938*

———

When this book by Frank Harris was first published twentytwo years ago I declared it the best literary portrait of Wilde in existence.[1] Never was there a more incendiary testimonial. Men began devoting their lives to proving it the worst biography ever written, and Frank Harris the prince of rascals. They felt that the staggered universe would not regain its stability until I was shamed into withdrawing everything I had said that was complimentary to Harris and standing in the pillory as a convicted logroller.

A minor grievance was that in a chapter I contributed to Harris's book describing my own few contacts with Oscar Wilde, I somewhat Pharisaically summed up his latest days in Paris as those of "an unprofitable drunkard and swindler." This deeply wounded Wilde's idolators. In their shrieks for its withdrawal they kept on repeating it, to my great annoyance, until their readers might have been excused for forgetting that Wilde's permanent celebrity belongs to literature, and only his transient notoriety to the police news. I did what I could to discourage the agitation by ignoring it; but it erupted again last year in a frantic book by Mr Robert Harborough Sherard entitled Bernard Shaw, Frank Harris, and Oscar Wilde,[2] introduced by the publishers

1. Harris's biography was published in 1916 as *Oscar Wilde: His Life and Confessions*. A letter from Shaw to Harris written in September 1916 for publication was incorporated in a second impression (1918) as an appendix (not, as Shaw misrecalled, as a chapter) to the second volume. In the letter Shaw expressed the conviction, '[Y]ou have written the best life of Oscar Wilde'. In 1934 he informed Hesketh Pearson it was 'still . . . by far the best literary portrait of Oscar in existence'.
2. Sherard, a devoted friend of Wilde (although opposed to homosexuality), published three studies of Wilde: *Oscar Wilde: The Story of an Unhappy Friendship* (1902), *The Life of Oscar Wilde* (1906), and *The Real Oscar Wilde* (1915). A fourth book, *Bernard Shaw, Frank Harris, and Oscar Wilde* (1937), was a disputatious condemnation of Harris's biography and its principal defender, motivated by a 1930 American reissue of the book. Shortly before his death in 1943 Sherard returned to the fray with a work listed in his *Who's Who* biography as *Ultima Thule: Reply to Shaw* (1940). Apparently this was a premature announcement for a work whose publication was interrupted by wartime conditions or by his final illness, for no copy has ever surfaced.

as "an exposure of THE GREATEST LITERARY IMPOSTURE OF ALL TIME IN THE HISTORY OF ENGLISH LETTERS." These capitals are the publisher's; and the IMPOSTURE is this pen portrait of Wilde by Frank Harris.

Now Mr Sherard is an author too engaging in his reckless way to be ignored. Oscar wrote to him from prison [16 April 1895] "Don't fight more than six duels a week." I describe his book as frantic because that is precisely what it is from beginning to end; but if I were to describe it as characteristically Sherardesque I should mean the same thing. He is the champion hurricane fighter of the Wilde fans. Great-grandson of Wordsworth, he comes to the fray trailing clouds of glory. His reckless impetuosity of attack, and the vitality and endurance with which he keeps it up through fifty thousand words of invective, produce an exhilarating impression of a man who lives in a permanent rage, and who, being gifted to superfluity with the necessary facility of literary expression, can put his rage red hot on record. And the more ungovernable his furies, the more impossible it is to dislike him. One cannot be angry with Don Quixote.

But until this preface was all but finished I did not know that Mr Sherard was a wizard. I had learnt from his latest explosion that he was the author of a biography of Wilde; but I had never read it, and, I swear, never possessed it. Yet the other day, when I was searching my bookshelves for another book on quite another matter, I found in my hand a smallish volume in a blue binding entitled Oscar Wilde, the Story of an Unhappy Friendship, by Robert H. Sherard, published [second edition] by Greening & Co. in 1905, a date at which only the bravest of the brave dared to proclaim himself a friend of Oscar, then under a cloud of a peculiar infamy that made it impossible to take his part without being suspected of being his accomplice. How Mr Sherard played this trick on me I do not know. I conclude that he is a magician. If not, let him explain it if he can.

The book is dedicated "to R.R. [Robert Ross[3]] in remembrance of his noble conduct towards the unhappy gentleman who is the subject of this memoir, whom in affliction he comforted, in prison he visited, and in poverty he succoured, thus showing his elevation of heart and loyalty of character." Mr Sherard could not have named Robbie at that time without doing him a wanton injury; but he sailed into the line of battle himself with all his colors flying and his own name blazoned on his shield. That was fine, was it not?

I liked the book so well that I immediately hunted up Mr Sherard's name

3. Another devoted friend of Wilde, who became the executor of his estate and first editor of Wilde's *De Profundis* (1905).

in the catalogue of the London Library, and found that in 1906 he had published a full dress biography of Wilde, which I at once devoured. Mr Sherard has apparently forgotten everything about it except the fact that he wrote it. Being myself an author I am not surprised at this. No man can be expected to remember what he wrote thirty years ago. But it follows that I, having read it all yesterday, have over Mr Sherard a considerable advantage, which I shall use unscrupulously.

For I found that all the things that Mr Sherard now denounces as malicious slanders of a great man may be read in his own book. And they are all true. From his pages you may learn that Oscar was a snob; that, literature apart, his pose as a connoisseur in painting and music was an imposture; that his father was no less notorious as a libertine than as an oculist and antiquary; that his mother "Speranza," famous as a patriot and poetess, was not only a political rebel but so strongly in reaction against Victorian prudery that she brought up her children as Immoralists; that his poems, to anyone acquainted with the works of William Morris, Swinburne and Rossetti, were *pastiche*; that his inheritance of excessive sexual sensibility and romantic lawlessness received at Oxford the turn that led to his downfall, Oxford being then half a nursery of scholarship and half a hotbed of classical vices; that though he was to the end an incomparable talker he drank himself into complete impotence as a writer; that after his imprisonment he lived recklessly on the contributions of his friends; that he took to drink with the success of his plays and was drunk when he laid a criminal information against Lord Queensberry;[4] and, generally, that "the demon" within him that sent him to a premature grave under a cloud of tragic infamy was a fatal inheritance that needed only the stimulus of alcohol to wake into one of those forms of epilepsy in which men commit the most frightful crimes unconsciously. Mr Sherard's plea for a scientific approach to Wilde's case is urgent and eloquent. When he penned it he must have been reading [Richard von] Krafft-Ebing and Sigmund Freud under the influence of Ibsen's Ghosts.

The book is so good, and as far as it goes, so true (it anticipates my own recorded impressions) that I may very well be asked whether it did not make Harris's book superfluous. Unfortunately it is incomplete and out of date. In 1906 the subject of homosexuality was quite unmentionable in decent literature. Militant Secularists accused the Bible of impropriety because it put into the minds of children the story of the cities of the plain [Sodom and Gomorrah: Genesis 19: 29]. Consequently it was impossible in 1906 for Mr Sherard

4. John Sholto Douglas, eighth Marquess of Queensberry, father of Lord Alfred Douglas, was noted as a patron of boxing, giving the sport nobility.

to tell the story of Wilde's downfall plainly. The book collapses at what should be its climax, leaving the reader informed only that Wilde was sentenced to two years imprisonment for a crime of unmentionable atrocity; recovered his health under prison discipline; and finally relapsed and died a diseased outcast in Paris.

There was no need for this obscurantism in 1916, when Harris's book appeared. The scientific indelicacies of Dr Sigmund Freud and his retinue of psychoanalysts, with the shock of the war, had made an end of Victorianism and substituted trench morals. Harris could tell the tale without reserve. Also he was by temperament and character able to do what Mr Sherard by temperament and character cannot do: that is, tell the tale unsentimentally. Harris admired Wilde as much as Mr Sherard; but he could see him objectively. He lost his head only when he was raging against the cruelty of the law and the prisons. Like Mr Sherard, he reviles the crowd that cheered the Marquess of Queensberry after his acquittal, forgetting that it was entirely natural and proper for the people to congratulate a father who had been impudently prosecuted for doing a public service, and triumphantly vindicated on standing his trial. But these outbursts of Harrisian scorn do not affect the portrait, which is not that of a hero and a martyred saint, but of a master talker and brilliant man of letters who came to grief through an unlucky sexual perversion and afterwards drank himself to death.

It is part of the tale that he should also have been able to enchant his friends to such an extent that they all, except Harris and Mr Arthur Ransome,[5] became more or less maudlin about him after his death. One of them, who had the misfortune to be imprisoned for six months for a patriotic libel totally unconnected with Wilde,[6] has declared that this happened to him providentially because he owed it to Wilde's memory to suffer as Wilde had suffered. The same fate overtook Harris; but he put no such mystical interpretation on it.

Then there were delicacies and touchinesses which Oscar had to consider when talking to Mr Sherard, to whom a duel was all in the day's work. The saddest page in his Story of an Unhappy Friendship is that on which he tells us that it ended by their passing oneanother in Paris with silently cool nods. Now on Harris delicacy was thrown away. He smashed through it with ten

5. Journalist and author, involved in a suit for libel lodged by Douglas, following publication of his *Oscar Wilde* (1912). Judgment was given in Ransome's favour (1915).
6. This was Douglas, whose conviction for libel is explained in footnote 39 on pp. 379–80.

scornful words (often unprintable) and forced you to play with all your cards on the table. Nothing was too fine for him and nothing too coarse. He was on your level instantly whether you were a master of literature or a hobo; and nothing can persuade me that he did not get out of Oscar all that was to be got, wheras there are a hundred things that nobody could say to Mr Sherard.

Naturally, Mr Sherard cannot abide Harris. Harris is to him that unpardonable character, a poacher; and he pillories me beside him because I spoke well of his trespass into the domain which Mr Sherard had pre-empted. In his fury he forgets that in 1906 he declared that "it is one of the most detestable axioms of commercial Philistinism that the exclusive right in a thought or comparison belongs to the man who has first voiced them. In the Republic of Letters no such proprietary instinct prevails." And again "the artist is entitled to appropriate for his own treatment the thoughts, the conceptions of others: it is a tribute to the man from whom the borrowing took place. It would be unfair to say that a *prima donna* who sings us the jewel song in Gounod's Faust ought not to be listened to because we have heard other *prime donne* sing that song before she came on the stage." But he will make no such concession to Frank Harris. He picks up any stick to belabor him with, and in pursuit of him plunges into such a morass of contradictions that he finally achieves a sort of impartiality perhaps more informative, as it is certainly more entertaining, than the most judicial summing-up could possibly be.

The main propositions in Mr Sherard's indictment of Harris, as well as I can disentangle them, are as follows:

1. That Harris's book is a gross plagiarism, all its facts being derived, not from his own knowledge, but, by a process of simple cribbing, from Mr Sherard's earlier work.

2. That Harris was a thoroughpaced liar whose book is a tissue of spiteful inventions and hypocritical falsehoods from beginning to end.

3. That Frank Harris, who wrote one book about Oscar Wilde, was basely trying to make money out of his friend's sensational misfortunes.

4. That Robert Harborough Sherard, who has written four, was fulfilling a disinterested duty to the memory of a martyr.

5. That Oscar Wilde was a man of spotless and almost angelic domestic character, rather like the Vicar of Wakefield, disinterestedly and happily married to a beautiful Irish girl without a penny in her pocket.

6. That Oscar Wilde broke off marital relations with his wife because he contracted syphilis in an *affaire de canapé* [casual sofa incident], and, being driven mad by this disease, committed offences in his dementia which landed

him in prison, leaving Mrs Wilde on the hands of her grandfather, from whom she had expectations that were fully realized.

7. That Oscar Wilde, being as innocent as a lamb of the practices charged against him, could not, as Harris asserts, have warned Harris that the facts in the case for the Crown were as stated.

8. That it was horribly cruel and unjust to punish Wilde for offences which, though actually committed, were entirely pathological, being hereditary and "epileptiform."

Mr Sherard is irrefutable: he has it both ways every time.

Frank Harris's admirers and champions, who are as numerous and fanatical as those of Wilde (Mr Sherard generously gives an imposing array of testimonials to this effect in the second chapter of his new book) will no doubt rush to cross-examine him. Their first question, as I guess, will be "Why did you, instead of attacking Harris's book immediately on publication, wait for twenty years until he was dead and could no longer defend himself?"

To this Mr Sherard has two quite valid replies. The first is that he did not read the book until 1928 (pp. 18–19). The second is that he refrained in sheer goodnature and regard for Harris and Mrs Harris (p. 32).

The second poser will probably be something like this. "You reproach Harris again and again for exploiting Wilde's notoriety to make money for himself, and contrast the sordidness of this motive with the purity of your own. Were you not the first to exploit Wilde's notoriety in this fashion? And are you not now flagrantly exploiting the publicity of Shaw by dragging his name into the title of a book with which he has no more to do than any other of Harris's friends?"

To this Mr Sherard might well reply that there was nothing but obloquy to be gained by championing Wilde. His reply on the other point I give verbatim. Here it is. "The idea of any pecuniary benefit from such a source is abhorrent to my nature," and, "as to Shaw, it is just these pronouncements of his—those imprimaturs which he delivers to Frank Harris on his biography of Wilde in general and on his portrayal of the man in particular—that have finally roused me to issue this book."

So it appears that I, Bernard Shaw, am the unfortunate cause of Mr Sherard's denunciation of poor Frank as "a man who has described himself with his own pen as seated between Gilles de Retz[7] and the Marquis de Sade in the lowest depths of Malebolge" [foul ditches in the eighth circle of Dante's *Inferno*].

7. Gilles de Laval, sire de Retz, comrade-in-arms of Joan of Arc and marshal of France, gave himself over to a life of debauchery and was judicially strangled and burned at Nantes.

This fiery sentence alone convinces me that Mr Sherard knows next to nothing about Harris. There are plenty of counts ready to the hand of the devil's advocate if anyone attempts to canonize Frank. But cruelty is not one of them. Harris was not merely accessible to pity: his transports of indignant scorn were always roused by cruelty, injustice, and oppression. He was not in the least perverted sexually: on the contrary, though he was conscientiously shameless where normal sexual adventures were concerned, he was, outside the straight line of sex, a prude. As to his being a hypocrite, his deficiency in this most necessary and invaluable art of social intercourse was equaled only by Mr Sherard's. Their inability to dissemble their likes and dislikes takes them to the verge of indecent exposure. A little polite hypocrisy would have made their lives far smoother.

Mr Sherard is madly determined to convict Harris of habitual and malicious mendacity. I would not undertake to find a page in his latest book on which he does not call Harris a liar. Now the trouble with Frank was not his dramatizations and imaginary conversations, which were all in the classic literary tradition, but his appalling and ruthless candors, delivered in a voice which filled the largest theatres and dominated the noisiest dinner parties. It was part of his unsuspected *naïveté* that he never knew and never learnt how much dissimulation is needed to make good society work smoothly; and it was this that finally made him impossible in any but the most Bohemian circles in London, though the best people had been quite ready to lionize him at his first impact on them as a Tory Democrat with a powerful pen. "Harris" said Wilde "has been at all the great houses—*once.*"

It was the rule at that time that you must not say anything to a young unmarried lady that could bring a blush to her cheek; yet Harris always assumed, in perfect good faith, that every young woman over fifteen knew the tales of [Guy de] Maupassant by heart; was as open to the discussion of sex in all its aspects as Mr Havelock Ellis; and had a portfolio of the etchings of Felicien Rops[8] on her bedroom bookshelf. This cannot have been the effect of any frequentation of low company on his part; for there is no company on earth, however abandoned, where young women entertain their views on sex as part of a fastidious literary and artistic culture. I cannot believe that there is one prostitute in every million in Europe who has ever heard of Maupassant or Rops. Harris's assumptions on the subject were purely imaginative, and therefore incurable by any pressure of remonstrance from his friends.

8. Controversial engraver and painter of erotic and sometimes pornographic themes of social decadence.

Add to this that if Harris suspected any fellow guest of not being soundly Harrisian on any point, he felt it to be his duty to challenge him defiantly on that point; that such business morals as his artistic temperament had permitted him to acquire were American in all respects in which American business morals differ from English: that he remained ridiculously incapable of the tactful dissimulation, hypocrisy, and polite mendacity which are needed to consolidate a position in the London governing class society to which he had effected an entrance; and you will understand how Harris, instead of consolidating that position, shattered it almost every time he opened his mouth.

In short, if ever there was a martyr to truth, that martyr was Saint Francis Harris.

Mr Sherard again goes wildly astray when he declares that Harris's favorite posture was that of "a pirate from the Spanish main."[9] It was I who fastened that aspect on him; and he was too astonished by it to be offended. He expostulated with me earnestly about it, asking me "Why do you persist in calling me a buccaneer?" He never could see himself in that light. His ideal character was Jesus, of whom he considered himself to some extent a reincarnation. In vain I urged his unprintable language, his scornful and deeptoned measured utterance, his genius for scandalizing respectable people (mostly through innocently assuming that they all thought exactly as he did), his dark hair, his challenging gaze, his irresistible suggestion of a Byronic pirate. He could not see himself in that way: to himself he was "Gentle Jesus, meek and mild" with overmuch of Mary Magdalen in the picture. When he sent me a copy of the first volume of his autobiography (My Life and Loves)[10] containing several careful clinical lectures on his early sexual adventures, he was extraordinarily surprised and hurt when I told him that it had to be destroyed lest it should be picked up by the maidens on our domestic staff. One of the clinical lectures concludes with a sentence beginning "What will my young lady readers think of me if &c. &c." He could not understand why the book should not be on the library table of every country house and even every convent. At all events the succeeding three volumes were not sent to me; and I remain to this day ignorant of their contents. But I gather that they scandalize nobody now save Mr Sherard.

9. In the Shaw letter published in 1918 as an appendix, he wrote: 'When people asked, "What has Frank Harris been?" the usual reply was, "Obviously a pirate from the Spanish Main."'
10. Four volumes of Harris's autobiography were privately printed in 1923 and a fifth, based on unpublished material, after his death.

The only person who understood this quaintly blind side of Harris was the late Mrs Julia Frankau ([a novelist who wrote under the name] "Frank Danby"), who remonstrated with me very seriously for being brutal in my handling of his sensitiveness. Mrs Frankau was quite right. I did deal with him as if he was a buccaneer, not then realizing what a daisy he really was.

I remember our first meeting. He was then editing the Fortnightly Review, and had invited me to see him with a view to my becoming a contributor. I found him engaged with a visitor to whom he was speaking in resounding and perfectly fluent German. This impressed me, as I am the worst of linguists. I also appreciated his fine elocution, though, being a public speaker and a producer of my own plays, I was an expert at this game and proof against its theatrical illusion. I told myself that this was the man for me as an editor, but that he would bully me if I did not bully him first. All the editors who were any use to me were men of this sort.

My bullying was very mild. He was telling me how he had upset himself by some athletic feat on the river. I immediately assumed the character of President of the Royal College of Physicians, and said severely "Do you drink?" He was taken aback for a moment. Then he accepted the situation and gave me quite a long account of his symptoms and diet and so forth. After that we were on quite unreserved and intimate terms.

Harris was also an artist with a personal style as imposing in its way as the style of Wilde, and much more trenchant. Both of them transformed crude statements of fact into polished works of art. But Wilde, the greatest *raconteur* in the world, never told stories about himself or about any identifiable real persons. Harris always romanced about himself and about real persons. He once described to me a supper party at which King Edward VII rose from the table and marched down the middle of the room with his arm round Frank's neck. Frank behaved admirably. In a noble Ciceronian oration, punctuated with the necessary number of "sirs," he remonstrated with the slightly intoxicated monarch for doing him an honor that must not only scandalize the court but bring down upon him, Harris, an avalanche of jealous envy and hatred. And there the scene ended.

Mr Sherard will dismiss this as a gross fabrication and plead his usual unanswerable proof of its falsehood: to wit, that the tale must be a lie because Harris, who told it, was a liar. But I have a special reason for cherishing a conviction that it must have happened, or at least ought to have happened. Let me explain.

There is a vulgar legend current that Edward VII was afflicted with a strong and incurable German accent. I know that he had nothing of the sort; for I had an opportunity, possibly unique, of hearing his voice for a considerable time before I knew who the speaker was. One summer day [5 May 1906] I was in the Paris Salon,[11] rather astonished to find that I was apparently the only person there. I had expected the sort of crowd to which we are accustomed at the shows of our Royal Academy.[12] But no: I wandered through roomful after roomful of mediocre paintings without meeting a soul. The silence and solitude were uncanny. They were broken by the irruption into the next room of an English party of gentlemen in noisy conversation. I could not see them, and, having no reason to suspect who they were, cursed their intrusion in the British manner until my ear was caught by a voice (I am, as I have already hinted, professionally sensitive to voices) unlike any speaking voice I had ever heard before. Its timbre was that of a bassoon. Not a common bassoon, but one of the choice old instruments which sell for fancy prices, like Stradivarius violins. I had never heard a voice exactly like it, and immediately coveted it for my stage dialogues and wondered whether the man could sing, as, if so, he must be a *basso cantante* [a flexible 'lyric' bass voice] of the first order. At last the party came through still talking, and I saw that the possessor of the remarkable voice was King Edward VII. I understood at once why people ignorant of German and of phonetics might suppose that the unusual quality of the voice was a German accent.

This incident made Harris's anecdote irresistible to me. What it conjured up was not merely a vision of a royal supper party, but a duet between a bassoon and an ophicleide by two consummate performers. It was too good to be rejected as a romantic invention. Besides, it was not impossible. The governing classes in London are experts in flattering people who are useful or might be dangerous to them, and quite reckless in petting those who amuse them.

As Mr Sherard may not know the difference between a bassoon and an ophicleide, and is in any case implacable in his determination to pillory Frank as a liar, let us, to please him, assume that the incident is a romantic invention, and that Frank Harris and Victoria's successor never met in their lives. The assumption does not take Mr Sherard a step further. This epithet of liar, liar, liar, which Mr Sherard seems unable to cease shouting, proves nothing for or against the character of the vituperated person. We are all liars as a matter of common civility. But there are liars and liars. Harris, I repeat, was ostracized in London because he was intolerably truthful. What Mr Sherard is trying to

11. The Société des Artistes Français (founded in 1872) held an annual salon or exhibition in May and June at the Palais d'Industrie, open to artists of all nationalities.
12. The Royal Academy was founded under the patronage of George III in 1768 for the annual exhibition of works of contemporary artists and for the establishment of a school of art.

establish is not that Harris, as an artist in Plutarchian biography, followed the practice of the classic historians in inventing imaginary conversations, but that he was a slanderer. Now there are in the literary profession satirists whose genius in that department carries them into a mania for calumny. Such a Thersites[13] was not far to seek in the circle which surrounded Harris and Wilde; for it included the late Thomas William Henry Crosland, whose passion for satire, invective, and denigration was unscrupulous and insatiable. His best friend, Lord Alfred Douglas, has immortalized him in a magnificent sonnet beginning "You were a brute and more than half a knave" [*Sonnets*, 1935: 'The Unspeakable Englishman']. Now Harris was not a bit like Crosland: his indignations were all generous and public spirited. Mr Sherard thunders on for pages against statements made by Harris which he denounces as lies on the simple but unsubstantial datum that he does not believe them and does not want to believe them. Some of them are to my knowledge true; others Harris may have honestly believed; and none are slanderous or malicious or in any way illnatured.

For example, the first count in the indictment, labored through a whole chapter, is that Harris told a friend that 40,000 copies of this book had been sold. Mr Sherard does not pretend to know whether this was true or false: he simply refuses to believe it. He cannot bear it. I am more credulous, because I contributed a chapter to it on the strength of which my name appeared in golden letters on the cover as if it were a book about Oscar Wilde by Bernard Shaw.[14] But suppose the real sale was 400 copies or 40, or 4! Does Harris's exaggeration imply any such rancorous depravity of character as Mr Sherard claims? Is anyone the worse? Was it worth raving about for so many pages?

Again, take the story about the steam yacht which Harris declares he had ready at Erith [in Kent, near Woolwich] to enable Oscar to escape to the continent! Mr Sherard makes malicious fun of this as a romantic flourish from the Spanish main, and an unnecessary one inasmuch as the authorities were much too anxious to get rid of Wilde to take any steps to prevent his leaving

13. Thersites was a deformed, scurrilous Grecian in Shakespeare's *Troilus and Cressida*. The name became Shaw's apt cognomen for T. W. H. Crosland, boorish assistant to Douglas on the *Academy* (1907–10).
14. While Harris's name and the title of the book were blocked on the spine, the upper cover bore only a prominent imprint 'WITH MEMORIES OF OSCAR WILDE By BERNARD SHAW'. Harris's rationale for this sales enhancement was that he had included in the second volume Shaw's lengthy letter, captioned by Harris 'My Memories of Oscar Wilde', and the comments (in footnotes) throughout the book that Shaw had provided on the page proof sent to him.

the country as an ordinary passenger. I have made too much fun of the incident myself [in the 1918 appendix] to grudge the joke to Mr Sherard; but he goes on recklessly to accuse Harris of having stolen the story from his 1906 biography, where it would have been just as absurd. I say would have been because there is not a word about it either in the story or the biography. As Harris tells it, however, it is not absurd. Harris had every reason to doubt whether the railway stations were as safe as Mr Sherard thinks; and Wilde was certain that he would be arrested there, and in any case recognized and mobbed. In his state of mind, as to which Mr Sherard and Harris are in agreement, nothing but the private carriage and the private yacht could have tempted him. The whole episode leaves such a strong impression of Wilde's immovable despair during the ordeal of the three trials that even as fiction it would justify itself artistically. Why then demur to it without any better reason than Mr Sherard's incredulity? It is not at all flattering to Harris; for it involves an admission that his alternative exhortation to Wilde to rouse himself and fight his case in court was blustering nonsense, and that Wilde was right in his conviction that he was doomed, as nothing could prevail against the hotel evidence in the hands of the Crown.

The truth is that Harris lost his head over the affair much more completely than Wilde, who did not lose his head at all. Harris raged at the cruelty of the law, the savagery of the sexually excited mob, the Press hue and cry against "the man Wilde" now that the journalists whom he had snubbed had got him down and could kick him with impunity, and the abandonment and repudiation of the reprobate by his eminent acquaintances. In transports comparable to Mr Sherard's at his hottest, he fills page after page with denunciations of judge and jury, of the entire British nation, and finally of pseudo-Christian civilization. He was amazed because Wilde would not rise up and echo his thunders: so abject an extremity of impugnacity he could not understand. All this was buccaneering froth. Wilde was right: he knew he was doomed and must go through with it, or else break his bail and run away: a course, as his silly brother ['Willie' (William)] put it, not open to an Irish gentleman. But in what way was Frank's bluster ungenerous?

I pass by the fearful disturbance Mr Sherard makes about Harris's alleged call at the Home Office on Sunday to remonstrate about Wilde's treatment in jail, and about [Commandant Ferdinand] Esterhazy,[15] the villain of the

15. The French army officer who perpetrated the espionage for which Alfred Dreyfus was wrongfully imprisoned escaped punishment, when the truth was uncovered, by fleeing abroad. Shaw confused him with Hubert-Joseph Henry, chief of intelligence in the French war office, who, after admitting he had forged documents that led to Dreyfus's condemnation and suppressed others, committed suicide in prison.

Dreyfus drama, openly admitting his guilt in a Paris Café before committing suicide. Does anyone whom Mr Sherard has persuaded that Harris was senselessly drawing the long bow infer that Harris was a calumnious scoundrel? Mr Sherard will reply that Harris imagined things that never occurred and recollected events that never happened.

Very well: let me try to move Mr Sherard to a little charity by comparing them with his own flights of imagination? He tells us (page 196) that "the Wilde scandal caused the collapse of the then Government, and brought about the General Election of 1895." Could Harris beat that? On page 266 he draws what he calls "the logical conclusion" that Wilde contracted a contagious disease in "some *affaire de canapé*." Where does the logic come in? On page 272 he "proves" his statement that Harris plundered Wilde shamefully and heartlessly by endorsing an opinion that Harris's play entitled Mr. and Mrs. Daventry was "entirely Wilde's production." This last is beyond my patience. If, as Mr Sherard admits, Harris paid Wilde two sums of £50 each for the plot of Daventry,[16] he paid him £99 19s. 10d. too much. As to a single line of the play having been by Oscar, either Mr Sherard does not know chalk from cheese, which seems improbable, or else he has never read a line of Daventry or seen it acted. If Oscar had written it, it would now be a classic.

Mr Sherard's virtuous indignation against Harris reaches one of its frequent climaxes in the case of a British General [Hector Macdonald] who committed suicide on being summoned to answer charges of the kind that Wilde had to answer. Harris alluded to him, but in ordinary consideration for his family did not mention his name. Mr Sherard gives the name quite unnecessarily, and then says that the General's death "should have muted the tongue even of a Frank Harris." He tells us how he himself met the General in the rue de Rivoli, whereupon the General went back to his hotel and shot himself. Why should this fatal encounter have muted the tongue of Harris, who knew nothing of it? On the essential point of the name Harris did mute his tongue. Nothing can mute Mr Sherard's.

But let us get to the counts in the indictment on which Harris, if found guilty, would be unpardonable. The gravest of these is that Wilde, being innocent of the charges on which he was convicted, could not possibly have told Harris that he was not innocent. Consequently we are to condemn Harris's use of the word Confessions in the original title of this book as a villainous catchpenny slander.

16. Wilde in the last year of his life sold to a number of acquaintances, among them Harris, the scenario of a play he had sketched out for George Alexander in 1894. Unaware of the subterfuge, Harris fleshed out the plot and sold it to Mrs Patrick Campbell, who appeared in it at the Royalty Theatre in October 1900.

Now it may be argued that the practices for which Wilde was punished are innocent practices, and should not be banned by the criminal law nor stigmatized as guilty in private conversation. Wilde went further, and held that homosexual love is a nobler mode of passion than the normal fertile form. This was his final considered opinion, as Harris shews in the discussion recorded hereinafter in chapter XXII. It is how all homosexualists strong-minded or lightminded enough to be proof against inculcated superstition think of it. As Mr Sherard puts it "after each crisis Oscar Wilde seems to have been totally unconscious of having done anything bad, detestable, shameful, or even unusual. Under no other condition could he have maintained the serene and tranquil dignity which stamped him in his sane moments."

Wilde could therefore plead Not Guilty with perfect sincerity, and indeed could not honestly put in any other plea. Guilty or not guilty is a question not of fact but of morals: the prisoner who pleads Not Guilty is not alleging that he did this or did not do that: he is affirming that what he did does not involve any guilt on his part. Mr Sherard, like too many jurymen, may have overlooked this distinction and taken Wilde's protestations of innocence, if he ever made any, to be a denial of the acts for which he was imprisoned.

But did he make any? I can testify from my own direct knowledge[17] that at the moment before the Queensberry trial, when a wrongfully accused man would have been indignantly vehement in his denial and wholly preoccupied with the marshaling of the facts to clear himself, Oscar assumed that Harris and I and the others present knew that he had no case. He admitted that his suit against the Marquess was an act of folly. Harris told him to drop the suit and leave the country there and then, as the trial would turn, not on a contest of epigrammatic repartee between Wilde and the Marquess's counsel, but on a mass of unpleasant evidence by hotel chambermaids and other quite unepigrammatic persons, in the face of which Wilde's counsel would surrender at discretion and practically oblige the police to arrest his client: in short, he foretold precisely what subsequently happened. It is true that Wilde did not endorse the presentation of the case against him by the police. Of the six counts in the indictment[18] he said, on the authority of a friend [unidentified]

17. Wilde and Douglas had joined Shaw and Harris at their table in the Café Royal, London, on 25 March or 1 April 1895. Harris lunched there every Monday with members of his staff, and apparently was sought out by Wilde to appear as a literary expert witness at the forthcoming trial.
18. According to contemporary reports the jury found Wilde guilty on seven counts, involving four sex partners, and found him 'not guilty' of sexual misconduct with a fifth party.

vouched for by Mr Sherard, "Five of the counts referred to matters with which I had absolutely nothing to do. There was some foundation for one of the counts. I could not tell my lawyers without betraying a friend." This is credible and indeed highly probable; but it means only that the police "constructed" their story confusedly, not that the charges were untrue or the verdict wrong. At the Café Royal both Wilde and Lord Alfred Douglas, who was present, reproached Harris for refusing to come into court and pay futile compliments to the purity of Wilde's novel, Dorian Gray, which Lord Alfred in his maturer wisdom has since described as an extraordinarily pernicious homily in its effect on young Oxford;[19] but not for a moment did either make any pretence that Queensberry had traduced Wilde.

Harris, by the way, has misplaced the conversation in which Wilde warned him not to assume his innocence. It must have preceded the first trial;[20] for at the Café Royal that day Frank was under no illusion, though, like most of Wilde's friends, he had had no suspicion of the truth until Lord Queensberry published it.

Harris's failure to rouse Wilde to any defensive effort, amply confirmed by Mr Sherard's account, meant simply that he knew that on the facts he had no defence. Yet Mr Sherard will have it that Oscar always most emphatically denied to everybody the charges he warned Harris not to dismiss as unfounded, though this does not prevent him from repeatedly urging that when Wilde committed his offences he had been driven mad by the *sequelae* of the hypothetical *affaire de canapé*! When he takes the warpath against Harris he rides two horses at once; and the fact that they charge in opposite directions does not discompose him in the least.

Wilde must have formally represented himself as innocent to his lawyers in his attack on Lord Queensberry; otherwise they could not have taken his

19. Douglas explained in his *Autobiography* (1929) that 'when all this happened I had been six years at school and at Oxford, and I had lost my moral sense and had no religion . . . Even before I met Wilde I had persuaded myself that "sins of the flesh" were not wrong, and my opinion was of course mostly strengthened and confirmed by his brilliantly reasoned defence of them . . . He went through life preaching the gospel which he puts into the mouth of Lord Henry Wotton in *Dorian Gray*.'
20. There were three trials: one civil and two criminal. The first was an action for libel brought by Wilde on 3 April 1895 against Queensberry in a civil court. Queensberry was found not guilty. The second ran from 26 April to 1 May in the criminal courts; the jury failed to reach a verdict. The third ran from 20 to 25 May, with Wilde found guilty of being, according to the judge in his sentencing speech, the 'centre of a circle of extensive corruption of the most hideous kind among young men'.

case into court. When it became apparent that their client had no case at all, and that the defendant's case was overwhelming, Wilde had to accept the surrender. I do not believe that he ever condescended to denials except when legal fictions were necessary. Like most similarly afflicted men of culture, he was not only unashamed of his reversed sex instinct but proud of it, and of its association with some great names. But he never thrust it upon those of his friends to whom it was repugnant. He therefore had two reputations: a black one and a white one. Mr Sherard shouts this down as impossible, forgetting, as usual, how he shouted it up in 1906 in an eloquent page (339) which culminates in the statement that "until the very day of Wilde's arrest his wife had not the faintest suspicion of anything wrong with his conduct." I was ordinarily acquainted with Wilde's reputation; but until he prosecuted Queensberry I had never heard a word about his homosexuality. The late Carlos Blacker,[21] an intimate friend of Wilde's who lent me a typescript of De Profundis when the last half of it was still kept secret, told me that he also had not had the faintest suspicion of anything of the kind, and was as amazed as I was when it came to light. And what says Mr Sherard himself in his first book on Wilde? "I can disregard, in writing of him, the cruel and devilish madness which, as people said and to their satisfaction proved, at times actuated him, with all the greater ease, that during the sixteen years of our friendship by not one word of his, by not one gesture, by not the fleeting shadow of one evil thought, did it betray itself to me in the radiant and pleasant gentleman that he was." And again "If behind the wonderful eyes a demon was indeed crouching, madness here too allied itself with such supreme cunning of dissimulation, that for me until the very end he remained the *beau idéal* of a gentleman in all that the word implies of lofty and serene morality."

Well, if Mr Sherard did not know, how should Harris, a comparative stranger, have known? I am convinced that he was as much in the dark as Mr Sherard; for, I repeat, Harris, in spite of, and perhaps because of his obsession with normal sex, was a prude as to its byways. In any case his ruthless bluntness in such matters made him the last person on earth whom Wilde would have taken into his confidence until it became necessary to enlighten him.

In spite of the prison cruelties as to which Mr Sherard and Harris are

21. A wealthy Englishman who continued to be a loyal friend of Wilde's wife Constance and their two sons, but turned against Wilde because of his resumed friendship with Douglas. Blacker, later a friend of the Shaws, probably had the copy from Robbie Ross.

entirely in sympathy, it cannot be said that the police did their worst to Wilde. Had they charged him directly with the Scriptural offence, a verdict against him would have obliged the judge to sentence him to twenty years penal servitude. Juries cannot now be depended on to find verdicts involving such sequels. There is a considerable prevalence of the Benthamite view that the policy of the State in dealing with private vices should be one of *Laissez-faire*.[22] This is quite in line with the view of the psychopathists that homosexuality is a disease for which its victim is not responsible, or a freak of nature, like having your heart on the right side instead of the left, and in both cases a misfortune calling for profound pity instead of execration and savage punishment. The legislation against it, called medieval but really dating from the irruption of the middle classes into Parliament in 1832, full of crass Bible fetichism and conviction of their mission to execute the wrath of God on the sins of the Cities of the Plain, had become ridiculous.

But *Laissez-faire* breaks down in practice. In Russia the Bolshevik revolution of 1917 wiped the slate as far as Scriptural superstitions were concerned, and produced a state of sexual liberty which gave a chance to the esthetic view, the Benthamite view, and the scientific view of homosexuality. The result was that without any relapse into bourgeois Bible fetichism, the Soviet government found it necessary to class homosexual practices as crimes punishable by four years imprisonment (the usual sentence for manslaughter in Russia) or eight years when the culprit was the official superior of the accomplice.

Nobody in England has yet explained why this was done, whether on the ground of sterilization, demoralization, abuse of authority in the public services, or what not. The fact remains that it was found necessary on its merits as a measure of social discipline without reference to the changing of Lot's wife into a pillar of salt [Genesis 19: 26]. It is gossiped that the mischief began in the British colony; but it is evident that the practice of a handful of temporary sojourners in Moscow could not be a ground for imposing a moral reform of such severity on a federation of oriental States covering a sixth of the globe and containing more than 160 millions of people. It must have been discovered in practice that unrestrained and unreprobated homosexuality acts as a plague spot with dangerous powers of infection. Whatever evidence

22. Jeremy Bentham, examining the issue of consensual sex in *An Introduction to the Principles of Morals and Legislation* (1789), argued (euphemistically) that an 'act', otherwise 'mischievous or disagreeable', was 'unmeet for punishment' if 'the person whose interest it concerns gave his *consent* to the performance of it', provided the consent 'be free, and fairly obtained'.

there may be for this, there is no need to go further than the nearest experienced policeman, or the keepers of public playgrounds and designers of blocks of working class dwellings, to know what an abiding terror the seducer of children is to parents who cannot afford nursemaids and governesses, or what a nuisance to the police. Alphonse Daudet, asked by Mr Sherard to intercede for Wilde, replied "You see, Sherard, you are not a parent."[23] Daudet knew what he was talking about, which is more than can be fully said for either Harris or Mr Sherard, or indeed for any of the literary enthusiasts who are so wrapped up in their vision of Oscar as a saint, a martyr, and a hero, that policemen and parents are ignored by them as vulgar and irrelevant intruders.

In England, when the law against homosexuality, like the law against apostasy, became unworkable through the extravagance of its penalties, the police soon discovered that, as Wellington said when challenged as to the barbarities of military discipline, "anything is better than impunity."[24] To protect children it was found necessary to pass the Criminal Law Amendment Act [1885]; and it was under this Act that Wilde was charged with indecency and corruption of the young, the extreme penalty being two years imprisonment with hard labor.

It was Oscar's ill luck to fall into the hands of a judge [Mr Justice Sir Alfred Wills] who, being ignorantly horrified by the case, not only did his worst but proclaimed his regret that his worst (the sentence of two years) was so

23. Wilde, who met the French writer Daudet in Paris early in 1883, subsequently became acquainted with his son Léon Daudet, then in his late teens, on several social visits to the apartment of a mutual friend Marcel Schwob. Léon Daudet recalled Wilde as one who 'attracted and repelled you at the same time . . . There was about him something morbid, unnatural . . . Finally I asked Schwob to try to avoid having me meet so fatiguing a character. Several years later, when I read the details of the trial, I appreciated the correctness of my early impressions' (*Memoirs*, tr. Arthur K. Griggs, 1926).

24. Iterated frequently by the Duke. In a despatch to the Rt. Hon. J. Villiers, from Badajoz, Spain, on 8 September 1809, he ordered punishment for a Portuguese miscreant as it was 'very desirable that the people of the country should know that they cannot be guilty of [misconduct] with impunity'. In a memorandum on 28 November 1812, following a disorderly retreat from Salamanca: 'I am concerned to have to observe that the army under my command has fallen off in the respect of discipline . . . to a greater degree than any army with which I have ever served . . . [I]rregularities and outrages were committed with impunity'. In a parliamentary discussion on flogging on 11 August 1846, the Duke insisted 'it is impossible to carry on the discipline of the British army without some punishment of that description which the individual shall feel'.

little. The police probably expected a sentence of six months, plus, of course, its inevitable sequel of a social ostracism that would drive Wilde into exile and rid the country of him. They could have done no less. And even this much they did not do until Queensberry took the bull by the horns and forced Wilde to defend himself or else clear out of London clubland and take refuge on the Continent. Howbeit the situation was exactly as Harris describes it. Wilde made no pretence of injured innocence in private when the veil was torn off. The discovery of his Scotland Yard reputation gave a rude shock to friends intimate enough to think that they had known all that was to be known about him. It horrified and disgusted the more distant circle of his social acquaintances just as it horrified and disgusted the judge who sentenced him.

I now come to the complaints not only of Harris but of myself. I cannot be forgiven, it seems, for saying, when I contributed a chapter to an early American edition of this book, that it was "the best life of Wilde, whose memory will have to stand or fall by it." I wrote this in ignorance of Mr Sherard's biographies, and therefore did not know what I was talking about. I apologize. Perhaps Mr Sherard will tell me that it is all very well to apologize; but what am I going to do about it? Now that I am better informed am I going to stick to my old estimate?

I am afraid my reply must be "More than ever." Wilde and Harris were to my personal knowledge human beings. They were remarkable specimens no doubt, distinctly supercharged; but still their species was unmistakable; each was *homo sapiens* (so called), authentic and possible. The figures labeled Wilde and Harris in Mr Sherard's last book are entertaining enough; but they are impossible. They are monsters. Wilde is an angelic monster, Harris a diabolical one. His address is given as Malebolge; and there is no such place on earth. He is blown about in the whirlwinds of Mr Sherard's vituperative rhetoric until prosaic Frank in the dock vanishes and is replaced by a doubly damned phantom from the Inferno. I can applaud Mr Sherard as an advocate. I cannot accept him as a biographer.

As to that soulless phrase of mine "an unproductive swindler and a drunkard," I withdraw swindler because it suggests business operations of which Wilde was quite incapable; though as a professional playwright I must insist that his sale to Harris of a stage plot which he had already sold to most of his theatrical friends was a very serious fraud, to be dismissed goodnaturedly with a laugh only because it was such a transparent excuse for begging. Where I was wrong was in describing Oscar as unproductive in his last phase. On the contrary, he had found his true vocation, and was incessantly industrious in its pursuit. He was the best company, the best English-speaking talker, of whom we have any record in his time; and all witnesses now agree that he performed with all his old brilliancy and pleasantness to the end, though for years we heard nothing but fictions invented to provide a crucificial ending to a spurious gospel.

The disadvantage of his conversational specialization was that when he had entertained his acquaintances as they had never been entertained before, he could not take round the hat and get paid for his labor on the spot. In fact he could not get directly paid at all unless he went to an agent and hired himself out for fifty guineas an evening like a musical virtuoso or any other sort of solo entertainer. And this can be done only in social circles to which agents must not introduce notorious ex-convicts. How then was Oscar to live? I will answer this presently. But first let me get rid of the word drunkard.

Mr Sherard scores a point when he cites the testimony of Oscar's gallant landlord. "I never saw him drunk" says the brave and kindly Dupoirier.[25] "Half seas over, perhaps, sometimes. But drunk, never."

Now if I withdraw the word drunkard to please Mr Sherard he may rush impetuously to the conclusion that Wilde was a teetotaller. So here I must drop the critic and put on the temperance lecturer.

There are two ways of setting in motion the mystical agency that changes a mere human animal into a writer, a composer, an actor, a painter, a poet or what not. There is the natural and sacred one, the way of the application of one's own inner force by one's own inner light. The other is the way of sorcery: the resort to stimulants and drugs. A writer, for instance, takes a cup of coffee or a glass of beer. Instantly his standard of self-criticism falls by, say, twenty per cent: a deliciously comforting sensation which makes the task of writing a chapter much pleasanter and easier, though the chapter is twenty per cent the worse for it. When the effect wears off the remedy is obvious: another cup or glass. But this time the effect wears off sooner by a degree so infinitesimal that it is not noticeable. Yet it is the beginning of a process in which the stimulant which at first produced a chapter produces only a few pages, then produces only a single page, then only a paragraph, and finally only a sentence, by which time the coffee or beer has long been replaced by whiskey, brandy, or (in France) absinthe. Finally the sorcerer cannot get through even a sentence, and dies. True, the process takes some time; and in most cases it is not carried out at full speed to the last extremity. But in all directions you

25. Proprietor of the Hôtel d'Alsace in Paris, where Wilde resided from August 1899 to April 1900. He liked Wilde and advanced him money to rescue his belongings from another hotel. Rupert Hart-Davis gives his Christian name as Jean, Richard Ellmann as Édouard.

may see people whose regular diet consists more or less of fermented or distilled liquor, and yet are never drunk, however saturated they may be. As Monsieur Dupoirier put it, they may be half seas over (*entre deux vins*), but drunk, never. They have drunk away even that rollicking privilege. Some of them come to loathe the stimulant they cannot do without. A friend of mine who reached this stage and died in it pleaded his loathing as a proof that as he was morally a teetotaller I had no right to class him as a drunkard.

Monsieur Dupoirier goes on to draw the complete picture. "Towards the end it became very difficult for Monsieur Melmoth[26] to write; and he used to whip himself up with cognac. A litre bottle would hardly see him through the night. And he ate little and took but little exercise. He used to sleep until noon, and then breakfast, and then sleep again until five or six in the evening."

Mr Sherard quotes this triumphantly as a complete refutation of my description of Wilde in his last days as a drunkard. So I withdraw the word very willingly. But what does Mr Sherard call him?

All Wilde's set, Harris included, ate and drank appallingly. Harris believed that his virility, of which he was inordinately proud, could be maintained only by lunching on at least two *entrecote* [sirloin] steaks and a mush of highly flavored cheese, with plenty of Burgundy to help them and several liqueurs to finish up with. I have heard him say to a lady after an exhibition of this kind "We do this for your sakes," which was his sort of Anacreontic gallantry. Yet I never saw Harris drunk. At the Saturday Review office every week whiskey was *ad libitum* [at pleasure] and though it had no more apparent effect on Harris than a can of beer on a sweating haymaker in a hot July, it changed J. F. Runciman,[27] his very promising music critic, from a sober young enthusiast into a fatal case of dipsomania in a year or two.

Now there was nothing extraordinary in all this. Because I knew enough of the rudiments of dietetics to avoid sorceries I was classed as a Puritan ascetic and suspected of sexual impotence. English education, and its American imitation, were such, that it was possible to become a Senior Wrangler, a double first[28], a Lord Chief Justice, or a Minister of Public Health with less

26. On leaving prison (18 May 1897) Wilde adopted the alias of Sebastian Melmoth, made up of the name of his favourite martyr and of the satanic hero of Revd Charles Maturin's *Melmoth the Wanderer* (1820). Maturin was Wilde's maternal great uncle.
27. Secretary of the Fabian Society's Southern Group, music critic, and Frank Harris's deputy on the *Saturday Review*.
28. At Cambridge (until 1910) a Senior Wrangler was one who attained first place on the honours list in the final mathematical tripos examination. A double first is one who attains first class honours in two different subjects or in Part I and Part II of the same subject.

knowledge of how to feed wholesomely than a monkey. Six leading physicians, invited to a symposium by the first editor [Sir James T. Knowles] of the Nineteenth Century, solemnly declared that alcohol was a necessary part of human nourishment.[29] Prescriptions of champagne jelly were fashionable; and wine was a common item in medical advice, as it is still.

It has been found impossible to define the word drunk with legal exactitude. The police are obliged in doubtful cases to apply tests in which any teetotaller might stumble. The army gets out of the difficulty by the rough and ready rule that a soldier is drunk when he is not sober. The extinct Royal Irish Constabulary always described the condition as being "under the influence." I should say that at the present moment as in the nineties the whole civilized world is more or less under the influence. I have personally known prominent statesmen and great artists whose consumption of whiskey dismayed their hostesses. And it was I with my glass of barley water or cup of postum, mistrusting even tea and coffee, who excited surprise and even reprobation whilst these tragic topers were destroying themselves before the whole miseducated world. The only consolation their wives and children have is that the Life Force is so inexhaustibly adaptable that our insides can accustom themselves to almost anything short of absolute prussic acid. De Quincey could write charmingly on a diet of fourteen thousand drops of laudanum a day; and Edmund Kean gave his contemporaries "Shakespear by flashes of lightning" through drinking unlimited brandy until he dropped dead on the stage.[30]

I conclude my temperance lecture by declaring my conviction that if Wilde and Harris had adopted my diet they might quite possibly have now been as alive as I. Mr Sherard, who survives in excessive vigor, must surely be a vegetarian.

Now comes a delicate question. Why has this book, published twentytwo years ago in America, not been published in the British Empire until today?

29. The recollection of a physicians' symposium on alcohol in an early number of *Nineteenth Century* is an aberration. In May 1885 (its ninth year) the journal published an attack by Archdeacon Frederick W. Farrar on a recently published pamphlet, 'Drink', by Lord Bramwell, extolling the nourishing properties of alcoholic beverages, which was reprinted in the same issue. This led to a rejoinder by Bramwell and a 'last word' by Farrar in June and July, and an article by Fortescue Fox on 'Stimulants and Narcotics' in December.
30. De Quincey recorded the dosage in his *Confessions of an English Opium Eater*. The description of Kean (dated 27 April 1823) appears in Coleridge's *Table Talk* (1836): '[T]o see him act is like reading Shakespeare by flashes of lightning.' Kean collapsed during a performance of *Othello*; but died in bed seven weeks later.

The technical answer is that in England it infringed certain copyrights that were not valid in the United States. The real answer is that it libeled Lord Alfred Douglas, whose audacity and success as a litigant had intimidated the publishers. He was a younger son of the Marquess.

The part played by Wilde in Lord Alfred's life was fateful. There had been nothing like it in literary history since the famous case of Mr W. H., the "onlie begetter" of Shakespear's sonnets. Without the tragedy of Lord Alfred the story would be impossible. For please let us hear no more of the tragedy of Oscar Wilde. Oscar was no tragedian. He was the superb comedian of his century, one to whom misfortune, disgrace, imprisonment were external and traumatic. His gaiety of soul was invulnerable: it shines through the blackest pages of his De Profundis as clearly as in his funniest epigrams. Even on his deathbed he found in himself no pity for himself, playing for the laugh with his last breath, and getting it with as sure a stroke as in his palmiest prime.

Not so the young disciple whose fortunes were poisoned and ruined through their attachment. The tragedy is his tragedy, not Oscar's.

It so happened that Lord Alfred Douglas in [his] twenties was gifted or cursed with the degree of personal beauty that, taking its possessor quite beyond the sphere of sex attraction, inspires affectionate admiration in men and women indiscriminately. Poets wrote sonnets praising his beauty as Shakespear praised Mr W. H's. Had there been a Shakespear among his acquaintances, the body of adoring verses he inspired would be as copious and as famous as the "sugred sonnets" about which books have been written by Tyler, by Samuel Butler, by Wilde, and finally by Lord Alfred himself, who being Mr W. H. *redivivus* [revived], alone understands them.[31]

Unfortunately, when beauty worship finds hyperbolical expression, it is always misunderstood by homosexuals who want to misunderstand it as well as by the much larger body who are not very susceptible to beauty and are very susceptible to sex. They forget that the new world of the cinema has shewn them a long train of world's sweethearts, from Mary Pickford onward, who are adored by women as well as by men, and that male political adventurers are cheered and adored by crowds of admirers of their own sex in ecstasies of sentiment in which sex has no part. Who has ever wanted to sleep with the Venus of Milo? Ninetynine hundredths of the sentiment in the world,

---

31. The 'Sug'red sonnets' description comes from Francis Meres in *Palladis Tamia* (1598). Thomas Tyler's study was an introduction to a facsimile of the first quarto of the *Sonnets* (1885). Butler's book was *Shakespeare's Sonnets Reconsidered* (1899); Wilde's, *The Portrait of Mr. W.H.* (1889); Douglas's, *The True History of Shakespeare's Sonnets* (1933).

including the maddest infatuations, are asexual. The fact is staring the psychoanalysts and the penners of redblooded thrillers in the face all the time; yet they
persist in hunting for what they call libido in every manifestation of it.

It was therefore very unlucky for Lord Alfred that the best known of the
attachments which he inspired and returned should have been with a man
who became notorious as a homosexualist, and that he remained faithful to
the attachment when Oscar came out of prison and was cut dead by most
of his respectable acquaintances; for it was immediately assumed, without a
scrap of evidence, that he was not only Wilde's closest friend but his accomplice. I have no doubt that Harris wrote this book under that impression.
Mr Sherard, in his 1906 book, alludes to Wilde's "evil genius," clearly meaning Lord Alfred. Mr Ransome's otherwise straightforward and judicial biography is spoilt by the same cruel mistake. Mrs Wilde's refusal to live with Wilde
when, after his imprisonment, he rejoined Lord Alfred at Naples, shews that
she was of the current opinion. What other objection could they have had
to the resumption of the old friendship? And, what mattered most, his father,
the Marquess of Queensberry, branded him with it publicly in the act of
branding Wilde. Until the publication of Lord Alfred's convincing and
extremely entertaining first hand account entitled *Without Apology* [1938],
deferred until this preface was already in print, there was no book available
which was not tainted more or less by the parental innuendo.

Now Lord Alfred resembled Shelley in two particulars. He was an authentic
poet, making language lyrical with a born mastery which shewed up the
artificiality of Wilde's metrical manufactures when the two were placed in
contrast. And, like Shelley again, he had come to hate his father, whom he
had idolized in his childhood as an amateur champion boxer and fearless
cross-country rider. He did not, as far as I know, entertain his schoolmates
with formal comminations of his parent as Shelley did; but as the Marquess
was far more vulnerable to criticism and even to invective than Timothy
Shelley, Lord Alfred was able to let him have both to an extent very far from
filial. "My father" he said "was an inhuman brute. He bullied and persecuted
and outraged my mother for years, long even before she divorced him seven
years before the Wilde case. He had for twenty years neglected and ill-treated
his children, and had forfeited all claim to a father's authority over them."
And again "My father was a madman and his mania was to persecute my
mother. My mother was and is an angel and a saint who has never done a
wrong thing or thought a wrong thought in her life."[32]

32. The quotations are from Douglas's *A New Preface to* [Harris's] *Life and Confession
of Oscar Wilde* (1925, reprinted as 'Full and Final Confession' in the 1930 American
edition of the biography). They appear also in the *Autobiography*.

The Marquess seems to have earned his son's opinion of him very thoroughly. He was a Scots Marquess, Earl, Viscount and Baron, with a fourfold contempt for public opinion, an ungovernable temper, and, after his divorce, a maniacal hatred of his family. His chief claim to respect was that he was an outspoken freethinker. He is still famous as the author of the rules[33] under which boxers have fought ever since boxing with gloves superseded the old prizefights with bare knuckles. Clearly not a man to be lightly braved by Wilde, who was no pugilist, or by the boldest of his friends. He was, when irritated, especially with his family, so foully abusive that his second son Percy was provoked to punch his head in broad daylight in Bond Street; and when the two were bound over to keep the peace in the police court nobody was surprised; for that was the sort of man the Marquess was known to be. [See p. 386 fn 46.]

It must be added that he and Lord Alfred were virtually strangers, a thing that happens easily in aristocratic families even when the father is not divorced. Consequently in Lord Alfred's intense dislike to his father, and in his father's inclusion of him in his feud against his family, there was nothing specially unnatural or surprising. What is both unnatural and surprising is that when Queensberry exposed and ruined Wilde by accusing him of having corrupted his son, the fact that he was ruining his son as well as Wilde was curiously overlooked, and has been so ever since. This may even have been his real object. Lord Alfred's own opinion on the point is unequivocal. "His pretended solicitude for his son and his alleged desire to save him were nothing but a hypocritical pretence, his real object being to do, what in effect he succeeded in doing, to ruin his son and finally break the heart of his martyred wife." [*New Preface*].

Certainly there was no doubt about his success. Without a particle of evidence the public rushed to the conclusion that Lord Alfred was Wilde's accomplice, and had in fact corrupted him. A juryman actually asked in court whether Lord Alfred was to be prosecuted, and, if not, why.[34]

33. The Queensberry Rules actually were devised, in 1867, by John Graham Chambers, founder of the Amateur Athletic Club.
34. This question was put by the foreman of the jury in the third trial. 'Quite so', replied Mr Justice Wills, 'but how does that relieve the defendant? Our present inquiry is whether guilt is brought home to the man in the dock . . . I believe that to be the recipient of such letters and to continue the intimacy is as fatal to the reputation of the recipient as to the sender. But you have really nothing to do with that at present.' A moment later Wills added, 'It is a thing we cannot discuss . . . [it] would be a prejudice of the worst possible kind' (*The Three Trials of Oscar Wilde*, ed. H. Montgomery Hyde, 1948).

Unfortunately Lord Alfred was too young (24) to take in the gravity of his situation. In point of contempt for Philistine opinion, of high temper and insensate courage, he was a chip of the old block; and though he knew that the libel on his father's visiting card could be justified, he was confident that he himself if called as a witness could give such an account of his father that no jury could give a verdict in his favor. He certainly proved afterwards that he was a champion client in getting round juries, and more than a match for the ablest cross-examiners and even the most prejudiced judges. It is true that the simple secret of his successes was his innocence; but as nobody believed in it (thanks to his father) it remained a secret.

Whether such a parricidal defence as he planned for the first trial would have met the views of a British jury cannot be decided, as Wilde's counsel did not think the case desperate enough to try it. He put Wilde in the box instead of Lord Alfred; and though Wilde held his own easily whilst his cross-examiner (Carson) was ill-advised enough to attempt a contest of repartee, the moment Carson came down to the flat facts of the case[35] Wilde collapsed; and his counsel,[36] who had evidently not known what was coming, had to surrender so completely that Wilde's arrest on the criminal charge became inevitable.

Why Wilde allowed Robert Ross to persuade him to prosecute the Marquess without consulting Lord Alfred is explicable partly by his swelled head, which had led him to believe that, as he himself put it, there was nothing which he could not carry through successfully: a delusion which seems to have taken possession of him when his success as a playwright brought him plenty of money for the first time;[37] and partly because Queensberry had got him in a cleft stick by obliging him either to fight or to be asked to resign from his club and be exiled. Harris's advice was sound, as it proved: he had better have faced his inevitable defeat at once and left the country; but there was something to be said for Lord Alfred's plan, which would at least have given the Queensberry family the satisfaction of exposing their unbearable progenitor as the monster he was to them, and discrediting his attack on his son's morals. But Douglas, being young, angry, and contemptuous of Harris

35. Queensberry's agents had been able to collect testimony over the previous several weeks, concerning intimacies at the Savoy Hotel and elsewhere, from hotel servants and male prostitutes, most of the latter provided by Alfred Taylor.
36. Sir Edward Clarke, eminent leader at the Bar and Solicitor-General under the Conservatives, 1886–92.
37. Wilde's *An Ideal Husband* and *The Importance of Being Earnest* opened six weeks apart and ran concurrently early in 1895.

and his guests, did not explain his plan. When the plan was dropped he agreed with Harris that there was no escape save by flight.

And so everything conspired to drive Oscar over the precipice and Lord Alfred with him. Lord Alfred, however, stuck to his guns and stuck to Oscar, who stuck to him when he came out of prison, with the result that Douglas was thoughtlessly rated as Oscar's evil genius, and Oscar given up as incorrigible. And wheras Oscar still had some friends and worshippers, including Mr Sherard, Frank Harris, Robert Baldwin Ross, Reginald Turner,[38] and others, Lord Alfred got fair play from nobody. When his father dropped out of notice and presently died, the son was cast for the villain of the piece; and every donkey had a kick at him until he set up a very effective terror by dragging his enemies into court, or defending himself when he was dragged in himself, with such prowess and success that at last no publisher or editor dared mention his name, and this book could not get into print in London. People complained that the son of a Marquess could do anything with impunity. Nobody except the juries with whom he came face-to-face realized that there was absolutely no case against him except a budget of old letters and sonnets in which his beauty was praised by male admirers. These things came up again and again; and Lord Alfred was quite willing that they should come up; for, not being at all ashamed of his personal beauty, he was quite willing that its trophies should be exhibited from time to time, all the more then the flowerlike youth hardened into the mature man and elicited no more such tributes. Yet it was just these tributes that kept alive the ill repute his father had fastened on him, and tempted his rivals in Wilde's affections to imagine that they could attack him with impunity. Out of court he hit back freely by establishing himself as editor and proprietor of a weekly paper [the *Academy*, 1907–10], and employing Thersites Crosland, whose harsh ul, he said, was sweet to him, as his lieutenant in a campaign in which ery vulnerable crown was rapped mercilessly and enemies were made in directions. At last, in a fit of quite conscientious war delirium, Douglas acked a man of his own rank, Mr Winston Churchill, and immediately lowed Oscar to prison for six months.[39]

A member of Wilde's circle who befriended him in France on his release from on and was with him when he died. He achieved a modest success as a novelist. In 1923 Douglas distributed a pamphlet claiming Churchill had manipulated s about the Battle of Jutland to allow stock-market profits to be made in New k by a small, powerful Jewish group. He further asserted that the sinking of the S *Hampshire* (5 June 1916) was the doing of Bolshevik Jewry supported by rchill, who promptly prosecuted him for libel, successfully. Douglas was

Wilde's friends were so contemptuous or jealous of oneanother that it is impossible to do anything but guess at the truth of their stories about him. In one respect they are unanimous: each one of them vouches for the shameless mendacity of all the others. For the moment there seems to be an alliance to crush Frank Harris; but the allies have long since crushed each other. Mr Sherard began by writing with marked respect about Harris and calling Lord Alfred Wilde's evil genius. Now Lord Alfred and Mr Sherard are united in a determination to prove that Harris's book is THE GREATEST LITER-ARY IMPOSTURE OF ALL TIME IN THE HISTORY OF ENGLISH LETTERS. Lord Alfred has gone farther. Having denounced Harris as a liar, and denounced Wilde as a liar in a pardonably angry book [*Oscar Wilde and Myself*, 1914] provoked by Ross's publication of the silly sequel to De Profundis,[40] he has finally denounced himself as a liar [in *Without Apology*], declaring that his book was written by Crosland and should never have been written at all. Mr Turner testified that Ross was a liar; and Lord Alfred had hardly epithets enough for Ross's mendacity, and only a very rude one for his homosexuality, finally driving him to take legal action[41] exactly as his father had driven Wilde, and winning a surrender in court almost as complete as Wilde's, but with the amazing result that Ross received a testimonial to his high character with over 300 distinguished signatures (including my own) and received a public appointment which he held to the day of his death,[42] the fact being that Robbie, though afflicted with a somewhat

sentenced to a prison term. In his preface to Sherard's book in 1937 Douglas wrote that, once Wilde had been sent to prison, this 'became the goal for any self-respecting English poet, and I never rested till I got there'. Shaw's remark that Lord Alfred 'immediately followed Oscar to prison' is subject to misconstruction. Douglas's imprisonment 'immediately followed' his conviction – in 1923.
40. Less than half of Wilde's letter to Douglas was published as *De Profundis* in 1905. A slightly enlarged text was included by Ross in his Collected Edition of Wilde's works, which in no way could be described as a 'silly sequel'. There was no further publication of the letter until 1949.
41. In the 1914 trial Douglas collected evidence against Ross from a number of young men, much as his father had done two decades earlier. The case was dismissed on Ross's plea of *nolle prosequi* after a jury had disagreed and failed to reach a verdict.
42. The public testimonial (to which Shaw contributed) was issued in March 1915, linked to a scholarship presented in Ross's name at the Slade School of Art. In the same year he was approached to allow himself to be put forward as candidate for the keepership of the National Gallery of Ireland, a post he would almost certainly have been offered. Concerned, however, about the volatile relationship between Britain and Ireland, he declined. Shaw's statement about the appointment is a misconception.

crapulous appearance which convinced everyone of us that Lord Alfred's worst epithet could be justified, was nevertheless so obliging and efficient in his business as an art dealer, and so pathetically grateful to us when we did not cut him dead, that he made friends everywhere by his very infamy.

As to Mr Sherard, he contradicts himself so recklessly on every second page that were it not for the passionate sincerity with which he pens both affirmations and contradictions he could easily be held up by an illnatured person—Crosland for example—as the prince of liars. And all this because Wilde had to beg from them, and therefore to pretend to each of them that he was getting no money from the others!

Outside this little circle there was a wider circle sorry for Wilde. Wilde's dignity did not permit him to beg from them crudely. He did therefore what Sheridan did under the same pressure. Sheridan did not beg and did not borrow from his more important friends: he only offered them Drury Lane Theatre debentures as an investment. Wilde, not owning Drury Lane or any other theatre, offered the plot of a play as an investment; and several among his real stage friends accepted the excuse and bought the plot, or a share in the plot, or however Wilde put it to them so as to make it appear that they were receiving a consideration for their generosities. At last the situation was changed by Harris, who not only bought the plot for £50 (plus another £50 later on) but took a theatre and produced a play founded on it, with a very popular actress in the title part. This was more than the other purchasers could stand. They had never dreamt of dunning Oscar for their money or taking the transaction seriously; but to allow Harris to get away with it and make lots of money out of it was quite another pair of shoes. They swept down on Harris, who had to buy them off as best he could. Harris gives a list of them; and they are all the sort of people who would be likely to give Oscar a lift for the sake of old times to the tune of a hundred pounds or less.

Mr Sherard shrieks that this is a malicious lie and that these transactions were invented by Harris in sheer spite against Wilde. He cannot possibly know anything about it unless he possesses the accounts of the Royalty Theatre (if any such exist); but he offers his usual unanswerable proof: the statement was made by Harris: Harris was a malicious liar: therefore the statement is a malicious lie. He forgets also, as usual, that he, Robert Harborough Sherard, in 1905 began the revelation of this side of Wilde's methods by his pitiable tale of how, at the moment of his utmost devotion to an unhappy friendship, he was sent by Oscar to Paris to try to extract some money from Sarah Bernhardt on the security of his play Salomé [1893], and desperately importuned that hardheaded lady until he had to be asked not to call again.

This story is far more likely to make Oscar's ghost wince than the later very pleasant and kindly account of the meeting with Ada Rehan, and her refusal to cut him dead in the days of his disgrace.

Then there is much intolerable stuff about Wilde's snobbery, meaning his love of aristocratic society and his resentment of any familiarity from the rank and file of the journalists of his day. Harris said that Wilde was a snob. I said that he was a snob (I, born in Dublin of a family of snobs, knew the Merrion Square variety only too well.) Douglas, who introduced him to the top layer of titled society in London, testifies that he was "in heaven" there. Mr Sherard protests before heaven and earth that we are all infamous liars and that Harris in particular is the Father of Lies. I refer him again to the foundations of Wilde's biography laid by himself in 1905. There he records how he dined with Wilde after the said ascent into heaven and found such a change in his host's manner that he did not repeat the experiment. In every case it is Mr Sherard who drives the criticism home by some stinging instance, and Harris who simply mentions the fact for what it is worth.

A more important matter in its bearing on the Queensberry case is the description given by Harris of Wilde's personal appearance. Wilde had an imposing presence, carrying himself always as a person of distinction. His eyes and forehead might be called beautiful. His nostrils were haughty, and proclaimed the snob, but not unpleasantly. But he inherited from his father an unsymmetrical mouth, and from his mother an acromegalic bulkiness[43] that looked obese as he developed into middle age. The point of this is that when he and Douglas met for the first time, he being Douglas's elder by 18 years, he must have appeared to Douglas as middle-aged and fat, and, however intellectually and histrionically attractive, physically repulsive. Beyond the suspicions of the crazy Marquess there is no reasonable ground for doubting Douglas's own statement that he made this repulsion so perceptible to Wilde that from many months before the Queensberry case to the end of Wilde's life it was understood that there should be no physical contacts between them. But Mr Sherard will have it that Wilde was an unblemished Apollo; that he was also a Samson who at Oxford vanquished four simultaneous assailants with contemptuous ease; and that anyone who records that the first impression Wilde made was slightly repulsive and had to be swept away as it always was by his charm of manner and wonderful conversation, is an infamous liar. And today he will not hear a word against Oxford during

43. Acromegalia is a chronic disease characterized by a gradual and permanent enlargement of the head, thorax, hands and feet, due to hyperactivity of the pituitary gland.

Wilde's residence there. Let him look at his 1905 book and read what he wrote about Oxford then. Here is what he wrote about Oscar. "Though in detail his clean-shaven face was not altogether comely, there was such beauty in the blazing intelligence of his fine eyes that if the first impression he produced was to startle, the second was one of entire admiration." Precisely.

As to Wilde himself, he had to lie or die when he could no longer live by his pen. His friends, tired, as Harris put it, of "holding up an empty sack" all urged him to write; but they forgot that his market was gone: no publisher or editor would have his name in his list: no manager would put it in his playbill. He had to beg; and he found that it was quite possible, with such friends as he had made, to live by begging whilst he was working hard as a conversationalist and humorist, which was his true vocation.

Now to get money out of Harris, Ross and Douglas, it was necessary to lie to them. When any of the three, on being asked to contribute, objected that Oscar was enjoying a pension from the others, he had to be assured that the others had not contributed a rap. Thus each of them was touched to the limit of his finances whilst being led to believe that all the others had deserted Wilde in his need. Naturally, after his death they accused oneanother freely of this heartlessness and then of lying about it.

The resultant quarrels were endless. Codlin and Short [itinerant showmen in *The Old Curiosity Shop*, 1841] both started from the silly notion that the Queensberry family was morally bound to support Wilde because it, especially Douglas, had ruined him by pushing him into the action against the Marquess to gratify the family hatred. Naturally Douglas, having a logical Scottish mind, and having given Wilde all he could spare, repudiated this claim so energetically that Harris was shocked, and assumed that Oscar had appealed to Douglas in vain. The claim was ridiculous because (a) Oscar's ruin was caused by his breach of the Criminal Law Amendment Act and by nothing else, (b) Douglas's advice to Wilde had been quite sound and disinterested, though he came round to Harris's counsel of flight when the lawyers had lost the day by refusing to fight the case on his lines, and (c) the Queensberry family, far from profiting by Oscar's disgrace, had themselves been disgraced by it, and must have detested him and deplored Douglas's continued attachment to him.

That attachment received a maddening blow, fortunately not permanent in its effect, when De Profundis, the excellent first half of which had produced a reaction in Wilde's favor and was understood to have a mysterious sequel at the British Museum which could not be published until everyone concerned was dead, was published by Ross in its entirety, when the sequel from which so much was expected turned out to be a letter addressed to Lord

Alfred of the most amazingly undignified kind, venting all sorts of petty grudges about the sharing of their expenses and omissions to visit Wilde when he had influenza and what not, trifles enough in themselves, but betraying the fact that Wilde, though he could inspire British friendships of the most devoted kind, was incapable of such friendships himself, though not, on occasion, of noble and generous gestures. In this connection it must not be forgotten that though by culture Wilde was a citizen of all civilized capitals, he was at root a very Irish Irishman, and, as such, a foreigner everywhere but in Ireland.

And so, after his death his friends began denouncing each other as liars, as deserters of their friend in his adversity, and even in some cases of complicity in his perversion. Lawsuits raged between them for years; and still, though we are now all old or elderly or dead, comes Mr Sherard's hysterical dithyramb to Wilde and anathematizing of Harris, to say nothing of myself.

It is time to put an end to these misunderstandings and recriminations by publishing Harris's book with the facts brought up to date, as he presumably would have corrected it were he still alive to do so. Lord Alfred's [1914] book, more than two thirds of which was written by Crosland, is withdrawn remorsefully. Mr Sherard's book of 1906 is out of fashion in its now unnecessary reticences. His 1937 volume is a masterpiece of confusion. There remains Harris, who, for the particular purpose of telling Wilde's story both artistically and sanely, was the noblest Roman of them all. He loved and admired Wilde, but always on this side idolatry: there is not in this book a line of the maudlin deification his British adorers wallow in. He confessed to a constitutional dislike of Douglas, though thanks to Lord Alfred's personal charm their contacts were very cordial except on one occasion when Harris was the nominal editor of a paper which tried to blackmail Lord Alfred.[44] Notwithstanding the dislike Harris placed Douglas as a poet on the level of Shakespear and

---

44. This is attempted whitewashing. Though nothing ever was proven, Harris had a reputation for blackmail. H. G. Wells, in *Experiment in Autobiography* (1934), expressed a belief that the 'blackmailer' image was 'pure romancing, for he achieved neither the wealth nor the jail that are the alternatives facing the serious blackmailer. He was . . . far too eager to create an immediate impression to be a proper scoundrel' (p. 441). Douglas, however, in a letter to Shaw on 20 April 1938 (*Bernard Shaw and Alfred Douglas*, ed. Mary Hyde, 1982) insisted Harris had attempted to blackmail him, and identified as the contact man the novelist Edgar Jepson, a staffer at *Vanity Fair* (of which Harris was co-editor, 1907–10). Harris had in 1907, according to Douglas in a letter to Elmer Gertz (published by Gertz in his Harris biography, 1931), communicated through Jepson a threat to publish in the next issue a sensational article about him, involving the Wilde scandal, but would consider quashing it for

Keats,[45] far above Wilde, and, though he did him some injustice (easily corrected now) did it without malice to the best of his information and belief, and with the further excuse that Lord Alfred during the Wilde episode did not lay himself out to be liked or even acquitted, belonging as he did to a generation of young bloods whose pet affectation it was to be steeped in impossible scarlet sins, and to *épater le bourgeois* not only by such paradoxes as they could invent, but by meeting every accusation of downright wickedness with an intimation that it was only half the terrible truth.

Douglas was still in this phase even in 1895; for though he was twentyfour [he became twenty-five on 22 October] he was a plant of very slow growth. When he was twentyseven he was refused admission to the gaming rooms at Monte Carlo on the ground that he was obviously younger than the manager's son, who was only sixteen. When the real disgrace brought on him by the Wilde affair cured him of the notion that shocking public opinion is splendid fun as well as an aristocratic privilege, he bought a moribund weekly paper called The Academy and made "the unspeakable Englishman" Crosland his chief of staff, with the result that the paper, well written and fearless enough to regain its circulation, seemed to be conducted with a view to giving the greatest offence to the greatest number. It perished, but had a successor called Plain English, in which the English was too plain to please everybody. It was killed by the patriotic delirium induced by the war: specifically by the battle of Jutland, which landed the editor in prison as aforesaid. Lord Alfred's career cannot, therefore, be classed as a conciliatory one; and as nothing corrupts justice so much as resentful dislike, he has suffered more than any of Wilde's friends from the campaigns of recrimination which will probably continue to rage round his memory until his last contemporary is dead. Finally, having joined the Roman Church, he relented greatly towards his dead father, whose quaint fate it was to have his head punched by his son and to be so far converted by his brother (a Catholic priest) from Atheism to faith in salvation by Jesus that he accepted conditional absolution and is

---

a few hundred pounds. When Douglas threatened to retaliate with a warrant for Harris's arrest for attempted blackmail and criminal libel, the article did not appear.
45. In *My Life and Loves* (vol. 4, chapter 1, 1923) Harris compared Douglas with Wordsworth as a high-ranking sonneteer, in a context that linked him also with Shakespeare. In *Oscar Wilde: His Life and Confessions* (vol. 2, chapter 25, 1916) Harris reproduced Douglas's sonnet written after Wilde's death, remarking that 'in sheer beauty and sincerity of feeling it ranks with Shelley's lament for Keats'. We are grateful to Fred D. Crawford for researching this for us.

therefore qualified to meet Lord Alfred in paradise.[46] Those of us who are not Catholics, and indeed some who are, cannot refrain from adding that we hope not. Not until 1935, forty years after his father struck him down, did Douglas play his ace of trumps by publishing his poems in two volumes [*Lyrics* and *Sonnets*, 1935] which his worst enemies cannot open without exclaiming almost at every page "For this be all thy sins forgiven thee" [Matthew 9: 2]. And at that I must leave him and return to Frank Harris.

It is still my opinion that though all Wilde's militant friends can write pretty well, none of them have Harris's trenchancy, his temperance, or his instinct for putting the truth of his portraiture before the indulgence of his likes and dislikes. Naturally his implied portrait of himself is not unflattering; but it is inimitably like him as he was in the nineties; and it is just the absence of Frank from the picture that makes all the other biographies incomplete. Only Harris could depict Harris: he, more than any man I have known, could give you in a single sentence a portrait of a contemporary which was also a portrait of himself. In literature he had a genuine hatred of falsehood as such, and, I repeat, got himself into trouble mainly by speaking his mind and finally by his efforts to break through the taboos that hampered literature in his time and thus to make honest writing possible for later realists like D. H. Lawrence and James Joyce. In the adversity which this brought on him he became fair game for Mr [Hugh] Kingsmill and the rest of his debunkers;[47] but with them this book has nothing to do: he had his hour of legitimate triumph as editor of the Saturday Review; and it is to that hour that the history of Oscar Wilde belongs. Of what he was in that hour Mr Sherard, ever chivalrous even in his utmost wrath, tells us that "he had much in him that I liked and admired." "As long as Harris was alive I allowed him to enjoy any happiness to the last minute of his life all the more readily because I heard that he was not very prosperous, that the man I remembered as

---

46. Lord Alfred's brother Percy (afterwards ninth Marquess of Queensberry) was a loyal supporter of both Alfred and Wilde. When he met his father in Piccadilly at the time of the disastrous last trial they exchanged words and blows until, finally, the police took them both into custody. When old Queensberry was on his deathbed he was visited by Lord Alfred's cousin, Archibald Douglas, a Catholic priest, who reported that the old man had renounced his atheism and professed his love for and faith in Jesus Christ to whom, he said, 'I have confessed all my sins.' Then, when Percy, his heir, approached the bedside he sat up and spat at him (Douglas, 'Full and Final Confession').

47. Hugh Kingsmill's debunking of Harris was in his *Frank Harris: A Biography* (1932). The deflation continued in his review of the 1938 edition of Harris's biography in the September issue of the *Fortnightly*.

buoyant, of radio-active vitality and an Ajax-like attitude towards the world, had come in his old age to no pleasant Latium, but, frail, feeble, and given to somnolence, was fighting an up-hill battle for existence (on lines of luxury certainly) for himself and the devoted wife whom he cherished."[48]

But this, handsome as it is from Mr Sherard, is but faint praise compared with the adulation of the young Harris fans, mostly American, who used to come to see me, not on my own account, but because I had once "seen Harris plain."[49] They were disgusted when I spoke of Harris as a mere human being and not as a demigod. Mr Sherard, in his very first chapter, quotes a string of tributes to Harris which will surprise many of his friends. They have, I confess, astonished me; for I have allowed myself to be persuaded that I was defending an underrated author. I thank Mr Sherard for enlightening me.

Accordingly, here is his book, with a few emendations which are now needed to prevent its misleading readers to whom the subject is new.

AYOT ST LAWRENCE.
9 January 1938.

---

48. Helen (Nellie) Harris, thirty years Frank's junior, was his second wife. Shaw's concern for the widow, who was in straitened circumstances, underlay his successful effort to win Douglas's approval for the first English publication of the book, and provision of a preface to increase its saleability.
49. An echo of Browning's 'Memorabilia' (1855): 'Ah, did you once see Shelley plain . . .'

# Pygmalion

*Spoken preface to the film version, 1938, for American audiences. First published in the* New York Times, *11 December 1938*

======

Oh, my American friends, how do you do? Now, since Ive got you all here, might I make a little speech? Right! I will. Do you mind if I sit down? I am very old.

Now, it's a delightful thing to sit here, and to think that although at this moment I'm sitting in London, I can talk in this way to an American audience. Oh—stop a minute—I quite forgot to tell you who I am. I am the author of the film that you are going to see, but I'm also Bernard Shaw.

Mind you, the Bernard Shaw. Your newspapers are so full of me that you must have heard about me. Now youve seen the animal. I hope you like it.

You know, Ive suffered a great deal from America in this matter of motion pictures. For years past youve been trying to teach me how to make a film. And I'm going to show you really how it should be done.

One thing that youve never dreamed of doing is—when you want to know how to make a film—send for the author. Youll never send for the author. Youll send for an electrician when the light goes wrong. Youll send for a photographic expert when the camera goes wrong. But when the play goes wrong, you send for anybody who happens to be about. Of course, I know it's not your fault. Youre not in this business. Well, thats the sort of thing that theyve been giving me in America, and the result is—my plays have not been filmed.

And, then, the American newspapers say that I dont want to have my plays screened and that Ive always refused to have them made. Ive never refused to have them filmed. I can do a great deal more with them on the screen than I can do on the stage. So dont you believe anything that you hear or read in the newspapers about me and about the film business. I know all about the motion picture business and I'm going to teach you—(I mean, of course, the gentlemen who make the films)—but I'm going to teach them what really a film should be like.

My friend, Mr Gabriel Pascal,[1] who has made this production, has tried

1. Hungarian film producer and director, whose production of *Pygmalion* (1938) was the first of four Shaw plays he brought to the screen, the others being *Major Barbara* (1941), *Caesar and Cleopatra* (1945) and *Androcles and the Lion* (1952).

the extraordinary experiment of putting a play on the screen just as the author wrote it and as he wanted it produced.

If you agree with me when you see this film of mine—if you enjoy it, very well. Youll shew it in the usual way by coming to see it—each of you—about twenty times. And then, if you do that, there will be other films. I'm thinking of doing an American play that I once wrote called The Devil's Disciple. Probably another play of mine, Cæsar and Cleopatra, you may see that on the film. But the really good thing about it is that when you have seen these on the screen—and if you like them—all the American films will become much more like my films. And that will be a splendid thing for America, and it wont be such a bad thing for me. Although, as you know, I'm pretty near the oldest writer here, and I shant have much enjoyment of them.

Youll have to make up your mind that youll lose me presently, and then, Heaven only knows what will become of America. I have to educate all the nations. I have to educate England. Several of the Continental nations require a little education, but America most of all. And I shall die before Ive educated America properly. But I'm making a beginning.

Now I think it's time for me to get out of the way. I was asked to say something to you. I'm always glad to say something to you. I was asked to say something very agreeable to you. Ive done my best. Thats my aged idea of an agreeable speech. But, I'm quite friendly. I think youve always heard that about me; at any rate, it's been written—you ought to.

# My Apology for This Book

*First published as 'The Autobiographer's Apology' in* Shaw Gives Himself Away,
*a limited edition issued by the Gregynog Press, 1939. Revised and retitled
for* Sixteen Self Sketches, *1949*

===

People keep asking me why I do not write my own biography. I reply that I am not at all interesting biographically. I have never killed anybody. Nothing very unusual has happened to me. The first time I had my hands examined by a palmist he amazed me by telling me the history of my life, or as much of it as he had time for. Apparently he knew about things I had never told to anyone. A few days later I mentioned in conversation with a friend (William Archer) that I had been dabbling in palmistry. He immediately put out his hand and challenged me to tell him anything in his life that I did not know from my acquaintance with him. I told him about himself exactly what the palmist had told me about myself.

He too was amazed, just as I had been. We had believed our experiences to be unique, wheras they were ninetynine-point-nine per cent the same; and of the point-one per cent the palmist had said nothing.

It was as if a couple of monkeys had believed their skeletons to be unique. To the extent of a bone or two they would have been right; for anatomists tell us that no two skeletons are exactly alike. Consequently a monkey is fully entitled to exhibit his unique bone or two as curiosities; but the rest of his skeleton he must reject as totally uninteresting. He must keep it to himself on pain of boring people with it intolerably.

And here comes my difficulty as an autobiographer. How am I to pick out and describe that point-five per cent of myself that distinguishes me from other men more or less fortunate than I? What earthly interest is there in a detailed account of how the illustrious Smith was born at Number Six High Street, and grew taller and taller until he was twenty, when the obscure Brown, Jones, and Robinson, born at Number seven, eight, and nine, went through exactly the same routine of growing, feeding, excreting, dressing and undressing, lodging and moving? To justify a biography Smith must have had adventures. Exceptional things must have happened to him.

Now I have had no heroic adventures. Things have not happened to me: on the contrary it is I who have happened to them; and all my happenings have taken the form of books and plays. Read them, or spectate them; and you have my whole story: the rest is only breakfast, lunch, dinner, sleeping, wakening, and washing, my routine being just the same as everybody's routine. Voltaire tells you in two pages all you need know about Molière's private life [in *Œuvres de Molière. Nouvelle édition*, ed. Voltaire, 1765]. A hundred thousand words about it would be unbearable.

Then there is the difficulty that when an adventure does come, somebody else is usually mixed up in it. Now your right to tell your own story does not include the right to tell anyone else's. If you violate this right, and the other party still lives, you are sure to be indignantly contradicted; for no two people recollect the same incident in the same way; and very few people know what has actually happened to them, or could describe it artistically. And biographies must be artistic if they are to be readable.

The best autobiographies are confessions; but if a man is a deep writer all his works are confessions. One of the greatest men who ever attempted an autobiography was Goethe [*My Life: Poetry and Truth*, 1811−22]. After his childhood, which is the readablest part of even the worst autobiography, his attempts to escape from his subject are pitiable. He takes refuge in sketches of all the Toms, Dicks, and Harrys he knew in his youth, persons utterly unmemorable, until the book drops from your hand and is not picked up again. I am one of the very few people who have read Rousseau's confessions [1782−9] through to the end, and can certify that from the moment when he ceases to be a rather rascally young adventurer, and becomes the great Rousseau, he might as well be anybody else for all one can grasp or remember of his everyday life.

Of Madame de Warens when he was sixteen I have a lively recollection. Of Madame d'Houdetot when he was fortyfive I have not the faintest impression, and remember only the name.[1] In short, the confessions tell us next to nothing of any importance about the adult Rousseau. His works tell us everything we need know. If Shakespear's everyday life from his birth to his death were to come to light, and Hamlet and Mercutio to be simultaneously lost, the effect would be to substitute a perfectly commonplace man for a very interesting one. In the case of Dickens so much is known about him that might have happened to Wickens or Pickens or Stickens that his

---

1. Louise de Warens was a young and pretty woman, at Annecy, who had deserted her husband and become a convert to Catholicism. In 1728 she became the boy Rousseau's first guiding spirit and lover, influencing him to embrace the faith. Later, his passion for Madame d'Houdetot, unreciprocated, provided an inspiration for his novel *La nouvelle Héloïse* (1761).

biographers have obliterated him for those who do not read his books, and for those who do, spoilt his portrait very painfully.

Therefore the autobiographical fragments which pad this volume do not present me from my own point of view, of which I am necessarily as unconscious as I am of the taste of water because it is always in my mouth. They tell you mostly what has been overlooked or misunderstood. I have pointed out, for instance, that a boy who knows the masterpieces of modern music is actually more highly educated than one who knows only the masterpieces of ancient Greek and Latin literature. I have illustrated the wretched lot in our society of the Downstart, as I call the boy-gentleman descended through younger sons from the plutocracy, for whom a university education is beyond his father's income, leaving him by family tradition a gentleman without a gentleman's means or education, and so only a penniless snob. I have thought it well to warn the young that it is as dangerous to know too much as to know too little, to be too good as to be too bad, and how Safety First lies in knowing and believing and doing what everyone knows and believes and does.

These things are mentioned not because I have been unbearably persecuted nor as yet assassinated, but because they concern my whole Downstart class, and, when intelligibly stated and understood, may help to make it class conscious and better behaved. Thus, being incorrigibly didactic, I violate the biographical laws I began this apology with by telling you little about myself that might not have happened to a thousand Shaws, and a million Smiths. Perhaps our psychoanalysts may find in such dull stuff clues that have escaped me.

To relieve the dulness there are tales of my relatives which must be read as ordinary fiction, the Irish Family Shaw having been occasionally funnier than [Johann Wyss's] the Swiss Family Robinson [English tr., 1820], and perhaps not less instructive to those who are capable of such instruction. As to myself, my goods are all in the bookshop window and on the stage: what is communicable has been already communicated in a long life of which, though I cannot say that no day of it has been left without a written line,[2] yet I have perhaps brought it as near to that Roman ideal as is healthily and humanly possible.

AYOT ST LAWRENCE.
15 January 1939.
Revised, 1947.

---

2. Condensation of a passage by Pliny the Elder in *Historia Naturalis*, Book XXXV, chapter 36, section 10.

# Major Barbara

*Spoken preface to the film version, 1941, for American audiences. First published in* PM's Weekly, *New York, 19 January 1941*

=====

Citizens of the United States of America, the whole 130 millions of you

I am sending you my old plays, just as you are sending us your old destroyers. Our government has very kindly thrown in a few naval bases as well; it makes the bargain perhaps more welcome to you.[1] Now, the German humorist, I think his name is Dr Goebbels,[2] he has got a great deal of fun out of that. He tells us—or rather he tells the rest of the world—that England has sold her colonies for scrap iron. Well, why shouldnt we? We are in very great need of scrap iron. We are collecting iron from door to door. Our women are bringing out their old saucepans; our men are bringing out their old bicycles, and you, with equal devotion, are bringing out your old destroyers. Well, a very good bargain for us. Every one of those destroyers will be worth much more to us than their weight in bicycles and saucepans.

And now, what about our colonies? Our colonies are always much the better when we have plenty of Americans visiting them. You see, in America you have all the gold in the world. We have to barter things for want of that gold, and accordingly, when we see Americans coming along with gold to spend, when we think of our colonies with American garrisons in them, we are delighted.

If you had only known, we would have given you those naval bases—Dr Goebbels calls them colonies, but let us be correct and call them naval bases—you could have had those naval bases for nothing but your friendship. Absolutely nothing. We should have been only too glad to have you. In fact, if you would like a few more, say in the Isle of Wight or the Isle of Man, or on the West Coast of Ireland, well, we shall be only too glad to welcome you. Delightedly!

Now, here I am in an English county, one of the counties that we call

---

1. In desperate need of escort vessels for convoys in the early stage of World War II, Britain leased a number of naval bases to the United States in September 1940 in return for fifty over-age destroyers.
2. Joseph Goebbels, Nazi Party minister for propaganda.

the home counties.[3] I am within forty minutes' drive of the center of London, and at any moment a bomb may crash through this roof and blow me to atoms, because the German bombers are in the skies. Now, please understand, I cant absolutely promise you such a delightful finish to this news item. Still, it may happen, so dont give up hope—yet. If it does happen, well, it will not matter very much to me. As you see, I am in my eightyfifth year. I have shot my bolt, I have done my work. War or no war, my number is up. But if my films are still being shewn in America, my soul will go marching on, and that will satisfy me.

When I was a little boy, a child, just taught to read, I saw in the newspaper every day a column headed The Civil War in America. That is one of my first recollections. When I grew up they told me that that war in America had abolished black slavery, so that job having been done, I determined to devote my life as far as I could to the abolition of white slavery. That is just as much in your interest as it is in my interest or that of England. I hope you will have a hand in that abolition as you had a hand in the last abolition.

And I dont think I need detain you any longer. Look after my plays and look after my films. They are all devoted to the abolition of that sort of slavery. And I should like to imagine that when my mere bodily stuff is gone, I should like to imagine that you are still working with me, with my soul—in your old phrase—at that particular job. That is all I have got to say. And so, farewell!

---

3. These are the counties – Middlesex, Surrey, Kent and Essex – that encircle the administrative county of London, all of them at least partially within the Greater London area. A few adjoining counties – Berkshire, Buckinghamshire, Hertfordshire and Sussex – are sometimes classified in this category.

# Major Barbara

*Written preface to the film version, 1941, for British audiences, reproduced on the screen calligraphically. First published in the* Daily Herald, *London, 21 February 1941*

———

Friend

What you are about to see is not an idle tale of people who never existed and things that could never have happened. It is a parable.

Do not be alarmed; you will not be bored by it. It is, I hope, both true and inspired. Some of the people in it are real people whom I have met and talked to.

One of the others may be YOU.

There will be a bit of you in all of them. We are all members one of another.

If you do not enjoy every word of it we shall both be equally disappointed.

Well, friend, have I ever disappointed you? Have I not been,

always your faithful servant
G. Bernard Shaw?

# The R.A.D.A. Graduates' Keepsake

*Graduates of the Royal Academy of Dramatic Art in 1941 (and for some years afterwards)
received a small book titled* The R.A.D.A. Graduates' Keepsake & Counsellor
*(privately printed, 1941, with two later printings), created and underwritten
by Bernard Shaw, who provided an unsigned preface and edited the dozen messages
from theatre luminaries and friends of the theatre that filled the remaining
pages of the slim volume*

======

With your diploma as a graduate of the Royal Academy of Dramatic Art
you now pass honorably into the ranks of an ancient and famous profession.
Your personal reputation and your professional achievements are henceforth
bound up with the credit not only of the Academy but with that of the
standing of theatrical art in the civilized world. The road is open for you to
the utmost that your ability can command or your ambition desire, including
a celebrity and popularity equal to and sometimes greater than that enjoyed
by the most eminent statesmen, scholars, soldiers, divines, or great public
servants of whatsoever degree.

Such a position has inestimable privileges; but it has also its strict obligations;
and it is in respect of these that we must not leave you to face them without
a word or two of counsel on points of conduct for which the technical skill
and practice we have given you may leave you unprepared.

Unless you have given some consideration to this, your first impulse may
be to say that your private conduct is your own affair. This is not so: you
are now a public servant in the widest sense; and in direct proportion to your
success will be the publicity given to the most intimate events in your life
off the stage. A successful player has no private life.

You may contend more reasonably that you have been sufficiently well
brought up to know how to behave yourself without any instruction from
the Academy. To a considerable extent this is true; and within that extent
we shall not presume to interfere with you. But it is not wholly true. In
every profession by which its members earn their living there are not only
the general morals of the community but a stringent professional etiquet to
which the general morality gives no clue and of which the best bred novice
may be blamelessly but completely ignorant. A disregard of this etiquet may
in extreme cases make it impossible for you to obtain engagements as a player.
You may find yourself blacklisted by managements and boycotted by your

fellow players without being guilty of any offence against the common code.

In the professions which are officially recognized and organized more or less by the State: for example the medical, legal, and clerical professions, the conditions are controled by law. A medical doctor cannot practise as qualified and privileged until he is inscribed on a register kept by the General Medical Council; and he may be struck off that register if he offends against professional etiquet. A barrister may not plead in the courts until he has been called to the Bar, and can be disbarred if he, too, is guilty of professional misconduct. A clergyman may not officiate in an established church until he is ordained; and he can be silenced or even unfrocked if he lives scandalously or alters the prescribed ritual according to his private fancy.

In these respects the artistic professions are apparently free. David Garrick was a stagestruck wine merchant who began his career as an actor without any qualifying process or ceremony whatever. You with your diploma would have been justified in dismissing him as an unqualified practitioner. Until the establishment of the Royal Academy of Dramatic Art in 1904,[1] British players, with or without a few lessons in elocution, picked up their profession on the stage as best they could; and it is still open to those who can to do the same. This is true also of the professions of literature, painting and statuary, music and the fine arts generally.

You must not, however, conclude that these professions, including your own, are completely anarchic because they are not legally organized. The competition among players for engagements would reduce their salaries to bare subsistence point, and even below it in the case of women, if there were not among them an understanding that they must not obtain employment by underselling oneanother or playing without payment for the fun of it.

And here you meet a difficulty peculiar to the artistic professions. It will be your privilege to find in the earning of your living the enjoyment of your greatest pleasure. Players seek their work for its own sake, and are unhappy as well as penniless when unemployed. A player with a private fortune will take a theatre and risk losing it all rather than do anything but act. A player with sufficient private means to be independent of salary is under a strong temptation to obtain engagements by consenting to play either without any salary or for less than a player in a less enjoyable position could live on.

You have only to imagine yourself having the bread taken out of your

---

1. The Academy of Dramatic Art (later royalized) was founded by the actor–manager H. Beerbohm Tree, who housed it in the upper reaches of His Majesty's Theatre. Shaw, appointed to its Council in 1911, served for thirty years, bequeathing to it one third of his residuary estate at his death in 1950.

mouth by a fellow player taking an engagement from you in this way to understand the intensity of the feeling against it. Women players stand in special need of this protection, as it is unfortunately possible for women without skill, talent, training or vocation as players to use the stage to advertize their real profession, with the connivance of managers whose theatres are not temples of the drama but houses of drink and disorder. These are disagreeable facts; but it is not yet possible to allow a woman to enter on a stage career without warning her that if she plays for less than a standard subsistence wage she will not only commit a grave professional misdemeanor, but class herself with disorderly persons who, when charged in the police courts, describe themselves as "actresses."

Male players are not placed in this situation, though it is most necessary that they should understand it; for they are equally bound, whatever their private means or necessities may be, never to obtain nor compete for employment by underselling a fellow player or accepting less than the standard salary. That standard salary is fixed by a professional association formed by the players for their own protection, all the members agreeing to accept the limits which the association sets to their individual liberty in business matters. This association is called the British Actors' Equity Association, called shortly Equity. Join it at once if you have not already done so.

The professional association cannot restrict increases in the remuneration of the player; for though it must set a limit below which the salary must not fall, there is no upper limit except that set by the money obtainable in the box offices and at the pay boxes when all the concurrent expenses of theatrical management have been deducted from it.

The effect of this is to confront the player with the problem of what salary to ask or accept over and above the prescribed minimum. This is made difficult by the impossibility of equating money with fine art. You will be tempted at first to hold that the different grades of your art should be paid according to their dignity; but you will soon find that on the stage the salary is often in inverse ratio to the dignity. The player most eminent in classical tragedy cannot hope to be paid as well as the most popular low comedian. Stepdancing[2] and singing vulgar trash at a variety theatre may bring the

2. Vigorous dancing with intricate steps, performed principally in music halls; described by Shaw as 'very rapid and neat bravura . . . [danced] with the feet alone, with spine rigid, shoulders pushed up to the top of it and nailed hard there, fists clinched, neck stiff as iron, and head held convulsively as if only the most violent effort of continence on the dancer's part could keep it from exploding' ('A Musical Farce', *Saturday Review*, 9 January 1897; reprinted in *Our Theatres in the Nineties*, 1932, 3: 10, 12).

performer a bigger and less precarious income than excellence in Shakespear or the great dramatic poets of ancient Greece. It may be more honorable to be great as Clytemnestra or Medea, Rosalynde or Lady Macbeth, Hamlet or Lear, than to be a very funny circus clown or pantomime dame; but it is not always more lucrative in the commercial theatre. You must therefore be content with what you are commercially worth, leaving the dignity of your repertory and your cultural value to your country out of the question. In view of the periods of unemployment you will have to face, and the style in which you will be expected and obliged to live, your bare subsistence wage may be much higher than that of educated persons in ordinary commercial employment where an engagement may last for thirty years; but over and above that your commercial value will be what you can draw: that is, the difference in money between the receipts when your name is in the bill and when it is not, less a profit to the management sufficient to make it worth while to collect it for you.

Passing now from such counsel as we have been able to give you for your guidance in your business affairs, a word or two as to your personal conduct may be of service to you. The player's art frequently involves actual physical contacts which the slightest personal carelessness on the part of the practitioner might make intolerably disagreeable. An author may smoke strong cigars, drink ardent spirits, wear unpleasantly shabby clothes, shun baths, and feed on tripe and onions without losing a single reader or offending a single member of an audience; but an actor who attempted to play Romeo under such conditions would not obtain a second engagement with the same management or the same Juliet, though she would not care how many cigars Mercutio smoked nor how many glasses of whiskey he shared with Tybalt. So far, Dean Swift's dictum that good manners are simply good sense[3] will serve you on the stage as elsewhere; yet the world behind the curtain is so secret and invisible that it is easy at first to conclude that manners and conventions there must be different. Beware of this error. Professional etiquet imposes additional obligations: it does not absolve you from those of ordinary social intercourse.

A player at work has to maintain a double consciousness, both as the character to be impersonated and imposed on the senses of the audience with all its illusions of imaginary time and space, and as a disguised player going through a prearranged set of movements on a stage, knowing exactly what is going to happen, including what is going to be said and replied, speaking so as to be heard in the back row of the pit and moving so as to be visible

---

3. Jonathan Swift, *A Treatise on Good Manners and Good Breeding* (*c.* 1720): 'I insist that good sense is the principal foundation of good manners.'

there, and perhaps simulating a tragic death whilst taking care not to fall where the curtain will descend across the apparently inanimate body. The players must never forget themselves in the heat of their dramatic imagination. A kiss must not be a real kiss, a blow a real blow, nor must Othello's fingers leave a bruise on Desdemona's or Iago's throat: such professional misdemeanors admit of no excuse.

For your own sake also remember that though tragedy may call for apparently superhuman violence and intensity, these must be illusions produced by the technical skill of perfectly selfpossessed players who would destroy themselves by any attempt at realism. The greatest actors can play the most arduous parts without turning a hair.

Double consciousness is natural to born players and playwrights: if not, it must be acquired as an indispensable sixth sense.

And here we must give you a special warning on a subject of which you may be entirely ignorant, as it belongs to the scientific rather than to the artistic side of the art of acting. Since Hypnotism, after a century of discreditable quackery, was placed on a scientific basis by a British doctor in 1841,[4] it has been known that many people, of whom you may be one, can be thrown into a condition in which they become, in effect, not themselves but quite different persons suggested to them by the hypnotist. They can be made to behave in ludicrously absurd ways for the entertainment of audiences; and this has been exploited by entertainers calling themselves electro-biologists and the like to such an extent that the practice has been made illegal on the Continent. It is used legitimately in surgery to enable patients to whom the ordinary anesthetics might prove fatal to endure operations without pain. It is used in maternity cases under the name of twilight sleep. Hypnotized persons have been known to exercise faculties and powers which in their normal condition they do not possess. The fiction of Svengali and Trilby [George du Maurier, *Trilby*, 1894] is founded on established facts; but Svengali is not indispensable; for it is now known that many persons can induce the hypnoidal condition in themselves by the exercise of their own imagination, prompted by circumstances and not by other individuals.

Perhaps the most astonishing omission in the study of this branch of psychology and its later developments in psychotherapy is that of the hypnosis of the player, whose profession it is to assume an imaginary personality at the suggestion of the playwright, and even to create one when the playwright has failed to suggest one. It is a fact well known in the theatre that players

4. Dr James Braid, a Manchester physician, explored the subject of mesmerism and originated the term 'hypnotism', which at first was known as 'neurohypnotism'.

disabled by illness or accident in their own persons can become unconscious of their disability on the stage and play as if they were in perfect health. The late Robert Loraine,[5] a soldier-actor, when so severely wounded in the knee that he walked very lamely with the aid of a stick, could and did, in the character of Cyrano de Bergerac, stride all over the stage and fence in stage duels without halting or feeling the slightest pain. Temperatures that would send unhypnotized people to bed, sciaticas, rheumatisms, even paralyses, have been forgotten when the player comes on the stage or is pushed on to it. This may seem incredible to you, because you may be one of those who cannot be hypnotized, and who acquire the art of acting with difficulty through a positiveness of character which resists any sort of transfiguration. But that it exists in various degrees is beyond all question. And there is a danger in it which you must never forget.

Just as a badly lamed man may on the stage dance and fence like a sound one, a hopelessly drunk player may on the stage be as sober as a judge. And just as the patients of Richet and Charcot[6] rose to powers that were quite beyond their normal capacities, an actor [Edmund Kean] stimulated with overdoses of brandy drew from so exacting a critic as Coleridge the tribute that to see him act was to see Shakespear's plays by flashes of lightning. But that great actor died before he was fifty, as others did who, not content with their natural powers, used up their vital capital for the sake of a few years of a fictitious glamor. This is the danger against which we feel bound to warn you. If you resort to an abuse of stimulants you will soon be unable to act without them; then without more and more of them; finally you will be blacklisted by managers as an undesirable, unless you forestall that tragedy by a premature death.

Note also that drugs more potent and more rapidly destructive than alcohol have been discovered. In spite of the most stringent laws they are offered for sale by secret agents. Be on your guard against them, and content yourself with your natural powers kept at their highest efficiency by taking care of your physical and mental health. Bear in mind, however, that the training undergone by professional athletes for short periods at long intervals is not suitable for players who have to perform their feats daily—sometimes twice nightly—all the year round.

5. British actor, who toured the United States and Canada for several years as Tanner in *Man and Superman*, was a close friend of Shaw.
6. Charles Richet, French physiologist, specialized in psychical phenomena. Jean Charcot, French neurologist, influenced one of his students, Sigmund Freud, through his work on hysteria and hypnotism.

Do not forget that though youth and the charm peculiar to it have their value in the theatre, yet, as they must pass so soon from you to the younger generation knocking at the door, the trade in them is a blind alley occupation, wheras good acting finds a market on the stage at all ages.

Among the professional relations which are sometimes difficult are those between the player, the producer, and the author. The producer, like the orchestral conductor, is a modern innovation. Until the last quarter of the XIX century his work was done, as far as it was done at all, by the stage manager, who addressed every actress as Darling and every actor as Old Boy, and swore freely at the extras, whom he called supers. What he was at his worst may be guessed from the caricatures of him in Pinero's Trelawny of the Wells.[7] His supersession by the modern producer is an advance; but producers must not forget that qualified players are neither marionettes, schoolchildren, nor employees with no interest in the directions they receive. They may have strong views of their own as to how parts and plays should be treated; and as authors may be misunderstood by producers, conflicts may arise which only the greatest tact on all sides can end agreeably. Production is part of the business of an author; but there are authors who cannot produce and will not learn, just as there are composers who cannot conduct. And authors are not always available for rehearsals. Shakespear and Eschylus may have been good producers; but they are both dead; and the treatment of their plays by producers and actor-managers has often been shocking. A tradition-ridden producer may insist that Roderigo [in *Othello*] is a low comedian and that all Sheridan's male characters should end their speeches with Ha ha ha; but no player is bound to accept such traditions. The producer must convince the players that his (or her) view is the right view.

Even when agreement is reached as to the view there is still room for disagreement as to the execution. A player may say to the producer "You are not here to teach me to act. That is my business, not yours. You will arrange the stage and its furniture. You will plan my exits and entrances and positions so that whatever I have to say or do will be said and done conveniently and effectively. That drudgery is your business, not mine; and beyond that you will please not interfere with me."

A player making such a speech to a producer would be entirely within his or her rights; but only a player of sufficient eminence to be indispensable as a public attraction could afford to make it in a commercial theatre, as producers have so much power there in the selection of casts that it is not wise to

---

7. One of Sir Arthur Pinero's few enduring plays (1898), a romantic comedy relating to a theatrical company.

quarrel with them. On the producer's part it would be disgraceful to provoke such an outburst, as it is part of a producer's art to know how far the players need direction and how much they are capable of. If the producer and the player know their places, and are tactful, matters will not come to this extreme.

But there is the opposite extreme, which is seldom reached except in the case of plays which reflect, not conventional morals, but the beginnings of a change in the world's mind on social questions. It may then happen that a player may say to a producer something like this. "I do not understand this play, and do not like it. The character I have to impersonate does not say anything that it would ever occur to me to say, nor think nor feel as I should if such things happened to me. I can memorize my lines. I can laugh or cry when you tell me to, though I can see nothing to laugh at or to cry about. I can pretend to be inspired by speeches that disgust me. If you insist I can wait for a derisive laugh when I say something I quite agree with. I will take your word for it that I can gain the sympathy of the audience by behaving like an eccentric and unaccountable cad. But as the whole affair seems to me to be nasty nonsense you must coach me in it line by line, and take the consequences."

You may say that a player who feels in this way about a play and part should not accept the engagement; but until you reach the very top of the tree you cannot make a living in the theatre if you confine yourself to parts in which you can be simply yourself under a fictitious name. In the historical drama a player can quite honestly impersonate Napoleon without being a military genius, Newton without mastering the infinitesimal calculus, Richelieu without being a Roman Catholic, and Florence Nightingale without being an anti-vaccinationist. All that can be said in that direction is that the more sympathetic a part is to a player the better it will be played; yet even this cannot be admitted by an actor who specializes in melodramatic villains or an actress who finds herself always engaged to play vampires or poisoners. Many players delight in parts that are as unlike themselves as possible; and some who excel in what are called character parts involving elaborate disguises are overcome with shyness and quite useless in "straight parts." In the pantomime of Puss in Boots the principal boy can and indeed must be her own charming self; but the cat must not be even human.

In any case the player needs a skilled observer and listener watching the rehearsals intently and critically, and noting every point at which the performance can be improved and the players helped. This is a service which a player has a right to expect; and to resent it as an interference would be silly. The best and most experienced players may drop a line, slur a key word, lose the full advantage of a position, distract the attention of the audience by some untimely movement from a fellow player who has to hold the stage for the moment, overlook something wrong with wig or makeup or costume, or in a dozen ways need a skilled watcher to detect the slip. Such skilled watching, though it is mainly concerned with trifles that have nothing to do with the meaning of the play or the appropriate conception of its parts, nevertheless makes all the difference between a finished metropolitan performance and a happy-go-lucky provincial one.

There are, however, matters in which the player's health and endurance may conflict with the convenience of the producer or the management. A producer or manager has no more right to prolong rehearsals beyond reason than the manager of a factory is permitted to by law. When such abuses become intolerable they should be dealt with collectively by the professional association and not by individual players as a personal grievance. Producers, like other directors, must attain their results within limits imposed by the welfare of their collaborators. If they cannot produce presentable results within these limits, they have mistaken their profession. A portrait painter cannot have unlimited sittings, nor a landscape painter elaborate his picture until autumn has become winter. An author cannot rewrite his chapters and revise his proofs until they reach ideal perfection. And producers cannot have a hundred rehearsals nor prolong them until the last trains and buses have gone, and the company is tired out and half asleep. Players who fear being blacklisted by producers if they refuse to comply with such unreasonable demands should remember that it is equally possible for producers to be blacklisted by the professional association, and that players who consent to work for excessive hours are as much enemies of their profession as those who accept less than standard subsistence salaries.

In any case an atmosphere of coercion in a theatre is as fatal to genuine artistic cooperation as an atmosphere of envy and jealousy. Players who cannot bear to hear other players praised, or will not loyally help other players as far as they can to make the best of their parts, may be good actors; but they also are wicked persons, bad comrades, and traitors in the battle for success all round, victory in which benefits the whole company. As between players of equal popularity engagements will always fall to the most helpful and considerate. When a gifted player complains of a difficulty in getting engagements whilst mediocrities and utilities apparently have a mysterious power of keeping in with the managements, the explanation is simply the likes and dislikes created by consideration for others and jealous selfishness.

Inexperienced authors must be borne with, as it is unwise to offend them, and there is no academy in which they can learn their stage business as you have learnt yours. They expect the first rehearsal to be a perfect performance, and, knowing all about the play themselves, are upset by finding that the players know comparatively nothing about it. They are dismayed when, after the preliminary book-in-hand rehearsals at which the stage business is settled, and in which the play shapes itself encouragingly, the books are banished and the acting suddenly lost in an agony of memorization in which the least interruption is unbearable, though the author wants to remonstrate at every line, and in extreme cases has to be kept out of the theatre or suppressed as a disorderly person. Also authors are apt to complain without knowing how to direct; they discourage without knowing what to expect and when to expect it; they worry about shortcomings that will cure themselves and disappear automatically. All this must be endured with what goodhumor is possible until the author learns his business by experience, and becomes, as every author should, a skilled producer.

In film work the extent to which the time and endurance of the players may be wasted through want of organization is so great that players must defend themselves vigorously through their professional association. No trade unionist workman will do a stroke of work that is not part of his particular technical job, nor tolerate such a proceeding on the part of a fellow worker; but a player may be called on to repeat a scene over and over until the words have lost all meaning to enable the producer and camera man to arrive by trial and error at the exact lighting they desire. The rebellion of the stars against this has produced the stand-in substitute; but much more could be done in this and other ways to relieve the players from mechanical drudgeries that spoil their artistic work and in any case are as foreign to their specific art as scene shifting or theatre cleaning. But such abuses cannot be remedied by individual complaints and "making scenes" at rehearsals. The electrician will not do the work of the scene shifter; but both would be helpless slaves without their trade unions; and the players must realize that unless and until they have a strong professional organization, providing for its funds and obeying its rules, they, too, will be slaves in the hands of their employers and directors. The unorganized strolling player is no longer classed by the magistrate as a masterless man, a rogue and a vagabond, nor need he belong to the household of a nobleman as Shakespear had to. Letters are no longer addressed "To Betterton the player"[8] without Mister or Esquire; but for all that the position of the average player is as precarious as the income; and the credit readily given by the shops to the barrister and the clergyman is denied

8. Thomas Betterton, a late seventeenth-century versatile actor, created about 130 new roles in addition to performing the standard 'classic' roles of Hamlet, Lear, Othello and Macbeth.

to customers who give the stage as their profession. Only by strong professional organization can the profession attain the social consideration and official recognition accorded without question to the "learned" professions.

Make the utmost possible use of the professional association in business dealings. For example, if a manager tries to induce you to play for less than the standard minimum salary, and uses the unpardonable argument that if you will not accept it he can easily find others who will, you may, according to your temperament, shrink from hurting his feelings or offending him by a flat refusal, or feel strongly tempted to tell him off as a sweater with a few expletives thrown in. The correct course is to regret politely that the rules of your professional association, in whose hands you are, do not allow you to accept his proposal.

Again, the manager may propose an adequate salary but ask you to sign a contract containing oppressive clauses. It is not necessary to tear up the contract and throw it in his face, however richly he may deserve it. Refer him to the professional association, which does not allow you to sign such clauses.

You should in any case submit all contracts to the association before signing them. You may easily try to impose clauses on the manager which are outside your powers as a citizen. Both managers and players, for lack of legal training, sometimes imagine that they can make laws and impose penalties by clauses in private contracts. The courts of justice make short work of such clauses. Penalties are the prerogative of the sovereign. You cannot throw any of your responsibilities as a citizen on to anyone else by private contract: for instance, a contract that if you commit a murder the manager shall be hanged for it, or vice versa, would only expose both you and the manager to prosecution for conspiracy to defeat the law. You are not likely to do this; but short of murder there are offences possible on the stage, such as the utterance of blasphemous, political, or obscene libels, responsibility for which you cannot transfer to the manager or author by any sort of contract. A contract is only a memorandum of an agreement between the parties to do certain things that are within the law. If you want to secure what you would perhaps call penalties for non-fulfilment, the professional association will shew you how to impose them under the heading of "liquidated damages." But woe to you if you sign a contract to break the law!

All the famous players whose names and experience entitle them to speak with authority to us are agreed as to the importance of good manners behind the curtain. You will like to have their counsel in their own words and with the weight of their own names. We now give them to you exactly as we have received them, with a reminder that on the stage class manners are out of place because every class is to be met with there. We must add that the worst manners to be dreaded are not the manners of the poorest class. The stage is very largely recruited from the Bohemian sections of society, in which the social pretensions of educated gentlefolk with strong artistic tastes are combined with absence of discipline and disregard for convention. To them especially we recommend the following warnings,[9] with an assurance that the opening of the road to fame depends far more on their strict observance than they can at present guess.

9. The messages of advice that followed the preface were provided by, among others, Dames Sybil Thorndike and Irene Vanbrugh, George Arliss, Cyril Maude, Athene Seyler, Sir Barry Jackson, William Bridges-Adams, the second Earl of Cromer (Rowland T. Baring), former Lord Chamberlain, and Kenneth Barnes (Principal of RADA).

# The Miraculous Birth of Language

*First published as a preface to a work by R. A. Wilson (1937) in a reprint in J. M. Dent's Guild Books series, 1941*

═══

This book by Professor [Richard Albert] Wilson[1] is one in which I should like everyone to be examined before being certified as educated or eligible for the franchise or for any scientific, religious, legal, or civil employment. My own profession is, technically, that of a master of language; and I have been plagued all my life by scientists, clergymen, politicians, and even lawyers, who talk like parrots, repeating words and phrases picked up from oneanother by ear without a moment's thought about their meaning, and accept mere association of ideas as an easy substitute for logic. They are often good fellows and even clever fellows; but they are not rational. And they are incurably addicted to their personal habits, which they call human nature.

The main controversy in my early days was about Evolution. It was started by Charles Darwin, a great naturalist, who upset both the Evolutionists and the Edenists (now calling themselves Fundamentalists) by bringing forward an array of instances in which the changes attributed to divinely purposed evolutionary developments could be accounted for by what he called Natural Selection: that is, by circumstances favoring the survival and multiplication of whatever natural varieties happened to be fittest to survive in the general struggle for subsistence. It was as if someone had shewn that the fact that most men's hats fit them, usually accounted for by the belief that they were made on purpose to fit them, could be accounted for on the hypothesis that hats occur in nature like wild strawberries, and that men picking them up discard those that do not fit and retain and wear those that do.

Such a suggestion would have been received, one would suppose, as a

---

1. Professor of English at the University of Saskatchewan, Saskatoon. The book, originally titled *The Birth of Language: Its Place in World Evolution and its Structure in Relation to Space and Time*, 'was so up to date and emancipated from the damnable post-Darwinian Materialism cum Determinism', Shaw informed Beatrice Webb on 17 February 1941, 'that I immediately urged Dent to publish a cheap edition, and offered to write a preface' (*Collected Letters 1926–1950*, 1988). It was Shaw who revised the title.

clever *jeu d'esprit*, to be taken seriously only to the extent of its calling attention to the fact that alongside evolutionary development has gone on the chapter of accidents and of changes forced on living creatures by the need to adapt themselves to external circumstances instead of obeying the evolutionary urge. Yet in the middle of the XIX century it produced an intellectual revolution in the biological, clerical, and philosophical professions generally. They had been compelled on pain of ostracism and financial ruin to work, write, and think on the assumption that the apologues in the book of Genesis are statements of scientific facts, and that the universe is the work of a grotesque tribal idol described in the book of Numbers as God, who resolves to destroy the human race, but is placated by a pleasant smell of roast meat brought to its nostrils by Noah.[2] Any baptized and confirmed person questioning this assumption could be, and still can be, indicted for apostasy, and sentenced to penalties as severe as those reserved for manslaughter and treason. The intensity of the revolt against this limitation among scientists, philosophers, and thinkers of all sorts can hardly be imagined nowadays.

Unfortunately, when a reaction is produced by unbearable persecution, people do not sit down to a judicial examination of their beliefs so as to retain what is valid in them. Instead, they perform the operation known as emptying the baby out with the bath. They do not weed the garden: they tear up everything that grows in it, flower and fruit and vegetable as well as weed, and throw them all on the compost heap. Much as the scientists and philosophers (the best of them were the same people) hated the Fundamentalist's God, they had never been able to dispose satisfactorily of Paley's puzzle [see vol. 2, p. 395]. If you find something as full of purpose and contrivance as a watch, he argued, you know that it did not make itself: somebody must have contrived it and made it. Napoleon pointed to the stars and asked "Who made all that?"[3] The only reply was "Well, who made the maker?" Such logic chopping is not solid enough to stand against the mass of facts which seem contrived and designed. When Charles Darwin pointed out a host of

2. Shaw appears to have conflated Moses's offering in Numbers 15: 1–16 with that of Noah in Genesis 8: 20–22.
3. Probably apocryphal. Archibald Primrose, fifth Earl Rosebery, in *Napoleon: The Last Phase* (1900), noted: 'We have ... often read anecdotes in which [Napoleon] is represented as pointing to the firmament, and declaiming a vague deism ... But the real Napoleon talked in a very different fashion. Gourgaud talks of the stars and their Creator in the way attributed to Napoleon, but the latter snubs him.' Gaspard Gourgaud, an army officer who accompanied Napoleon into exile voluntarily, was author of *Sainte-Hélène: journal inédit de 1815 à 1818* (1847).

instances in which a semblance of design had been produced by the chapter of accidents, the scientists embraced him as their deliverer. They threw over not only Noah's idol but all the other Scriptural attempts to personify or allegorize a creator as well.

They went further—far beyond Darwin, who was never a Darwinian. They lost their tempers if anyone hinted that there was any purpose or design in the universe at all. They set up a creed called Determinism, compared to which the story of Noah was cheerful and encouraging. One of its tenets was a topsyturvy view of Causation in which the cause was itself an effect, and could not help itself. Samuel Butler, a sheepfarmer turned painter and painter turned philosopher, perceiving that Darwin had "banished mind from the universe," made war on him with all the literary weapons at his command, which were considerable; but he was immediately ostracized as maliciously unscientific. Challenged to explain the difference between a live body and a dead one, the physiologists declared that there was no difference. Not only mind, but life of any sort, was banished from the universe; and Materialism went stark raving mad. The author of this book calls it Mechanistic; but the Materialists dislike the term; for a machine, like Paley's watch, is a product of purpose and design; and this the ultra-Darwinians would not tolerate at any price.

The man in the street did not care. To him Darwin was a crank accusing him of being a developed ape. The religious sects found Genesis and St Paul more comforting than pessimistic godlessness. A human society which, very wicked and evil in many ways, was redeemable by a blood sacrifice, and, since it was managing to survive, must be led in the long run by its saints rather than by its sinners, could at least bear thinking of, especially when it was borne in mind that our human life was only a brief purgatorial prelude to an eternity of bliss. But a wicked, evil, cruelly disease-ridden world which was also entirely senseless was a horror beyond words.

No matter. The most unwholesome food is welcome to the starving; and the scientific world gorged itself with Natural Selection. For the Bible was smashed at last. The 39 articles were reduced to absurdity. People stopped going to church in all directions. Hell was abolished. Jehovah was exposed as an impostor whose real name was Jarvey.[4] Science said so; and everything that Science said was true, and everything that the clergy said was false. Talk of emptying the baby out with the bath! Babies were emptied out by the dozen with the deluge. Herod's massacre of the innocents was a joke in comparison.

4. A variant of Jahve(h), believed by some to be the original name of Jehovah.

Of course this was great nonsense; but it occurred for all that among people who were mentally active enough to be capable of a revolution in thought. A handful of people like Butler and myself saw that Natural Selection, far from being, as the public supposed, a discovery of something new called Evolution, was in fact a repudiation and castration of Evolution, depriving it of its moral basis in faith, hope, and charity; but our view went beyond the comprehension of the public, and some of our conclusions seemed irreconcilable. Though we were as anti-Edenist and anti-Paul as the crudest atheists and agnostics, we were classed with them and at the same time repudiated by them. Rousseau had said to the Churches, "Get rid of your miracles and the whole world will fall at the feet of Christ" [see vol. 2, pp. 177–8]; but we insisted that the world was full of miracles: for instance, the resurrection of life every spring was a miracle so stupendous that the cures of lameness and blindness, and even the raising of Lazarus of which Rousseau was thinking, were mere conjuring tricks in comparison.

It was very puzzling. How could people who were "infidels" believe in miracles and go far beyond the Bible in wonders and visions and prophecies? Infidels were people who did not believe in anything: how then could they have the face to call for an oceanic credulity as to the vital possibilities of the future? They do not believe in God, these people; yet here is this man Shaw telling us that if God becomes convinced that Man is a political failure, incapable of solving the problems raised by his own powers of reproduction and aggregation, God will supersede him by a new species as surely as the dinosaurus was superseded by Tom, Dick and Harry, Jill, Jane and Kate. What do they mean by God? What do we mean by God? The 39 articles tell us that God has neither body, parts, nor passions, and that we must accept the Bible as His word, though it describes Him as having all three. We shall lose caste if we dont go to church; but we shall gain it if we buy a motor car and drive in the country in it on Sunday; and, after all, the Smiths and Joneses have bought cars and have not been to church since; and no one has cut them for it.

As a run in the country brings better sermons from Nature than most persons can preach, perhaps the cars did more good than harm; but the balance was not always on that side. When Ibsen shewed that our ideals were often poisonous, when the Socialists shewed that our morals and economics were out-of-date and stale, when the Evolutionists and ultra-Darwinists alike made it impossible for any instructed person to accept the books of Moses as the work of a competent astrophysicist, over went all the baths and out went all the babies. Vivisectors claimed that science acknowledged no morals; plutocrats held that business is business and nothing else; Anacreontic writers

412 The Complete Prefaces: Volume 3

put vine leaves in their hair and drank or drugged themselves to death; sadists and flagellomaniacs outfaced the humanitarians in the criminal courts; bright young things daubed their cheeks with paint and their nails and lips with vermilion, made love to soldiers, kept up their spirits with veronal tablets [hypnotic barbitol], and changed into battered old demireps [courtesans] in their twenties; adult suffrage tore the mask from the fabulous public opinion and democracy which Lincoln believed in and made the centre of his millennial hopes; statesmen found that the way to the Treasury bench was to "stoke up" public meetings with bunk, and get photographed smoking briarwood pipes or nursing babies whilst convincing the bankers and financiers that they could be trusted to change nothing; dictators superseded parliaments all over Europe, proscribing their enemies like [Lucius Cornelius] Sulla,[5] and organizing troops of young ruffians armed with irresistible modern weapons to impose their wills effectively: in short, all the aberrations that can occur in the absence of a common faith and code of honor occurred and are still occurring, including a monstrous war which no armistice can stop for longer than time enough for the disillusioned combatants to be superseded by a new generation of young dupes.

This very onesided statement leaves out all that we have gained by our liberation from the pseudo-religious superstitions and pseudo-decent taboos and pruderies that had produced the reaction against Jehovah. That reaction was so monstrously overdone that, being itself a reaction, it produced a counter-reaction which is now taking the upper hand. It is not too much to say that St Thomas Aquinas has now a wider vogue as a fashionable philosopher than he ever enjoyed before. The Church of England, which disgraced itself utterly during the Four Years War [World War I, 1914–18] by turning its vestries into Jingo recruiting stations, has redeemed itself by behaving very much better since the resumption of that war in 1939. Psychology, which had belied itself by treating belief in the existence of such a thing as a soul as quite as superstitious as a belief in the existence of God, is becoming really psychological, just as biology is becoming really biological. Even medicine is following the lead of Scott Haldane,[6] and beginning to regard a healthy body as a product of a healthy mind instead of the other way about. Butler, could he revisit us, would no longer find himself a boycotted crank. Even my own

5. In 82 BC Sulla declared himself 'dictator' of Rome and the Roman world, instituting a proscription list of men declared to be outlaws and public enemies, whom he massacred, exacting revenge with pitiless and calculated cruelty.
6. Scottish physiologist and philosopher, author of The Sciences and Philosophy (1929) and The Philosophy of a Biologist (1935).

claims to be a biologist might not now be received with contemptuous incredulity by the biological profession. Obviously a playwright working on the Shakespearean plane in the great laboratory of the world with its uncontrived conditions, its innumerable untampered-with animals (mostly human) under observation, and its recorded history as I am, must be a biologist. Anyhow he can claim to know as much about the origins of life as the professionals, this being exactly nothing.

When I said many years ago ['The Revolutionist's Handbook', *Man and Superman*] that the Holy Ghost is the sole survivor of the Trinity, and that it is far more scientific to describe Man as the Temple of the Holy Ghost than as an automaton made of a few chemicals in which some carbon got mixed accidentally, I was accused of advertizing myself by uttering paradoxes of the same order as the statement that black is white, which is not a paradox but a lie. Now that I am old and obsolescent, young people who happen to have heard about the paradoxical Shaw from their elders, and are tempted to read him, cannot find anything startling in me. If they have the requisite erudition, they point out that what I have said had been said long ago by St Augustine and all the great spiritual leaders of mankind before and after him. They class me as a Quaker of sorts, and are not puzzled as their fathers were by the fact that Sir Arthur Eddington, great as an astronomer, is a professed Friend, that [Michael] Faraday and Darwin were members of religious sects,[7] and that the now somewhat forgotten Lucretian Irishman [John] Tyndall,[8] who startled the world at Belfast in 1874 by declaring that he saw in matter the promise and potency of all forms of life, is represented today by De Broglie, who scandalizes nobody by demonstrating what was plain enough to me in my

7. Eddington was Professor of Astronomy at Cambridge University, noted for researches into the constitution of stars and contributions to the theory of relativity. Embracing the faith of his parents he was a lifetime Quaker, whose spiritual insights are evident in his *Science and the Unseen World* (1929) and the chapter ('The Domain of Physical Science') he contributed to *Science, Religion and Reality*, ed. Joseph Needham (1925). Faraday was an English physicist, discoverer of magnetic-electricity, who from childhood attended meetings of a minuscule Christian sect known as Sandemanians, founded by Robert Sandeman, who observed a strict, primitive Christanity. Darwin attended Christ's College, Cambridge, as a student of divinity, but (as indicated in his posthumously published autobiography) gradually moved from theism to agnosticism, and finally to atheism, though – presumably to spare his wife's sensibilities – he did not publicly proclaim it.
8. A zealous advocate of the doctrine of materialism, which he upheld in his presidential address to the British Association in Belfast, 1874. Also see vol. 2, p. 414.

teens: to wit, that if a dissolved salt can crystallize itself into a solid stone it is as much alive as the nearest squalling baby.[9]

The Materialists, in fact, are faced with the discovery that there is no such thing as matter: a much greater advance than their grandfathers' discovery that there is no such person as Old Nick with his horns, tail, cloven hoof, and pitchfork. As to the belief of the physicists, which so discouraged Dean Inge, one of the best brains of my time, that the sun is cooling and the earth must therefore end as a frozen lifeless moon strewn with the bones of the Last Men [*God and the Astronomers*, 1933] Sir James Jeans,[10] our Superphysicist, has suggested that the continuous slowing down of the heavenly bodies by the tides must finally stop them in their orbits, whereupon, I suppose, they will all crash into oneanother as disabled airplanes crash to earth, and form a giant globe at a temperature never before reached, in which life will carry on its work just as it does on the floor of the ocean under pressures that no dryland animal could endure for a moment.

It is a great relief to me to find that even the choice spirits among the college professors (still a literally Godforsaken lot) are ceasing to parrot obvious anticlerical nonsense in the firm belief that they are teaching science. Imagine my delight when I received a copy of the first edition of this book inscribed by its author as "an instalment of interest on an old debt." His name being unknown to me, I hastened to ascertain whether his chair was at Oxford or Cambridge, Owen's or Edinburgh, Dublin or Birmingham. I learnt that it was at Saskatoon, a place of which I had never heard, and that his university was that of Saskatchewan, which was connected in my imagination with ochred and feathered Indians rather than with a university apparently half a century ahead of Cambridge in science and of Oxford in common sense.

Now I had noticed for some years past that American culture, which forty years ago seemed to subsist mentally on stale British literary exports, was more and more challenging our leadership, especially in science. When I learned that provincial Canada had drawn easily ahead of Pasteurized Pavloffed Freudized Europe, and made professors of men who were in the vanguard instead of among the stragglers and camp followers, I found myself considering

9. Prince Louis de Broglie, French physicist, noted for investigations of the wave theory of matter, for which he was awarded the Nobel Prize for physics (1929), was a younger brother of Duc Maurice de Broglie, also a physicist, whose early work included a thesis (1908) on ionic mobilities. It is not clear here to which brother Shaw alluded.
10. English astronomer, physicist, mathematician and philosopher, author of *Problems of Cosmogony and Stellar Dynamics* (1919) and *The Universe Around Us* (1929).

seriously, especially when the German airmen dropped a bomb near enough to shake my house, whether I had not better end my days in Vancouver, if not in Saskatoon. Meanwhile I urged, as strongly as I could, the reprinting of Professor Wilson's treatise in a modestly priced edition baited for the British book market with a preface by myself: an overrated attraction commercially, but one which still imposes on London publishers.

But I did not look at it commercially. I had an axe of my own to grind; and I thought Professor Wilson's book might help me to grind it. I am not a professor of language: I am a practitioner, concerned with its technique more directly than with its origin. Professor Wilson described how Man was a baby, to whom Time and Space meant no more than the present moment and the few feet in front of his nose, until writable language made Time historical and Thought philosophical. Thought lives on paper by the pen, having devized for itself an immortal and evergrowing body. You will understand this when you have read the book; and I hope you will appreciate its importance, and the magnitude of the service its author has done you.

Meanwhile, where do I come in? Solely as a technician. Professor Wilson has shewn that it was as a reading and writing animal that Man achieved his human eminence above those who are called beasts. Well, it is I and my like who have to do the writing. I have done it professionally for the last sixty years as well as it can be done with a hopelessly inadequate alphabet devized centuries before the English language existed to record another and very different language. Even this alphabet is reduced to absurdity by a foolish orthography based on the notion that the business of spelling is to represent the origin and history of a word instead of its sound and meaning. Thus an intelligent child who is bidden to spell debt, and very properly spells it d-e-t, is caned for not spelling it with a b because Julius Cæsar spelt the Latin word for it with a b.

Now I, being not only a scribe but a dramatic poet and therefore a word musician, cannot write down my word music for lack of an adequate notation. Composers of music have such a notation. Handel could mark his movements as *maestoso* [stately], Beethoven as *mesto* [sad], Elgar as *nobilmente* [nobly], Strauss, as *etwas ruhiger, aber trotzdem schwungvoll und enthusiastich* [somewhat quieter but yet lively and enthusiastic].[11] By writing the words *adagio* [slowly] or *prestissimo* [very rapid], they can make it impossible for a conductor to mistake a hymn for a hornpipe. They can write *ritardando* [becoming slower], *accelerando* [gradually faster] and *tempo* over this or that passage. But I may have my best scenes ridiculously ruined in performance for want of such

11. Prologue to *Ariadne auf Naxos* (1912), op. 60, rehearsal no. 114.

indications. A few nights ago [25 January 1941] I heard a broadcast recital of The Merchant of Venice ['In Belmont is a Lady: a Romantic Chronicle'] in which Portia [Fay Compton] rattled through "How all the other passions fleet to air!" [III: ii] exactly as if she were still chatting with Nerissa and had been told by the producer to get through quickly, as the news had to come on at nine o'clock sharp. If that high spot in her part had been part of an opera composed by Richard Strauss a glance at the score would have saved her from throwing away her finest lines.

These particular instances seem impertinent to Professor Wilson's thesis; but I cite them to shew why, as a technician, I am specially concerned with the fixation of language by the art of writing, and hampered by the imperfections of that art. The Professor's conspectus of the enormous philosophical scope of the subject could not condescend to my petty everyday workshop grievances; but I may as well seize the opportunity to ventilate them, as they concern civilization to an extent which no layman can grasp. So let me without further preamble come down to certain prosaic technical facts of which I have to complain bitterly, and which have never as far as I know been presented in anything like their statistical magnitude and importance.

During the last 60 years I have had to provide for publication many millions of words, involving for me the manual labor of writing, and for the printer the setting up in type, of tens of millions of letters, largely superfluous. To save my own time I have resorted to shorthand, in which the words are spelt phonetically, and the definite and indefinite articles, with all the prepositions, conjunctions and interjections, as well as the auxiliary verbs, are not spelt at all, but indicated by dots and ticks, circles or segments of circles, single strokes of the pen and the like. Commercial correspondence is not always written: it is often spoken into dictaphones which cost more than most private people can afford. But whether it is dictaphoned or written in shorthand it has to be transcribed in ordinary spelling on typewriters, and, if for publication, set up from the typed copy on a printing machine operated by a stroke of the hand for every letter.

When we consider the prodigious total of manual labor on literature, journalism, and commercial correspondence that has to be done every day (a full copy of the London Times when we are at peace and not short of paper may contain a million words) the case for reducing this labor to the lowest possible figure is, for printers and authors, overwhelming, though for lay writers, most of whom write only an occasional private letter, it is negligible. Writers' cramp is a common complaint among authors: it does not trouble blacksmiths.

In what directions can this labor be saved? Two are obvious to anyone interested enough to give half an hour's thought to the subject. 1. Discard useless grammar. 2. Spell phonetically.

Useless grammar is a devastating plague. We who speak English have got rid of a good deal of the grammatic inflections that make Latin and its modern dialects so troublesome to learn. But we still say I am, thou art, he is, with the plurals we are, you are, they are, though our countryfolk, before school teachers perverted their natural wisdom, said I be, thou be, he be, we be, you be, they be. This saved time in writing and was perfectly intelligible in speech. Chinese traders, negroes, and aboriginal Australians, who have to learn English as a foreign language, simplify it much further, and have thereby established what they call business English, or, as they pronounce it, Pidgin. The Chinese, accustomed to an uninflected monosyllabic language, do not say "I regret that I shall be unable to comply with your request." "Sorry no can" is quite as effective, and saves the time of both parties. When certain negro slaves in America were oppressed by a lady planter who was very pious and very severe, their remonstrance, if expressed in grammatic English, would have been "If we are to be preached at let us not be flogged also: if we are to be flogged let us not be preached at also." This is correct and elegant but wretchedly feeble. It says in twentysix words what can be better said in eleven. The negroes proved this by saying "If preachee preachee: if floggee floggee; but no preachee floggee too." They saved fifteen words of useless grammar, and said what they had to say far more expressively. The economy in words: that is, in time, ink and paper, is enormous. If during my long professional career every thousand words I have written could have been reduced to less than half that number, my working lifetime would have been doubled. Add to this the saving of all the other authors, the scribes, the printers, the paper millers, and the makers of the machines they wear out; and the figures become astronomical.

However, the discarding of verbal inflections to indicate moods, tenses, subjunctives, and accusatives, multiplies words instead of saving them, because their places have to be taken by auxiliaries in such a statement as "By that time I shall have left England." The four words "I shall have left" can be expressed in more inflected languages by a single word. But the multiplication of words in this way greatly facilitates the acquisition of the language by foreigners. In fact, nearly all foreigners who are not professional interpreters or diplomatists, however laboriously they may have learnt classical English in school, soon find when they settle in England that academic correctness is quite unnecessary, and that "broken English," which is a sort of home-made pidgin, is quite sufficient for intelligible speech. Instead of laughing at them and mimicking them derisively we should learn from them.

In acquiring a foreign language a great deal of trouble is caused by the irregular verbs. But why learn them? It is easy to regularize them. A child's "I thinked" instead of "I thought" is perfectly intelligible. When anybody says "who" instead of "whom" nobody is the least puzzled. But here we come up against another consideration. "Whom" may be a survival which is already half discarded: but nothing will ever induce an archbishop to say at the lectern "Who hath believed our report? and to who is the arm of the Lord revealed?" [Isaiah 53: 1].

But it is not for the sake of grammar that the superfluous m is retained. To pronounce a vowel we have to make what teachers of singing call a stroke of the glottis. The Germans, with their characteristic thoroughness, do this most conscientiously: they actually seem to like doing it; but the English, who are lazy speakers, grudge doing it once, and flatly refuse to do it twice in succession. The Archbishop says "To whom is" instead of "to who is" for the same reason as the man in the street, instead of saying Maria Ann, says Maria ran. The double *coup de glotte* [glottal stop] is too troublesome. No Englishman, clerical or lay, will say "A ass met a obstacle." He says "A nass met a nobstacle." A Frenchman drops the final t in "*s'il vous plaît,*" but pronounces it in "plaît-il?" Euphony and ease of utterance call for such interpolations.

I can give no reason for the cockney disuse of final l. Shakespear, accustomed to be called Bill by Anne Hathaway, must have been surprised when he came to London to hear himself called Beeyaw, just as I was surprised when I came to London from Ireland to hear milk called meeyock. Final r does not exist in southern English speech except when it avoids a *coup de glotte.* In that case it is even interpolated, as in "the idear of." French, as written and printed, is plastered all over with letters that are never sounded, though they waste much labor when they are written.

The waste of time in spelling imaginary sounds and their history (or etymology as it is called) is monstrous in English and French; and so much has been written on the subject that it is quite stale, because the writers have dwelt only on the anomalies of our orthography, which are merely funny, and on the botheration of children by them. Nothing has been said of the colossal waste of time and material, though this alone is gigantic enough to bring about a reform so costly, so unpopular, and requiring so much mental effort as the introduction of a new alphabet and a new orthography. It is true that once the magnitude of the commercial saving is grasped the cost shrinks into insignificance; but it has not been grasped because it has never yet been stated in figures, perhaps because they are incalculable, perhaps because if they were fully calculated, the statisticians might be compelled to make the unit a billion or so, just as the astronomers have been compelled to make their unit of distance a lightyear.

In any case the waste does not come home to the layman. For example, take the two words tough and cough. He may not have to write them for years, if at all. Anyhow he now has tough and cough so thoroughly fixed in his head and everybody else's that he would be set down as illiterate if he wrote tuf and cof; consequently a reform would mean for him simply a lot of trouble not worth taking. Consequently the layman, always in a huge majority, will fight spelling reform tooth and nail. As he cannot be convinced, his opposition must be steam-rollered by the overworked writers and printers who feel the urgency of the reform.

Though I am an author, I also am left cold by tough and cough; for I, too, seldom write them. But take the words though and should and enough: containing eighteen letters. Heaven knows how many hundred thousand times I have had to write these constantly recurring words. With a new English alphabet replacing the old Semitic one with its added Latin vowels I should be able to spell t-h-o-u-g-h with two letters, s-h-o-u-l-d with three, and e-n-o-u-g-h with four: nine letters instead of eighteen: a saving of a hundred per cent of my time and my typist's time and the printer's time, to say nothing of the saving in paper and wear and tear of machinery. As I have said, I save my own time by shorthand; but as it all has to go into longhand before it can be printed, and I cannot use shorthand for my holograph epistles, shorthand is no remedy. I also have the personal grievance, shared by all my namesakes, of having to spell my own name with four letters instead of the two [diphthongs] a Russian uses to spell it with his alphabet of 35 letters. All round me I hear the corruption of our language produced by the absurd device of spelling the first sound in my name with the two letters sh. London is surrounded by populous suburbs which began as homes or "hams" and grew to be hamlets or groups of hams. One of them is still called Peter's Ham, another Lewis Ham. But as these names are now spelt as one word this lack of a letter in our alphabet for the final sound in wish, and our very misleading use of sh to supply the deficiency, has set everyone calling them Peter Sham and Louis Sham. Further off, in Surrey, there is a place named Cars Halton. Now it is called Car Shallton. Horse Ham is called Hor-shm. Colt Hurst, which is good English, is called Coal Thirst, which is nonsense. For want of a letter to indicate the final sound in Smith we have Elt Ham called El Tham. We have no letter for the first and last consonant in church, and are driven to the absurd expedient of representing it by ch. Someday we shall have Chichester called Chick Hester. A town [Cirencester] formerly known as Sisseter is so insanely misspelt that it is now called Siren.

But the lack of consonants is a trifle beside our lack of vowels. The Latin alphabet gives us five, wheras the least we can write phonetically with is eighteen. I do not mean that there are only eighteen vowels in daily use: eighteen hundred would be nearer the truth. When I was chairman [1930–37] of the Spoken English Committee of the British Broadcasting Corporation it was easy enough to get a unanimous decision that exemplary and applicable should be pronounced with the stress on the first syllable, though the announcers keep on putting the stress on the second all the same; but when the announcers asked us how they should pronounce cross or launch there were as many different pronunciations of the vowels as there were members present. I secured a decision in favor of my own pronunciation of launch by the happy accident that it was adopted by King George the Fifth when christening a new liner on the Clyde. But the members were perfectly intelligible to oneanother in spite of their ringing all the possible changes between crawz and cross, between lanch and lawnch. To get such common words as son and science phonetically defined was hopeless. In what is called the Oxford accent son and sun became san; sawed and sword are pronounced alike; and my native city becomes Dabblin. In Dublin itself I have heard it called Dawblin. The Oxford pronunciation of science is sah-yence: the Irish pronunciation is sŭ-yence. Shakespear pronounced wind as wined; and as late as the end of the XVIII century an attempt to correct an actor who pronounced it in this way provoked the retort "I cannot finned it in my minned to call it winned."[12] Rosalind is on the stage ridiculously pronounced Rozzalinned though Shakespear called her Roh-za-lined, rhyming it to "If a cat will after kind" [*As You Like It*, III: ii]. Kind, by the way, should logically be pronounced kinned. The word trist is again so far out of use that nobody knows how to pronounce it. It should rhyme to triced, but is mostly supposed to rhyme to kissed. The first vowel in Christ and Christendom has two widely different sounds, sometimes absurdly described as long i and short i; but both are spelt alike.

I could fill pages with instances; but my present point is not to make lists of anomalies, but to shew that (a) the English language cannot be spelt with five Latin vowels, and (b) that though the vowels used by English people are as various as their faces yet they understand oneanother's speech well enough

---

12. A couplet (author unknown), the second line of which reads: 'But I can fined it in my mined to call it wined.' In a letter to Shaw on 12 September 1941, Edward McNulty ascribed it to Swift (see McNulty, 'Memoirs of G.B.S.', *SHAW: The Annual of Bernard Shaw Studies*, XII (1992), p. 43). It does not, however, appear in editions of Swift's complete poems.

for all practical purposes, just as whilst Smith's face differs from Jones's so much that the one could not possibly be mistaken for the other yet they are so alike that they are instantly recognizable as man and man, not as cat and dog. In the same way it is found that though the number of different vowel sounds we utter is practically infinite yet a vowel alphabet of eighteen letters can indicate a speech sufficiently unisonal to be understood generally, and to preserve the language from the continual change which goes on at present because the written word teaches nothing as to the pronunciation, and frequently belies it. Absurd pseudo-etymological spellings are taken to be phonetic, very soon in the case of words that are seldom heard, more slowly when constant usage keeps tradition alive, but nonetheless surely. When the masses learn to read tay becomes tee and obleezh becomes oblydge at the suggestion of the printed word in spite of usage. A workman who teaches himself to read pronounces semi- as see my. I myself, brought up to imitate the French pronunciation of envelope, am now trying to say enn-velope like everybody else.

Sometimes the change is an esthetic improvement. My grandfather swore "be the varchoo" of his oath: I prefer vert-yoo. Edge-i-cate is less refined than ed-you-cate. The late Helen Taylor,[13] John Stuart Mill's stepdaughter, who as a public speaker always said Russ-ya and Pruss-ya instead of Rusher and Prussher, left her hearers awestruck. The indefinite article, a neutral sound sometimes called the obscure vowel, and the commonest sound in our language though we cannot print it except by turning an e upside down, was always pronounced by Mrs Annie Besant, perhaps the greatest British oratress of her time, as if it rhymed with pay. In short, we are all over the shop with our vowels because we cannot spell them with our alphabet. Like Scott, Dickens, Artemus Ward and other writers of dialect I have made desperate efforts to represent local and class dialects by the twentysix letters of the Latin alphabet, but found it impossible and had to give it up. A well-known actor [Nigel Playfair], when studying one of my cockney parts [Hodson, in *John Bull's Other Island*, 1904], had to copy it in ordinary spelling before he could learn it.

My concern here, however, is not with pronunciation but with the saving of time wasted. We try to extend our alphabet by writing two letters instead of one; but we make a mess of this device. With reckless inconsistency we write sweat and sweet, and then write whet and wheat, just the contrary. Consistency is not always a virtue; but spelling becomes a will o' the wisp

---

13. Woman's rights advocate, who served on the London School Board 1876–84, and was a founder of the [Social] Democratic Federation.

without it. I have never had much difficulty in spelling, because as a child I read a good deal, and my visual memory was good; but people who do not read much or at all, and whose word memory is aural, cannot spell academically, and are tempted to write illegibly to conceal this quite innocent inability, which they think disgraceful because illiteracy was for centuries a mark of class.

But neither speech nor writing can now be depended on as class indexes. Oxford graduates and costermongers alike call the sun the san and a rose a rah-ooz. The classical scholar and Poet Laureate John Dryden said yit and git where we say yet and get: another instance of spelling changing pronunciation instead of simply noting it. The Duke of Wellington dropped the h in humble and hospital, herb and hostler. So did I in my youth, though, as we were both Irish, h-dropping as practised in England and France was not native to us. I still say onner and our instead of honour and hour. Everybody does. Probably before long we shall all sing "Be it ever so umbl theres no place like ome," which is easier and prettier than "Be it evvah sah-oo hambl *etc.*"

I have dealt with vowels so far; but whenever an Englishman can get in an extra vowel and make it a diphthong he does so. When he tries to converse in French he cannot say *coupé* or *entrez*: he says coopay and ongtray. When he is in the chorus at a performance of one of the great Masses—say Bach's in B minor—he addresses the Almighty as Tay instead of making the Latin e a vowel. He calls gold gah-oold. I pronounce it goh-oold. Price, a very common word, is sometimes prah-ees, sometimes prawce, sometimes proyce, and sometimes, affectedly, prace. That is why our attempts to express our eighteen vowels with five letters by doubling them will not work: we cannot note down the diphthongal pronunciation until we have a separate single letter for every vowel, so that we can stop such mispronunciations as reel and ideel for real and ideal, and write diphthongs as such. The middle sound in beat, spelt with two letters, is a single pure vowel. The middle sound in bite, also spelt with two letters, is a diphthong. The spelling l-i-g-h-t is simply insane.

The worst vulgarism in English speech is a habit of prefixing the neutral vowel, which phoneticians usually indicate by e printed upside down, to all the vowels and diphthongs. The woman who asks for "e kapp e te-ee" is at once classed as, at best, lower middle. When I pass an elementary school and hear the children repeating the alphabet in unison, and chanting unrebuked "Ah-yee, Be-yee, Ce-yee, De-yee" I am restrained from going in and shooting the teacher only by the fact that I do not carry a gun and by my fear of the police. Not that I cannot understand the children when they speak; but their speech is ugly; and euphony is very important. By all means give us an adequate alphabet, and let people spell as they speak without any nonsense about bad or good or right or wrong spelling and speech; but let them remember that if they make ugly or slovenly sounds when they speak they will never be respected. This is so well known that masses of our population are bilingual. They have an official speech as part of their company manners which they do not use at home or in conversation with their equals. Sometimes they had better not. It is extremely irritating to a parent to be spoken to by a child in a superior manner; so wise children drop their school acquirements with their daddies and mummies. All such domestic friction would soon cease if it became impossible for us to learn to read and write without all learning to speak in the same way.

And now what, exactly, do I want done about it? I will be quite precise. I want our type designers, or artist-calligraphers, or whatever they call themselves, to design an alphabet capable of representing the sounds of the following string of nonsense quite unequivocally without using two letters to represent one sound or making the same letter represent different sounds by diacritical marks. The rule is to be One Sound One Letter, with every letter unmistakably different from all the others. Here is the string of nonsense. An alphabet which will spell it under these conditions will spell any English word well enough to begin with.

> Chang at leisure was superior to Lynch in his rouge, munching a lozenge at the burial in Merrion Square of Hyperion the Alien who valued his billiards so highly.
>
> Quick! quick! hear the queer story how father and son one time sat in the house man to man eating bread and telling the tale of the fir on the road to the city by the sea following the coast to its fall full two fathoms deep. There they lived together served by the carrier, whose narrower mind through beer was sore and whose poor boy shivered over the fire all day lingering in a tangle of tactless empty instinct ineptly swallowing quarts of stingo [zesty beer].

As well as I can count, this sample of English contains 372 sounds, and as spelt above requires 504 letters to print it, the loss in paper, ink, wear and tear of machinery, compositors' time, machinists' time, and author's time being over 26%, which could be saved by the use of the alphabet I ask for. I repeat that this figure, which means nothing to the mass of people who, when they write at all, seldom exceed one sheet of notepaper, is conclusive for reform in the case of people who are writing or typing or printing all day. Calligraphers intelligent enough to grasp its importance will, if they have read these pages, rush to their drawingboards to seize the opportunity.

The first question that will occur to them is how many letters they will have to design; for it will seem only commonsense to retain the 26 letters of the existing alphabet and invent only the ones in which it is deficient. But that can only serve if every letter in the 26 is given a fixed and invariable sound. The result would be a spelling which would not only lead the first generation of its readers to dismiss the writers as crudely illiterate, but would present unexpected obscenities which no decent person could be induced to write. The new alphabet must be so different from the old that no one could possibly mistake the new spelling for the old.

This disposes of all the attempts at "simplified spelling" with the old alphabet. There is nothing for it but to design 24 new consonants and 18 new vowels, making in all a new alphabet of 42 letters, and use it side by side with the present lettering until the better ousts the worse.

The artist-calligraphers will see at first only an opportunity for 42 beautiful line drawings to make a printed book as decorative as a panel by Giovanni da Udine,[14] and a handwritten sonnet as delightful visually as one by Michael Angelo, the most perfect of all calligraphers.[15] But that will never do. The first step is to settle the alphabet on purely utilitarian lines and then let the artists make it as handsome as they can. For instance, a straight line, written with a single stroke of the pen, can represent four different consonants by varying its length and position. Put a hook at the top of it, and you have four more consonants. Put a hook at the lower end, and you have four more, and put hooks at both ends and you have another four; so that you have 16 consonants writable by one stroke of the pen. The late Henry Sweet [see vol. 2, p. 261], still our leading authority on British phonetics, begins his alphabet in this way, achieving at one stroke p, t, k, and ch; b, d, g (hard) and j; m, n, ng and the ni in companion; kw, r, Spanish double l and the r in superior. He takes our manuscript e and l (different lengths of the same sign) and gets f, s, and zh. Turning it backwards he gets v, z, and sh. He takes our c and o, and gets dh and th. A waved stroke gives him l; and thus, borrowing only four letters from our alphabet, he obtains the required 24 consonants, leaving 22 of our letters derelict. For vowels he resorts to long and short curves at two levels, with or without little circles attached before or after, and thus gets the requisite 18 new letters easily. Thus the utilitarian task of inventing new letters has already been done by a firstrate authority. The artists have only to discover how to make the strokes and curves pleasing to the eye.

14. Italian painter, decorative artist and architect. Inspired by archaeological discoveries in Rome, he evolved a light and graceful decorative style in stucco and fresco.
15. Many examples of Michelangelo's fine writing hand survive, including more than three hundred sonnets, madrigals and other verse forms, and hundreds of his letters.

At this point, however, the guidance of Henry Sweet must be dropped; for when he had completed his alphabet he proceeded to bedevil it into an instrument for verbatim reporting, which is the art of jotting down, not all the sounds uttered by a public speaker, which is beyond manual dexterity, but enough of them to remind the practised reporter of the entire words. He writes zah and depends on his memory or on the context to determine whether this means exact or example or examine or exasperate or what not. After seven years practice Sweet became so expert at this sort of guessing that the specimens he gives in his Manual of Current Shorthand (published by the Clarendon Press) are unreadable by anyone lacking that experience.

This is true of all reporting systems. There are dozens of them in existence; and they are all efficient enough; for the debates of Cromwell's Ironsides[16] and the cross-examinations of St Joan are on record. Charles Dickens was a competent verbatim reporter before any of the systems now in use were invented. Sweet's contractions and guessings were therefore quite superfluous: what was needed from him was an alphabet with which the English language could be unequivocally spelt at full length, and not a new reporting shorthand.

Now Sweet, being a very English Englishman, was extremely quarrelsome. Being moreover the brainiest Oxford don of his time, he was embittered by the contempt with which his subject, to say nothing of himself, was treated by his university, which was and still is full of the medieval notion, valid enough for King Richard Lionheart but madly out of date today, that English is no language for a gentleman, and is tolerable only as a means of communication with the lower classes. His wrath fell on his forerunner Isaac Pitman,[17] whose shorthand he called the Pitfall system. Pitman had anticipated Sweet's strokes; but he made their interpretation depend on their thickness and the direction in which they were written. Thus a horizontal stroke meant k, and a vertical one t. The strokes slanting halfway between meant p and ch. The same strokes thickened gave him g, d, b, and j, with the addition of r for ch written upward instead of downward. Thus he got nine letters from the single

---

16. Shaw is misapplying the term 'Ironsides' here. This was the nickname bestowed upon Cromwell by Prince Rupert after the latter's defeat near York in 1644 (*DNB*). The term soon was applied to the crack cavalry troops of the Independents, in the Civil War. The debates relate to the parliaments of the Protectorate, which were accessible to Shaw in Cobbett's *Parliamentary History of England: From the Norman Conquest in 1066 to the Year 1803*, II (1808).

17. Inventor of a shorthand system of phonography. He published his *Stenographic Sound-Hand* in 1837.

stroke, and would have got ten if an upstroke could be thickened, which is not possible as a feat of penmanship. Sweet discarded these distinctions because, as no two people write at the same slant, the stroke should have only one meaning no matter at what slant it is written. Making strokes at different slants is drawing, not writing; and Sweet insisted that writing must be *currente calamo* [the pen flowing unhesitatingly]: hence he called his script Current Shorthand. Thick and thin he discarded as unpractical for upstrokes and pencil work. His getting rid of these elaborations was an important improvement. The distinctions he substituted were those to which the old printed alphabet has accustomed us. In it the stroke projects sometimes above the line of writing as in the letter l, sometimes below it as in the letter j, sometimes neither above nor below as in the letter i, sometimes both above and below as in our manuscript p, f and capital j. This gave Sweet only four letters per simple stroke instead of Pitman's nine; but four are more than enough. Also much of the pen work imposed by our alphabet is unnecessary: for instance, m and w take twice as long to write as l though they can be indicated quite as briefly; and p and q could be indicated by their projecting strokes alone without attaching an n to the p and an o to the q.

I take it then that the new English alphabet will be based on Sweet, and not on Pitman, though I am writing this preface in Pitman's shorthand and not in Sweet's, having discarded Sweet's reporting contractions as unnecessary for my purpose and puzzling for my transcriber. The designer of the new alphabet will find that Sweet has done all the preliminary study for him, and solved its utilitarian problems.

What remains to be done is to make the strokes and hooks and curves and circles look nice. If very young, the designer may ask me indignantly whether I think of the beauty sought by artists as something to be stuck on to the inventions of the pedant. In this case it is. An architect has to make a house beautiful; but the house, if it is to be lived in, must be dictated by the needs of its inhabitants and not by the architect's fancies. The great printers, Jensen, Caslon, Morris, did not invent letters:[18] they made the old ones pleasing as well as legible, and made books worth looking at as well as reading. What they did for the old alphabet their successors must do for the new. There is plenty of scope for invention as well as for decoration: for instance, Sweet's alphabet has no capitals nor has Pitman's. Neither has any italics. Since Morris

18. Nicolas Jenson, who worked with Gutenberg, is known chiefly as the introducer of roman type. William Caslon, London typefounder, created simple 'old-style' typefaces that are still much used. William Morris revived typographical art at his Kelmscott Press, designing typefaces, ornamental initials and borders.

revived printing as a fine art, scores of new types have come into the market. Morris himself designed several.

The new alphabet, like the old, will not be written as printed: its calligraphers will have to provide us with a new handwriting. Our present one is so unwritable and illegible that I am bothered by official correspondents asking me to write my name "in block letters, please," though a good handwriting is more legible and far prettier than block, in which the letters, being the same height, cannot give every word a characteristic shape peculiar to itself. Shakespear's signature, though orthographically illegible, is, when once you have learnt it, much more instantaneously recognizable and readable than SHAKESPEAR, which at a little distance might be CHAMBERLAIN or any other word of eleven letters.

Other changes and developments in the use of language and the art of writing may follow the introduction of an English alphabet. There is, for instance, the Basic English of the Orthological Institute[19] at 10, King's Parade, Cambridge, by which foreigners can express all their wants in England by learning 800 English words. It is a thought-out pidgin, and gets rid of much of our grammatical superfluities. The Institute is, as far as I know, the best live organ for all the cognate reforms, as the literary Societies and Academies do nothing but award medals and read historical and critical lectures to oneanother.

The various schools of shorthand teach new alphabets; but they are wholly preoccupied with verbatim reporting, which is a separate affair. Their triumphs are reckoned in words per minute written at speeds at which no language can be fully written at all. They train correspondence clerks very efficiently; but they should pay more attention to authors and others whose business it is to write, and who cannot carry secretaries or dictaphones about with them everywhere. Such scribes can write at their own pace, and need no reporting contractions, which only waste their time and distract their attention, besides presenting insoluble puzzles to the typist who has to transcribe them. I have long since discarded them. On these terms shorthand is very easy to learn. On reporting terms it takes years of practice to acquire complete efficiency and then only in cases of exceptional natural aptitude, which varies curiously from individual to individual.

The only danger I can foresee in the establishment of an English alphabet

19. Charles Ogden, creator of Basic English, organized the Orthological Institute in 1927. In June 1946 he was requested to assign to the Crown his copyright in Basic English, with a grant from the Minister of Education, with which he created the Basic English Foundation.

is the danger of civil war. Our present spelling is incapable of indicating the sounds of our words and does not pretend to; but the new spelling would prescribe an official pronunciation. Nobody at present calls a lam a lamb or pronounces wawk and tawk as walk and talk. But when the pronunciation can be and is indicated, the disputable points will be small enough for the stupidest person to understand and fight about. And the ferocity with which people fight about words is astonishing. In London there is a street labeled Conduit Street. When the word conduit, like the thing, went out of use, cabmen were told to drive to Cundit Street. They are still so told by elderly gentlemen. When modern electric engineering brought the word into common use the engineers called it con-dew-it. A savage controversy in the columns of The Times ensued. I tried to restore good humor by asking whether, if the London University decided to pay a compliment to our Oriental dominions by calling one of its new streets Pundit Street it would be spelt Ponduit Street.[20] I had better have said nothing; for I was instantly assailed as a profane wretch trifling with a sacred subject. Englishmen may yet kill oneanother and bomb their cities into ruin to decide whether v-a-s-e spells vawz or vahz or vaiz. Cawtholic or Kahtholic may convulse Ireland when the national question is dead and buried. We shall all agree that h-e-i-g-h-t is an orthographic monstrosity; but when it is abolished and we have to decide whether the official pronunciation shall be hite or hyth, there will probably be a sanguinary class war; for in this case the proletarian custom is more logical than the Oxford one.

Still, we must take that risk. If the introduction of an English alphabet for the English language costs a civil war, or even, as the introduction of summer time did, a world war,[21] I shall not grudge it. The waste of war is negligible in comparison to the daily waste of trying to communicate with oneanother in English through an alphabet with sixteen letters missing. That must be remedied, come what may.

Ayot St Lawrence.
23 February 1941.

20. The controversy arose when Shaw's letter 'B.B.C. Pronunciation' was published in *The Times* on 2 January 1934. The 'Pundit' jest appeared in Shaw's second letter, 'B.B.C. English', in *The Times* on 25 January. Both letters are reprinted in Shaw, *Agitations* (1985).
21. The Germans adopted daylight saving in 1915. British Summer Time was first effected on 21 May 1916.

# An Explanatory Word

*Prefatory note to* Florence Farr, Bernard Shaw and W. B. Yeats:
A Correspondence, *ed. Clifford Bax, 1941*

========

I made the acquaintance of Florence Farr in the eighteen eighties, when the Socialist revival of those years, in which I took an active part as one of the Fabian leaders and as an indefatigable platform orator, took me on many Sundays to the house of William Morris on the Mall in Hammersmith to lecture there in the converted coach house which served as a meeting hall for Morris's followers.

Florence was the daughter of Dr William Farr,[1] famous as a sanitary reformer in the mid-XIX century when he and Sir Edwin Chadwick[2] were forcing us to realize that England was dying of dirt.

Florence had been born unexpectedly long after her mother had apparently ceased childbearing: she was possibly indulged as a welcome surprise on that account. Though Dr Farr survived his wits and lost most of his means by senile speculations before his death in 1883, he left enough to enable Florence to live modestly without having to sell herself in any fashion, or do anything that was distasteful to her.

She went on the stage and married a clever actor [Edward Emery], who was a member of the well-known histrionic Emery family. There was some trouble (not domestic) that ended in his emigrating to America and passing out of Florence's life. She attached so little importance to the incident, being apparently quite content to forget him, that I had some difficulty in persuading her to divorce him for desertion by pointing out that as long as their marriage remained undissolved, he might turn up any moment with very serious legal claims on her.

Whatever the trouble was that took him out of the country Florence gave up the stage for the moment, and set herself to learn the art of embroidery

---

1. English statistician, known for his contribution (1839–80) to the annual report of the Registrar-General on the cause of the year's deaths in England.
2. Social reformer, commissioner of the Board of Health 1848–54, among whose writings is the *Report . . . into the Sanitary Condition of the Labouring Population of Great Britain* (1842).

under Morris's daughter May. She acted [1889] in an entertainment at the house on the Mall; and on this occasion I made her acquaintance, and had no difficulty in considerably improving it. She set no bounds to her relations with men whom she liked, and already had a sort of Leporello list of a dozen adventures, none of which, however, had led to anything serious. She was in violent reaction against Victorian morals, especially sexual and domestic morals; and when the impact of Ibsen was felt in this country, and I wrote somewhere that "home is the girl's prison and the woman's workhouse" ['Maxims for Revolutionists', *Man and Superman*] I became *persona grata* with her; and for some years we saw a great deal of oneanother, and I wrote the letters which follow. It was a one-sided correspondence; for I cannot remember that she ever wrote to me.

She played the heroine [Blanche] in my first play [*Widowers' Houses*] in 1892. In 1894 the late Miss Horniman gave her money to produce modern plays at the old Avenue Theatre, now replaced by the Playhouse. The first production, inadequately cast and acted, failed; and Florence was about to replace it by my first play, when I wrote Arms and the Man for her instead, selecting the cast myself. With Yeats's Land of Heart's Desire as an exquisite curtain raiser it had a startling first night success, and kept the theatre open (average receipts £17) until Miss Horniman's money was exhausted.

Being bound to secrecy to avoid shocking Miss Horniman's Puritan family, Florence could not tell me who was backing her. Years later I had a dream in which I went into a room and found Miss Horniman sitting there, whereupon I exclaimed "YOU were the backer at the Avenue." Next day I wrote to her and asked her whether this revelation had any foundation. The allusion to this in the letters suggests that she was displeased; but that was only her way: she was one of those good women who do things, but are also incorrigibly cantankerous.

I made desperate efforts to work up Florence's technique and capacity for hard professional work to the point needed for serious stage work; but her early life had been too easy. I failed, and had to give up worrying and discouraging her. She found the friend she really needed in Yeats. What she called "cantilating"[3] for him was within her powers. We detached ourselves from oneanother naturally and painlessly; and presently I got married.

I heard about her departure for the East, but had no suspicion that her health was impaired in any way until I heard that she had undergone an

---

3. A technique of chanting, accompanied by a psaltery, that Florence had developed under the tutelage of Yeats.

operation. I telegraphed urgently for full information. My anxiety pleased her; and I learnt from her that the operation had been, so far, "successful." Months later [1917], her sister wrote to me that she was dead.

G. B. S.

# The Webbs

*Preface to Sidney and Beatrice Webb's* The Truth about Soviet Russia, *1942*

The Webbs, Sidney and Beatrice, officially the Right Honorable the Baron and Lady Passfield, are a superextraordinary pair. I have never met anyone like them, either separately or in their most fortunate conjunction. Each of them is an English force; and their marriage was an irresistible reinforcement. Only England could have produced them. It is true that France produced the Curies, a pair equally happily matched; but in physics they found an established science and left it so, enriched as it was by their labors; but the Webbs found British Constitutional politics something which nobody had yet dreamt of calling a science or thinking of as such.

When they began, they were face to face with Capitalism and Marxism. Marxism, though it claims to be scientific, and has proved itself a mighty force in the modern world, was then a philosophy propounded by a foreigner without administrative experience, who gathered his facts in the Reading Room of the British Museum, and generalized the human race under the two heads of *bourgeoisie* and proletariat apparently without having ever come into business contact with a living human being.

## THE QUARREL WITH CAPITALISM

Capitalism was and is a paper Utopia, the most unreal product of wishful thinking of all the Utopias. By pure logic, without a moment's reference to the facts, it demonstrated that you had only to enforce private contracts and let everybody buy in the cheapest market and sell in the dearest to produce automatically a condition in which there would be no unemployment, and every honest and industrious person would enjoy a sufficient wage to maintain himself and his wife and reproduce his kind, whilst an enriched superior class would have leisure and means to preserve and develop the nation's culture and civilization, and, by receiving more of the national income than they could possibly consume, save all the capital needed to make prosperity increase by leaps and bounds.

## WHAT KARL MARX DID

Karl Marx's philosophy had no effect on public opinion here or elsewhere; but when he published the facts as to the condition to which Capitalism had reduced the masses, it was like lifting the lid off hell. Capitalism has not yet recovered from the shock of that revelation, and never will.

Sixty years ago, the Marxian shock was only beginning to operate in England. I had to read Das Kapital in a French translation, there being no English version as yet. A new champion of the people, Henry Mayers Hyndman, had met and talked with Karl Marx. They quarreled, as their habit was, but not before Hyndman had been completely converted by Marx; so his Democratic Federation presently became a Social-Democratic Federation. Socialism, in abeyance since the slaughter of the Paris Commune in 1871, suddenly revived; but Marx, its leader and prophet, died at that moment and left the movement to what leadership it could get.

Socialism was not a new thing peculiar to Marx. John Stuart Mill, himself a convert, had converted others, among them one very remarkable young man and an already famous elderly one. The elderly one was the great poet and craftsman William Morris, who, on reading Mill's early somewhat halfhearted condemnation of communism,[1] at once declared that Mill's verdict was against the evidence, and that people who lived on unearned incomes were plainly "damned thieves." He joined Hyndman, and when the inevitable quarrel ensued, founded the Socialist League.

## SIDNEY WEBB, THE PRODIGY

The younger disciple had followed Mill's conversion and shared it. His name was Sidney Webb. He was an entirely unassuming young Londoner of no extraordinary stature, guiltless of any sort of swank, and so naïvely convinced that he was an ordinary mortal and everybody else as gifted as himself that he did not suffer fools gladly, and was occasionally ungracious to the poor things.

The unassuming young cockney was in fact a prodigy. He could read a book as fast as he could turn the leaves, and remember everything worth remembering in it. Whatever country he was in, he spoke the language with perfect facility, though always in the English manner. He had gone through

1. Presumably Mill's *Principles of Political Economy* (1848).

his teens gathering scholarships and exhibitions as a child gathers daisies, and had landed at last in the upper division of the civil service as resident clerk in the Colonial Office. He had acquired both scholarship and administrative experience, and knew not only why reforms were desirable but how they were put into practice under our queer political system. Hyndman and his Democratic Federation were no use to him, Morris and his Socialist League only an infant school. There was no organization fit for him except the Liberal Party, already moribund, but still holding a front bench position under the leadership of Gladstone. All Webb could do was something that he was forbidden to do as a civil servant: that is, issue pamphlets warning the Liberal Party that they were falling behind the times and even behind the Conservatives.[2] Nevertheless he issued the pamphlets calmly. Nobody dared to remonstrate.

### G.B.S. Meets the Man he Sought

This was the situation when I picked him up at a debating society which I had joined to qualify myself as a public speaker. It was the year 1879, when I was 23 and he a year or two younger. I at once recognized and appreciated in him all the qualifications in which I was myself pitiably deficient. He was clearly the man for me to work with. I forced my acquaintance on him; and it soon ripened into an enduring friendship. This was by far the wisest step I ever took. The combination worked perfectly.

We were both in the same predicament in having no organization with which we could work. Our job was to get Socialism into some sort of working shape; and we knew that this brainwork must be done by groups of Socialists whose minds operated at the same speed on a foundation of the same culture and habits. We were not snobs; but neither were we mere reactionists against snobbery to such an extent as to believe that we could work in double harness with the working men of the Federation and the League, who deeply and wisely mistrusted us as "bourgeois," and who would inevitably waste our time in trying to clear up hopeless misunderstandings. Morris was soon completely beaten by his proletarian comrades: he had to drop the League, which immediately perished. The agony of the Social-Democratic Federation was longer drawn out; but it contributed nothing to

2. Only one pamphlet was published: *Wanted, A Programme; An Appeal to the Liberal Party* (1888, for private circulation only).

the theory or practice of Socialism, and hardly even pretended to survive the death of Hyndman.

## The Fabian Society's Rise to Power

One day I came upon a tract entitled Why Are The Many Poor?[3] issued by a body of whom I had never heard, entitled the Fabian Society. The name struck me as an inspiration. I looked the Society up, and found a little group of educated middle-class persons who, having come together to study philosophy, had finally resolved to take to active politics as Socialists. It was just what we needed. When I had sized it up, Webb joined, and with him Sydney Olivier, his fellow resident clerk at the Colonial Office. Webb swept everything before him; and the history of the Fabian Society began as the public knows it today. Barricades manned by Anarchists, and Utopian colonies, vanished from the Socialist program; and Socialism became constitutional, respectable, and practical. This was the work of Webb far more than of any other single person.

## Marriage to Beatrice Potter

He was still a single person in another sense when the Fabian job was done. He was young enough to be unmarried when a young lady as rarely qualified as himself decided that he was old enough to be married. She had arrived at Socialism not by way of Karl Marx or John Stuart Mill, but by her own reasoning and observation. She was not a British Museum theorizer and bookworm; she was a born firsthand investigator. She had left the West End, where she was a society lady of the political plutocracy, for the East End, where she disguised herself to work in sweaters' dens and investigate the condition of the submerged tenth just discovered by Charles Booth and the Salvation Army. The sweaters found her an indifferent needlewoman, but chose her as an ideal bride for Ikey Mo: a generic name for their rising sons.[4] They were so pressing that she had to bring her investigation to a

---

3. Fabian Tract No. 1, drafted in 1884 by Frederick Keddell and William L. Phillips. Shaw revised the tract in 1889, reducing the rhetoric and fine-tuning the phraseology, but leaving the substance unaltered.

4. A derogatory but commonly used nineteenth-century term for a Jew: abridgement of Isaac and Moses. See also p. 350.

hasty end, and seek the comparatively aristocratic society of the trade union secretaries, with whom she hobnobbed as comfortably as if she had been born in their houses. She had written descriptions of the dens for Booth's first famous Enquiry, and a history of Co-operation which helped powerfully to shift its vogue from producers' co-operation to consumers' co-operation. Before her lay the whole world of proletarian organization to investigate.

It was too big a job for one worker. She resolved to take a partner. She took a glance at the Fabian Society, now two thousand strong, and at once dismissed nineteen hundred and ninetysix of them as negligible sheep; but it was evident that they were not sheep without a shepherd. There were in fact some halfdozen shepherds. She investigated them personally one after the other, and with unerring judgment selected Sidney Webb, and gathered him without the least difficulty, as he had left himself defenseless by falling in love with her head over ears.

### Their Literary Partnership

And so the famous partnership began. He took to her investigation business like a duck to water. They started with a history of trade unionism so complete and intimate in its information that it reduced all previous books on the subject to waste paper, and made organized labor in England class conscious for the first time. It traveled beyond England and was translated by Lenin. Then came the volume on Industrial Democracy which took trade unionism out of its groove and made it politically conscious of its destiny. There followed a monumental history of Local Government which ran into many volumes, and involved such a program of investigations on the spot all over the country, and reading through local archives, as had never before been attempted. Under such handling not only Socialism but political sociology in general became scientific, leaving Marx and Lassalle almost as far behind in that respect as they had left Robert Owen. The labor of it was prodigious; but it was necessary. And it left the Webbs no time for argybargy [haggling] as between Marx's Hegelian metaphysics and Max Eastman's[5] Cartesian materialism. The question whether Socialism is a soulless Conditioned Reflex *à la* Pavlov or the latest phase of the Light of the World announced by St John [John 9], did not delay them: they kept to the facts and the methods suggested by the facts.

5. American socialist editor of *The Masses*, 1912–17, and *The Liberator*, 1918–22.

Finally came the work in which those who believe in Divine Providence may like to see its finger. The depth and genuineness of our Socialism found its crucial test in the Russian revolution, which changed crude Tsarism into Red Communism. After the treaty of Brest Litovsk,[6] Hyndman, our arch-Marxist,[7] denounced it more fiercely than Winston Churchill. The history of Communist Russia for the past twenty years in the British and American Press is a record in recklessly prejudiced mendacity. The Webbs waited until the wreckage and ruin of the change was ended, its mistakes remedied, and the Communist State fairly launched. Then they went and investigated it. In their last two volumes they give us the first really scientific analysis of the Soviet State, and of its developments of our political and social experiments and institutions, including trade unionism and co-operation, which we thought they had abolished. No Russian could have done this all-important job for us. The Webbs knew England, and knew what they were talking about. No one else did.

They unhesitatingly gave the Soviet system their support, and announced it definitely as a New Civilization.

It has been a wonderful life's work. Its mere incidental by-blows included Webb's chairmanship of the London County Council's Technical Education Committee, which abolished the old school board, the creation of the London School of Economics, the Minority Report which dealt a death blow to the iniquitous Poor Law, and such comparative trifles as the conversion of bigoted Conservative constituencies into safe Labor seats, and a few years spent by Webb in the two Houses of Parliament.[8] They were the only years he ever wasted. He was actually compelled by the Labor Government to accept a peerage [1929]; but nothing could induce Beatrice to change the name she had made renowned throughout Europe for the title of Lady Passfield, who might be any nobody.

For the private life of the Webbs, I know all about it, and can assure you that it is utterly void of those scandalous adventures which make private lives readable. Mr Webb and Miss Potter are now Darby and Joan: that is all.

6. The treaty completely dismembered European Russia for the benefit of the Central Powers of Germany, Austria-Hungary and Turkey, as well as exacting a reparation payment of six billion marks.
7. Hyndman in his late years became a virulent anti-Bolshevik, expounding strong views on nationalism in his last work, *The Evolution of Revolution* (1920).
8. Webb served as chairman of the Technical Education committee 1892–1903. He and Beatrice founded the LSE in 1895; they co-drafted the Minority Report in 1909. Sidney represented the Seaham Division, Durham, in Parliament 1922–9.

# Hitler Has Won!

*Shaw's brief foreword (with another by C. E. M. Joad[1]) was published on a singleton leaf inserted loosely into copies of a pamphlet* Hitler Has Won! *published by Fact Service, Glasgow, 1946*

＝＝＝

Compulsory military service is the most complete form of personal slavery possible in a modern civilized country where the soldier has to be discharged as an efficient civilian at the end of his service. In the old days of horse drawn trams it paid best to work the horses to death in four years. In certain cotton districts in America it paid best to work the negroes to death in seven years. From this sort of profiteering the soldier is free; but on the other hand a certain statistical percentage are enlisted to be killed; and all are enlisted to kill, burn and destroy ruthlessly. To call this democratic because a majority can and does impose it on a minority is nonsense. When it is imposed by a disciplined minority commanded by one man; say by Marlborough or Wellington, it may be more bearable; but even under such commanders every sergeant is a Hitler.

Yet voluntary armies do not lack recruits. In Germany, when military service was compulsory in peace time, I never met a Prussian who regretted his period of service. But that meant, not that soldiering made barrack life heavenly but that poverty and ignorance made home life hellish. And there are many men who, under daily tutelage, with their meals, clothes and lodgings provided for them, are well conducted winners of Victorian Crosses and the like: but throw them on their own resources as free men and they are presently in the dock as criminals.

What has not yet been discussed, is whether soldiering is really a whole-time job. I am not convinced that it is. Waterloo was won by raw recruits against Napoleon's veterans. It is true that it was very nearly lost; but the bayoneting was as effective one way as the other. Cæsar and Cromwell picked up their soldiering in middle life very quickly. Bayoneting is not much use against atomic bombs. Now that shorter hours for civilians are possible, our

1. British philosopher, chairman of the department at Birkbeck College, University of London; author of many works on theology and ethics, including *Matter, Life and Value* (1929) and a study of Shaw (1949).

young men could all play at soldiers in the evenings for a few months and do better in the field than the trained Old Soldier (not, by the way, a title of honor).

May, 1946.                                                 George Bernard Shaw.

# Geneva

*First published in the collective edition of* Geneva, Cymbeline Refinished, *and* 'In Good King Charles's Golden Days', *1947*

=====

When I had lived for 58 years free from the fear that war could come to my doorstep, the thing occurred. And when the war to end war had come to a glorious victory, it occurred again, worse than ever. I have now lived through two "world wars" without missing a meal or a night's sleep in my bed, though they have come near enough to shatter my windows, break in my door, and wreck my grandfather clock, keeping me for nine years of my life subject to a continual apprehension of a direct hit next time blowing me and my household to bits.[1]

I cannot pretend that this troubled me much: people build houses and live on the slopes of Etna and Vesuvius and at the foot of Stromboli as cheerfully as on Primrose Hill. I was too old to be conscripted for military service; and the mathematical probabilities were enormously against a bomb coming my way; for at the worst of the bombardments only from ten to fifteen inhabitants of these islands were killed by air raids every day; and a dozen or so out of fortyfive millions is not very terrifying even when each of us knows that he or she is as likely as not to be one of the dozen. The risk of being run over by a motor bus, which townsmen run daily, is greater.

1.  A series of German air strikes in autumn 1917 caused minor damage to the Shaws' London residence in Adelphi Terrace. On 31 October Charlotte Shaw wrote to her Ayot neighbour Apsley Cherry-Garrard: 'We had the father and mother of a raid here last night . . . The gun flashes were lovely: the searchlights completely "dowsed" by the fog. The eerie thing was the whirl of the shells overhead, on 3 occasions the beat & buzz of the aircraft' [HRC]. During the 1940 blitz (the Shaws were in Ayot at the time) two windows and a door panel at Whitehall Court were smashed. In 1944 a blast from a V–bomb blew in Shaw's study window, shattering a grandfather clock in the hall. Again he was absent; but the bombing caught up with him in the country shortly thereafter when, near midnight on the eve of his 88th birthday, a V–bomb landed in a nearby coppice, its blast decimating a pane of glass in his bedroom window.

### Hoodwinked Heroism

It was this improbability which made pre-atomic air raiding futile as a means of intimidating a nation, and enabled the government of the raided nation to prevent the news of the damage reaching beyond its immediate neighborhood. One night early in the resumed war I saw, from a distance of 30 miles, London burning for three hours. Next morning I read in the newspapers that a bomb had fallen on the windowsill of a city office, and been extinguished before it exploded. Returning to London later on I found that half the ancient city had been leveled to the ground, leaving only St Paul's and a few church towers standing. The wireless news never went beyond "some damage and a few casualties in Southern England" when in fact leading cities and seaports had been extensively wrecked. All threatening news was mentioned only in secret sessions of parliament, hidden under heavy penalties until after the victory. In 1941, after the Dunkirk rout,[2] our position was described by the Prime Minister to the House of Commons in secret session as so desperate that if the enemy had taken advantage of it we should have been helplessly defeated; and it is now the fashion to descant dithyrambically on the steadfast heroism with which the nation faced this terrible emergency. As a matter of fact the nation knew nothing about it. Had we been told, the Germans would have overheard and rushed the threatened invasion they were bluffed into abandoning. Far from realizing our deadly peril, we were exulting in the triumph of our Air Force in "the Battle of Britain"[3] and in an incident in South America in which three British warships drove one German one into the river Plate. Rather than be interned with his crew the German captain put to sea again against hopeless odds; scuttled his ship; and committed

2. The miraculous deliverance of 233,000 members of the British Expeditionary Force and 112,500 French and other allied troops in an evacuation across the Strait of Dover from northern France by hundreds of military and hastily commandeered civilian small craft, occurred on 26 May to 3 June 1940.
3. On 10 July 1940 the *Luftwaffe* commenced air attacks that targeted convoys in the English Channel; they extended this in August with attacks on fighter airfields in southern England. On 7 September the Germans commenced a devastating series of raids on London, hoping to break morale. When they sustained heavy losses (more than 1600 planes) they switched to a blitz of night raids. The defensive RAF, however, destroyed so many of the invading aircraft and, as well, enemy landing craft and barges at sea, that the Germans in 1941 were forced to alter their strategy, ending the 'Battle of Britain' and defeating Hitler's project for invading the British island by sea.

suicide.[4] The British newspapers raved about this for weeks as a naval victory greater than Salamis, Lepanto, and Trafalgar rolled into one.

Later on our flight from Tobruk[5] to the border of Egypt did not disturb us at home: it was reported as a trifling setback, whilst trumpery captures of lorries or motor bicycles by British patrols figured as victories. After major engagements German losses were given in figures: Allies' losses were not given at all, the impression left being that the Allies had killed or taken prisoner tens of thousands of Axis troops without suffering any casualties worth mentioning. Only by listening to the German broadcasts, similarly cooked, could the real facts and fortunes of the war be estimated. Of course the truth leaked out months later; but it produced only a fresh orgy of bragging about our heroic fortitude in the face of the deadly peril we knew nothing of.

All this was necessary and inevitable. It was dangerous to tell the truth about anything, even about the weather. The signposts on the roads had to be taken down and hidden lest they should help an invader to find his way. It was a crime to give an address with a date, or to scatter a few crumbs for the birds. And it was an act of heroic patriotism to drop a bomb weighing ten thousand pounds on dwellings full of women and children, or on crowded railway trains. Our bombing of foreign cities not only in Germany but in countries which we claimed to be "liberating" became so frightful that at last the word had to be given to two of our best broadcasters of war reports to excuse them on the ground that by shortening the war they were saving the lives of thousands of British soldiers.[6]

4. In an encounter in the South Atlantic on 13 December 1939 the British cruisers *Ajax*, *Exeter* and *Achilles* heavily damaged the German pocket battleship *Graf Spee*, whose captain, Hans Langsdorff, sought momentary refuge in the neutral port of Montevideo. The crew of the ship, which was scuttled two days later, were rescued and interned.

5. In the third Axis offensive in North Africa (1943) Field Marshal Erwin Rommel's Afrika Korps captured the Libyan coastal town of Tobruk, long a symbol of resistance. Although Tobruk 'fell' on 30 May, the Australian garrison fought a desperate holding action until 21 June.

6. One of the broadcasters was the BBC's chief announcer, Stuart Hibberd. 'Anthony Weymouth' (Ivo Geikie Cobb), a member of the BBC's Programmes Department, noted in his diary on 9 August 1942: 'There has been a good deal of fuss about Air-Marshal [Arthur] Harris's broadcast to the German people in which he told them that we and the Americans were going to blast their country from one end to the other', as the RAF had pulverized Cologne in a thousand-plane attack on 30 May. On 31 May the diarist had written: 'I can't say I feel in any way jubilant

Meanwhile nobody noticed how completely war, as an institution, had reduced itself to absurdity. When Germany annexed Poland in 1939, half of it was snatched out of her jaws by Soviet Russia. The British Commonwealth, having bound itself to maintain inviolate the frontiers of Poland as they were left after the fighting of 1914–18 with a Polish corridor cut right through Prussia to the Baltic, was committed to declare war on Germany and Russia simultaneously. But the British people and their rulers were in no mood to black out their windows and recommence the Four Years War in defence of this distant and foreign corridor. Being, as usual, unprepared for war, we tried to appease Germany and yet keep the peace with Soviet Russia.

## ENGLAND FRIGHTENED AND GREAT

Nations should always be prepared for war, just as people with any property to leave should always have made their wills. But as most of them never do make their wills, and the rest seldom keep them revised and up to date, States, however militarist, are never fully prepared for war. England will do nothing outside her routine until she is thoroughly frightened; but when England is frightened England is capable of anything. Philip II of Spain frightened her. Louis XIV of France frightened her. Napoleon frightened her. Wilhelm II of the German Reich frightened her. But instead of frightening the wits out of her they frightened the wits into her. She woke up and smashed them all. In vain did the Kaiser sing *Deutschland über Alles*, and Hitler claim that his people were the *Herrenvolk* created by God to rule the earth. The English were equally convinced that when Britain first at Heaven's command arose from out the azure main she was destined to rule the waves, and make the earth her footstool. This is so natural to Englishmen that they are unconscious of it, just as they cannot taste water because it is always in their mouths. Long before England first sang Rule Britannia at Cliveden[7] she had

---

at the thought of the hundreds of killed and thousands of injured people which will result from an attack on this scale . . . [A]s our own people have experienced intensive air attack first-hand, they understand exactly what it entails. Perhaps that's one reason why there is no jubilation here over the bombing of German towns' (*Journal of the War Years (1939–1945) and One Year Later*, 1948). Air-Marshal Harris was chief of Bomber Command.

7. Shaw is stretching things a bit. Cliveden, in Buckinghamshire, is on the Thames opposite Maidenhead, where in 1740 at the residence of Frederick, Prince of Wales, the song was first performed in *The Masque of Alfred*, with words by James Thomson and David Mallet and music by Thomas Arne.

annihilated Philip's Invincible Armada to the music of the winds and waves, and, after being defeated again and again by General Luxemburg, made hay of the French armies at Blenheim, Ramilies, and Malplaquet to the senseless gibberish of Lillibullerobullenalah.[8] She not only took on Hitler singlehanded without a word to the League of Nations nor to anyone else, but outfought him, outbragged him, outbullied him, outwitted him in every trick and turn of warfare, and finally extinguished him and hanged his accomplices.

## ENGLAND SECURE AND LAZY

The drawback to England's capacity for doing impossible things when in danger is her incapacity for doing possible things (except repeating what was done last time) in security. The prefabrication in England of harbors for France[9] and planting them there as part of the baggage of the allied invading armies, was a feat which still seems incredible even now that it has actually been achieved; yet during the 20 years armistice England could not bridge the Severn below Gloucester, harness the Pentland tides, nor tap the volcanic fires of the earth's boiling core, much less mechanize the coalmines or even design an alphabet capable of saving billionsworth of British time, ink, and paper, by spelling English speech sounds unequivocally and economically. The moment the Cease Fire is sounded England forgets all the lessons of the war and proves the truth of Dr Inge's old comment on the Anglo-Irish situation as illustrating the difficulty of driving in double harness people who remember nothing with people who forget nothing.[10] Still, as forgetful people

8. François de Montmorency-Bouteville, Duc de Luxembourg, was a French marshal who thrice defeated William III in battle. British and allied armies defeated the French at Blenheim, a Bavarian village; at Ramillies (which Shaw misspelled), a Belgian village in Brabant; and at Malplaquet, a French village near Mons. The 'senseless gibberish' is an early nursery song that gained popularity at the end of the seventeenth century with new doggerel verses satirizing English politics in Ireland. The air was introduced by John Gay in *The Beggar's Opera* (1728).
9. Artificial ports fabricated in England were set up within two weeks after D-Day.
10. The statement (a variant of which appears in the preface to *Farfetched Fables*, p. 525), is another instance of Shavian epigrammatic enhancement. Inge, rigidly anti-Irish and arrogantly, smugly English, was rather more verbose in his *England* (1926): 'Akin to [our English] humanity is an absence of vindictiveness. We have short memories when we have been wronged, and never make long plans for revenge . . . An Englishman is simply unable to comprehend the brooding hatred of the Irishman, which has no better ground than that Cromwell exercised the laws of war somewhat

ff.?

who act in the present can master vindictive people who only brood on the past there is much to be said for England's full share of human thoughtlessness. It is sometimes better not to think at all than to think intensely and think wrong.

Statesmen who know no past history are dangerous because contemporary history cannot be ascertained. No epoch is intelligible until it is completed and can be seen in the distance as a whole, like a mountain. The victorious combatants in the battle of Hastings did not know that they were inaugurating feudalism for four centuries, nor the Red Roses on Bosworth Field and the Ironsides at Naseby know that they were exchanging it for Whig plutocracy.[11] Historians and newspaper editors can see revolutions three centuries off but not three years off, much less three hours. Had Marx and Engels been contemporaries of Shakespear they could not have written the Communist Manifesto, and would probably have taken a hand, as Shakespear did, in the enclosure of common lands [see vol. 2, p. 115] as a step forward in civilization.

### HISTORY STOPS YESTERDAY: STATECRAFT WORKS BLINDFOLD

This is why history in our schools stops far short of the present moment, and why statesmen, though they can learn the lessons of history from books, must grope their way through daily emergencies within the limits of their ignorance as best they can. If their vision is vulgar and vindictive the guesses they make may be worse than the war. That vision has not widened nor that ability grown of late. But the perils of the situation have increased enormously. Men are what they were; but war has become many times more destructive, not of men, who can be replaced, but of the plant of civilization, the houses and factories, the railways and airways, the orchards and furrowed fields, and

severely against the Irish rebels, and that William III won the battle of the Boyne' (pp. 54–5). '[C]ool practicality has led the English to show almost inexhaustible patience with the treasons, insults, and outrages of the Irish' (p. 66).

11. These are three of the most decisive battles in British history. The defeat of Harold, king of England, at Hastings, on 14 October 1066 by William, duke of Normandy. The defeat of the usurper Richard III of York by the 'Red Roses' (the Lancastrians in the civil wars known as the Wars of the Roses) led by Henry Tudor, on 22 August 1485. The defeat of the Royalist army of Charles I on 14 June 1645 by the New Model army of Parliament under its commander-in-chief Sir Thomas Fairfax, in a battle in which the double cavalry regiment known as the 'Ironsides' played a major role. On this occasion, however, Cromwell (as Fairfax's lieutenant-general) led a regiment of foot soldiers.

the spare subsistence which we call capital, without which civilized mankind would perish. Even the replacement of the slain is threatened because the latest bombs are no respecters of sex; and where there are no women there will soon be no warriors. In some of the air raids, more women were killed than men. The turning point of the war was the siege of Stalingrad, written up by the newspapers more dithyrambically than any siege in history since the siege of Troy. But when the Greeks captured Troy they had the city for their pains as well as the glory. When the Red Army triumphed at Stalingrad[12] they had nothing but festering corpses to bury, heaps of rubble to clear away, and a host of prisoners to feed. Meanwhile the British and American armies were "liberating" French cities, Dutch cities, Belgian cities, Italian cities: that is, they were destroying them exactly as they were destroying German cities, and having to house and feed their surviving inhabitants after wrecking their water mains, electric power stations, and railway communications. From the national point of view this was conquest, glory, patriotism, bravery, all claiming to be necessary for security. From the European wider angle it was folly and devilment, savagery and suicide. The ready money collected for it (wars cannot be fought on credit) was called Savings: a barefaced wicked lie. All the belligerents have been bled white, and will find, when they claim their "savings" back from their governments, that their Chancellors of the Exchequer will reply, like the juvenile spendthrift exhorted to pay his debts by Richelieu in Lytton's play, "Willingly, your Eminence: where shall I borrow the money?";[13] for not a farthing of it (say 12 millions shot away every day for six years) remains; and all of it that achieved its purpose of ruin has imposed on us the added burden of repairing what we have destroyed.

So much for England frightened into fighting. The question now is has war become frightful enough to frighten her out of it? In the last months the bombs launched by young British warriors from airplanes at the risk of their lives grew to such prodigious weight and destructiveness that they wrecked not merely houses but whole streets, and scattered blazing phosphorus and magnesium on such a scale that the victims, chiefly women with children who could not escape by flight as a few of the men did, were stifled by having nothing to breathe but white hot air, and then burnt to cinders

12. The German army at Stalingrad, under the command of General Friedrich Paulus, surrendered to the Russians on 2 February 1943 after five months of futile combat.
13. The Chevalier de Mauprat is admonished in Act I, scene 2, of Edward Bulwer-Lytton's play *Richelieu* (1839).

and buried under the piles of rubble that had been their houses.[14] We rained these monster bombs on Germany until the destruction of their railways and munition factories made retaliation in kind impossible. Our flame-throwing from tanks finished the fugitives.

## We Split the Atom

But the resources of decivilization were not exhausted. When we were exulting in our demolition of cities like Cologne and Hamburg we were very considerably frightened by the descent on London of new projectiles, unmanned yet aimed and guided, which demolished not only streets but districts.[15] And when we and our allies "liberated" German-occupied territory (blowing its cities to smithereens largely in the process) we discovered that the manufacture of these new horrors had been planned for on such a scale that but for their capture in time the tables might have been turned on us with a vengeance.

But we had another card up our sleeve: this time a trump so diabolical that when we played it the war, which still lingered in Japan, was brought to an abrupt stop by an Anglo-American contrivance which may conceivably transform the globe into a cloud of flaming gas in which no form of life known to us could survive for a moment. That such explosions have visibly occurred on other stars (called novas) is vouched for by our astronomers, who have seen them with their naked eyes and studied their photographs and spectrographs for years past. When England and the United States of North America got ahead of Germany and Japan with this terrific weapon all their opponents at once surrendered at discretion.

## An Amoral Victory

This time there could be no sustainable pretence of a moral victory, though plenty were made as usual; for nothing yet discovered has cured mankind of

14. These were incendiary bombs, called 'block-busters', rained down on cities such as Hamburg in the final months of 1944 in a pattern that produced 'fire storms', a phenomenon that created simultaneous fires over a large area, which would merge to produce more heat and destructive power than in ordinary conflagrations.
15. 'V-1' jet-propelled flying bombs in June to September 1944, supplanted, to the end of the year, by 'V-2' rockets faster than the speed of sound.

lying and boasting. It was what Wellington called Waterloo, a very near thing;[16] for had the Germans not concentrated on the jet propulsion of pilotless aeroplanes instead of on the atomic bomb, they might have contrived it before us and made themselves masters of the situation if not of the world. They may yet cheapen and improve on it. Or they may discover a gas lighter than air, deadly but not destructive. And then where shall we be? Ethical victories endure. Discoveries cannot be guaranteed for five minutes.

Still, though the victory was not a triumph of Christianity it was a triumph of Science. American and British scientists, given *carte blanche* in the matter of expense, had concentrated on a romantic and desperate search for a means of harnessing the mysterious forces that mould and hold atoms into metals, minerals, and finally into such miracles as human geniuses, taking some grains of metal and a few salts purchasable at the nearest oilshop and fashioning with them the head of Shakespear, to say nothing of my own. It is already known that the energy that makes uranium out of molecules, escapes by slow radiation and both kills and cures living organisms, leaving behind it not radium but lead. If this disintegration could be speeded up to instantaneousness it would make a heat so prodigious that a couple of morsels of uranium dropped from a plane and timed to collide and disintegrate above a city could convert that city and its inhabitants into a heap of flaming gas in a fraction of a second. The experiment was tried on two Japanese cities. Four square miles of them vanished before the experimenters could say Jack Robinson.

There is no getting away from the fact that if another world war be waged with this new weapon there may be an end of our civilization and its massed populations. Even for those philosophers who are of opinion that this would not be any great loss there is a further possibility. An atomic bomb attached to a parachute and exploded in the air would devastate only as many square miles as it was meant to; but if it hung fire and exploded in the earth it might start a continuous process of disintegration in which our planet would become a *nova* to astronomers on Mars, blazing up and dimming out, leaving nothing of it and of us in the sky but a gaseous nebula.

It seems that if "the sport of kings" [William Somerville, *The Chase*, 1735] is to continue it must be fought under Queensberry rules classing atomic bombs with blows below the belt, and barring them. But it was the British

16. 'It has been a damned serious business', Wellington told Thomas Creevey shortly after the battle. 'Blücher and I have lost 30,000 men. It has been a damned nice thing – the nearest run thing you ever saw in your life . . .' (*Creevey Papers*, ed. John Gore, London: revised edn., 1963, chapter 7, p. 133).

refusal to bar aerial bombardment that made the air battles of the world war lawful; and these air battles had already reduced war to economic absurdity before the atomic bomb came into action. War had become logical: enemies were massacred or transported: wayleave was abolished. Thus the victors were left with the terror of their own discovery, and the vanquished with the hope that they may soon discover for themselves how to disintegrate uranium or perhaps some other element with ten times its energy. And two of the great allies, England and America, flatly refuse to share the secret of the new bomb with Russia, the third. Villages in India are still wiped out to "larn" their mostly harmless inhabitants not to snipe at British soldiers. The alarm is general: the cry of all hands, the triumphant even more than the subjugated, is that there must be an end of war. But all the other cries are as warlike as ever. The victorious Allies agree in demanding that Germans and Japanese must be treated as Catholic Ireland was treated by England in the XVII century.[17]

Some of them are now consoling themselves with the hope that the atomic bomb has made war impossible. That hope has often been entertained before. Colonel Robinson, in the Nineteenth Century and After,[18] has given a list of previous discoveries, dating back to B.C., which have developed the technique of killing from the single combats of the Trojan war, fought man to man, to artillery operations and air raids in which the combatants are hundreds of miles apart on the ground or thousands of feet up in the air dropping bombs and flying away at a speed of ten miles per second, never seeing oneanother nor the mischief they do. At every development it is complained that war is no longer justifiable as a test of heroic personal qualities, and demonstrated that it has become too ruinous to be tolerated as an institution. War and imperialist diplomacy persist nonetheless.

17. Presumably Shaw is speaking of confiscated land, more than 750,000 acres of Catholic-owned Irish estates having been transferred to a conquering army of Protestants. In other respects, Irish Catholics received more severe treatment than did modern Germany and Japan. By the end of the seventeenth century they had been excluded from the Dublin parliament; their middle classes debarred from trades and professions; conscientious Catholics denied the right to wear arms or own a horse, to teach publicly or to practise law. At the start of the eighteenth century they were excluded from public office, jury service and the electoral vote.

18. Major-General H. Rowan-Robinson, 'The Atomic Bomb', September 1945.

## CIVILIZATION'S WILL TO LIVE ALWAYS DEFEATED
### BY DEMOCRACY

Mankind, though pugnacious, yet has an instinct which checks it on the brink of selfdestruction. We are still too close to the time when men had to fight with wild beasts for their lives and with oneanother for their possessions, and when women had to choose fighters for their mates to protect them from robbery and rapine at their work as mothers, nurses, cooks, and kitchen gardeners. There are still places in the world where after tribal battles the victors eat the vanquished and the women share the feast with the warriors. In others foreign explorers, visitors, and passengers are killed as strangers.[19] The veneer of civilization which distinguishes Europeans from these tribesmen and their wives is dangerously thin. Even English ladies and gentlemen "go Fantee"[20] occasionally. Christmas cards will not prevent them from using atomic bombs if they are again frightened and provoked. But the magnitude of the new peril rouses that other instinct, stronger finally than pugnacity, that the race must not perish. This does not mean that civilization cannot perish. Civilizations have never finally survived: they have perished over and over again because they failed to make themselves worth their cost to the masses whom they enslaved. Even at home they could not master the art of governing millions of people for the common good in spite of people's inveterate objection to be governed at all. Law has been popularly known only as oppression and taxation, and politics as a clamor for less government and more liberty. That citizens get better value for the rates and taxes they pay than for most other items in their expenditure never occurs to them. They will pay a third of their weekly earnings or more to an idle landlord as if that were a law of nature; but a collection from them by the rate collector they resent as sheer robbery: the truth being precisely the reverse. They see nothing extravagant in basing democracy on an assumption that every adult native is either a Marcus Aurelius or a combination of Saint Teresa and Queen

19. Cannibalism survived into the present century in several remote areas of the world, from west and central Africa to Sumatra and Fiji, ritually, with head-hunters and warriors consuming bits of flesh of their dead enemies. In the interior of New Guinea as late as the 1960s strangers and interlopers were devoured; one of these presumed victims was a scion of the Nelson Rockefeller family.
20. That is, to go native and, by implication, savage. The Fanti were a nation of black people inhabiting a portion of the coastal region of the Gold Coast colony in British West Africa.

Elizabeth Tudor, supremely competent to choose any tinker tailor soldier sailor or any goodlooking well dressed female to rule over them. This insane prescription for perfect democracy of course makes democracy impossible and the adventures of Cromwell, Napoleon, Hitler, and the innumerable conquistadores and upstart presidents of South American history inevitable. There never has been and never will be a government which is both plebiscitary and democratic, because the plebs do not want to be governed, and the plutocrats who humbug them, though they are so far democratic that they must for their own sakes keep their slaves alive and efficient, use their powers to increase their revenues and suppress resistance to their appropriation of all products and services in excess of this minimum. Substitute a plebeian government, and it can only carry on to the same point with the same political machinery, except that the plunder goes to the Trade Unions instead of to the plutocrats. This may be a considerable advance; but when the plebeian government attempts to reorganize production collectively so as to increase the product and bring the highest culture within the reach of all who are capable of it, and make the necessary basic material prosperity general and equal, the dread and hatred of government as such, calling itself Liberty and Democracy, reasserts itself and stops the way. Only when a war makes collective organization compulsory on pain of slaughter, subjugation, and nowadays extinction by bombs, jet propelled or atomic, is any substantial advance made or men of action tolerated as Prime Ministers. The first four years of world war [1914–18] forced us to choose a man of action as leader; but when the armistice came we got rid of him and had a succession of premiers who could be trusted to do nothing revolutionary.[21] Our ideal was "a commonplace type with a stick and a pipe and a half bred black and tan."[22] Even Franklin Roosevelt won his first presidential election more by a photograph of himself in the act of petting a baby than by his political program, which few understood: indeed he only half understood it himself. When Mr Winston Churchill, as a man of action, had to be substituted for the *fainéants* [idlers] when the war was resumed, his big cigars and the genial romantic oratory in which

21. Lloyd George (Shaw's 'man of action') lost his Liberal majority in Parliament in the General Election of December 1918; but his ministry survived in a coalition government, dominated by Conservatives, until October 1922, when he was succeeded by Bonar Law, who won a General Election a month later. Shaw may have been thinking of the succession of Law, MacDonald and Baldwin in the early and middle 1920s.
22. From a duet, 'When I go out of door', in Act II of Gilbert and Sullivan's *Patience* (1881).

he glorified the war maintained his popularity until the war was over [in Europe] and he opened the General Election [5 July 1945] campaign by announcing a domestic policy which was a hundred years out of fashion, and promised nothing to a war weary proletariat eager for a Utopia in which there should be no military controls and a New World inaugurated in which everybody was to be both employed and liberated.

Mr Churchill at once shared the fate of Lloyd George; and the Utopians carried the day triumphantly. But the New World proved the same as the old one, with the same fundamental resistance to change of habits and the same dread of government interference surviving in the adult voter like the child's dread of a policeman.

It may be asked how it is that social changes do actually take place under these circumstances. The reply is that other circumstances create such emergencies, dangers, and hardships, that the very people who dread Government action are the first to run to the Government for a remedy, crying that "something must be done." And so civilization, though dangerously slowed down, forces its way piecemeal in spite of stagnant ignorance and selfishness.

Besides, there are always ancient constitutions and creeds to be reckoned with; and these are not the work of adult suffrage, but inheritances from feudal and ecclesiastical systems which had to provide law and order during the intervals between dominating personalities, when ordinary governments had to mark time by doing what was done last time until the next big boss came along and became a popular idol, worshipped at the polls by 99 per cent majorities.

All the evidence available so far is to the effect that since the dawn of history there has been no change in the natural political capacity of the human species. The comedies of Aristophanes and the Bible are at hand to convince anyone who doubts this. But this does not mean that enlightenment is impossible. Without it our attempts at democracy will wreck our civilization as they have wrecked all the earlier civilizations we know of. The ancient empires were not destroyed by foreign barbarians. They assimilated them easily. They destroyed themselves: their collapse was the work of their own well meaning native barbarians. Yet these barbarians, like our own at present, included a percentage of thinkers who had their imaginations obsessed by Utopias in which perfectly wise governments were to make everybody prosperous and happy. Their old men saw visions and their young men dreamed dreams just as they do now. But they were not all such fools as to believe that their visions and dreams could be realized by Tom, Dick, and Harriet voting for Titus Oates, Lord George Gordon, Horatio Bottomley, Napoleon, or Hitler. My experience as an enlightener, which is considerable, is that what is wrong with the average citizen is not altogether deficient political capacity. It is largely ignorance of facts, creating a vacuum into which all sorts of romantic antiquarian junk and cast-off primitive religion rushes. I have to enlighten sects describing themselves as Conservatives, Socialists, Protestants, Catholics, Communists, Fascists, Fabians, Friends (Quakers), Ritualists, all bearing labels which none of them can define, and which indicate tenets which none of them accept as practical rules of life and many of them repudiate with abhorrence when they are presented without their labels. I was baptized as a member of the then established Protestant Episcopal Church in Ireland. My religious education left me convinced that I was entitled to call myself a Protestant because I believed that Catholics were an inferior species who would all go to hell when they died; and I daresay the Roman Catholic children with whom I was forbidden to play believed that the same eternity of torment awaited me in spite of Pope Pius the Ninth's humane instruction to them to absolve me on the plea of invincible ignorance.[23] We were both taught to worship "a tenth rate tribal deity" of the most vindictive, jealous, and ruthless pugnacity, equally with his Christlike son. Just so today Conservatives know nothing of the Tory creed, but are convinced that the rulers of Russia are bloodstained tyrants, robbers and murderers, and their subjects slaves without rights or liberties. All good Russians believe equally that the capitalist rulers of the Western plutocracies are ruthless despots out for nothing but exploiting labor in pursuit of surplus value, as Marx called rent, interest, and profit. They group themselves in political parties and clubs in which none of them knows what he or she is talking about. Some of them have Utopian aspirations, and have read the prophets and sages, from Moses to Marx, and from Plato to Ruskin and Inge; but a question as to a point of existing law or the function of a County Council strikes them dumb. They are more dangerous than simpletons and illiterates because on the strength of their irrelevant schooling they believe themselves politically educated, and are accepted as authorities on political subjects accordingly.

Now this political ignorance and delusion is curable by simple instruction as to the facts without any increase of political capacity. I am ending as a sage with a very scrappy and partial knowledge of the world. I do not see

23. Pope Pius IX's encyclical, *Singulari Quidem*, of 17 March 1856 stipulates: 'The Church clearly declares that the only hope of salvation for mankind is placed in the Christian faith, which teaches the truth, scatters the darkness of ignorance by the splendour of its light, and works through love . . . Outside of the Church, nobody can hope for life or salvation unless he is excused through ignorance beyond his control.'

why I should not have begun with it if I had been told it all to begin with: I was more capable of it then than I am now in my dotage. When I am not writing plays as a more or less inspired artist I write political schoolbooks in which I say nothing of the principles of Socialism or any other Ism (I disposed of all that long ago), and try to open my readers' eyes to the political facts under which they live. I cannot change their minds; but I can increase their knowledge. A little knowledge [learning] is a dangerous thing [Pope, *An Essay on Criticism*, 1711]; but we must take that risk because a little is as much as our biggest heads can hold; and a citizen who knows that the earth is round and older than six thousand years is less dangerous than one of equal capacity who believes it is a flat groundfloor between a first floor heaven and a basement hell.

## INCOMPETENT GOVERNMENTS ARE THE CRUELEST

The need for confining authority to the instructed and capable has been demonstrated by terrible lessons daily for years past. As I write [November 1945], dockfuls of German prisoners of war, male and female, are being tried on charges of hideous cruelties perpetrated by them at concentration camps. The witnesses describe the horrors of life and death in them; and the newspapers class the accused as fiends and monsters. But they also publish photographs of them in which they appear as ordinary human beings who could be paralleled from any crowd or army.

These Germans had to live in the camps with their prisoners. It must have been very uncomfortable and dangerous for them. But they had been placed in authority and management, and had to organize the feeding, lodging, and sanitation of more and more thousands of prisoners and refugees thrust upon them by the central government. And as they were responsible for the custody of their prisoners they had to be armed to the teeth and their prisoners completely disarmed. Only eminent leadership, experience, and organizing talent could deal with such a situation.

Well, they simply lacked these qualities. They were not fiends in human form; but they did not know what to do with the thousands thrown on their care. There was some food; but they could not distribute it except as rations among themselves. They could do nothing with their prisoners but overcrowd them within any four walls that were left standing, lock them in, and leave them almost starving to die of typhus. When further overcrowding became physically impossible they could do nothing with their unwalled prisoners but kill them and burn the corpses they could not bury. And even this they could not organize frankly and competently: they had to make their victims die of illusage instead of by military law. Under such circumstances any miscellaneous collection of irresistibly armed men would be demoralized; and the natural percentage of callous toughs among them would wallow in cruelty and in the exercise of irresponsible authority for its own sake. Man beating is better sport than bear baiting or cock fighting or even child beating, of which some sensational English cases were in the papers at home at the time. Had there been efficient handling of the situation by the authorities (assuming this to have been possible) none of these atrocities would have occurred. They occur in every war when the troops get out of hand.


## HITLER

The German government was rotten at the centre as well as at the periphery. The Hohenzollern monarchy in Germany, with an enormous military prestige based on its crushing defeat of the Bonapartist French Army in 1871 (I was fifteen at the time, and remember it quite well) was swept away in 1918 by the French Republic. The rule of the monarch was succeeded by the rule of anybody chosen by everybody, supposed, as usual, to secure the greatest common measure of welfare, which is the object of democracy, but which really means that a political career is open to any adventurer. It happened that in Munich in 1930 there was a young man named Hitler who had served in the Four Years War. Having no special military talent he had achieved no more as a soldier than the Iron Cross and the rank of corporal. He was poor and what we call no class, being a Bohemian with artistic tastes but neither training nor talent enough to succeed as an artist, and was thus hung up between the bourgeoisie for which he had no income and the working class for which he had no craft. But he had a voice and could talk, and soon became a beer cellar orator who could hold his audience. He joined a cellar debating society (like our old Coger's Hall)[24] and thereby brought its numbers up to seven. His speeches soon attracted considerable reinforcements and established him as a leading spirit. Much of what he spouted was true. As a soldier he had learnt that disciplined men can make short work of mobs; that party parliaments on the British model neither could nor would abolish the

24. The 'cellar' society was a tiny political group, the National Socialist German Workers Party, in Munich (1919). The Honourable Society of Cogers (from the Latin *cogito*), established in 1755 in Shoe Lane, London, was a debating society, whose members consisted principally of young barristers, law students and politicians.

poverty that was so bitter to him; that the Treaty of Versailles under which Germany, defeated and subjected far beyond the last penny she could spare, could be torn up clause by clause by anyone with a big enough army to intimidate the plunderers; and that Europe was dominated economically by a plutocracy of financiers who had got the whip hand even of the employers. So far he was on solid ground, with unquestionable facts to support him. But he mixed the facts up with fancies such as that all plutocrats are Jews; that the Jews are an accursed race who should be exterminated as such; that the Germans are a chosen race divinely destined to rule the world; and that all she needs to establish her rule is an irresistible army. These delusions were highly flattering to Hans, Fritz, and Gretchen at large as well as to the beer drinkers in the cellar; and when an attempt was made to silence the new Hitlerites by hired gangsters, Hitler organized a bodyguard [storm-troopers, also known as Brown Shirts, 1923] for himself so effectively that the opposition was soon sprawling in the street.

With this stock in trade Hitler found himself a born leader, and, like Jack Cade, Wat Tyler, Essex under Elizabeth Tudor, [Robert] Emmet under Dublin Castle, and Louis Napoleon under the Second Republic, imagined he had only to appear in the streets with a flag to be acclaimed and followed by the whole population. He tried the experiment with a general from the Four Years War at his side and such converts to his vogue and eloquence as his beer cellar orations had made. With this nucleus he marched through the streets. A rabble gathered and followed to see the fun, as rabbles always will in cities. In London I have seen thousands of citizens rushing to see why the others were rushing, and to find out why. It looked like a revolutionary *émeute* [uprising]. On one occasion it was a runaway cow. On another it was Mary Pickford, "World's [America's] Sweetheart" of the old silent films, driving to her hotel in a taxi.

For a moment Hitler may have fancied that a success like that of Mussolini's march to Rome (he went by train) was within his grasp. He had the immediate precedent of Kurt Eisner's successful *Putsch* to encourage him. But Eisner was not resisted.[25] When Hitler and his crowd came face to face with the Government troops they did not receive him as the *grognards*[26] of the Bourbon

25. In November 1918 Kurt Eisner, a Bavarian socialist and journalist, proclaimed Bavaria a republic and assumed the position of prime minister. Three months later, however, he was assassinated.

26. The Grognards (grumblers) were veterans of Napoleon's army. On his return from Elba and entry into Paris, 20 March 1815, the troops sent against him joined his standard.

army received Napoleon on his return from Elba. They opened fire on him. His rabble melted and fled. He and General Ludendorff had to throw themselves flat on the pavement to avoid the bullets. He was imprisoned for eight months for his escapade,[27] not having frightened the Government enough to be considered worth killing as Cade, Tyler, and Essex were killed. In prison, he and his companion-secretary [Rudolf] Hess,[28] wrote a book entitled *Mein Kampf* (My Struggle, My Program, My Views or what you please).

Like Louis Napoleon he had now learnt his lesson: namely, that *Putsches* are a last desperate method, not a first one, and that adventurers must come to terms with the captains of finance and industry, the bankers, and the Conservatives who really control the nations wherever the people choose what rulers they please, before he can hope to be accepted by them as a figurehead. Hitler had sufficient histrionic magnetism to strike this bargain even to the extent of being made perpetual chancellor of the German Realm with more than royal honors, though his whole stock in trade was a brazen voice and a doctrine made up of scraps of Socialism, mortal hatred of the Jews, and complete contempt for pseudo-democratic parliamentary mobocracy.

## PSEUDO MESSIAH AND MADMAN

So far he was the creature and tool of the plutocracy. But the plutocracy had made a bad bargain. The moment it made Hitler a figurehead, popular idolatry made a prophet and a hero of him, and gave him a real personal power far in excess of that enjoyed by any commercial magnate. He massacred all his political rivals not only with impunity but with full parliamentary approval. Like St Peter on a famous earlier occasion the German people cried "Thou art the Christ" [Matthew 16: 16], with the same result. Power and worship turned Hitler's head; and the national benefactor who began by abolishing unemployment, tearing up the Treaty of Versailles, and restoring the selfrespect of sixty millions of his fellow countrymen, became the mad Messiah who, as lord of a Chosen Race, was destined to establish the Kingdom of God on earth—a German kingdom of a German God—by military

27. An aborted beer-hall *Putsch* in Munich, 8–9 November 1923, in an attempt by Hitler and Ludendorff to overthrow the Bavarian government. Ludendorff's reputation saved him from any consequences; Hitler was imprisoned for nine months (out of a five-year sentence).
28. German National Socialist, who assisted in the Munich *Putsch*, and who took Hitler's dictation of *Mein Kampf* in Landsberg prison.

conquest of the rest of mankind. Encouraged by spineless attempts to appease him he attacked Russia [22 June 1941], calculating that as a crusader against Soviet Communism he would finally be joined by the whole Capitalist West.

But the Capitalist West was much too shortsighted and jealous to do anything so intelligent. It shook hands with Stalin and stabbed Hitler in the back. He put up a tremendous fight, backed by his fellow adventurers in Italy and Spain; but, being neither a Julius Cæsar nor a Mahomet, he failed to make his initial conquests welcome and permanent by improving the condition of the inhabitants. On the contrary he made his name execrated wherever he conquered. The near West rose up against him, and was joined by the mighty far West of America. After twelve years of killing other people he had to kill himself, and leave his accomplices to be hanged.

The moral for conquerors of empires is that if they substitute savagery for civilization they are doomed. If they substitute civilization for savagery they make good, and establish a legitimate title to the territories they invade. When Mussolini invaded Abyssinia [3 October 1935] and made it possible for a stranger to travel there without being killed by the native Danakils he was rendering the same service to the world as we had in rendering by the same methods (including poison gas[29]) in the north west provinces of India, and had already completed in Australia, New Zealand, and the Scottish Highlands. It was not for us to throw stones at Musso, and childishly refuse to call his puppet king [Victor Emmanuel III] Emperor. But we did throw stones, and made no protest when his star was eclipsed and he was scandalously lynched in Milan [28 April 1945]. The Italians had had enough of him; for he, too, was neither a Cæsar nor a Mahomet.

Contemplating the careers of these two poor devils one cannot help asking was their momentary grandeur worth while? I pointed out once [preface to *The Millionairess*, pp. 262–3] that the career of Bourrienne, Napoleon's valet-secretary for a while, was far longer, more fortunate, easier and more comfortable in every commonsense way, than that of Napoleon, who, with an interval of one year, was Emperor for fourteen years. Mussolini kept going for more than twenty. So did Louis Napoleon, backed by popular idolization of his uncle, who had become a national hero, as Hitler will become in Germany presently. Whether these adventurers would have been happier in obscurity hardly matters; for they were kept too busy to bother themselves about happiness; and the extent to which they enjoyed their activities and

29. Chemical warfare was introduced by German use of chlorine at Ypres in April 1915. There is no evidence of earlier British use. Possibly Shaw is classifying as 'poison' the toxic agents, such as tear gas, employed for irritant effect.

authority and deification is unknown. They were finally scrapped as failures and nuisances, though they all began by effecting some obvious reforms over which party parliaments had been boggling for centuries. Such successes as they had were reactions from the failures of the futile parliamentary talking shops, which were themselves reactions from the bankruptcies of incompetent monarchs, both mobs and monarchs being products of political idolatry and ignorance. The wider the suffrage, the greater the confusion. "Swings to the Left" followed by "swings to the Right" kept the newspapers and the political windbags amused and hopeful. We are still humbugging ourselves into the belief that the swings to the Left are democratic and those to the Right imperial. They are only swings from failure to failure to secure substantial democracy, which means impartial government for the good of the governed by qualified rulers. Popular anarchism defeats them all.

Upstart dictators and legitimate monarchs have not all been personal failures. From Pisistratus to Porfirio, Ataturk, and Stalin, able despots have made good by doing things better and much more promptly than parliaments. They have kept their heads and known their limitations. Ordinary mortals like Nero, Paul of Russia, our James the Second, Riza Khan in Iran, and some of the small fry of degenerate hereditary tribal chiefs like Theebaw[30] in Burma have gone crazy and become worse nuisances than mad dogs. Lord Acton's[31] dictum that power corrupts gives no idea of the extent to which flattery, deference, power, and apparently unlimited money, can upset and demoralize simpletons who in their proper places are good fellows enough. To them the exercise of authority is not a heavy and responsible job which strains their mental capacity and industry to the utmost, but a delightful sport to be indulged for its own sake, and asserted and reasserted by cruelty and monstrosity.

30. Peisistratus, tyrant of Athens (560–559, 556–555, 546–527 BC), commissioned a definitive text of the *Iliad* and the *Odyssey*. Porfirio Diaz, president (1877–80, 1884–1911) and dictator of Mexico, achieved financial and political reform. Kemal Atatürk, first president of the Republic of Turkey (1923–38), modernized legal and educational systems and instituted cultural reforms. Theebaw was the last king of Burma, 1878–85.
31. John Emerich Dalberg-Acton, first Baron Acton of Aldenham, was Regius Professor of History at Cambridge University. 'Power tends to corrupt; absolute power corrupts absolutely,' he wrote to Bishop Mandell Creighton, 3 April 1887 (Louise Creighton, *Life and Letters of Mandell Creighton*, 1904).

## DEMOCRACY MISUNDERSTOOD

Democracy and equality, without which no State can achieve the maximum of beneficence and stability, are still frightfully misunderstood and confused. Popular logic about them is, like most human logic, mere association of ideas, or, to call it by the new name invented by its monstrous product Pavlov, conditional reflex. Government of the people for the people, which is democracy, is supposed to be achievable through government by the people in the form of adult suffrage, which is finally so destructive of democracy that it ends in a reaction into despot-idolatry. Equality is supposed to mean similarity of political talent, which varies as much as musical or mathematical or military capacity from individual to individual, from William Rufus [William II of England] to Charles II, from Nero to Marcus Aurelius, from Monmouth and Prince Charlie to Alexander and Napoleon. Genuine democracy requires that the people shall choose their rulers, and, if they will, change them at sufficient intervals; but the choice must be limited to the public spirited and politically talented, of whom Nature always provides not only the necessary percentage, but superfluity enough to give the people a choice. Equality, which in practice means intermarriageability, is based on the hard facts that the greatest genius costs no more to feed and clothe and lodge than the narrowest minded duffer, and at a pinch can do with less, and that the most limited craftsman or laborer who can do nothing without direction from a thinker, is, if worth employing at all, as necessary and important socially as the ablest director. Equality between them is either equality of income and of income only or an obvious lie.

Equality of income is practicable enough: any sporting peer with his mind bounded by the racecourse can dine on equal terms with an astronomer whose mental domain is the universe. Their children are intermarriageable without misalliance. But when we face the democratic task of forming panels of the persons eligible for choice as qualified rulers we find first that none of our tests are trustworthy or sufficient, and finally that we have no qualified rulers at all, only bosses. The rule of vast commonwealths is beyond the political capacity of mankind at its ablest. Our Solons, Cæsars and Washingtons, Lenins, Stalins and Nightingales, may be better than their best competitors; but they die in their childhood as far as statesmanship is concerned, playing golf and tennis and bridge, smoking tobacco and drinking alcohol as part of their daily diet, hunting, shooting, coursing, reading tales of murder and adultery and police news, wearing fantastic collars and cuffs, with the women on high heels staining their nails, daubing their lips, painting their faces: in short, doing all sorts of things that are child's play and not the exercises or recreations of statesmen and senators. Even when they have read Plato, the Gospels, and Karl Marx, and to that extent know what they have to do, they do not know how to do it, and stick in the old grooves for want of the new political technique which is evolving under pressure of circumstances in Russia. Their attempts at education and schooling end generally in boy farms and concentration camps with flogging blocks, from which the prisoners when they adolesce emerge as trained and prejudiced barbarians with a hatred of learning and discipline, and a dense ignorance of what life is to nine tenths of their compatriots.

## "GREAT MEN"

Here and there, however, cases of extraordinary faculty shew what mankind is capable of within its existing framework. In mathematics we have not only Newtons and Einsteins, but obscure illiterate "lightning calculators," to whom the answers to arithmetical and chronological problems that would cost me a long process of cyphering (if I could solve them at all) are instantly obvious. In grammar and scripture I am practically never at a loss; but I have never invented a machine, though I am built like engineers who, though they are never at a loss with machinery, are yet so unable to put descriptions of their inventions into words that they have to be helped out by patent agents of no more than common literary ability. Mozart, able in his infancy to do anything he pleased in music, from the simplest sonata to the most elaborate symphony or from the subtlest comic or tragic opera to fugal settings of the Mass, resembled millions of Austrians who could not to save their lives hum a line of *Deutschland über Alles* nor compose a bar of music playable by one finger, much less concerted for 30 different orchestral instruments. In philosophy we spot Descartes and Kant, Swift and Schopenhauer, Butler and Bergson, Richard Wagner and Karl Marx, Blake and Shelley, Ruskin and Morris, with dozens of uncrucified Jesuses and saintly women in every generation, look like vindictive retaliators, pugnacious sportsmen, and devout believers in ancient tribal idols.[32] The geniuses themselves are steeped in vulgar superstitions and prejudices: Bunyan and Newton astound us not only by their specific talents but by their credulity and Bible fetichism. We prate gravely of their achievements and faculties as attainments of mankind, as if every Italian were Michael Angelo and Raphael and Dante and Galileo rolled

32. The text in this sentence is garbled; no manuscript text survives.

into one, every German a Goethe, and every Englishman a compound of Shakespear and Eddington. Of this folly we have had more than enough. The apparent freaks of nature called Great Men mark not human attainment but human possibility and hope. They prove that though we in the mass are only child Yahoos it is possible for creatures built exactly like us, bred from our unions and developed from our seeds, to reach the heights of these towering heads. For the moment, however, when we are not violently persecuting them we are like Goldsmith's villagers [in *The Deserted Village*], wondering how their little heads can carry all they know and ranking them as passing rich on four hundred pounds a year when they are lucky enough to get paid for their work instead of persecuted.


## WE CAN AND MUST LIVE LONGER

Considering now that I have lived fourteen years longer than twice as long as Mozart or Mendelssohn, and that within my experience men and women, especially women, are younger at fifty than they were at thirty in the middle of the XIX century, it is impossible to resist at least a strong suspicion that the term of human life cannot be fixed at seventy years or indeed fixed at all. If we master the art of living instead of digging our graves with our teeth as we do at present we may conceivably reach a point at which the sole cause of death will be the fatal accident which is statistically inevitable if we live long enough. In short, it is not proved that there is such a thing as natural death: it is life that is natural and infinite.

How long, then, would it take us to mature into competent rulers of great modern States instead of, as at present, trying vainly to govern empires with the capacity of village headmen. In my Methuselah cycle I put it at three hundred years: a century of childhood and adolescence, a century of administration, and a century of oracular senatorism.

But nobody can foresee what periods my imaginary senators will represent. The pace of evolutionary development is not constant: the baby in the womb recapitulates within a few months an evolution which our biologists assure us took millions of years to acquire. The old axiom that Nature never jumps[33] has given way to a doubt whether Nature is not an incorrigible kangaroo. What is certain is that new faculties, however long they may be dreamt of and desired, come at last suddenly and miraculously like the balancing of the

33. Scottish adage: 'Nature hates all sudden changes.' In the poem 'Providence' (1633), George Herbert wrote: 'Thy [i.e., nature's] creatures leap not . . .'

bicyclist, the skater, and the acrobat. The development of *homo sapiens* into a competent political animal may occur in the same way.

## THE NEXT DISCOVERY

Meanwhile here we are, with our incompetence armed with atomic bombs. Now power civilizes and develops mankind, though not without having first been abused to the point of wiping out entire civilizations. If the atomic bomb wipes out ours we shall just have to begin again. We may agree on paper not to use it as it is too dangerous and destructive; but tomorrow may see the discovery of that poisonous gas lighter than air and capable before it evaporates through the stratosphere of killing all the inhabitants of a city without damaging its buildings or sewers or water supplies or railways or electric plants. Victory might then win cities if it could repopulate them soon enough, wheras atomic bombing leaves nothing for anyone, victor or vanquished. It is conceivable even that the next great invention may create an overwhelming interest in pacific civilization and wipe out war. You never can tell.

AYOT ST LAWRENCE.
1945.

# 'In Good King Charles's Golden Days'

*First published in the collective edition of* Geneva, Cymbeline Refinished, *and* 'In Good King Charles's Golden Days', *1947*

=====

In providing a historical play for the Malvern Festival[1] of 1939 I departed from the established practice sufficiently to require a word of explanation. The "histories" of Shakespear are chronicles dramatized; and my own chief historical plays, Cæsar and Cleopatra and Saint Joan, are fully documented chronicle plays of this type. Familiarity with them would get a student safely through examination papers on their periods.

## STAGE CHAPTERS OF HISTORY

A much commoner theatrical product is the historical romance, mostly fiction with historical names attached to the stock characters of the stage. Many of these plays have introduced their heroines as Nell Gwynn, and Nell's principal lover as Charles II. As Nell was a lively and lovable actress, it was easy to reproduce her by casting a lively and lovable actress for the part; but the stage Charles, though his costume and wig were always unmistakeable, never had any other resemblance to the real Charles, nor to anything else on earth except what he was not: a stage walking gentleman with nothing particular to say for himself.

Now the facts of Charles's reign have been chronicled so often by modern historians of all parties, from the Whig Macaulay to the Jacobite Hilaire Belloc,[2] that there is no novelty left for the chronicler to put on the stage. As to the romance, it is intolerably stale: the spectacle of a Charles sitting with his arm round Nell Gwynn's waist, or with Moll Davis seated on his

1. The Malvern Festival was inaugurated in 1929, created by Barry Jackson of the Birmingham Repertory Theatre as a showcase for Shaw's plays and, at Shaw's later insistence, those of his contemporaries. It ran annually in July and/or August until interrupted by war in 1939, and once more in Shaw's lifetime in 1949.
2. Roman Catholic idealist, disciple of Herbert Spencer, whose simplistic religious views reached back to the Middle Ages for tradition and order.

knee, with the voluptuous termagant Castlemaine raging in the background,[3] has no interest for me, if it ever had for any grown-up person.

But when we turn from the sordid facts of Charles's reign, and from his Solomonic polygamy, to what might have happened to him but did not, the situation becomes interesting and fresh. For instance, Charles might have met that human prodigy Isaac Newton. And Newton might have met that prodigy of another sort, George Fox, the founder of the morally mighty Society of Friends, vulgarly called the Quakers. Better again, all three might have met. Now anyone who considers a hundred and fiftieth edition of Sweet Nell of Old Drury[4] more attractive than Isaac Newton had better avoid my plays: they are not meant for such. And anyone who is more interested in Lady Castlemaine's hips than in Fox's foundation of the great Cult of Friendship should keep away from theatres and frequent worse places. Still, though the interest of my play lies mainly in the clash of Charles, George, and Isaac, there is some fun in the clash between all three and Nelly, Castlemaine, and the Frenchwoman Louise de Kéroualle,[5] whom we called Madame Carwell. So I bring the three on the stage to relieve the intellectual tension.

## NEWTON'S RECTILINEAR UNIVERSE

There is another clash which is important and topical in view of the hold that professional science has gained on popular credulity since the middle of the XIX century. I mean the eternal clash between the artist and the physicist. I have therefore invented a collision between Newton and a personage whom I should like to have called Hogarth; for it was Hogarth who said "the line of beauty is a curve" [in *The Analysis of Beauty*, 1753], and Newton whose first dogma it was that the universe is in principle rectilinear. He called straight lines right lines; and they were still so called in my school Euclid eighty years

3. All three were mistresses of Charles II and mothers of several of his fourteen acknowledged illegitimate children. Eleanor (Nell) Gwynn's son was created Duke of St Albans. Mary (Moll) Davis (or Davies), who was, like Nell, an actress, had a daughter Lady Mary Tudor. Barbara Villiers, Lady Castlemaine, Duchess of Cleveland, bore Charles's sons, the Dukes of Cleveland, Grafton and Northumberland.
4. A popular play by Paul Kester, first produced at the Theatre Royal, Haymarket, in 1900 and revived in London in 1901, 1902, 1911, 1915 and 1934.
5. Duchess of Portsmouth and Aubigny, Breton noblewoman who became a mistress of Charles and bore him a son, Charles Lennox, who was created Duke of Richmond.

ago.[6] But Hogarth could not by any magic be fitted into the year 1680, my chosen date; so I had to fall back on Godfrey Kneller.[7] Kneller had not Hogarth's brains; but I have had to endow him with them to provide Newton with a victorious antagonist. In point of date Kneller just fitted in.

But I must make an exception to this general invitation. If by any chance you are a great mathematician or astronomer you had perhaps better stay away. I have made Newton aware of something wrong with the perihelion of Mercury.[8] Not since Shakespear made Hector of Troy quote Aristotle [*Troilus and Cressida*, III: ii] has the stage perpetrated a more staggering anachronism. But I find the perihelion of Mercury so irresistible as a laugh catcher (like Weston-super-Mare [Somerset]) that I cannot bring myself to sacrifice it. I am actually prepared to defend it as a possibility. Newton was not only a lightning calculator with a monstrous memory: he was also a most ingenious and dexterous maker of apparatus. He made his own telescope; and when he wanted to look at Mercury without being dazzled by the sun he was quite clever enough to produce an artificial eclipse by putting an obturator [baffle or shutter] into the telescope, though nobody else hit on that simple device until long after. My ignorance in these matters is stupendous; but I refuse to believe that Newton's system did not enable him to locate Mercury theoretically at its nearest point to the sun, and then to find out with his telescope that it was apparently somewhere else.

For the flash of prevision in which Newton foresees Einstein's curvilinear universe I make no apology. Newton's first law of motion is pure dogma. So is Hogarth's first law of design. The modern astronomers have proved, so far, that Hogarth was right and Newton wrong. But as the march of science during my long lifetime has played skittles with all the theories in turn I dare not say how the case will stand by the time this play of mine reaches its thousandth performance (if it ever does). Meanwhile let me admit that Newton in my play is a stage astronomer: that is, an astronomer not for an age but for all time. Newton as a man was the queerest of the prodigies; and I have chapter and verse for all his contradictions.

6. Newton's first law – the Law of Inertia – states that if a body is at rest or moving at a constant speed in a straight line, it will remain at rest or keep moving in a straight line at constant speed unless it is acted upon by a force.
7. German-born portraitist famous for his likenesses of ten reigning sovereigns. He painted Charles II, much to his satisfaction, several times.
8. There is a slight irregularity in the orbit of Mercury at its closest approach to the Sun (perihelion) that can not be explained by the theory of gravity proposed by Newton. In 1915 Albert Einstein demonstrated that the treatment of gravity in his general theory of relativity could explain the small discrepancy.

## CHARLES'S GOLDEN DAYS

As to Charles, he adolesced as a princely cosmopolitan vagabond of curiously mixed blood, and ended as the first king in England whose kingship was purely symbolic, and who was clever enough to know that the work of the regicides could not be undone, and that he had to reign by his wits and not by the little real power they had left him. Unfortunately the vulgarity of his reputation as a Solomonic polygamist has not only obscured his political ability, but eclipsed the fact that he was the best of husbands. Catherine of Braganza,[9] his wife, has been made to appear a nobody, and Castlemaine, his concubine, almost a great historical figure. When you have seen my play you will not make that mistake, and may therefore congratulate yourself on assisting at an act of historical justice.

Let us therefore drop the popular subject of The Merry Monarch[10] and his women. On the stage, and indeed off it, he is represented as having practically no other interest, and being a disgracefully unfaithful husband. It is inferred that he was politically influenced by women, especially by Louise de Kéroualle, who, as an agent of Louis XIV, kept him under the thumb of that Sun of Monarchs as his secret pensioner. The truth is that Charles, like most English kings, was continually in money difficulties because the English people, having an insuperable dislike of being governed at all, would not pay taxes enough to finance an efficient civil and military public service. In Charles's day especially they objected furiously to a standing army, having had enough of that under Cromwell, and grudged their king even the lifeguards which were the nucleus of such an army. Charles, to carry on, had to raise the necessary money somewhere; and as he could not get it from the Protestant people of England he was clever enough to get it from the Catholic king of France; for, though head of the Church of England, he privately ranked Protestants as an upstart vulgar middle-class sect, and the Catholic Church as the authentic original Church of Christ, and the only possible faith for a gentleman. In achieving this he made use of Louise: there is no evidence that she made use of him. To the Whig historians the transaction makes Charles a Quisling in the service of Louis and a traitor to his own country. This is mere Protestant scurrility: the only shady part of it is that Charles,

9. Portuguese-born wife of Charles, whom he married on 21 May 1662. Her continued childlessness militated against her at the English court.
10. An appellation in 'A Satyr on Charles II', first published in 1697 by John Wilmot, Earl of Rochester, in his *Poems on Affairs of State*.

spending the money in the service of England, gave *le Roi Soleil* [the Sun King] no value for it.

The other mistresses could make him do nothing that his goodnature did not dispose him to do, whether it was building Greenwich Hospital[11] or making dukes of his bastards. As a husband he took his marriage very seriously, and his sex adventures as calls of nature on an entirely different footing. In this he was in the line of evolution, which leads to an increasing separation of the unique and intensely personal and permanent marriage relation from the carnal intercourse described in Shakespear's sonnet [129]. This, being a response to the biological decree that the world must be peopled [*Much Ado about Nothing*, II: iii], may arise irresistibly between persons who could not live together endurably for a week but can produce excellent children. Historians who confuse Charles's feelings for his wife with his appetite for Barbara Villiers do not know chalk from cheese biologically.

## THE FUTURE OF WOMEN IN POLITICS

The establishment of representative government in England is assumed to have been completed by the enfranchisement of women in 1928. The enormous hiatus left by their previous disenfranchisement is supposed to have been filled up and finished with. As a matter of fact it has only reduced Votes For Women to absurdity; for the women immediately used their vote to keep women out of Parliament. After seventeen years of it the nation, consisting of men and women in virtually equal numbers, is misrepresented at Westminster by 24 women and 616 men.[12] During the Suffragette revolt of 1913 I gave great offence to the agitators by forecasting this result, and urging that what was needed was not the vote, but a constitutional amendment enacting that all representative bodies shall consist of women and men in equal numbers, whether elected or nominated or co-opted or registered or picked up in the street like a coroner's jury.

11. This occupied the site of a royal palace removed during the Commonwealth, rebuilt in the reigns of Charles II and William III, and in 1694 converted into a sailors' hospice.
12. The disproportion remains great, the last figures available (as of mid-September 1996) indicating 588 men and 63 women (Conservative, 18; Labour, 38; Liberal Democrat, 4; Scottish Nationalist, 2, and the Speaker).

## THE COUPLED VOTE

In the case of elected bodies the only way of effecting this is by the Coupled Vote. The representative unit must be not a man *or* a woman but a man *and* a woman. Every vote, to be valid, must be for a human pair, with the result that the elected body must consist of men and women in equal numbers. Until this is achieved it is idle to prate about political democracy as existing, or ever having existed, at any known period of English history.

It is to be noted that the half-and-half proportion is valid no matter what the proportion of women to men is in the population. It never varies considerably; but even if it did the natural unit would still be the complete couple and not its better (or worse) half.

The wisdom or expediency of this reform is questioned on various grounds. There are the people who believe that the soul is a masculine organ lacking in women, as certain physical organs are, and is the seat of male political faculty. But, so far, dissection, spectrum analysis, the electronic microscope, have failed to discover in either sex any specific organ or hormone that a biologist can label as the soul. So we christen it the Holy Ghost or the Lord of Hosts and dechristen it as a Life Force or *Élan Vital*. As this is shared by women and men, and, when it quits the individual, produces in both alike the dissolution we call death, democratic representation cannot be said to exist where women are not as fully enfranchised and qualified as men. So far no great harm has been done by their legal disabilities because men and women are so alike that for the purposes of our crude legislation it matters little whether juries and parliaments are packed with men or women; but now that the activities of government have been greatly extended, detailed criticism by women has become indispensable in Cabinets. For instance, the House of Lords is more representative than the House of Commons because its members are there as the sons of their fathers,which is the reason for all of us being in the world; but it would be a much more human body if it were half-and-half sons and daughters.[13]

All this went on with the approval of the women, who formed half the community, and yet were excluded not only from the franchise but from the professions and public services, except the thrones. Up to a point this also did not matter much; for in oligarchies women exercise so much influence

13. This changed with the introduction of men and women under the Life Peerage Act of 1958, and the Peerage Act of 1963 which admitted women peers in their own right to sit in the House of Lords, subject to the same qualifications as men.

privately and irresponsibly that the cleverest of them are for giving all power to the men, knowing that they can get round them without being hampered by the female majority whose world is the kitchen, the nursery, and the drawingroom if such a luxury is within their reach.

But representation on merely plangent Parliamentary bodies is not sufficient. Anybody can complain of a grievance; but its remedy demands constructive political capacity. Now political capacity is rare; but it is not rarer in women than in men. Nature's supply of five per cent or so of born political thinkers and administrators are all urgently needed in modern civilization; and if half of that natural supply is cut off by the exclusion of women from Parliament and Cabinets the social machinery will fall short and perhaps break down for lack of sufficient direction. Competent women, of whom enough are available, have their proper places filled by incompetent men: there is no Cabinet in Europe that would not be vitally improved by having its male tail cut off and female heads substituted.

But how is this to be done? Giving all women the vote makes it impossible because it only doubles the resistance to any change. When it was introduced in England not a single woman was returned at the ensuing General Election, though there were women of proved ability in the field. They were all defeated by male candidates who were comparative noodles and nobodies.

Therefore I suggest and advocate The Coupled Vote, making all votes invalid except those for a bisexed couple, and thus ensuring the return of a body in which men and women are present in equal numbers. Until this is done, adult suffrage will remain the least democratic of all political systems. I leave it to our old parliamentary hands to devize a plan by which our electorate can be side-tracked, humbugged, cheated, lied to, or frightened into tolerating such a change. If it has to wait for their enlightenment it will wait too long.

MALVERN. 1939.
AYOT ST LAWRENCE. 1945.

# *Against Corporal Punishment in Schools*

*Foreword to a pamphlet, 1947*

The difficulty is that there are not enough humane qualified teachers to go round, and classes are too large. Any callous fool with a cane in his (or her) hand can terrorize a child into learning the alphabet and the multiplication table; and that process does all the mischief. Are we prepared to say that it is better to leave a child unschooled than intimidated physically? I am. Fear compels children to learn, but also to hate learning and teachers. The qualified teacher can interest pupils and is respected by them and not disliked.

8 April 1947.                                                    G. Bernard Shaw.

# Pugilism

*Shaw informed his publisher in August 1947 that he was preparing*
*a new volume for the Collected Edition, to contain 'my old articles on Pugilism*
*and Painting', for which he had drafted prefatory notes. The volume was not published.*
*The corrected typescript of this prefatory note is in the British Library*
*(Add. Mss. 50664, fos. 152–3)*

======

I have been asked how it is that I, a critic and playwright whose interests, taste, and practice are ultra-classical, should concern myself with anything so barbarous as boxing. I have even had to ask myself that question.

The best reply I can make is that all forms of personal combat are interesting not only technically as exhibitions of skill but because they are also exhibitions of character concentrating into minutes differences that years of ordinary intercourse leave hidden. And we are not yet so civilized as to have no interest in being able to defend ourselves against physical assault, nor even, on the Continent, sure that we may not have to figure in a duel. Joseph Conrad, a Pole, was restrained from challenging me to a duel on Calais sands by being assured by H. G. Wells that some remark of mine was allowable according to the British code of humor.[1] My Austrian translator, Siegfried Trebitsch, during his military service, was obliged to fight three duels[2] without the least desire to do so by social pressure which included the ostracism on default of all his nearest relatives. As I write these lines (1947) the newspapers

1. H. G. Wells related in *Experiment in Autobiography* (1934): 'When Conrad first met Shaw in my house, Shaw talked with his customary freedoms. "You know, my dear fellow, your books won't *do*" – for some Shavian reason I have forgotten – and so forth. I went out of the room and suddenly found Conrad on my heels, swift and white-faced. "Does that man want to *insult* me?" he demanded. The provocation to say "Yes" and assist at the subsequent duel was very great, but I overcame it. "It's humour," I said, and took Conrad out into the garden to cool. One could always baffle Conrad by saying "humour." It was one of our damned English tricks he had never learnt to tackle.'
2. These duels, in his youth, were reported by Trebitsch in *Chronicle of a Life* (1953); one of them provided the basis for his novel *Genesung* (1902).

contain the report of a duel between two French politicians[3] which, though it cost no bloodshed, must have cost both of them a considerable sum of money. Millions of young men have been trained, and are still being trained, in bayonet fighting and marksmanship as conscripted infantry soldiers. It is still as possible for me to be interested in boxing, wrestling, fencing, and shooting, as it was for Byron to take boxing lessons from Gentleman Jackson [see vol. 1, p. 96].

I myself never had any lessons; but a friend of mine, Pakenham Beatty, a minor poet, went crazy about boxing, and insisted on my sparring with him, which I did after studying a brief handbook on the subject by his instructor, Ned Donnelly.[4] And as an economist with a strong sense of comedy, I was amused by the contrast between the popular romantic conception of famous professional boxers as heroes and champions, and their dominance by commercial motives and betting odds. Some boxers made more money by selling their fights: that is, agreeing to lose them, such bargains being called crosses or barneys, than by winning them.

Anyhow pugilism became one of my subjects; and I can invent no further nor better excuses for that lapse from my dignity as a dramatic poet and artist-philosopher.

March, 1947.

3. The duel, reported in *The Times*, 31 March 1947 (5: 4), resulted from an exchange of blows on 28 March in the lobbies of the French National Assembly when a socialist deputy, former under-secretary of state, boxed the ears of a radical, former minister of commerce (no names supplied). The bullets fired during a rainstorm missed their mark, being embedded instead in tree trunks in the Forest of Rambouillet.
4. Instructor of boxing at the London Athletic Club and author of *Self-Defence; or, The Art of Boxing* (1879), who was Shaw's model for Ned Skene, the fight trainer in *Cashel Byron's Profession* (1882).

# Pictures

*Prefatory note for an aborted volume in the Collected Edition, 1947.*
*The corrected typescript is in the British Library (Add. Mss. 50664, fos. 158–61).*
*First published in* Bernard Shaw on the London Art Scene 1885–1950,
*ed. Stanley Weintraub, 1989*

———

William Morris was fond of saying that no man could pass a shop window with a picture in it without stopping to look at it.[1] This is not completely true: there are people who are picture blind just as there are people who are tone deaf; but it is true enough to be worth saying. I was certainly born with an interest in pictures: I had no literary ambitions, but wanted intensely to be a Michael Angelo. As I could not remember anything that did not interest me I could not pass the simplest examination; but I never forgot that Domenicho's[2] name was Zampieri and Raphael's Sanzio. I haunted the National Gallery in Dublin and seldom found anyone else there.[3] When as a child I possessed as much as sixpence (usually my mother's bribe to induce me to submit to a mustard plaster on a sore throat) I bought a box of water colors with it. But though I could write by nature I could not draw nor paint presentably; and nobody ever dreamt of teaching me; so I perforce became an eminent writer instead of a mediocre painter.

Nevertheless I began as an author with years of complete and apparently hopeless failure. When from 1879 to 1883 I wrote five full dress novels no

1. Shaw made frequent reference to views held by Morris, most of them coming, not from written sources, but from conversation. 'I need hardly say', wrote Shaw in an appreciation ('William Morris as Actor and Playwright', *Saturday Review*, 10 October 1896), 'that I have often talked copiously to him on many of his favorite subjects, especially the artistic subjects. What is more to the point, he has occasionally talked to me about them. No art was indifferent to him. He declared that nobody could pass a picture without looking at it – that even a smoky cracked old mezzotint in a pawnbroker's window would stop you for at least a moment.' (See also p. 272.)
2. Seventeenth-century Italian painter, a student of the Baroque eclectic school of the Carraccis; known as Domenichino.
3. As a 'day boy' at school, Shaw was not required to return to classes after lunch hour, which afforded him time for frequent visits to the National Gallery and for exploring his native city.

publisher would accept them. The first and longest of them did not get into print for fifty years. I was in the very trough of failure when I made the acquaintance of William Archer, a leading theatre critic on the staff of The World, then the most fashionable weekly magazine of the day. Like most of my few friends we were attracted to oneanother by being "infidels," the name by which at that time were described all who were at all sceptical as to the articles of the religious creeds and the absolute and final historical and scientific authority of the Bible. Voltaire, Rousseau and Tom Paine were presented to us as blasphemous scoundrels whose deathbeds were made frightful by the imminence of eternal burning in a brimstone hell; and even Bishop Colenso was excommunicated for questioning the actual occurrence of the Resurrection. Archer, piously brought up, was an irreconcilable atheist; and I called myself one publicly whenever the situation called for a stroke of bravado.

It happened that the picture critic of The World died;[4] and the editor, Edmund Yates, asked Archer to take his place. Archer put it to me whether he could honestly undertake this duty in view of the fact that he knew nothing about pictures and could not keep awake in a gallery. I told him to take it by all means, as I knew all about pictures and would go with him to the exhibitions and tell him what to say until he picked up his job.

We tried the experiment until Archer, making no progress, found it unbearable and told Yates so, adding that his notices, with which Yates was quite satisfied, were being written by me. And so I became picture critic to The World, writing paragraphs about the exhibitions for fivepence a line, and articles on the Royal Academy on great occasions. My success led to my becoming music critic to the paper when that too presently fell vacant; but I still wrote about pictures until I discovered that the fivepence a line was earning me only £35 a year. Yates, shocked and apologetic, handed the post over to Lady Colin Campbell.[5] I returned briefly to the galleries as picture critic to Truth [eight notices: 20 March–22 May 1890] and later on to The Observer [one notice: 3 May 1891]; but Truth, under a now forgotten editor [Henry Labouchère], required me to praise his friends' pictures instead of criticizing them, with freedom to do the same for my own friends. I walked out; and that editor presently died [twenty-two years later], some said of

4. No Shaw researcher has yet been able to identify him.
5. Irish-born Gertrude Blood, judicially separated from her husband Lord Colin Campbell (who died in 1895), earned her livelihood as a journalist, moving in literary and art circles.

shock and surprise at the refusal of what seemed to him an entirely reasonable request on a subject of no importance.

The Observer episode was even briefer. The paper had just been bought by a lady [Rachel Beer] who interpolated my first Academy article with eulogies of painters of no account who had invited her to tea; so again I burnt my boats and left the galleries for ever. I must add that these two magazines [the *Observer* was a Sunday newspaper, as it still is] were passing through phases of which there is now no trace left, whilst The World has long since ceased to exist.

I do not pretend that these youthful criticisms of mine are of any artistic importance; but they illustrate to some extent the evanescence of fashionable reputations in art, and also the growth of unfashionable ones; so here they are for what they are worth.

[*c.* March, 1947.]                                        G. Bernard Shaw.

# Some Impressions

*Preface to* Sydney Olivier: Letters and Selected Writings, *edited with a memoir by Margaret Olivier, 1948*

———

I first met Sydney Olivier when we were both in our twenties, and had from different directions embraced Socialism as our creed. I had come by the way of Henry George and Karl Marx. He had begun with the Positivist philosophy of Auguste Comte, and was, as far as I know, the only Fabian who came in through that gate.

He and Sidney Webb, Comtist at secondhand through John Stuart Mill, shared the duty of resident clerk at the Colonial Office. Both of them had passed into the upper division of the Civil Service, Olivier heading the competition list, apparently so easily that I never heard either of them speak of it, though to me it was a wonder, as the passing of even an elementary school examination has always been for me an impossible feat. There was no question then of peerages to come for either of them: by plunging into Socialism they were held to be burning their boats as far as any sort of official promotion was concerned, though as founders of Fabian Socialism they soon took The Cause off the barricades, and made it constitutional and respectable.

Olivier was an extraordinarily attractive figure, and in my experience unique; for I have never known anyone like him mentally or physically: he was distinguished enough to be unclassable. He was handsome and strongly sexed, looking like a Spanish grandee in any sort of clothes, however unconventional. He was not interested in athletics; but his college chum, Graham Wallas, who stood six foot two (or was it four?) in his socks, told me that once when he alluded to Miss Margaret Cox, now Lady Olivier, as if she were no more than any other young lady, Olivier threw him across the room. I believe he could have carried a cottage piano upstairs; but it would have cracked in his grip.

It was fortunate for mankind that he was a man of good intent and sensitive humanity; for he was a law to himself, and never dreamt of considering other people's feelings, nor could conceive their sensitiveness on points that were to him trivial. He once paid a call on a family after an interval of some years, and immediately (he was very observant) remarked, "I see you have moved that carpet: the hole in it is now under the sofa." He had no apparent conscience, being on the whole too well disposed to need one; but when he had a whim that was flatly contrary to convention he gratified it openly and unscrupulously as a matter of course, dealing with any opposing prejudice by the method recommended by the American Mrs Stetson, of "walking through it as if it wasnt there."

This freedom from the tangle of inhibitions which go to the makeup of a typical Englishman made him as foreign as his name and his Huguenot ancestry, which gave him also the invaluable power of taking an objective view of his employer the British Empire, now reluctantly rechristened the British Commonwealth. It helped him to get on very well with me; for I, being Irish, am more a foreigner in England than any man born in Wiltshire could possibly be.

Though Olivier came to positions of authority by sheer gravitation, he could never have become a popular idol, because his mental scope, like that of a champion chess player, enabled him to see the next five or six steps in an argument so clearly and effortlessly that he could not believe that anything so obvious need be stated. I found this out when I edited Fabian Essays in 1889. To that epoch-making volume, Olivier contributed the essay on the Moral Basis of Socialism. On reading his manuscript I found a hiatus in his argument which convinced me at first that a couple of pages must have dropped out. But as the hiatus occurred in the middle of a page I had to reconsider this. I had to think out the missing links for myself: and finally I wrote the page and a half needed to fill the gap in the argument, and brought it to Olivier to rewrite in his own fashion. He said that my chain of reasoning was all right; but I could not persuade him that it was not too obvious to need mentioning, nor to take the trouble to translate my version into his own language. I could stick it in just as it was for the benefit of readers (if any) imbecile enough to be unable to follow the argument without it. Which I accordingly did.

This excess of mental and muscular power was accompanied by an excess of nervous power which hampered him as a public speaker. He spoke only on special provocation, and always had to wrestle with his speeches rather than deliver them comfortably. I once asked the chief of the Observatory on Mount Vesuvius why the energy wasted by the burning mountain was not utilized for industrial purposes. He replied that there was too much of it to be manageable. That was Olivier's case; but once I heard it serve him in good stead.

It was at the International Socialist Congress at Zurich, where he and I were the Fabian delegates.[1] As usual, the Congress, instead of getting at once

1. The Conference convened on 7 August 1893; Shaw reported on it as a special correspondent to the *Star*, London, 8–12 and 14 August.

to real business, fell back on the old controversy between Marx and Bakunin, and began disputing whether anarchists should be expelled or not. Day after day was wasted in endless orations by the opposing windbags, followed by tedious translations into two languages, which, being made by amateur interpreters, who were also strong and eloquent partisans, either improved the originals recklessly or guyed them mercilessly. This went on and on, and was all the fun of the fair for most of the delegates; but to us Fabians, out for business, it became at last quite unbearable; and I was on the point of attempting some sort of protest when suddenly the silent Olivier shot up from his chair, and Vesuvius went into full eruption. In a voice like the roaring of a safety valve releasing a thousand horsepower, he discharged his impatience in a speech such as I had never heard before nor have heard since. It left me amazed, and the Congress stunned. When we recovered sufficiently to take action the Congress closed the discussion by throwing the Anarchists out. Once safely outside they produced credentials as trade unionists, and came back and resumed their seats unchallenged. That was what Socialist Congresses were like in those days.

Olivier began his official career overseas by being sent to straighten out the finances of British Honduras. He found that his success in the entrance examinations for the upper division of the Civil Service had left him so ignorant that he had to discover the art of bookkeeping by double entry and learn it on his outward voyage. This revolutionary stroke established him as a great financial authority and business head in Downing Street. When he had balanced the Honduras books by double entry he was made Auditor General of the Leeward Islands. When they too were successfully straightened he was pushed into one post after another in which some capacity for figures as well as an imposing presence was indispensable. Thus his freedom from vulgar ambition did not retard his career: distinction and promotion came to him unasked.

In Honduras his habit of observation came into play. He noticed when he bathed in the sea that there was a plank missing in a palisade meant to keep out sharks. When he pointed this out, much as he had pointed out the hole in the carpet, the local authorities, instead of mending the palisade, instructed a native to bathe always with the Colonial Office gentleman, as sharks preferred colored diet to white.

But there is a snag in eminent success as a civil servant. Efficient men of action, though they are indispensable when the mere routineers land their departments in intolerable messes, terrify their ministries as dangerous innovators and upsetters. An official capable of discovering and learning bookkeeping by double entry may be capable of anything: he cannot be trusted to do always what was done last time. Certainly Olivier could not. He went his own way politically, just as he did privately. When in 1884 I discovered a little bud of middle-class social compunction which had been happily inspired to call itself the Fabian Society, and induced Olivier and Webb to join and capture it, we were so preoccupied with industrial problems that we left colonial and foreign policy out of the question until the South African War forced it on us in 1899; and even after we had said our say on that subject in Fabianism and the Empire [see vol. 1, p. 53], we dropped it until 1913, when the rumblings of the coming European earthquake came to me, not in our Fabian councils, but through an attack made by an English critic on the music of Richard Strauss.[2] We had got only so far as that colonial government should be democratized by the formation of local and native councils, with our viceroys and governors working with them as Prime Ministers rather than as despots.

When Olivier was Governor of Jamaica I visited him there,[3] and one day asked him whether he had tried our democratic plan, and if so, how did it work. He replied that he had tried it, and found that whenever he proposed a measure intelligible only to people who could see further than the ends of their noses he was invariably opposed by his democratic councils. "I now" he went on "do not consult them. I do what is needed. In eighteen months or so they see that I was right, and stop howling about it."

Hitler could say no more; and it is a pity that Hitler had not Olivier's brain and kindly objectivity. The trouble in Jamaica just then was that the Americans had a way of behaving as if the island belonged to the United States. In particular, their color prejudice demanded satisfaction in a colony in which blood was so mixed that no matter how white your host might be, you never could be sure that his father was not as brown as a berry. Olivier consulted the Americans as little as he consulted his infantile councils, and gave an important public appointment to a colored native over their heads. He understood thoroughly the conflict of economic interests between the planters and the black proletariat, sympathizing with the oppressed negroes; but these easygoing and likeable darkies understood nothing but their immediate grievances. They made no trouble until their tram fares were raised, when they immediately revolted and confronted their Governor with riots which

2. Ernest Newman, 'The Strange Case of Richard Strauss', the *Nation* (London), 27 June 1914 (reprinted in *Shaw's Music*, 1981, vol. 3), which led to an epistolary debate by Shaw and Newman in the same journal for several succeeding weeks.
3. The Shaws, who sailed from England on 24 December 1910, visited Olivier 6–12 January 1911.

he had to suppress. In one of these, when an insurgent negro was battering in the door of a newspaper office, Olivier handled him as he had handled Graham Wallas in his college days.

Later on the rioters got a bit of their own back. They managed to launch a heavy stone which struck their high-handed Governor flush on his occiput. The same thing happened to Nelson at the Battle of the Nile. For a year or two after, in Naples, Nelson's insubordinate Nelsonism got out of hand to an extent that cost the life of [Francesco] Caracciolo.[4] Olivier's head being stronger he did not hang anybody: but he was not quite unaffected by the injury. He was none the less Olivier; but he was more talkative, and, if possible, more indifferent to the effect of what he said on his hearers. This, I think, made the Foreign Office afraid of him, and might have prevented his promotion to any of the few governorships that could be considered more important than that of Jamaica, had he not himself had enough of colonial exile and pressed for central work.

Although he always held steadily by the Colonial Office as the only power that stood between the black proletariats and their pitiless exploitation by the West Indian planters and the diamondocracy in Africa, he had no Kiplingesque idolatry of the Empire, and said, quite openly, that its breakup would not be the end of the world. After one of these utterances he expressed to me, without any bitterness, some surprise at being left for the moment without a special job; for he still expected his jobs to come to him unasked for as they had always done. I reminded him that it was hard for any British government to select for an imperial job a man who had just been reported as saying, in effect, that the British Empire might break up for all he cared. He was taken aback for a moment. It had never occurred to him to consider the feelings of the Foreign Office, or the Colonial Office, or anyone else's. His Fabian grasp of the appalling social danger of the imperial instincts that were keeping Downing Street under the thumb of a handful of planters in the face of millions of black proletarians, reduced official Kiplingism, in his view, to negligible poppycock.

But this general statement cannot convey any impression of Olivier's idiosyncrasy, nor of the effect his reports must have made on the routineers of the Colonial Office. He wrote and thought, and could only write and think, clean over their heads. Let me quote a typical letter he wrote me in 1932, when I had just published a story with a negress as its heroine.

4. Neapolitan admiral, who successfully prevented the landing of the British and Sicilian fleet at Naples in 1799, hanged at Nelson's order after the eventual capture of the city.

10th December, 1932

Dear Shaw,

I think your Black Girl, in her full dress, is charming, and ought to be influential as a mild diaphoretic. The problem for the missionary is an acute one. The lady missionary whom you begin by caricaturing—for I can hardly believe your account of her engagements to be authentic—finds herself capable, by influences (emanating through her) which she associates with certain formulas, of producing a really vivifying and stimulating effect upon the African temperament, hitherto protected from the impact of European spiritual and intellectual development. That has also been the case in the West Indies, and especially in Jamaica, where the ex-slaves were helped only by Christian missionaries, and with great profit to their development: but with the result that all the best people in such a community (for instance, the late Archbishop [Enos] Nuttall,[5] who was a really great man) are frightfully bigoted evangelical formalists, and indeed, practically fundamentalists: so that I find it very difficult to write honestly and conscientiously about civilization in Jamaica as I am trying to do. However, I have just sent out a copy of the *Outline of Knowledge for Young People* to a club of young Jamaicans formed for education and study. I am hesitating whether also to send them a copy of *The Black Girl*.

The Black Girl's observation that it is impossible to get Europeans to understand what is "less than enough" for Africans, is a thing I have been up against all my life. The political economy of Colonial Government is founded upon the obvious fact that an African or a negro can, apparently, consider himself well-off with much less than a white man, and therefore, that no wrong is done him by exploiting him to the full surplus value that can be extracted from his labour over and above that limit: and that if he grumbles about the difficulty of paying taxes, he is a lazy hypocrite. And it is impossible for a white employer, and almost insuperably difficult for a European official, to apprehend that these people are really very *poor* and suffer hardship from poverty, and that what they manage to produce for themselves and are satisfied with, costs them a physical and intellectual labour of which any white man would be simply incapable under similar conditions, and that the reason why they perspire freely is not merely because they have large sweat glands, but because they are effecting a high quantity of metabolism. The only people whom I have found capable of appreciating the facts of the black man's economy in that aspect are missionaries, who believe they

5. A leader in the reorganization of the disestablished Church of England in Jamaica, who became primate and first archbishop of the West Indies.

can only give the black man what he wants by means of their fundamentalist formulas.

Whence did you get your idea of calling the writer of the Revelations a drug-addict? The book is an elaborate and deliberate cryptogram embodying Chaldaeo-Egyptian astrology: all its forms and figures, dragons, archers, centaurs, virgins, etc., are sublimations of the imagery of the constellations. The souls under the Altar are the souls that form the Milky Way in which is the constellation Ara which was the habitat of released souls awaiting reincarnation – *i.e.*, in purgatory. As the Christian church formulated that doctrine I think it is a blunder to speak of John of Patmos as a drug-addict. He was a mystical symbolist in the line of Blake; and he had a very clear idea of the theories he wanted to symbolise.

Many years ago, writing an essay on the idea of the Significance of Bodily Form and of its persistence after terrestrial death, I struck out in the precise argument (from the nature of form and matter) which you do, and declared I felt myself perfectly capable of continuing my life in the sun, also anticipating your observation that the inventors of a material fiery hell apprehended that possibility quite rationally. I have been trying to look up what I wrote, which was curiously coincident and identical in idea, but I cannot find it. But I have never seen it said anywhere else.

I am in a state of complete deflation following influenza and pneumonia, which has stopped my finishing a book I wanted to get off before Christmas, hoping then to get away into some sunshine. The devil caught me (visiting Oxford Gaol as a Justice). I have been dictating this letter to you because I cannot force myself to the labour of composition devoid of internal stimulus: by which you may understand the Black Girl has afforded a pleasant stimulus. Under present circumstances I devote myself to writing unnecessary letters to people who have written to me, but whom I have not replied to so long as I found I could be better employed. As you will be better employed in digging your garden, please don't regard this as imposing on you any obligation of commentary or reply.

Margaret has gone off today to see Margery, otherwise she would send her love to Charlotte and you. Mine please.

Yours sincerely,<br>Olivier

P.S.—The Black Girl's observation "why are you surprised at a thing like that?" is very pertinent to the psychology of the unsophisticated African in contact with the sophisticated civilized man. He constantly detects the obvious which is concealed from the civilized man by the very formula which has been built up from observation of it. Of course, you may find the same quality in really unsophisticated country peasants where they survive. They are realists; and the lady ethnologist has sound reason for her theory that the next great civilization will be a black civilization. The white man will be destroyed by his idols if he doesn't look out: and I see little sign of his doing so. Lala Lajpat Rai[6] once asked me "Why do English people make such a fuss about a few of them being killed?" It was apropos of the Amritsar Massacre, which English imperialist opinion, exemplified by Mr Justice McCardie, thought reasonable and laudable.[7] Indian opinion thought it unbalanced; and it was in fact the crucial event in Indian Constitutional history. Similarly, when the peasants of St Thomas in the East were fed up with their magistrates, and after resisting arrest, went down to demonstrate that they would stand no nonsense, and when a shindy broke out, they clubbed some of the magistrates to death and burnt the courthouse, Eyre thought it quite reasonable that 450 peasants should be killed and 600 flogged and a thousand houses burnt in compensation for the deaths of 15 Europeans.[8]

The Jamaica black people were shocked at the clubbing, and, having a respect for Law, condemned it; but they positively considered that the retaliation exacted was entirely out of proportion!

6. Indian nationalist and dramatist, deported (*c.* 1908) after a trial for sedition. His books include *Young India* (1916) and *The Political Future of India* (1919).
7. The Amritsar massacre, on 13 April 1919, occurred when a brigade commander in India, General Reginald Dyer, ordered a military detachment to fire on a crowd of unarmed native protesters who had assembled, in defiance of his orders, in an enclosed park square. It resulted in 379 deaths. Sir Henry (the Hon. Mr Justice) McCardie, was a judge of the High Court in Britain who, in 1924, presiding over a libel action arising from the Amritsar affair, gave 'his considered opinion' in instructing the jury on the evidence, 'that the action of [Dyer] was correct, and that the secretary of state for India had acted wrongly [in 1920] in removing him from the army' (*DNB*). The statement made McCardie a target of much political rancour at home and abroad.
8. The Jamaican uprising in the parish of St Thomas in the East, on 11 October 1865, was a local riot by discontented black peasantry, quickly suppressed by troops under orders of the colonial governor, Edward Eyre. In a reign of terror in the weeks following, several hundred Jamaicans were slain, a larger number subjected to torture and flogging, and over a thousand of their homes destroyed. The uprising and its shockingly repressive aftermath, including execution of George Gordan, a radical coloured representative of the Jamaican House of Assembly, whose vehement denial of involvement was ignored by the governor in an apparent desire to be rid of a personal enemy, were debated in heated division in the English Parliament and in the world press. Eyre was recalled for questionable conduct.

It is amusing that General [Luke Smythe] O'Connor[9] (the O.C.T.), an Irishman, frankly told Eyre, at an early date in the business, that he was making much too heavy weather about it, and that from his experiences in Belfast and for many years in the West Indies he did not think this was very much of a riot and was certainly not an insurrection. Anyhow, it had been put down in three days, so why worry? Eyre, however, thought that "justice must be done" and condign punishment (his favourite expression) inflicted. So did Mr. Justice McCardie and the people who canonised General Dyer in England. But the fun of the thing is that we learn from Edward Thompson's last book[10] that Dyer himself acknowledged that the Amritsar Massacre was an appalling mistake, because he had had no intention of killing all those people, but expected them to run away, which they would have done if they had not had a stone wall all round them, a fact he was not aware of! Which leaves Justice McCardie rather in the air!

It will now, I think, be pretty clear why none of Olivier's later appointments were governorships nor had anything to do with the treatment of subjugate native races, although it was just here that his exceptional character and ability had asserted itself most conspicuously.

This did not prevent him from writing books about the blacks unlike any that had been written about them before.[11] There was an arresting freshness about his analysis of the much decried half-breed, comparing him to a black and white sugarstick, in which the black threads and the white, however finely and intimately drawn out, never mixed, preserving their integrity side by side, so that in dealing with a half-breed you were dealing, not with a shifty rogue, but with a man of two different moralities, who would slip from one to the other without notice, and with a suddenness very disconcerting to a white European with a single-track mind. The more Olivier wrote, the plainer it was in Downing Street that he was pro-negro and not pro-planter, and that he must be kept out of the colonies at all cost. But as this was what he himself desired, he made no trouble about it and was in fact not conscious of it. He was never that most tiresome of public nuisances, a man with a personal grievance.

Accordingly, after Jamaica, he found himself not in Ceylon, Australasia or

9. Officer in command of troops in Jamaica, a veteran of African warring and a former Governor of the Gambia.
10. Radical journalist, poet, playwright and historian, author of *The Making of the Indian Princes* in 1943.
11. Olivier's writings included *White Capital and Black Labour* (1906), *The Anatomy of African Misery* (1927) and *Imperial Trusteeship* (Fabian Tract No. 230, 1929).

Canada, but safe at home, first as Secretary to the Board of Agriculture and Fisheries, and finally, until his superannuation in 1920, as Assistant Comptroller and Auditor to the Exchequer. Here he found that the British Empire was keeping its accounts exactly as they were kept in the reign of King John, except that they were recorded by ink marks in cashbooks instead of by notches in sticks called tallies. Even tallies had been used as recently as the beginning of the XIX century. The method was so crude that though it could record the issue of stores to a Navy ship, it could not grapple with any return of them. Consequently our cruisers, when their commissions were fulfilled and they came back home, had to throw all their remaining stores overboard. The English Channel is paved with ropes and barrels of paint, ship's biscuit and salt horse, deposited there by many generations of the mariners of England whose flag had braved a thousand years the battle and the breeze.

When the new Labor Party reached the Treasury Bench under the banner of Socialism, but under the thumb of Trade Unionism, its lack of representation in the House of Lords compelled it to hand out peerages to any presentable members within its reach who were not needed in the House of Commons: and Olivier, being eminently presentable and much more aristocratic-looking than most of the hereditary nobles, became Lord Olivier. Being also the only available overseas diplomat, he was made Secretary of State for India.

But here, knowing too much, he could do nothing fundamental, and did not pretend that he could. British Secretaries for India, like the old Secretaries for Ireland, were only scapegoats. On the rare occasions when the Houses of Parliament discussed Indian or Irish affairs, the Secretary's duty was to whitewash the Government. For this the only talent needed was for eloquently pouring out at the greatest bearable length phrases that told the House nothing that it did not know better than it knew the Chaplain's prayers. In short, he had to be an accomplished bunk merchant. Ramsay MacDonald, the Prime Minister, who made Olivier Secretary for India, was easily the champion bunk merchant of his day; and he finally fell back on this gift of his so shamelessly that after his last two November performances at the Guildhall[12] he became negligible even in the House of Commons, and was dismissed from history as what Beatrice Webb had long before dismissed him from Fabian consideration, as "a façade."

Now the accomplishment which Olivier most conspicuously lacked was that of bunk merchant. He never spoke when he had nothing to say; and

---

12. Ramsay MacDonald's last two speeches at the Guildhall, London, on peace and disarmament, the League of Nations, the European situation, and Britain's foreign policy, were reported in *The Times* on 26 October and 10 November 1934.

even when he had he did not speak easily. Often the ellipses in his reasoning (like the one in his Fabian Essay) made him hard to follow. And even had he been a spellbinder like Bebel, Jaurès, or Lloyd George, it would never have occurred to him to whitewash the Government or anyone else: he would have pointed out the black spots instead, making him, from the party point of view, utterly impossible as a deadhead secretary. After ten months of this, his last official job, MacDonald's short-lived Government collapsed before Olivier had had time to do anything except establish his impossibilities as a parliamentary hack careerist and scapegoat. He was then sixtyfive and had retired from the Civil Service, where his great practical ability and authority had been needed, and proficiency in the parliamentary game of marking time was not expected from him. His life lasted nineteen years longer (death has a long struggle with men of his vitality); and he employed them in writing on the problems raised by the subjugated colored races in Africa and the West Indies. He kept educating himself and learning from his experience to the last. Out of official harness and out of politics, he could indulge his distaste for conventionally-minded company to the full. In his last letter to me he said that he never went out of doors.

I have enjoyed (or suffered) much more celebrity, or as they call it now, publicity, than this old Fabian colleague of mine, though as a man of action I was not qualified to tie his shoestrings. Nothing can be more unfair and dangerous than the enormous excess of popularity, or at least of notoriety, lavished on playwrights, novelists, artists and actors, as compared with our rarer Oliviers. Only victorious soldiers can compete with them in that respect. And their celebrity is long deferred unless they are also incorrigible actors. My friend H. G. Wells has complained that it is impossible to move about without being confronted with some effigy of my "wicked old face" in painting or sculpture or photography: and though this is true only dramatically, my aspect is much better known than Olivier's. But Olivier had a single and real self and never exploited it histrionically. My portraits are not all portraits of the same person. There are many portraits of my reputation, and so few of my real self that without them I should doubt, like Peer Gynt when he peeled the onion, whether I have any real self. Rodin, when he modeled me in plaster, said to my wife, when she began to explain to him who and what I was: "I know nothing of Monsieur Shaw, but what there is I will give you." And he did, so exactly that none of the dupes of my reputation could see any likeness to me in the bust. Many years later, when Dame Laura Knight,[13] whose nature is so entirely frank and direct that no reputation can

13. English painter, who worked in the tradition of nineteenth-century British realism, and did a portrait of Shaw in 1932.

blind her, painted a portrait of me into which, as all true artists do, she substituted her own simple sincerity for my artificiality, my wife said, "It's not a bit like you: you're always acting." But I knew better. I recognized in Rodin's bust and Laura's portrait the simple truth about myself.

Now Olivier has no double set of portraits. There was only one Olivier. However many abusive names he was called by the planters and Unsocialists he was never called a humbug. His success as a Civil Servant was not in the least illusory. His air of being a Spanish grandee was not an affectation: it was entirely natural. I am glad I retained his friendship to the last; for he did not give his friendship for nothing. I hope his biographers will rate him as highly as I do.

22 September 1944.

# Buoyant Billions

*The preface was first printed in a 1947 rough proof rehearsal copy of the play.
Play and preface were first published, in German translation, 1948, and in English
in a limited edition, 1950 (though dated 1949)*

———

I commit this to print within a few weeks of completing my 92nd [91st] year. At such an age I should apologize for perpetrating another play or presuming to pontificate in any fashion. I can hardly walk through my garden without a tumble or two; and it seems out of all reason to believe that a man who cannot do a simple thing like that can practise the craft of Shakespear. Is it not a serious sign of dotage to talk about oneself, which is precisely what I am now doing? Should it not warn me that my bolt is shot, and my place silent in the chimney corner?

Well, I grant all this; yet I cannot hold my tongue nor my pen. As long as I live I must write. If I stopped writing I should die for want of something to do.

If I am asked why I have written this play I must reply that I do not know. Among the many sects of Peculiar People which England produces so eccentrically and capriciously are the Spiritualists. They believe in personal immortality as far as any mortal can believe in an unimaginable horror. They have a cohort of Slate Writers and Writing Mediums in whose hands a pencil of any sort will, apparently of its own volition, write communications, undreamt-of by the medium, that must, they claim, be supernatural. It is objected to these that they have neither novelty, profundity, literary value nor artistic charm, being well within the capacity of very ordinary mortals, and are therefore dismissed as fraudulent on the ground that it is much more probable that the mediums are pretending and lying than performing miracles.

As trueblue Britons the mediums do not know how to defend themselves. They only argue-bargue. They should simply point out that the same objection may be raised against any famous scripture. For instance, the Peculiars known as Baconians believe, with all the evidence against them, that the plays attributed to Shakespear must have been written by somebody else, being unaccountably beyond his knowledge and capacity. Who that somebody else was is the mystery; for the plays are equally beyond the capacity of Bacon and all the later rival claimants. Our greatest masterpiece of literature is the

Jacobean translation of the Bible; and this the Christian Churches declare to be the word of God, supernaturally dictated through Christian mediums and transcribed by them as literally as any letter dictated by a merchant to his typist.

Take my own case. There is nothing in my circumstances or personality to suggest that I differ from any other son of a downstart gentleman driven by lack of unearned income to become an incompetent merchant and harp on his gentility. When I take my pen or sit down to my typewriter, I am as much a medium as Browning's Mr Sludge or Dunglas Home, or as Job or John of Patmos.[1] When I write a play I do not foresee nor intend a page of it from one end to the other: the play writes itself. I may reason out every sentence until I have made it say exactly what it comes to me to say; but whence and how and why it comes to me, or why I persisted, through nine years of unrelieved market failure, in writing instead of in stockbroking or turf bookmaking or peddling, I do not know. You may say it was because I had a talent that way. So I had; but that fact remains inexplicable. What less could Mr Sludge say? or John Hus, who let himself be burnt rather than recant his "I dont know. Instruct me"?[2]

When I was a small boy I saw a professional writing medium, pencil in hand, slash down page after page with astonishing speed without lifting his pencil from the blank paper we fed on to his desk. The fact that he was later transported for forgery did not make his performance and his choice of mediumship as his profession less unaccountable.[3] When I was an elderly man, my mother amused herself with a planchette and a ouija, which under her hands produced what are called spirit writings abundantly. It is true that these screeds might have been called wishful writings (like wishful thinkings) so clearly were they as much her own storytelling inventions as the Waverley novels were Scott's. But why did she choose and practise this senseless activity? Why was I doing essentially the same as a playwright? I do not know. We both got some satisfaction from it or we would not have done it.

1. Dunglas Home, Browning's model for 'Mr Sludge the Medium' (1864), was a Scottish spiritualist, noted for seances across Europe. The apostle John, according to legend, saw visions of the Apocalypse in a cave on the Greek island of Patmos.
2. At his third hearing before the Council of Constance on 8 June 1415, John Hus made the appeal, 'I came here freely, not to defend anything obstinately, but that if in some matters I had stated anything not quite well or defectively . . . [and] if my reasons and Scripture will not suffice, I wish to submit humbly to the instruction of the Council' (Matthew Spinks, *John Hus at the Council of Constance*, 1965, p. 214).
3. The medium has not been identified. Charles Bateson in *The Convict Ships* (1974) indicates transportation to the colonies did not cease until 1868.

This satisfaction, this pleasure, this appetite, is as yet far from being as intense as the sexual orgasm or the ecstasy of a saint, though future cortical evolution may leave them far behind. Yet there are the moments of inexplicable happiness of which Mr J. B. Priestley spoke in a recent broadcast as part of his experience.[4] To me they have come only in dreams not oftener than once every fifteen years or so. I do not know how common they are; for I never heard anyone but Mr Priestley mention them. They have an exalted chronic happiness, as of earth become heaven, proving that such states are possible for us even as we now are.

The happiest moment of my life was when as a child I was told by my mother that we were going to move from our Dublin street to Dalkey Hill in sight of the skies and seas of the two great bays between Howth and Bray, with Dalkey Island in the middle. I had already had a glimpse of them, and of Glencree in the mountains, on Sunday excursions; and they had given me the magic delight Mr Ivor Brown has described as the effect on him of natural scenery.[5] Let who can explain it. Poets only can express it. It is a hard fact, waiting for some scientific genius to make psychology of it.

The professional biologists tell us nothing of all this. It would take them out of the realm of logic into that of magic and miracle, in which they would lose their reputation for omniscience and infallibility. But magic and miracle, as far as they are not flat lies, are not divorced from facts and consequently from science: they are facts: as yet unaccounted for, but none the less facts. As such they raise problems; and genuine scientists must face them at the risk of being classed with [Alessandro di Conte] Cagliostro instead of with [James]

4. 'Moments of Happiness', 1 July 1947, in a series of Priestley's talks called *Pot Luck*. 'The most mysterious things in life', he began, 'are to me its moments of happiness. And when I say moments, I mean moments. I am not discussing whole periods of well-being, after you have had some piece of luck, finished a fine job of work, or are enjoying the holiday that happens to come right from beginning to end. I mean something quite different, the moments that arrive quite unexpectedly, that appear, give us their blessing and vanish, all while you could count ten' (Written Archives Centre, BBC).
5. In a BBC radio series on 'What I Believe' the critic Ivor Brown gave a talk on 15 July 1947 (published as 'Ethics of the Golden Mean', the *Listener*, 24 July): 'I was in North Wales and the sight of that majestic mountain, Tryfan . . . rearing its proud cone into a fleecy sky gave me ecstasy: I use the word deliberately. It was the same ecstasy that great poetry or great beauty in any of the arts can give. If the man of reason does not share in religious rapture, he is not therefore a joyless clod, I assure you. His delight in beauty of nature or the arts and in human affection, can be as rich, I am sure, as anything which comes to the devotee of a religion.'

Clerk-Maxwell[6] and Einstein, Galileo and Newton, who, by the way, worked hard at interpreting the Bible,[7] and was ashamed of his invention of the Infinitesimal Calculus until Leibniz made it fashionable.[8]

Now Newton was right in rating the Calculus no higher than a schoolboy's crib, and the interpretation of the Bible as far more important. In this valuation, which seems so queer to us today, he was not in the least lapsing from science into superstition: he was looking for the foundation of literary art in the facts of history. Nothing could be more important or more scientific; and the fact that the result was the most absurd book in the English language (his Chronology[9]) does not invalidate in the least his integrity as a scientific investigator, nor exemplify his extraordinary mental gifts any less than his hypothesis of gravitation, which might have occurred to anyone who had seen an apple fall when he was wondering why moving bodies did not move in straight lines away into space. Newton was no farther off the scientific target in his attribution of infallibility to Archbishop Ussher than most modern biologists and self-styled scientific socialists in their idolatry of Darwin and Marx. The scientist who solves the problem of the prophet Daniel and John of Patmos, and incidentally of Shakespear and myself, will make a longer stride ahead than any solver of physical problems.

My readers keep complaining in private letters and public criticisms that I have not solved all the problems of the universe for them. As I am obviously

6. Cagliostro was an Italian charlatan who travelled across Europe practising forms of soothsaying and alchemic trickery. Clerk-Maxwell, a Scottish physician, was the first Professor of Experimental Physics at Cambridge University, author of a *Treatise on Electricity and Magnetism* (1873).

7. As Newton kept his religious convictions secret, very few of his utterances on religion were published in his lifetime. These are collected in *Theological Manuscripts*, ed. H. MacLachlan (1950).

8. Though Newton had in 1665–6 invented a method of fluxions (differentials) and a form of integral calculus, using these in the preparation of his *Philosophae Naturalis Principia Mathematica* (1687), he kept them secret in the belief that the established geometrical methods of the ancients would be more acceptable to readers. When Leibniz, who had in 1675 apparently independently laid the foundations of integral and differential calculus, published *Calculus Differentialis* (1684), Newton was forced to establish his priority in Book II of the *Principia* (issued in three volumes) and in *Opticks* (1704). The claims of and acrimony between the two men led to enormous controversy in scholarly circles.

9. The full title of the work is *Chronology of Ancient Kingdoms Amended, to which is prefixed a short Chronicle from the First Memory of Kings in Europe to the Conquest of Persia by Alexander the Great* (1728).

neither omnipotent, omniscient, nor infallible, being not only not a god nor even the proprietor of The Times (as they all assume), they infuriate me. Instead of reminding them calmly that, like Newton, all I know is but a grain of sand picked up on the verge of the ocean of undiscovered knowledge,[10] I have some difficulty in refraining from some paraphrase of "An evil and idolatrous generation clamors for a miracle" [Matthew 12: 39]. But as Mahomet kept his temper under the same thoughtless pressure, so, I suppose, must I.

This is all I can write by way of preface to a trivial comedy which is the best I can do in my dotage. It is only a prefacette to a comedietta. Forgive it. At least it will not rub into you the miseries and sins of the recent wars, nor even of the next one. History will make little of them; and the sooner we forget them the better. I wonder how many people really prefer bogus war news and police news to smiling comedy with some hope in it! I do not. When they begin I switch off the wireless.

AYOT ST LAWRENCE.
July, 1947.

10. Newton's actual words allegedly were, 'I don't know what I may seem to the world, but, as to myself, I seem to have been only like a boy playing on the sea shore, and diverting myself in now and then finding a smoother pebble or prettier shell than ordinary, whilst the great ocean of truth lay all undiscovered before me' (Joseph Spence, *Anecdotes, Observations, and Characters, of Books and Men*, second edition, 1828).

# Farfetched Fables

*First published in 1951*

═══

As I have now entered my 93rd year, my fans must not expect from me more than a few crumbs dropped from the literary loaves I distributed in my prime, plus a few speculations as to what may happen in the next million light years that are troubling me in the queer second wind that follows second childhood.

Being unable to put everything in the heavens above and on the earth beneath into every page I write, as some of my correspondents seem to expect, I have had to leave some scraps and shavings out; and now I gather up a few of them and present them in the childish form of Farfetched Fables. Philosophic treatises, however precise and lucid, are thrown away on readers who can enjoy and sometimes even understand parables, fairy tales, novels, poems, and prophecies. Proverbs are more memorable than catechisms and creeds. Fictions like The Prodigal Son, The Good Samaritan, The Pilgrim's Progress, and Gulliver's Travels, stick in minds impervious to the Epistles of Paul, the sermons of Bunyan, and the wisecracks of Koheleth and Ecclesiasticus. Hard workers who devour my plays cannot all tackle my prefaces without falling asleep almost at once.

The Panjandrums of literature will no doubt continue to assume that whoever can read anything can read everything, and that whoever can add two and two, bet on a horse, or play whist or bridge, can take in the tensor calculus.[1] I know better, and can only hope that a batch of childish fables may stick in some heads that my graver performances overshoot.

---

1. This is defined mathematically, in *Webster's New World Dictionary*, as 'an abstract object representing a generalization of the vector concept and having a specified system of components that undergo certain types of transformation under changes of the coordinate system'.

## The New Psychobiology

Nowadays biology is taking a new turn in my direction. What I called metabiology when I wrote The Doctor's Dilemma has made a step towards reality as psychobiology. The medical profession has split violently into psychotherapists and old-fashioned pill and bottle prescribers backed by surgeons practising on our living bodies as flesh plumbers and carpenters. When these surgeons find a tumor or a cancer they just cut it out. When your digestion or excretion goes wrong the bottlemen dose you with hydrochloric acid or chalk-and-opium ("the old mixture"[2]) as the case may be. When these treatments fail, or when they are impracticable, they tell you sympathetically that you must die; and die you do, unless you cure yourself or are cured by a disciple of Mrs Eddy practising Christian Science.

The more intelligent, observant, and open-minded apothecaries and Sawboneses, wakened up by an extraordinarily indelicate adventurer named Sigmund Freud, and by the able Scotch doctor Scott Haldane (J. B. S. Haldane's[3] father), become more and more sceptical of the dogma that a healthy body insures a healthy mind (*mens sana in corpore sano*) and more and more inclined to believe that an unhealthy body is the result of a diseased mind. As I write, a treatise on Mental Abnormality by Dr Millais Culpin has just been published.[4] It would have been impossible when I wrote The Doctor's Dilemma. In spite of its author's efforts to be impartial, it is convincing and converting as to his evident belief that the old mechanistic surgery and *materia medica* [remedial substance used in medicine] cost many lives.

## Am I a Pathological Case?

This leads my restlessly speculative mind further than Dr Culpin has ventured. Is literary genius a disease? Shakespear, Walter Scott, Alexandre Dumas, myself: are we all mental cases? Are we simply incorrigible liars? Are players

2. Variant of 'the mixture as before', written or printed in earlier years on labels of medicine bottles.
3. Marxist geneticist and popularizer of science, author of *New Paths in Genetics* (1941), was Professor of Biometry at London University until he emigrated and took Indian citizenship.
4. Ophthalmic surgeon at London Hospital and Professor of Medical-industrial Psychology at the University of London; author of *Mental Abnormality* (1948).

impostors and hypocrites? Were the Bible Christians right when they disowned Bunyan because the incidents he described had never occurred nor the characters of whom he told such circumstantial tales ever existed? He pleaded that Jesus had taught by parables; but this made matters worse; for the Bibliolators never doubted that the Prodigal Son and the Good Samaritan were historical personages whose adventures had actually occurred. To them Bunyan's plea, classing the parables with Esop's Fables and the stories of Reynard the Fox, was a blasphemy. The first Freudians used to recite a string of words to their patients, asking what they suggested, and studying the reaction, until they wormed their way into the sufferer's subconscious mind, and unveiled some forgotten trouble that had been worrying him and upsetting his health. By bringing it to light they cured the patient.

When this Freudian technique was tried on me it failed because the words suggested always something fictitious. On the salt marshes of Norfolk I had been struck by the fact that when the horses stood round timidly at a distance, a handsome and intelligent donkey came and conversed with me after its fashion. I still have the photograph I took of this interesting acquaintance.[5] The word Ass would have recalled this experience to any normal person. But when it was put to me, I immediately said Dogberry. I was once shewn the dagger with which Major Sirr killed Lord Edward Fitzgerald;[6] but the word dagger got nothing from me but Macbeth. Highway or stile produced Autolycus, Interpreter the Pilgrim's Progress, blacksmith Joe Gargery. I was living in an imaginary world. Deeply as I was interested in politics, Hamlet and Falstaff were more alive to me than any living politician or even any relative. Can I then be given credit for common sanity? Can I make any effective excuse except Bunyan's excuse, which is no excuse at all? If I plead that I am only doing what More and Bunyan, Dickens and Wells did I do not exonerate myself: I convict them.

5. Hundreds of photographs taken by Shaw on his travels, and a large number of negatives, have been placed by the National Trust on permanent loan in the British Library of Political and Economic Science, in the London School of Economics. Albums of Shaw travel photos are on display at Shaw's Corner in Ayot St Lawrence.
6. Irish MP and member (1796) of the United Irishmen, whose aim was the establishment of an independent Irish republic. Shaw is confused about the dagger. On 19 May 1797 Major Henry Sirr, police chief of Dublin city, seeking to arrest Fitzgerald at his home, disabled him with a pistol bullet in the shoulder after Fitzgerald fatally stabbed an accompanying official with a dagger. Fitzgerald died of his wound ignominiously in Newgate jail twelve months later.

All I can plead is that as events as they actually occur mean no more than a passing crowd to a policeman on point duty, they must be arranged in some comprehensible order as stories. Without this there can be no history, no morality, no social conscience. Thus the historian, the storyteller, the playwright and his actors, the poet, the mathematician, and the philosopher, are functionaries without whom civilization would not be possible. I conclude that I was born a storyteller because one was needed. I am therefore not a disease but a social necessity.

## DIVINE PROVIDENCE

Providence, which I call the Life Force, when not defeated by the imperfection of its mortal instruments, always takes care that the necessary functionaries are born specialized for their job. When no specialization beyond that of common mental ability is needed, millions of "hands" (correctly so called industrially) are born. But as they are helpless without skilled craftsmen and mechanics, without directors and deciders, without legislators and thinkers, these also are provided in the required numbers. Chaucer and Shakespear, Dante and Michael Angelo, Goethe and Ibsen, Newton and Einstein, Adam Smith and Karl Marx arrive only once at intervals of hundreds of years, whilst carpenters and tailors, stockbrokers and parsons, industrialists and traders are all forthcoming in thousands as fast as they are needed.

I present myself therefore as an instrument of the Life Force, writing by what is called inspiration; but as the Life Force proceeds experimentally by Trial-and-Error, and never achieves a 100 per cent success, I may be one of its complete failures, and certainly fall very short not only of perfection but of the Force's former highest achievements. For instance I am much less mentally gifted than, say, Leibniz, and can only have been needed because, as he was so gifted as to be unintelligible to the mob, it remained for some simpler soul like myself to translate his monads[7] and his universal substance, as he called the Life Force, into fables which, however farfetched, can at least interest, amuse, and perhaps enlighten those capable of such

---

7. According to Leibniz in *La Monadologie* (written in 1714; first published in Latin, 1721) a monad is an unextended, indivisible and indestructible entity that is the basic or ultimate constituent of the universe and a microcosm of it. In the original edition (1951) of the volume containing *Farfetched Fables*, which Shaw may not have proofread before his final illness, the word is misprinted as 'nomad'.

entertainment, but baffled by Leibniz's algebraic symbols and his philosophic jargon.

Here I must warn you that you can make no greater mistake in your social thinking than to assume, as too many do, that persons with the rarest mental gifts or specific talents are in any other respect superior beings. The Life Force, when it gives some needed extraordinary quality to some individual, does not bother about his or her morals. It may even, when some feat is required which a human being can perform only after drinking a pint of brandy, make him a dipsomaniac, like Edmund Kean, [Frederick] Robson,[8] and Dickens on his last American tour. Or, needing a woman capable of bearing firstrate children, it may endow her with enchanting sexual attraction yet leave her destitute of the qualities that make married life with her bearable. Apparently its aim is always the attainment of power over circumstances and matter through science, and is to this extent benevolent; but outside this bias it is quite unscrupulous, and lets its agents be equally so. Geniuses are often spendthrifts, drunkards, libertines, liars, dishonest in money matters, backsliders of all sorts, whilst many simple credulous souls are models of integrity and piety, high in the calendar of saints.

## MENTAL CAPACITY DIFFERS AND DIVIDES

When reading what follows it must not be forgotten that though we differ widely in practical ability and mental scope, the same basic income, or ration, or minimum wage, or national dividend, or whatever the newspapers call it for the moment, will suffice for mayor and scavenger, for admiral and cabin boy, for judge and executioner, for field marshal and drummer boy, for sexton and archbishop, bank manager and bank porter, sister of charity and prison wardress, and who not. What is more, they are all equally indispensable. An industrial magnate once wrote asking me did I realize that his army of laborers would be destitute and helpless without him. I replied that if he did not realize that without them he would be a nobody he was no gentleman. This closed the correspondence.

Equality of income is an obvious corollary. Yes; but how much income? A national dividend of, say, thirteen shillings a week per family, which was the share agricultural laborers got in the XIX century, kept them alive for

8. Celebrated tragicomic performer, destroyed at 43 by alcoholism. Shaw, in 'Rules for Producers' (*Strand Magazine*, July 1949), described Edmund Kean and Robson as actors who 'drank themselves into heroic fame and premature death'.

thirty years or so, but left no surplus for education and culture: in short, for civilization. Now without cultured homes civilization is impossible. Without culture possible in every home democratic civilization is impossible, because equality of opportunity is impossible. The present combination of class culture and general savagery produces civil war, called class war, until strikes, lockouts, and police batons are succeeded by shot and shell. Then the final destruction of civilization is threatened.

Consequently the basic income to be aimed at must be sufficient to establish culture in every home, and wages must be leveled up, not down, to this quota by increased production. When the quota is achieved, arithmetical inequality will no longer matter; for the eugenic test is general intermarriageability; and though the difference between £5 a week and £50 makes the recipients practically exogamous, millionaires could not marry at all if they scorned brides from homes with £5000 a year. There is no harm in a few people having some spare money, called capital, to experiment with; for the basic income will keep them in the normal grooves.

So much for the economics of the situation produced by differences in mental capacity! Having dealt with it in former writings, I mention it here only for new readers saturated with the common notion that income ought to vary with mental capacity, personal talent, and business ability. Such equations are wildly impossible, and have nothing to do with the insane misdistribution of national income produced by XIX century plutocracy. And so I pass on to political ethics.

Most of us so far are ungovernable by abstract thought. Our inborn sense of right and wrong, of grace and sin, must be embodied for us in a supernatural ruler of the universe: omnipotent, omniscient, all wise, all benevolent. In ancient Greece this was called making the word flesh, because the Greeks did not then discriminate between thought and the words that expressed it. The Bible translators have Englished it too literally as the word made flesh [John I: 14].

But as the minds of the masses could not get beyond their trades and their localities, their God could not be omnipresent; and a host of minor gods sprang up. The Greeks added to Zeus and Chronos [Titan ruler of the universe, dethroned by Olympian Zeus] vocational deities: Vulcan the blacksmith, Athene (Minerva) the thinker, Diana the huntress, Aphrodite (Venus) the sexmistress. They reappear in Christianity as Peter the fisherman, Luke the painter, Joseph the carpenter, Saint Cecilia the musician, and the rest.

But this also was too wide a classification for the very simple souls, who carried the localization of their gods to the extent of claiming exclusive property for their own city in each saint, and waging civil war in the name of the black image of the Blessed Virgin in their parish church against the worshippers of her white image in the next village.[9]

## SATANIC SOLUTION OF THE PROBLEM OF EVIL

A difficulty was raised by the fact that evil was in the world as well as good, and often triumphed over the good. Consequently there must be a devil as well as a divinity: Poochlihoochli as well as Hoochlipoochli, Ahriman as well as Ormudz, Lucifer Beelzebub and Apollyon[10] as well as the Holy Trinity, the Scarlet Woman [Revelation 17: 3–6] as well as Our Lady: in short as many demons as saints.

At first, however, this setting up against God of a rival deity with a contrary ideology was resented as a Manichean heresy,[11] because plague, pestilence and famine, battle, murder and sudden death [Anglican *Book of Common Prayer*: Litany], were not regarded with horror as the work of Shelley's Almighty Fiend [*Queen Mab* (1813), canto IV: 211; canto VI: 222], but with awe as evidence of the terrible greatness of God, the fear of him being placed to his credit as the beginning of wisdom. The invention of Satan is a heroic advance on Jahvism.[12] It is an attempt to solve the Problem of Evil, and at least faces the fact that evil *is* evil.

Thus the world, as we imagine it, is crowded with anthropomorphic supernatural beings of whose existence there is no scientific proof. Nonetheless, without such belief the human race cannot be civilized and governed, though the ten per cent or so of persons mentally capable of civilizing and

9. The Black Virgin of Kazan, a town of eastern Russia, was reputed to be a miracle-working image. It was transferred to Moscow in 1612. Abbe M. Osini, in *The Life of the Blessed Virgin Mary* (1874), recorded, 'At the foot of the Vosges, on the frontiers of Lorraine, an enormous Gallic oak . . . held in its centre, softly carpeted with moss, a mysterious white image of the Blessed Virgin, before which Jane d'Arc, the holy maid, devoutly went to pray against the English.'

10. Hoochlipoochli, the 'source of all creation', is the God of the Native in *Buoyant Billions*; his opposite, the God of the nether regions, is Poochlihoochli. Ormudz, in the Zoroastrian religion, is god of goodness and light, in eternal battle with Ahriman, spirit of darkness. In *Pilgrim's Progress* Apollyon is the angel of the bottomless pit.

11. A religion founded by Mani, a Persian who lived in the third century AD. It is a dualistic theology contrasting God and Satan, the soul and the body, light and darkness.

12. Jehovism: one Supreme Being, called God or Jehovah.

governing are mostly too clever to be imposed on by fairy tales, and in any case have to deal with hard facts as well as fancies and fictions.

MENDACITY COMPULSORY IN KINGCRAFT AND PRIESTCRAFT

This lands them in the quaintest moral dilemmas. It drives them to false-hoods, hypocrisies, and forgeries most distressing to their intellectual con-sciences. When the people demand miracles, worship relics, and will not obey any authority that does not supply them, the priest must create and nourish their faith by liquefying the blood of Saint Januarius, and saying Mass over a jawbone labeled as that of Saint Anthony of Padua. When the people believe that the earth is flat, immovable, and the centre of the universe, and Copernicus and Leonardo convince both Galileo the scientist and the Vatican that the earth is a planet of the sun, the Pope and the cardinals have to make Galileo recant and pretend that he believes what the people believe, because, if the Church admits that it has ever been mistaken, its whole authority will collapse, and civilization perish in anarchy. If Joshua could not make the sun stand still [Joshua 10: 12–13], there is a blunder in the Bible. When the Protestants blew the gaff to discredit the Vatican, and the secret could no longer be kept by forbidding Catholics to read the Bible, the people were not logical enough to draw subversive inferences. They swallowed the contra-diction cheerfully.

Meanwhile the people had to be threatened with a posthumous eternity in a brimstone hell if they behaved in an uncivilized way. As burning brim-stone could not hurt a spirit, they had to be assured that their bodies would be resurrected on a great Day of Judgment. But the official translators of the Bible in England were presently staggered by a passage in the Book of Job, in which that prophet declared that as worms would destroy his body, in the flesh he should not see God. Such a heresy, if published, would knock the keystone out of the arch of British civilization. There was nothing for it but to alter the word of God, making Job [19: 26] say that though worms would destroy his body yet in his flesh he should see God. The facts made this forgery necessary; but it was a forgery all the same.

A later difficulty was more easily got over. The apostles were Communists so Red that St Peter actually struck a man and his wife dead for keeping back money from the common stock. The translators could not pretend that St Peter was a disciple of the unborn Adam Smith rather than of Jesus; so they let the narrative stand, but taught that Ananias and Sapphira were executed for telling a lie and not for any economic misdemeanor. This view was impressed on me in my childhood. I now regard it as a much graver lie than that of Ananias.

"The lie" said Ferdinand Lassalle "is a European Power." He might, however, have added that it is none the worse when it does a necessary job; for I myself have been a faker of miracles. Let me tell one of my old stories over again.

### G.B.S. Miracle Faker

When I was a vestryman I had to check the accounts of the Public Health Committee. It was a simple process: I examined one in every ten or so of the receipted accounts and passed it whilst my fellow members did the same; and so enough of the accounts got checked to make their falsification too risky.

As it happened, one which I examined was for sulphur candles to disinfect houses in which cases of fever had occurred. I knew that experiments had proved that the fumes of burning sulphur had no such effect. Pathogenic bacilli like them and multiply on them.

I put the case to the Medical Officer of Health, and asked why the money of the ratepayers should be spent on a useless fumigant. He replied that the sulphur was not useless: it was necessary. But, I urged, the houses are not being disinfected at all. "Oh yes they are" he said. "How?" I persisted. "Soap and water and sunshine" he explained. "Then why sulphur?" "Because the strippers and cleaners will not venture into an infected house unless we make a horrible stink in it with burning sulphur."

I passed the account. It was precisely equivalent to liquefying the blood of Saint Januarius.[13]

Some twenty years later I wrote a play called Saint Joan in which I made an archbishop explain that a miracle is an event that creates faith, even if it is faked for that end. Had I not been a vulgar vestryman as well as a famous playwright I should not have thought of that. All playwrights should know that had I not suspended my artistic activity to write political treatises and work on political committees long enough to have written twenty plays, the Shavian idiosyncrasy which fascinates some of them (or used to) and disgusts the Art For Art's Sake faction, would have missed half its value, such as it is.

13. Shaw served (1897–1903) as a vestryman for St Pancras and as a councillor when the vestry became a borough in 1900, his principal assignment being to the health committee. See also vol. 1, p. 401, where Shaw speaks of a yet earlier account of the sulphur incident (in 'The Revolutionist's Handbook', *Man and Superman*).

## PARENTAL DILEMMAS

The first and most intimate of the moral dilemmas that arise from differences in mental ability is not between classes and Churches, but in the daily work of bringing up children. The difference between Einstein and an average ploughman is less troublesome than the difference between children at five, at ten, and at fifteen. At five the Church catechism is only a paradigm: I learnt it at that age and still remember its phrases; but it had no effect on my conduct. I got no farther with it critically than to wonder why it obliged me, when asked what my name was, to reply that it was N or M,[14] which was not true.

What did affect my conduct was my nurse's threat that if I was naughty or dirty the cock would come down the chimney. I confidently recommend this formula to all parents, nurses, and kindergarten teachers, as it effects its purpose and then dies a natural death, fading from the mind as the child grows out of it without leaving any psychic complexes.

But the same cannot be said for more complicated schemes of infant civilization. If they begin with Law's Serious Call [see vol. 2, p. 39], as many pious parents think they should, they may be worse than no scheme at all. I knew a man whose youth was made miserable by a dread of hell sedulously inculcated from his infancy. His reaction against it carried him into Socialism, whereupon he founded a Labor Church[15] in which all the meetings began by calling on the speakers to pray: a demand which so took aback my Fabian colleagues that one of them began with "Heavenly Father: unaccustomed as I have been many years to address you, I *etc. etc.*" The Labor Church did not last; but the reaction did; and the last I heard of its founder was that he was helping the movement against Victorian prudery in a very practical way as a Nudist photographer, the basis of that prudery being the fact that the clothing, or rather upholstering, of Victorian women was much more aphrodisiac than their unadorned bodies.

As to the Socialist orator who parodied "Unaccustomed as I am to public speaking," he died in the bosom of the Roman Catholic Church.

14. In the original Catechism 'name or names' (*nomen vel nomina*) was abbreviated as 'N' or 'NN', the latter (a Latin doubled initial) being misread as M, until, in the marriage service, they came to be used as M (*maritus*, bridegroom) and N (*nuptia*, bride). At present the initials are equalized as N and N.
15. Revd John Trevor, a Unitarian minister, was founder of the first Labour Church, in Manchester, 1891.

I tell these anecdotes because they give an impression, better than any abstract argument could, of the way in which highly intelligent children of pious families, or of irreligious ones capable of nothing more intellectual than sport and sex, reacted against their bringing-up. One day, at a rehearsal of one of my plays, an actress who was a Roman Catholic consulted me in some distress because her adolescent son had become an atheist. I advised her not to worry; for as family religions have to be cast off as thoughtless habits before they can be replaced by genuine religious convictions, she might safely leave her son's case to God.

Edmund Gosse was the son of a Plymouth Brother, and was baptized by total immersion, of which he wrote a highly entertaining description in his book called Father and Son [1907]. The immersion had washed all the father's pious credulity out of the son.[16] George Eliot, also piously brought up, began her reaction by translating Emil Strauss's Life of Jesus [1846], which divested the worshipped Redeemer of supernatural attributes, and even questioned the sanity of his pretension to them.

## THE ALL OR NOTHING COMPLEX

In those days we were all what I called Soot or Whitewash[17] merchants, pilloried as All or Nothings in Ibsen's Brand. When one link in our mental chain snapped we did not pick up the sound links and join them, we threw the chain away as if all its links had snapped. If the story of Noah's Ark was a fable, if Joshua could not have delayed the sunset in the Valley of Ajalon, if the big fish could not have swallowed Jonah nor he survive in its belly, then nothing in the Bible was true. If Jehovah was a barbarous tribal idol, irreconcilable with the God of Micah, then there was no God at all, and the heavens were empty. On the other hand if Galileo, the man of science, knew better than Joshua, and Linneus and Darwin better than Moses, then everything that scientists said was true. Thus the credulity that believed in the Garden of Eden with its talking serpent, and in the speeches of Balaam's ass [Numbers 22: 29–30], was not cured. It was simply transferred to Herbert Spencer and John Stuart Mill. The transfer was often for the worse, as when baptism by water and the spirit, consecrating the baptized as a soldier and a

16. Gosse was a poet and man of letters, who introduced Ibsen to the British. His father Philip, a zoologist, was the central character in his autobiographic work.
17. We can find no earlier usage of this terminology by Shaw than in Act 3 of *Buoyant Billions* (1950).

servant of the Highest, was replaced by the poisonous rite of vaccination on evidence that could not have imposed on any competent statistician, and was picked up by Jenner from a dairy farmer and his milkmaids.

## CATHOLICISM IMPRACTICABLE

The lesson of this is that a totally Catholic Church or Communist State is an impossible simplification of social organization. It is contrary to natural history. No Church can reconcile and associate in common worship a Jehovah's Witness with William Blake, who called Jehovah Old Nobodaddy. Napoleon, who pointed to the starry sky and asked "Who made all that?" did not kneel beside those who replied that it made itself, or retorted "We dont know: and neither do you." I, as a Creative Evolutionist, postulate a creative Life Force or Evolutionary Appetite seeking power over circumstances and mental development by the method of Trial and Error, making mistake after mistake, but still winning its finally irresistible way. Where in the world is there a Church that will receive me on such terms, or into which I could honestly consent to be received? There are Shaw Societies; but they are not Catholic Churches in pretence, much less in reality. And this is exactly as it should be, because, as human mental capacity varies from grade to grade, those who cannot find a creed which fits their grade have no established creed at all, and are ungovernable unless they are naturally amiable Vicars of Bray[18] supporting any government that is for the moment established. There are hosts of such creedless voters, acting strongly as a conservative force, and usefully stabilizing government as such. But they make reforms very difficult sometimes.

## THE TARES AND THE WHEAT

I therefore appreciate the wisdom of Jesus's warning to his missionaries that if they tore up the weeds they would tear up the wheat as well [Matthew 13: 29], meaning that if they tried to substitute his gospel for that of Moses instead of pouring the new wine into the old bottles (forgive the Biblical

18. 'The Vicar of Bray' is an anonymous song dating from the eighteenth century, depicting a time-serving parson who adjusts to the religious view of whoever is in power. From it Shaw derived the title of his play *'In Good King Charles's Golden Days'*.

change of metaphor) nothing would be left of either Jesus or Moses. As I put it ['Maxims for Revolutionists', *Man and Superman*], the conversion of savagery to Christianity is the conversion of Christianity to savagery.

This is as true as ever. Not only are the immediate black converts of our missionaries inferior in character both to the unconverted and the born converted, but all the established religions in the world are deeply corrupted by the necessity for adapting their original inspired philosophic creeds to the narrow intelligences of illiterate peasants and of children. Eight thousand years ago religion was carried to the utmost reach of the human mind by the Indian Jainists, who renounced idolatry and blood sacrifice long before Micah,[19] and repudiated every pretence to know the will of God, forbidding even the mention of his name in the magnificent temples they built for their faith.

But go into a Jainist temple today:[20] what do you find? Idols everywhere. Not even anthropomorphic idols but horse idols, cat idols, elephant idols and what not? The statues of the Jainist sages and saints, far from being contemplated as great seers, are worshipped as gods.

## THE THIRTYNINE ARTICLES

For such examples it is not necessary to travel to Bombay. The articles of the Church of England begin with the fundamental truth that God has neither body, parts, nor passions, yet presently [article 6] enjoin the acceptance as divine revelation of a document alleging that God exhibited his hind quarters to one of the prophets [Exodus 33: 23], and when he had resolved to destroy the human race as one of his mistakes, was induced to make an exception in the case of Noah and his family by a bribe of roast meat [Genesis 8: 20–22]. Later articles [12–13] instruct us to love our fellow-creatures, yet to obey an injunction to hold accursed all who do good works otherwise than in the name of Christ, such works being sinful. In one article [28] it is at first assumed that the swallowing of a consecrated wafer is only the heathen rite of eating the god (transubstantiation) and as such abominable, and then that it is holy as a memorial of the last recorded supper of Jesus. No man can be ordained a minister of the Church of England unless he swears without any mental reservation that he believes these contradictions. I once held

19. Micah allegedly prophesied in the eighth century BC. Vardhamana Juatiputra, called 'Mahavira' ('great hero'), a contemporary of Buddha, founded the present form of Jainism in the sixth century BC.
20. Shaw visited two Jain temples in January 1933, during a week's stay in Bombay.

lightly that candidates of irresistible vocation might swear this blamelessly because they were under duress. But one day I was present at the induction of a rector. When the bishop asked the postulant to tell a flat lie which both of them knew to be a lie, and he told it without a blush, the impression made on me was so shocking that I have felt ever since that the Church of England must revise its articles at all hazards if it is to be credited with the intellectual honesty necessary to its influence and authority. Shake that authority, and churchgoing will be nothing more than parading in our best clothes every Sunday.

## A Hundred Religions and only One Sauce

As it is, Christianity has split into sects, persuasions, and Nonconformities in all directions. The Statesman's Year-Book has given up trying to list them. They range from Pillars of Fire,[21] Jehovah's Witnesses, Plymouth Brothers, and Glasites [see vol. 2, pp. 560–1], to Presbyterians, Methodists, Congregationalists, Baptists, Friends (Quakers), and Unitarians. Within the Established Church itself there are Ritualists,[22] Anglo-Catholics who call their services Masses and never mention the Reformation, Laodicean Broad Churchmen, and Low Church Protestants. The Friends abhor ritual and dictated prayers, and repudiate cathedral services and Masses as playacting, whilst the Anglo-Catholics cannot think religiously without them. Presbyterians and Congregationalists differ from the clergy of the Established Church on the political issue of episcopal or lay Church government. The Unitarians reject the Trinity and deny deity to Jesus. Calvinists deny universal atonement, preached by our missionaries, who are practically all Independents.[23]

Common to these irreconcilable faiths is the pretension that each is the true Catholic Church, and should hand over all whom it cannot convert to the State (the Secular Arm) to be exterminated for the crime of heresy by the cruelest possible methods, even to burning alive. This does not mean that all rulers who order such extermination are horribly cruel. "Bloody Mary"

21. An offshoot of the Methodist Church, founded by Mrs Alma White in 1901, emphasizing divine healing and full ministerial orders for women.
22. Those in the churches of the Anglican Communion who use the six points of ritual: altar lights, eucharistic vestments, eastward position, wafer bread, mixed chalice and incense.
23. Those who believe that the local Christian church is independent of all external ecclesiastical authority.

[Tudor] believed that heretics must be liquidated; but she was not responsible for the political circumstance that the secular criminal law was atrociously cruel, and that no other agency could effect the liquidation. Calvin agreed that Servetus must be killed; but he objected humanely to his being burned.[24] Charles II, humane (indeed, as some think, too humane in his kindness to his dozen dogs and half dozen mistresses), could not question the necessity for punishing the Regicides with death;[25] but he loathed the butchering of them in the hideous manner ordained centuries earlier for the punishment of William Wallace, and stopped it as soon as he dared. It was still unrepealed during my own lifetime; and has only just (1948) been repealed in Scotland.

So far I have not been imprisoned, as poorer men have been in my time, for blasphemy or apostasy. I am not technically an apostate, as I have never been confirmed; and my godparents are dead. But having torn some of the Thirtynine Articles to rags, I should have been pilloried and had my ears cropped had I lived in the days of the British Inquisition called the Star Chamber [see vol. 1, p. 519]. Nowadays Nonconformity and Agnosticism are far too powerful electorally for such persecution. But the Blasphemy Laws are still available and in use against obscure sceptics, whilst I suffer nothing worse than incessant attempts to convert me. All the religions and their sects, Christian or Moslem, Buddhist or Shinto, Jain or Jew, call me to repentance, and ask me for subscriptions. I am not so bigoted as to dismiss their experiences as the inventions of liars and the fancies of noodles. They are evidence like any other human evidence; and they force me to the conclusion that every grade of human intelligence can be civilized by providing it with a frame of reference peculiar to its mental capacity, and called a religion.

24. Calvin declared that death by burning was an 'atrocity' for which he sought to substitute death by the sword. (Letter to Guillaume Farel, 20 August 1553.) For Servetus, see p. 201.
25. Eighty-four men, following the Restoration, were named as 'Regicides', responsible for the execution of Charles I. Many escaped abroad, but thirty-five were tried before a court of commissioners in October 1660. Although twenty-nine of these were condemned to death, and the others to life imprisonment, only ten of the condemned were immediately executed, at Charing Cross or Tyburn, the sentences of the others being commuted subsequently to life imprisonment.

## The Marxist Church

The Marxist Church, called Cominform, is like all the other Churches. Having ceased to believe in the beneficently interfering and overruling God of Adam Smith and Voltaire, no less than in the vicarage of the Pope and his infallibility in council with the College of Cardinals, Cominform makes Karl Marx its Deity and the Kremlin his Vatican. It worships his apostles at its conventicles and in its chapels, with Das Kapital as its Bible and gospel, just as Cobdenist Plutocracy used to make a Bible of Adam Smith's Wealth of Nations [1776] with its gospel of the Economic Harmonies[26] and its policy of Free Trade.

I am myself much idolized. I receive almost daily letters from devout Shavians who believe that my income is unlimited, my knowledge and wisdom infinite, my name a guarantee of success for any enterprize, my age that of Jesus at his death, and the entire Press at my command, especially The Times, of which I am assumed to be the proprietor.

If this is not idolatry the word has no meaning. The fact that I am ascertainably, and indeed conspicuously, only a superannuated (not supernatural) journalist and playwright does not shake the faith of my idolaters in the least. Facts count for nothing. I am told that I should be shot in Russia if I dared to pontificate against the Government there as I often do here, and that Freedom of the Press, the glory of England, does not and cannot exist under Communist tyranny.

## Should I be Shot in Russia?

As a matter of fact the Russian newspapers are full of complaints and grievances. There is a Government Department whose function it is to receive and deal with such complaints. Here in England I, an old journalist and agitator, know only too well that both platform and press are gagged by such an irresponsible tyranny of partisan newspaper proprietors and shamelessly mendacious advertizers, and by the law against seditious and blasphemous libel, that my speeches were never reported, and my letters and articles inserted only when I could combine what I believed and wanted to say with something that the paper wanted to have said, or when I could disguise it as an attractively

26. An allusion to *Les Harmonies économiques* (1849) by Claude-Frédéric Bastiat, a French political economist who advocated Free Trade.

readable art criticism, the queer result being that my reputation was made in Conservative papers whilst the Liberal, Radical, and Socialist editors dared not mention my name except in disparagement and repudiation. I owe more of my publicity to The Times than to any other daily newspaper. The same is true of my Fabian colleagues. The Webbs, now in Westminster Abbey, never could get into the British daily newspapers. In Russia, when Fabians were despised there as bourgeois Deviators, the Webbs were translated by Lenin.[27]

As a playwright I was held up as an irreligious pornographer, and as such a public enemy, not to say a thoroughpaced cad, for many years by an irresponsible censorship which could not be challenged in parliament or elsewhere. No such misfortune has happened to me in Russia.

What damns our foreign policy here is our ignorance of history of home affairs. In the imagination of our amateur politicians England is a Utopia in which everything and everybody is "free," and all other countries "police States." I, being Irish, know better.

To return to the inveteracy of idolatry. Ten years ago disciples of a rival celebrity were sending me portraits of an Austrian Messiah named Hitler, described by Mr Winston Churchill as a bloodthirsty guttersnipe,[28] yet more fanatically deified in Germany than Horatio Bottomley in England.[29]

One of the puzzles of history is whether Jesus, denounced by the ladies and gentlemen of his time as a Sabbath breaker, a gluttonous man, and a winebibber, and finally executed for rioting in the temple, really believed in his claim to be Messiah, or was forced to assume that character because he could not make converts on any other terms, just as Mahomet found that he could not govern the Arabs without inventing a very sensual paradise and a very disgusting hell to keep them in order. Whether he invented his conversations with the Archangel Gabriel, or, like Joan of Arc, really heard voices when he listened for the voice of God, we shall never know. I have just had

27. Lenin translated vol. 1 and edited the translation of vol. 2 of the Webbs' *Industrial Democracy* (1899), published in Russia as *The Theory and Practice of English Trade Unionism* (1900–01).
28. A speech broadcast by the BBC on 22 June 1941, following Germany's sudden air attack on Russia and violation of Russian frontiers without declaration of war: '[T]his bloodthirsty guttersnipe launches his mechanized armies upon new fields of slaughter, pillage and devastation' (*The Times*, 23 June 1941).
29. During the First World War Bottomley, as publisher of the journal *John Bull*, was adulated by the British masses for his fanatical patriotism and aggressive anti-Germanism.

a letter from a man who, having made repeated attempts to give up smoking, had failed, until one day, walking through Hyde Park, he heard a Gospel preacher cry "Listen for the voice of God and it will come to you." This stuck in his mind. He listened, not piously but experimentally; and sure enough a voice said to him "Quit smoking: quit smoking." This time he quitted without the smallest difficulty.

## COMPATIBILITIES

Differences of creed must be tolerated, analyzed, discussed, and as far as possible reconciled. My postulate of a provident and purposeful Life Force that proceeds by trial-and-error, and makes mistakes with the best intentions, is not in effect irreconcilable with belief in a supernatural benignant Providence at war with a malignant Satan. We cannot "make our souls" in the same assembly; but in the same building we can. Therefore if our cathedrals and churches are to be open to all faiths, as they in fact are, for contemplation and soul making, their different rituals must be performed at different hours, as they are at the Albert Hall in London, the Usher Hall in Edinburgh, the Free Trade Hall in Manchester, the Montford Hall in Leicester, and wherever two or three gathered together [Matthew 18:20] may hear Messiah or the great Masses of Bach and Beethoven on Sunday or Monday, and watch a boxing show on Tuesday or Wednesday. The rituals differ, but not enough to provoke their votaries to burn oneanother at the stake or refuse to dine together on occasion. The sporting peer who becomes famous as the owner of a Derby winner meets the winner of a Nobel Prize without the least embarrassment; and I have never suffered the smallest discourtesy except once in a Manchester club, and then only because my criticisms of Shakespear stopped this side of idolatry.

It may seem that between a Roman Catholic who believes devoutly in Confession and a modern freethinking scientist there can be neither sympathy nor cooperation. Yet there is no essential difference between Confession and modern Psychotherapy. The post-Freudian psychoanalyst relieves his patient of the torments of guilt and shame by extracting a confession of their hidden cause. What else does the priest do in the confessional, though the result is called cure by one and absolution by the other? What I, a Freethinker, call the Life Force, my pious neighbors call Divine Providence: in some respects a better name for it. Bread and wine are changed into living tissue by swallowing and digestion. If this is not transubstantiation what *is* transubstantiation? I have described the surprise of a Fabian lecturer on being asked to open a political meeting with prayer. When I was invited to address the most important Secular Society in England[30] I found that I had to supply the sermon in a ritual of hymns and lessons in all respects like a religious Sunday service except that the lessons were from Browning and the hymns were aspirations to "join the choir invisible."[31] Later on [5 April 1929], when I attended a church service in memory of my wife's sister [Mary Cholmondeley], and was disposed to be moved by it, the lesson was the chapter from the Bible [Exodus 12: 35–6] which describes how the Israelites in captivity were instructed by a deified Jonathan Wild[32] to steal the jewelry of the Egyptians before their flight into the desert. The Leicester Atheists were in fact more pious than the Shropshire Anglicans.

## BOHEMIAN ANARCHISM

The anarchy which the priests feared when they gagged Galileo actually came to pass much more widely than the epidemics which the Medical Officer of Health dreaded when he gagged me about the sulphur candles. In my early days as a Socialist lecturer I was once opposed by a speaker who had been an apostle of Robert Owen's New Moral World, the first version of British Socialism. His ground was that too many of his fellow apostles took the new moral world as an emancipation from all the obligations of the old moral world, and were dishonest and licentious. Prominent in my own generation of Marxists was one who, I believe, would have gone as a martyr to the scaffold or the stake rather than admit that God existed, or that Marx and Darwin were fallible. But when money or women were concerned, he was such a conscienceless rascal that he was finally blackballed by all the Socialist societies.[33]

Do not misunderstand me. I am not stigmatizing all Owenites, Marxists,

30. To Shaw the 'most important' Secular Society was not the National Secular Society in London, which he addressed on 'Freethinking, New and Old', in the Hall of Science on 22 February 1891; but the Leicester Secular Society, to which he lectured on 'Progress in Freethought' on 1 November 1891.
31. 'May I join the Choir Invisible', in George Eliot's *The Legend of Jubal and Other Poems* (1874).
32. Head of a large corporation of thieves in eighteenth-century London. Henry Fielding fictionalized him in a satirical romance *The Life of Jonathan Wild the Great* (1743).
33. This presumably was Edward Aveling.

and Darwinists as immoral; but it must be borne in mind that all revolutionary and reform movements are recruited from those who are not good enough for the existing system as well as those who are too good for it. All such movements attract sinners as well as saints by giving them a prominence as platform orators and pamphleteers out of all proportion to their numbers and deserts. They justify their delinquencies as assertions of principle, and thus give Socialism a reputation for anarchism, irreligion, and sexual promiscuity which is association of ideas, not logic. No eminence in a specific department implies even ordinary ability in any other, nor does any specific personal depravity imply general depravity. I may fairly claim to be an adept in litera-ture; but in dozens of other departments I am a duffer. I have often quoted a certain ex-Colonel who said to me "I know for certain that the Rector is the father of his housemaid's illegitimate child; and after that you may tell me that the Bible is true: I shall not believe you." It does not follow that the Colonel was not a military genius, nor the Rector an eloquent preacher and efficient clergyman.

Nevertheless we cannot legislate for every individual separately, nor provide a special policeman to keep him (or her) in order. All civilized persons except certified lunatics and incorrigible criminals must for elementary purposes be held equally capable and responsible. Those who cannot read any book more abstruse than Esop's Fables, nor get beyond the multiplication table (if so far) in mathematics, can understand the Ten Commandments well enough to be legislated for in the mass.

## SHAM DEMOCRACY

In the face of these hard facts most of the current interpretations of the word Democracy are dangerous nonsense. The fundamental notion that the voice of the people is the voice of God is a sample. What people? Were Solon and Sully,[34] Voltaire and Adam Smith, Plato and Aristotle, Hobbes and Tom Paine and Marx, the people? Were Lord George Gordon, Titus Oates, and Horatio Bottomley the people? Were General Roberts and Henry Irving, nominated by Gallup poll as ideal rulers, the people? Am I the people? Was Ruskin? Were Moses, Jesus, Peter and Paul, Mahomet, Brigham Young? If their voices were all voices of God, God must be a very accomplished ventriloquist.

34. Maximilien de Béthune, Duc de Sully, French statesman and Huguenot, a princi-pal adviser to France's Henry IV (Henry of Navarre).

Democracy means government in the interest of everybody. It most emphatically does not mean government BY everybody. All recorded attempts at that have not only failed but rapidly developed into despotisms and tyrannies. The trade union secretary elected by everybody in his Union, the pirate captain whose crew can make him walk the plank at any moment, are the most absolute despots on earth. Cromwell tried government by a parliament of elected saints and had to turn it into the street[35] as Bismarck turned the Frankfort Parliament in 1862.[36] He tried an oligarchy of majors general, but finally had to make himself Lord Protector and govern despotically as much as it was possible to govern Englishmen at all, which, as he bitterly complained, was not very much.[37] Much or little, votes for everybody, politically called Adult Suffrage, always produces anarchy, which, being unbearable, produces by reaction overwhelming majorities in favor of Regressions called Restorations, or Napoleonic Emperors and South American dictator-presidents. Democratic government of the people by the people, professed ideologically nowadays by all Governments and Oppositions, has never for a moment existed.

Real democracy leaves wide open the question as to which method best secures it: monarchies, oligarchies, parliaments nominated or elected with or without proportional representation, restricted franchise, intervals between general elections, or other "checks and balances" devized to prevent glaring abuses of virtually irresponsible power. None of them has ever made Voltaire's

35. Oliver Cromwell, on 20 April 1653, used force to dissolve the so-called 'Long' (later 'Purged' or 'Rump') Parliament as they were about to pass a bill that would ensure their tenure, thus himself becoming the sole authority in the State.

36. When the German parliament in 1862 refused the request of King William I for military funds, Otto von Bismarck ruled as minister-president without a budget, by taking advantage of an omission in the constitution, which did not specify what was to happen in the event crown and parliament could not agree.

37. The complaint was implicit, reflected in frequent querulous and despairing utterances in correspondence and in angry dissolutions of successive parliaments to rid himself of self-perpetuating 'ambitious and troublesome' men (speech to first Protectorate Parliament, 12 September 1654). He struck out at Anabaptist Levellers as 'a company of men like briers and thorns' on 22 January 1654–5; and, as reported by Clement Walker (*History of the Independency 1640–60*, 1660–61), asked God in a sermon as early as 1 April 1648 'to take off from him the government of this mighty People of England, as being too heavy for his shoulders to bear . . .' In dissolving the second Protectorate Parliament (4 February 1657–8), seven months before his death, he brusquely informed its members 'you are not satisfiable'. Texts and dates extracted from Cromwell's *Letters and Speeches*, ed. Thomas Carlyle (1845).

*Monsieur Tout le Monde*[38] master of the situation. Adult suffrage did not prevent two so-called world wars and a royal abdication on which the people were no more consulted than I was. Political adventurers and "tin Jesuses" rose like rockets to dictatorships and fell to earth like sticks, or were succeeded, as Napoleon was, by Bourbonic bosses. The Russian Bolsheviks, having invented the Soviet System, and brought their country to the verge of ruin and a little over by All or Nothing Catastrophism, were forced by the facts to make room in Bolshevism for more private enterprize than there is in England. The moment it did so, the basic difference between British and Russian economic policy vanished or criss-crossed. Lenin and Stalin had to cry *Laisser-faire* to all the enterprizes not yet ripe for nationalization. The Labor Party in England nationalized as many industries as it could manage, and regulated private employers, controled prices, rationed food and clothing, imposed purchase taxes on luxuries, and increased the bureaucracy both in numbers and power whilst jealously restricting official salaries more grudgingly with a view to equality of income than the Kremlin. Stalin's Russo-Fabian slogan, Socialism in a Single Country, is countered by Churchill's manifestos of Plutocratic Capitalism Everywhere and Down with Communism,[39] which is more than Trotsky claimed for international Marxism.

With all this staring them in the face, and no intention whatever of going back to turnpike roads, toll bridges, private detectives and prizefighters for police, sixpenny linkmen [torch carriers] for municipal electric lighting, cadis under palm trees for judges, *condottieri* [mercenaries] and privateers for national defence, profiteers for Exchequer Chancellors: in short, the substitution of private enterprize for the omnipresent Communism without which our civilization could not endure for a week, our politicians and partisans keep shouting their abhorrence of Communism as if their Parties were cannibal tribes fighting and eating oneanother instead of civilized men driven by sheer pressure of facts into sane co-operation.

38. There is a common misconception that Voltaire created a Monsieur Tout le Monde. Shaw made frequent allusion to this mythic character, unaware that the source was Prince Talleyrand, who, on 24 July 1821, in a speech condemning the existing censorship in France, said: 'There is someone smarter than Voltaire, smarter than Bonaparte, smarter than each of the directors, than each of the past, present, and future ministers: it is Everybody.' We are indebted to Jacques Barzun for this information.

39. Churchill, who consistently contrasted Capitalism with Socialism rather than with Communism, claimed in a speech in the House on 22 October 1945 that 'the inherent vice of Capitalism is the unequal sharing of blessings; the inherent virtue of Socialism is the equal sharing of miseries' (Hansard).

## THE POLITICAL TIME LAG

The worst features of our sham-democratic misgovernment are caused, not by incurable mental incapacity, but by an ignorance that is essentially mathematical. None of our politicians seems to know that political action, like all earthly action, must take place in a world of four dimensions, not three. The fourth dimension is that of Time. To ignore it is to be pre-Einstein, which is as out-of-date as to be pre-Marx. Fortunately it can be taught, just as the theories of rent and value can be taught; and those who learn it see that our British parliamentary system is far too slow for XX century social organization. The Soviet system in Russia outstrips it because, being faster, it is more immediately responsive to the continual need for reforms and adaptations to changing circumstances. It includes all the conventional democratic checks and safeguards against despotism now so illusory, and gives them as much effectiveness as their airy nature is capable of. Incidentally it gives Stalin the best right of any living statesman to the vacant Nobel peace prize, and our diplomatists the worst. This will shock our ignoramuses as a stupendous heresy and a mad paradox. Let us see.

When the horrors of unregulated selfish private enterprize forced both Conservatives and Cobdenists to devize and pass the Factory Acts, it took the British Parliament a time lag of 50 years [see vol. 2, p. 30 fn 18] to make them effective. Home Rule for Ireland took thirty years to get through Parliament, and was decided after all by a sanguinary civil war.

In the simplest home affairs the time lag extends to centuries. For instance, the practice of earth burial, with its cemeteries crowding the living out by the dead, its poisonous slow putrefactions, its risk of burial alive, and its cost, should be forbidden and replaced by cremation. It was discussed 80 years ago when I was a boy. Yet not even the cremation of an Archbishop [of Canterbury] ([William] Temple: one of our best) has overcome our dread of doing anything that everyone else is not yet doing, nor the bigoted opposition of the Churches which preach the Resurrection of the Body without considering that a body can be resurrected from dust and ashes as feasibly as from a heap of maggots. Our crematory gardens of rest are still countable only in dozens, and cremations only in thousands, even in big cities. In lesser towns the figure is zero.

## ADULT SUFFRAGE IS MOBOCRACY

Adult Suffrage is supposed to be a substitute for civil war. The idea is that if two bodies of citizens differ on any public point they should not fight it out, but count heads and leave the decision to the majority. The snag in this is that as the majority is always against any change, and it takes at least thirty years to convert it, whilst only ten per cent or thereabouts of the population has sufficient mental capacity to foresee its necessity or desirability, a time lag is created during which the majority is always out-of-date. It would be more sensible to leave the decision to the minority if a qualified one could be selected and empanelled. Democratic government needs a Cabinet of Thinkers (Politbureau) as well as a Cabinet of Administrators (Commissars). Adult Suffrage can never supply this, especially in England, where intellect is hated and dreaded, not wholly without reason, as it is dangerous unless disciplined and politically educated; whilst acting and oratory, professional and amateur, are popular, and are the keys to success in elections.

## THE MARXIST CLASS WAR

The conflict of economic interest between proprietors and proletarians was described by H. G. Wells as past and obsolete[40] when it had in fact just flamed up in Spain from a bandying of strikes and lockouts into raging sanguinary civil war, as it had already done in Russia, with the difference that in Russia the proletarians won, wheras in Spain they were utterly defeated through lack of competent ministers and commanders.

The struggle is confused by a cross conflict between feudal and plutocratic ideologies. The feudal proprietariat is all for well policed private property and *Laisser-faire*, the proletariat all for State industry with abolition of feudal privilege and replacement of private or "real" property by property on social conditions; so that a proprietor shall hold his land, his shares, his spare money

40. In *Experiment in Autobiography* Wells wrote: 'But it has been the refrain of my lifetime that Marx antagonized property and the expropriated too crudely, and that he confused mere limitation and unhappiness with the rarer and more precious motive of creative discontent ... Most men are ready to sympathize with the under-dog but few will allow they are themselves under-dogs. Nor did Marx realize how acutely people who have wealth and position can be bored and distressed by the existing state of affairs' (New York, 1934, pp. 625–6).

(called capital) on the same terms as his umbrella: namely that he shall not use it to break his neighbor's head nor evict him from his country and homestead to make room for sheep or deer.

Both parties insist on the supreme necessity for increased production; but as the Plutocrats do all they can to sabotage State industry, and the Proletarians to sabotage private enterprize, the effect is to hinder production to the utmost and demonstrate the vanity of two-party government.

## What Is To Be Done?

I am asked every week what is my immediate practical remedy for all this. Also what is my solution of the riddle of the universe? When I reply that I dont know, and have no panacea, I am told that I am not constructive, implying that practical people are constructive and do know. If they are and do, why are we in our present perilous muddle?

I can only suggest certain definite and practicable experiments in social organization, on a provisional hypothesis or frame of reference (a necessary tool of thought) that will serve also as a credible religion. For nomenclatory purpose I may be called a Fabian Communist and Creative Evolutionist if I must have a label of some sort. At present I am stuck all over with labels like a tourist's trunk. I cannot call myself the Way and the Life, having only a questionable hypothesis or two to offer; but that is the heroic label that all Worldbetterers aspire to, and some have even dared to claim.

Some 30 years or so ago I wrote a play called As Far As Thought Can Reach [Part V of *Back to Methuselah*]. Perhaps I should have called it as far as my thought could reach; but I left this to be taken for granted.

## Political Mathematics

What we need desperately is an anthropometric sliderule by which we can classify and select our rulers, most of whom are at present either rich nonentities, venal careerists, or round pegs in square holes. Now it is no use my singing at the top of my voice that democracy is impossible without scientific anthropometry. I might as well be the Town Crier offering a reward for an imaginary lost dog. How are we to begin?

Sixty years ago Sidney Webb created a Progressive Party on the new County Councils by sending to all the candidates at the first election a catechism setting forth a program of Socialist reforms, and demanding whether they were in favor of them or not.[41] As Nature abhors a vacuum the program flew into empty heads and won the election for them. This, as far as I know, was the first non-party test ever applied to membership of a public authority in England since benefit of clergy was legal, and the professions were closed to all but members of the Church of England. This at least provided some evidence as to whether the candidate could read, write, and even translate a little dog Latin. It was better than no test at all.

But it is now quite insufficient in view of the enormous increase of public functions involved by modern Socialism. We already have in our professional and university examinations virtual panels of persons tested and registered as qualified to exercise ruling functions as Astronomers Royal, Archbishops, Lord Chief Justices, and public schoolmasters. Even police constables are instructed. Yet for the ministers who are supported to direct and control them we have no guarantee that they can read or write, or could manage a baked potato stall successfully.

Now people who cannot manage baked potato stalls nor peddle bootlaces successfully cannot manage public departments manned with school-tested permanent executives. Consequently these executives constitute a bureaucracy, not a democracy. Elections do not touch them: the people have no choice. When they have passed the competitive examinations by which they are tested, they are there for life, practically irremovable. And so government goes on.

Unfortunately the tests tend to exclude born rulers. Knowledge of languages, dead and foreign, puts a Mezzofanti [half-savage], useless as a legislator or administrator, above a Solon who knows no language but his own. It puts facility in doing set sums in algebra by rule of thumb above inborn mathematical comprehension by statesmen who cannot add up their washing bills accurately. Examinations by elderly men of youths are at least thirty years

---

41. Shaw confused the first council election (1889) with the second (1892). The theorist who 'created' the Progressive Party was J. F. B. Firth, head of the London Municipal Reform League. It was he who most strongly influenced the first election of the newly founded London County Council, in which no Fabian gained a seat. Following his death in 1889 the Fabians successfully employed their 'permeation' strategy to gain a foothold among the Progressives, masterminded by Webb, who drafted (1891) the Fabian tract *The London Programme* and several 'Questions' leaflets to be addressed to candidates for the LCC, town councils, Parliament and school boards. In the 1892 election six Fabians, including Webb, attained seats as Progressives, and in 1901 gained control of municipal government by a sweeping victory over the Moderates.

out of date: in economics, for instance, the candidate who has been taught that the latest views are those of Bastiat and Cobden, ignoring those of Cairnes and Mill, is successful, especially if he ranks those of Karl Marx as blasphemous, and history as ending with Macaulay. The questions that will be asked and the problems set at the examinations, with the answers and solutions that will be accepted by the elderly examiners, soon become known, enabling professional crammers to coach any sixth form schoolboy to pass in them to the exclusion of up-to-date candidates who are ploughed because they know better than their examiners, yet are as unconscious of their mental superiority as a baby is of the chemistry by which it performs the complicated chemical operation of digesting its food.

Evidently the present curriculum and method should be radically changed. When I say this, the reply is "Granted; but how?" Unfortunately I dont know; and neither does anyone else; but as somebody must make a beginning here are a few of the best suggestions I can think of.

### RENT AND VALUE THE ASS'S BRIDGES

First, there is the economic Ass's Bridge:[42] the theory of rent, and with it inextricably the theory of exchange value. Unless a postulant for first class honors in politics can write an essay shewing that he (or she) has completely mastered these impartial physical and mathematical theories, the top panel must be closed against him. This would plough Adam Smith, Ricardo, Ruskin, and Marx; but they could read up the subject and return to the charge. [William] Stanley Jevons would pass it, though after he had knocked out Ricardo and the rest with his correct mathematical theory he taught that a State parcel post is an impossibility.[43] For when he returned to England after

---

42. Novices in the study of Euclidean geometry often stumbled in their effort to master the fifth proposition (the isosceles triangle) of the first book of his *Elements*. The theorem thus became known as the *pons asinorum* (ass's bridge), separating dunces from scholars.

43. If Jevons did teach this, he altered his view in his later years, as attested by his *Political Economy* (one of Macmillan's Science Primers, 1878), in which he opined: 'Great economy would rise . . . if an establishment like the post-office were created in Great Britain in order to convey small goods and parcels. If a government postal system undertook the work [of independent carters in the large towns], there would be an almost incredible saving in the distance travelled and the time taken up. This illustrates the economy which may arise from government management.'

serving in the Gold Escort in Australia, and became a university professor,[44] he taught anything and everything the old examiners expected him to teach, and so might have failed in a character test.

## STATISTICS VITAL

The panel for health authorities should require a stringent test in statistics. At present the most unbearable tyranny is that of the State doctor who has been taught to prescribe digitalis and immobilization, plus a diet of alcoholic stimulants, for heart disease, and to amputate limbs and extirpate tonsils as carpenters and plumbers deal with faulty chair legs and leaking pipes. He may, like Jenner, be so ignorant of the rudiments of statistics as to believe that the coincidence of a decrease in the number of deaths from a specific disease following the introduction of an alleged prophylactic proves that the prophylactic is infallible and that compulsion to use it will abolish the disease. Statisticians, checking the figures by the comparisons they call controls, may prove up to the hilt that the prophylactic not only fails to cure but kills. When vaccination was made compulsory as a preventive of smallpox the controls were cholera, typhus, and endemic fever: all three rampant when I was born. They were wiped out by sanitation; whilst under compulsory vaccination, enforced by ruthless persecution, smallpox persisted and culminated in two appalling epidemics (1871 and 1881) which gave vaccination its deathblow, though its ghost still walks because doctors are ignorant of statistics, and, I must add, because it is lucrative, as it calls in the doctor when the patient is not ill. In the army some thirty inoculations are practically compulsory; and vaccination is made a condition of admission to the United States and other similarly deluded countries. The personal outrage involved is so intolerable that it will not be in the least surprising if vaccination officers are resisted, not with facts and figures but with fists, if not pistols.

The remedy, however, is not to compel medical students to qualify as statisticians, but to establish a Ministry of Statistics with formidable powers of dealing with lying advertisements of panaceas, prophylactics, elixirs, immunizers, vaccines, antitoxins, vitamins, and professedly hygienic foods and drugs and drinks of all sorts. Such a public department should be manned not by

---

44. In 1854, at nineteen, Jevons was appointed assayer to the new mint in Sydney, Australia, a position he held for five years. In 1866 he was appointed Professor of Logic, Political Economy and Philosophy at Owens College, University of Manchester, and in 1876 Professor of Political Economy at University College, London.

chemists analyzing the advertized wares and determining their therapeutical value, but by mathematicians criticizing their statistical pretensions. As there is an enormous trade in such wares at present the opposition to such a Ministry will be lavishly financed; but the need for it is too urgent to allow any consideration to stand in its way; for the popular demand for miracles and deities has been transferred to "marvels of science" and doctors, by dupes who think they are emancipating themselves from what in their abysmal ignorance they call medieval barbarism when they are in fact exalting every laboratory vivisector and quack immunizer above Jesus and St James. Mrs Eddy, a much sounder hygienist than Jenner, Pasteur, Lister, and their disciples, had to call her doctrine Christian Science instead of calling the popular faith in pseudo-scientific quackery Anti-Christian Nonsense.

## THE ESTHETIC TEST

The next test I propose may prove more surprising. For the top panel I would have postulants taken into a gallery of unlabeled reproductions of the famous pictures of the world, and asked how many of the painters they can name at sight, and whether they have anything to say about them, or are in any way interested in them. They should then be taken into a music room furnished with a piano, and asked to sing or whistle or hum or play as many of the leading themes of the symphonies, concertos, string quartets, and opera tunes of Mozart and Beethoven, and the *Leitmotifs* of Wagner, as they can remember. Their performances may be execrable; but that will not matter: the object is not to test their executive skill but to ascertain their knowledge of the best music and their interest in and enjoyment of it, if any.

I would have them taken then into a library stocked with the masterpieces of literature. They should be asked which of them they had ever read, and whether they read anything but newspapers and detective stories. If the answer be Yes, they can be invited to indicate the books they know.

I am quite aware of the possibility of misleading results. Dr Inge, an unquestionably top notcher, when he was Dean of St Paul's and had to deal with the music there, expressed a doubt whether the Almighty really enjoys "this perpetual serenading."[45] William Morris, equally *honoris causa* [worthy

45. We can find no instance of Inge speaking specifically of 'perpetual serenading' (which may be Shaw's phrase, not Inge's), but his attitude towards church music is discernible in the remark: '[T]he true mystic cares little about symbolism, and often dislikes it. His inner world is so rich in forms, sounds, and colours that he objects

of honour], could not tolerate a piano in his house. When one was played in his hearing by his neighbors, he would throw up his window and roar curses at them.

But if Dr Inge had been brought up on Beethoven instead of on [William] Jackson's Te Deum [see vol. 2, p. 77 fn 36], he might have preferred Wagner to Plotinus; and Morris was deeply affected by medieval music, and quite right in loathing the modern steel grand piano of his day as a noisy nuisance. Still, some of the postulants will be tone deaf or color blind. Their comments may be none the less valuable as evidence of their mental capacity.

## SUBCONSCIOUS CAPACITIES

More baffling at present are the cases in which the judges will be faced with apparently vacant minds, and met, not with an epigram of which no mediocrity would be capable, but with a blank "I dont know what you are talking about." This will not prove that the postulant is a nitwit: it will raise the question whether the question is beyond his mental powers or so far within them that he is unconscious of them. Ask anyone how water tastes, and you will get the reply of Pinero's Baron Croodle [in *The Money Spinner*, 1880] "Water is a doglike and revolting beverage" or simply "Water has no taste," or, intelligently, "Water has no taste for me, because it is always in my mouth." Ask an idle child what it is doing, and it will not claim that it is breathing and circulating its blood: it will say it is doing nothing. When we coordinate our two eyes to look at anything we do not notice that the images of everything else within our range of vision are doubled. When we listen to an orchestra or an organ we are deaf to the accompanying thunder of beats, partials, and harmonics. Attention is a condition of consciousness. Without it we may miss many "self-evident truths."[46] How then are we to distinguish between the unconscious genius and the idiot?

Again, I do not know; but we can at least call in the professional psycho-therapists whose business it is to dig up the buried factors of the mind and bring them to light and consciousness. The technique of this therapy has

---

to having poor imitations of the sublime thrust upon his senses while he is communing with the Eternal. While the music of the spheres is ringing in his ears he would rather not hear an organ' ('Day-Dreaming', *More Lay Thoughts of a Dean*, 1931).
46. The phrasing echoes the American Declaration of Independence (4 July 1776): 'We hold these truths to be self-evident . . .'

developed since the days when, being asked what the word Ass suggested to me, I replied Dogberry and Balaam. It suggested, not facts and experiences, but fictions. Put the word calculus to a surgeon and he will name the disease called stone, from which Newton suffered. Put it to a mathematician and he will cite the method of measurement Newton and Leibniz elaborated.

## EXAMINATIONS AND SCHOOLMASTERS

I avoid calling the tests examinations because the word suggests the schoolmaster, the enemy of mankind at present, though when by the rarest chance he happens to be a born teacher, he is a priceless social treasure. I have met only one who accepted my challenge to say to his pupils "If I bore you you may go out and play" [see vol. 2, p. 22]. Set an average schoolmaster or schoolmarm to test for the panels, and the result will be a set of examination papers with such questions and problems as "Define the square root of minus one in [Giuseppe] Peano[47] terms; and if an empty aeroplane traveling at supersonic speed takes a thousand light years to reach the nearest star, how long will it take a London motor bus keeping schedule time to travel from Millbank to Westminster Bridge with a full complement of passengers? Give the name, date, and locality of the birth of Beethoven's greatgrandmother's cousin's stepsister; and write a tonal fugue on the following theme. Give the family names of Domenichino and Titian; and write an essay not exceeding 32 words on their respective styles and influence on Renaissance art. Give the dates of six of Shakespear's plays, with the acreage occupied by (*a*) the Globe Theatre, (*b*) the Shoreditch Curtain theatre, and (*c*) the Blackfriars theatre. Estimate the age of Anne Hathaway at her marriage with Shakespear. Enumerate the discrepancies between the narratives of Homer, Plutarch, Holinshed, and Shakespear. Was Bacon the author of Shakespear's plays (5000 words)?"

## THE WRONG SORT OF MEMORY

And so on. The schoolmaster does not teach. He canes or impositions or "keeps in" the pupils who cannot answer pointless questions devized to catch them out. Such questions test memory, but secure victory in examinations

47. Italian mathematician, noted particularly for his work in vector algebra, formal logic and geometric calculus. His work in symbolic logic is paralleled by his invention (1903) of a proposed international language, Interlingua.

for the indiscriminate encyclopedic memory, which is the most disabling of all memories. Universities are infested with pedants who have all recorded history at their tongues' ends, but can make no use of it except to disqualify examinees with the priceless gift of forgetting all events that do not matter. Were I to keep always in mind every experience of my 93 years living and reading I should go mad. I am often amazed when, having to refer to old papers filed away and forgotten, I am reminded of transactions which I could have sworn had never occurred, and meetings with notable persons I have no recollection of having ever seen. But this does not disconcert me. Kipling's "Lest we forget" ['Recessional', 1897] is often less urgent than "Lest we remember."

Certainly, those who forget everything are impossible politically; and I have often wished I had the memory of Macaulay or Sidney Webb, or the patience of my player collaborators who have to memorize speeches I have myself written but of which at rehearsal I cannot quote two words correctly; but on the whole the people who remember everything they ought to forget are, if given any authority, more dangerous than those who forget some things they had better remember. Dr Inge, commenting on the Irish question, pointed out how difficult is the common government of a nation which never remembers and one which never forgets.

Anyhow, we must keep schoolmasters away from the panel tests. My own school experience has biased me on this point. When the time came to teach me mathematics I was taught simply nothing: I was set to explain Euclid's diagrams and theorems without a word as to their use or history or nature. I found it so easy to pick this up in class that at the end of the half year I was expected to come out well in the examinations. I entirely disgraced myself because the questions did not pose the propositions but gave only their numbers, of which I could recollect only the first five and the one about the square of the hypothenuse.

The next step was algebra, again without a word of definition or explanation. I was simply expected to do the sums in Colenso's schoolbook.[48]

Now an uninstructed child does not dissociate numbers or their symbols from the material objects it knows quite well how to count. To me $a$ and $b$, when they meant numbers, were senseless unless they meant butter and eggs and a pound of cheese. I had enough mathematical faculty to infer that if $a = b$ and $b = c$, $a$ must equal $c$. But I had wit enough to infer that if a quart

48. As a Fellow of St John's College, Cambridge, John W. Colenso taught and wrote mathematical books on algebra (1841) and arithmetic (1843).

of brandy equals three Bibles, and three Bibles the Apostles' Creed, the Creed is worth a quart of brandy, manifestly a *reductio ad absurdum*.

My schoolmaster was only the common enemy of me and my schoolfellows. In his presence I was forbidden to move, or to speak except in answer to his questions. Only by stealth could I relieve the torture of immobility by stealthily exchanging punches (called "the coward's blow"[49]) with the boy next me. Had my so-called teacher been my father, and I a child under six, I could have asked him questions, and had the matter explained to me. As it was, I did exactly what the Vatican felt everybody would do if Galileo picked a hole in the Bible. I concluded that mathematics are blazing nonsense, and thereafter made a fool of myself even in my twenties when I made the acquaintance of the editor of Biometrika, Karl Pearson, who maintained that no theory could be valid until it was proved mathematically. I threw in his teeth my conviction that his speciality was an absurdity. Instead of enlightening me he laughed (he had an engaging smile and was a most attractive man) and left me encouraged in my ignorance by my observation that though he was scrupulous and sceptical when counting and correlating, he was as credulous and careless as any ordinary mortal in selecting the facts to be counted. Not until Graham Wallas, a born teacher, enlightened me, did I understand mathematics and realize their enormous importance.[50]

## SOME RESULTS

Is it to be wondered at that with such school methods masquerading as education, millions of scholars pass to their graves unhonored and unsung whilst men and women totally illiterate or at most selftaught to read and write in their late teens, rise to eminence whilst "university engineers" are drugs in the labor market compared to those who go straight from their elementary schools to the factory, speaking slum English and signing with a mark. Experienced employers tell us they prefer uneducated workmen. Senior

49. 'A blow given to provoke a boy to fight or be branded a coward' (*English Dialect Dictionary*, 1981).
50. On 22 August 1887 Shaw had an impulse to purchase a second-hand copy of Lewis Hensley's *The Scholar's Algebra* (1880), and for a year or so worked sporadically at mastering the subject. During this period he and Wallas were almost inseparable: attending lectures, sharing meals, walking country miles, swimming at the baths, and, presumably, discussing algebra. The volume is now at Cornell.

Wranglers and Double-Firsts and Ireland Scholars[51] see no more than costermongers in the fact that a saving of 1 per cent per minute of time in writing
English means 525,000 per cent per year, and that ten times that much could
be saved by adding 15 letters to the alphabet. It took a world war to establish
summer time after it had been contemptuously rejected by our pundits as a
negligible fad. The fact that by adding two digits to our arithmetic tables we
could make 16 figures do the work of twenty (a colossal saving of time for
the world's bookkeeping) appeals no more to winners of the mathematical
tripos than the infinitesimal calculus to a newly born infant. Political controversy is now (1949) raging on the nationalization of our industries;[52] yet not
one word is said nor a figure given as to its basic advantage in the fact that
coal can be had in Sunderland [Tyne & Wear, north-east England] for the
trouble of picking it up from the sands at low tide, whilst in Whitehaven
[Cumbria, north-west England] it has to be hewn out under the sea, miles
from the pit head, or that land in the City of London fetches fabulous prices
per square foot and twenty miles off will hardly support a goose on the
common, thus making it impossible without nationalization to substitute
cost-of-production prices, averaged over the whole country, for prices loaded
with enormous rents for the proprietors of London land and Seaham mines
[County Durham], not equivalently surtaxed. Doctors and dental surgeons[53]
who excuse their high fees on the ground that they are working until half
past four in the afternoon earning rent for their landlords, and only the rest
of the day for themselves and their families, are so incapable of putting two
and two together politically that they vote like sheep for the landlords, and
denounce land municipalization as robbery. Had the late famous President
Franklin Roosevelt, a thoroughly schooled gentleman-amateur Socialist, been
taught the law of rent, his first attempts at the New Deal would not have
failed so often. I could cite dozens of examples of how what our Cabinet
ministers call Democracy, and what I call Mobocracy, places in authority
would-be rulers who assure us that they can govern England, plus the

51. The Ireland classical scholarship at Oxford bears the name of John Ireland, Dean
of Westminster.
52. There was much dissension between the Conservatives and Labour in the late
1940s as the post-war Labour Government (in its first term of office, 1945–50)
nationalized the coal mines, iron and steel industries, gas and electricity, inland
transport, civil aviation and the Bank of England.
53. Medicine was not fully nationalized until the National Health Acts of 1951 and
1952.

Commonwealth, plus Western Europe, and finally the world, when as a matter of fact they could not manage a village shop successfully.

## CAPITAL ACCUMULATION

Capital is spare money saved by postponement of consumption. To effect this in a private property system some people must be made so rich that when they are satiated with every purchasable luxury they have still a surplus which they can invest without privation. In the XIX century this arrangement was accepted as final and inevitable by able and benevolent public men like Thomas de Quincey, Macaulay, [John] Austin, Cobden, and [John] Bright,[54] until Karl Marx dealt it a mortal blow by shewing from official records that its delusive prosperity masked an abyss of plague, pestilence and famine, battle, murder, compulsory prostitution, and premature death. Ferdinand Lassalle in Germany had already demonstrated the injustice of its "iron law of wages."[55]

## ENGLAND'S SHAMEFACED LEADERSHIP

England was by no means silent on the subject. Marx's invective, though it rivaled Jeremiah's, was pale beside the fierce diatribes of Ruskin, who puzzled his readers by describing himself [in *Fors Clavigera*] as an old Tory and the Reddest of Red Communists.[56] Carlyle called our boasted commercial prosperity shooting Niagara, and dismissed Cobdenist Free Trade as God-

54. De Quincey was author of *The Logic of Political Economy* (1844). Austin, an English jurist and educator, wrote *The Province of Jurisprudence Determined* (1832), in which he advocated a variation of Bentham's theory of utilitarianism. Bright, a liberal statesman, was a free-trader who fought for fiscal and electoral reform and for religious tolerance.

55. A now discarded theory (borrowed from David Ricardo but popularized in Lassalle's phrasing) that wages tend towards subsistence level despite any efforts to improve the real income of workers. It was pronounced in Lassalle's *The Open Answer*, an open letter dated 1 March 1863, arising from his trial and conviction a month earlier for 'inciting to hatred and contempt' of the Government by publication of his lecture 'The Workers' Programme' (1861). The letter is considered to be the first charter of German Social Democracy.

56. This 'puzzling' dichotomy was alluded to by Shaw also in his 1921 lecture *Ruskin's Politics* (reprinted in *Platform and Pulpit*, 1962).

forsaken nonsense.[57] The pious Conservative Lord Shaftesbury and the Radical atheist demagogue Bradlaugh were at one in their agitation for Acts in restraint of the prevalent ruthless exploitation of labor. Robert Owen had called for a New Moral world as loudly as any of our present postwar Chadbands.[58] It was he who made current the word Socialism as the alternative to Capitalist plutocracy. When the Russian Bolsheviks went ruinously wrong by ignoring "the inevitability of gradualness"[59] and attempting a catastrophic transfer of industry and agriculture from private to public ownership, it was the Englishman Sidney Webb and his Fabians who corrected them and devized the new economic policy Lenin had to announce, and Stalin to put in practice.[60] Thus

57. 'Shooting Niagara: and After?' (Carlyle's last published utterance on British politics, in *Macmillan's Magazine*, August 1867, and, amended, as a pamphlet in the same year) was his polemical response to the introduction by the Conservatives of the Second Reform Bill of that year. Angrily he aspersed 'traitorous politicians, grasping at votes, even votes from the rabble', and predicted the dilution and decay of religious and moral restraint, ending in the new religion of 'Free Trade, in all senses, and to all lengths: unlimited Free Trade – which some take to mean, "Free racing, ere long with unlimited speed, in the career of *Cheap and Nasty*" . . .' As Disraeli's Government prepared to shoot the Niagara rapids, the contemptuous Carlyle saw no hope left for 'poor Old England': it was the beginning of her political downfall, in 'ignominious Farce'.
58. Fat and hypocritical minister much given to platitudes, in *Bleak House*.
59. A phrase coined by Sidney Webb to describe the evolutionary (rather than revolutionary) principle of the Fabian Society in its drive towards a socialist society.
60. In the New Economic Policy (1921) Lenin sought to stimulate the Soviet economy by introducing a degree of private enterprise, enabling him to come to terms with capitalist governments. Though Shaw, an avowed communist in late years, exulted in 1948 in the image of Russian Communism saved by Webb and the Fabians, the picture he created here is a distorted and inaccurate one, far removed from his 1921 attitude and position. That individual Fabians were directly involved in the creation of the NEP is almost certain, but not Webb and not the Fabian Society. In 1912 a completely autonomous Fabian Research Department was created by Beatrice Webb, with Shaw elected chairman and G. D. H. Cole, a bright young Fabian economist, vice-chairman. In ensuing years the Webbs, who had declined to accept office as elected members of the Executive, gave little more than moral support to the Department, and when it metamorphosed in 1918 into the Labour Research Department, in tandem with the Labour Party, they became even less involved.

When the Russians established the NEP the Webbs expressed disapproval, Beatrice in her diary on 7 December 1921 seeing the policy as a blow to 'international socialism'. Shaw was equally disturbed, especially when Webb broke the news that young communist members of the LRD Executive, led by Cole, were talking of negotiations with Leonid Krassin, head of the Russian trade delegation in London,

Englishmen can claim to have been pioneers in the revolutionary development of political organization since Cobdenism conquered us.

Unfortunately, whenever English parties effect an advance, they are so ashamed of it that they immediately throw away all credit for it by protesting that they are respectable citizens who would never dream of changing anything, and shouting their abhorrence of all the wicked foreigners who are in effect taking their advice. And then they are surprised when their disciples, especially in Russia, regard them as enemies, and the Marxist Left wins more and more votes from them.

## THE THREATENING FUTURE: HOMILIES NO USE

While the time lag lasts the future remains threatening. The problem of optimum wealth distribution, which Plutocracy, with its inherent class warfare, has hopelessly failed to solve, will not yield to the well-intentioned Utopian amateurs who infest our parliaments and parties, imagining that it

---

to obtain a subvention of £6000 in return for information and assistance. Though Krassin balked at the arrangement, it is likely smaller sums were paid to members of the Department for personal services rendered. Shaw on 16 October 1921 informed Webb he had burst in on a General Purposes Committee meeting and made 'short work' of it, warning that 'every public man of us would have to resign if as much as a five pound note changed hands between us and Moscow'. If the Department, he threatened, 'give information to *any* foreign government' he would resign (TLS: London School of Economics, Webb Papers). On 21 October he attended an Executive Meeting, at which he offered the Department a resolution: 'That in view of the constitution of the L.R.D. and of the diplomatic and legal questions raised by any sort of traffic in information with Foreign States, it be a standing instruction to the staff . . . not to supply information to, accept Research Commissions or subscriptions or donations from, or enter into committal official relations of any kind with Foreign States, allied, hostile or neutral.' The resolution, Shaw reported to Webb later that night, was defeated, following which 'they resolved to instruct the Finance Committee to arrange the job as with the Russian co-operators (trade delegation), not with the Government. My resignation goes in by this post' (TLS: LSE, Webb Papers).

The Webbs, too, recognized that the situation required a 'final break' with the Department. 'To take your livelihood from the Russian government', Beatrice lamented on Christmas Eve 1921, 'when millions of Russians are starving, for services which are obviously unreal or, at any rate, irrelevant to famine, is rather a poor business. But it was not the thing itself which disgusted us: it was the surreptitious way in which it was done' (*Diaries 1921–1924*, 1952).

can be solved by giving all of us according to our needs and balancing the account by taking from each of us according to our productive capacity. They might as well decree that we shall do unto others as we would have them do to us, or achieve the greatest good for the greatest number, or soothe our souls with exhortations to love oneanother. Homilies cut no ice in administrative councils: the literary talent and pulpit eloquence that has always been calling for a better world has never succeeded, though it has stolen credit for many changes forced on it by circumstances and natural selection. The satirical humor of Aristophanes, the wisecracks of Confucius, the precepts of the Buddha, the parables of Jesus, the theses of Luther, the *jeux d'esprit* of Erasmus and Montaigne, the Utopias of More and Fourier and Wells, the allegories of Voltaire, Rousseau, and Bunyan, the polemics of Leibniz and Spinoza, the poems of Goethe, Shelley, and Byron, the manifesto of Marx and Engels, Mozart's Magic Flute and Beethoven's Ode to Joy, with the music dramas of Wagner, to say nothing of living seers of visions and dreamers of dreams: none of these esthetic feats have made Reformations or Revolutions; and most of them, as far as they have been thrown into the hands of the common people as the Protestant Reformation threw the Bible, have been followed by massacres, witch hunts, civil and international wars of religion, and all forms of persecution, from petty boycotts to legalized burnings at the stake and breakings on the wheel, highly popular as public entertainments. The XIX century, which believed itself to be the climax of civilization, of Liberty, Equality, and Fraternity, was convicted by Karl Marx of being the worst and wickedest on record; and the XX, not yet half through, has been ravaged by two so-called world wars culminating in the atrocity of the atomic bomb.

As long as atomic bomb manufacture remains a trade secret known to only one State, it will be the mainstay of Peace because all the States (including the one) will be afraid of it. When the secret is out atomic warfare will be barred as poison gas was in 1938–45; and war will be possible as before. How that may happen is the subject of the first two farfetched fables that follow.

Ayot St Lawrence.
1948–9.

# Shakes versus Shav

*First published in 1951*

This in all actuarial probability is my last play and the climax of my eminence, such as it is. I thought my career as a playwright was finished when Waldo Lanchester of the Malvern Marionette Theatre, our chief living puppet master, sent me figures of two puppets, Shakespear and myself, with a request that I should supply one of my famous dramas for them, not to last longer than ten minutes or thereabouts. I accomplished this feat, and was gratified by Mr Lanchester's immediate approval.[1]

I have learnt part of my craft as conductor of rehearsals (producer, they call it) from puppets. Their unvarying intensity of facial expression, impossible for living actors, keeps the imagination of the spectators continuously stimulated. When one of them is speaking or tumbling and the rest left aside, these, though in full view, are invisible, as they should be. Living actors have to learn that they too must be invisible while the protagonists are conversing, and therefore must not move a muscle nor change their expression, instead of, as beginners mostly do, playing to them and robbing them of the audience's undivided attention.

Puppets have also a fascination of their own, because there is nothing wonderful in a living actor moving and speaking, but that wooden headed dolls should do so is a marvel that never palls.

And they can survive treatment that would kill live actors. When I first saw them in my boyhood nothing delighted me more than when all the puppets went up in a balloon and presently dropped from the skies with an appalling crash on the floor.

Nowadays the development of stagecraft into filmcraft may destroy the idiosyncratic puppet charm. Televised puppets could enjoy the scenic backgrounds of the cinema. Sound recording could enable the puppet master to give all his attention to the strings he is manipulating, the dialogue being spoken by a company of firstrate speakers as in the theatre. The old puppet master spoke all the parts himself in accents which he differentiated by Punch-

1. The Lanchester Marionette Theatre was for many years an adjunct of the Malvern Festival. For Shaw's views on puppets see also p. 114 and *Collected Letters 1911–1925* (1985), pp. 182–4, for a 1913 letter to the itinerant puppeteer Clunn Lewis.

and-Judy squeaks and the like. I can imagine the puppets simulating living performers so perfectly that the spectators will be completely illuded. The result would be the death of puppetry; for it would lose its charm with its magic. So let reformers beware.

Nothing can extinguish my interest in Shakespear. It began when I was a small boy, and extends to Stratford-upon-Avon, where I have attended so many bardic festivals that I have come to regard it almost as a supplementary birthplace of my own.

No year passes without the arrival of a batch of books contending that Shakespear was somebody else. The argument is always the same. Such early works as Venus and Adonis, Lucrece, and Love's Labour's Lost, could not possibly have been written by an illiterate clown and poacher who could hardly write his own name. This is unquestionably true. But the inference that Shakespear did not write them does not follow. What does follow is that Shakespear was not an illiterate clown but a well read grammar-schooled son in a family of good middle-class standing, cultured enough to be habitual playgoers and private entertainers of the players.

This, on investigation, proves to be exactly what Shakespear was. His father, John Shakespear, Gent, was an alderman who demanded a coat of arms which was finally granted. His mother was of equal rank and social pretension. John finally failed commercially, having no doubt let his artistic turn get the better of his mercantile occupation, and leave him unable to afford a university education for William, had he ever wanted to make a professional scholar of him.

These circumstances interest me because they are just like my own. They were a considerable cut above those of Bunyan and Cobbett, both great masters of language, who nevertheless could not have written Venus and Adonis nor Love's Labour's Lost. One does not forget Bunyan's "The Latin I borrow."[2] Shakespear's standing was nearer to Ruskin's, whose splendid style owes much more to his mother's insistence on his learning the Bible by heart than to his Oxford degree.

So much for Bacon-Shakespear and all the other fables founded on that entirely fictitious figure Shaxper or Shagsper the illiterate bumpkin.

Enough too for my feeling that the real Shakespear might have been myself, and for the shallow mistaking of it for mere professional jealousy.

AYOT ST LAWRENCE.
1949.

2. This was Bunyan's admission in *Pilgrim's Progress* that his formal education was minimal.

# Salt and His Circle

*Preface to a biography of Henry S. Salt[1] by Stephen Winsten, 1951*

━━━

I was always happy at the Salts. We never talked politics but gossiped endlessly about our friends and everything else. The bond between us was that we were Shelleyans and Humanitarians. He was also a keen Meredithian; but I disliked upper ten[2] ladies and gentlemen so much (they bore me) that I could not read Meredith's novels (except the Tragic Comedians [1880] which was about Lassalle). We agreed about Herman Merivale's [error for Melville's][3] Moby Dick, another of his pets.

Kate (Mrs Salt) loved me as far as she could love any male creature. Once, towards her end, when I had been absent for years and turned up unexpectedly after they had moved to Carpenter's neighborhood in Yorkshire, she actually flung her arms round me. She was a queer hybrid. I never met anyone in the least like her, though another friend of mine, the Christian Socialist parson, Stewart Headlam,[4] also had a wife who was a homo.

He married again [Catherine Mandeville, 1927] after Kate's death and it was, as far as I know, a comfortable normal marriage. I have never met her.

As his last two books shew Salt liked Cambridge.[5] But he hated being

1. Classical scholar, teacher, writer, founder of the Humanitarian League, introduced to Shaw by James Leigh Joynes, Jr., brother of Salt's wife Kate.
2. Upper ten thousand, meaning the aristocracy; comparable to New York's elitist 'four hundred'.
3. One of a number of names and places that Shaw invariably muddled, as in his confusion of Twain's Tom Sawyer with Dickens's medical student Bob Sawyer in *Pickwick Papers*, and in his frequent misrecollection of Edward Carpenter's residence as in Yorkshire (see below) rather than in Derbyshire. Herman Merivale was co-author of an oft revived drama *Forget-Me-Not* (1879). Shaw's first stage performance (Socialist League, 30 January 1885) was in a comedy-drama *Alone* by Merivale and Palgrave Simpson.
4. Open-minded founder of the Guild of St Matthew, who raised the bail money for Oscar Wilde in 1895.
5. Error for Eton College, which Salt attended on a scholarship, and to which he returned as an assistant master (later housemaster) after graduating from King's College, Cambridge, in 1875. Among his last works were *Memories of Bygone Eton* (1928) and *Company I Have Kept* (1930); his last book was *The Creed of Kinship* (1935).

Housemaster and kept saving enough to buy a pension of £800 a year which
was then considered a minimum on which a Housemaster could retire. When
he read a book in which Edward Carpenter advocated "the simple life,"[6] and
said that it could be lived on £160 a year, which was just what Salt had by
that time accumulated, he instantly shook the dust of Cambridge [Eton] off
his feet and took the Tilford cottage where I first met him. See my article
in the Pall Mall Gazette entitled "A Sunday on the Surrey Hills."[7]

Salt's tragedy was that his wife (born Kate Joynes, and half German) would
not consummate their marriage, calling herself an Urning.[8] She got it from
her close friend Edward Carpenter who taught Kate that Urnings are a chosen
race. Carpenter and I used to meet at Salt's cottage at Tilford. We all called
him "The Noble Savage," and wore the sandals he made. He and I played
piano duets with Kate, making a fearful noise with Wagner's Kaisermarch
and The Ring, and shared her friendship about equally. We were "Sunday
husbands" to her. Salt was quite in the friendship.

Though Kate would not sleep with Salt she was always falling in love with
some woman, among others with Mrs Francis Adams,[9] widow of an American
poet of some note who had committed suicide. She was a proletarian, and
an inveterate and fluent romancer. She claimed to have helped her husband
to kill himself, not knowing that if she had really done so she would have
been indicted for manslaughter, if not for murder. Kate swallowed her stories
greedily and adoringly. When I, on being introduced to her in Tilford, treated
her not as a heroine but as a vulgar liar and a rapscallion she did not deny
it. She laughed and took me as one of her own kidney. Kate was amazed,

6. Poet (*Towards Democracy*, 1883–1902) and socialist (*Civilisation: Its Cause and Cure*, 1889), a British Whitman-cum-Thoreau, who envisioned a primitivistic democratic society.
7. Shaw's essay was published on 25 April 1888; reprinted in *The Black Girl in Search of God and Some Lesser Tales*.
8. Urning, a term coined by K. H. Ulrichs, in *Numa Numantius* (1864), originally in reference to a male homosexual. J. A. Symonds, however, in *A Problem in Modern Ethics* (1881) defined it as 'either a male or a female in whom we observe a real and inborn, not an acquired or a spurious inversion of [sexual] appetite'.
9. Edith Goldstone Adams was second wife of an Australian poet and novelist, Francis W. L. Adams, who, tubercular and despondent, committed suicide in 1893. Shaw met the Adamses on 1 April 1893 at the rural home of the Salts, in Oxted, not Tilford. Her remarks about having 'assisted' her husband in destroying himself, if Shaw reported her accurately, would have been no more than normal guilt reactions, for a coroner's jury had cleared her of any complicity. Our thanks to Stanley Weintraub for this information.

536	The Complete Prefaces: Volume 3

staggered and disillusioned. Such escapades were bad for her, as what she really needed was children; and I told her to get a job in a factory to bring her to her senses. To my surprise she actually did so, and became an employee in my friend Emery Walker's engraving works.[10] But as she could not engrave she was set to work in the office. She soon left it and worked for me as unpaid typist secretary [1897–8] until my marriage. Finally she went back to Salt and lived with him until she faded out mentally and died. Unless you know this background to Salt you know nothing.

When they moved from Tilford to a lodging in Gloucester Road in London, their landlord was a Keeper at the Zoo. One evening he came home utterly exhausted. Salt asked why. The reply was "He had been beating the elephant." That's exactly what we had been doing.

Salt, like Samuel Butler, was at war implacably with his father because he considered that his mother had been ill-treated by him and he represented me as saying something unfeeling about my mother to Robert Buchanan.[11] He had mixed Buchanan up somehow with the scandal given by Cashel Byron's "I hate my mother" which so shocked Mrs R. L. Stevenson that she shut the book with a bang and flung it away. All heroes in 1882 had to love their mothers and in due degree the rest of their relatives. I broke that convention partly because I knew H. W. Massingham,[12] who hated his mother and was hated by her, but also because my father's relatives, though they quarreled between themselves, combined against my mother, who one day, calling on one of my aunts, overheard her exclaiming to the servant who announced her "Oh, that bitch!" After that we all boycotted oneanother; and I came to regard all paternal relatives as obnoxious persons, and to make a joke of it. My own memory is not too good; and though I see where he

10. Engraver and type-designer, associated with Morris in the Kelmscott Press and later with T. Cobden-Sanderson in the Doves Press.
11. Salt in a late memoir (inserted as an appendix in *Salt and His Circle*) misrecalled and muddied the incident. In a letter to Buchanan, after reading his poetic work *The Devil's Case*, Shaw had stated, 'If my mother dies before me, I am quite sure that I shall not be moved by it as much as I was moved by your poem on the death of your mother. The inevitable does not touch me . . . I really care deeply for nothing but *fine work*.' Buchanan published an extended extract in a pamphlet *Is Barabbas a Necessity?* (1896), without authorization, but also without identification of the 'distinguished man of letters' who penned it. Reprinted in *Collected Letters 1874–1897* (1965), pp. 584–5.
12. Assistant editor of the *Star* during Shaw's association with the paper; later editor of the *Daily Chronicle* and the *Nation*.

has mixed up quite different events I cannot always remember what actually happened.

I never met the Reverend Joynes (Swinburne's tutor at Eton) and neither Butler nor Olivier ever met Salt or knew anything about him.[13] It was J. L. Joynes, Junior, son of the Reverend, and brother-in-law to Salt, who introduced me to Salt. He also was an Eton master (not a Housemaster). He wore his red hair in long curls hanging round his neck and down his back and wrote some very good translations of the revolutionary poems of [Ferdinand] Freiligrath.[14] He went to Ireland, spoke for the Land League there and was arrested, but released apologetically on pleading his Eton credentials. His heart failed; and he was murdered by the doctors, in whom his father believed fanatically. They immobilized him and fed him on whiskey until he became a mere lump and died after writing some wretched verses in imitation of William Morris. This began my feud with the doctors, who are doing that still.

My visit to Swinburne [on 22 May 1890] at Putney was with Salt. It began with Salt and myself taking a walk over the common with Watts [-Dunton], who talked all the time about the great authors he had discovered and who were totally unknown to anyone else. The totally unknown were Meredith and Merivale, about whom Salt had written a lot. At the Putney villa we found Swinburne, whom Watts treated as a kindly tutor treats a promising small boy, making him shew us a worthless shilling chap-book that he had bought. I terrified Swinburne so utterly that I had to do all the talking; but Salt had some conversation with him afterwards of which I heard nothing. He was a pitiable old creature with eyes like shirt buttons.

As to Meredith, whom Salt admired, and who was a famous talker who never let anyone else get in a word edge-wise, it was proposed by Salt and (I think) Clement Shorter[15] that I should visit him and talk him off the stage. I had just spoken for four hours to a crowd in Salford [Lancashire]. This plot

---

13. Shaw's dimming memory failed him in all three instances. Stephen Winsten in *Salt and His Circle* related an anecdote recorded somewhere by Salt that indicated he and Shaw had visited the senior Joynes. Samuel Butler and the Sydney Oliviers were close acquaintances of Salt; Butler had been introduced to Salt by Shaw over luncheon at Adelphi Terrace on 24 January 1902.

14. Joynes's *Songs of a Revolutionary Epoch*, reviewed by Shaw in the *Star*, 3 April 1888, and in the *Pall Mall Gazette*, 16 April 1888 (both unsigned), was a translated collection of German political poems and patriotic songs, principally by Freiligrath and Georg Herwegh, nationalists of the '48 period.

15. Editor and journalist, one of Shaw's colleagues on the *Star* (1888).

did not come off; but years later when I last visited Meredith at Box Hill [Surrey] he was shoved into a corner by his family, who wanted to hear *me* all the time. He was deaf and disabled by locomotor ataxy; but I had half an hour of private talk with him in his study before lunch. He had supported the reactionary candidate at a recent election, imagining that he represented the principles of the French Revolution, and Meredith was apologetic when I explained to him that my Fabianism was the latest thing. He was a relic of the Cosmopolitan Republican Gentleman of the previous generation, and must have contracted V. D. in his youth: hence the locomotor.

But he was still brightly blue eyed.

The man who was supreme in the Salt household was Edward Carpenter, "The Noble Savage."

Salt was a born Naturalist and never went out of doors without a binocular to watch the birds. His pet authors were [W. H.] Hudson and [Richard] Jefferies;[16] and it was with them that Wordsworth falls in, just as Ruskin's Praeterita would have done if he had ever read it. He never to my knowledge thought of Francis Adams as a great poet nor did he think anything of Tennyson, whose first enormous popularity was followed by a strong reaction in favor of Browning, and a disgust at his political renague.[17] Salt felt about him as Browning did about Wordsworth when he wrote "Just for a handful of silver he left us" [from 'The Lost Leader', 1845]. But we must stop trying to treat Salt as a mere precipitate of the literary celebrities of his time.

I remember basking in the heath outside his cottage and writing The Philanderer when I was staying with them. And it was Salt who, hearing me read Candida, exclaimed after the third act "Why, the man is a poet" meaning *me*. I did not use Salt for a model for any of my characters.

I do not think that Salt would have disagreed with Tolstoy's true statement that the urge of the artist is to communicate his views to the others and propagate them.[18] That was what Morris was always trying to do and what Ruskin's failure to accomplish drove him out of his wits. Like Morris and Ruskin, Salt was a Humanitarian. The only author he celebrated and translated

16. Naturalists and authors. The first specialized in ornithology, and is known for his popular romance *Green Mansions* (1904). The second concentrated on Wiltshire country folk and their habits.
17. A dialectic noun form of the verb 'renegue' or 'renege', an archaism favoured by Shaw, meaning renunciation or withdrawal.
18. In *What is Art?* (1898) Tolstoy observed: 'Art is an activity by means of which one man, having experienced a feeling, intentionally transmits it to others.'

was Virgil, whom, like Ruskin,[19] I could not read through, though I paid for the printing and publication of the translation[20] on the understanding that I was to have half the profits until I was paid off. There were never any profits. I knew there would not be with Dryden and Morris in the field.

When Salt and Carpenter contemplated setting up land colonies, I explained that the socialist colonies in America failed except when they were monastically celibate. The Oneida Creek Community was founded in 1847 by John Humphrey Noyes, the Perfectionist, who dissolved it when he was past his work. The sexual arrangements were quite abnormal and gave as great scandal in the U.S.A. as the Mormons did. The young men slept with the old women who were past child-bearing. Noyes's son, though bred carefully to succeed his father, became a hard-bitten manufacturer of steel traps to catch oppossums: a cruel trade. Any colony however is better than the damned Bohemian anarchism which never succeeds anywhere. Salt went with me to the John Burns and [R. B.] Cunninghame Graham demonstration in Trafalgar Square on Bloody Sunday.[21] All the Labor Forces marched to hold a meeting there and were broken up in every avenue to it by squads of police, and a detachment of cavalry kept riding round it with a magistrate in front to read the Riot Act. Carpenter was clubbed, as in his fury he wrote, "by that crawling thing a policeman." Salt had his watch pickpocketed but he could not appeal to the police! I, with the scattered remnants of the procession, made my way to the Square, and kept "moving on" without moving off. Burns and Graham tried to break into the Square and were arrested. Graham also was clubbed and spent his prison time in hospital.

It was Salt who introduced William Archer to me.[22] Both of them were Thoreau specialists: Salt wrote the life of Thoreau and William Archer called

19. Ruskin in his autobiography *Praeterita* (1885–9) confessed, 'I had nominally read the whole Æneid, but thought most of it nonsense.' In a section called 'Oxford Studies', found among his notes and inserted posthumously by his editors (1907) in an appendix to vol. 4, he noted: 'Both Virgil and Milton were too rhetorical and parasitical for me'; but he admitted (vol. 2, chapter 3) that eventually the legends 'became all at once true'.
20. *The Story of Aeneas: Virgil's Aeneid Translated into English Verse* (1928).
21. Legendary street fracas, on 13 November 1887, between the London mounted police and socialists/anarchists demonstrating against the Government's Irish policy. It resulted in the securing of the right of free speech in Trafalgar Square. Cunninghame Graham was a socialist MP, who deliberately provoked arrest to obtain a court test.
22. This may have been a formal introduction; the two were, however, already casually acquainted from their proximity as researchers in the British Museum's library from February 1883.

his cottage Walden. It was through this introduction that I started writing plays. He was also one of the witnesses of my marriage. He introduced me to Olive Schreiner who was like what she wrote.[23] She astonished me by writing that I was the only man she was ever afraid of. Why, God knows!

As my friends lived in different worlds and I rarely introduced one to the other they did not necessarily know oneanother. Webb and Salt didnt. Neither Samuel Butler nor Olivier ever met Salt or knew anything about him as far as I know. On the other hand, I did not know Hudson and Salt never succeeded in persuading me to read Thoreau or Jefferies; I never was of the bird-watching or flower-hunting group but followed Thoreau and Carpenter in having a hut well away from the house in which to do my writing.[24] My reason however was of a more practical kind. No woman likes a man about the house: men-in-house is a worse disease than meningitis. Neither Thoreau nor Carpenter had this difficulty.

We were Shelleyans and Humanitarians. I was not present with Salt at the Shelley Centenary Celebration at Horsham.[25] Edmund Gosse *was*. It presented Shelley as a Church of England country gentleman whose pastime was writing sermons in verse. My pastime has been writing sermons in plays, sermons preaching what Salt practised.

Salt was original and in his way unique.

G. B. S.

23. South African feminist and author, celebrated for her *Story of an African Farm* (1883), which Shaw found 'fascinating' when he read it in 1888. In his diary on 29 September 1891 he indicated he had written 'a note to Olive Schreiner to remind her of my existence before she leaves England' (*Diaries*, ed. Stanley Weintraub, 1986).
24. The 64-square-foot hut in Shaw's back garden at Ayot, which pivoted on a socket to enable its occupant to shift it to follow the sun, was designed by Shaw at his wife's request for *her* use. He soon, however, usurped it for his own comfort and convenience.
25. Another lapse of memory. Shaw, Archer and Salt attended the Horsham celebration in the afternoon of 4 August 1892, at which the speaker was Edmund Gosse. They were obliged to leave before the talk had ended to catch a train back to London, where Shaw, with Salt in the audience, delivered a centenary address on Shelley in the Hall of Science. See his report 'Shaming the Devil about Shelley', in the *Albemarle*, September 1892; reprinted in *Pen Portraits and Reviews*, 1931.

# APPENDIX

# Communism

*Editor's note by Shaw to a lecture by William Morris, delivered on 10 March 1893;
published as Fabian Tract No. 113 in March 1903*

======

The Fabian Society is indebted to the Trustees of William Morris for permission to include the following paper in its series of Tracts. It was written
for delivery as a spoken address to the members of the Hammersmith Socialist
Society in 1893. By that time Morris had acquired an intimate knowledge
of the attempt to organize Socialism in this country which began in the early
eighties. He had himself undertaken and conducted that part of the experiment
which nobody else would face: namely, the discovery and combination,
without distinction of class, of all those who were capable of understanding
Equality and Communism as he understood it, and their organization as an
effective force for the overthrow of the existing order of property and privilege. In doing so he had been brought into contact, and often into conflict,
with every other section of the movement. He knew all its men and knew
all their methods. He knew that the agitation was exhausted, and that the
time had come to deal with the new policy which the agitation had shaken
into existence. Accordingly, we find him in this paper doing what he could
to economize the strength of the movement by making peace between its
jarring sections, and recalling them from their disputes over tactics and programs to the essentials of their cause.

The Socialist agitation in Morris's time had divided itself into three clearly
defined sections. His own section, organized as the Socialist League, broke
down because there was only one William Morris. Those who combined
any real understanding of his aims or his view of our commercial civilization
with high personal character and practical ability were too few and far between
to effect a political revolution. The other two sections survived. One of them,
the Social-Democratic Federation, concerned itself very little with Morris's
fundamental conceptions of Equality, Communism, and the rediscovery under
Communism of Art as "workpleasure." It set itself frankly to organize the
proletariat as a single class for the purpose of wresting the material sources
of production from the hands of the proprietary class; or, in the well worn
phrases of the older Social-Democrats, to make the workers "class-conscious"
of themselves, and to organize "the class war." The third section was the

Fabian Society, which aimed simply at the reduction of Socialism to a constitutional political policy which, like Free Trade or Imperial Federation or any other accepted parliamentary movement, could be adopted either as a whole or by instalments by any ordinary respectable citizen without committing himself to any revolutionary association or detaching himself in any way from the normal course of English life.

The Fabian project was, of course, enormously more acceptable to a timidly Conservative nation than its two rivals. It also called for a good deal of administrative knowledge and parliamentary ingenuity, and so selected automatically for its membership the politically clever and officially experienced Socialists. It is not surprising, therefore, that the Fabians alone made any headway; that the Socialist League was abandoned by Morris as a failure after a patient and laborious trial; that the Independent Labor Party, a later formation, adopted parliamentary methods; and that the Social-Democratic Federation, after keeping up the struggle for a declaration of the class war for years, had finally to choose between assimilating its methods to those of the Independent Labor Party and being crowded out of the field of Labor agitation.

It is unnecessary to say that Morris was from the first impatient of Fabianism as an essentially superficial movement. But he was fundamentally the most practical of all the Socialists. When he quarreled with facts, he set to work at once to alter them. He was quite accustomed to be laughed at and explained away in a superior manner, both from the popular and the academic point of view. In all the arts and crafts which he had touched with his own hands, the laughter and the superior explanations had been hastily checked by the discovery that he had effected a revolution whilst his critics were idly chattering. But the same qualities which enabled him to alter unpleasant facts when he could, enabled him to face them when he could not. When he found after trying his hardest that the English people would not join the Socialist League or allow the Social-Democratic Federation to convince them that they belonged to an ungentlemanly class, he accepted the situation and considered how to make the best of it. His inevitable isolation as a man of genius was of course not less among avowed Socialists than elsewhere; but it compelled all the sections to listen to him when they would not listen to oneanother; and the Hammersmith Socialist Society, a faithful bodyguard surviving from the extinct Socialist League, provided for him within his own curtilage a platform on which every Socialist was proud to speak.

What he himself said to the sections from this platform will be found in the following pages. It gives his reasons for advising the other Socialists not to quarrel with the Fabians. And it gives his warning to the Fabians that it is one thing to formulate on paper a constitutional policy, and another thing to induce people to carry it out when the Equality and Communism to which it leads are abhorred instead of desired by them.

I must add a word of editorial explanation. It was Morris's habit, fortunately for posterity, to write his lectures at full length instead of trusting to extemporization. How he found time to write so many, even when he was reviving the lost art of fine printing in his spare time, I cannot imagine. He certainly did not find time to revise them. Besides, he seems to have had the Shakespearean habit of never blotting a line, perhaps as part of his general rule not to waste time in cobbling a bad job, but to do it over again. The manuscript consists of fourteen pages of white foolscap. There are words scored through and replaced by others before the ink was dry, but no reconstructions made on revision, a ceremony which was clearly never gone through. The last half of the paper must have been written against time in great haste: more words are left out than in the earlier pages; and occasionally a sentence becomes a hopeless no-thoroughfare. The grammar, too, is hasty: the verb agrees with the nearest noun, which is not always its subject. The ands are sometimes written at full length, and sometimes indicated by ampersands, just as we have printed them. The spelling is for the most part conventional; but the s is always doubled in disappear and disappoint, and there is never more than one g in aggressive. The italics represent Morris's own underscoring. The punctuation is very hasty; but as the sense never depends on the position of a stop, I have altered or supplemented it freely for the sake of clearness. I have been very reluctant to meddle with the words; but on page 10, line 48, I have changed "anything" to "like everything"; the footnote on page 11 occurs in the manuscript as a rather obstructive parenthesis; on page 12, line 48, I have been Vandal enough to alter the characteristic phrase "their wealth—nay their riches" into "their wealth—or rather their riches" because I found that the "nay" in this passage conveyed to a typical reader the impression that Morris thought more of riches than of wealth (a misunderstanding which would almost bring him back from the grave to protest);* on page 14, line 4, I have altered "which doesn't involve" into "which will then no longer involve"; and on page 15, line 4, I have changed "as they are now and probably must be to be successful under the guidance of one man" to "as they are now (and, to be successful, must probably remain) under the guidance of one man." To Morris's friends, as to myself, these changes will seem mere impertinences; but others will find the meaning made clearer by the changes. At all events, those who are offended can correct

---

* See the paper on 'Art, Wealth and Riches' in the volume of Morris's essays entitled *Architecture, Industry and Wealth* (London, 1902: Longmans; 6s. net). [GBS]

their copies. The rest of the very few departures from the manuscript are only replacements of obviously dropped articles or prepositions, and need no apology. I believe that the words "of making" on page 11, line 5, should be "to make"; but I have not altered them, as such a change would affect the meaning. Finally, I may say that the back of the manuscript, which lay before Morris as he sat listening to the debate on the platform after his lecture, is adorned with decorations in pencil, which began, schoolboy fashion, with several arrows—not, it must be confessed, the clothyard shafts he describes in A Dream of John Ball, but fat, short, heavy-headed bolts for a medieval machine gun. Then comes a sort of fishing rod with Gothic crockets—or perhaps it is a conventionalized lily leaf. The rest is the familiar decoration of flower and scroll and leaf with which his hand was so often busy in idle moments. His notes of the discussion run as follows: "old age pensions—Mordhurst one road—means—luxury or necessity—opponent—come Bradlaugh—Bullock—workman."

Morris bibliographers should note that the title Communism is not distinctive of this lecture, as he used it on other occasions on the Hammersmith platform and elsewhere.

G. B. S.

# Man and Superman

*A foreword to the Popular Edition, 1911, issued in paper wrappers
in Constable's Sixpenny Series*

———

I have a special reason for making this book more widely accessible than it can be, even in these days of free libraries, at the customary price of my books.[1] It is described on the title page as "A Comedy and a Philosophy." It might have been called a religion as well; for the vision of hell in the third act, which has never been performed on the stage except as a separate work,[2] is expressly intended to be a revelation of the modern religion of evolution.

Putting it roughly and briefly, the discovery and vogue of evolution, from 1790 to 1830, made an end, for the pioneers of thought, of XVIII century rationalist atheism and deism on the one hand, and, on the other, of what may be called Garden-of-Edenism. In the middle of the XIX century the discovery by Darwin and Wallace of Natural Selection, which might have had as its subtitle "The revelation of a method by which all the appearances of intelligent design in the universe may have been produced by pure accident," practically destroyed religion in cultured Europe for a whole generation, in spite of Darwin's and Wallace's own reservations and the urgent warnings and fierce criticisms of Samuel Butler. With the beginning of the present century the return swing of the pendulum has inaugurated a counterfashion of saying that Natural Selection, instead of accounting for everything, accounts for nothing. That it accounts for nothing in any religious sense is of course true; for it leaves untouched the whole sphere of will, purpose, design, intention, even consciousness; and a religion is nothing but a common view of the nature of will, the purpose of life, the design of organism, and the intention of evolution. Such a common view has been gradually detaching itself from the welter of negation provoked by the extremely debased forms

1. The standard trade edition of Shaw's plays and novels in Britain remained constant at six shillings from 1901 to 1916.
2. The play was first performed in its entirety by Esmé Percy and Kristeen Graeme with their Travelling Repertory Company at the Lyceum Theatre, Edinburgh, on 11 June 1915. An instant success, it was performed with great frequency by Percy in later years when he toured with the Macdona Players.

of religion which have masqueraded as Christianity in England during the period of petty commercialism from which we are emerging. The time has come for an attempt to formulate this common view as a modern religion, and to provide it with a body of doctrine, a poesy, and a political and industrial system. Shelley and Wagner made notable attempts to provide it with materials for a Bible; and I, with later lights of science to guide me than either of these prophets had, have made a further attempt in this Man and Superman. As I have not been sparing of such lighter qualities as I could endow the book with for the sake of those who ask nothing from a play but an agreeable pastime, I think it well to affirm plainly that the third act, however fantastic its legendary framework may appear, is a careful attempt to write a new Book of Genesis for the Bible of the Evolutionists; and as it is recognized that no matter how highly priced other works of art may be, Bibles must be cheap, I have consented to the issue of this edition at the lowest price possible in the book market today.

22 March 1911.

# A Word going to Press
## (War Issues for Irishmen)

*Brief foreword for an appeal drafted in the form of a letter to Col. Arthur Lynch,*
*commander of British forces in Ireland, intended to assist the Irish recruiting programme.*
*Shaw had received proof of the letter in October 1918, by which time some of the text*
*had become obsolete. To keep pace with recent events Shaw in October*
*drafted the prefatory 'Word', which he pre-dated 10 November, the intended date of*
*publication. Just as the book went to press the Armistice was declared; all but*
*a handful of copies were pulped. First published in Shaw,* The Matter with Ireland, *eds. Dan H. Laurence and David H. Greene (1962)*

═══

In war, when events move in earnest, they move so much faster than the brains of the fastest thinker or the pen of the fastest writer that every really well considered utterance arrives the day after the fair. They have certainly moved with a vengeance since conscription was threatened in Ireland. That threat was made in a moment of panic so acute that the British Government actually announced that it was abandoning the English harvest, and tearing its necessary cultivators from the fields regardless of consequences, to meet the military emergency created by the rout of the Fifth Army. Compared to this desperate and suicidal demand on the English nation the demand for conscription in Ireland was moderate and pardonable. Any special bitterness on our side concerning it seems to me to be inhuman. Both demands were, from the military point of view, insane: neither of them could have operated in time to save the situation. Both had to be dropped rather shamefacedly when the scare subsided. But they shew how appallingly close to the brink of utter defeat the Government believed us then to be.

That was only a few moments ago as moments are counted in this war. Yet as I write these last few hurried words before going to press the German Empire is in the dust; the Austro-Hungarian Empire is changed, as if by an enchanter's wand, into three Republics and a Revolution; the Ottoman Empire is suing for mercy on its knees; and the fact that Bulgaria is out of the war and, with Roumania, declared a Republic, is hardly worth noticing in the general political metamorphosis. The difficulty now is to persuade the

Allied nations that the war is not yet over, and that the European chaos, though a necessary accompaniment of a huge transition from what we in Ireland call Castle rule[1] to popular rule, is for the moment a danger that calls, even more urgently than the mere struggle to avoid defeat of the last four years, for the resolute unification and military organization of Western democracy. That the Hohenzollern and Hapsburg empires have fallen may fitly be received here with exultant cheers. But if you go deeper and put it that the whole centre of Europe has fallen to pieces politically, the wise man in the West will look to his arms more anxiously than before.

Still, it is a glorious day for Democracy; and it is fortunate for us that there are enough Irishmen in the Democratic army, and enough soldiers' widows and orphans in Ireland, to make it impossible for Democracy to turn a cold shoulder to us in the hour of her triumph and say, "No thanks to you Irish." But some of us are still open to that reproach. Out of five hundred thousand farmers and farmers' men in England, two hundred thousand who had never dreamt of soldiering before volunteered for service at the beginning of the war to fight for the ideals which Nationalist Ireland has professed in season and out of season. There are Irishmen who plead that we might have done equally well in proportion to our numbers if the English Ascendancy had let us. I do not like the excuse, because I do not see why we need have let the British Ascendancy hinder us; and I could tell stories of how some of the first English volunteers were received when they rushed to the colors, which would set Ireland wondering that England ever raised an army at all. But however that may be, the fact remains that we are allowing England to beat us in her contribution to the victory of Democracy, and that America, whose subsidies have kept our Nationalist party in parliamentary existence for thirty years on the understanding that we Irish are all born soldiers of freedom, is reminding us that if we are too poor to pay we are not too poor to fight, and asking us pretty emphatically which side we are on. Sinn Fein, replying through the mouth of its Congress the other day that it will "make itself felt at the Peace Conference"[2] (whatever that may be), apparently by some mysti-

1. The seat of British rule in Ireland was in Dublin Castle, headquarters of the Lord-Lieutenant of Ireland.
2. Sinn Féin had in 1917 determined on a policy of presenting its case for independence, not at Westminster, but to the Peace Conference that would follow the war, 'where the Bench will not be packed against us' (*Clare Champion*, 7 July 1917). At a meeting in Dublin on 25 October 1917 it amended its constitution to make its principal aim 'international recognition of Ireland as an independent Irish Republic'. It commenced at the same time a campaign of vigorous opposition to Irish military conscription and recruiting.

cal force inherent in doing nothing, has made itself so acutely ridiculous that it had really better elect the ex-Kaiser Grand Master of its Order, and retire with him to Dalkey Island, which he would doubtless prefer to Saint Helena as a jumping-off place for any future operations his enthusiasm for Irish liberty may suggest.

There is still time for more Irishmen to affirm their true allegiance to Democracy. They will find in the following pages no attempt to confuse that allegiance with the false allegiance which is only the bargain of Esau. And I am happy to be able to add that they will find no argument which is weakened, and some which are strengthened, by the astonishing turn which Europe has taken since my letter to Colonel Lynch was penned six weeks ago.

AYOT ST LAWRENCE.
10 November 1918.

# On Ritual, Religion, and the Intolerableness
## of Tolerance

*Shaw's publisher in 1920 persuaded him to undertake a Collected Edition of his work. In the following year he drafted a preface for his unpublished first novel* Immaturity *and began compiling lists and gathering cuttings and tearsheets of his critical journalism. Surviving in the British Library's Shaw archive is a folder (Add. Mss. 50663) labelled 'Religion and Religions', which contains several typescripts (with holograph corrections) of materials that appear to have been intended for a preface to an eventually abandoned volume. These include two copies, each dated 'Ayot St Lawrence. 16/10/22', with the second (fos. 67–92) being a revision of the first (fos. 39–66). The earlier version (signed by Shaw) is captioned 'On Ritual, Religion and the Intolerableness of Tolerance', which we believe Shaw intended to be the title of the preface; the second bears the caption 'The Church Versus Religion', which presumably was to be a sectional sub-head. Another, shorter, piece 'The Infancy of God', neither signed nor dated (fos. 23–33), has been placed arbitrarily following the principal section. Lacking corroborative evidence for our hypothesis, we have cautiously relegated the material to the appendix. The texts were published as 'essays' in* Shaw on Religion *(1967), edited by the late Warren Sylvester Smith*

=====

## THE CHURCH VERSUS RELIGION

Such a caption as The Church Versus Religion begs the question whether the Churches are really opposed to religion. Proverbs like "The nearer the Church, the further from God," or, "Heaven for holiness: hell for company" are happy as witticisms; but no statesman could legislate on them, nor any Churchman apostatize on them, unless both had given up religion altogether as a bad job. Tolstoy, whose letters to certain churchmen[1] have provoked

---

1. A letter of 4 April 1901 in answer to a decree of Excommunication issued on 22 February by the Holy Synod of the Orthodox Russian Church stated: 'I have renounced the Church which calls itself Orthodox . . . because . . . I became convinced that Church doctrine is theoretically a crafty and harmful lie, and practically a collection of the grossest superstitions and sorcery, which completely conceals the whole meaning of Christ's teaching.' In another letter, on 26 August 1901, Tolstoy informed a sympathetic French pastor: 'I do not agree with you . . . of the necessity of the church, and, therefore, of pastors . . . [T]he chief meaning of the Christian teaching is the establishment of a direct communion between God and men' (both letters are in Tolstoy's *Letters and Essays*, ed. Leo Wiener, 1904).

the present discussion, did not shake the dust of the Greek Church off his feet because it was religious, nor even because, on its political side, it was violently and shockingly irreligious. On that ground he would have had to leave, not only the Greek Church, but the world. Churches can repent and can reform; can purify their hearts and ennoble their rituals; can defy ambitious and tyrannical princes and either make them come to Canossa[2] or suffer the worst they can inflict; can, in short, raise themselves from "harmful sects," as Tolstoy rightly called the Church he left,[3] to mighty spiritual powers, without committing suicide and abandoning their flocks to the world, the flesh, and the devil.

Tolstoy's real reason for leaving the Church was that he had no personal use for it. Its ritual, which helped others to a religious mood, only exasperated him, much as Jackson's Te Deum might have exasperated Beethoven. The preacher who seemed to the moujik and the little shopkeeper a wise and holy man must have often seemed to Tolstoy a noodle making an absurd mess of his job.

But even if the music had been by Beethoven, and the preacher another Peter or even another Christ, Tolstoy would have appreciated them only as a connoisseur appreciates a masterpiece of art. He would not have needed them for the making of his soul. That was his own business, which he could do so well for himself that a ritual and a priest could only distract him. For this reason he was an anti-Ritualist, and in England or America would have been a Quaker if he could have endured even a Quakers' meeting.

He need not have gone far to find men no less religious than himself to whom the forms in which he apprehended his religion seemed as idolatrous as the ikons of the Greek Church seemed to him. "I believe", said Tolstoy, "in God the Father, who sent me into this world so that I should fulfil His law."[4] A Bergsonian evolutionist would have replied, "This conception of a

2. The excommunicated emperor Henry IV came to the castle of Canossa in 1077 to kneel before Pope Gregory VII as a simple penitent, to receive absolution.
3. In *The Spirit of Christ's Teachings* (tr. V. Tchertkoff, 1899) Tolstoy wrote of 'a large number of hostile sects, whose formation can only be prevented by a reconciliation of all the varied revelations, or by a right conception of the teaching of one man, believed to be God'.
4. In the 4 April letter to the Holy Synod, Tolstoy added: 'I believe in God, whom I understand as Spirit, as Love, as the beginning of everything . . . and see the whole meaning of life only in the fulfilment of God's will, as expressed in the Christian teaching. I believe that the greatest true good of man is the fulfilment of God's will' (Wiener).

Father is the superstition of a cottager. The *élan vital* in which I believe cannot be represented by anything so corporeal, though as I, too, believe that it sent me into the world to do its will, I am as religious a man as you."

Beside the Bergsonians he might have found many people at the opposite extreme of intellectual development, to whom even so familiar a concept as a Father is no use unless he is seen and felt as well as conceived. They can pray to some material object only, were it only a stone that overhangs them threateningly or has something uncanny about its shape.

All the religious conflicts and bigotries and persecutions and wars of religion and *autos da fé* and so forth are misunderstandings between the men who apprehend God directly and intimately in the abstract (say Platonically), and those who can reach him only through symbols and ceremonies.

Let me state the case in due order from the beginning, using for convenience sake the term Quaker (it is more homelike than Platonist) to denote the man at one end of the scale, and the term Ritualist to denote the man at the other.

There has always been, and always will be, a division between the Ritualist and the Quaker. There is no reason for quarreling over it. There is room in the world for George Fox and the Pope. The trouble begins only when an attempt is made to force ritual on Fox, or to smash the statues and extinguish the candles in the Pope's chapel. Religion takes different men in different ways; and if they would accept that fact instead of trying to force their ways on oneanother, a process which involves the utter extinction of the religious spirit the moment it is even contemplated, both the Ritualist and the Quaker would be free to develop their states of grace to the utmost.

The first thing to grasp is that ritual is not religion, nor the absence of ritual irreligion. One man will not enter a church on any persuasion: he will not even call it a church: he calls it a steeplehouse. Another man haunts churches because he finds that in them he can meditate or pray better than anywhere else; but he flies from them the moment he is interrupted by the entry of the priest and the choristers in procession. Yet another man goes to church for the service alone: he never dreams of entering a church at any other time; and until the ritual begins he will busy himself disposing of his hat and umbrella, and noting that old Jones must be still down with lumbago as he has not come to church, and that young Smith has bought a new coat at last. But at the first word of the service he will buckle-to and be as pious as he can. Far from feeling that the priest and the service are coming between him and his God, and resenting them as a distracting intrusion, he clings to them because they are doing for him something that he cannot do for himself. The fact that the priest is there, and is not dressed as men of the world are dressed, and does not speak as they do, makes him feel that God must be there in the background, just as the sight of a liveried butler on the doorstep of a great man, and of the sentries at the palace gates, convinces him that the great man exists, and that the king is a reality. For what more convincing proof of a nearness of God can there be than the bodily vision of His house and of His servants?

Now it is very hard for these three different men to believe in oneanother's religiousness. To Number Three Number One must be an atheist, because he not only does not go to church, but denies its sacredness. Number Two, who prowls about churches when there is no service going on, and leaves them when the congregation arrives, is clearly either a lunatic or a thief watching for an opportunity to break open the money boxes or steal the Communion plate. Number One and Number Two regard Number Three as a Pharisee and a hypocrite. Number One suspects Number Two, who prays in the steeplehouse, of being half ritualist, half dilettant. When they go to extremes, Number One becomes an iconoclast, smashing everything in the cathedrals that he can reach, and insulting and murdering priests; and Number Three makes laws that Number One shall come to church whether he likes it or not, on pain of pillory, mutilation, outlawry, or the stake. Number Two is never powerful enough to go to extremes. If he were, he would keep Number Three and his priests out of the church, and keep Number One in the county jail.

When this sort of thing begins, there is an end of religion. Number Three, who, being usually in the majority, has most power of social and political coercion, attacks not only the man who does not go to church, but the man who goes to church at which the service differs in the slightest detail from that at his own church. In Ulster, men who go to the Protestant church throw bombs into groups of little children because the parents of those children go to the Roman Catholic church. They do so as champions of God, to the great amusement of the devil. They are provoked to this by the records of the Holy Office, or Inquisition, the proceedings of which moved the humane and genuinely religious Voltaire, who himself erected a church to God, to exclaim, as he contemplated the established Church of his country, *Écrasez l'infâme!* Whereupon Number Three concluded that Voltaire must be an atheist, and believed that he died in horrible terror and remorse, not because this was true, but because Number Three liked to believe that an atheist died that way, even when he also believed that God had warned him that there are no bands in death for the wicked; that their strength is firm; that they are not troubled as other men [Psalms 73: 4–5].

Number One cannot mistake Number Three for an atheist. He mistakes him for something much more revolting than an atheist: an idolator. An Ulster Protestant, when he sees a Papist (as he calls him) lighting a candle before a statue of the Blessed Virgin, feels exactly as Robinson Crusoe did when he burnt the tribal idol, or as Moses did when he found his people worshipping the golden calf. Mahomet in his reaction against idolatry stamped on Islam a law that makes it impossible today to place any image of man or beast in a mosque. Machiavelli, an ultra-Ulsterman, though he was never in Ulster, hated priests with a mortal hatred, and might logically have adopted the creed of Mahomet, who excluded priests from his system as religiously as images. In vain does the Laodicean man of the world, the Gallio [Acts 18: 12–17], or the impatiently Protestant Jonathan Swift, ask what these people are quarreling about? what it matters whether a man prays and preaches in a black gown or a white vestment? whether he raises a winecup above his head before drinking or not? whether the wafer is regarded as bread eaten in memory of the bread that Christ broke at his last supper or as the body of God? Men who understand the issues behind the symbolism are not indifferent: their intense abhorrence of idolatry on the one hand, and of atheism on the other, is at stake on every one of these details; and they will slaughter and lay waste, burn women alive, beat children savagely, sink and demolish, act so as to make the tiger and the serpent, the lightning and the earthquake, seem beneficent in comparison; and all this with the name of God not only on their lips, but in their hearts.

When we have the two extremes of a case clearly in mind, we have no difficulty in understanding the position of the persons who are somewhere on the scale between them. These are the great majority; for there are relatively few out-and-outers in religion. Anyone who has been in a mosque can testify that though there is nominally no priest there, the Imaums who lead the prayers and conduct the ceremonies fill, in the imagination of the worshippers of Allah, the place of the clergy and priests in the Christian churches, and that a Moorish Marabout [Muslim holy man] has all the powers and all the sanctity of a medieval Christian bishop. True, there are no graven images or likenesses of anything that is in heaven above or in the earth beneath or in the water under the earth; but the elaborate decoration, the symbols and texts, the majestic architecture that is made homelike for Allah by the carpeted floor, are capable of influencing the mind of the spectators quite as powerfully as the imagery in Christian cathedrals.

The mass of mankind must have something to worship that the senses can apprehend. The Church of England began with a resolute effort to repudiate the anthropomorphic conception of God: its first article of belief is that God is a spirit without body, parts, or passions. Yet if it were to exclude from its communion today the people to whom God is the figure we see in Raphael's Vision of Ezekiel, and in Blake's illustrations to the Book of Job, it would be a negligible sect instead of a national Church. The four articles numbered 28 to 31 were a desperate attempt to make room in the same Church for Puritans who, though they lived too soon to read Sir James Frazer's Golden Bough, yet identified the Mass with the heathen Mexican ceremony of eating the god, and for Catholics who believed literally in transubstantiation.[5] There are High churches to please the Anglican Catholics and Low churches to please the Protestants. Those who cannot stomach prelacy will not join an Episcopalian Church; but they can become Presbyterians. The last straw that breaks the churchgoer's back is often a very light one. A single candle on the Communion table, or a right or left turn of the celebrant reading the service, may drive one worshipper away to a church where there is neither candle on the table nor pivot in the parson, and attract another to it.

The persecuting spirit acts in opposite directions. At first it meant an attempt to force heretics into churches. Charlemagne offered his heathen prisoners of war the choice between baptism and death. Queen Elizabeth told the Catholics and Puritans that she had done her best to make a Church that would satisfy both of them, and that they must come to it every Sunday or go to prison.[6] As she overlooked the fact that there was a third alternative, America, Puritan Massachusetts and Catholic Maryland were among the consequences; but the point is that she wanted to compel people to come to her Church, not to repel them from its doors. Yet the inevitable result of treating as enemies the people who will not come to your Church is that you end by refusing to let them come even when they want to. Mahomet summoned the whole world to Mecca; but when Captain [Sir Richard]

5. The four articles address themselves to the ceremony of the Lord's Supper. Articles 28 and 29 could be read as holding contradictory views about the actual presence of Christ's body and blood in the bread and wine of the ceremony.
6. In a 1559 parliamentary Act of Religious Uniformity, subjects were required to attend Anglican church service. In June 1570, before the Star Chamber, the queen declared: 'Her Majesty would have all her loving subjects to understand that as long as they shall openly continue in the observation of her laws and shall not wilfully and manifestly break them by their open acts, her Majesty's meaning is not to have any of them molested by an inquisition or examination of their consciences in causes of religion . . .' The next year she vetoed a Bill to increase fines for non-attendance and to compel participation in communion, declaring the latter an invasion of conscience (J. E. Neale, *Elizabeth I and Her Parliaments: 1559–1581*, 1953, pp. 349, 370).

Burton[7] went there in 1853 he did so at the risk of his life, carefully disguised as a Mussulman. I have seen an Englishman in Tangiers dragged violently away from the door of a mosque into which he was peeping. Thus the heretic is so hated that he is denied his right to conversion and salvation: he is killed because he will not worship in the temple, and killed equally if he attempts to enter it.

The evils of intolerance are so monstrous and so well advertized that the Laodicean Centre, as we may call the easygoing majority, have set up Toleration as a virtue, and established it in law to some extent. But their success is only apparent. What is called Toleration is only submission to the fact that after many bloody trials Catholics and Protestants, Churchmen and Dissenters, Hindus and Mahometans, Buddhists and Shintos, have found that they cannot exterminate oneanother, and must agree to live and let live until luck gives one of them a decisive upper hand. The Laodiceans have never been able to prevent the religious people from dragging them sooner or later into wars of religion; and civilization does nothing to diminish the ferocity of these wars. The British Empire is specially hampered by the number and variety of its fanaticisms. White Christians are only about 11 per cent of the population. In India alone 33 native languages are more spoken than English. In addition to the 17-or-so varieties of Christians which the United States have to handle, the British Empire has to drive in single harness hundreds of millions of Hindus, Sikhs, Jains, Buddhists, Parsees, and Mahometans, to say nothing of divisions that the compilers of western books of reference have been unable to classify. The Jew is everywhere; and the attempt to shepherd him into a definitely localized Zion in Palestine has only brought his faith into a definitely localized conflict with the Islam of its native Arabs. It is natural for the American to preach Toleration to all these fanatics, because his very existence is due to a flight of persecuted but utterly intolerant men from intolerance; but his sermons are wasted breath. We must face the fact that no man will tolerate what he believes to be a false and mischievous religion whilst he has the means of persecuting and suppressing it.

Let the American who, fancying himself tolerant, is surprised by this statement, consider a little. If he were ruling India, would he tolerate Suttee and the car of Juggernaut? Would he tolerate Thuggee, the worship of Kali, goddess of blood, who demands from her devotees, not prayers and good

7. In his *Personal Narrative of a Pilgrimage to El-Medinah and Meccah* (1855–6, 3 vols.) Burton related that he travelled in July–September 1853 in the guise of Al-Haj Abdullah, a Pathan (Indian-born Afghan) educated at Rangoon, to account for speech peculiarities.

works, but murders?[8] Does he tolerate Voodoo? These questions answer themselves in the negative: nobody but a lunatic dreams of toleration for such beliefs in practice.

Bring it nearer home. If he is a materialist atheist, would he tolerate the Plymouth Brethren if he could help it? If he is a Plymouth Brother, would he tolerate atheism if he could help it? Is he quite sound on the Jewish question? Even if he is a Laodicean, and is prepared to tolerate all religions and irreligions for the sake of a quiet life, is that a reason for tolerating Ulster Calvinism and Ultramontanism [doctrine of papal supremacy]? I cannot exhaust all the particular cases which raise the question of toleration; but I do not believe there is a man or woman on earth who cannot be fitted with a case in the which he or she is an uncompromising advocate of ruthless persecution. To be convinced of this it is only necessary to turn from the adults to the children. Granted that your neighbor must be left undisturbed in his belief that he may be predestined to spend eternity in boiling brimstone, driving himself half mad by continually thinking about it, is he to be allowed to lay his children's souls waste by urging that doctrine on them before they are old enough to dare go upstairs by themselves in the dark? If Shelley's children were taken away from him because he held that the god of Calvinistic Predestination is a fable, and if he were not, would be a fiend, are the people who agree with Shelley now that he is accepted as a prophet and a saint, likely to allow Calvinism to be taught to infants as divine truth in the public elementary schools for which they have to pay?

No. Toleration as an expediency may be very advisable; but as a principle it is out of the question. Persecution may be so inexpedient in many cases that no sane person would insist on it; but when expediency is on the side of persecution, as, for example, on the Prohibition issue, everyone can see that there is not the smallest difference in principle between persecuting a toper and persecuting a Thug. In prejudice, of course, there is all the difference in the world. Speaking as a man of prejudice I should say that when you prevent me from doing anything I want to do, that is persecution; but when I prevent you from doing anything you want to do, that is law, order, and morals. After 1917 in America there was a savage persecution of Bolshevism. Several of its victims are still in prison. Do you, respectable Yankee, call that

---

8. Juggernaut is the incarnation of the Hindu god Vishnu, whose idol was transported on a car at religious rites. Zealous devotees were known to throw themselves under its wheels in sacrifice. The Thugs were members of a semi–religious cult in India that murdered and pillaged in the name of Kali, in Hindu mythology a black goddess of death and destruction.

persecution? Are you going to have those victims released? Of course not. You believe in Toleration; but you draw the line at Bolshevism. I blame you for this; but I am not blaming your intolerance: I am blaming your ignorance. If you believe that Bolshevism means theft, murder, communism in women, and everything horrid (your English great-grandfather believed the same things about Jacobinism, and talked about Washington as you do about Lenin) why, then you are right to persecute Bolshevism. But you are not right to believe such manifest guff and bugaboo.

Is there then no remedy for the evils brought on us by our bigotry? None, in my opinion, except a hair of the dog that bit us. What we need is more religion to get us to the root of the matter. There is a science of religion in which we should all be instructed. When Mrs Eddy set up the Church of Christ Scientist, she was very well inspired indeed. Christ was not tolerant: he was not prepared to tolerate money changers and traders in sacrificial beasts in the Temple. He warned the Pharisees that there were blasphemies that are unpardonable, and denounced them as vipers [Matthew 12: 31–2, 34]: that is, creatures whom the most tolerant cannot tolerate. But he refused altogether to make any distinction on the point of eligibility for salvation between Jew and Gentile, baptized and circumcized. He not only refrained from proselytizing, but expressly warned the proselytizers that a man's religious consciousness is like a fertile field, so that if they tried to root up the tares in it they would root up the wheat as well and leave him without any religion at all [Matthew 13: 24–30]. It never occurred to him to ask a Jew to cease being a Jew:[9] he simply exhorted him to become a Christian as well as a Jew. Christianity as Christ preached it is applicable to all the Churches and religions that are consistent with human society. A Thug cannot be a Christian; but a Mahometan can: a Buddhist can: a Parsee can: a Jain can; and though there are greater difficulties in the case of the varieties of pseudo-Christians now overrunning the world outside Asia, there is hope even for them.

When men are united in a common religion, there will be no persecution problem. What we have to deal with now is the fact that they cannot be so

9. In a lecture he delivered for the Fabian Society on 10 May 1918, 'The Climate and Soil for Labour Culture', Shaw stated: 'Jesus, who was a Jew living among Jews, never suggested that any Jew should cease to be a Jew, and never abjured the Jewish faith. He declared emphatically that if you rooted up a man's native form of religion to substitute your own form, you would rout up his soul in the process: the wheat, he said, would come up with the tares. His view was that there were certain truths that all men must recognize and act on if they are to find salvation, whether they be Jews or Gentiles' (Shaw, *The Road to Equality*, ed. Louis Crompton, 1971).

united until the common religion presents itself to them in many different forms. If you ask me why not, I reply that all men's minds have not the same scope. The form of worship that brings one man into communion with God may move another to impatient derision as a childish mummery or even as a blasphemy. God without body, parts or passions, though legally the God of the Church of England, is no god at all to the man who can apprehend no moral force that is not anthropomorphic. Rousseau told us that if we would only get rid of our miracle stories the whole world would fall at the feet of Christ; but he was wrong: there are multitudes of simple people—Italian peasants for example—who cannot be induced to worship any saint or Savior who does not prove his title to their veneration by performing miracles; so that their Church has actually to provide sham miracles to save their souls. The popular fiction of hell is a very horrible one: so much so that if it were not tacitly dropped in cultured urban congregations, the Churches would die of it; but Mahomet, though personally humane to a degree that makes his personal career somewhat scandalous to Western tastes, was forced to elaborate the story of the brimstone lake by the most ingeniously disgusting inventions, knowing that men who are morbidly attracted by tragically terrible punishments, will recoil from the ridicule that attends squalor, dirt, stench, and infirmity.[10] And what drove him to this was that he had to govern men of whom many were quite incapable of conceiving divine displeasure unless it had what modern diplomatists call sanctions: that is, unless it was visited on those who incurred it in extremely unpleasant ways.

These are only the more obvious cases of the rule that no two men can have exactly the same faith unless they have exactly the same mental capacity. St Thomas Aquinas was an Italian Catholic; and the peasants of the Abruzzi were Italian Catholics; but as St Thomas was a very subtle schoolman, and the peasants were very superstitious fieldmen, they understood Catholicism quite differently, and had not in fact the same religion at all; whilst the avowed differences between the Italian peasant and the Tibetan peasant, between St Thomas and Plato or Aristotle, were no deeper than differences of dialect.

To take a less extreme contrast, there are men of wide culture and reading,

---

10. See vol. 1, p. 317, where Shaw speaks of 'the false doctrine of a material hell which Mahomet was driven to invent . . .' Neither in J. M. Rodwell's 1861 translation of the Koran, which Shaw sought around 1908–9 to have reprinted, nor in more modern translations do we find anything so graphic as the 'brimstone lake' of which Shaw speaks. In the present Penguin edition (fifth revised, 1990) N. J. Dawood renders the description of hellfire in Sura 67: 'When they are flung into its fire, they shall hear it roaring and seething, as though bursting with rage.'

and of considerable achievement in physical science, who are so matter-of-fact in their mental constitution that they can see nothing in the Athanasian Creed but an arithmetical impossibility. They say that if there is one god there is one god, and if there are three gods there are three gods, but there cannot be one and three at the same time. But the three in one and the one in three presented no difficulty to Athanasius: it seemed so simple to him that he went the length of declaring that anyone with so little intellect as to boggle at it would be damned. To many of us the notion of a man being damned for purely intellectual inadequacy is revolting: we feel that everything will be forgiven to him whose heart is in the right place, and that Athanasius himself deserved to be damned for his uncharitableness, in spite of his having written the most intellectually subtle page in the Prayer Book of the Church of England;[11] but there is a great deal to be said for a sharp reminder to us that good intentions are no excuse for stupidity, and that if people are to be damned at all, it had better be the fools than the rascals.

If we try to group all these differences, and scores of others which it would be wearisome to state, so as to arrive at some generalization by which our mind can deal compendiously with them, we will find that, as to worship, they arrange themselves along the scale at one end of which is the Quaker and at the other the Ritualist, and, as to belief, along the scale from the abstract to the concrete. At one end of this scale of belief is a Creative Spirit, a Force of Nature, as immaterial until incarnated in its living works as a part without an actor; and at the other the visible corporal humanly-emotional figure depicted by Blake and Raphael, or fashioned with a hundred hands and an elephant's trunk by Hindoo artificers, or as a man with a hawk's head by the Egyptians, until you come to the mere block of stone on which the human imagination fastens as sacred in the stage in which it must have something concrete to cling to to save it from madness.

In the understanding and recognition of this inequality of apprehension between men lies the secret of tolerance. Take my own case. When my affairs do not oblige me to be in London, I live in a little village of 130 scattered inhabitants. It has a church and a Rector. My own house was for

11. Athanasius, as Bishop of Alexandria, was imperious and inflexible, having to flee in 335 when charged with cruelty and possible murder. He is no longer believed to be the author of the so-called Athanasian Creed, which appears in the Anglican prayer book. It is subtle in the attention it gives to the mysteries of the Trinity and the Incarnation, explaining that 'Christ is equal to the Father in His divinity and less than the Father according to His humanity'.

a long time the Rectory; and my tenancy of it endowed the church.[12] When the churchwardens apply to me at the usual seasons I contribute; and when the hat goes round for special expenses for repairs to the building, I pay my share of what may be necessary to keep it standing. I am on intimate terms with the Rector. I am, in short, a local pillar of the Church; and I visit it occasionally. But I have never attended a service there. Whether from defect or excess of intellect, I cannot use the Church of England ritual either as spiritual food or to express and demonstrate my religion. The last time I tried it was when [1913] my mother died. She was not a Church of England ritualist; but she had no prejudices nor bigotries; and she would have agreed with me that when there was a chaplain attached to the crematorium, it would have been a little shabby to save his fee and consign her body to the fire without any ceremony at all. And so the Church of England burial service was read. But I found it morbid and heathenish. It was all wrong for my mother and all wrong for me. Later on [1920], my sister [Lucy] followed my mother; and she left a will in which she expressly barred any ritual. But here I found myself up against a religious need. When I found myself in the chapel of the crematorium surrounded by her friends, many of them suffering from a distress that needed some recognition and expression, I found that it was not possible to order the officials to dispose of the remains that still had my sister's shape as if they were a scuttleful of coals. I had to improvize a ceremony which was none the less a funeral ceremony because it consisted of an address by myself in my own words. This was possible for me: I am a practised public speaker, and by profession an author. But of the relatives of those who die not one in a thousand could compose a suitable address, or dare utter it in public if he or she could. For the vast majority there must be a form of words provided and a professional speaker to utter them impressively. To bury without a word or gesture would be to them to bury "like a dog." How then could I possibly live in a village and refuse my share in the provision of a ceremony to my neighbors merely because the ceremony did not fit my own case, and I was able to supply one for myself? It would be the act not merely of a bigot, but of a curmudgeon.

Later still [1921] a friend of mine [Robert Loraine] induced me to go to the nuptially famous London church of St George's, Hanover Square, to see him married. Here my feelings were quite decisive. I felt that I would live

12. The Shaws first occupied the New Rectory at Ayot St Lawrence, on a rental basis, on 3 November 1906. The twelve-room house on two acres of ground was eventually purchased, in June 1920, for £6300. A year later Shaw added a strip of land from Ayot Farm, purchased from his neighbour Apsley Cherry-Garrard.

and die celibate rather than take part in such a ceremony and thereby seem to assent to its unwholesome and nonsensical comparison of my mating to the mystical union of Christ with the Church, and to that very disingenuous reference to St Paul[13] by which the authors of the Prayer Book tried to make the best of what they evidently considered (as he did) a rather questionable business. I congratulated myself on having had the alternative of civil marriage open to me. But in the view of strict Catholics, Anglican or Roman, I am not married at all. Only, they need not go on to say that I am living in sin; for on my part the sin would lie in giving a false expression to my religious feeling. But what is false for me may be true for another; and I have not the smallest objection to its being provided for him out of the common funds to which I contribute. He has to contribute to the common fund out of which the civil registrar who marries me is paid; and if this reciprocal fiscal toleration works smoothly I do not see why reciprocal spiritual toleration should be impossible.

If I were asked to fill up an ordinary official form containing a column for my religion I should probably save the officials trouble by writing the Episcopal Church of Ireland, of which I am a member by baptism. But if I were asked to describe myself for the purposes of a serious investigation of the religious condition of the country, I should call myself a Creative Evolutionist for reasons which I have already sufficiently explained in my preface to Back to Methuselah; but I might quite fairly write myself down a Platonist or amateur Quaker, using the word amateur to imply that I am not an enlisted member of the Society of Friends, in which, by the way, genuine Quakers are hardly commoner than they are elsewhere, because, as membership of the Society is largely hereditary, and genuine Quakerism is a gift of God, I suspect that in most Quaker meetings, if the Spirit moved a young man to get up and say anything unexpected, or indeed to say anything at all, there

---

13. The reference is to an exhortation in the Holy Eucharist ceremony: 'But if we are to share rightly in the celebration of those holy Mysteries, and to be nourished by that spiritual Food, we must remember the dignity of that holy Sacrament. I therefore call upon you to consider how Saint Paul exhorts all persons to prepare themselves carefully before eating of that bread and drinking of that cup.' Paul's exhortation in I Corinthians 10: 6–21 includes, however, a request to 'Behold Israel [Abraham] after the flesh: are not they which eat of the sacrifices partakers of the altar?' (10: 18). Thus, Shaw clarifies in a related essay, after the bridegroom has given a pledge of lifetime monogamy he is instantly urged 'to take for his model in domestic conduct a polygamous oriental patriarch', shared by Sarah and Hagar in a *ménage à trois* ('A Note on the Prayer Book', *Shaw on Religion*, 1967).

would be as much scandalized indignation as if he had "brawled" in a cathedral. In essentials I am Protestant and Quaker, because the intervention of any priest between me and my God would be to me the most unbearable of impertinences, and because I need no visible image, no temple made with hands, no acted fable, to enable me to apprehend as much of my relation to the universe as is humanly apprehensible. Nor do I use or need forms of prayer. When I was a child, and said my prayers at night as I had been taught to do, I composed my own prayers, ending up with the Lord's Prayer: rather, I think, as a gesture of politeness to its author, than as a prayer. Thus, even in my nonage, I was independent of the set forms of heavenly communion; and my religion, for what it is worth, needs no ceremonial aid from writer, builder, musical composer, priest, or Church, though nobody has been more nourished by their works than I. Nothing must come between me and the spirit that moves within me; and though I do not walk by the inner light alone, but by all the light I can get, from without or within, yet I must interpret what I see for myself. And if that is not the quintessence of Quakerism, and indeed of genuine Quakerism, I do not know what Quakerism means.

But what could be more unreasonable and cruel than for me to try to deprive my ritualist neighbors of their set prayers, their praises, their legends, their temples and masses, their anthems, their colored windows, their pictures and statues, and their hierarchies of vestured priests, especially as all these give extraordinary delight to my sense of art when their poets and painters and sculptors and orators have been religiously inspired, and often awaken my religious sense as sun and rain awaken seed? It would be no less unreasonable and cruel on their part to force their ritual on me and persecute me because another fashion of religion is natural to me.

The mischief of persecution lies, not in our different ways, but in the unfounded inferences we draw from them. A friend of mine, since dead, an army officer with the education and knowledge and experience of the world implied by that position, once said to me, "Well, Shaw, I dont know what you think about religion; but I know for a fact that the son of the Vicar up at —— is the father of the housemaid's illegitimate child; and you may tell me that the Bible is true after that if you like; but I shant believe you." To this man the whole validity of his religion, and indeed of all religion, depended on the success of one of its ministers in imposing conventional chastity on his son. We cannot laugh at him because we all know that such grotesque tests of religion are too common to be a laughing matter. Immense numbers of people would conclude unhesitatingly that because I do not attend Church services I can have no religion and therefore no conscience. Of these numbers many believe that if a man prays to the Blessed Virgin to intercede for him with God, he is an idolator who, if he had the power, would consign thousands of his fellow citizens to the rack and stake. To such sophisticated souls it is not enough to believe in God: you must call him God and nothing else: if you call him Allah or Vishnu or (of late years) even Gott, you are a heathen.

The difficulty is an old one. Everybody is sincerely in favor of religion, of duty, of goodness and justice, of all things that are lovely and of good report; but it is not enough to be in favor of these things: you must be able to recognize them when you meet them. Annas and Caiaphas had a remarkable opportunity in that way; but they missed it because they mistook a man more religious than themselves, though in a different fashion, for a blasphemer and a scoundrel.

Nowadays intolerance is rife between sects so anti-clerical that the mere suggestion of their possibility would have made Caiaphas tear himself beardless and naked. Take for example the formulas of the Church of Christ Scientist as prescribed by Mrs Eddy. Mrs Eddy, as it is now appearing, was much sounder in her science than the medical profession in her day, with its materialistic view of the living body as a purely mechanical and chemical phenomenon; yet she is denounced and reviled not only by the materialistic doctors and surgeons, but by the disciples of M. [Émile] Coué,[14] who makes invalids cure themselves by the formula "I am getting better and better every minute." The cures of Christian Science are obviously fundamentally identical with the cures of M. Coué; but Mrs Eddy's formula will not start the self-healing process in Smith, who is subsequently cured triumphantly by M. Coué; and Jones, who has told himself in vain for weeks that he is getting better from hour to hour, is no sooner taken in hand by one of Mrs Eddy's ministers than he makes a perfect recovery. The plan of St James, as practised by the Peculiar People, succeeds where both Mrs Eddy and M. Coué's plan fail. Even a doctor's prescription has been known to succeed with people who have faith in it, and would succeed much oftener if doctors did not persist in poisoning the chalice by putting drugs into it. None of these plans cure me, because they have not found the exact sort of hocus-pocus that starts the miracle of healing and recreation in me; but I owe a great deal to the fact that having in my happily irreverent youth dismissed all the religions, and subsequently the scientific formulas as hocus-pocus, there was nothing to hinder me from going on to discover that all the hocus-pocuses are equally good for the people whose capacities and idiosyncrasies they hit off. Thus they are at once all wrong and all right; and he who calls his brother a fool

14. French psychotherapist, who encouraged auto-suggestion through his famous though often ridiculed simplistic formula.

for clinging to one of them is a fool himself. The texts to hang out like banners to confound bigots are (from Tennyson) "God fulfils himself in many ways," ['The Passing of Arthur', *Idylls of the King*, 1859] and (my favorite Scripture) "What doth the Lord require of thee but to do justly, and to love mercy, and to walk humbly before thy God?" [Micah 6: 8].

Though the moral of all this is that you must suffer your neighbor to serve God in his own way, however different it may be from yours, let no Church lazily conclude that its ritual needs no revision merely because it is sure to supply somebody's want. If the Church of England, for example, consoles itself for the loss of another hundred of the British intelligentsia by the accession of another million Polynesian and African converts from crude anthropophagy, her state will not be the more gracious. I take, after my manner, the extreme instance to make the position clear; but the danger lies in more insidious changes. If the Church is losing its hold on relatively clever and cultured people and filling their pews with relatively stupid and ignorant people, then, however slight the difference may be from year to year, it will tell perceptibly from lustrum to lustrum. The Dean of St Paul's, himself the greatest Platonist of us all, has said that if ordination be refused to all candidates who do not believe literally and unequivocally what they now have to profess to believe before they can be ordained, the ministry will presently consist exclusively of fools, bigots, and liars.[15] This, which is so obviously true that the Church dares not rebuke the Dean for affirming it, however much it may wish he had said nothing, is not a wholesome state of things. And the Prayer Book has gone bad in the course of three centuries in other places

15. Another instance of Shavianized 'improvement'. What Inge wrote, in 'Bishop Gore and the Church of England', *Outspoken Essays*, First Series (1919), was: 'A general assent to the Articles does not mean that the man who gives that assent is free to repudiate any "particular phrases or expressions" which do not please him. A witness who admitted having signed an affidavit with this intention would cut a poor figure in a law court . . . There are some honourable men who have abstained from entering the service of the Church on account of these requirements. But there are many others who recognise that knowledge grows and opinions change, while formularies for the most part remain unaltered; and who consider that, so long as their general position is understood by those among whom they work, it would be overscrupulous to refuse an inward call to the ministry because they know that they will be asked to give a formal assent to unsuitably worded tests drawn up three centuries ago. Dr Gore himself would probably have been refused ordination fifty years ago on the ground of his lax views on inspiration . . . [A]n obstinate persistence in that kind of honesty would have excluded from the ministry all except fools, liars, and bigots.'

than in the creeds and articles. The people they are good enough for are not good enough for a Church aiming at representing what is best in Christendom.

Then there is the quaint anarchy of the parsons by whose conduct most of their neighbors judge the Church. The Rector is the freeholder of his Rectory; and he may also be a rampant freethinker in politics and sociology. He claims and exercises all the liberties of a country gentleman, and wallows openly in class prejudices. Often he snubs the poor, and sides with the squire against them; he sees to it that servility and imperialist militarism are inculcated in the Church schools; he pitches the emblems of Christian peace into the cellar and waves the Union Jack the moment there is any question of war; he supports the way of the police as God's appointed way of dealing with crime; and he is equally free to preach the most extreme Bolshevist views in opposition to all this if his congregation will stand it. In the late war British clergymen who had to bury certain German soldiers who were killed in aeroplane raids actually altered the words of the burial service to express their personal refusal to admit that Englishmen and Germans, as the children of the Father of us all, are brothers; and though this was clearly either treachery to Christ or cowardice in the face of the mob: that is to say, a betrayal of duty for which a soldier would be shot, it was taken as a matter of course that a clergyman should behave like any irresponsible tramp if he had a mind to. It was this sort of thing that made Tolstoy so bitter against the Greek Church, and which makes all the revolutionary movements anti-clerical, in spite of the fact that Socialism, the main revolutionary movement of today, bases its policy on the conception of a truly Catholic Church for the workers of all nations.

There is, in fact, no effective modern discipline in any of the Churches. A Roman Catholic priest can be silenced; but he is much more likely to be silenced for advocating the wholesome practice of cremation, or declaring that animals have quite soul enough to have rights as against cruel and thoughtless men, than for making his Church ridiculous or odious by insisting on such crudely literal acceptance of all the Church's dogmas as must put them in the light of silly superstitions before reasonably humane and well informed people. As to a Church of England rector, he cannot be silenced at all: his rectory is his castle; and he can be driven from it only by general social pressure.

Up to a certain point this freedom of the individual priest or minister, unless he is a hopeless crank, does more good than harm. And beyond a certain point Churches will be what their members, clerical and lay, make them, no matter what their creeds, articles, and disciplines may be. But the same may be said of any human organization; and yet an organization that does not draw certain lines in faith and conduct is not an organization at all, but a mob. The British navy allows its admirals a latitude in writing to The Times which can be explained only by its recognition of the fact that no man can go through the ordeal of the quarter-deck without becoming more or less crazy; but an admiral who altered the Articles of War to suit his own political prejudices, or who allowed rich officers to shirk their share of the risks run by those who were the sons of parsons and suchlike hard-ups (like Nelson), would be dismissed from the service or certified as insane and sent to Copenhagen Hospital.[16] You may be a very eccentric naval officer: you may swear like a fighting mate on an ocean tramp, and shake your fist in the king's face, and even flatly disobey orders if you can win a battle thereby; but you may not fight for the enemy when the battle is joined (however much you may sympathize with him), nor, in time of peace, may you, by example and precept, devote yourself to the subversion of the principles of national defence and the encouragement of the slackers and shirkers as the most respectable persons in the ship. Consequently the navy has never fallen into contempt in England as the Church has, and as the courts have; and the explanation is that clergymen are not effectively restrained from bringing religion, nor judges from bringing the law, into contempt. To the naval and military officer we do effectively and convincingly say, "Be faithful to your profession, or get out." To the officers of the Church and the Law, we say, "Do what you please, and be damned." With the result that it is we who are damned, unless we keep carefully out of the churches and out of the courts. And it is not possible for all of us to keep out of either.

The end of the discussion then is, for the present, that as some of the most religious men in the world have been mistaken for atheists, like Voltaire, for mere gluttonous winebibbers, like Christ, for impostors, like Mahomet, and for superstitious humbugs, like many very honest nameless parsons and priests, we had better be careful how we judge oneanother, or put ourselves in the place of God by dictating how our neighbor should serve Him. And also that any Church which makes a great fuss when a cathedral pillar sinks or a

16. Neither the British Library nor the Wellcome Institute for the History of Medicine has been able to locate a Copenhagen Hospital in the British Isles. There was a naval hospital of that name in Denmark, but it did not specialize in psychiatric cases. Shaw may have been introducing playfully a fabulous medical institution in the time of Nelson and the Battle of Copenhagen (1801). An earlier reference to the hospital, in the same vein, will be found in Shaw's polemic 'What is to be Done with the Doctors?' (*English Review*, December 1917–March 1918; reprinted in *Doctors' Delusions*, 1931).

wall cracks, and collects a great sum to have the building underpinned and made safe, but sees its creeds and services going crazy with age, and sinking and rifting and tumbling in all directions without saying a word about them except to swear that they are as safe as the Pyramids, and that those who are complaining that they will presently fall and bury the nation in their ruins are disreputable liars, that Church will end, as many churches have ended in England, in having buildings without congregations. Also, since people want up-to-date creeds and rituals, but care for nothing later than the XV century in architecture (or, if they are connoisseurs, the XII), the carefully "restored" churches will not attract even the better sort of sightseeing tourists to fill the places of the worshippers their obsolete rituals have driven away.

[AYOT ST LAWRENCE.
16 October 1922.]

## THE INFANCY OF GOD

I wish at the outset to clear myself of all suspicion of that confusion of religion with Veneration which enables most men to imagine themselves religious when they are only reverent. I am myself, and always have been, as religious a man as Voltaire; but as I have also been, like him, an extremely irreverent one, most Englishmen are unable to conceive me as religious. I have no power to alter this state of things. Many years ago I found myself in a vegetarian restaurant in Barbican, sitting opposite a man who began to discuss religion with me. Before I had at all shewn my hand on the subject, he said: "I can see you are a sceptic." "How do you know?" said I. "I am a bit of a phrenologist," said he. "Oh," said I, "have I no bump of venera- tion?" "Bump of veneration!" he exclaimed: "Why, it's a hole."[17] And as a matter of fact that part of the scalp which in very devout worshippers and very obedient moralists rises into a dome or a ridge like a church roof, is on my scalp a majestic plain with a slight depression in the centre.

To ask me to be reverent, with whatever moving appeals to good taste, is like asking me to hang from a tree by my tail. In me nature has discarded the tail, having higher uses for me than hanging on trees upside down. She has also discarded the bump of veneration, having nobler attitudes for me

17. Reported by Frederic Whyte in 'Bumps and Brains: "G. B. S." on the Imperfec- tions of the Phrenologists', *Daily Graphic*, 7 January 1907; reprinted in Whyte, *A Bachelor's London* (1931). See also vol. 2, p. 294.

than kneeling and groveling. I have achieved at least one of the characteristics of the Superman: the upright posture of the soul; and I am as proud of it as the first monkey who achieved the upright posture of the body, and so felt himself a stage nearer the Supermonkey, man.

Yet I am not so far evolved that I cannot understand veneration. It is important that every statesman (and I write always for statesmen) should know that veneration is a passion; and that its satisfaction brings a comfort so ineffable that its voluptuaries never stop to think out what it implies, and are consequently not degraded by it as they would be if they had thought it out—as I should be by it, for example. Let me think it out for the purpose of this book, on paper. To venerate, you must have something higher than yourself before you. To obtain the utmost satisfaction for your passion of veneration, you conceive a God who is omnipotent, omniscient, and infinitely good. And you think no more about it, but worship and are happy. But I, having no such use for this ideal, and having, instead, an instinct for criticism, immediately begin to reflect. I see that the veneration scheme implies that an all-powerful God, to whom nothing is impossible, has deliberately created something lower than himself for the sake of enjoying his own superiority to them, just as a snob surrounds himself with footmen or an unkingly king with flatterers. Immediately my chin goes up; and my back stiffens. I, with all my faults and follies, am at least better than this; for, being man, I strive to surpass myself and produce Superman; whilst this God of the people with ridged and domed heads, does not try to produce a Supergod, but produces subgods, giving them all sorts of ridiculous and disastrous weaknesses so that he may despise them. This God will not do for me at all: to be quite frank, I consider him a cad. Unless I can bring you to the knowledge of some higher divinity than that, I may as well shut up my treatise on religion, and write farces.

Yet such a God is at present indispensable to the statesman, and, as I have said, to the venerators also. To the statesman, because the ridged and domed men, of whom there are many, will not obey laws or officials through a comprehension of the need for subordinators, but only through veneration for the lawgiver and the official. To induce them to do anything subordinate, you have to set up a golden calf for them to adore, and persuade them that your officials are its ministers, to which end you must deck the officials in the best trappings your stage managers can devize, and set them apart by every device of caste and money that can make them appear awful and venerable. And you will find the task a very easy one; for the passion of veneration is so strong that the ridged heads and what Shakespear called the pregnant knees [*Hamlet*, II: ii] will bend and crook before the most pitiful and grotesque makeshifts. Humanity has not yet produced a creature so cruel, so disgusting, so silly, or even so common, but it will find adorers as loyal as the noblest kings and bishops known to history. Just as the amorous voluptuary soon comes to care nothing for the lover and everything for the passion, so the ridged and domed care everything for loyalty and piety and nothing for the king or bishop. Nero will serve their turn as well as Alfred. The blacking on the shoes of "Great Catherine, whom the world still adores"[18] is as sweet to their lips as that on the shoes of the virgin Elizabeth. Neither their loyalty nor their devotion affords the smallest guarantee of good government or lofty religion. It guarantees nothing but its idol; and if its idol deepens the emotional effect from time to time by some appalling crime, his hold is all the surer; the cult of pleasure is near akin to the cult of pain. What finally wrecks all republics, and is now struggling fiercely with Democracy, is this Idolatry, abhorred of all the prophets. The English Commonwealth of the XVII century failed because it starved the idolator; it took away his king and his bishop; and Cromwell, had he lived, would have had to crown himself or perish; for he could not have gone on much longer with his armed heel on the throat of an idolatrous nation without pretending that he was something more than a man of like passions to themselves.

Democracy is fundamentally a proposal that we should live without idols, obeying laws and doing justly because we understand the need for doing so, and making an end of purely lascivious veneration and idolatry. In every democratic revolution the democrats instinctively begin by rushing to the cathedral and knocking off the heads of the statues. It then proceeds to the residences of the human idols—the official persons—and knocks off their heads also. When, as often happens, these unlucky living idols are excellent functionaries and estimable, kindly, or at worst quite commonplace individuals, such acts of mob violence seem as senseless as they are cruel. Even those who care little about the slaughter of men are infuriated by the destruction of priceless works of art. All the same, there must be some logic in the action of a thousand men who all do the same thing without stopping to paralyze thousands with inept arguing. In Paris, in 1789, there was not in the Bastille a single prisoner about whom the mob cared a rap; and the governor was no worse a man than any other military gentleman with a good place. But when the mob demolished the Bastille and hacked off Delaunay's

18. Misreading of Byron's *Don Juan* (Canto VI, stanza 92): 'In Catherine's reign, whom Glory still adores'. The final four words are accurately quoted on titles or fly-titles of editions of Shaw's play *Great Catherine* (1919).

head,[19] they were demonstrating that the Bastille was only a heap of stones and its governor only a man who would die when you cut his throat: a demonstration which had been made necessary by the success with which the Bastille had been imposed on France as the inviolate temple of a terrible and irresistible idol called the King, and the Governor as a High Priest wielding the idol's power vicariously. In the same way, if no one had ever thought Charles I more than a man, Cromwell would never have taken the trouble to prove that his neck, at all events, was mortal, and that one could shear through it without being struck by lightning. And when Cromwell, having in due course become something of an idol, was dug out of his grave and hung up in chains, that, too, was thought necessary to shew people that what he had done was no more than any common criminal could have done. It is but a few years since, in the Sudan, we desecrated the tomb of the Mahdi, and mutilated his corpse[20] to prove that Mahomet would not avenge him; and no doubt we shall yet see the statue of Gordon we set up in his place duly defiled and decapitated by the next Mahometan conqueror to prove that it, too, is under no special supernatural protection.

All these tides of idolatry and iconoclasm are to me, and therefore presumably to many other people, stupid and disgusting. To us idolatry, though easy, and, for the mere mechanical purposes of law and order, effective, is a rotten and degrading basis for society, and reduces religion to "a rhapsody of words" [*Hamlet*, III: iv], as Shakespear put it. We want intelligent obedience instead of idolatrous obedience, as that is our only guarantee against the abuse of power for the private ends of those whom we must trust with it.

So far, this is mere political commonplace. The need for political intelligence in order to secure rebellion the moment our governors betray their trust has been demonstrated quite often enough, in spite of the fact that the Ridged and Domed remain constitutionally impervious to it. What has been less noticed is the danger that arises from the fact that idolators always expect too much from their idols, and in the fury of their disappointment often outdo the iconoclasts when an insurrection is provoked by famine or defeat.

19. Bernard Jourdan, Marquis de Launay, governor of the Bastille, was slain and decapitated, his head exhibited on a pike, in the storming of the prison on 14 July 1789.

20. When Sir Herbert Kitchener's Anglo-Egyptian army in 1898 defeated the Mahdists in the Sudan, the tomb of Mohammed Ahmed (the Mahdi), Muslim hero of the 1885 capture of Khartoum, was desecrated and destroyed. See Shaw's letter, 'The Mahdi's Skull', *Morning Leader*, 6 October 1898; reprinted in Shaw, *Agitations: Letters to the Press 1875–1950* (1985).

Anatole France tells the story of a peasant who, praying before a statue of
the Virgin and Child, addressed the latter in these terms: "It is not to thee,
son of a wanton, that I offer my prayer, but to thy sainted mother."[21] On a
previous occasion he had made his petition to the Infant Christ without
success; and when it was not granted he abused the obdurate deity just as
Russian peasants, when they have prayed in vain for good weather to their
Ikons, take them into the fields and beat them.

We have the same phenomenon in politics, where it takes the form of
"the swing of the pendulum" at general elections. Our Party leaders are
idolized. The inevitable consequence is that impossibilities are expected from
them. They are held accountable for the harvests, for the fluctuations of trade,
for the fortune of war, for every private mishap and every public calamity,
whilst at the same time they get no credit for beneficial measures that are
beyond the comprehension of their idolators. Consequently they are thrown
down and smashed, and the Opposition set up on their pedestals and worshipped until the pendulum swings again, when they are set up again and
given another turn. At last the governing classes become entirely cynical as
to democracy and set themselves deliberately to perfect themselves in the art
of exploiting idolatry.

This also is something of a commonplace as far as politics are concerned.
But its application to religion is less familiar. How about the man who expects
too much from his God?

How are atheists produced? In probably nine cases out of ten, what happens
is something like this. A beloved wife or husband or child or sweetheart is
gnawed to death by cancer, stultified by epilepsy, struck dumb and helpless
by apoplexy, or strangled by croup or diphtheria; and the looker-on, after
praying vainly to God to refrain from such horrible and wanton cruelty,
indignantly repudiates faith in the divine monster, and becomes not merely
indifferent and sceptical, but fiercely and actively hostile to religion. This
result is inevitable when once the level is passed beneath which idolatry is
intensified by cruelty. For all people are not driven from religion by calamity:
many are driven just the other way by it. Whilst their circumstances are
happy they never think of religion; but "plague, pestilence and famine, battle,
murder, and sudden death" impress them with such a dread of the majesty
and power of God, that they spend the rest of their lives in worship and
propitiation. It is the stronger spirits, the thinkers, those with a high ideal of

21. Also alluded to in Shaw's letter to Gilbert Murray on 5 November 1914 (*Collected
Letters 1911–1925*, 1985), in which the pejoration 'whore' is substituted for 'wanton'.
Source not located.

God and the power and courage to criticize and judge God by the standard of that high ideal, who revolt against his cruelty, denouncing him as "the Almighty Fiend" of Shelley; and finally rejecting the tale of his existence as a hideous dream. Although atheism may be mere stupidity, yet the intelligent atheist is generally superior to the average worshipper in intellect, and in character as well. When the Westminster and Fortnightly Reviews were distinctly atheistic reviews, they were as superior to their orthodox competitors in intelligence and culture as the extinct National Reformer and the Freethinker of today to the Parish Magazine. The association of scepticism with high mental gift soon became so firmly established that orthodoxy was a positive disadvantage in a scientific career, a useless qualification in medicine and law, and a thing not to be too strongly insisted on even by clergymen and schoolmasters. The Bishop who reminded people, however unintentionally, of the sceptical abbés of the French salons of the XVIII century, was much more fashionable than any of his evangelical colleagues could hope to be. It became necessary to invent a polite euphemism for the terms atheist and atheism; and we now speak of Agnostics and Agnosticism, representing sometimes, no doubt, an entirely honest confession of ignorance as to the ultimate problems of existence, but mostly the state of mind of those who have neither faith to believe nor courage to deny. But whether the attitude was frankly and boldly negative or timidly non-committal, what was at the back of it in nine cases out of ten was the horror of a God who was not only the God of honor, of love, and of light, but also the God of epilepsy, of cancer, of smallpox, of madness, of war, of poverty, of tyranny: in short, of the huge burden of pain and evil under which the world has always groaned and is still groaning more pitifully than ever. In vain did the orthodox attempt to propitiate the agnostics by throwing over the imaginary hell of everlasting brimstone: they could not throw over the real hell which was flaming all round them. And so, as Nietzsche put it, the news went round that God was dead.[22]

Now this whole difficulty was created by the idolatry which conceives God as perfect and omnipotent. If he is omnipotent, then he is a hopeless puzzle. He is not the Almighty Fiend of Shelley's Queen Mab, because he is also the God of veracity, honor, and kindness. And he is not the God of love and mercy because he is also the god of the tubercle bacillus, and the guilty butt of the sarcasms of Mephistopheles. Now a God who is a puzzle is no use. It is easy to say "If I could understand him, he would not be a

22. 'Zarathustra's Prologue', II, *Thus Spake Zarathustra*, tr. Thomas Common, first published in the *Eagle and the Serpent*, No. 5 (1 November 1898).

God: how can a creature understand the creator?"; but if you do not understand God, you may as well be an atheist for all practical purposes, because you must leave the thing you do not understand out of account. The moment you make any law or give any counsel on the ground that the thing you enjoin or forbid will please him or offend him, you are pretending to understand him to that extent: that is, you are treating him, not as a puzzle, but as a consistent, understood, ascertained character. And with what assurance can you undertake to say that any given conduct will please or displease a deity who is responsible for all the cruelty and evil of life as well as for all the good? It ends inevitably, as it always has ended, either in ignoring him altogether or making him the excuse for whatever you feel inclined to do, whether it happens to be a crime or a benefaction. The latter course, which prevailed as long as God was exempt from criticism, is now so revolting to the Opposition that God is never mentioned in Parliament, and very seldom out of it, except to give emphasis to an expletive.

In the old times, God was not really conceived as omnipotent, but as the divine antagonist of a malign power which wrestled with him for the souls of men. The Father of Lies and the Author of Evil was not God but Satan, who was so vividly imagined that Luther threw his inkpot at him. Fortunately a malignant god—a devil—is too grotesquely horrible a thing to be believed in. A god with horns and a tail is ridiculous; and a fallen archangel is not really a devil: people began to defend him and make him the hero of the piece instead of the villain.

The moment this point is reached it is all over with the old childish way of accounting for evil as the work of Old Nick the mischief maker. And yet that nurse's tale has made us familiar with a conception of immeasurable value. When he wanted to do anything he had to tempt a man or woman to do it. Failing that instrument, he could do nothing. Now one glance at the world as it exists, or at the pages of history, will shew that this is also the method of God. You may call it inspiration in the one case and temptation in the other, out of politeness to God; but the two things are as identical as steadfastness and obstinacy. When a hungry and penniless man stands between his good and his bad angel in front of a baker's shop, the good angel cannot seize and drag him away, nor can the bad angel thrust the loaf into his hands. The victory of honesty or the consummation of a theft must be effected by the man; and his choice will depend a good deal on the sort of man he is. Not only is he an indispensable agent; not only is he the vehicle of the force that moves him; but he is also the vehicle of the force that chooses. He is, in the old phrase, the temple of the Holy Ghost. He has, in another old phrase, the divine spark within him.

Now, to the extent that a man is the temple of the Holy Ghost and the agent of the Holy Ghost, he is necessarily also the limitation of the Holy Ghost. Not even the Holy Ghost can lift ten pounds with a baby's arm or ten tons with a man's. Not even the divine spark can solve a problem in fluxions with the brain of an actor, or play Hamlet with the brain of a mathematician. When "the word became flesh" it had to take on all the weaknesses of flesh. In all ages the saints and prophets have had to protest against the demand made on them for miracles. John Bunyan's inspiration could make him write better than Shakespear; but it could not make him write always grammatically. It could nerve Mahomet to convert the fierce tribes of Arabia from worshipping stones to an exalted monotheism; but it could not make him say No to a pretty woman. The sword will snap in the hand of God at just the point at which it will snap in a testing machine; and all the swords of God bend and snap at one point and another, or cut the wrong throats at the bidding of the ape or tiger from whom they are evolved.

Now if God (so to speak) were omnipotent, it is clear that he would provide himself with a perfectly fashioned and trustworthy instrument. And it is also clear that such an instrument would be nothing less than God himself incarnate. The fact that man is his best instrument so far on this planet, and that 999 out of every 1000 men are so stupid and cruel, so clumsy and imbecile, that they drive the thousandth to despair even when they do not murder him in sheer dread and hatred of his superiority, proves that God is as yet only in his infancy.

[?1922]

# The Author's Apology

*Prefatory note to 'Still after The Doll's House', in* Short Stories,
Scraps and Shavings, *1932. Shaw's narrative sequel was first published
in* Time (*London*), *n.s. I, February 1890*

=====

I hope I need not apologize for assuming that the readers of this story are
familiar with Ibsen's epoch-making play A Doll's House, which struck
London in the year 1889 and gave Victorian domestic morality its deathblow.

Unfortunately I cannot claim an equal renown for the sequel written by
the late Sir Walter Besant[1] in the sincere belief that he was vindicating that
morality triumphantly against a most misguided Norwegian heretic. Nor may
I reproduce it here, as the copyright does not belong to me. And I am sorry
to say I do not remember a word of it, and can only infer its incidents from
the allusions in my own sequel to it.

I am therefore as much in the dark as my readers: a poor excuse, but the
best I have to offer.

1931.                                                                    G. B. S.

---

1. Popular novelist, a founder of the Society of Authors in 1894. His sequel to *A
Doll's House* appeared in the *English Illustrated Magazine*, January 1890.

# Index to Volume 3

*by David Bowron*

Other than in the entry under his name, Shaw is referred to as S. Insignificant references to persons or works mentioned in Shaw's text and/or in the footnotes have not been indexed.

Education – *cont.*
  schoolmasters as enemies, 526
  secondary, 23
  secular, 233
  training to mistake evil for good, 100
  *see also* Universities
Edward III, King, (1312–77), 242
Edward VII, King, (1841–1910),
    361–2
Einstein, Albert (1879–1955), 118, 139,
    166, 178, 204, 257, 266, 461, 466,
    492, 497
Eisner, Kurt (1867–1919), 456 *and* n.
Elections
  acting and oratory keys to success in,
    517
  divine right of election winners, 179
  Eatanswill (Dickens), 300, 301
  failings of, 46–7
  most are nothing but stampedes, 50
  as public auctions, 52
  swing of the pendulum, 574
  testing capacity of candidates, 55–6,
    173, 518–25
  time-wasting, 103
  *see also* Government; Parliament;
    Power
Elgar, Sir Edward (1857–1934), 293,
    317–18, 339, 342, 415
Eliot, George (Mary Ann Evans) (1819–
    80), 504
Elizabeth I, Queen, (1533–1603), 43,
    246, 283, 346–7, 557
Ellis, W. Ashton (1853–1919), 341
Emery, Edward (1861–1938), 429
Eminescu, Mihail (1850–89), 37–8
    *and* n.
Emmet, Robert (1778–1803), 456

Empires: replaced by republics, 88, 92;
    *see also* British Empire
Engels, Friedrich (1820–95), 260, 531
England
  difficulty in governing English, 514
    *and* n.
  English have an insuperable dislike of
    being governed, 467
  English humour, 472n.
  intellect hated and dreaded, 517
  lessons of war forgotten, 444–5
  S a foreigner, 478
  shamefaced leadership, 528–30
  Utopia in eyes of amateur politicians,
    510
  when frightened, is capable of any-
    thing, 443
English language, *see* Language
Epstein, Sir Jacob (1880–1959), 228 *and*
    n., 229
Equality
  blitherings about the impossibility of,
    267
  and Communism, 543
  of income, 460, 498–9
  lack of, in mental capacity, 498–500
Equity (British Actors' Equity Associ-
    ation), 398, 405–6
Erasmus, Desiderius (1466?–1536), 531
Essex, Robert Devereux, 2nd Earl of
    (1566–1601), 456–7
Esterhazy, Ferdinand (1847–1923), 364
    *and* n.
Eton College, 88
Euripides (*c.*484–407 BC), 215, 229
Europe
  chaos following World War I, 90–
    91, 549–50

The Complete Prefaces: Volume 3

Vincent de Paul, Saint, (1576–1660), 171

Virgil (Publius Vergilius Maro) (70–19 BC), 539

Vivisection, 316, 332

*The Voice* (Lee), 329 *and* n.

Voltaire (1694–1778), 103, 129, 229, 391, 475, 509, 513, 514–15 *and* n., 531, 555, 569

   'Monsieur Tout le Monde' wrongfully ascribed to him, 515 *and* n.

Vril, 266 *and* n.


W. H., Mr, 347, 375

Wagner, Richard (1813–83), 107, 271, 279, 315, 318 *and* n., 319, 324, 329, 461, 522–3, 531, 535

   pre- and pro-Wagner, 341–2

   ridiculed by Anti-Wagnerites, 341

   on singers, 147

   supplanted old-fashioned Italian opera, 142–3

   works: *Lohengrin*, 338; *Ring* Cycle, 339

Walker, Sir Emery (1851–1933), 536

Wallace, Alfred Russel (1823–1913), 547

Wallace, Sir William (1272–1305), 183, 508

Wallas, Graham (1858–1932), 477, 481, 526

Walters, Revd Charles Ensor (1872–1938), 295–6

Walton, Sir William (1902–83), 342

Warren, Samuel (1807–77), 156

Wars

   borrowing to pay for, 446

   chemical warfare, 458 *and* n.

   Church of England's attitude to, 412, 568

   compulsory military service, 438

   destructiveness of, 445–7

   economic absurdity, 449

   force Socialist production systems, 264

   great generals of the past, 250

   killing techniques, 449

   modern war impossible, 250–51

   nations should always be prepared for, 443

   no armistice can stop, 412

   as popular diversion, 263–4

   of religion, 121–2, 554, 558

   whether soldiering a whole time job, 438–9

   wiping out, 463

   *see also* World War I; World War II

Waterloo, Battle of (1815), 250, 438, 448 *and* n.

Watts, George Frederic (1817–1904), 69

Watts-Dunton, Theodore (1832–1914), 288 *and* n.

Wealth

   anti-labour creed, 233–4

   consolations of landed gentry, 160–61

   of Empire, 168

   game of making money, 155

   lady of fashion never has a moment off, 155

   landed gentry, 160–61, 234, 261

   meanest creature can become rich, 247

   miseries of vagrant, rootless rich, 161–2